The
Handbook
of Lifespan
Communication

LIFESPAN
COMMUNICATION
Children, Families, and Aging

Thomas J. Socha
GENERAL EDITOR

Vol. 2

The Lifespan Communication series
is part of the Peter Lang Media and Communication list.
Every volume is peer reviewed and meets
the highest quality standards for content and production.

PETER LANG
New York • Bern • Frankfurt • Berlin
Brussels • Vienna • Oxford • Warsaw

The
Handbook
of Lifespan
Communication

Edited by Jon F. Nussbaum
Amber Worthington, Editorial Assistant

PETER LANG
New York • Bern • Frankfurt • Berlin
Brussels • Vienna • Oxford • Warsaw

Library of Congress Cataloging-in-Publication Data

The handbook of lifespan communication / edited by Jon F. Nussbaum.
pages cm. — (Lifespan communication: children, families, and aging; vol. 2)
Includes bibliographical references and index.
1. Interpersonal communication. 2. Communication—Psychological aspects.
3. Developmental psychology. I. Nussbaum, Jon F.
BF637.C45H259   153.6—dc23   2014012237
ISBN 978-1-4331-2266-8 (hardcover)
ISBN 978-1-4331-2265-1 (paperback)
ISBN 978-1-4539-1367-3 (e-book)
ISSN 2166-6466

Bibliographic information published by **Die Deutsche Nationalbibliothek.**
Die Deutsche Nationalbibliothek lists this publication in the "Deutsche
Nationalbibliografie"; detailed bibliographic data are available
on the Internet at http://dnb.d-nb.de/.

Cover photo: "The Climb of Life" by Amber Worthington

The paper in this book meets the guidelines for permanence and durability
of the Committee on Production Guidelines for Book Longevity
of the Council of Library Resources.

© 2014 Peter Lang Publishing, Inc., New York
29 Broadway, 18th floor, New York, NY 10006
www.peterlang.com

Printed in the United States of America

Dedication

This Handbook is dedicated to Aoife Elizabeth Bacon.
Her lifespan was brief. Her impact is immense.

Contents

Part Three: Childhood Communication

Part Four: Adolescent Communication

Part Five: Emerging Adulthood Communication

Part Six: Middle Adulthood Communication

Part Seven: Older Adulthood Communication

Lifespan Communication

Children, Families, and Aging

THOMAS J. SOCHA

The *Handbook of Lifespan Communication* represents a signficant milestone in the history of the development of ideas about communication. Milestones, intended to mark distances along thoroughfares, also highlight important vistas along the way. Decades ago, the Editor of this volume, Professor Jon Nussbaum, regarded as the father of lifespan communicaton, offered the communication discipline the most expansive view of communication possible: the study of communication across the entire human lifespan. Since then, Professor Nussbaum and a host of colleagues have amassed an important body of knowledge under the auspices of lifespan communication that features an extensive focus on communication in later life. In other parts of the communication field, communciation scholars who study families, for example, have also been developing bodies of knowledge (mostly focused on young adults), alongside of those studying communication in relationships, groups, and orgnizations as well as in public and mass-mediated contexts. In fact, scholars representing at least 57 different divisions, sections, and caucuses of the National Communication Association (www.natcom.org) have all been been working to advance the field of communication.

Inspired in part by Professor Nussbaum's work, this book series invites all communication scholars to view communication through a panoramic lens, from first words to final conversations—a comprehensive communication vista that brings children, adolescents, adults, and those in later life as well as lifespan groups such as the family into focus. By viewing communciation panoramically it is also my hope that communication scholars and educators will incorporate into their work the widely accepted idea that communication develops, that is, it has a starting point and a developmental arc, changing as we change over time. And further, that developmental communication arcs are historically contextualized. As infants we begin our communication education in unique historical contexts that shape our early communication learning as well as the foundations of our communication values. Children born in 2014, for example, will begin their communication learning in a time that can be thought of as a golden age of digital media, where society is attempting to manage a rapid influx of a dizzying array of new communciation technologies into everyday life. Of course the parents of these children—who could have been born anytime between the 1960s to the late 1990s—have experienced vastly different developmental communication arcs, but yet must span the generations and pass along their communciation knowledge and values as well as teach their children how to communicate effectivively within the current historical context, if they are to be successful later in life as adults. Historically contextualized lifespan thinking also raises important new questions, such as what is to be passed along from one generation to the next as "timeless" communication knowledge and practices, or in contemporary digital parlance, what becomes memetic, that is, analogous to genetic information, what survives to become the communication inheritance of future generations.

It is my hope that the *Handbook of Lifespan Communication* and all of the books published in the *Lifespan Communication: Children, Families, and Aging* series will offer the communication field new understandings and deeper appreciation of the complexities of all forms of communciation as it develops across the lifespan as well as raise important questions about communication for current and future generations to study.

—Thomas J. Socha

Introduction

JON F. NUSSBAUM AND AMBER K. WORTHINGTON

The lifespan communication perspective evolved from the fundamental notion that a true understanding of human communication can only be realized by investigating communication throughout the entire lifespan. Communication scholars began to adopt a lifespan perspective that recognizes the dynamic and evolving nature of communication within their theories and methodologies during the last few decades of the 20th century. Termed "developmental" or "lifespan" communication, this approach mirrors the lifespan perspective movements within the sister disciplines of psychology and sociology, which focus on the study of behavioral change across time. Communication scholars publically showed their interest in a lifespan perspective by organizing a caucus on communication and aging during the 1979 National Communication Association convention (Nussbaum & Friedrich, 2005). Just over 10 years later, notable Communication scholars including Nikolas and Justine Coupland, Howard Giles, John Wiemann, Gary Kreps, Mary Ann Fitzpatrick, Lynne Webb, Mark Knapp, Jon Nussbaum, and numerous others responded to this surge of interest in a lifespan communication perspective with a summer conference, a Fulbright International Colloquium, and several books and articles. These not only showcased a developmental approach to communication scholarship but also illuminated the need to appreciate more fully the communication changes that occur as a function of a developmental process over the entirety of the lifespan (Nussbaum et al., 2002; Nussbaum & Friedrich, 2005). It should be noted that mass communication scholars have investigated the usage and effects of media consumption by children, adolescents, and older adults beginning in the 1950s. To date, developmental communication research—with interdisciplinary studies in familial relationships, media effects, entertainment, education, and health—have produced a substantial amount of knowledge at the individual, relational, and societal levels addressing communication changes over time.

At the present time, the lifespan communication perspective has become a significant and impactful contributor to the knowledge base within communication scholarship. The purpose of this *Handbook* is to highlight the breadth and depth of the exceptional scholarship that has been produced over the past few decades within the general domain of lifespan communication and to point each of us to future discoveries within lifespan communication.

My (Jon Nussbaum) interest in investigating communication from a lifespan perspective began in the early 1970s as a developmental psychology major at Marquette University. At that time, studying developmental psychology meant studying children. It can be stated without any hesitation that the dominant thinking of the time was that all significant development within humans occurred within the first 12 years of life. Searching for developmental change after childhood was often looked upon as a waste of time. I began my graduate career within the psychology department at West Virginia University (WVU) in 1976 within the newly formed lifespan developmental psychology emphasis. Morgantown was the unlikely epicenter of lifespan developmental psychology with a number of the most respected scholars (e.g., Paul Baltes, K. Warner Schaie, Hayne Reese, and John Nesselroade) spending some of their academic careers supervising numerous lifespan developmental gatherings and producing many of the foundational lifespan developmental theoretical and methodological articles and edited books. Ironically, during my first year at WVU, I was assigned to a research project investigating 5- and 6-year-old children who had experienced the federally funded Head Start program. I quickly realized that I was not meant to study children and began my scholarly interest in studying individuals at different points within the lifespan. I met and began studying the communication processes of older individuals within the Department of Speech Communication at WVU before moving to Purdue University to earn my doctorate. While at Purdue, I was fortunate to study and serve as a research assistant under the direction of Victor Cicirelli within the Department of Psychological Sciences and with Mark Knapp, Bob Norton, Don Ellis, and others within the Department of Communication. My dissertation focused on the interactive behavior of older adults living within three environments (home, a retirement center, and a nursing home). My study predicted communicative behavior and life satisfaction as a function of living environment with older adulthood. The dissertation was solidly grounded within the theory and methodology of the lifespan perspective and has ultimately shaped my scholarship for over 35 years.

I edited my first book focusing on the lifespan communication perspective, *Lifespan Communication: Normative Processes*, in 1989. Since that time, the lifespan communication perspective has evolved and grown within the discipline of communication and now is a healthy component of numerous undergraduate and graduate curricula. Recently, the Department of Communication and Theatre Arts within Old Dominion University has created the first graduate degree program offering an advanced degree in lifespan and digital communication. This *Handbook* is meant to reflect this growth and presents numerous important scholarly contributions written by distinguished scholars.

I have organized the *Handbook* into separate life stages with the first two chapters dedicated to lifespan communication theory and lifespan communication methodology. A major limitation of lifespan communication research is the lack of large, funded, longitudinal investigations of how our interpersonal, family, health, or media-related communication behaviors change over the course of the lifespan. Numerous psychological, sociological, and health-related investigations throughout the technologically advanced world have utilized longitudinal methodologies to investigate various human activities for the past 60 or 70 years. While at times these longitudinal investigations have collected data on some very simple notions of frequency of interaction or on interactive networks, high-quality, longitudinal data related to communication change across the lifespan are not available. Thus, at this point I feel the life stage organization of this initial issue of the *Handbook* is optimal to capture and to imitate the flow of communicative change across the lifespan. The life stages (Early Childhood, Childhood, Adolescence, Emerging Adulthood, Middle Adulthood, and Older Adulthood) utilized as organizational parts of this *Handbook* are generally recognized markers of development by lifespan scholars across the social sciences. Each chapter is also written to stand on its own as a valuable reference source for content contextualized within a specific life stage.

The initial two chapters of the *Handbook* cover the fundamental dynamics of lifespan communication theory and lifespan communication methodology. Jake Harwood introduces the basic lifespan communication principles, influences, and theoretical perspectives that relate communication to the aging process throughout the lifespan. In addition, he highlights those communicative processes that may mediate or moderate lifespan development in his chapter, "Lifespan Communication Theory." Maggie Pitts and Mary Lee Hummert review the unique methodologies in their chapter, "Lifespan Communication Methodology," which captures communication change across the lifespan. Quantitative methodologies that typically include cross-sectional and longitudinal designs as well as qualitative methodologies utilizing field observations, diaries, and interviews are discussed.

Early Childhood is the initial life stage covered within the *Handbook*. It is fair to note that communication within early childhood has not received the scholarly attention within the communication discipline as compared to our sister disciplines. However, the research both within the communication discipline and within related disciplines has contributed significantly to our understanding of the process of communication with lifelong implications. Carol Miller and Laura DeThorne, in their chapter, "Communication Development: Distributed Across People, Resources, and Time," describe the development of intentionality, the growing awareness of the mental states of self and others, and the increasing use of linguistic forms for communication within early childhood. Beth Haslett and Wendy Samter highlight the importance of eye gaze, touch, gesture, turn taking, and the joint focus of attention as infants establish trust, attachment, and relational connections throughout infancy and toddlerhood that serve as the foundation to enable communication in their chapter, "Parent-Infant Communication."

Part Two of the *Handbook* focuses on **Childhood Communication**. Childhood is a time of dramatic communication change and consequence. Children spend significant time interfacing with various forms of media. Children explore their developing social skills outside of their immediate family and children also begin a multi-decade process of formal schooling. Helen Vossen, Jessica Piotrowski, and Patti Valkenburg explore the effects and use of the media within childhood in their chapter, "Media Use and Effects in Childhood." Robert Duran and Diane Prusank concentrate on the development of pro-social skills within childhood and discuss how these early peer relationships set the stage for childhood friendships that can have both positive and negative consequences for future relationship competencies in their chapter, "Children's Peer Relationships Outside the Family." Jennifer Waldeck overviews the aspects of human communication that research indicates impact education in her chapter, "Communication and Learning." Areas of importance that are addressed include student communication apprehension and quietness, student/teacher interaction patterns, student-student communication, teacher power, and classroom climate and the use of technology and social media.

Adolescent Communication is the focus of Part Four of the *Handbook*. Adolescents are avid media users who spend significant time listening to music, watching television, playing video games, or producing and sharing digital media via online applications. Piotr Bobkowski and Autumn Shafer, in their chapter, "The Digital Bridge into Adulthood: Media Use and Effects in Adolescence," utilize the Media Practice model to focus on the intersections between media use and four areas of adolescent well-being: aggressive behavior, sexual identity and behavior, body image and eating disorders, and substance abuse. Adolescence is also a time of emerging identities separate from family that influence decisions to experiment with substance abuse. Michael Hecht, in his chapter, "Adolescent Identity and Substance Use Prevention," examines how identity research grounded with Communication Identity Theory was used to develop the substance prevention program *keepin' it REAL* to influence adolescent health choices and behavior. Kevin Wright and Shawn King focus on adolescent social media use and its impact on relationship development, relational maintenance, computer-mediated social support, and social/psychological outcomes in their chapter, "Adolescent Online Friendship and Peer Relationships."

Lifespan developmental scholars have uncovered a distinct life stage, emerging adulthood, which has emerged within advanced technological societies because of the changing dynamics of financial realities, the lengthening of educational responsibilities, downturns within job possibilities, and a reframing of the parent-child relationship (Arnett, 2004). Part Five of the *Handbook*, **Emerging Adulthood Communication**, begins with the chapter authored by Alyssa Ann Lucas titled "Emerging Adults in College: Communication, Friendships, and Risky Sexual Behaviors." This chapter unpacks the unique dangers associated with participating in risky sexual behaviors, drug use, and alcohol abuse. Tara McManus focuses her chapter, "Commitment and Marriage," on the meaning of commitment and marriage for emerging adults and examines the primary ways they express commitment within their romantic relationships and the possible impact on relational satisfaction and marriage. "Communication and Workplace Socialization: A Lifespan Examination of the Work-Life Interface," written by Michael Kramer and Karen Myers, examines the socialization/assimilation process of joining organizations with a primary focus on individuals in their late teens and early twenties who are entering the workforce for the first time. Part Five of the *Handbook* concludes with "Friend Me, Poke Me, Then Comfort Me: An Exploration of Supportive Communication in Online Social Networking Sites," by Andy High. The chapter draws from theories of mediated interpersonal communication and research about online venues to develop a framework to integrate the theoretical and empirical implications of online social networking sites for the provision and reception of social support.

Part Six of the *Handbook* concentrates on **Middle Adulthood Communication**. Jordan Soliz and Craig Fowler focus their chapter, "Sandwich Relationships: Intergenerational Communication," on the communication dynamics that differentiate positive and negative family and relational functioning within multigenerational families. This chapter also discusses custodial grandparents and the nature of the caregiving roles they assume for their grandchildren. Dennis Gouran concentrates on career choice and organizational life for individuals within middle adulthood in his chapter, "Communicating in Professional Life: The Nature and Evolution of Superior-Subordinate Interactions." He explores superior-subordinate relationships and the impact that interactions within them have on how one negotiates various aspects of his or her professional life, performs, and derives such satisfaction as he or she may experience during the period ranging from middle to late adulthood. "Spouse and Parent: Television Images of Major Roles of Adulthood," by Diane Prusank, examines the media portrayals of socially approved enactments of spousal and parenting roles, as well as the implications for media audiences of these portrayals.

Older Adulthood Communication is the final part of this *Handbook*. James Robinson and Kathleen Watters examine the media usage habits of older adults, the types of content older adults consume, the reason for such consumption with a special focus on health information, and the dominant theories of media effects and implications of media use on older adult audience members in their chapter, "Media Use and Effects in Older Adulthood." Fran Dickson and Patrick Hughes, in their chapter, "The Socially and Sexually Active Later-Life Family Member," explore the communication challenges associated with living with older family members, the intergenerational communication between family members, the challenges associated with older family members providing care, the negotiation of new familial roles, and the interesting dynamics of dating in older adulthood for the family. The chapter by Carla Fisher and Mollie Rose Canzona, "Health Care Interactions in Older Adulthood," reviews the significance and prominence of health care interactions within older adulthood with emphasis on caregiving, future planning, medical decision making, conflict management, geriatric medicine, and social support. The final chapter of the *Handbook* is co-authored by Howie Giles, Chan Thai, and Abby Prestin, titled "End-of-Life Interactions." This chapter expresses the firm ideological conviction that the inability to manage death's challenges seriously impoverishes lifespan adaptations. Topics covered within the chapter include theories of death and dying; palliative care and education; topic avoidance of death; and a proposed set of integrative principles with a focus on processual ways in which death, dying, and communication can be empowering and lead to exciting prospects for future scholarship.

The *Handbook* highlights several content areas or themes of communication research that differentially impact individuals or relationships at different life stages. Media and social media consumption, usage, and effects as well as various relationship dynamics are common areas of focus throughout many of the life stages. I envision numerous editions of this *Handbook* that may eventually reframe its organization in which each chapter covers more numerous areas of significance within communication research and traces the development of each particular area throughout the lifespan. This first edition marks the scholarly significance of lifespan communication and offers a solid foundation on which to further our investigations into communication change throughout the entire lifespan.

REFERENCES

Arnett, J. J. (2004). *Emerging adulthood: The winding road from late teens through the twenties*. New York, NY: Oxford University Press.

Nussbaum, J. F., & Friedrich, G. (2005). Instructional/developmental communication: Current theory, research and future trends. *Journal of Communication, 55*, 578–593.

Nussbaum, J. F., Pecchioni, L., Baringer, D., & Kundrat, A. (2002). Lifespan communication. In W. B. Gudykunst (Ed.), *Communication yearbook 26* (pp. 366–389). Mahwah, NJ: Erlbaum.

PART ONE

Theory and Methods in Lifespan Communication

CHAPTER ONE

Lifespan Communication Theory

JAKE HARWOOD

We age not only chronologically, but also communicatively. Our chronological progression is marked and shaped by communicative actions (sometimes congratulatory, often commiserative), and our communication styles and preferences change as a result of aging (our own and others'). In this chapter, I examine how existing lifespan theory can be expanded by incorporating a communication focus and the ways in which contemporary communication theory utilizes or would benefit from a lifespan perspective. The scope here is obviously huge, and hence I consider only a subset of the potentially relevant theories. Broader reviews of theory and the empirical literature are available, and interested readers should view those as complementary sources (e.g., Harwood, 2007; Nussbaum, Pecchioni, Baringer, & Kundrat, 2002; Pecchioni, Wright, & Nussbaum, 2005). Other chapters in this handbook also address additional perspectives that are equally interesting and valid. This chapter will focus on the later portion of the lifespan. Most of the general principles could be addressed to lifespan development at any age, but the specifics pertain primarily to older adulthood.

The chapter begins by outlining the broad parameters of a lifespan perspective (derived from multiple sources, notably P. Baltes, 1987), and then delineating specific roles that communication can be seen as playing in social life. Then, I discuss specific theoretical issues in a manner organized by place of communication in the perspective. In closing, I briefly describe how one theoretical perspective (communication accommodation theory: Giles, Coupland, & Coupland, 1991) offers particular promise in addressing multiple areas related to communication and aging.

LIFESPAN PRINCIPLES

Development Can Occur at All Ages

Historically, developmental psychologists (among others) were guilty of viewing development as something that happened only during childhood and adolescence. In recent years, both research findings and an ideological shift against ageist assumptions have led to broad acceptance of the notion that development occurs at all ages. People at all ages may experience decline and deficit on certain fronts, but growth is always possible on other fronts. Understanding the resources that we draw on to attain and sustain such growth is a sensible focus for research. Most theory since at least the time of Erikson (1968) acknowledges this. Research on communication processes is also consistent with this assumption, demonstrating that some communicative phenomena remain stable or improve into late adulthood—vocabulary and narrative complexity, for example (Kemper, Rash, Kynette, & Norman, 1990; Pennebaker & Stone, 2003).

Change Across the Lifespan Is Nonlinear and Multidimensional

The most stereotypical accounts of the lifespan express it as an inverted U-shaped progression, with rapid early growth and then a slow (but perhaps accelerating) decline through middle age and into older adulthood. While such accounts are overly simplistic and widely discredited, they do illustrate the nonlinear nature of change through the lifespan. On any given dimension, it is likely that abilities and motivations increase and decrease at different life stages, and that no two dimensions will follow the same trajectory. Things like perceptual processing speed decline at a very steady and constant rate throughout the adult lifespan, verbal ability increases and then levels off or declines slightly very late in life (Hedden & Gabrieli, 2004), and communicative phenomena related to semantic knowledge and wisdom increase throughout the lifespan in the absence of pathological processes (Nussbaum, 2012). Antonucci's convoy model provides a nice illustration; the model recognizes that our social networks are multidimensional and multifaceted entities that follow us through life, constantly changing, but also serving as a source of stability (Antonucci & Akiyama, 1995). Indeed, the simultaneous experience and interplay of stability and change is perhaps the fundamental dynamic necessary to understand the development of any individual.

Age Constrains but Doesn't Control Development

Age-related changes in physical and cognitive functioning are described in detail in other sources (e.g., Masoro & Austad, 2011; Schaie & Willis, 2010). These changes undoubtedly place constraints on activities at different ages. Few professional athletes (except golfers, perhaps) perform at the highest level beyond age 40, and most people in very advanced old age are subject to substantial constraints across multiple areas of functioning. However, the vast majority of individuals retain a wide array of options in many arenas throughout their lives. This flexibility is particularly apparent in discussions of communication: communication is not hugely dependent on physical speed or strength, and hence strong communication skills can be retained (and improved) long after specific physical declines are noticeable. Indeed, communication can be a means by which other declines are compensated for and by which control over one's life circumstances can be maintained when challenges occur. For instance, individuals marshal assistance, maintain social and emotional support, seek medical care, and assert their independence through communicative channels (Haase, Heckhausen, & Wrosch, 2013). In other words, thinking about communicative processes forces us to recognize that age is not simply something that "happens" to us, but rather something we can manage and over which we can exert considerable control.

Individual Differences Coexist with Differences in Age-Based Averages

Whatever the broad age-based patterns that we identify and theorize about, there are substantial individual differences that must be considered. At times, the interesting questions for theorists might be how these standard deviations change over time (e.g., examining whether there is more *variability* on certain dimensions among certain age groups: Rabbitt, 2011; cf. Salthouse, 2011)—questions that haven't been given as much attention as questions about mean differences (Hedden & Gabrieli, 2004). One person may experience a challenging old age beset by physical and cognitive problems; another may have a vigorous retirement characterized by leisure, travel, and giving back to the community. The source of those individual differences resides in social and interactional processes (including communication), biological (including genetic) variables, and economic disparities that deny some people the resources required to age successfully (Giles, Davis, Gasiorek, & Giles, 2013; Rowe & Kahn, 1998). In terms of communicative processes, those of us interested in aging should not lose track of the literatures explaining communication processes through other mechanisms; just because we are examining older adults does not mean that our other theories lose their explanatory power and age suddenly explains most of the variance.

Aging Is an Ambiguous Word

The term "aging" is understood in many different ways in many different contexts. As lifespan theorists, we are interested in almost all uses of the term, but we need to be careful when using it. The term can be used to understand the changes that occur (or are perceived to occur) with chronologically advancing (year to year) throughout life; some of these changes are normal, and some are pathological. It is also used in more restrictive ways to describe getting older only in the second half (or final third) of the lifespan (so one is "aging" when moving from 65–70, but not when moving from 10–15). Aging can also represent the state of being old (someone of 85 might be described as "aging," perhaps because we think it sounds better than "old"). Aging, of course, is also interesting as a subjective experience and impression; that is, there is variability in the extent to which we feel that we are "aging" and the extent to which we perceive others to be doing so. These subjective dimensions of aging are critical elements in the larger picture of how people experience and anticipate getting older. As communication theorists, we are interested in the connections between communication and those subjective facets of aging, including the many ways in which communication might serve to construct both perceptions and the very experience of aging (N. Coupland, 2004; Hepworth, 2004).

Communication Principles

The discipline of communication centers on processes surrounding human message exchange. This section considers briefly the various roles or positions into which communication is placed as part of the research and theory process. Clearly, in a chapter concerning lifespan issues, age-related variables would be the critical "other" variables in the following descriptions. Sometimes we consider communication as a *dependent variable*. Personality, the immediate interaction partner, a preceding message, conversational goals (and any number of other considerations) all affect the nature of the messages we generate. Other times we place communication in the causal position as the *independent variable*. When communication is understood as an independent variable, we are interested in the manner in which it influences other phenomena. How do our messages (unmediated or mediated) influence emotional, cognitive, or physiological responses, subsequent messages, or how we organize our worlds? Again, the effect of communication on age-related phenomena is critical here in the current chapter; to what extent does communication shape our experience or perceptions of the aging process?

At other times, communication variables are considered as *mediators or moderators*. When communication serves as a mediator, it is affected by some other phenomenon and it subsequently affects something else; often the mediator role is an explanatory one. For instance, if people with a particular personality type are less likely to have successful romantic relationships, communication might explain that by demonstrating that the personality trait leads to communication behaviors (e.g., poor conflict management skills) that result in the relevant outcome. In a moderating position, communication changes the relationship between other variables. For instance, the effect of a negative trait on relational outcomes might be moderated by a *partner's* communication. A partner who says the right thing to *elicit* appropriate conflict management might break the personality → relational failure connection; a different partner message might exacerbate the connection. Hayes (2013) provides an in-depth discussion of the theoretical role of mediators and moderators, as well as access to sophisticated analytical tools to investigate such relationships.

These are crude sketches, but they should illustrate that the questions we ask about communication place it in many positions in social processes. It should be clear that (a) communication could simultaneously be functioning in multiple causal positions (e.g., we might study the effect of one message on another message, and that effect might be moderated by some other communication phenomenon in the environment), but (b) given that theories tend to be designed to explain some specific phenomenon, it is unlikely that a single theory will be equally sensitive to each of these roles of communication. Figure 1 illustrates this broad conceptualization of interconnections between communication and aging. At a fundamental level, given the objective and inevitable fact of the passing of time, chronological progression (objective aging) is framed as the starting point of the model; neither communication (nor anything else) influences this most basic process. However, not all theory or research need include chronological age as a primary variable; different perspectives would incorporate only portions of the framework, as elaborated next.

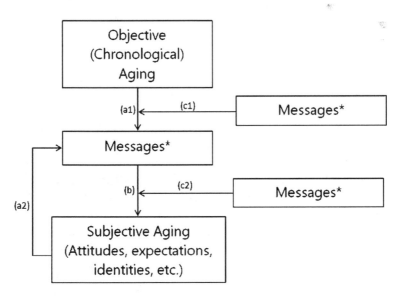

Figure 1. Conceptual model illustrating various roles played by communication in a lifespan-oriented model. As indicated by the asterisks, messages need not inhabit all of the positions indicated, but communication research and theory should include a message-relevant variable in at least one of the positions indicated.

Broad Approaches Linking Communication and Aging

Building on these "positionings" of communication, the next sections consider how age and communication might interact within these broad patterns. To begin, I consider communication as a dependent variable. In so doing, I examine how age influences communication phenomena, including the effects of sender and receiver age on the production and reception of communication.

Aging Influences Communication (Communication as DV)

Age of sender. The core research in this area examines the effects of various age-related declines on communication production and reception. For instance, the vocal characteristics of speech change with old age due to physiological changes in the vocal chords (Hooper & Cralidis, 2009). Older people also produce syntactically simpler speech, a phenomenon that has been explained as a function of normal declines in short-term memory function with old age (Rabaglia & Salthouse, 2011). Hearing loss similarly influences not just reception, but also message production. Villaume et al. (1997), for instance, discuss the effects of normal age-related high-frequency hearing loss (presbycusis) on turn taking in conversation. They suggest that presbycusis can shift conversational patterns in old age into exchanges whereby control over topic is exchanged between participants in longer turns, rather than the typical young-person pattern in which topics are quickly negotiated. In other words, age-related physiological changes can change the very structure of conversation.

Chronological age also influences communication processes via more subtle emotional processes. Older adults send messages differently within their social networks (Luong, Charles, & Fingerman, 2011). They respond differently to conflict situations in marriage, for instance, by letting things go or by engaging negative communication with positive responses (Levenson, Carstensen, & Gottman, 1994). Such responses fit within the scope of socioemotional selectivity theory (SST: Carstensen, 1992), which suggests that this change reflects a shift in the emotional regulatory focus of older adults. The theory suggests that older adults have a shorter time horizon than younger people (they recognize they do not have as long to live), and therefore their priorities in social relationships change. While younger people might acknowledge the utility of social relations that they don't enjoy (e.g., in career advancement), older adults focus on the relationships that provide the broadest emotional rewards and jettison relationships that are peripheral, unrewarding, or stressful. Perhaps related to some of these socioemotional processes, communicative phenomena like storytelling also change with age. Young couples describing a vacation, for instance, will give more itinerary-like descriptions of the experience; older adults focus to a greater degree on the emotional dimensions of the experience (Gould & Dixon, 1993; Nussbaum & Bettini, 1994). The processes described thus far (and undoubtedly others) fit within path (a1) of Figure 1. Research examining childhood development in the production of language and more sophisticated social messages would also fit within this broad area.

Communication may also serve age-related functions concerning survival and well-being. Heckhausen, Wrosch, and Schulz (2010) argue that primary control capacity declines in older adulthood—our ability to directly and personally control some outcomes is diminished by physiological and societal influences. We respond to this both with compensatory strategies (attempting to regain primary control) and secondary control (attempting to come to terms with the loss of primary control). The integration of communication into these areas has not been directly examined, but is fundamentally relevant. Communication is sometimes a focal primary control concern. For instance, the ability to communicate clearly and effectively is made salient after experiencing a stroke that impairs communication. Perhaps more interestingly, however, communication is also a fundamental concern in the areas of compensation and secondary control. The ways in which people seek out help with tasks, for instance, falls squarely in the area of compensatory control strategies, and seeking help typically involves communication. Knowing how, when, and from whom to seek help deserves more attention as a lifespan communicative phenomenon. Similarly, the process by which people come to terms with their own aging and resolve their primary control losses is undoubtedly in part a communicative process—goal disengagement in Heckhausen's terms (Gill & Morgan, 2011). Uncertainty reduction and social comparison mechanisms, for instance, surround events wherein people talk about their age in order to understand more about what it means, how they are doing relative to other people of similar ages, and the extent to which their experience is "normal" (J. Coupland, Coupland, Giles, & Henwood, 1991). Secondary control processes also typically involve communicative phenomena as people attempt to motivate themselves to pursue a valued goal, avoid distractions, and the like. This should at times occur through interpersonal processes—particularly insofar as social processes sometimes remove control and hence decrease volition to pursue specific goals (M. Baltes & Wahl, 1996; Langer & Rodin, 1976; Rodin & Langer, 1977).

Chronological age also brings with it an aging identity; age is freighted with subjective meaning that manifests in specific communication behaviors and activities (path (a2) in Figure 1). For instance, once people self-categorize as old, they might be inclined to behave in ways consistent with the self-categorization (Turner, Hogg, Oakes, Reicher, & Wetherell, 1987) and talk in group-related ways (e.g., storytelling, dispensing advice, discussing health problems: J. Coupland et al., 1991). This includes phenomena such as age-b(i)ased accounting and attribution (Erber & Prager, 2000). Hence, theorizing in this area should consider the multifarious effects of objective and subjective aging on message production.

To provide just one more example, the SST processes described earlier probably operate at an intersection of subjective and objective age, being influenced both by absolute position in the lifespan as well as each individual's specific feelings and interpretations of that position.

Age of receiver. The age of the communication receiver also influences aspects of the communication process. Starting in a similar place to the previous subsection, short-term memory processes have effects here: older adults have a harder time understanding complex syntax (Kemper & Harden, 1999). Similarly, the previously discussed hearing loss in older adulthood affects message reception (particularly in noisy environments). Older people can have trouble identifying who said what in a multi-party conversation and have particular problems distinguishing the direction from which sounds are coming (Abel, Giguère, Consoli, & Papsin, 2000). This again fits within path (a1) in Figure 1; in this case the message variable is comprehension. Normal aging's effects on comprehension have influenced the development of practical tools designed to help professionals work effectively with aging populations (e.g., Gerontological Society of America, 2012). One theoretical area engaging with these issues is research on compensation strategies. For instance, P. Baltes's (1997) selective optimization and compensation (SOC) framework explains various ways in which older adults compensate for declining function in one area, while simultaneously optimizing function in areas that retain strength.

When we consider the age of the receiver, we should also consider that recipients of communication are active participants who seek out (and avoid) specific messages. Substantial recent work on media processes demonstrates that older adults seek out different media messages and appear to get different rewards from consuming those media compared to younger people (Harwood, 1997). To understand such age-related changes in message behavior, we need to examine age-related change in motivations, desires, perceived gratifications related to the media, as well as the broader social context. Riggs's (1996) ethnographic work on media consumption in a retirement community provides a rich illustration of such a conceptualization. She demonstrates connections between lifespan position, social context, background variables like socioeconomic status, and the critical links between interpersonal and mass communication. Given that this work extends beyond the influence of chronological age and into the subjective meaning of aging, it fits within path (a2) of Figure 1.

The age of the receiver also influences the nature of messages directed *toward* older adults. Models and theories in this area focus on how people (typically younger people) talking *to* older people will make adjustments to their speech as a function of recipient age (path (a2)). Grounded in communication accommodation theory, this research has resulted in multiple models of the communication and aging process (e.g., Hummert, 1994; Ryan, Giles, Bartolucci & Henwood, 1986). These models emphasize the ways in which speech directed at older adults is sometimes grounded in stereotypes; the recipient's age elicits cognitive representations of decrement, for instance, and so a simplified message is produced. Hummert (1994) notes that stereotypes can be positive or negative, and that communication reflects the specific content of the cognitive representation.

A complex model in this broad region is the social input model (Fingerman, Miller, & Charles, 2008; Luong et al., 2011). This model suggests that features associated with age (sociostructural factors, time horizons, and positive stereotypes) lead older adults to seek out positive interactions. The same features establish a more positive social environment *for* older adults (e.g., via younger people treating them more positively: paths (a1) and (a2)). The more positive communication experienced by older adults in that environment feeds into more satisfying conversations and relationships for older people.

Communication Influences Aging (Communication as IV)

This section outlines theoretical perspectives bearing on the constructive influence of communication in shaping beliefs about, or the actual experience of, aging (path (b)).

Beliefs about aging. The most straightforward theoretical frame for understanding the influence of communication on aging comes from work in the contact theory paradigm. Work in this area suggests that interpersonal contact (from our perspective, contact = communication) with older people will influence attitudes about older adults and aging (Allport, 1954; Harwood, 2010).

Interpersonally, work has demonstrated that contact has positive effects, and that they appear to occur via processes of reducing uncertainty and increasing accommodative communication (Harwood, Hewstone, Paolini, & Voci, 2005). Effects of interpersonal contact are enhanced when group memberships are salient (e.g., when a grandparent is viewed as a typical older person), but group salience also has downsides in terms of increasing the likelihood of negative interaction (Barlow et al., 2012).

While originally grounded in interpersonal communication, the theory has expanded to consider contact through traditional and new media channels (Harwood, 2010). The content analytic literature has convincingly demonstrated that media portrayals of aging are rare, and that when they occur they are negative (Robinson & Anderson, 2006). Such portrayals, at least under some circumstances, have the capacity to influence people's stereotypes and attitudes about old age (Donlon, Ashman, & Levy, 2005). Early work on this was grounded in cultivation theory (Gerbner, Gross, Signorielli, & Morgan, 1980; see Passuth & Cook, 1985, for debate about these effects). More broadly, perspectives involving priming, framing, and indeed any perspective on message effects could conceivably and usefully be extended to understanding the effects of messages on beliefs and attitudes about aging.

The experience of aging. Communication is powerful; it can profoundly affect our mood, and long-term communication serves as the primary medium through which our social relationships prosper or perish. As such, it is not surprising that communication has been linked to fundamental aspects of function and survival in old age. In a nursing home context, for example, subtle differences in communication about self-efficacy and dependency can affect physical health in ways that are traditionally seen as symptoms of aging (Rodin & Langer, 1977). Communication serves to construct and reinforce age-related *identities* and indeed the "presence" of age in a given context. For instance, from different perspectives both N. Coupland, Coupland, and Giles (1989; J. Coupland et al., 1991) and Harwood, Raman, and Hewstone (2006) note that specific ways of talking can increase or decrease the relevance of age in a given exchange. Understanding communication as the mechanism by which age is viewed as *relevant* puts communication in a very powerful position; it is the source of subsequent age-related psychological, behavioral, and physiological processes.

In other words, when we consider communication as an independent variable, it sensitizes us to how aging itself is socially constructed. The decline and decrement traditionally (and stereotypically) associated with old age may occur as a function of some of the ways in which we communicate about, and to, older adults.

There is considerable potential here for the integration of additional areas of study from within the field of communication. Notably, research on uncertainty-related processes is burgeoning in psychology and communication, with implications for aging. Boundaries between age groups are by definition fuzzy, and talk about aging must be, in part, an attempt to reduce uncertainty about where I belong (am I middle-aged? old?) as well as negotiating the meaning of that age categorization (Bytheway, 2005), or negotiating specific age-related challenges (Gill & Morgan, 2011). In other words, communication constructs the boundaries between age groups and the ensuing self- and other categorizations (Giles & Reid, 2005). Communication may also be strategically used to maintain uncertainty about age categories and boundaries, for instance, when a particular categorization is undesirable (Brashers et al., 2000). Such approaches place communication as the fundamental process variable determining the meaning of age and aging.

Communication as Mediator

The two previous sections actually cover considerable ground concerning the role of communication as mediator. In a sense, those sections have artificially sliced up the message process into digestible chunks, but in fact simply combining the two results in some sophisticated perspectives on mediation. Returning to Figure 1, if chronological aging influences communication (a1), and communication influences subjective aging (b), then communication is positioned as a mediator. For instance, chronological age might lead to a more easygoing communication style, which in turn might improve a hearer's attitudes about aging. Of course, communication could mediate between age and some non-age-related variable (e.g., age → easy-going communication style → more satisfying conversation). Likewise, some non-age-related variable could influence communication, which subsequently influences an aging process (e.g., physician authoritarianism → patronizing communication style to older adult → older adult passive approach to health care).

One widely used theoretical model in the communication and aging area that incorporates a sophisticated mediation model is the communication predicament of aging model (Ryan et al., 1986). This model notes that (chronological) age provides cues (e.g., older people's physiognomy) that activate age-related stereotypes in younger people. Those stereotypes influence the communication used by the young person toward the older person—often in ways that are patronizing to the older person or involve "elderspeak" (Kemper & Harden, 1999; Nussbaum, Pitts, Huber, Krieger, & Ohs, 2005). This in turn influences the (subjective) experiences associated with aging for the older person. As such, the model integrates the effects of chronological aging on communication (as facilitated by age-related stereotyping), while simultaneously demonstrating the effects of communication on age-related processes at the individual and societal levels.

A brief mention of macro-level communication processes is warranted here. For instance, sociologists and anthropologists have considered the role of modernization in social stratification processes related to age (Diamond, 2012, Chapter 6). In more complex modern societies, they argue that age loses prestige. For instance, when an oral culture is replaced by a literate one, the value of older people's knowledge declines because the knowledge can be codified and accessed without the need to personally consult with an older person. Technological developments marginalize older adults by rendering their expertise in old technologies obsolete (Hagestad & Uhlenberg, 2005). Communication is deeply involved in many of these processes: modernization results in new forms, styles, and media of communication, and these processes ultimately marginalize older people. The extent to which broader social processes precipitate marginalization of older people via symbolic representations of age hence emerges as a mediated process.

Communication as Moderator

Existing models of communication and aging have not considered communication primarily in the moderator role; hence this section is a little more speculative than the previous sections. At least two broad conceptual roles for communication fit this position in the model. Communication is a moderator to the extent that it affects relationships between aging and other variables (including, of course, other communication variables) (path (c1) in Figure 1), or when it moderates the association between a variable (including a communication-related variable) and subjective aspects of age (path (c2)).

In the former position, we should be concerned about the multifarious ways in which communication moderates what might typically be seen as "effects" of aging. For example, as described earlier, socioemotional selectivity theory suggests that aging leads to shorter time horizons and an emphasis on closer and more positive social interactions and relationships. Communication would moderate this process to the extent that messages shifted the time horizon for older people. Such messages could have critically important consequences in decision making concerning retirement planning or adjustments in living situations. A message that lengthens one's time horizon, for instance, might change associations between chronological aging and emphasis on retirement planning, decisions to move in with one's adult children, or willingness to engage problematic areas in relationships (rather than avoiding conflict). Messages having these effects might include simple life-expectancy statistics tailored to the individual—the time-horizon effects of feeling "old" at age 70 might be shifted by being made aware of the relatively high probability of living another 20 years. Other parallel effects could be imagined wherein communication might reduce or enhance the effects of aging on other phenomena. Löckenhoff and Carstensen (2004) address these issues in the context of the impact of older adults' positivity bias in health decision making, noting that appropriate message construction could be used to counter biases introduced by socioemotional selectivity issues.

The latter position (c2) would concern the ways communication might change the association between some other phenomenon and subjective beliefs or perceptions of aging. Earlier, I discussed the application of contact theory to aging, noting the ways in which contact with older people affects attitudes about aging. Contact effects are moderated by group typicality—contact with members of a group has stronger effects when the contacted group members are seen as typical or representative of their groups (Brown & Hewstone, 2005). Contact with an older adult who is perceived to be a typical older adult has stronger effects on ageist attitudes than contact with an unusual old person (Harwood et al., 2005). If typicality is a moderator, then communication phenomena that enhance perceptions of typicality should also serve as moderators in this position; research suggests that explicit disclosure of age, painful self-disclosures about health, and communicative manifestations of cognitive or sensory deficits all enhance age salience (Harwood et al., 2006). Given the negative tone of many of these, seeking potentially positive salience-enhancing communicative phenomena should be a focus for future work in this area (Paolini, Harwood, & Rubin, 2010).

An Exemplar: Communication Accommodation Theory

One theoretical approach that has appeared in multiple places throughout this chapter is communication accommodation theory (CAT; Giles, Coupland, & Coupland, 1991). This theory provides unique opportunities for development of a true lifespan communication framework, one that incorporates the multiple roles communication can play in a social process, as well as the multiple positions of age and aging within social interaction. To give a sense of this promise, the following represent four processes incorporating complex interrelationships of age and communication that are squarely within the remit of CAT.

Categorization

CAT considers objective communication changes that occur as a function of objective aging, as well as the consequences of those for social categorization. At the core of accommodation theory is the idea that we respond to others based on cues that lead to categorization. The role of communication in that categorization has been apparent since very early CAT research looking at the effects of accent and language on categorization and subsequent interpersonal behavior. As a result, accommodation theory is well equipped to form a bridge between the physiological and socio-psychological factors that influence changing communication style with age and the interpersonal consequences of those changes.

Stereotyping and Attitudes

As discussed at some length earlier, accommodation theory explains considerable variance in intergenerational behavior and the ways in which communication is shaped by perceptions of aging. Hence, CAT makes straightforward and specific predictions of how people's attitudes and stereotypes influence their interpersonal behavior. Younger people with more paternalistic attitudes would be more likely to engage in overaccommodative and dependence-supportive behaviors toward older people; contexts and older adult targets that enhance the salience of more negative or dependent stereotypes would enhance the effects of stereotyping (Hummert, 2010). This work has extended to analyses of how older adults might effectively respond to such communication (Ryan, Kennaley, Pratt, & Shumovich, 2000) and the physical and contextual characteristics that ameliorate or encourage it (Hummert, 2010).

Levels of Analysis

With its extensions into vitality and ethnolinguistic identity, CAT is more flexibly applied across levels of analysis than many other theories (e.g., Giles & Johnson, 1987). For instance, contemporary discourse features distinct foreboding about the effect of the aging population on macroeconomic factors. Incorporating these discourses of intergenerational competition and shifting age group vitality, CAT would predict shifts toward more divergent intergenerational communication, and broader societal shifts in generationally specific language use (e.g., youth argots incomprehensible to older people).

Lifespan Changes

CAT has not explicitly considered lifespan development in accommodative tendencies (indeed it has remained relatively underdeveloped in terms of individual and "demographic" differences overall). However, SST and selective optimization and compensation approaches suggest a strong theoretical basis for examining age-related trends in accommodation. Specifically, SST would predict that older adults have more sophisticated accommodation skills, and that they will put more energy and activity into accommodation. The lifespan experience of social relations (behavioral practice), adjusting time horizons (motivation), and increasing knowledge (wisdom) suggest that older people should be able to manage complex social moments with more skill (Hess & Auman, 2001; Luong et al., 2011). Data from older marriages support this contention (Carstensen, Gottman, & Levenson, 1995; Hatch & Bulcroft, 2004). Similarly, the control strategies literature mentioned earlier suggests that control motivations become more urgent and complex with advanced age (Heckhausen et al., 2010). A number of these concerns can easily be framed as accommodation issues. For instance, Heckhausen et al. (2010) would suggest that accommodative practices should follow control motivations, with more attention paid (and presumably more successful accommodation achieved) in contexts in which the interaction is serving an important control motivation.

In other words, accommodation theory comfortably recognizes both objective and subjective aspects of aging. It acknowledges the ways in which aging affects communication as a function of physiological and psychological processes and also handles the identity and categorization processes associated with old age and intergenerational relations. It fully incorporates the interpersonal and societal levels of analysis. This is not to suggest that CAT is fully developed; as noted above, it could benefit from more attention in terms of individual differences in accommodative skills, motivations, and propensities. The theory would also benefit from more explicit attention to hypothesis generation in the newer areas of its development. Since the introduction of concepts like overaccommodation and underaccommodation to the theory (N. Coupland, Coupland, Giles, & Henwood, 1988), there have been relatively few attempts to develop specific hypotheses as to the circumstances that might lead to such behaviors. The overaccommodation literature has flourished in examining patronizing talk (elderspeak, secondary baby talk) to older adults (Hummert & Ryan, 2001), but beyond this, there has not been extensive development of the construct. Underaccommodation work remains largely restricted to a limited literature on painful self-disclosure (J. Coupland, Coupland, Giles, & Wiemann, 1988). The intergenerational context, as the origin of the development of these terms, would be a reasonable place to start in terms of generating specific hypotheses for when and where underaccommodation and overaccommodation would be most likely and elaborating on the specific communication dynamics surrounding them.

CONCLUSIONS

This chapter has provided a structure for various positions in which communication can be understood in relation to aging and lifespan development: communication as independent, dependent, moderator, and mediator variable. On one level, placing communication in all these positions dilutes our ability to develop singular coherent theoretical positions on communication and the lifespan. On another level, it is itself a theoretical testament to communication as fundamental to human aging. Communication is the water and we are the fish (Carey, 1989). We swim through it, sometimes actively seeking certain areas, and at other times passively absorbing it. It changes us, while we often barely notice it. At times, aging is fundamental to how we conceive of and present ourselves communicatively. As noted by N. Coupland (2004), the "discursive negotiation of the life course" (p. 77) is an ongoing project for all of us; our language does not merely reflect our age, it constructs who we are for others and ourselves.

Psychologists and biologists sometimes appear to have co-opted the lifespan territory, and particularly old age. In some communication research, the psychological and biological changes are treated as the "real" stuff of lifespan development, with communication serving as a symptom of such changes or perhaps as contributing to such changes. This chapter has by no means avoided this trap. But for a true *communication-based* lifespan theory to take hold and contribute, communication needs to take a more central place in the theoretical structure. We need to discover ways of writing and talking that make communication the phenomenon *central* to our discussions. Perhaps explaining and understanding communication must be more of an end in itself and less of a means to understanding biological and psychological issues. One of the best illustrations of this sort of work comes from research on conversational (collaborative) remembering. Pasupathi (2001) describes how *conversations* about the past embody memory processes in ways that are more accurate and more meaningfully connected to people's real lives than traditional "memories" in the brain. Memories are meaningful to the extent that they are presented, shared, and transformed within our personal relationships, and it is in the study of communication that we can fully appreciate how such processes occur.

REFERENCES

Abel, S. M., Giguère, C., Consoli, A., & Papsin, B. C. (2000). The effect of aging on horizontal plane sound localization. *Journal of the Acoustical Society of America, 108,* 743–752.

Allport, G. W. (1954). *The nature of prejudice.* Reading, MA: Addison-Wesley.

Antonucci, T. C., & Akiyama, H. (1995). Convoys of social relations: Family and friendships within a life span context. In R. Blieszner & V. H. Bedford (Eds.), *Handbook of aging and the family* (pp. 355–372). Westport, CT: Greenwood Press.

Baltes, M. M., & Wahl, H. (1996). Patterns of communication in old age: The dependence-support and independence-ignore script. *Health Communication, 8,* 217–232.

Baltes, P. B. (1987). Theoretical propositions of life-span developmental psychology: On the dynamics between growth and decline. *Developmental Psychology, 23,* 611–626.

Baltes, P. B. (1997). On the incomplete architecture of human ontogeny: Selection, optimization and compensation as foundation of developmental theory. *American Psychologist, 52,* 366–380.

Barlow, F. K., Paolini, S., Pedersen, A., Hornsey, M. J., Radke, H. R. M., Harwood, J., Rubin, M., & Sibley, C. G. (2012). The contact caveat: Negative contact predicts increased prejudice more than positive contact predicts reduced prejudice. *Personality and Social Psychology Bulletin.* doi:10.1177/0146167212457953

Brashers, D. E., Neidig, J. L., Haas, S. M., Dobbs, L. K., Cardillo, L. W., & Russell, J. A. (2000). Communication in the management of uncertainty: The case of persons living with HIV or AIDS. *Communication Monographs, 67,* 63–84.

Brown, R., & Hewstone, M. (2005). An integrative theory of intergroup contact. In M. P. Zanna (Ed.), *Advances in experimental social psychology* (Vol. 37, pp. 255–342). San Diego, CA: Elsevier.

Bytheway, B. (2005). Ageism and age categorization. *Journal of Social Issues, 61*(2), 361–374.

Carey, J. W. (1989). *Communication as culture: Essays on media and society.* Winchester, MA: Unwin Hyman.

Carstensen, L. L. (1992). Social and emotional patterns in adulthood: Support for socio-emotional selectivity theory. *Psychology and Aging, 7,* 331–338.

Carstensen, L. L., Gottman, J. M., & Levenson, R. W. (1995). Emotional behavior in long-term marriage. *Psychology and Aging, 10,* 140–149.

Coupland, J., Coupland, N., Giles, H., & Henwood, K. (1991). Formulating age: Dimensions of age identity in elderly talk. *Discourse Processes, 14*(1), 87–106.

Coupland, J., Coupland, N., Giles, H., & Wiemann, J. M. (1988). My life in your hands: Processes of self-disclosure in intergenerational talk. In N. Coupland (Ed.), *Styles of discourse* (pp. 201–253). London, England: Croom Helm.

Coupland, N. (2004). Age in social and sociolinguistic theory. In J. F. Nussbaum & J. Coupland (Eds.), *Handbook of communication and aging research* (2nd ed., pp. 69–90). Mahwah, NJ: Erlbaum.

Coupland, N., Coupland, J., & Giles, H. (1989). Telling age in later life: Identity and face implications. *Text, 9*, 129–151.

Coupland, N., Coupland, J., Giles, H., & Henwood, K. (1988). Accommodating the elderly: Invoking and extending a theory. *Language in Society, 17*, 1–41.

Diamond, J. (2012). *The world until yesterday.* New York, NY: Viking.

Donlon, M. M., Ashman, O., & Levy, B. R. (2005). Re-vision of older television characters: A stereotype-awareness intervention. *Journal of Social Issues, 61*, 307–319.

Erber, J. T., & Prager, I. G. (2000). Age and excuses for forgetting: Self-handicapping versus damage-control strategies. *International Journal of Aging and Human Development, 50*, 201–214.

Erikson, E. H. (1968). *Identity: Youth and crisis.* New York, NY: Norton.

Fingerman, K. L., Miller, L., & Charles, S. (2008). Saving the best for last: How adults treat social partners of different ages. *Psychology and Aging, 23*(2), 399–409.

Gerbner, G., Gross, L., Signorielli, N., & Morgan, M. (1980). Aging with television: Images on television drama and conceptions of social reality. *Journal of Communication, 30*(1), 37–48.

Gerontological Society of America. (2012). *Communicating with older adults: An evidence-based review of what really works.* Washington, DC: Author.

Giles, H., Coupland, J., & Coupland, N. (1991). Accommodation theory: Communication, context, and consequence. In H. Giles, J. Coupland, & N. Coupland (Eds.), *Contexts of accommodation* (pp. 1–68). Cambridge: Cambridge University Press.

Giles, H., Davis, S. M., Gasiorek, J., & Giles, J. (2013). *Successful aging: A communication guide to empowerment.* Girona, Spain: Editorial Aresta.

Giles, H., & Johnson, P. (1987). Ethnolinguistic identity theory: A social psychological approach to language maintenance. *International Journal of the Sociology of Language, 68*, 66–99.

Giles, H., & Reid, S. A. (2005). Ageism across the lifespan: Towards a self-categorization model of ageing. *Journal of Social Issues, 61*(2), 389–404.

Gill, E. A., & Morgan, M. (2011). Home sweet home: Conceptualizing and coping with the challenges of aging and the move to a care facility. *Health Communication, 26*, 332–342.

Gould, O. N., & Dixon, R. A. (1993). How we spent our vacation: Collaborative storytelling by young and old adults. *Psychology and Aging, 8*, 10–17.

Haase, C. M., Heckhausen, J., & Wrosch, C. (2013). Developmental regulation across the life span: Toward a new synthesis. *Developmental Psychology, 49*, 964–972. doi:10.1037/a0029231

Hagestad, G. O., & Uhlenberg, P. (2005). The social separation of old and young: A root of ageism. *Journal of Social Issues, 61*, 343–360.

Harwood, J. (1997). Viewing age: Lifespan identity and television viewing choices. *Journal of Broadcasting and Electronic Media, 41*, 203–213.

Harwood, J. (2007). *Understanding communication and aging: Developing knowledge and awareness.* Thousand Oaks, CA: Sage.

Harwood, J. (2010). The contact space: A novel framework for intergroup contact research. *Journal of Language and Social Psychology, 29*, 147–177.

Harwood, J., Hewstone, M., Paolini, S., & Voci, A. (2005). Grandparent-grandchild contact and attitudes towards older adults. *Personality and Social Psychology Bulletin, 31*, 393–406.

Harwood, J., Raman, P., & Hewstone, M. (2006). Communicative dynamics of age salience. *Journal of Family Communication, 6*, 181–200.

Hatch, L. R., & Bulcroft, K. (2004). Does long-term marriage bring less frequent disagreements? Five explanatory frameworks. *Journal of Family Issues, 25*, 465–495.

Hayes, A. F. (2013). *Introduction to mediation, moderation, and conditional process analysis: A regression-based approach.* New York, NY: Guilford.

Heckhausen, J., Wrosch, C., & Schulz, R. (2010). A motivational theory of life-span development. *Psychological Review, 117*, 32–60.

Hedden, T., & Gabrieli, J. D. E. (2004). Insights into the ageing mind: A view from cognitive neuroscience. *Nature Reviews Neuroscience, 5*, 87–96. doi:10.1038/nrn1323

Hepworth, M. (2004). Images of ageing. In J. Nussbaum & J. Coupland (Eds.), *Handbook of communication and aging research* (pp. 3–29). Mahwah, NJ: Erlbaum.

Hess, T. M., & Auman, C. (2001). Aging and social expertise: The impact of trait-diagnostic information on impressions of others. *Psychology and Aging, 16*, 497–510.

Hooper, C. R., & Cralidis, A. (2009). Normal changes in the speech of older adults: You've still got what it takes; it just takes a little longer! *Perspectives on Gerontology, 14*(2), 47–56.

Hummert, M. L. (1994). Stereotypes of the elderly and patronizing speech. In M. L. Hummert, J. M. Wiemann, & J. F. Nussbaum (Eds.), *Interpersonal communication in older adulthood: Interdisciplinary theory and research* (pp. 162–184). Newbury Park, CA: Sage.

Hummert, M. L. (2010). Communicating across generations. In H. Giles, S. Reid, & J. Harwood (Eds.), *Dynamics of intergroup communication* (pp. 41–52). New York, NY: Peter Lang.

Hummert, M. L., & Ryan, E. B. (2001). Patronizing. In W. P. Robinson & H. Giles (Eds.), *The new handbook of language and social psychology* (pp. 253–270). Chichester, England: John Wiley.

Kemper, S., & Harden, T. (1999). Experimentally disentangling what's beneficial about elderspeak from what's not. *Psychology and Aging, 14*, 656–670.

Kemper, S., Rash, S., Kynette, D., & Norman, S. (1990). Telling stories: The structure of adults' narratives. *European Journal of Cognitive Psychology, 2*, 205–228.

Langer, E. J., & Rodin, J. (1976). The effects of choice and enhanced personal responsibility for the aged: A field experiment in an institutional setting. *Journal of Personality and Social Psychology, 34*, 191–198.

Levenson, R. W., Carstensen, L. L., & Gottman, J. M. (1994). The influence of age and gender on affect, physiology, and their interrelations: A study of long-term marriage. *Journal of Personality and Social Psychology, 67*, 56–68.

Löckenhoff, C. E., & Carstensen, L. L. (2004). Socioemotional selectivity theory, aging, and health: The increasingly delicate balance between regulating emotions and making tough choices. *Journal of Personality, 72*, 1395–1424.

Luong, G., Charles, S. T., & Fingerman, K. L. (2011). Better with age: Social relationships across adulthood. *Journal of Social and Personal Relationships, 28*(1), 9–23.

Masoro, E. J., & Austad, S. N. (Eds.). (2011). *Handbook of the biology of aging* (6th ed.). New York, NY: Academic Press.

Nussbaum, J. F. (2012). The communication of wisdom: The nature and impact of communication and language change across the life span. *Journal of Language and Social Psychology*. Advance online publication. doi:10.1177/0261927X12463009

Nussbaum, J. F., & Bettini, L. (1994). Shared stories of the grandparent-grandchild relationship. *International Journal of Aging and Human Development, 39*, 67–90.

Nussbaum, J. F., Pecchioni, L. L., Baringer, D. K., & Kundrat, A. L. (2002). Lifespan communication. In W. B. Gudykunst (Ed.), *Communication yearbook 26* (pp. 366–389). Mahwah, NJ: Erlbaum.

Nussbaum, J. F., Pitts, M. J., Huber, F. N., Krieger, J. L. R., & Ohs, J. E. (2005). Ageism and ageist language across the life span: Intimate relationships and non-intimate interactions. *Journal of Social Issues, 61*, 287–305.

Paolini, S., Harwood, J., & Rubin, M. (2010). Negative intergroup contact makes group memberships salient: Explaining why intergroup conflict endures. *Personality and Social Psychology Bulletin, 36*, 1723–1738. doi:10.1177/0146167210388667

Passuth, P. M., & Cook, F. L. (1985). Effects of television viewing on knowledge and attitudes about older adults: A critical reexamination. *The Gerontologist, 25*, 69–77.

Pasupathi, M. (2001). The social construction of the personal past and its implications for adult development. *Psychological Bulletin, 127*, 651–672. doi:10.1037//0033-2909.127.5.651

Pecchioni, L. L., Wright, K. B., & Nussbaum, J. F. (2005). *Life-span communication*. Mahwah, NJ: Erlbaum.

Pennebaker, J. W., & Stone, L. D. (2003). Words of wisdom: Language use over the lifespan. *Journal of Personality and Social Psychology, 85*, 291–301.

Rabaglia, C. D., & Salthouse, T. A. (2011). Natural and constrained language production as a function of age and cognitive abilities. *Language and Cognitive Processes, 26*, 1505–1531.

Rabbitt, P. (2011). Between-individual variability and interpretation of associations between neurophysiological and behavioral measures in aging populations: Comment on Salthouse (2011). *Psychological Bulletin, 137*, 785–789. doi:10.1037/a0024580

Riggs, K. (1996). Television use in a retirement community. *Journal of Communication, 46*, 144–156.

Robinson, T., & Anderson, C. (2006). Older characters in children's animated television programs: A content analysis of their portrayal. *Journal of Broadcasting and Electronic Media, 50*, 287–304.

Rodin, J., & Langer, E. J. (1977). Long-term effects of a control-relevant intervention with the institutionalized aged. *Journal of Personality and Social Psychology, 35*, 897–902.

Rowe, J. W., & Kahn, R. L. (1998). *Successful aging*. New York, NY: Random House.

Ryan, E. B., Giles, H., Bartolucci, G., & Henwood, K. (1986). Psycholinguistic and social psychological components of communication by and with the elderly. *Language and Communication, 6*, 1–24.

Ryan, E. B., Kennaley, D. E., Pratt, M. W., & Shumovich, M. A. (2000). Evaluations by staff, residents, and community seniors of patronizing speech: Impact of passive, assertive, or humorous responses. *Psychology and Aging, 15*, 272–285.

Salthouse, T. A. (2011). All data collection and analysis methods have limitations: Reply to Rabbitt (2011) and Raz and Lindenberger (2011). *Psychological Bulletin, 137*, 796–799. doi:10.1037/a0024843

Schaie, K. W., & Willis, S. L. (Eds.). (2010). *Handbook of the psychology of aging* (7th ed.). New York, NY: Academic Press.

Turner, J. C., Hogg, M. A., Oakes, P. J., Reicher, S. D., & Wetherell, M. (1987). *Rediscovering the social group: A self-categorization theory*. Oxford, England: Basil Blackwell.

Villaume, W. A., Brown, M. H., Darling, R., Richardson, D., Hawk, R., Henry, D. M., & Reid, T. (1997). Presbycusis and conversation: Elderly interactants adjusting to multiple hearing losses. *Research on Language & Social Interaction, 30*, 235–262.

CHAPTER TWO

Lifespan Communication Methodology

MARGARET J. PITTS AND MARY LEE HUMMERT

As early as the mid-1970s, researchers began to note both the potential for and naissance of a lifespan perspective in social sciences and especially lamented the insufficiency of methods developed to investigate continuity and change (Baltes, Reese, & Nesselroade, 1977). More than two decades later, Bronfenbrenner (1999) referred to the "evolution" of the lifespan approach as it developed within disciplines, especially with regard to psychology, that begins with the recognition and scholarly curiosity of a lifespan perspective and then moves to the evolution of the scientific models and measures used to explore developmental phenomena. In this way, the communication discipline follows suit. What communication lacks is a systematic way of thinking about and measuring communication as a developmental process. This is perhaps because of the relative newness of the scientific study of communication in comparison to its more established sister fields of psychology and sociology, for example, which have developed measurement tools and techniques for the study of lifespan processes. In writing this chapter, we borrow some methods and analytical tools from psychology, sociology, and other fields, but propose that the process of communication must be uniquely studied. Indeed, with the National Communication Association having reached its centennial year in 2014 and Eastern Communication Association (our oldest professional association) having reached the centennial milestone in 2010, it is time for those of us in the field to place human development at the foreground of our studies.

Placing a lifespan perspective at the center of communication research means recognizing and planning research that captures the notion that "any communicative event or series of events is made clearer when studied as a progression of events rather than as an isolated event.… [A] communicative event is often given meaning by the communicative events that have occurred previously" (Pecchioni, Wright, & Nussbaum, 2005, p. 261). Our ability to communicate develops as we age, and it is imperative that the field of communication begin to seek out, recognize, and study the gains and losses that accompany that development, as well as continuity and change, across the lifespan. The trend has been to equate aging with decline and create studies designed to capture/expose/accentuate declines rather than gains—such as improved storytelling capabilities (Kemper, Kynette, Rash, O'Brien, & Sprott, 1989). But when we consider communication as a developmental process that is deeply influenced by contextual features (family, culture, resources, ability, etc.), then we become more aware of the potential for positive change as well as declines over time. Indeed, the process starts before a child is born—as that child is born into a communication context—and continues through the end of life and beyond through conversations and the stories and legacies that are left behind.

Individuals build a communication repertoire with every interaction from childhood through older adulthood. Our socioemotional development occurs throughout the lifespan as people create, experience, and plan for important, meaningful, and engaging events. Communication has much to offer the developmental sciences, but its potential is still untapped. Like other disciplines, the traditional methods applied in research are not designed to capture change. Thus, we take our cue from Pecchioni et al. (2005) who write that "unique research methodologies are required to capture the nature of change across the lifespan" (p. 254). Toward this end, our chapter is organized under two main headings—qualitative methods/methodology and quantitative methods/methodology. We use this organizational structure only because it allows for clarity in describing different methods, not because we intend to identify one approach as more valid than the other. Indeed, we recognize a methodological continuum from qualitative to quantitative, rather than dichotomy, and agree with Pecchioni et al. that the multiple influences involved in development are not likely to be captured by one method. Ideally, data should be both qualitative and quantitative, at both micro and macro levels, and include both retrospective and prospective designs (Giele & Elder, 1998). Thus we include a discussion of mixed methods approaches as a third section of the chapter.

QUALITATIVE APPROACHES TO LIFESPAN RESEARCH

There are, of course, many approaches toward and philosophies of qualitative methodology making it difficult to provide a succinct overview. Yet, among the many possibilities for the collection and analysis of qualitative data, there are several threads that unify the process and purpose of qualitative research at its core (see Lindlof & Taylor, 2011; Miller, 2007). Generally speaking, qualitative research is subjective in nature, focusing on the lived experiences and practices of humans engaging in daily routines. It privileges in situ research occurring in natural contexts over controlled environments. It focuses on depth of understanding over breadth. One of the central goals of qualitative research is to offer a nuanced description of human interaction. In this way, it offers more explanatory power than predictive. Qualitative researchers often embrace the notion of multiple socially constructed realities and an understanding that what is known (truth) cannot be separated from the knower. Most important, qualitative research tends to privilege participants' knowledge, reasoning, and experiences over the researcher's.

Qualitative inquiry has much to offer lifespan communication. For example, qualitative research seeks out, recognizes, and values individual experiences and idiosyncratic lifespan trajectories providing increased insight into unique paths for human development. It allows scholars to look around the edges of "normative trajectories" and identify areas of enrichment, concern, and neglect not captured in standardized models of development. Qualitative methods are also uniquely designed to capture the contexts, content, and process of communication as well as people's communicative experiences. Qualitative methods also bring to the surface the process of meaning making and negotiation through numerous types of talk (e.g., storytelling, argumentation) and non-talk (e.g., silences, gestures) that might otherwise be overlooked. These advantages of approaching lifespan communication from a qualitative perspective can be roughly categorized into three broad approaches: Calendar and Diary Methods, Field Observations and Archival Methods, and Narrative and Interview Methods.

Calendar and Diary Methods

Within communication, and across sister disciplines, there are numerous labels for qualitative methods and analysis that make use of the meaning and interpretation assigned to life events. We have chosen to represent these here under "Calendar and Diary Methods" because of the use of significant dates and life events as central to data collection. Regardless of the specific terminology used (life history calendar, turning points, life events), "the use of life events and their timing as a means of organizing data on the life course makes sense both theoretically and practically" (Giele & Elder, 1998, p. 11).

The qualitative investigation of lifespan turning points is a meaningful way to collect lifespan data. Turning points can be conceptualized as "points of transformation" that may over time lead to a major transformation (personal or interpersonal change) through the sequencing of small turning points (Bolton, 1961). Although they may not be "dramatic" life events, upon reflection people are generally good at pinpointing turning points in one's life that influenced its trajectory. Turning points often include changes in role expectations that affect not only the developmental changes of individuals, but also the social systems in which they are involved (Bronfenbrenner, 1999). Indeed, many of our role transitions are predictable and therefore become important/meaningful entry points for the study of lifespan communication. Turning points allow researchers to examine the significance, meanings, and patterns of event history, the accumulation of experiences over time, and the subjective evaluation or interpretation of the event and experiences (Scott & Alwin, 1998). This can be done once or ongoing.

The family system, in particular, is a rich context for the study of lifespan turning points because of the many natural transitions and life situations that occur across the lifespan of the family (Hummert, 2007). Consider Dun's (2010) study on the transition from the child-parent relationship to a parent-grandparent relationship among first-time parents. For many couples the transition into parenthood is an expected role transition that has significant intergenerational implications. By charting the turning points experienced by new parents, Dun was able to identify communicative and relational events that led to role transitions and relational changes.

Similar to the turning points analyses often used in communication, Scott and Alwin (1998) support the use of life-history calendars (LHC) or event history data in which individuals record personal and family events and transitions. Although traditionally LHCs have been used in large-scale quantitative research, Nelson (2010) articulated its strengths as means to qualitatively capture nuanced longitudinal accounts of subjective experiences across the life course. In this strategy, participants indicate precise or general time frames of events and experiences, as well as phases and states of life transitions. Nelson described the standard LHC as "a printed matrix with temporal cues running horizontally and domain cues listed vertically. Researchers may partition temporal cues into months, years, or any time unit. Domain cues encompass indicators applicable to the study at hand. Common domain categories include births, marriages, living arrangements, and educational transitions" (p. 415). However, using the LHC in a more subjective manner offers greater flexibility in choosing time cues, domain cues, and starting points that optimize engaged participation with an interviewee. While the majority of LHC and turning point analyses are retrospective in nature (often employing the Retrospective Interview Technique; Huston, Surra, Fitzgerald, & Cate, 1981), they can also be prospective, asking people to chart out their expected or desired life course over the next several years. Moreover, written documents, such as calendars, scrapbooks, and diaries, can be collected from past events as well as the present part of an ongoing study (Rosenblatt & Fischer, 1993).

Recognizing the potential of both retrospective and prospective accounts puts into perspective the notion that "any point in the life span must be viewed dynamically as the consequence of past experience and future expectation as well as the integration of individual motive with external constraint" (Giele & Elder, 1998, p. 19). Moreover, as Clausen (1998) notes, a life events review or turning points analysis should not imply that respondents are in their later years of life, but rather that retrospective insight can occur at any time along the life course. Despite a clear preference for prospective accounts in lifespan research with a focus on present circumstances, retrospective accounts offer recollections about the past (see Scott & Alwin, 1998), which are not only frequently easier to obtain when considering important life events, but are also meaningful in their own right. Although Scott and Alwin describe retrospective reports as often being the result of "failed opportunities, lack of resources, or poor planning" (p. 100), when used with intention, good retrospective studies capitalize on opportunities and involve a good bit of planning, organization, and resources. Retrospective accounts are relevant to study, because (1) people often use present understandings of past events to make sense of both the present and future, and (2) retrospective accounts play a significant role in lifespan and intergenerational communication through storytelling and advice.

Finally, investigating turning points and life transitions can be a means of "compressing" and "traveling through" time. For example, using life course trajectories, we can anticipate many lifespan transitions and turning points. These present researchers with the opportunity to engage in (the admittedly oxymoronic) "short" longitudinal studies by examining events, experiences, and episodes leading up to an event, through the event, and following the event. Examples might include graduations, marriage, becoming a parent/grandparent, transition into or out of workplace, school grade transitions, military, international deployment or sojourns, retirement, death and dying, and so forth. Because these life events are frequently associated with developmental change, the span of time necessary to examine both continuity and change with respect to a particular life event can be significantly compressed.

Field Observations and Archives

Qualitative research on lifespan development and communication benefits from participation and observation in the natural environments or contexts in which interactions occur. Using field observation techniques and archives that document human experiences or milestones, the researcher is given access to the sites, processes, and repositories of meaning making. In other developmental fields, as well as communication, the family serves as an important unit of observation (Hummert, 2007), but other groups and social settings can be equally insightful. Indeed ethnographic field methods are especially suited to examining developmental processes of social groups and networks (see Brown 1999). This is in part because participant observation makes available the sequencing of events that might be useful in identifying developmental trends or influence strategies (Bradley, 1999).

Nevertheless, we use the family unit as our point of departure in this section. Families provide a unique context for lifespan studies not only because of the natural developmental cycle of a family,[1] but also because of the duration of many family relationships. It is well documented that some marital dyads and parent-child relationships can persist more than 60 years, and sibling relationships may live on even longer (Hummert, 2007; Menaghan & Godwin, 1993). Moreover, the family offers a bounded system (whether loosely connected or deeply enmeshed) that offers unique insight into the intergenerational process of development, although research rarely examines developmental processes for all family members simultaneously. Some of the studies on the "sandwich generation" take this into account, but do so primarily from the position of the adult child and less so from the important developmental stages of the children (maybe grandchildren) and elder parent (see Riley & Bowen, 2005). Extending research into three or more family generations is an important move forward (Hummert, 2007). It is important to recognize the system itself as well as the individual members of a system are all in some phase of development, continuity, and change.

Studying families also offers insight into the ways in which lifespan development is influenced by stereotypes and expectations of development and aging across the lifespan, for it is within this context that we can study the types of communication that facilitate or limit positive growth and development in later life (Hummert, 2007) as well as types of communication that facilitate or inhibit earlier developmental stages. Observing the family system makes it possible to see how individual and group development is mutually influential. One of the challenges, however, is that methods of data collection must change as humans age—researchers cannot collect the same types of data in the same ways from humans at varying stages of development. While direct observation of parent-infant interactions is feasible and would generate meaningful data, direct observation of parent-adolescent interactions or adult child–aging parent interactions is difficult and would not likely yield meaningful data without accompanying measurements such as interviews and observations of peer groups (Bradley, 1999).

Home or family observations are often quite restricted due to the fact that many make use of only a limited set of indicators in the environment and a single type of data (e.g., one interview with one family member or observing from only one vantage point; Bradley, 1999). Yet, in-home visits can provide a good opportunity to include process and environmental features necessary to capture and measure development. Bear in mind that participant observers must be able to establish a sense of household regularity, be free from interruption, and gain access to view the extent to which activities and interactions become more and more complex over time (Bronfenbrenner, 1999). Specifically, as Bradley noted, the same environment must be studied over time in multiple ways. The researcher must observe multiple indicators within the home environment including interactions (i.e., observations, interviews, narratives), archives (i.e., photos, documents, toys, books, resources available to members of the family), and living spaces (places of work, leisure, sleep). The observer must be present at different places/spaces in the environment, at different times, and for differing spans of time. This requires frequency, rapport, flexible spans of time, and multiple tools for collecting and measuring data from multiple data points. Researchers may also wish to collect diaries or provide workbooks or guided activities/programs for family members to complete.

Keep in mind that archival materials and other documents can be collected both retrospectively as well as part of an ongoing study (Rosenblatt & Fischer, 1993). Personal documents (love letters, diaries, photos, etc.) give insight into the past and processes of thought, behavior, interactions, and so forth occurring over time conveyed in the participants' own voice and without the restrictions or interference of a researcher. Archival data are also available to researchers through the Library of Congress as well as at university and historical archives such as the Murray Research Center at Radcliffe College. Communication scholars can even consider less traditional sources such as the archived interviews by Studs Terkel (http://www.studsterkel.org) or Storycorps (www.storycorps.org).

Narrative and Interview

Walter Fisher (1984) described humans as homo narrans—storytelling man—because of our natural capacity and drive to engage in narrative, stories, and storytelling in everyday speech. Indeed, from this perspective much of the way we make sense of our world and our experiences is through narrative including both traditional storytelling and the more abstract notion that all communication is narrative. Because narrative is so much a part of the human experience, narrative research is an especially powerful tool for the study of lifespan communication, as it can be successfully applied across all phases of the lifespan from infancy and toddlerhood to elder adulthood (Miller, 2007). Inviting narratives from research participants offers insight into the ways in which they make sense of their own lives, but also how they might imagine their future. A life story interview, for example, provides respondents opportunities to look at their life from "within, backward, and forward" (Clausen, 1998, p. 194). Life reviews are not necessarily factual accounts, but rather a reflection of a constellation of variables including the context and circumstances under which the story was prompted, the respondent's current life positionings and relationships, accumulation of other life experiences and knowledge, and accuracy of memories, among other things. Still, the facticity of such accounts is not necessarily the most important element. As Clausen writes, life reviews provide

> Knowledge of how the person sees his or her past and present life and the influences that helped to shape it. [This entails] a person's presentation of self and, potentially, may reveal how that self developed over time, especially if the accounts have a longitudinal perspective. There is, indeed, no better way to get at the elements that have become most firmly integrated into a person's sense of identity than a thoughtful account, whether spontaneous or elicited by prolonged, empathic interviewing. (p. 191)

Although the life review or life story interview reveals much about the individual and their development, there are many types of interviews, each yielding a subtly different outcome. Ethnographic interviews, for example, allow the researcher to learn about the interviewee, but the real target of the interview is to learn about the culture or social system in which the interviewee inhabits (Super & Harkness, 1999).

Like observational studies, longitudinal research that uses narratives and interviews benefits from supplementary materials such as diaries, newspaper clippings, school papers, letters, photographs, and so forth. Use of personal documents can stimulate and add depth to the discussion, as well as offer opportunities to triangulate data for accuracy and to look for points of intrigue or gaps in knowledge or narrative threads.

QUANTITATIVE APPROACHES TO LIFESPAN RESEARCH

Three primary characteristics have come to describe research endeavors from a life course perspective: process, change, and continuity. The qualitative methods discussed in the previous section of this chapter will enable researchers to investigate these factors, providing useful knowledge for understanding perceptions about the relationship between past and current communication phenomena and how those relationships might influence future communication. However, Baltes et al. (1977) suggest that it is not enough to account for change through naturalistic description of events and phenomena. Instead, they believe that scholars must also inquire about the determinants and mechanisms that contribute to change, tasks which demand a focus on measurement and quantitative analysis. Achieving these goals entails the use of experiments and surveys, the basics of which are well described elsewhere (Campbell & Stanley, 1963; Cook & Campbell, 1979; Crano & Brewer, 2002). Here we address two topics: (1) cross-sectional and longitudinal research designs to study development, including archival resources for longitudinal data sets; and (2) statistical methods that can reveal inter-individual and intra-individual change.

Study Designs: Cross-Sectional Versus Longitudinal

One of the first decisions in designing a study of lifespan communication involves determining whether the phenomena of interest can be identified by comparing performance of those in different age groups at a single point in time (a cross-sectional design) or whether they can be identified only by following individuals over time (a longitudinal design). Each approach to design has its advantages and disadvantages. Cross-sectional designs have the advantage of economy of resources in that they enable investigation of the performance of people in different age groups within a limited time frame without any need to maintain contact with the participants after the study is completed. However, cross-sectional designs may lead researchers to mistakenly attribute cohort differences between those in different age groups to developmental differences (Baltes et al., 1977; Miller, 2007).

Hummert and Nussbaum (2013) outline several strategies for designing cross-sectional research to assess existence of developmental differences, two of which are highlighted here. First, design the study to rule out alternative theoretical explanations (including cohort) for the developmental hypotheses. Second, carefully select the measurement strategies and materials to ensure that age differences in physical status (e.g., response time) or familiarity with the measurement strategy (e.g., computer games) are not confounded with the variables of interest. As an example of the first strategy, Nussbaum and Hummert cite a study of age group differences in stereotypes of older people (Hummert, Garstka, Shaner, & Strahm, 1994), which found that the complexity of age stereotypes was lower among young adult participants than among older adult participants. These differences between young and older participants could reflect developmental processes relating to integration of life experiences into age stereotype schemas, or, alternatively, intergroup processes (Linville, 1982) related to older adults having more complex perceptions of their age group (ingroup) than do young adults for whom older adults are an outgroup. The researchers were able to establish the greater validity of the developmental hypothesis over the intergroup hypothesis because the design included a group of middle-aged participants. Consistent with developmental theory, the complexity of middle-aged participants' age stereotypes fell between that of the young and older participants, whereas intergroup theory would predict no differences in the complexity of young and middle-aged adults' age stereotypes.

Although it is possible to study developmental hypotheses using a cross-sectional design, many scholars point to longitudinal designs as the preferred approach because such designs allow for the examination of continuity and change in individuals' performance over time (Ferraro & Kelley-Moore, 2003; Nesselroade & Baltes, 1979; Schaie & Hofer, 2001). Yet, like cross-sectional designs, longitudinal designs are not immune to problems that can affect the validity of interpretations and conclusions from study results. Campbell and Stanley (1963) identified several challenges to internal validity in experiments and quasi experiments to which longitudinal researchers must pay attention. These include measurement variance, practice effects due to repeated testing on the same measures, and loss of participants over time. For example, just as differences between participants of different ages in a cross-sectional study could be misinterpreted as the result of the process of development when the differences could be due to cohort effects, the observed changes in an individual's performance in a longitudinal study could be misinterpreted as the result of development when the changes could be due to repeated testing on the same measures. Missing data, which occurs when participants drop out of a study, miss a session, or fail to complete all measures, create yet another challenge for longitudinal research.

Ferrer and Ghisletta (2011) suggest that the shortcomings and potential misinterpretations of longitudinal research can be reduced through careful planning, checking data to ensure they meet psychometric standards over time; monitoring participant performance for retest effects and individual differences that lead to attrition; using appropriate statistics to deal with missing data; and employing complex designs such as time-lag, measurement bursts, and longer sequences of cross-sectional and longitudinal studies. As one example, they argue that factorial invariance over time is essential, but difficult to achieve especially as new measures are included in later waves of data collection. One solution they propose is to look for invariance at a higher level, specifically in the inter-factor relationships which are likely to be more stable than the individual factors. To check for retest effects, they suggest two strategies. The first is to recruit a "refreshment" sample matched on key characteristics to the longitudinal sample. Differences in performance between the refreshment and longitudinal samples may be signs of retest effects. In the absence of a refreshment sample, Ferrer and Ghisletta state that a statistical approach provides the only alternative. In this approach, the researcher examines the effects of maturation (i.e., age) and retest effects separately to see whether different patterns exist (e.g., declines with age but increases with repeated testing).

Despite these challenges, the number of longitudinal studies of human development has grown since the mid-20th century to today. In the field of gerontology, Ferraro and Kelley-Moore (2003) attribute this growth to several factors: (1) a paradigm shift from "the study of *older people* to the *process of aging* ... as a *lifelong process*"; (2) increased availability of federal funding for longitudinal research; (3) establishment of public archives that provide investigators with access to longitudinal data; and (4) the "revolution in statistical computing" that created new "*analytic resources* for longitudinal data" (emphasis in the original; pp. S264–S265). We consider the first three factors in the context of lifespan research on communication next and will discuss the statistical resources in the section on analytical methods.

The paradigm shift to a focus on the lifelong process of development noted by Ferraro and Kelley-Moore (2003) in gerontology has had more impact in encouraging longitudinal research in some communication fields than in others. While language scholars have long been asking questions about the process of language development and decline from infancy through older adulthood and pursuing longitudinal research to address those questions, scholars of interpersonal and organizational communication have only recently begun to pose developmental questions that require longitudinal designs. For instance, a search conducted in November 2013 of peer-reviewed articles indexed in *PsychInfo* over the past 30 years yielded 3,602 *longitudinal* studies of *children or infant language* and 268 *longitudinal* studies of *aging or elderly language* (search terms in italics). In contrast, the number of peer-reviewed articles reporting *longitudinal* studies of *children or infant interpersonal communication* over the same 30-year time frame was only 166 and the number reporting *longitudinal* studies of *aging or elderly interpersonal communication* was only 21. Further, the articles identified in all four of the searches were published primarily in journals within the fields of psychology, speech pathology, and audiology. Clearly there is a need for such longitudinal research on development in the broader communication discipline, and we encourage communication scholars to strive toward building communication-centered longitudinal data sets for sharing and collaboration with scholars within and beyond our field (Hummert, 2007).

While it will take considerable time and funding for communication scholars to develop the longitudinal data sets that will best meet their needs going forward, there are some existing longitudinal studies whose data could be tapped for secondary analyses addressing communication questions. Table 1 provides information about nine of these longitudinal studies, their purpose, and some of the variables they contain. Many are publicly available while others are available only through an application process.

Table 1. Longitudinal Data Sets of Interest to Lifespan Communication Scholars.

Study Name	Years	Description
Age and Generations Study, 2007–2008 PIs Pitt-Catsouphes, M., Smyer, M. ICPSR 34837 Available at: http://www.icpsr.umich.edu/ icpsrweb/ICPSR/	2007–2008	Online survey of 2,195 employees in multigenerational work teams in 9 organizations representing 5 industries. Second surveys occurred 6 months after first. Includes data on intergenerational relationships and work outcomes, employee satisfaction, opportunities for learning and development, health and well-being.

Study Name	Years	Description
Assessment of Doctor-Elderly Patient Encounters (ADEPT) Contact the PI: Mary Ann Cook JVCRadiology@sbcglobal.net	1998–2001	A database of approximately 435 audiotapes and videotapes of visits of 65+-year-old patients (N=46) to their physicians. Sponsored by the National Institute on Aging.
Health and Retirement Study PIs: Juster, F. T., Willis, R. J. Available at: http://hrsonline.isr.umich.edu/index.php	1992–Present	The HRS is a longitudinal panel study that surveys a representative sample of more than 26,000 Americans over the age of 50 every 2 years. Includes survey and interview data. Funded by the National Institute on Aging (NIA U01AG009740) and the Social Security Administration.
Iowa Youth and Families Project PIs: Conger, R. D., Lasley, P., Lorenz, F. O., Simons, R., Whitbeck, L. B., Elder, G. H., Jr., Norem, R. ICPSR 26721 Available at: http://www.icpsr.umich.edu/icpsrweb/ICPSR/	1989–1992	Panel study of 471 7th graders in 2-parent families in rural Iowa. Includes parent and child survey data on family relationships and family interaction tasks, and interviewers' observations of interaction tasks. Funded by the National Institutes of Health and the MacArthur Foundation.
Longitudinal Study of Generations PI: Bengston, V. L. ICPSR 22100 Available at: http://www.icpsr.umich.edu/icpsrweb/NACDA/	1971, 1985, 1988, 1991, 1994, 1997, 2000	Initially a survey of intergenerational relations among 300 three-generation families in California that now includes a fourth generation. Includes data on intergenerational solidarity, conflict, marital relationships, role importance, family structure, attitudes, values, socioeconomic changes, etc. Funded by the National Institute on Aging (2R01AG00799-21A2)
Marriage Matters Panel Survey of Newlywed Couples PIs: Nock, S. L., Sanchez, L., Wright, J. D. ICPSR 29582 Available at: http://www.icpsr.umich.edu/icpsrweb/ICPSR/	1998–2004	Survey of 1,310 couples who participated in Louisiana covenant marriages, which required pre-marital counseling. Includes three waves of data collection with data on marital satisfaction, marital problems, political and social views, health and well-being, children, etc. Funded by the National Science Foundation.

Midlife in the United States, (MIDUS II, 2004–2006) PIs: Ryff, C. D., Almeida, D. M., Ayanian, J. S., Carr, D. S., Cleary, P. D., Coe, C., Davidson, R., Krueger, R. F., Lachman, M. E., Marks, N. F., Mroczek, D. K., Seeman, T., Seltzer, M. M., Singer, B. H., Sloan, R. P., Tun, P. A., Weinstein, M., Williams, D. ICPSR 4652 Available at: http://www.icpsr.umich.edu/ icpsrweb/NACDA/	1995–2006	Survey of 7,108 participants aged 25 to 74 in 1995, including a twin sub-sample. Longitudinal follow-up (MIDUS II) began in 2004 reaching 4,963 original participants, a 75% response rate adjusting for mortality. Includes data on marital relations, parent-child relationships, social support, etc. MIDUS I funded by the MacArthur Foundation and MIDUS II by the National Institute on Aging (5-PO1-AG20166-04).
NICHD Study of Early Child Care and Youth Development (SECCYD) Series PI: U. S. Department of Health and Human Services. National Institutes of Health. Eunice Kennedy Shriver National Institute of Child Health and Human Development ICPSR Series 00233 Available at: http://www.icpsr.umich.edu/ icpsrweb/ICPSR/	1991–2009	Survey of 1,361 newborn infants and their families in 1991 through age 4 in 1995, with three subsequent survey waves: 1996–1999, 2000–2004, 2005–2008. Includes data on parent-child interactions, marital relationships, parents' values and beliefs, etc. Funded by National Institute on Child Health and Human Development (U01 HD019897)
Welfare, Children, and Families: A Three-City Study PIs: Angel, R., Burton, L., Chase-Lansdale, P. L., Cherlin, A., Moffitt, R. ICPSR 4701 Available at: http://www.icpsr.umich.edu/ icpsrweb/ICPSR/	1999–2006	Survey of 2,400 families in Boston, Chicago, San Antonio beginning in 1999 when children were either 0–4 or 10–14. Focus on child and primary female caregiver with teachers included in Wave 3. Includes data on parent-child relationships, family routines, parenting style, marital relationships, psychological and health variables. Funded by the Eunice Kennedy Shriver National Institute of Child Health and Human Development (R01 HD036093)

Note: These studies may include some data that are subject to restricted use.

The majority of the studies listed in Table 1 are archived at the Inter-university Consortium for Political and Social Research (ICPSR) at the University of Michigan. The consortium includes 700 universities and colleges as members, providing faculty and researchers from the member institutions with access to over 500,000 data sets for secondary analysis. Located within ICPSR is the National Archive of Computerized Data on Aging (NACDA), funded by the Behavior and Social Research division of the National Institute on Aging. NACDA includes not only U.S. longitudinal data but also data from many countries around the world. Scholars with a focus on communication and child development can access the online archive at Childcare and Early Education Research Connections (http://www.researchcon nections.org/childcare/datasets-instruments.jsp), funded by the Office of Planning, Research and Evaluation, Administration for Children and Families of the U.S. Department of Health and Human Services, but administered through ICPSR. For data sets that are available for use, Childcare and Early Education Research Connections provides the option to download data or use an online analysis tool.

ICPSR has been in existence for over 50 years, as have other, smaller data archives such as the Murray Research Center at Radcliffe College. A newer development is Harvard's open source Dataverse Network (DVN) (http://thedata.harvard.edu/dvn/), initiated in 2006, which accepts data from social science researchers in order to support data sharing, reproducibility of research results, and good archival practices. The DNV is a project of the Harvard University Library and the Harvard Institute for Quantitative Social Science, and, according to its website, has "the world's largest collection of social science research data." This site can also be searched for longitudinal data of interest to communication scholars. While the open source nature of the DNV may require more careful scrutiny than an archive such as ICPSR, both, along with other archives, provide rich resources for communication scholars.

Statistical Methods to Assess Change

As Ferraro and Kelley-Moore (2003) noted, there has been significant growth in the statistical computing tools available to analyze longitudinal data. Thirty years ago time series analyses and repeated measures analysis of variance procedure provided the ability to analyze whether performance differed significantly from one data collection point to a second, third, etc. According to Ferrer and Ghisletta (2011), these approaches are still used, but do not provide the insights into change processes offered by newer methods such as latent growth curve modeling, multilevel modeling, and dynamic factor analysis. These methods build on earlier mathematical models, but their development and application in research has been made possible due to advances in computing capabilities and statistical software. Table 2 provides a description of the statistical approaches which Ferrer and Ghisletta see as most useful and the advantages they offer in investigating change at the intra-individual and inter-individual levels.

Table 2. Statistical Approaches to Measuring Change.

Statistical Tool	Uses and Advantages
Latent Growth Curve Models (LGC)	Used to identify within-individual change; Advantages include the ability to test different models of changes, incorporate covariates into the model, assess retest effects, and compare groups.
Multilevel Models (MLM)	Used to analyze data with a hierarchical structure (e.g., members within families, repeated measures within individuals); Advantages include the ability to analyze nonlinear change such as that before and after an event, such as birth of a child.
Latent Change Score Models (LCS)	Used to analyze the interrelationship of two processes over time; Advantages include the ability to analyze the interrelationship of intra- and inter-individual change such as in the study of marital dyads.
Dynamic Factor Analysis (DFA)	Used to analyze intra-individual variability over time; Advantages include the ability to identify processes at the level of the individual allowing for an assessment of the stability of the process, e.g., emotional regulation, at the individual level.
Joint Longitudinal + Survival Analysis	Used to predict an event from repeated measurement of change over time; Advantages include the ability to incorporate change in multiple predictors into the equation.

Note: Descriptions summarized from Ferrer, E., & Ghisletta, P. (2011). Methodological and analytical issues in the psychology of aging. In K. W. Schaie & S. L. Willis (Eds.), *Handbook of the psychology of aging* (7th ed., pp. 25–39). San Diego, CA: Academic Press.

MIXED METHODS AND "CATCH-UP" APPROACHES

Like Laub and Sampson (1998) we believe that "merging quantitative and qualitative data analysis provides important clues for explaining the processes of continuity and change in human behavior over the life course" (p. 214). Mixed methods allow for the powerful combination of the flexibility of qualitative designs with the stability of quantitative designs in longitudinal studies capturing both the richness of detail as well as breadth of experiences. See Talbert and McLaughlin (1999) for an excellent example of mixed methods lifespan developmental research within the school environment that uses both large-scale survey research and in-depth case studies.

Many of the methods discussed above can be used for the collection and analysis of qualitative and quantitative data. Turning points events, for example, can be both quantifiable and qualitative (Scott & Alwin, 1998). Moreover, it should not be overlooked that life story data can be quantified for generalizability and to provide concrete findings for future research if used as a "catch-up" study. This involves the systematic collection and analysis of life story data through the development of elaborate coding books and coding schemes, but does not lessen the importance of the subjective and nuanced nature of the original data (Clausen, 1998). Applying mixed-methods techniques in this manner provides full breadth and depth of the phenomenon under study at the present time, as well as opens opportunities for future analyses and comparisons.

Many, if not all, of the places where we do our living and interacting are part of a greater socio-environmental system where micro environments are nested within macro or meso environments located within a larger exosystem (Bronfenbrenner, 1999). Thus, one area to consider mixed methods is within nested social systems where it might be beneficial to apply qualitative methods and measures to understand phenomena at the more abstract exosystem level and quantitative techniques to measure specifics at the micro level (Bradley, 1999). Super and Harkness (1999) argued that studying the "developmental niche" requires a combination of techniques and the interweaving of qualitative and quantitative methods (p. 295). They noted also that a technique such as participant observation can also be usefully employed at all three levels of social organization to fully explore the developmental niche.

Before we close, we wish to point our readers toward an additional, creative opportunity for lifespan research called "catch-up studies." Catch-up studies make use of previously conducted cross-sectional and/or longitudinal research by seeking participants and/or their family members from the original study and inviting them to participate in a follow-up study. Scholars looking for an insightful chapter with abundant resources and inspirational anecdotes about research experiences and techniques for following up with participants even decades after an initial investigation should consult Dempster-McClain and Moen (1998). These authors write about the possibilities of using archival data and initial research investigations to locate participants for a follow-up study. Indeed, they report extensively on the serendipitous finding of meticulous participant records and data from a study conducted 25 years earlier. Dempster-McClain and Moen not only provide tips and resources for how to conduct a catch-up study and follow leads to locate and contact former participants, but also give useful information about collecting and maintaining respondent data on the chance that future researchers might wish to follow up with that study years in the future. Some of the tips Dempster-McClain and Moen offer for finding past participants include organized and meticulous searches of telephone directories; historical society records; obituary records; birth, death, and wedding certificates; hospital records; city directories;

motor vehicle records; family of origin addresses and neighbors; local informants; high school and college records; inquiring with former employers, clubs, organizations, churches, military, and so forth; and walking through neighborhoods.

FUTURE RESEARCH DIRECTIONS
AND CONCLUDING THOUGHTS

As of yet, there appears to be no gold standard of measurement for assessing continuity and change across or among the disciplines that take a lifespan, life course, or developmental approach toward social sciences (see Wachs, 1999). Indeed, it is a highly complex matter involving the study of time, process, environment, and those complex and oftentimes surprising creatures—humans! Nevertheless, we attempted here to provide some framework from which to begin building lifespan studies.

Because the field of communication is still in the formative stages of building methods to measure communication as a developmental process, our first recommendation is aimed broadly at the field. Developmental change and lifespan communication are relevant across all areas and interests of communication. As a field, we must continue to engage in dialogue about lifespan communication as this *Handbook* has begun to do. Our core methods texts, professional associations, and scholarly journals (e.g., *Communication Methods and Measures*) must take seriously the notion of lifespan communication and we must strive to make it a central feature in our pedagogy and research. Most important, we must move beyond merely acknowledging the importance of lifespan communication toward developing and engaging methods that will test and measure it. We must also recognize that while phases and stages of the lifespan (e.g., early childhood, emerging adulthood, older adulthood) offer deep wells to draw from in order to better understand communication in these specific developmental periods, it is equally important to go beyond the boundaries of developmental stages to consider the broader lifespan trajectory (i.e., implications for communication at emergent adulthood based on communication patterns formed during early childhood). This last point gets at Marshall's (2000) distinction between communication research that takes a "lifespan documentation" approach and one that takes a "lifespan explication" approach in which she advocates for more studies that embrace a lifespan explication framework.

Second, we must fully document steps taken to include a developmental approach within communication research. This will facilitate replication opportunities for similar studies and also has the potential to lay a foundation for possible catch-up studies. Such documentation should provide detailed reports on methodological successes and failures or challenges.

Third, while building rigorous longitudinal and/or cross-sectional research should be a priority for lifespan communication research, we must also seek out opportunities to investigate developmental change and continuity in a compressed manner. Time series designs, analyses of turning points, and a focus on lifespan transitions offer unique opportunities to study continuity and change in a short span of time. Similarly, scholars can study bounded, enduring social systems such as families or other organizations in which various stages and phases of developmental communication can be observed and recorded simultaneously.

Fourth, advancing a lifespan developmental perspective in communication requires us to think and act collaboratively. To achieve this, scholars can take advantage of publically and privately available archives and databases, can seek out opportunities for collaborative longitudinal research projects, and can be generous with data and collaborations as much as feasible within boundaries of ethical human research.

Finally, in order to advance research methods in lifespan communication, we must take risks and think creatively. This might include engaging mixed methods designs that allow for the collection of retrospective and prospective data through narratives and survey research. Longitudinal studies can be launched that capitalize on micro analyses made possible through observations and interviewing and macro analyses that involve and advance newer statistical modeling designed to measure change and continuity at the intra-individual and inter-individual levels. Likewise, we need to develop a new set of methodological skills to capture communication change across time (e.g., decades) and standardize them as part of a graduate curriculum (Nussbaum, 2007; Nussbaum & Fridrich, 2005).

In sum, we advocate for thinking and methods that move beyond a "cross-sectional slice of life." This must include the important communication groundwork that is evidenced in early life as it begins the foundation for communication across the lifespan. It must also consider communication across generations through passing down family norms, cultural patterns, and perhaps also genetic predispositions. We must not be focused on the potential for development, adaptation, or change across the lifespan, but the inevitability of it. Embedding a lifespan approach to communication scholarship will drive the future development of the field, contributing solidly to the knowledge of human processes and to the betterment of human experiences.

REFERENCES

Angel, R., Burton, L., Chase-Lansdale, P. L., Cherlin, A., & Moffitt, R. (2009-02-10). *Welfare, children, and families: A three-city study*. ICPSR04701-v7. Ann Arbor, MI: Inter-university Consortium for Political and Social Research [distributor]. doi:10.3886/ICPSR04701.v7

Baltes, P. B., Reese, H. W., & Nesselroade, J. R. (1977). *Life-span developmental psychology: Introduction to research methods*. Monterey, CA: Brooks/Cole.

Bengtson, V. L. Longitudinal Study of Generations, 1971, 1985, 1988, 1991, 1994, 1997, 2000 [California] (2009-05-12). ICPSR22100-v2. Ann Arbor, MI: Inter-university Consortium for Political and Social Research [distributor]. doi:10.3886/ICPSR22100.v2

Bolton, C. D. (1961). Mate selection as the development of a relationship. *Marriage and Family Living, 23*, 234–40.

Bradley, R. H. (1999). The home environment. In S. L. Friedman & T. D. Wachs (Eds.), *Measuring environment across the life span: Emerging methods and concepts* (pp. 31–58). Washington, DC: American Psychological Association.

Bronfenbrenner, U. (1999). Environments in developmental perspective: Theoretical and operational models. In S. L. Friedman & T. D. Wachs (Eds.), *Measuring environment across the life span: Emerging methods and concepts* (pp. 3–28). Washington, DC: American Psychological Association.

Brown, B. B. (1999). Measuring the peer environment of American adolescents. In S. L. Friedman & T. D. Wachs (Eds.), *Measuring environment across the life span: Emerging methods and concepts* (pp. 59–90). Washington, DC: American Psychological Association.

Campbell, D. T., & Stanley, J. C. (1963). *Experimental and quasi-experimental designs for research.* Boston, MA: Houghton Mifflin.

Clausen, J. A. (1998). Life reviews and life stories. In J. Z Giele & G. H. Elder Jr. (Eds.), *Methods of life course research: Qualitative and quantitative approaches* (pp. 189–212). Thousand Oaks, CA: Sage.

Colby, A. (1998). Foreword: Crafting life course studies. In J. Z Giele & G. H. Elder Jr. (Eds.), *Methods of life course research: Qualitative and quantitative approaches* (pp. viii–xii). Thousand Oaks, CA: Sage.

Conger, R. D., Lasley, P., Lorenz, F. O., Simons, R., Whitbeck, L. B., Elder, G. H., Jr., & Norem, R. (2011-11-03). *Iowa youth and families project, 1989–1992.* ICPSR26721-v2. Ann Arbor, MI: Inter-university Consortium for Political and Social Research [distributor]. doi:10.3886/ICPSR26721.v2

Cook, M. A. (1998–2001). *Assessment of doctor-elderly patient encounters (ADEPT).* St. Louis, MO: St. Louis University Library [distributor].

Cook, T. D., & Campbell, D. T. (1979). *Quasi-experimentation: Design & analysis for field settings.* Boston, MA: Houghton Mifflin.

Crano, W. D., & Brewer, M. B. (2002). *Principles and methods of social research* (2nd ed.). Mahwah, NJ: Erlbaum.

Dempster-McClain, D., & Moen, P. (1998). Finding respondents in a follow-up study. In J. Z Giele & G. H. Elder Jr. (Eds.), *Methods of life course research: Qualitative and quantitative approaches* (pp. 128–151). Thousand Oaks, CA: Sage.

Dun, T. (2010). Turning points in parent-grandparent relationships during the start of a new generation. *Journal of Family Communication, 10*, 194–210.

Ferraro, K. F., & Kelley-Moore, J. A. (2003). A half century of longitudinal methods in social gerontology: Evidence of change in the *Journal. Journal of Gerontology: Social Sciences, 58B*, S264–S270.

Ferrer, E., & Ghisletta, P. (2011). Methodological and analytical issues in the psychology of aging. In K. W. Schaie & S. L. Willis (Eds.). *Handbook of the psychology of aging* (7th ed., pp. 25–39). San Diego, CA: Academic Press.

Fisher, W. (1984). Narration as a human communication paradigm: The case of public moral argument. *Communication Monographs, 51*, 1–22.

Giele, J. Z, & Elder, G. H., Jr. (1998). Life course research: Development of a field. In J. Z Giele, & G. H. Elder Jr. (Eds.), *Methods of life course research: Qualitative and quantitative approaches* (pp. 5–27). Thousand Oaks, CA: Sage.

Hummert, M. L. (2007). As family members age: A research agenda for family communication. *The Journal of Family Communication, 7*, 3–21.

Hummert, M. L. (2009). Not just preaching to the choir: Communication scholarship does make a difference. *Journal of Applied Communication Research, 37*, 215–224.

Hummert, M. L., Garstka, T. A., Shaner, J. L., & Strahm, S. (1994). Stereotypes of the elderly held by young, middle-aged, and elderly adults. *Journal of Gerontology: Psychological Sciences, 49*, P240–P249.

Hummert, M. L., & Nussbaum, J. F. (2013). Developmental methods. In J. F. Nussbaum (Ed.), *Readings in communication research methods: From theory to practice* (pp. 75–82). San Diego, CA: Cognella.

Huston, T. L., Surra, C., Fitzgerald, N., & Cate, R. (1981). From courtship to marriage: Mate selection as an interpersonal process. In S. Duck & R. Gilmour (Eds.), *The emerging field of personal relationships* (pp. 53–88). New York, NY: Academic Press.

Kemper, S., Kynette, D., Rash, S., O'Brien, K., & Sprott, R. (1989). Lifespan changes to adults' language: Effects of memory and genre. *Applied Psycholinguistics, 10*, 49–66.

Laub, J. H., & Sampson, R. J. (1998). Integrating quantitative and qualitative data. In J. Z Giele & G. H. Elder Jr. (Eds.), *Methods of life course research: Qualitative and quantitative approaches* (pp. 213–230). Thousand Oaks, CA: Sage.

Lindlof, T. R., & Taylor, B. C. (2011). *Qualitative communication research methods* (3rd ed.). Los Angeles, CA: Sage.

Linville, P. W. (1982). The complexity-extremity effect and age-based stereotyping. *Journal of Personality and Social Psychology, 42*, 193–211.

Marshall, L. J. (2000). Toward a life-span perspective on the study of message production. *Communication Theory, 10*, 188–199.

Menaghan, E. G., & Godwin, D. D. (1993). Longitudinal research methods and family theories. In P. G. Boss, W. J. Doherty, R. Larossa, W. R. Schumm, & S. K. Steinmetz (Eds.), *Sourcebook of family theories and methods: A contextual approach* (pp. 259–273). New York, NY: Plenum Press.

Miller, S. A. (2007). *Developmental research methods* (3rd ed.). Los Angeles, CA: Sage.

Nelson, I. (2010). From quantitative to qualitative: Adapting the life history calendar method. *Field Methods, 22*, 413–428.

Nesselroade, J. R., & Baltes, P. B. (Eds.). (1979). Longitudinal research in the study of behavior and development. New York, NY: Academic Press.

Nock, S. L., Sanchez, L. A., & Wright, J. D. (2012-06-29). *Marriage matters panel survey of newlywed couples, 1998–2004, Louisiana.* ICPSR29582-v1. Ann Arbor, MI: Inter-university Consortium for Political and Social Research [distributor]. doi:10.3886/ICPSR29582.v1

Nussbaum, J. F. (2007). Life span communication and quality of life [Presidential Address]. *Journal of Communication, 57*, 1–7. doi:10.1111/j.1460-2466.2006.00325.x

Nussbaum, J. F., & Friedrich, G. (2005). Instructional/developmental communication: Current theory, research, and future trends. *Journal of Communication, 55*, 578–593

Pecchioni, L. L., Wright, K. B., & Nussbaum, J. F. (2005). *Life-span communication.* Mahwah, NJ: Erlbaum.

Pitt-Catsouphes, M., & Smyer, M. (2013-10-07). *Age and generations study, 2007–2008.* Ann Arbor, MI: Inter-university Consortium for Political and Social Research [distributor]. doi:10.3886/ICPSR34837.v1

Riley, L. D., & Bowen, C. P. (2005). The sandwich generation: Challenges and coping strategies of multigenerational families. *The Family Journal: Counseling and Therapy for Couples and Families, 13*, 52–58.

Rosenblatt, P. C., & Fischer, L. R. (1993). Qualitative family research. In P. G. Boss, W. J. Doherty, R. Larossa, W. R. Schumm, & S. K. Steinmetz (Eds.), *Sourcebook of family theories and methods: A contextual approach* (pp. 167–177). New York, NY: Plenum Press.

Ryff, C., Almeida, D.M., Ayanian, J. S., Carr, D. S., Cleary, P. D., Coe, C., ... Williams, D. (2012-04-18). *National survey of midlife development in the United States (MIDUS II), 2004–2006.* ICPSR04652-v6. Ann Arbor, MI: Inter-university Consortium for Political and Social Research [distributor]. doi:10.3886/ICPSR04652.v6

Schaie, K. W., & Hofer, S. M. (2001). Longitudinal studies in aging research. In J. E. Birren & K. W. Schaie (Eds.), *Handbook of the psychology of aging* (5th ed., pp. 53–77). San Diego, CA: Academic Press.

Scott, J., & Alwin, D. (1998). Retrospective versus prospective measurement of life histories in longitudinal research. In J. Z Giele & G. H. Elder Jr. (Eds.), *Methods of life course research: Qualitative and quantitative approaches* (pp. 98–127). Thousand Oaks, CA: Sage.

Super, C. M., & Harkness, S. (1999). The environment as culture in developmental research. In S. L. Friedman & T. D. Wachs (Eds.), *Measuring environment across the life span: Emerging methods and concepts* (pp. 279–323). Washington, DC: American Psychological Association.

Talbert, J. E., & McLaughlin, M. W. (1999). Assessing the school environment: Embedded contexts and bottom-up research strategies. In S. L. Friedman & T. D. Wachs (Eds.), *Measuring environment across the life span: Emerging methods and concepts* (pp. 197–227). Washington, DC: American Psychological Association.

United States Department of Health and Human Services. National Institutes of Health. Eunice Kennedy Shriver National Institute of Child Health and Human Development (2010-01-26). *NICHD Study of early child care and youth development: Phase IV 2005–2008* [United States]. ICPSR22361-v1. Ann Arbor, MI: Inter-university Consortium for Political and Social Research [distributor]. doi:10.3886/ICPSR22361.v1

Wachs, T. D. (1999). Celebrating complexity: Conceptualization and assessment of the environment. In S. L. Friedman & T. D. Wachs (Eds.), *Measuring environment across the life span: Emerging methods and concepts* (pp. 357–392). Washington, DC: American Psychological Association.

NOTE

1 While longitudinal studies that commence with infancy suffer from great challenges in getting a suitable sample, once the sample is established, longitudinal studies among this group are more feasible because of their rapid growth and how quickly they hit developmental milestones. But, because of this rapidity, the issue of measurement equivalence is perhaps greater during infancy than at other points (Miller, 2007).

PART TWO

Early Childhood
Communication

CHAPTER THREE

Communication Development

Distributed Across People, Resources, and Time

CAROL A. MILLER AND LAURA S. DeTHORNE

Note: The authors contributed equally to this chapter.

Communication, the cornerstone of human relationships, develops long before young children begin to master a linguistic code. Definitions of communication vary, ranging from all human behavior to specification of conventional forms. For the purposes of this chapter, we refer to communication as the intentional exchange of ideas across individuals, including both verbal and nonverbal behavior (cf. Ciccia, Step, & Turkstra, 2003; Haslett & Samter, 1997). As such, speech and language can serve as powerful resources for communicative purposes, but are not themselves synonymous with communication. Speech refers to the sensory-motor process of talking, whereas language encompasses the cognitive-linguistic conventions of vocabulary, grammar, and phonology. Neither is sufficient in understanding the rich landscape of social interaction. Take, for example, the 6-month-old infant who is repeating "dadada" while in his crib. Such babbling represents the early sensory-motor building blocks of speech, but is not *communicating* until someone receives the babble and attributes meaning to it. As such, communication is always dependent upon receipt and interpretation by others (i.e., distributed across people). Similarly, the interpretation of "dadada" is shaped by additional resources and aspects of the environment (i.e., distributed across resources). For example, whether the infant is looking up at his dad or down at the dog on the floor is likely to affect how the message is taken up. Nonverbal resources, such as gesture, eye gaze, facial expression, and objects in the environment serve as powerful influences on communicative success. Finally, communication is shaped by past interactions and influenced by projections for the future. For example, imagine the infant in the above scenario is babbling at bedtime. As such, this interaction will be shaped by the routines and relationship this father and child have developed over time, as well as the aspirations they both have for future interactions (i.e., distributed across time). The scenario is likely to unfold very differently if this is the first time the infant's father has heard him babble "dadada" versus if the father commonly hears the child repeat this sequence of sounds as he falls asleep every night.

The view of communication as a multimodal exchange of ideas that is distributed across people, resources, and time is adapted from prior work by Hengst and colleagues (DeThorne, Hengst, Fisher, & King, 2013; Hengst & Miller, 1999) and draws heavily on situated social theories of communication (e.g., Wertsch, 1991). In addition, we recognize the importance of cognitive approaches to communication that highlight the development of children's perspective-taking, as in the case of Constructivism (Burleson, 1984; Delia & O'Keefe, 1979), and the interconnectedness of children's linguistic and social-emotional expression, as in the Intentionality Model (Bloom & Tinker, 2001). Although this chapter has not fully captured a systems approach to communication development, our perspective also has much in common with systems models, such as those described by Stafford and Dainton (1995) that highlight interdependence among family members (i.e., communication as distributed across people). Together these models underscore the complexity of human communication and emphasize the critical role of context within a child's development.

For the purpose of this chapter, we have chosen to focus on three critical elements of a child's communication system: people, resources, and time. In addition, we have drawn on our particular experience in communication sciences and disorders (CSD) to support each of these elements. In fact, we claim that the cases of communication disruption and marked extreme developmental trajectories studied in CSD offer an insightful and unique glimpse into the complexities of human interaction.

COMMUNICATION IS DISTRIBUTED ACROSS PEOPLE

Communication, by definition, requires an exchange of ideas. Therefore, at the most basic level communication requires both a sender and a receiver. However, in this section we discuss the more nuanced notion of how children's communicative partners shape communication development as both senders and receivers of information, not only during specific communication events, but also throughout the entirety of development. In particular we highlight three key contributions of children's communication partners: exposure, presumed competence, and interpretation. Though it may seem self-evident, providing exposure to language and other communicative resources within meaningful activities is a critical role of children's potential communication partners. It is from such everyday exposure that infants emerge from the womb already familiar with their mother's voices and some aspects of their home's spoken languages (Kisilevsky et al., 2003; Nazzi, Bertoncini, & Mehler, 1998; Socha & Yingling, 2010). Similarly, from an early age children are observing the repertoire of actions, sounds, and symbols that tend to occur and co-occur in their everyday environments. As an example, newborns will copy gestures such as mouth opening and tongue protrusion from adults (Meltzoff & Moore, 1998). Such gestures are not random but derived from the people in that baby's immediate environment. When recognized by caregivers, such imitation sets the stage for early turn taking and communicative exchange (Yingling, 1995). Of particular interest, evidence suggests that at least by 18 months infants are not strictly mimicking isolated behaviors but recognizing and attempting to replicate the intended goals of behaviors (Meltzoff, 1995). In short, the people in a child's life provide critical information about communication just by being nearby and "doing what people do."

In addition to exposure, partners contribute to children's communication development by granting them presumed competence, sometimes from a very young age (Dunst & Lowe, 1986; Ochs & Schieffelin, 1994). By presumed competence, we refer here to an individual's willingness to attribute meaning to a child's actions, whether or not intent is readily apparent. Infants, like anyone, can communicate without intending to. The newborn cries, gurgles, burps, and yawns, and the caregiver may choose to interpret these behaviors as communicating a message (I'm hungry, I'm tired, My tummy hurts) and to respond accordingly (offering food, a bed, soothing). We claim that it is actually through the process of presuming competence that communicative intention and shared meanings unfold. To illustrate, consider the emergence of what has been dubbed "protoconversation" between infants and caregivers around the age of 2 to 3 months (Trevarthen, 1998). This is an interaction in which adult and infant take turns vocalizing and/or gesturing. The adult responds to the infant's coos, gurgles, smiles, and so on, as if they were intended as messages and interprets them accordingly. By responding to infants' behavior as if it were communicative, caregivers, in a sense, create and shape communicative intent (Adamson, 1995; Ochs & Schieffelin, 1994; Prizant, Wetherby, Rubin, Laurent, & Rydell, 2006).

Intertwined with the process of presumed competence is the act of interpretation. With the assumption of intent, communication partners are then in the position to interpret potential messages. As an example, consider the development of "protowords" as children begin to speak. These are relatively consistent phonological forms that are used in a way that appears to be referential, although the forms do not correspond to a word that adults use (e.g., Vihman & Miller, 1988). For example, an infant might routinely produce the syllable "kah" while holding or reaching for her favorite blanket. Caregivers may interpret "kah" as the infant's way of referring to the blanket, thereby demonstrating how reference works. The specific interpretations caregivers offer vary based on their cultural values and expectations (cf. Ochs & Schieffelin, 1994).

The process of presuming competence and offering interpretations leads to the creation of shared meaning, the very essence of communication. Over time, interpretations can become increasingly specified and symbolic. A child's utterance of "Dad" paired with a glance out the window might suggest to his mother, "Where is Dad? Isn't it time for him to come home?" to which she may simply respond, "Soon." Presuming competence and offering interpretation provide an essential foundation for communication development.

Work with children who have communication differences and impairment has underscored the critical role that partners have in providing accessible exposure, presuming competence, and offering interpretation. Interventions for children with various physical and cognitive impairments, such as cerebral palsy or autism, have underscored the importance of presumed competence and interpretation. Marked impairments may disrupt communication development in part because communication partners have more difficulty recognizing communicative intent and extending children with marked disorders the same benefit of presumed competence that is often granted to very young infants. Accordingly, many naturalistic or developmental treatment approaches, such as responsivity education and prelinguistic milieu teaching, have focused on instructing caregivers to presume and interpret early communicative intents (DeThorne et al., 2013; Warren et al., 2006).

COMMUNICATION IS DISTRIBUTED ACROSS RESOURCES

Both children and their communication partners are able to utilize a diverse array of communicative resources that expand as children develop. Traditionally, overviews of children's communication development include an explicit focus on milestones for producing and comprehending speech (see reviews in Hopper & Naremore, 1978; Hulit, Howard, & Fahey, 2011; Pence & Justice, 2008; Socha & Yingling, 2010; Wood, 1976). In this chapter, we emphasize not only that speech and language develop in the context of communication, but also that communication is distributed across many types of resources that may compete with and/or facilitate one another. Speech and language are extremely powerful resources for communication, but they develop in a rich, multimodal communicative milieu. In this section we focus on resources for communication considered intrinsic to the child. Figure 1 provides a visual guide to the developmental timeline of resources in three key domains: speech and language; gesture; and social-emotional expression. Although such delineation across domains is admittedly somewhat arbitrary, the intent was to underscore the multimodal nature of communication and to illustrate how development across modalities may inter-relate. It is also worthy of note that Figure 1 focuses almost exclusively on production. Although comprehension is an equally important aspect of development, there are two primary reasons for subordinating comprehension to production in our discussion. First, the research literature provides more data on production, in part because it is easier to observe than comprehension. Second, what we do know about comprehension suggests that it unfolds in a very similar sequence to production, but usually precedes it. We will highlight comprehension separate from production when deemed necessary.

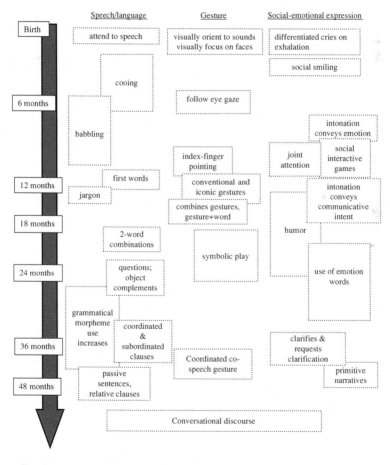

Figure 1. Developmental timeline of communicative resources.

Sources: Adamson, 1995; Bartsch & Wellman, 1995; Bates & Dick, 2002; Dunn, 1988; Hoff, 2009; Hulit, Howard, & Fahey, 2011; Iverson & Goldin-Meadow, 2005; Messinger & Fogel, 2007; Nicoladis, Mayberry, & Genesee, 1999; Pence & Justice, 2008; Snow & Balog, 2002; Socha & Yingling, 2010; Vasilyeva, Waterfall, & Huttenlocher, 2008.

A final note about Figure 1 and the associated text: both are organized chronologically. It is important to emphasize that there is a great deal of individual variation with regard to the timing of developmental milestones. For this reason, research on communicative development tends to focus on the sequence of acquisition rather than the average age at which a particular achievement is reached. For the purposes of this chapter, we offer age ranges when possible, but we encourage readers to view them as approximate.

Birth to 9 months

Infants' earliest vocalizations are cries, which start to become differentiated within the first few weeks of life, in a way that caregivers can distinguish how distressed the infant is (Adamson, 1995). Cooing—non-cry vocalization using an open vocal tract—begins at around 2 to 3 months. Infants begin to produce increasingly speech-like vocalizations by approximately 6 months of age. At this time, not only does the larynx move downward to form the mature human vocal tract configuration that allows a wide variety of sounds to be produced, but infants are able to hold their trunks, necks, and heads stable, allowing for better control of respiration and the vocal apparatus (Seikel, King, & Drumright, 2010; Socha & Yingling, 2010). These diverse early vocalizations are characterized as vocal play because they include a wide variety of sounds including squeals, growls, and "raspberries" (lip vibration). As consonant- and vowel-like sounds become recognizable and more prevalent, the vocalizations are described as babbling.

The infant in the second half of the first year has a rapidly expanding repertoire of sounds that become increasingly similar to the sounds of speech that they are exposed to; the possibilities for communication increase accordingly. Babbling often begins as repetition of the same syllable, becoming increasingly diversified until it includes many of the sound patterns and intonation contours of adult speech. In parallel with the development of speech, gesture is also increasingly used in the service of communication. Rhythmic hand-banging is coordinated with babbling at 6 to 8 months (Bates & Dick, 2002). Also at around the middle of the first year, infants respond to their name and the word "no" and become adept at following another's eye gaze (Gredebäck, Fikke, & Melinder, 2010). By 9 months, most infants can follow single-step commands.

As speech and gesture develop, they are used to express emotions. However, infants express emotions from birth through crying, whining, and other vocalizations, as well as facial expressions and gross motor movements (e.g., kicking). Social smiling—the payoff many parents receive for all those sleepless nights—emerges in the second month of life in response to the caregiver's smiling, vocalization, or other stimulation. "Although neonatal smiling has no clear emotional content, social smiling emerges out of attentive engagement with an interactive caregiver" (Messinger & Fogel, 2007, p. 357).

9 to 12 months

For most children, several very important developmental changes occur at the end of the first year. Beginning at around 9 or 10 months, infants bring together key resources in the language, gesture, and social-emotional domains to become communicators on a new level.

In the domain of language, babbling begins to give way to words. Around the end of the first year, some infants produce "jargon" babbling, which follows the intonation contours of adult language and may include a few recognizable words. Adults listening to jargon are often very engaged and have the strong impression that the toddler is speaking in sentences that they are not quite able to understand (Pence & Justice, 2008). On average, shortly before the first birthday children produce their first words that are recognized as such by listeners (Fenson et al., 1994, 2000).

In the domain of gesture, at about 10 months, infants begin showing objects to others, pointing to objects, and coordinating these gestures with eye gaze (Haslett & Samter, 1997). In time, such conventional gestures become embedded in communicative routines such as waving goodbye (Bates & Dick, 2002; Goldin-Meadow & Iverson, 2010). In addition to such gestures, iconic gestures (e.g., flapping hands for "bird") are often used by infants earlier than words (Acredolo & Goodwyn, 1988), and word plus gesture combinations not only precede but also predict later word combinations (Iverson & Goldin-Meadow, 2005). As typically developing children's vocabularies increase, they rely less on pointing and iconic gestures relative to speech; however, such gestures continue to be important for communication.

Social-emotional expression, integrated with speech and gesture, is a key part of the communicative changes at the end of the first year. Nine-month-olds engage in social interactive games (e.g., peek-a-boo, pattycake) that integrate speech, gesture, positive emotion, and social interaction (Dunst & Lowe, 1986). Likewise, social-emotional expression is central to joint attention, a key communicative development in the first year. Joint attention is multimodal and may involve not only gestures, words, and eye gaze, but also laughter, smiles, and other facial expressions (joy, surprise, trepidation) on the part of both infant and caregiver. Joint attention is demonstrated when the infant and another person are both attending to the same thing at the same time—and crucially, both are aware that they are attending to the same thing (Carpenter, Nagell, & Tomasello, 1998; Moore & Dunham, 1995; Mundy et al., 2007). In a classic joint attention episode, the infant points to an interesting object, and looks, smiling and laughing, from the object to the partner and back again. The partner also alternates gaze between the infant and the object, smiling and saying something like, "Wow, isn't that cool!" This shared experience is essential for reciprocal intentional communication, and ultimately for linguistic communication.

12 to 24 months

The second year of life is marked by tremendous vocabulary growth and a period of overt playfulness. Infants' receptive vocabulary grows steadily starting in the first year, and by about 18 months it becomes impractical to count the number of words they understand. Initially, productive vocabulary grows slowly during the first half of the second year, but many children experience a so-called vocabulary spurt when they have about 50 words in their repertoire. At that point, productive vocabulary grows more quickly, and children begin producing two-word utterances. By the end of the second year, almost all toddlers are combining words (Fenson et al., 1994, 2000). Also during the first half of the second year, children become able to comprehend more diverse sentence types, such as simple wh-questions, so called because they use question words that usually begin with *wh-* in English.

There is a great deal of individual variation encompassed in typical development. Not only do children develop at different rates, they also differ in what some call individual style. One of the best-known attempts to characterize style differences among children is Nelson's (1973) distinction between *referential* and *expressive* children. Nelson's research showed that the 50-word vocabularies of expressive children had a higher proportion of personal-social and function words (such as question words), whereas the vocabularies of referential children included a higher proportion of general nominals, especially words for objects, substances, animals, and people. Expressive children also produced more stereotyped phrases during the early word-learning period (e.g., stop it, thank you). A similar distinction in early word learning has been noted by Prizant et al. (2006) in relation to analytic versus gestalt learning styles, with the former being associated with early single-word productions and latter being linked to early use of larger linguistic chunks such as phrases (e.g., what's-that? Stop-it). Pine and Lieven (1993) argued that the learning strategy of first producing unanalyzed phrases and then breaking them down into smaller units may be quite common.

A notable aspect of vocabulary growth across children is the use of emotion words (e.g., *happy, like, mad, scared*) during their second year, a skill that continues to blossom and consolidate in later years (Bretherton & Beeghly, 1982; Fenson et al., 1994). Related both to vocabulary growth and emotional expression are the development and diversification of pitch patterns. Whereas familiarity with pitch contours likely helps substantially with parsing speech into meaningful chunks during early development, the expressive use of pitch is utilized during the first year and a half to express emotion—primarily through pitch height, as well as rising and falling pitch patterns. After that, pitch is used increasingly to express different communicative intentions, such as questions with rising intonation (American Speech-Language-Hearing Association, 2013; Snow & Balog, 2002).

Children's increasing breadth of vocabulary and familiarity with prosodic cues undoubtedly contributes to their transparent sense of humor during the second year of life. Specifically, children smile and laugh in response to incongruous situations (e.g., mother standing on kitchen counter) and create such situations themselves (e.g., putting potty chair on head) (Dunn, 1988). In addition, language is used in the service of humor. For example, toddlers may call people or things by the wrong name, clearly understanding and enjoying this sort of teasing (Shatz, 1994). Related to their expanding playfulness, children during this stage are expanding their use of pretend play. By 18 months, children imitate household activities, can pretend to pour liquid, feed a doll or comb its hair, and so on. Pretend play is also called symbolic play, because it is thought to draw on the same resources of symbolic representation as language does (Leslie, 1994).

24 to 36 months

By the end of the second year, the linguistic resources that children have available are quite formidable. Two-year-olds are able to comprehend most of what is said to them and by their third birthday can request clarification and also provide it if needed (Pence & Justice, 2008), and they can produce sentences that are well-integrated with gesture, facial expressions, and intonation to express a wide range of meanings and feelings. At around the second birthday, almost all sentences are simple, and those are mostly imperatives. Over the next few months, declaratives become the most common type of simple sentence. During this time, the complexity of the sentences produced by children increases, as does the diversity of sentence structures used, and both simple and complex sentences more closely approximate adult grammatical norms (Vasilyeva, Waterfall, & Huttenlocher, 2008). By the time they reach their third birthday, most children are producing utterances that are on average three linguistic units long (Hoff, 2009).

Vasilyeva et al. (2008) documented the emergence of complex sentence structures during the second year (examples are from Vasilyeva et al.). The earliest and most frequently used complex structure was the object complement (e.g., *Want you draw that for me; Make her eat*). By 26 months, other structures were being used, the most frequent of which were coordinated sentences (e.g., *You will be the prince, and I will be the princess*). Starting at 34 months, subordinated clauses (e.g., *They go to sleep when it's bedtime*) were about as frequent as coordinates.

The sentences produced by toddlers often are not fully fleshed out with function morphemes—the "little words" and suffixes that form the structural framework of language. For example, a 2-year-old might say, "Puppy want cookie," when an adult would say, "The puppy wants my cookie." However, the repertoire of morphemes expands rapidly in the third year. The order in which morphemes are acquired is quite consistent for English-speaking children, as observed by Roger Brown and his students in case studies (Brown, 1973) and supported by a large-scale normative study (Fenson et al., 1994). Among the earliest suffixes produced are the present progressive *–ing*, the plural and possessive *–s*, and the regular past tense *–ed*. Some of the earliest prepositions produced are *up*, *down*, *in*, and *out*. Irregular forms of verbs—past tense (e.g., *broke, went*) and third-person singular present tense (e.g., *has, does*)—are usually acquired before regular forms. Pronouns (e.g., *he, she, it, them*) are used consistently by about 40 months. Auxiliary and copula verb forms (*am, is, are, was, were*) emerge later in the third year.

3 to 5 years

The preschool years are a time of continued learning, as well as consolidation of earlier-acquired skills. Mastery of function morphemes is a protracted process. Children use these morphemes inconsistently for some time, for example, saying, "He is running" one moment and "He running" the next. By about the fourth birthday, however, most children are using function morphemes correctly almost all of the time.

At the same time that children are mastering the use of morphemes, they also continue to produce different types of sentences. Children also produce more questions, including yes/no questions (e.g., *Are we there yet?*) and wh-questions (e.g., *What is that one called?*). Questions using *what*, *where*, and *who* usually precede questions using *when, how,* and *why* (Zukowski, 2013). Some types of sentences have a protracted developmental course that continues through the pre-school years and even beyond. For English-speaking children, the comprehension and production of passive sentences (e.g., *The cow was kicked by the horse*) is a slow process. Relative clauses, especially so-called object-gap relative clauses (e.g., *There is the girl that the clown frightened*) also continue to develop during the preschool years (Zukowski, 2013).

Preschoolers are in the process of bringing together all of their communicative resources to become conversationalists and storytellers. For example, during this period, children increasingly integrate iconic and "beat" gestures—the nonsymbolic, up-down movements of arms and hands that serve to emphasize speech—with their utterances (Nicoladis, Mayberry, & Genesee, 1999). They produce narratives that, although still far from being mature, follow a temporal or causal sequence, and begin to take into account other people's perspectives (Pence & Justice, 2008).

Related to taking perspectives is the continuing development of "theory of mind." This term refers to the understanding that people have mental states (beliefs, desires, thoughts, wishes, etc.) and that behavior can be explained and predicted in terms of these mental states. Much research has investigated children's understanding of others' false beliefs. Imagine a scenario in which a boy has placed his chocolate bar in a drawer and then gone out to play. While he is out, his mother moves the chocolate bar to the refrigerator. When the boy comes back, ready to eat the chocolate, where will he look for it? A typical 3-year-old will respond that he will look in the refrigerator—the true location, known to the 3-year-old but not the child in the scenario. A typical 5-year-old will predict that the boy will look for the chocolate bar in the drawer—the location that accords with the supposed belief of the boy in the scenario, which is now false. Researchers have found that language ability and false belief understanding are closely related (de Villiers, 2007). The precise nature of the relation is still unresolved, but it is clear that a competent communicator must be able to take into account the knowledge and beliefs of his interlocutor.

Literature in CSD has highlighted that communication is distributed across linguistic, gesture, and social-emotional resources for all individuals, including children with linguistic impairments. For example, children with Asperger's syndrome or high-functioning autism often have strong linguistic skills but continue to struggle within the complex multimodal landscapes of social interactions. On a related note, forms of speech-generating technologies that have attempted to serve as substitutes for speech in children with speech-language impairments have proven powerful in some contexts, such as scripted performances, but have often lacked the flexibility needed for spontaneous exchanges that are often quick and richly multimodal. To illustrate, a case study by Mellman, DeThorne, and Hengst (2010) of three school-age boys with speech-generating devices revealed that only one of the children appeared to be using his device in the classroom, and in that case, the most frequent category of device use was responses prompted by an adult (e.g., "What number comes after six?"). In addition, peer interactions were notably limited across the three participants and seemed to rely on a combination of facial expressions, eye gaze, gesture, and speech/vocalization. In sum, both through their strengths and weaknesses, children with speech-language impairments have illuminated the importance of conceptualizing communication as a richly multimodal phenomenon.

COMMUNICATION IS DISTRIBUTED ACROSS TIME

In addition to people and resources, communication is invariably distributed across time. Although the construct of time can be considered from many perspectives, including the historical perspective of cultural traditions (cf. Nasir & Hand, 2006; Ochs & Schieffelin, 1994), we focus here on the course of individual development.

It is common to talk about how intrinsic abilities, such as language, gesture, and social-emotional expression, are shaped by the passing of time due to children's physiological maturation and accrued experiences. However, here we highlight the less transparent point that communication, as a broader phenomenon that is distributed across people and resources, is also distributed across time. Across time, the child and his communication partners are creating a shared history and future narrative. This shared history means that each communication act is enmeshed in a network of shared knowledge, expectations, emotions, and associations—what is sometimes called "common ground" (Tomasello, Carpenter, & Liszkowski, 2007). Participants in the interaction know what worked before and what didn't work, how they felt about it, how their partner responded, what the partner knows and doesn't know, and so on. As a result, patterns of communication shift and often condense across time with familiar partners, particularly within the context of familiar routines. Think of an inside joke you share with a friend. Over time, the two of you can likely elicit reference to such a memory with little more than a glance, a gesture, or a single word. This same process is also evident in young children in their interactions with familiar caregivers, which is what frequently makes parents such effective interpreters for their children. Take as an example an interaction recently observed during data collection of an ongoing treatment study of young children with impaired speech-language development. The 3-year-old pointed to the clock on the wall, looked at his examiner, and said, "mauw." The meaning was lost on the unfamiliar examiner who guessed that perhaps the child was saying "now." However, the mother interpreted for us that the child was saying "mouse" in reference to a children's book that the two often read together that includes a mouse in a clock. Although both the examiner and the caregiver were relying on their prior experiences to interpret the interaction (i.e., in the case of the examiner, she was linking the clock to her concepts of words that associate with time), the example highlights that communication is often facilitated when individuals' experiences become aligned.

It would be shortsighted to acknowledge the role of the past in shaping communication without also noting the role of our anticipated futures. To illustrate, consider how differently you might respond to a tedious conversation with an unfamiliar partner at a party if you never anticipated seeing this person again versus if you knew the colorless conversationalist had just been appointed as your new boss. In the former case you might be more apt to make an abrupt comment to facilitate a quick getaway, whereas in the latter you might be more apt to feign interest and nod politely. So, too, children's interactions with others are shaped by future expectations for the relationship—both by the child and by the child's communication partner. For example, a parent's patience for an extended bedtime routine is likely to vary depending on how much work she needs to get done after the child is asleep. A child may cry longer and harder when being dropped off at childcare if she has not yet noted the pattern of her mother's unfailing return.

In sum, any single communicative exchange can be thought of as one intersection in a complex array of behavioral trajectories. Consequently, one's behavior is shaped by both where one has been and where one intends to go—both for the child and the child's communication partner. Recognizing that communication is distributed across time highlights the value of familiar partners in the development of children's communication. Mothers as communication partners have traditionally received most of the attention in the research literature, often to the exclusion of others (cf. Ochs & Schieffelin, 1994). Without disparaging the crucial role mothers play, our perspective on communication across time emphasizes that children build shared histories with a variety of partners, some more communicatively skilled than the child, and some, like peers and siblings, equally or less skilled. All communication partners are important influences on the nature of the child's developmental trajectory.

Work related to communication impairments has highlighted the role of both familiarity and relationship. In particular, multiple articles have underscored the importance of including caregivers in the assessment and treatment process. In particular, a study by Bornstein, Haynes, Painter, and Genevro (2000) found that 2-year-olds produced more utterances and used more different words when interacting with their mothers than with a less familiar examiner. Similarly, numerous studies have emphasized the effectiveness of parent-implemented interventions (Girolametto & Weitzman, 2006). Such interventions capitalize on the familiarity and investment of parent-child relationships and, as previously mentioned, capitalize on the role of caregivers as proficient interpreters. As a specific example, consider a 9-year-old boy with autism and apraxia of speech who was recently observed rolling up his babysitter's pant legs. When asked what was happening, the babysitter interpreted with a smile, "He likes to imitate a tough guy by rolling up his sleeves before throwing a pretend punch. Since I'm wearing a shirt without sleeves, he is helping me prepare for a pretend fight with him by rolling up my pant legs." Without a shared history, this child's communicative intent would not likely have been fully available to his communication partner. Over time, all children establish many such shortcuts and routines with their caregivers and other familiar partners, but they may not be recognized as such because they are so much a part of the natural ebb and flow of communication.

FUTURE DIRECTIONS IN COMMUNICATION DEVELOPMENT

Communication interactions, when successful, often appear so effortless that the complexity is lost to the casual observer. We suggest that future research needs to embrace ethnographic approaches and use situated theories of children's communication development to directly study and document the complexity of social interactions. To paraphrase a point made by Ochs and Schieffelin (1994), language structure and use have been a long-standing focus of investigation; however, the child as language user is a relatively unexamined focus of scholarly interest (p. 471). Ten years later, literature in the field of family communication is still markedly missing research on children's lived experiences as communicators (Miller-Day, Pezalla, & Chesnut, 2013). Similarly, literature in communication sciences and disorders has focused almost exclusively on experimental group designs to describe the nature of children's linguistic impairments. Little attention has been given to the complexity and resilience of the children's communicative interactions in everyday life. We recommend ethnographic approaches, not to replace reductionist experimental models, but as a means to augment, enrich, and contextualize them (cf. Miller, Hengst, & Wang, 2003; Miller-Day et al., 2013).

Ethnographic methods also offer the opportunity to build appreciation for the heterogeneity of child language development and the richness of everyday communicative practices across diverse communities (Harris, 1996; Ochs & Schieffelin, 1994). To date, much of the literature on child communication development has focused on what Ochs and Schieffelin (1994) referred to as the "white middle-class developmental story." Such cultural monocentrism has perpetuated the myth of language homogeneity and led to the reliance on deficit-based models to describe cultural-linguistic variation (Harris, 1996; Lane, Pillard, & Hedberg, 2011; Straus, 2013). Consequently, future research needs to illustrate communication practices across various cultural groups that will help us understand the complexities of children's communication development across the full spectrum of our increasingly diversified and globalized society (Blommaert & Rampton, 2011; Socha, Sanchez-Hucles, Bromley, & Kelly, 1995; West & Turner, 1995). Understanding individual and cultural differences in communication practices will ultimately lead us to a more complete account of the development of human communication.

REFERENCES

Acredolo, L. P., & Goodwyn, S. W. (1988). Symbolic gesturing in normal infants. *Child Development, 59,* 450–466.

Adamson, L. B. (1995). *Communication development during infancy.* Madison, WI: Brown & Benchmark.

American Speech-Language-Hearing Association (ASHA). (2013). *How does your child hear and talk?* Retrieved August 20, 2013, from http://www.asha.org/public/speech/development/chart.htm

Bartsch, K., & Wellman, H. (1995). *Children talk about the mind.* Oxford, England: Oxford University Press.

Bates, E., & Dick, F. (2002). Language, gesture, and the developing brain. *Developmental Psychobiology, 40,* 293–310.

Blommaert, J., & Rampton, B. (2011). Language and superdiversity. *Diversities, 13*(2), 1–21.

Bloom, L., & Tinker, E. (2001). The Intentionality model and language acquisition. *Monographs of the Society for Research in Child Development, 66*(4), 1–90.

Bornstein, M. H., Haynes, O. M., Painter, K. M., & Genevro, J. L. (2000). Child language with mother and with stranger at home and in the laboratory: A methodological study. *Journal of Child Language, 27*, 407–420.

Bretherton, I., & Beeghly, M. (1982). Talking about internal states: The acquisition of an explicit theory of mind. *Developmental Psychology, 18*, 906–921.

Brown, R. (1973). *A first language: The early stages.* Cambridge, MA: Harvard University Press.

Burleson, B. R. (1984). Comforting communication. In H. E. Sypher & J. L. Applegate (Eds.), *Communication by children and adults: Social cognitive and strategic processes: Vol. 5 in Sage series in interpersonal communication* (pp. 63–104). Beverly Hills, CA: Sage.

Carpenter, M., Nagell, K., & Tomasello, M. (1998). Social cognition, joint attention, and communicative competence from 9 to 15 months of age. *Monographs of the Society for Research in Child Development, 63*(4), 1–143.

Ciccia, A. H., Step, M., & Turkstra, L. (2003, December). Show me what you mean: Nonverbal communication theory and clinical application. *ASHA Leader, 22*(8) 4–5, 34.

Delia, J. G., & O'Keefe, B. J. (1979). Constructivism: The development of communication in children. In E. Wartella (Ed.), *Children communicating: Media and development of thought, speech, understanding: Vol. 7 in Sage annual reviews of communication research* (pp. 157–185). Beverly Hills: Sage Publications.

DeThorne, L., Hengst, J. A., Fisher, K., & King, A. (2013). Keep your eye on the prize: Implementing AAC within the broader context of communicative competence. *Young Exceptional Children.* doi:10.1177/1096250613485453

de Villiers, J. (2007). The interface of language and Theory of Mind. *Lingua, 117*, 1858–1878.

Dunn, J. (1988). *The beginnings of social understanding.* Cambridge, MA: Harvard University Press.

Dunst, C. J., & Lowe, L. W. (1986). From reflex to symbol: Describing, explaining, and fostering communicative competence. *Augmentative and Alternative Communication, 2*, 11–18.

Fenson, L., Dale, P. S., Reznick, J. S., Bates, E., Thal, D., & Pethick, S. J. (1994). Variability in early communicative development. *Monographs of the Society for Research in Child Development, 59*(5), 1–173.

Fenson, L., Pethick, S. J., Renda, C., Cox, J. L., Dale, P. S., & Reznick, J. S. (2000). Short-form versions of the McArthur Communicative Development Inventories. *Applied Psycholinguistics, 21*, 95–116.

Girolametto, L., & Weitzman, E. (2006). It takes two to talk—The Hanen Program for parents: Early language intervention through caregiver training. In R. J. McCauley & M. E. Fey (Eds.), *Treatment of language disorders in children* (pp. 77–104). Baltimore, MD: Brookes.

Goldin-Meadow, S., & Iverson, J. (2010). Gesturing across the life span. In R. M. Lerner, M. E. Lamb, & A. M. Freund (Eds.), *The handbook of life-span development* (pp. 754–791). Hoboken, NJ: John Wiley & Sons.

Gredebäck, G., Fikke, L., & Melinder, A. (2010). The development of joint visual attention: A longitudinal study of gaze following during interactions with mothers and strangers. *Developmental Science, 13*, 839–848.

Harris, J. L. (1996). Issues in recruiting African American participants for research. In A. G. Kamhi, K. E. Pollock, & J. L. Harris (Eds.), *Communication development and disorders in African American children: Research, assessment, and intervention* (pp. 19–34). Baltimore, MD: Brookes.

Haslett, B. B., & Samter, W. (1997). *Children communicating: The first 5 years.* Mahwah, NJ: Erlbaum.

Hengst, J. A., & Miller, P. J. (1999). The heterogeneity of discourse genres: Implications for development. *World Englishes, 18*, 325–341.

Hoff, E. (2009). *Language development* (4th ed.). Belmont, CA: Wadsworth.

Hopper, R., & Naremore, R. J. (1978). *Children's speech: A practical introduction to communication development* (2nd ed.). New York, NY: Harper & Row.

Hulit, L. M., Howard, M. R., & Fahey, K. R. (2011). *Born to talk: An introduction to speech and language development* (5th ed.). Boston, MA: Pearson.

Iverson, J. M., & Goldin-Meadow, S. (2005). Gesture paves the way for language development. *Psychological Science, 16*, 367–371.

Kisilevsky, B., Hains, S., Lee, K., Xie, X., Huang, H., Ye, H. H., Zhang, K., & Wang, Z. (2003). Effects of experience on fetal voice recognition. *Psychological Science, 14*, 220–224.

Lane, H., Pillard, R. C., & Hedberg, U. (2011). *The people of the eye: Deaf ethnicity and ancestry.* New York, NY: Oxford University Press.

Leslie, A. M. (1994). *Pretending* and *believing*: Issues in the theory of TOMM. *Cognition, 50*, 211–238.

Mellman, L. M., DeThorne, L. S., & Hengst, J. A. (2010). "Shhhh! Alex has something to say": AAC-SGD use in the classroom setting. *Perspectives on Augmentative and Alternative Communication, 19*, 108–114. doi:10.1044/aac19.4.108.

Meltzoff, A. (1995). Understanding the intentions of others: Re-enactment of intended acts by 18-month-old children. *Developmental Psychology, 31*, 838–850.

Meltzoff, A., & Moore, M. K. (1998). Infant intersubjectivity: Broadening the dialogue to include imitation, identity, and intention. In S. Braten (Ed.), *Intersubjective communication and emotion in early ontogeny* (pp. 47–62). Cambridge, England: Cambridge University Press.

Messinger, D., & Fogel, A. (2007). The interactive development of social smiling. In R.V. Kail (Ed.), *Advances in child development and behavior* (Vol. 35, pp. 327–366). London, England: Academic Press.

Miller, P. J., Hengst, J. A., & Wang, S. (2003). Ethnographic methods: Applications from developmental cultural psychology. In P. M. Camic, J. E. Rhodes, & L. Yardley (Eds.), *Qualitative research in psychology: Expanding perspectives in methodology and design* (pp. 219–242). Washington, DC: American Psychological Association.

Miller-Day, M., Pezalla, A., & Chesnut, R. (2013). Children are in families too! The presence of children in communication research. *Journal of Family Communication, 13*(2), 150–165.

Moore, C., & Dunham, P. J. (Eds.). (1995). *Joint attention: Its origins and role in development.* Hillsdale, NJ: Erlbaum.

Mundy, P., Block, J., Delgado, C., Pomares, Y., Van Hecke, A. V., & Parlade, M. V. (2007). Individual differences and the development of joint attention in infancy. *Child Development, 78*, 938–954.

Nasir, N., & Hand, V. (2006). Exploring sociocultural perspectives on race, class, and learning. *Review of Educational Research, 74*(4), 449–475.

Nazzi, T., Bertoncini, J., & Mehler, J. (1998). Language discrimination by newborns: Toward an understanding of the role of rhythm. *Journal of Experimental Psychology: Human Perception and Performance, 24*, 756–766.

Nelson, K. (1973). Structure and strategy in learning to talk. *Monographs of the Society for Research in Child Development, 38*(1–2), 1–135.

Nicoladis, E., Mayberry, R. I., & Genesee, F. (1999). Gesture and early bilingual development. *Developmental Psychology, 35*, 514–526.

Ochs, E., & Schieffelin, B. B. (1994). Language acquisition and socialization: Three developmental stories and their implications. In B. G. Blount (Ed.), *Language, culture, and society: A book of readings* (2nd ed., pp. 470–512). Prospect Heights, IL: Waveland.

Pence, K. L., & Justice, L. M. (2008). *Language development from theory to practice.* Upper Saddle River, NJ: Pearson.

Pine, J. M., & Lieven, E. V. M. (1993). Reanalysing rote-learned phrases: Individual differences in the transition to multi-word speech. *Journal of Child Language, 20,* 551–571.

Prizant, B. M., Wetherby, A. M., Rubin, E., Laurent, A. C., & Rydell, P. J. (2006). *The SCERTS model: A comprehensive educational approach for children with autism spectrum disorders* (Vol. 1, *Assessment*). Baltimore, MD: Brookes.

Seikel, J. A., King, D. W., & Drumright, D. G. (2010). *Anatomy and physiology for speech, language, and hearing* (4th ed.). Clifton Park, NY: Delmar Cengage Learning.

Shatz, M. (1994). *A toddler's life: Becoming a person.* New York, NY: Oxford University Press.

Snow, D., & Balog, H. L. (2002). Do children produce the melody before the words? A review of developmental intonation research. *Lingua, 112,* 1025–1058.

Socha, T. J., Sanchez-Hucles, J., Bromley, J., & Kelly, B. (1995). Invisible parents and children: Exploring African-American parent-child communication. In T. J. Socha & G. H. Stamp (Eds.), *Parents, children, and communication: Frontiers of theory and research* (pp. 127–145). Mahwah, NJ: Erlbaum.

Socha, T. J., & Yingling, J. (2010). *Families communicating with children: Building positive developmental foundations.* Cambridge, England: Polity Press.

Stafford, L., & Dainton, M. (1995). Parent-child communication within the family system. In T. J. Socha & G. H. Stamp (Eds.), *Parents, children, and communication: Frontiers of theory and research* (pp. 3–21). Mahwah, NJ: Erlbaum.

Straus, J. N. (2013). Autism as culture. In L. J. Davis (Ed.), *The disability studies reader* (4th ed., pp. 460–484). New York, NY: Routledge.

Tomasello, M., Carpenter, M., & Liszkowski, U. (2007). A new look at infant pointing. *Child Development, 78,* 705–722.

Trevarthen, C. (1998). The concept and foundations of infant intersubjectivity. In S. Braten (Ed.), *Intersubjective communication and emotion in early ontogeny* (pp. 15–46). Cambridge, England: Cambridge University Press.

Vasilyeva, M., Waterfall, H., & Huttenlocher, J. (2008). Emergence of syntax: Commonalities and differences across children. *Developmental Science, 11,* 84–97.

Vihman, M. M., & Miller, R. (1988). Words and babble at the threshold of language acquisition. In M. D. Smith & J. L. Locke (Eds.), *The emergent lexicon: The child's development of a linguistic vocabulary* (pp. 151–183). San Diego, CA: Academic Press.

Warren, S. F., Bredin-Oja, S. L., Escalante, M. R., Finestack, L. H., Fey, M. E., & Brady, N. C. (2006). Responsivity education/Prelinguistic milieu teaching. In R. J. McCauley & M. E. Fey (Eds.), *Treatment of language disorders in children* (pp. 47–76). Baltimore, MD: Brookes.

Wartella, E. (1979). *Children communicating: Media and development of thought, speech, understanding: Vol. 7. Sage annual reviews of communication research.* Beverly Hills, CA: Sage.

Wertsch, J. V. (1991). *Voices of the mind: A sociocultural approach to mediated action.* Cambridge, MA: Harvard University Press.

West, R., & Turner, L. H. (1995). Communication in lesbian and gay families: Building a descriptive base. In T. J. Socha & G. H. Stamp (Eds.), *Parents, children, and communication: Frontiers of theory and research* (pp. 147–169). Mahwah, NJ: Erlbaum.

Wood, B. S. (1976). *Children and communication: Verbal and nonverbal language development.* Englewood Cliffs, NJ: Prentice-Hall.

Yingling, J. (1995). The first relationship: Infant-parent communication. In T. J. Socha & G. H. Stamp (Eds.), *Parents, children, and communication: Frontiers of theory and research* (pp. 23–41). Mahwah, NJ: Erlbaum.

Zukowski, A. (2013). Putting words together. In J. Berko Gleason & N. Bernstein Ratner (Eds.), *The development of language* (pp. 120–162). Boston, MA: Pearson.

CHAPTER FOUR

Parent-Infant Communication

BETH BONNIWELL HASLETT AND WENDY SAMTER

Note: The authors contributed equally to this chapter

It is no exaggeration to say that children's earliest communicative interactions have lifetime implications for their future success—in terms of social and emotional well-being, as well as academic and career achievement. In what follows, we explore the capacities infants and young children bring to interaction, and how parents and other caretakers respond to them—it is this give-and-take that forms the foundation of communicative and social development (Yingling, 1995).

At the outset, we need to acknowledge that there is significant diversity in the configuration of families today—single-parent families, traditional families, blended families, homosexual families, and families with adopted children. By 2015, one-third of the U.S. population will be composed of people of color (Sherif & Haemon, 2007). Amid these population shifts also comes more varied communication and cultural practices, and many will be reflected in family interaction patterns. Moreover, it is important to note that increasing diversity in cultural practices is not just a U.S. phenomenon. Globalization is a major factor transforming life across developing and developed nation-states (Trask, 2010) and influences how families are configured, their child-rearing practices, and thus their children's social, emotional, and physical well-being (Shaffer, Joplin, & Hsu, 2011). While the scope of this chapter prohibits us from tackling any of these issues in depth, we will discuss, whenever possible, cultural and family diversity in how early interactions are developed. Acknowledging that one model does not fit all in effective family and parenting styles has significant implications for social values, attitudes, and public policy.[1]

CONCEPTUAL, COGNITIVE, AND PERCEPTUAL CAPABILITIES IN INFANTS

For our purposes, we view communication as a standardized, organized, culturally patterned system of behavior that makes possible human relationships (Scheflen, 1972). Important aspects of communication include its multimodal nature and its cultural underpinning. Both verbal and nonverbal dimensions of communication need to be mastered by young children as well as an appreciation of its contextual and contingent nature (Cameron-Faulkner, 2013). Acquiring these skills rests upon the considerable cognitive and perceptual abilities of infants and young children. What then are the capacities of infants for language and communicative acquisition? Below, we focus specifically on those nonverbal capabilities that are closely intertwined with verbal communication, such as vision, vocalization, gesture, touch and facial expressiveness (Haslett & Samter, 1997).[2]

Vision

Gaze plays an important role in attention, learning, and interacting (McGarvey, 2013). An infant is born with the capacity to focus about eight inches away—the approximate distance to his/her mother's eyes when in a normal bottle or breast feeding position. Thus, newborns' vision develops from close-up to more distant visual acuity, and they prefer to look at complex pictures or designs. In particular, infants tend to focus on human faces, which allows them to process various mouth and eye movements used in interaction. Studies also show that infants respond to different facial expressions exhibited by their caretakers. Their focus on the human face facilitates their early interactions with others, and infants frequently respond by imitating or mirroring others' facial expressions.

Vocal Stimuli

Vocal stimuli are processed in utero, and almost immediately after birth, infants orient to the sound of human voices. At two months, infants respond uniquely to their mother's voice and to different sounds of a language. In addition infants are much more likely to be soothed by a human voice than by other sounds. Infants can produce a wide range of sounds, but gradually focus on those unique to their native language. Infants also respond to caretakers' utterances by re-vocalizing them, using different intonational patterns, thus displaying early recognition of emotional signaling (Haslett & Samter, 1997).

Bodily Control

Coordination of the eyes and gestures requires considerable muscular acuity by young children and is necessary for pointing, reaching, and touching behavior—all important components of nonverbal communication. Daum, Sommerville, and Prinz (2009) suggest that

> young infants must rely primarily on the production and perception of bodily states and movements in self and others to navigate their social world ... [and they] also provide ideal models for studying the way in which emerging *symbolic modes* (language-based) of inter- action and communication co-exist and cross talk with embodied (body-based) modes. (p. 1196)

Facial Expressions

Facial expressions are key features of interaction. Ekman (1982) suggests that some basic emotions, like fear and surprise, are nonverbal universals that are sig- naled in similar ways across all cultures. Facial expressions can indicate discrete emotions, such as fear, or affective-cognitive blends such as sadness (Izard, 1994). As early as three months, infants imitate facial expressions and engage in face-to- face reciprocal exchanges with adults. Around this same time, the infant's smile becomes typically elicited by familiar others (Stern, 1977).

Thus, babies come into this world with considerable cognitive and perceptual capabilities that lay the foundation for communicative development. Given these capacities, how do parents and other significant adults respond to and engage in- fants? In general, parents establish coordinated activities with infants and thus help them focus attention on ongoing activities. Such skills as timing, scaffolding, reinforcement, social learning, and modeling occur during these coordinated ac- tivities (Bruner & Watson, 1983; Butler & Markman, 2012). Especially important are the development of preverbal routines which help provide stable, recurrent be- havioral patterns and a sense of a secure, safe environment; at nine months, infants often initiate preverbal routines. In what follows, we discuss these communicative rituals and routines.

ADULT-INFANT INTERACTIONS

In this section, we overview some of the more important forms of interaction in which parents and their youngsters engage throughout infancy and early childhood.

Much of this work—especially that examining the first year of life—has focused on mother-child interactions and our review will necessarily reflect that fact. However, subsequent research has shown that what seems to matter most to a child's successful development is the presence of a consistent, supportive, and responsive caretaker—whether father, uncle, aunt, or grandparent.

Mothers and Infant Communication: Infant Elicited Social Behaviors and Attunement

Infant elicited social behaviors. Nearly four decades ago, Stern (1977) used the term "infant elicited social behaviors" to denote the overblown expressions we almost automatically direct toward babies. A classic example of an infant elicited social behavior is baby talk or "motherese" (often referred to as adult-child language [ACL] or child-directed speech [CDS]). ACL is marked by simplified syntax, short length of utterance, nonsense syllables, raised pitch, increased loudness, altered speed, and longer vowel duration. In general, maternal child-directed speech, "including vocabulary, complexity and speech clarity, is related to children's early language development…. [P]arents progressively increase the complexity of their language to encourage the child to produce slightly more complex structures" (Majorano, Rainieri, & Corsano, 2012, pp. 2–3).

Gaze is another infant elicited behavior that is critical for infant engagement. During play interactions, mothers not only simultaneously gaze and vocalize at them, but also spend upward of 70% of the time looking at their infants, with an average gaze duration of about 20 seconds; this is significantly longer than gaze patterns in "normal" adult conversations. Exaggeration is also typical of the facial expressions mothers employ when interacting with their infants. These expressions are slow to form, held for several seconds, and limited in scope. In fact, Stern (1977) argues that caretakers typically limit their repertoire to a small number of facial displays that facilitates infant engagement; these include mock surprise, smile, frown, what Stern calls the "oh you poor dear" expression of concern, and a neutral expression.

The attunement of what mothers naturally do with their babies—and the innate capabilities with which infants are born—has been referred to as co-regulation, coordination, attunement, synchrony, reciprocal engagement, and, in attachment terms, maternal sensitivity. Such exchanges become increasingly complex across development. For instance, very young infants display mutual attention and interest in a social partner by imitating facial expressions (Meltzoff & Moore, 1977), and by two months, babies engage in mutual regulation of attention, emotions, and behavior in face-to-face interactions (Trevarthen, 1977). Studies further demonstrate that young babies typically produce speech-like vocalizations when interacting with their mothers, and after four months, when they explore the environment in the presence of the mother (Hsu & Fogel, 2001). As Haapakoski and Silven (2009) explain, "Infants respond, for example, with mounting arousal, happy vocalizations, and enthusiastic body movements to mother's greeting behavior" (p. 197).

With the youngster's increasing hand-eye coordination, the nature of mother-infant interaction changes as well. As Stern explains, "Their play interactions become a more triadic affair among mother, infant, and object. Different behaviors with different goals come into being" (p. 37). The second half of the first year is also marked by the emergence of infants' more systematic use of communicative gestures and their first words. Throughout this time period, the mother's ability to follow the infant's line of regard in joint attention episodes is related to enhanced vocabulary development (Tomasello & Farrar, 1986).

Protoconversations also emerge at this time. Infants initiate, maintain joint orientation, greet, produce some dialogue, and disengage—all of which is accomplished by both nonverbal and verbal means. Protoconversations lay out some of the fundamental features of subsequent interaction such as turn taking. Through such activities, infants learn that communication carries both an affective (relational) and referential aspect. They also learn to control their communication and to respond appropriately in context (Dore, 1983).

A systematic program of research from a social constructivist framework, by Burleson, Delia, and Applegate and others, links important aspects of parental communication to their influence on children's social-cognitive and communicative skills. Their perspective identifies the complexity in family patterns of interaction and argues that person-centered strategies by parents lead to more skills in perspective-taking and recognition of contextual complexity among children (Burleson, Delia, & Applegate, 1995).

A brief tour of language acquisition. In fact, this developmental period is marked by several important milestones in language acquisition, all of which are facilitated by joint attention episodes between mothers and their children. For example, for most youngsters, evidence of word *comprehension* appears between 8 and 10 months of age and word recognition grows rapidly (Bates, Dale & Thal, 1995). Children begin to *produce* words anywhere between the ages of 8 and 16 months, although most do not show signs of expressive language before 12 months. Development in word production is slow, with a mean of 1.8 words at the start of this period and a gradual increase to a mean of 534 words at 30 months (Bates, Benigni, Bretherton, Camaioni, & Volterra, 1979).

In sum, then, there can be little doubt that the verbal and nonverbal exchanges between parents and children are crucial to a youngster's development in multiple domains. The quality of one-to-one interactions children experience with a caretaker is related to their language development, as we have just seen, but it is also associated with their emerging sense of self, and their social, emotional, and cognitive growth. The nature and function of the mother-child bond are at the core of Attachment Theory, a theory that attempts to explicate individual differences in dyadic "attunement" or "synchrony" and its effects. Next, we briefly trace the ontogeny of this theory, discuss various ways of categorizing attachments and the role maternal sensitivity plays in their development, and overview some of the correlates and consequences of various types of attachment bonds.

Before concluding our discussion of parent-infant interaction, however, a brief word about gender differences is in order. Most studies investigating this topic were conducted in the 1970s and 1980s among Western, middle-class families. This work revealed, among other things, that compared to fathers mothers more often hold, vocalize, stimulate, express positive affection, and respond to their infants (Lamb, 1977). Studies also demonstrated that fathers engage infants in more stimulating physical play, whereas mothers involve their infants in more verbal and object-mediated play.

A good deal has changed in Western society in the forty years since these early investigations were performed. If nothing else, as we alluded to earlier, "traditional mothering and fathering roles in the nuclear family have dramatically changed due to the increased participation of women in work outside the home" (Haapakoski & Silven, 2009, p. 197). As a result, there appears to be increasing evidence that mothers and fathers are not as different in their childcare competencies as studies once indicated. For example, today's generation of fathers not only report feeling closer to their sons than they did with their own fathers, but also say that they engage in more verbal and nonverbal displays of affection (Mormon & Floyd, 2002).

ATTACHMENT THEORY

Bowlby and Ainsworth

Drawing on ethological studies of primates, John Bowlby (1969/1982), the author of Attachment Theory, argued that all humans have a fundamental fear of being alone in infancy and throughout life. From this perspective, people come into the world prewired to seek out and establish close relationships with others (called attachment figures) who support and protect them. Such relationships form the basis for "internal working models" (or IWMs), which are composed of the individual's beliefs about whether he/she is worthy (or unworthy) of love and whether others are available, responsive, and trustworthy. Evidence suggests that IWMs are established as early as one to two years of age and can remain relatively stable across the lifespan. Because IWMs serve as "prototypes of human beings," attachment researchers consider them to be a powerful determinant of people's expectations for and behaviors in future relationships.

Mary Ainsworth (1985), Bowlby's colleague for more than 30 years, developed the Strange Situation Paradigm. In the Strange Situation Paradigm, mother-child dyads are placed in a novel setting (hence the name); how toddlers react to the introduction of interesting toys, a stranger, and temporary separation from their mothers is then observed and recorded.

Based on studies utilizing the Strange Situation Paradigm, Ainsworth identified three distinct types of mother-infant attachments: secure, insecure/anxious-ambivalent, and insecure/avoidant. Securely attached youngsters are effective explorers. They use their mothers as a base for investigating the novel playroom and proceed on their mother's encouragement, whereas anxious-ambivalent children demonstrate little interest in exploring the environment and were extremely wary of adult strangers. Although they cry intensely when separated from their mothers, these infants often throw tantrums when she re-enters the playroom. Unlike secure infants, anxious-ambivalent children are not comforted by the reintroduction of their mothers who, in fact, seem to increase their distress and anger. Finally, avoidant infants show premature independence and pay little attention to their mothers while exploring the play area.

Since Ainsworth's seminal work, researchers have not only developed a variety of instruments for assessing attachment in children and adults (Shaver & Hazan, 1994), but also presented other schemes for classifying various attachment bonds, the most notable being the addition of a disorganized attachment (Main & Cassidy, 1988). Most recently, researchers have begun to array attachment along two major dimensions rather than as categorical styles. Underlying the dimension of "attachment related anxiety" is a working model of others as unpredictable sources of support and comfort. In contrast, people scoring high on the dimension of "attachment avoidance" have an internal working model of others as threatening, unworthy, or unavailable (Trillingsgaard, Elklit, Shevlin, & Maimburg, 2011).

Maternal Sensitivity in Attachment

Although researchers have differing perspectives on how best to categorize various forms of attachment, there is little disagreement regarding what fosters such bonds. As Belsky and Fearon (2008) explain,

> Individual differences in attachment security are systematically related to the quality of care that an infant or toddler experiences with a particular caregiver; ... [research demonstrates] that it is both correlational and experimental in nature; longitudinal as well as cross-sectional; apparently cross-culturally generalizable; and derived of studies of fathers and child care providers as well as mothers. (p. 304)

In general, maternal sensitivity involves an understanding of the child's unique attributes, an acceptance of his/her individual behavioral proclivities, a willingness to respond to the infant's signals promptly and efficiently, and the capacity to engage in harmonious interactions, especially during times when the infant is distressed and needs soothing.

Mothers of securely attached infants have been found to react quickly to their children's distress and to engage in warm and affectionate behaviors when their babies seek physical contact; they also strike a balance between responding to infants' signals for stimulation and recognizing when they need a time out to rest and regroup. In contrast, mothers of youngsters exhibiting insecure avoidant attachments have been shown to be intrusive, engage in excessive stimulation, and have a controlling interaction style, whereas mothers of children with insecure resistant attachments have been found to take an unresponsive and under involved approach to caregiving. Finally, mothers of youngsters with disorganized attachments often exhibit contradictory affective cues, role confusion, and/or verbal and physical withdrawal from their children.

It is important to note that the strength of the association between maternal behaviors and attachment security is not large. Various meta-analyses place the effect size somewhere between .17 and .24 (e.g., Goldsmith & Alansky, 1987). However, evidence from several intervention studies suggests that, although somewhat more modest than might be anticipated, the influence of maternal sensitivity on the development of secure attachments does seem to be causal in nature (Bakermans-Kranenburg, van Ijzendoorn, & Juffer, 2003).

The Consequences of Attachment: Individual and Relational Effects

The fact that interventions have been found to increase a mother's ability to form a secure attachment with her infant is encouraging given the profound implications inherent in the absence of a safe and reliable attachment figure. Attachment bonds are thought to be relatively stable, with some research suggesting that attachment styles have trait-like characteristics (e.g., Banai, Weller, & Mikulincer, 1998). Among young children, for example, significant associations have been observed between attachment security and (among other things) emotional regulation, emotional understanding, self-concept, and social competence.

Emotional regulation. As Thompson (2008) explains, one of the functions of attachment relationships is to help the child regulate emotional arousal. Moreover, by accepting and openly communicating about children's feelings, especially those that might be disturbing or threatening, parents in secure relationships "foster the children's developing emotional self-awareness and scaffold the growth of competent, flexible skills in emotion regulation" (p. 356). Studies (e.g., Kochanska, Coy, & Murray, 2001) show that, over time, insecurely attached children demonstrate not only progressively greater fear and anger, but also diminished happiness compared to securely attached youngsters. Such demonstrations can take the form of increased cortisol levels following exposure to moderate stressors among 18-month-old infants (Nachmias, Gunnar, Mangelsdorf, Parritz, & Buss, 1996), to the use of fewer constructive anger management techniques at age 3-and-a-half (Gilliom, Shaw, Beck, Schonberg, & Lukon, 2002), to inappropriate coping methods in middle childhood (Contreras, Kerns, Weimer, Gentzler, & Tomich, 2000).

Emotional understanding. Research shows that securely attached youngsters are better able than their insecurely attached counterparts to identify emotions in others and appear to be particularly adept at understanding negative emotions. Bretherton (1993) has argued that this is because the communication between securely attached children and their parents is open and flexible, and thus encourages the discussion and sharing of various feeling states. Perhaps as the result of such an approach, preschoolers in secure relationships have been found to spontaneously talk about emotions in everyday conversations with their mothers (Raikes & Thompson, 2006) more than preschoolers in insecure relationships.

Self-concept. Bowlby (1969/1982) was the first to contend that attachment influences children's self-concepts, especially with respect to their views of themselves as loved and lovable. A good deal of evidence confirms Bowlby's original hypothesis. Among young children, attachment security has been linked to positive self-esteem (Harter & Pike, 1984), to self-descriptions that have been labeled flexible (Cassidy, 1988), and to self-perceptions as "more agreeable and as expressing less negative affect" (Goodvin, Meyer, Thompson, & Hayes, 2008). In contrast, youngsters with insecure attachment bonds have been found to express more self-doubt and negative appraisals of their abilities when attempting to solve both easy and difficult puzzle tasks (Colman & Thompson, 2002).

Social competence. Many researchers argue that secure children's advanced social cognitive functioning in the areas of emotional regulation and emotional understanding—and the confidence that results from their positive self-image—are at least partially responsible for the quality of relationships they appear to enjoy with peers. A 2001 meta-analysis by Schneider, Atkinson, and Tardif revealed a combined effect size of .20 between parent-child attachment and children's peer relationships. Interestingly, when only close friendships were considered in the meta-analysis, the combined effect size increased to .24; this confirms Bowlby's original assertion that attachment security exerts its strongest effects in close relationships. It is generally believed that the sophisticated social cognitive abilities the securely attached youngsters bring to their social interactions enable them to behave in ways that peers find attractive. As Berlin, Cassidy, and Appleyard (2008) explain, "Although findings are not completely uniform, they are strikingly consistent in illustrating a relation between a secure child-mother attachment and more harmonious interactions with peers, higher regard from peers, and fewer behavioral problems in preschool and elementary school classrooms" (p. 337).

Correlates of Maternal Sensitivity and Attachment Security

At about the same time that interest in the foundations of attachment security was growing, Bronfenbrenner (1979) introduced his ecological perspective on development in an effort to move beyond the mother-child relationship and call attention to the broader context in which children mature. As Belsky and Fearon (2008) explain, "Whereas attachment theory is essentially a theory of the microprocesses of development, emphasizing the daily interactional exchanges between parent and child and the developing internal working model of the child, the ecological/ social contextual perspective draws attention to the contextual factors and processes likely to influence these micro-developmental processes" (p. 296).

One such factor includes gene-environmental interactions. In a recent study, for example, Gervai et al. (2005) found that among children who experienced significant disruptions in maternal communication, only those who had a particular dopamine receptor gene (DRD4) developed the expected disorganized attachment; there was no relationship between disrupted maternal communication and attachment disorganization in youngsters without this receptor gene.

Other factors involve the psychological attributes of the mother, her relationship with her partner, her access to important forms of support, and cultural variation in child-rearing practices. For instance, studies of non-clinical samples indicate that secure relationships are more likely to develop when mothers are psychologically healthy (Maslin & Bates, 1983), claim relatively low levels of prenatal anxiety (Del Carmen, Pedersen, Huffman, & Bryan, 1993), and describe themselves (among other things) as self-confident, independent, cheerful, and adaptable (O'Connor, 1997). Other work suggests that couple functioning also affects the extent to which mothers develop secure attachments with their infants. Both cross-sectional (e.g., Jacobsen & Frye, 1991) and longitudinal investigations (e.g., Howes & Markman, 1989) indicate that children growing up with mothers who perceive their partner relationships as satisfying and supportive tend to develop more secure attachments than children whose mothers feel less supported by and satisfied with partners.

In addition, research has demonstrated a link between the nature and amount of support that parents, especially mothers, experience from significant others and the way they interact with their infants. More specifically, increased maternal responsiveness has been found among middle income European American mothers who reported high levels of prenatal support, among lower income African American mothers who reported larger social networks, and among poor Hispanic women who received help from family and friends when interacting with their three-month-old premature infants. Researchers argue that, in most cases, a mediational model explains the effects of these correlates. As Belsky and Fearon (2008) argue, mediational thinking [generally] stipulates that even though maternal psychological well-being, as well as a mother's marital/couple relationship and social support, may directly affect attachment insecurity (through some unspecified process), most of the effect of such distal factors will flow through their impact on the quality of care the mother actually provides. (p. 307)

Finally, there is some evidence of cross-cultural differences in the overarching attachment goals mothers may develop for their children, as well as the distribution of attachment styles and their effects. For instance, Brown, Hawkins-Rogers, and Kapadia (2008) argue that, whereas Western goals for attachment "move the individual from reliance on a safe base to personal exploration encompassing a wider and wider periphery, with the ultimate goal of autonomy" (p. 358), many Eastern cultures may foster reliance on the collective and "mutual effort" (p. 358). Moreover, studies in Japan (Takashi, 1986) and Israel (Sagi et al., 1985) have yielded different distributions of attachment styles, and among Puerto Ricans increased maternal control does not appear to be associated with insecure attachments as it is in other cultures (Carlson & Harwood, 2003). In many ways, cross-cultural differences make sense because, according to van Ijzendoorn and Sagi-Schwartz (2008), "if all infants used the same fixed strategies to deal with attachment challenges, it would leave no room for adaptation to dynamic changes of the environment" (p. 900). These authors further argue, however, that what does appear to be universal are (a) cultural pressure toward selection of secure attachments in the majority of children, and (b) parental preference for this attachment type.

To summarize briefly, one of the most important aspects of early infant development, according to Attachment Theory, is the sense of trust and security children establish in the first few months of life with their caretakers; this provides a basic sense of their own value, the predictability and security in their world, and the confidence to interact with others. Given the consistent—albeit modest— associations between attachment and a child's well-being, it is important to understand not only what attachment is, but also the myriad factors impacting the development of secure maternal-infant bonds.

COMMUNICATION BETWEEN PARENTS AND YOUNG CHILDREN

As children mature, more and more attention is paid to socialization (Koback & Madsen, 2008), a process that "transpires through interpersonal transactions as people are exposed to and adopt ways of understanding and acting that reflect the norms of their social group" (Bornstein, Mortimer, Lutfey, & Bradley, 2011, p. 27). Researchers generally agree that there are two processes by which youngsters are socialized: one occurring in the context of parent-child relationships and one occurring in the context of peer relationships, particularly friendships. According to Youniss's (1980) seminal work on socialization, in the first process, parents act as "society's agents" who attempt to bring their youngsters' idiosyncratic (and often egocentric) behavior in line with accepted standards. In the second process, termed "reciprocity," youngsters learn that individuals bring unique meanings and desires to their interactions with one another. Within this context, there is a focus on *interaction*; views must be presented, objections must be acknowledged, and a compromise must be worked out. Reciprocity thus leads to what Youniss called a "cooperative production of meaning" which teaches children significant lessons about equality, mutual understanding, and negotiation. It is to this socialization process that we turn first.

Peers as Socializing Agents

By the early part of the second year of life, children begin to direct social behaviors to one another (Brownell & Carriger, 1990). Relatively quickly, they are combined to form complex routines that contain all of the basic features of adult interaction. By age two-and-a-half, children can signal interest in one another, exchange roles, sustain a common focus in play, and make repeated efforts to gain each other's attention (Haslett, 1983; Rubin, 1980). It is through such primitive "conversation" that youngsters develop specialized patterns of interaction leading to their earliest friendships. By age four, children actually begin to use the word "friend" to distinguish between familiar and unfamiliar peers (Hartup, 1983).

Over the next several years, what it means to be a friend—and the specific functions that friendship serves in children's lives—will change. What remains constant across the lifespan, however, is the significance of friendship to a youngster's physical and emotional well-being. Studies show that children who lack friends experience a variety of concurrent and long-term adjustment problems, including academic failure, truancy, school dropout, drug and alcohol abuse, antisocial conduct, juvenile delinquency, and suicidal ideation (for a review, see Ladd, 1999).

Research also demonstrates that parents can employ strategies to enhance their children's social competence. For instance, children whose parents nurture their contact with peers have been found to have a larger number of playmates, spend more time playing in friends' homes, show increased sociability in preschool classrooms, and exhibit higher levels of peer acceptance among boys (Ladd & Gloter, 1988; Ladd & Hart, 1992). According to Hart, Newell, and Olsen (2003), "Involvement, particularly on the part of mothers, is most effective when parents play a mediating role by 'scaffolding' (e.g., verbally coaching about how to extend invitations to play) their child's peer engagements" (p. 773). In addition, the ways parents supervise peer-group activities (Mize, Petit, & Brown, 1995), and advise their children on how to initiate friendships, manage conflicts, and address inter-personal problems have all been shown to facilitate successful negotiation of the peer-group culture (Flannagen, 1996).

Parents as Socializing Agents

Over the past 25 years, evidence has accrued to suggest that various forms of par-enting interact with a youngster's biological predisposition. In particular, work by Belsky and colleagues (e.g., Belsky, Fish, & Isabella, 1991) has shown that a neg-ative temperament can either be enhanced or diminished in difficult children—or evoked in easier ones—when parental responsiveness and involvement are lack-ing. Several schemes exist for capturing how parents socialize their youngsters. In general, almost all reflect the extent to which parents balance the dimensions of control and warmth when interacting with children.

Baumrind's parenting styles. Baumrind (1967) developed what is perhaps one of the most widely recognized schemes for classifying general styles of parenting. Based on extensive observations of parents and their three- and four-year-old chil-dren, Baumrind initially identified three primary parenting types: authoritative, authoritarian, and permissive; later a fourth category, called neglecting, was added.

The authoritative parenting style is responsive, supportive, and flexible. Par-ents are demanding and firm, yet also display warmth and receptivity to children's views. In this style, discipline is accompanied by an account of the transgression that gives children a clear understanding of rules and expectations. In contrast, the authoritarian parenting style is characterized by detached, controlling parental be-haviors; little warmth is apparent, and behavioral rules are strict. Individuals who exhibit this style emphasize power differences in the parent-child relationship, and compliance appears to be a major goal. Discipline is hostile and critical and fails to provide a clear explanation of the youngster's wrongdoing. At the other end of the spectrum, a permissive parenting style is, in Baumrind's words, "nontraditional and lenient." In general, permissive parents are nurturing and communicative with their children, but have low expectations for maturity and self-control. Finally, the uninvolved or neglectful parenting style is marked by very few parental demands, very low responsiveness, and little communication. While the child's basic needs may be met, this type of parent remains largely detached and indifferent.

Not surprisingly, authoritative parenting is generally regarded as the most ef-fective way of "molding competent and content children" (Segrin & Flora, 2011, p. 145); children who are more self-reliant, have more self-control, experience more positive moods, and enjoy a greater degree of social acceptance than those raised in authoritarian, permissive, or neglectful environments. In particular, Baumrind (1995) and others (e.g., Stormshak, Bierman, McMahon, & Lengua, 2000) have found a strong connection between punitive parenting and elevated rates of child disruptive behavior, including oppositional behaviors and aggression. These findings have been observed across different family structures, different races, education levels, genders, and ethnicities (Amato & Fowler, 2002)—although some work does indicate that authoritarian parenting is more common among African Americans and Mexican Americans than it is among European Americans (Driscoll, Russell, & Crockett, 2008). Extant evidence also indicates that, in general, fathers tend to parent with a more authoritarian style, whereas mothers tend to utilize a more authoritative style (McKinney & Renk, 2008).

Ritchie and Fitzpatrick's family orientations. Another scheme was advanced by McLeod and Chaffee (1972), who introduced the idea that, over time, families develop a communication climate. Later, Ritchie and Fitzpatrick (1990) identified two orientations that contribute to this climate: conformity and conversation. The conformity orientation captures the degree to which families emphasize homogeneity (versus heterogeneity) in beliefs, attitudes, and values. The conversation orientation refers to the extent to which family members are encouraged to participate "freely and frequently in interaction without limitations regarding time spent and topics discussed" (Segrin & Flora, 2011, p. 50). Several specific communicative acts germane to parenting and socialization have been linked to each orientation. For instance, families high on conformity tend to use more advice, ask more questions, and communicate for the purpose of personal influence, whereas families high on conversation employ more acknowledgments, reflection, and confirmation, and communicate for relationship reasons (Koerner & Cvancara, 2002). Interestingly, studies show important differential effects of family orientations on children's social competence. Youngsters from high conformity families appear to be most vulnerable; they have been found to be more susceptible to peer pressure, and to exhibit poorer social skills in friendships than children from high conversational families (Koesten, 2004).

The distinct influence of parents and peers in the ongoing socialization of children cannot be underestimated. Researchers from diverse theoretical perspectives have argued that each socializing agent teaches youngsters different lessons about the social world, and thus provides a unique context for cognitive, emotional, and social development.

Before concluding this discussion, however, two points are important to note. First, the increasing diversity in family structures has given rise to a literature on gay and lesbian parenting. If child outcomes are a legitimate estimate of parenting skills, then the results of this work show conclusively that good parenting is not inherently linked to gender. Children of homosexual parents do not differ from children of heterosexual parents on measures of adjustment, nor are they any more likely to experience gender confusion or become homosexual themselves (Meezan & Rausch, 2005).

Second, while there is a conceptual consensus on the positive outcomes associated with warm and responsive parenting throughout early childhood, the empirical effect sizes remain modest (Maccoby, 1992). Consequently, researchers have begun to shift from exploring the main effects of parenting to considering more complex moderators, including the parent-child relationship itself. From this perspective, attachment and later parenting strategies act as separate, but functionally related processes. Kochanska, Aksan, Knaack, and Rhines elegantly describe it in this manner:

> One process involves security, whose fundamental function is to instill trust in the caregiver and confidence in her availability in the event of a threat, stress, or distress…. Security, then, represents a socialization capital, which renders the child receptive to the second process—the parent's specific influence strategies, typically studied in the parenting and discipline research. (2004, p. 1237)

Clearly, parent-infant communication is a crucial ingredient for a child's successful emotional, social, and cognitive well-being. This interactional foundation provides the infant with the necessary trust in the social world and in social relationships so that she or he can negotiate further encounters and experiences.

DIRECTIONS FOR FUTURE RESEARCH

There are important areas for further exploration in parent-infant research. First, we suggest that more types of family structures and nurturing support systems be explored. What are patterns of family interactions in single-parent families? In families where multiple generations live together? In multicultural or multiethnic families? What impact do nannies and daycare workers have on infant and young children's development? What connections between families and society facilitate communicative development (Socha & Stamp, 2009)? We know relatively little about the variety of family and nurturing support systems that exist today. Increasing knowledge about the multiple ways in which parents and infants interact will lead to a richer understanding of developmental processes and the factors that may enhance development.

A related area of investigation would be exploring different cultural patterns of family interaction and looking at how culture is transmitted across the generations. Many of our socialization models are dominated by research done primarily in developed countries—our research models need to be expanded and to look at factors influencing parent-infant interaction in a wide variety of cultures.

Finally, we encourage scholarship in the emerging area of new technologies and their influence on parent-infant interaction. We already have research and anecdotal evidence that the presence of technology is altering interpersonal relationships—the ubiquitous cell phone being a prime example of mediated communicative presence in everyday life. TVs and iPads may serve as electronic "babysitters" and infants and young children are increasingly exposed to a wide range of electronic toys. Exploring the impact of mediated communication in parent-infant interaction and, more broadly, in family patterns of interaction will be a critical area to explore (Jennings & Wartella, 2004). In particular, we need to understand the ways in which mediated and non-mediated communication are integrated in and influence children's socio-cognitive and communicative abilities.

REFERENCES

Ainsworth, M. (1985). Patterns of attachment. *Clinical Psychologist, 38,* 27–29.

Amato, P. R., & Fowler, F. (2002). Parenting practices, child adjustment, and family diversity. *Journal of Marriage and Family, 65,* 1–22.

Bakermans-Kranenburg, M. J., van Ijzendoorn, M. H., & Juffer, F. (2003). Less is more: Meta analysis of sensitivity and attachment interventions in early childhood. *Psychological Bulletin, 129,* 195–215.

Banai, E., Weller, A., & Mikulincer, M. (1998). Interjudge agreement in evaluation of adult attachment style: The impact of acquaintanceship. *British Journal of Social Psychology, 37,* 95–109.

Bates, E., Benigni, L., Bretherton, I., Camaioni, L., & Volterra, V. (1979). *The emergence of symbols: Cognition and communication in infancy.* New York, NY: Academic Press.

Baumrind, D. (1967). Child-care practices anteceding three patterns of preschool behavior. *Genetic Psychology Monographs, 75,* 43–88.

Baumrind, D. (1995). *Child maltreatment and optimal caregiving social contacts.* New York, NY: Garland.

Belsky, J., & Fearon, R. M. P. (2008). Precursors of attachment security. In J. Cassidy & P. R. Shaver (Eds.), *Handbook of attachment: Theory, research and clinical applications* (2nd ed., pp. 295–316). New York, NY: Guilford Press.

Belsky, J., Fish, M., & Isabella, R. (1991). Continuity and discontinuity in infant negative and positive emotionality: Family antecedents and attachment consequences. *Developmental Psychology, 27,* 421–431.

Berlin, L. J., Cassidy, J., & Appleyard, K. (2008). The influence of early attachments on other relationships. In J. Cassidy & P. R. Shaver (Eds.), *Handbook of attachment: Theory, research, and clinical applications* (pp. 333–347). New York, NY: Guilford Press.

Bornstein, M. H., Mortimer, J. T., Lutfey, K., & Bradley, R. H. (2011). Theories and processes in life-span socialization. In K. L. Fingerman, C. A. Berg, J. Smith, & T. C. Antonucci (Eds.), *Handbook of life-span development* (pp. 27–56). New York, NY: Springer.

Bowlby, J. (1969/1982). *Attachment and loss: Vol. 1. Attachment.* London, England: Basic.

Bretherton, I. (1993). From dialogue to internal work models: The co-construction of self in relationships. In C. A. Nelson (Ed.), *Minnesota Symposium on Child Psychology: Vol. 26. Memory and affect in development* (pp. 237–263). Hillsdale, NJ: Erlbaum.

Bronfenbrenner, E. (1979). *The ecology of human development.* Cambridge, MA: Harvard University Press.

Brown, D., Hawkins-Rodgers, Y., & Kapadia, K. (2008). Multicultural considerations for the application of attachment theory. *American Journal of Psychotherapy, 62,* 353–363.

Brownell, C., & Carriger, M. (1990). Changes in cooperation and self-other differentiation during the second year. *Child Development, 61,* 1164–1174.

Bruner, J., & Watson, R. (1983). *Child's talk: Learning to use language.* New York, NY: Norton.

Burleson, R., Delia, J., & Applegate, J. (1995). The socialization of person-centered communication: Parents' contributions to their children's social-cognitive and communication skills. In M. Fitzpatrick & A. Vangelisti (Eds.), *Explaining family interactions*. Thousand Oaks, CA: Sage.

Butler, L., & Markman, E. (2012). Preschoolers use intentional and pedagogical cues to guide inductive inferences and exploration. *Child Development, 83*(4), 1416–1428.

Cameron-Faulkner, T. (2013). The interaction of gestures, intonation, and eye-gaze on proto imperatives. *Journal of Child Language, 38*, 1–19.

Carlson, V., & Harwood, R. (2003). Attachment, culture, and the caregiving system: The cultural patterning of everyday experiences among Anglo and Puerto Rican mother infant pairs. *Infant Mental Health Journal, 24*, 53–73.

Cassidy, J. (1988). Child-mother attachment and the self in six-year-olds. *Child Development, 59*, 121–134.

Colman, R. A., & Thompson, R. A. (2002). Attachment security and the problem-solving behaviors mothers and children. *Merrill-Palmer Quarterly, 48*, 337–359.

Contreras, J. M., Kerns, K. A., Weimer, B. L., Gentzler, A. L., & Tomich, P. L. (2000). Emotion regulation as a mediator of association between mother-child attachment and peer relationships in middle childhood. *Journal of Family Psychology, 14*, 111–124.

Daum, M., Sommerville, J., & Prinz, W. (2009). Becoming a social agent: Developmental foundations of an embodied social psychology. *European Journal of Social Psychology, 39*, 1196–1206.

Del Carmen, R., Pedersen, F., Huffman, L., & Bryan, Y. (1993). Dyadic distress management predicts security of attachment. *Infant Behavior and Development, 16*, 131–147.

Dore, J. (1983). Feeling, form, and intention in the baby's transition to language. In R. Golinkoff (Ed.), *The transition from prelinguistic to linguistic communication* (pp. 167–188). Hillsdale, NJ: Erlbaum.

Driscoll, A. K., Russell, S. T., & Crockett, L. J. (2008). Parenting styles and youth well-being across immigrant generations. *Journal of Family Issues, 29*, 185–209.

Ekman, P. (1982). *Emotion in the human face*. New York, NY: Cambridge University Press.

Flannagen, D. (1996). Mothers' and kindergartners' talk about interpersonal relationships. *Merrill-Palmer Quarterly, 42*, 519–536.

Gervai, G., Nemoda, A., Lakatos, K., Ronai, Z., Toth, I., Ney, K., et al. (2005). Transmission disequilibrium tests confirm the link between DRD4 gene polymorphism and infant attachment. *American Journal of Medical Genetics, Part B (Neuropsychiatric Genetics), 132B*, 126–130.

Gilliom, M., Shaw, D. S., Beck, J. E., Schonberg, M. A., & Lukon, J. L. (2002). Anger regulation in disadvantaged preschool boys: Strategies, antecedents, and the development of self-control. *Developmental Psychology, 38*, 222–235.

Goldsmith, H. H., & Alansky, J. A. (1987). Maternal and infant temperamental predictors of attachment: A meta-analytic review. *Journal of Consulting and Clinical Psychology, 55*, 805–816.

Goodvin, R., Meyer, S., Thompson, R. A., & Hayes, R. (2008). Self-understanding in early childhood: Associations with child attachment security and maternal negative affect. *Attachment and Human Development, 10*, 433–450.

Haapakoski, M., & Silven, M. (2009). Families, not parents, differ: Development of communication in Finnish infants. *Infancy, 14*, 195–221.

Hart, C. H., Newell, L. D., & Olsen, S. F. (2003). Parenting skills and social-communicative competence in childhood. In J. O. Greene & B. R. Burleson (Eds.), *Handbook of communication and social interaction skills* (pp. 753–797). Mahwah, NJ: Erlbaum.

Harter, S., & Pike, R. (1984). The Pictorial Scale of Perceived Competence and Social Acceptance for Young Children. *Child Development, 55*, 1969–1982.

Hartup, W. W. (1983). Peer relations. In E. M. Hetherington (Ed.), *Handbook of child psychology: Vol. 4. Socialization, personality, and social development* (pp. 103–196). New York, NY: John Wiley & Sons.

Haslett, B. (1983). Preschoolers' communicative strategies in gaining compliance from peers: A developmental study. *Quarterly Journal of Speech, 69,* 84–99.

Haslett, B., & Samter, W. (1997). *Children communicating: The first 5 years.* Mahwah, NJ: Erlbaum.

Howes, C., & Markman, H. J. (1989). Marital quality and child functioning: A longitudinal investigation. *Child Development, 60,* 1044–1051.

Hsu, H., & Fogel, A. (2001). Infant vocal development in a dynamic mother-infant communication system. *Infancy, 2,* 87–109.

Izard, C. (1994). Innate and universal facial expressions: Evidence from developmental and crosscultural research. *Psychological Bulletin, 115,* 288–299.

Jacobson, S. W., & Frye, K. F. (1991). Effect of maternal social support on attachment: Experimental evidence. *Child Development, 62,* 572–582.

Jennings, N., & Wartella, E. (2004). Technology and the family. In A. Vangelisti (Ed.), *Handbook of family communication.* Mahwah, NJ: Erlbaum.

Kobak, R., & Madsen, S. (2008). Disruptions in attachment bonds: Implications for theory, research, and clinical interventions. In. J. Cassidy & P. R. Shaver (Eds.), *Handbook of attachment: Theory, research, and clinical applications* (pp. 23–47). New York, NY: Guilford Press.

Kochanska, G., Aksan, N., Knaack, A., & Rhines, H. M. (2004). Maternal parenting and children's conscience: Early security as moderator. *Child Development, 75,* 1229–1242.

Kochanska, G., Coy, K. C., & Murray, K. T. (2001). The development of self-regulation in the first four years of life. *Child Development, 72,* 1091–1111.

Koerner, A. F., & Cvancara, K. E. (2002). The influence of conformity orientation on communication patterns in family conversations. *Journal of Family Communication, 2,* 133–152.

Koesten, J. (2004). Family communication patterns, sex of subject, and communication competence. *Communication Monographs, 71,* 226–244.

Ladd, G. W. (1999). Peer relationships and social competence during early and middle childhood. *Annual review of psychology* (Vol. 50, pp. 333–359). Palo Alto, CA: Annual Reviews.

Ladd, G. W., & Gloter, B. S. (1988). Parents' management of preschooler's peer relations: Is it related to children's social competence? *Developmental Psychology, 24,* 109–117.

Ladd, G. W., & Hart, C. H. (1992). Creating informal play opportunities: Are parents' and preschoolers' initiations related to children's competence with peers? *Developmental Psychology, 28,* 1179–1187.

Lamb, M. E. (1977). Father-infant and mother-infant interaction in the first year of life. *Child Development, 48,* 167–181.

Maccoby, E. E. (1992). The role of parents in the socialization of children: An historical overview. *Developmental Psychology, 28,* 1006–1117.

Main, M., & Cassidy, J. (1988). Categories of response to reunion with the parent at age six: Predictable from infant attachment classifications and stable over a one-month period. *Developmental Psychology, 24,* 415–426.

Majorano, M., Rainieri, C., & Corsano, P. (2012). Parents' child-directed communication and child language development: A longitudinal study with Italian toddlers. *Journal of Child Language, 37,* 1–24.

Maslin, C. A., & Bates, J. E. (1983, April). *Precursors of anxious and secure attachments: A multivariate model at age 6 months.* Paper presented at the biennial meeting of the Society for Research in Child Development, Detroit, MI.

McGarvey, K. (2013, September–October). Here's looking at you, kid. *Rochester Review, 2013*, 24–25

McKinney, C., & Renk, K. (2008). Differential parenting between fathers and mothers: Implications for late adolescents. *Journal of Family Issues, 29*, 806–827.

McLeod, J. M., & Chaffee, S. H. (1972). The construction of social reality. In J. Tedeschi (Ed.), *The social influence process* (pp. 50–59). Chicago, IL: Aldine-Atherton.

Meezan, W., & Rauch, J. (2005). Gay marriage, same-sex parenting, and America's children. *The Future of Children, 15*, 97–115.

Meltzoff, A. N., & Moore, M. K. (1977). Imitation of facial and manual gestures by human neonates. *Science, 198*, 75–78.

Mize, J., Petit, G. S., & Brown, G. (1995). Further explorations of family-peer connections: The role of parenting practices and parenting style in children's development of social competence. In P. T. Slee & K. Rigby (Eds.), *Children's peer relationships* (pp. 31–44). New York, NY: Routledge.

Mormon, M. T., & Floyd, K. (2002). A "changing culture of fatherhood": Effects on affectionate communication, closeness, and satisfaction with men's relationships with their fathers and sons. *Western Journal of Communication, 66*, 395–411.

Nachmias, S., Gunnar, M., Mangelsdorf, S., Parritz, R. H., & Buss, K. (1996). Behavioral inhibition and stress reactivity: The moderating role of attachment security. *Child Development, 67*, 508–522.

O'Connor, M. (1997, March). *Maternal personality characteristics on the MMPI and infant attachment.* Paper presented at the biennial meeting of the Society for Research in Child Development, Washington, DC.

Raikes, H. A., & Thompson, R. A. (2006). Family emotional climate, attachment security, and young children's emotional understanding in a high-risk sample. *British Journal of Developmental Psychology, 24*, 89–104.

Ritchie, D. L., & Fitzpatrick, M. A. (1990). Family communication patterns: Measuring intrapersonal perceptions of interpersonal relationships. *Communication Research, 17*, 523–544.

Rubin, Z. (1980). *Children's friendships.* Cambridge, MA: Harvard University Press.

Sagi, A., Lamb, M., Lewkowicz, K., Shoham, R., Dvir, R., & Estes, D. (1985). Security of infant-mother, -father, and -metapelet attachments among kibbutz-reared Israeli children. *Monographs for the Society for Research in Child Development, 50*(1–2), 257–275.

Scheflen, A. (1972). *Body language and the social order.* Edgewood Cliffs, NJ: Prentice-Hall.

Schneider, B., Atkinson, L., & Tardif, C. (2001). Child-parent attachment and children's peer relations: A quantitative review. *Developmental Psychology, 37*, 86–100.

Segrin, C., & Flora, J. (2011). *Family communication* (2nd ed.). New York, NY: Taylor & Francis.

Shaffer, M., Joplin, J., & Hsu, Y. (2011). Expanding the boundaries of work-family research: A review and agenda for future research. *International Journal of Cross Cultural Management, 11*, 221–268.

Shaver, P. R., & Hazan, C. (1994). Attachment. In A. L. Weber & J. H. Harvey (Eds.), *Perspectives on close relationships* (pp. 110–130). Needham Heights, MA: Allyn & Bacon.

Sherif, B., & Haemon, N. (2007). *Cultural diversity in families.* Thousand Oaks, CA: Sage.

Socha, T., & Stamp, G. (2009). *Parents and children communicating with society.* New York, NY: Routledge.

Stern, D. (1977). *The first relationship.* Cambridge, MA: Harvard University Press.

Stormshak, E. A., Bierman, K. L., McMahon, R. J., Lengua, L., & Conduct Problems Prevention Research Group. (2000). Parenting practices and child disruptive behavior problems in early elementary school. *Journal of Clinical Child Psychology, 29*, 17–29.

Takashi, K. (1986). Examining the strange-situation procedure with Japanese mothers and 12-month-old infants. *Developmental Psychology, 22*, 265–270.

Thompson, R. A. (2008). Early attachment and later development: Familiar questions, new answers. In. J. Cassidy & P. R. Shaver (Eds.), *Handbook of attachment: Theory, research, and clinical applications* (pp. 348–365). New York, NY: Guilford Press.

Tomasello, M., & Farrar, M. J. (1986). Joint attention and early language. *Child Development, 57,* 1454–1463.

Trask, B. S. (2010). *Globalization and families: Accelerated systemic social change.* New York, NY: Springer.

Trevarthen, C. (1977). Communication and cooperation in early infancy: A description of primary intersubjectivity. In M. Bullowa (Ed.), *Before speech: The beginning of human communication.* Cambridge, England: Cambridge University Press.

Trillingsgaard, T., Elklit, A., Shevlin, M., & Maimburg, R. (2011). Adult attachment at the transition to motherhood: Predicting worry, health care utility and relationship functioning. *Journal of Reproductive & Infant Psychology, 29,* 354–363.

van Ijzendoorn, M. H., & Sagi-Schwartz, A. (2008). Cross-cultural patterns of attachment: Universal and contextual dimensions. In J. Cassidy & P. R. Shaver (Eds.), *Handbook of attachment: Theory, research, and clinical applications* (pp. 880–905). New York, NY: Guilford Press.

Yingling, J. (1995). The first relationship: Infant-parent communication. In T. Socha & G. Stamp (Eds.), *Parents, children, and communication: Frontiers of theory and research.* Mahwah, NJ: Erlbaum.

Youniss, J. (1980). *Parents and peers in social development: A Sullivan-Piagetian perspective.* Chicago, IL: University of Chicago Press.

NOTES

1 Space prohibits our covering the burgeoning research on developmental delays and deficits in infant and young children's language and communicative skills.

2 There is considerable theoretical controversy surrounding the mechanisms by which an infant's cognitive and perceptual capabilities develop. There is also a substantial literature on the impairments to normal development such as hearing loss, blindness, or lack of oxygen during prenatal growth.

PART THREE

Childhood Communication

CHAPTER FIVE

Media Use and Effects in Childhood

HELEN G. M. VOSSEN, JESSICA TAYLOR PIOTROWSKI,
AND PATTI M. VALKENBURG

The children's media landscape has changed dramatically over the past few decades. The explosive growth of the Internet and digital media platforms has given rise to a new digital media culture. At the same time, media content itself has evolved dramatically. Today's media are more complex, more arousing, and more fast-paced that ever before (e.g., Koolstra, van Zanten, Lucassen, & Ishaak, 2004). This has led researchers, health practitioners, and public policy makers to ask how these changes may be influencing children's development. And while these questions are critical, it is also important to recognize that the relationship between media and child development is not unidirectional, but rather is bidirectional. As a result, not only should we ask how children's media use influences their development, but also how children's development may influence their media use. To that end, this chapter presents both sides of this discussion, paying explicit attention to several key theories that have been used to explain the reciprocal relationship between child development and media.

DEVELOPMENTAL PATTERNS IN MEDIA USE AND MEDIA PREFERENCES

The media children use and prefer are predicted largely by their developmental capabilities. Children have a preference for media that can at least be partly incorporated into their existing framework, and show less preference for extremely simple or extremely complex stimuli (e.g., D. R. Anderson & Lorch, 1983). This *moderate-discrepancy hypothesis* (Valkenburg & Cantor, 2000) predicts that at any given age, a moderate level of stimulus complexity is preferred and that this level increases as the child matures. This hypothesis offers a viable explanation for why the media preferences of children in various age groups differ so greatly. After all, the perceived simplicity and complexity of media content changes dramatically as children mature.

As such, in order to understand children's media usage and preferences, it is important to understand how children typically develop. Here we present a brief review of key developmental characteristics of three periods across childhood (infants and toddlers, early childhood, and middle childhood) and hypothesize how these characteristics influence media use and preferences. We also present statistics regarding the amount of media that is typically consumed during each period, relying primarily on American media use studies. However, in other in-dustrialized countries, children's media use patterns are comparable to the ones presented in this chapter (Beentjes, Koolstra, Marseille, & van der Voort, 2001; Szybist, 2011).

Infants and Toddlers

This age group involves children between birth and 2 years. When children are around 4 months of age, they begin to exhibit interest in television watching. Around this time, their ability to detect cues in their environment has matured, as has their ability to locate a sound in space by turning their head or eyes in the direction of the sounds (Field, Muir, Pilon, Sinclair, & Dodwell, 1980). In the first year of life, the orienting reflex mainly predetermines attention. Infants are typically interested in sudden and novel sounds and movements along with bright colors. In the second year, attention becomes somewhat less influenced by novelty and more influenced by relevant and interesting content. By 18 months, they begin to experi-ence a word spurt of nearly 20 new words per week (Bukatko, 2007). At this point, they enjoy verbally labeling familiar objects (boat, house, train) that they recognize when presented with a storybook or audiovisual media.

Media use for this age group is a rather controversial topic. Beginning with the introduction of *Baby Einstein* in the late 1990s, media for the infant and tod-dler demographic have become an enormous international industry (Christakis, 2009). And yet, many health care practitioners argue that we do not yet know enough about the (potentially negative) influence of media on this audience (e.g., Christakis, 2009). These and other similar concerns have brought about several public policy initiatives. For example, in the United States, the American Acad-emy of Pediatrics discourages screen media exposure in the first 2 years of life

(Council on Communications and Media, 2013). Yet, despite these efforts, recent data show that the average child under 2 years of age is exposed to over an hour of screen time daily (Wartella, Rideout, Lauricella, & Connell, 2013).

Despite the debate on whether or not media are appropriate for this young audience, we do know that infants and toddlers exhibit distinct media preferences. For example, they prefer content that relies heavily on music and song and content with salient formal features is best able to hold their attention. This preference wanes slightly as children become older toddlers (around 18 months old) and is replaced by an interest in simple narratives. Given their limited cognitive and verbal skills, content which relies on slow pacing and familiar contexts, incorporates significant repetition, provides opportunities for verbal labeling, and incorporates simple characters is also appealing for this group.

Early Childhood

Early childhood covers children between 3 and 6 years old. During this period of time, children typically demonstrate egocentrism (i.e., an inability to separate their own perspective from the perspectives of others), as well as perceptual boundedness (i.e., tendency to focus on immediately perceptible attributes of an object) and centration (i.e., tendency to focus on an individual, striking feature of an object) (Bukatko, 2007). Early childhood is characterized by an inability to distinguish between fantasy and reality, as well as by rapid emotional developments (Thomas, 2005). While newborns can produce facial expressions associated with primary emotions such as joy, sadness, and anger, by early childhood, children start to experience conscious emotions such as envy, guilt, and embarrassment. Conscious emotions differ from primary emotions in that they require perspective-taking skills. By age 4, children are able to understand conscious emotions in others. However, their detection of emotions is still perceptually bounded in such a way that they are only able to recognize emotions based on external cues (e.g., crying, sad face).

Today's early childhood media market is one of the most competitive and crowded markets across the media landscape. Children between 3 and 6 years old spend over 3 hours per day using media (Wartella et al., 2013). Younger children (3 years) spend the majority of their media time using television, while older children (4 to 6 years) also begin to add video games to their daily media diet (approximately 30 minutes per day). Finally, in this age group the use of mobile devices such as tablets and smartphones is increasingly used (approximately 30 to 45 minutes per day) but they are not yet using social media.

During early childhood, attention to media content increases dramatically (Valkenburg & Vroone, 2004). This reflects the rapid increase in children's information processing skills and their improved vocabulary. However, their cognitive and emotional capacity is still limited. Children in early childhood lack experience and semantic knowledge, which can make processing new media content challenging. As a result, they typically prefer media content that relies on slow pacing, incorporates repetition, and contains simple characters in familiar contexts. These preferences may change at the end of early childhood when children, especially boys, become more attracted to fast-paced media, more complicated characters, and adventurous contexts. The perceptual boundedness in early childhood leads children to judge media characters by perceptually salient features, thus character appearance and perceptually visible motives and emotions are important. And, because of their inability to distinguish fantasy from reality in media, fantasy characters are just as attractive and engaging as real-life characters.

Middle Childhood

Middle childhood involves children between 7 and 11 years old. During this stage, thought processes become more mature and adult-like. Although children are still unable to engage in abstract thinking, they are now able to think and solve problems in a logical fashion so long as the problems apply to concrete events or objects. Children can now clearly distinguish between fantasy and reality, and as a result, their admiration for cartoon characters decreases dramatically (Valkenburg & Cantor, 2000). Children's ability to understand their own emotions and the emotions of others is continuing to improve. Relatedly, children are increasingly able to understand the perspective of others. The combination of formal school entry during this period and understanding others' perspectives results in an important focus on peer relationships.

Children in middle childhood incorporate media into their daily lives at relatively high rates. In the beginning of middle childhood, we see estimates similar to early childhood with approximately 3 hours per day spent using media, most of which is predominantly television. By about age 8, children spend nearly 4 hours per day viewing television, 1 hour per day playing video games, and 30 minutes per day using social media sites (Rideout, Foehr, & Roberts, 2010). These estimates highlight an increased interest in and use of interactive media.

During this period, children lose their interest for slow-paced educational programs and develop a preference for entertainment media that is faster and more complex, and contains action and violence (Valkenburg, 2004). Children also begin to "decentrate" and develop an interest in detail. As a result, they prefer more complicated media characters and more sophisticated plotlines. However, given that they still struggle with abstract thinking, they prefer content that focuses on concrete problems and objects (e.g., the quest for a treasure). Although children now understand the difference between fantasy and reality, not all children are equally interested in realistic content at this age. Whereas girls typically develop an interest in real-life entertainment, boys more often remain attracted to fantasy content (e.g., Teenage Mutant Ninja Turtles). There is also a change in character preference. While early childhood was characterized by a focus on character appearance, the increased emotional development of middle childhood results in a greater focus on the psychological characteristics of media characters. Children now enjoy characters with which they can psychologically identify, for example, characters with an attractive sense of humor.

THEORIES OF MEDIA EFFECTS DURING CHILDHOOD

Given the amount of time that children spend using media across childhood, it is unsurprising that many researchers have investigated how this media use may impact children's development. These inquiries have been guided by several theories to explain how children are affected by media. Here we present two theoretical models that are commonly used to explain media effects in childhood: Social Cognitive Theory and the Capacity Model. Additionally, we introduce a new theory of media effects, the Differential Susceptibility to Media Effects Model, that represents an integration of several media effects theories to help predict for whom, and when, media effects occur.

Social Cognitive Theory

Social cognitive theory (previously referred to as social learning theory, Bandura, 1977) is one of the most commonly used theories to explain why and how media can influence the behavior of children. The theory posits that behavior is not only learned by one's own experience, but also by observing others (observational learning). Just as children can learn behavior by observing their parents, siblings, and peers, children can also learn new behaviors by observing characters in the media. Social learning theory argues that consequences of the behavior that is portrayed influences whether the behavior will be replicated. Behavior that is rewarded is more likely to be modeled than behavior that is punished (Bandura, 1977). Children will also imitate behaviors that receive no consequences because the lack of punishment is interpreted as tacit reward (Bandura, 1965).

Bandura observed, however, that not all children imitate rewarded behaviors, and not all observed behaviors are immediately performed. This observation led him to incorporate cognitive variables into his theoretical model. This newer perspective, which led to the name social cognitive theory (Bandura, 1986), states that several mental processes are involved in observational learning. As a result, a child's ability to engage in observational learning is dependent upon his/her cognitive development. For successful observational learning, social cognitive theory posits that four sequential cognitive processes must occur.

First, in order to learn behavior through observation, *attention* to the model and the model's behavior is critical. Television characters, in particular, have many distinctive and engaging features which easily attract attention (e.g., bright colors). Attention is also influenced by characteristics of the observer, such as her/his own needs and interests. Second, *retention* is a key cognitive process. Often there is a significant time lag between the observation of the behavior and the performance of the behavior. The observer can model the behavior only if s/he has retained the information. Following retention, the observer must also be able to engage in *motoric reproduction*. Motoric reproduction is a cognitive process in which the stored information is translated into motoric actions. And lastly, *motivation* is an important factor in whether or not the observer reproduces the behavior. In addition to one's personal values, motivation comes from reinforcement that a person receives either directly or vicariously (by observing someone else receiving reinforcement).

Although social cognitive theory was developed from a psychological perspective, this theory has served as an important framework for communication researchers to understand how various media affect their users, particularly children. In particular, this theory has helped researchers understand when children are most likely to imitate behaviors they see in the media (e.g., aggressive behavior and prosocial behavior).

Capacity Model

Despite the large body of research that has investigated the educational potential of television for children (e.g., *Sesame Street*, Fisch & Truglio, 2001), many scholars have noted that there is a dearth of theoretical approaches available to explain how viewers comprehend educational content. In response to this, Fisch (2000) presented the capacity model—a systematic model of comprehension with its roots in information processing research. Central to the model is the idea that working memory is limited and for content to be processed effectively, viewing demands cannot exceed working memory resources.

The capacity model focuses on children's allocation of cognitive resources during television viewing, with specific attention paid to the degree to which working memory resources are allocated to comprehension of narrative versus embedded educational content. Fisch (2000) defines narrative content as content that presents the story in the program, whereas educational content is the underlying educational concept or message that the program is intended to convey.

In the capacity model, demands for cognitive resources are said to come from three basic elements: (1) processing the narrative storyline, (2) processing the educational content, and (3) the distance between the two. In terms of distance, when the educational content and the narrative are divergent, the two comprehension processes are said to compete for limited working memory resources and result in impaired comprehension of the educational content. However, when the educational content is integral to the narrative, comprehension processes are said to become complementary, and comprehension of the educational content will likely be strengthened. The capacity model further predicts that factors that allow for more efficient processing of either the narrative or educational content will reduce the demands associated with processing that type of information and subsequently increase comprehension.

Although the allocation of working memory resources to narrative and educational processing is a function of the demands of each, the capacity model specifies several governing principles that help determine the allocation of resources (Fisch, 2000). First, because television is primarily an entertainment medium, the model posits narrative dominance (i.e., priority is given to comprehension of narrative content). Second, the amount of cognitive resources available to process educational content is a function of the amount of resources not already committed to the narrative. Lastly, the capacity model posits that viewers can choose to allocate resources differentially among the processing of narrative and educational content, although narrative can never entirely be abandoned.

The model indicates several ways in which the comprehension of educational television content can be increased (Fisch, 2000, p. 82), for example, by reducing the demand of processing the narrative or by minimizing the distance between the narrative and the education demand. These tenets gives rise to empirical predictions regarding the conditions under which comprehension of educational content will be strongest, as well as practical implications for the design of effective educational programming. And while the capacity model was originally designed to address educational television, researchers argue it can be applied to other educational media as well (e.g., video games, Kirkorian & Anderson, 2011).

Differential Susceptibility to Media Effects Model

The Differential Susceptibility to Media Effects Model (DSMM, Valkenburg & Peter, 2013a) is one of the most recently developed models to explain media effects. It incorporates many of the propositions of earlier media effects theories including social cognitive theory (Bandura, 1986), the (limited) capacity model (Fisch, 2000; Lang, 2000), and the reinforcing spiral model (Slater, 2007). The DSMM was designed to explain why some individuals are more susceptible to media effects than others. This model has four core propositions: (1) media effects are conditional, (2) media effects are indirect, (3) differential susceptibility factors have multiple roles, and (4) media effects are transactional (see Figure 1).

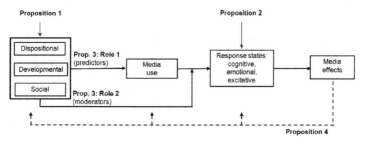

Proposition 1: Media effects depend on three types of susceptibility.
Proposition 2: Three media response states mediate the relationship between media use and effects.
Proposition 3: The differential susceptibility variables have two roles; they act as predictors and moderators.
Proposition 4: Media effects are transactional.

Figure 1. Differential Susceptibility to Media Effects Model.
(reprinted with permission from the Journal of Communication)

Proposition 1: Media effects are conditional. The DSMM posits that media effects are conditional and that they depend on three types of differential-susceptibility variables: dispositional, developmental, and social. *Dispositional* susceptibility refers to all personal factors that can determine selection of and response to media, such as personality, temperament, and existing schemata. *Developmental* susceptibility denotes the selective use and responsiveness to media due to cognitive, emotional, and social development. *Social* susceptibility consists of all the social-contexts factors that can influence the use and effects of media.

Proposition 2: Media effects are indirect. The DSMM states that all media effects are indirect and mediated by cognitive, emotional, and excitative response states. The cognitive response state includes the processing of attention, retention, and absorption of the media content. The emotional response state incorporates all affectively valenced reactions to media content (e.g., sadness, fear, happiness). The excitative response state refers to one's physiological arousal in response to the media. Each of these is expected to vary individually in response to different media. This proposition illustrates that how individuals process media content is critical to the influence of that media content. A child who experiences a significant physiological response to fearful content, for example, is expected to be affected differently when compared to a child who does not experience a similar physiological response.

Proposition 3: Differential susceptibility factors have multiple roles. The three types of differential susceptibility (dispositional, developmental, and social) mentioned in proposition 1 have two conceptual roles. First, they predict selection and exposure to media. Second, they can also strengthen or weaken the effect of media on behavior, through their influence on the response states mentioned in proposition 2.

These two conceptual roles can occur simultaneously. For example, children (and adults) tend to seek out media content that matches their dispositions, developmental level, and the norms that dominate in their social environment (Oliver, Kim, & Sanders, 2006). At the same time, these individual characteristics may influence how a person responds to media content, for example, because media content that is congruent with one's disposition or developmental level is processed faster and more easily than incongruent media content (Valkenburg & Peter, 2013b).

Proposition 4: Media effects are transactional. The final proposition of the DSMM is that media effects are transactional—media effects can have a reciprocal causal effect on media response states, media use, and on the differential susceptibility factors. For example, undesirable media effects on children may lead parents to restrict certain media content. Alternatively, frequent consumption of media violence has been argued to change personality (C. A. Anderson & Bushman, 2002).

The DSMM in future research. Although the DSMM is not designed specifically to assess media effects in childhood, it is a comprehensive media effects model that is suitable for inclusion in research investigating media effects on children. It places a significant emphasis on developmental susceptibility to media content, a critical variable when considering how media may affect children. Further, it builds upon existing theory by recognizing that media effects are dependent upon developmental, dispositional, and social factors. And lastly, it is not medium-specific. The DSMM can be used to guide research on the influence of traditional media such as television and books, as well as the influence of new media such as digital games and social media.

MEDIA EFFECTS ACROSS CHILDHOOD

Many researchers are concerned about the potential influence of media on children. In fact, these concerns have fueled more than 50 years of research on the role that media exposure plays in children's lives (e.g., Pecora, Murray, & Wartella, 2007). Although a complete review on the influences of media is beyond the scope of this chapter, we present an overview of the negative as well as positive effects of media that are most prominent in the public debate.

Negative Effects

Aggressive behavior. When it comes to the effects of media on children, the influence of violent media on aggressive behavior has received the most research attention. Hundreds of studies have investigated whether and how violent media exposure is related to subsequent aggression. These studies have looked at the influence of violent media exposure in middle childhood (e.g., Huesmann, Moise-Titus, Podolski, & Eron, 2003) and early childhood (e.g., Christakis & Zimmerman, 2007). The majority of studies have evaluated the influence of violent television content (e.g., Bushman & Huesmann, 2001) on aggression, although in recent years the influence of violent interactive media (e.g., video games and computer games) has received increased attention (e.g., C. A. Anderson & Dill, 2000).

Some studies have suggested no relationship between violent media exposure and aggression (e.g., Ferguson, San Miguel, Garza, & Jerabeck, 2011); however, most demonstrate that violent media exposure is positively related to aggressive behavior and may even lead to aggressive behavior later in life (e.g., Huesmann et al., 2003). Several meta-analyses on the effect of violent television and violent video games support this argument (C. Anderson & Bushman, 2001; Bushman & Huesmann, 2006; Paik & Comstock, 1994), suggesting small to moderate effects ($r = .19$ to $.31$) of violent media on aggressive behavior.

The most widely used theory explaining the influence of media violence on aggressive behavior in children is the social cognitive theory (Bandura, 1977). Children can learn aggressive behavior by watching media characters perform violent acts and not being punished for this behavior or even being rewarded for it (e.g., Wilson et al., 2002). In fictional media productions, physical aggression is often portrayed as the only means to solve interpersonal problems. Heroes are often just as violent as the villains. Children learn from this that physical violence is an effective and appropriate way to solve conflicts.

Most media researchers today accept that violent media exposure plays a role in children's aggressive tendencies, yet many nuanced questions remain unanswered. For example, which children are most susceptible to violent media exposure? Research that seeks to identify who is most susceptible to violent media is a critical area for future research.

ADHD-related behaviors. Attention-deficit hyperactivity disorder (ADHD) is a behavioral disorder characterized by elevated levels of inattentiveness, hyperactivity, and impulsivity (DSM-IV-TR, American Psychiatric Association, 2000). Although ADHD is a clinical diagnosis, many consider ADHD as the extreme end on a continuum of behaviors.

There have been recurrent claims that specific features of entertainment media may cause children's ADHD-related behaviors (Christakis, 2009; Nigg, 2009). Most of the claims focus upon children in early and middle childhood, as these are the periods in which ADHD diagnoses typically occur. While the research investigating these claims remains limited, existing research supports the argument that time spent with media (television and video games) may play a role in subsequent ADHD and ADHD-related behavior (Swing, Gentile, Anderson, & Walsh, 2010). Other researchers have gone beyond global exposure amounts to investigate the relationship between specific media content and ADHD-related behaviors. This research has shown that *violent* media content is related to more attention problems (Kronenberger et al., 2005) and impulsivity (C. Anderson & Maguire, 1978).

There are few theoretical mechanisms that explain how media content is related to ADHD-related behaviors. The DSMM (Valkenburg & Peter, 2013) may be a potential way to understand this relationship. Researchers have argued that media, particularly violent media, can negatively influence the arousal level (i.e., excitative response state) of children which may subsequently lead to ADHD-related behaviors (Arousal-Habituation Hypothesis; Huizinga, Nikkelen, & Valkenburg, 2013). Other researchers have suggested that media is a *function* of ADHD, where levels of ADHD-related behaviors determine the exposure to media (DSMM proposition 1). For example, low baseline arousal (which is typical in children with ADHD-related behavior) leads children to seek out arousal-enhancing activities because low arousal is experienced as an unpleasant physiological state (Eysenck, 1997).

Although the existing literature suggests a positive relationship between (violent) media exposure and ADHD-related behaviors, research in this field is very limited and there remain many gaps in our understanding of this relationship. For example, most studies mainly focused on the direct relationship between media use and ADHD-related behaviors. Future research should investigate whether and if arousal is the underlying mechanism of this relationship. Evaluating the role of individual differences is also an important next step.

Materialism, parent-child conflict, and childhood overweight. Children's media environment has become increasingly commercialized. More than ever, advertisers view children as an important and relevant target group. And advertisers now rely on a host of technologies to reach these young audiences—ranging from traditional television commercials to branded websites and brand placement in video games. Relatedly, there are concerns associated with the negative influence of advertising on children's behavior and well-being. These concerns have predominantly focused on the negative influence of child-directed advertising on *materialism, parent-child conflict*, and *childhood overweight*. Research investigating these outcomes has typically looked at the effects of television advertising (e.g., Halford, Gillespie, Brown, Pontin, & Dovey, 2004), although newer interactive advertising formats (e.g., Henry & Story, 2009) are receiving increased attention.

In terms of materialism, scholars have argued that the inherent nature of advertising makes children more materialistic. Empirical studies have indeed demonstrated that advertising leads to an increase in materialism in children (Buijzen & Valkenburg, 2012; Opree, Buijzen, van Reijmersdal, & Valkenburg, in press). Empirical evidence also shows that advertising exposure leads to increased parent-child conflict because children ask for the advertised products and parents do not want to comply (Buijzen & Valkenburg, 2003).

In recent years, advertising has also been implicated as an important factor in children's likelihood to become overweight or obese. Researchers argue that the preponderance of junk food advertisements has created a generation of children who expect a heavy presence of these foods in their diets, and parents who opt against this practice are thought to act outside the norm (Jordan, 2007). Advertising exposure is said to stimulate intake of high-calorie and low-nutrient food and beverages among children, which subsequently leads to overweight and obesity (Food Advertising Effects Hypothesis; Gantz, Schwartz, Angelini, & Rideout, 2007). A growing body of empirical research supports this contention (e.g., Borzekowski & Robinson, 2001).

The evidence for the negative influences of advertising on children is rather convincing. While more studies are needed to identify those children who are most susceptible to the negative effects of advertising, it is also important to recognize that advertising is part of today's consumer culture. Although one can imagine taking steps to limit children's exposure to violent media content, for example, it is harder to imagine ways to limit children's exposure to advertising content. Perhaps as a result of this fact, scholars are now investigating ways to help children become more resistant to advertising messages (e.g., by teaching advertising literacy) as well as identifying how the power of advertising can be used to promote healthier outcomes in childhood (e.g., healthier eating).

Positive Effects

All too often, discussions surrounding the effects of media in childhood focus upon negative effects. Far less attention has been paid to the role of developmentally appropriate media in supporting positive outcomes among children. Yet, as Fisch (2004) has observed, if we believe that children can learn negative lessons from media, it stands to reason that they can learn positive lessons too. To that end, we review the existing research on the positive impacts of media on prosocial behavior, school readiness skills, and core subject knowledge.

Prosocial behavior. Prosocial behavior refers to a range of positive behaviors including positive interactions (e.g., friendly play or peaceful conflict resolutions), altruism (e.g., sharing, offering help), and behaviors that reduce stereotypes (Mares & Woodard, 2007). Researchers who believe that media can influence prosocial behavior argue that depictions of prosocial behavior in the media are more consistent with social norms than antisocial behavior, and as a result, imitations of these behaviors are more likely to be received positively than imitation of antisocial acts (Rushton, 1979).

More than 30 studies have been conducted to identify whether and how prosocial media content (mostly television) might contribute to prosocial behavior. A meta-analysis by Mares and Woodard (2007) revealed that children who watched more prosocial television content exhibited significantly more prosocial behavior. The overall effect size (Z_{Fisher} = .27) is similar to that found in meta-analyses of the relationship between violent television content and subsequent aggression. Television is therefore just as prone to fostering prosocial behavior as it is to fostering aggression (Mares & Woodard, 2007). In line with social cognitive theory, the relationship reported by Mares and Woodward was strongest when prosocial behaviors were explicitly modeled in the television show. Moreover, children's age moderated this relationship in such a way that the effect of prosocial content increased sharply during early childhood, peaked at age 7, and then declined until and throughout the teen years. Mares and Woodard posit that the peak in middle childhood suggests that younger children may lack the cognitive ability to fully understand prosocial acts on television. More research is needed to understand why the relationship weakens after middle childhood. A possible explanation is that this decrease is due to a dearth of developmentally appropriate prosocial television content available for older children.

Recent studies also suggest that interactive media that are designed to support prosocial behavior do work. In a series of studies conducted in three countries across three different age groups (i.e., middle childhood, adolescence, adults), researchers found robust evidence to support the argument that playing video games in which characters model prosocial behavior does increase short- and long-term prosocial behaviors (Gentile et al., 2009). Similar findings support the relationship between prosocial video game play and subsequent prosocial behavior (Saleem, Anderson, & Gentile, 2012).

Overall, the literature indicates that exposure to media that explicitly depict prosocial behavior does result in children enacting this behavior. This effect is most typically explained via social cognitive theory (Bandura, 2001). And while this theory has helped us understand why prosocial media content can be beneficial for children, there remain unanswered questions. In particular, more research is needed to identify best practices when creating prosocial media content for children. We also know little about the role of individual differences in determining who is exposed to prosocial content and how individual differences impact processing of this content.

School readiness. School readiness refers to children's abilities to engage in and benefit from formal schooling. This concept encompasses early academic skills as well as social and emotional development. The majority of research on media and school readiness has focused on the role of television in early childhood. More than 1,000 studies, for example, have examined the influence of the television program *Sesame Street* on children's school readiness (for review, see Fisch, 2004). Results have consistently indicated that exposure to *Sesame Street*, and its international co-productions, is beneficial for young viewers' school readiness skills (Fisch, 2004; Mares & Pan, 2013). *Sesame Street*, however, is only one example of a program that has been shown to support school readiness. There are many others such as *Barney & Friends* (Singer & Singer, 1994) and *Pinky Dinky Doo* (Linebarger & Piotrowski, 2009). What these shows, and others like them, have in common is that they were developed with the *explicit* intent to support school readiness skills. Building upon formative and summative research, these programs merge best pedagogical practices with an understanding of the needs and preferences of young audiences.

The mechanisms to explain *how* media affect school readiness skills are less frequently discussed in the literature. When discussed, researchers typically proscribe to the capacity model (Fisch, 2004) or to social cognitive theory (Bandura, 2001). The notable theoretical consistency across studies investigating school readiness is the recognition that young children are active viewers that use the formal features embedded within media to guide their attention and comprehension (D. R. Anderson & Lorch, 1983). However, more research is needed to understand the theoretical mechanisms to explain when, and for whom, media can support school readiness.

Core subject knowledge. Core subject knowledge refers to a broad array of information and skills that children are introduced to during formal schooling including literacy, mathematics, and science. The majority of research looking at the relationships between media use and core subject knowledge has focused on the role of television in middle childhood. For example, research with the literacy-based program *Between the Lions* found that daily exposure to the program, over the course of 4 weeks, resulted in significant literacy gains (Linebarger, Kosanic, Greenwood, & Doku, 2004). Similarly, exposure to the math-focused television show *Cyberchase* supported children's mathematical problem-solving skills (Fisch, 2003), and research looking at the influence of television on science skills has shown that programs designed to support science knowledge (e.g., *The Magic School Bus*) do support viewers' understanding of scientific concepts as well as how to engage in the process of scientific discovery (ARC Consulting LLC, 1995; Rockman et al., 1996). These findings illustrate that developmentally appropriate media content designed with the explicit intent to support children's core subject knowledge is effective.

The available research also suggests that interactive media can support core knowledge. For example, children who actively used the website corollary of the program *Cyberchase* demonstrated gains in their mathematical problem-solving skills, particularly when used in combination with the television program (Fisch, Lesh, Motoki, Crespo, & Melfi, 2010). Similarly, electronic storybooks can support children's reading comprehension (Doty, Popplewell, & Byers, 2001) and phonics skills (McKenna, Reinking, & Bradley, 2003), and using interactive media to demonstrate scientific concepts results in better concept comprehension when compared to standard lessons (Ardac & Akaygun, 2004).

The mechanisms to explain *how* media support core subject knowledge are less known. The capacity model (Fisch, 2004) and social cognitive theory (Bandura, 2001) emerge as the two most prevalent explanations for these effects. However, the paucity of theoretical research on why and how media can affect core knowledge skills highlights a critical area for future research.

CONCLUSION

Media use and child development are reciprocally linked processes. This chapter has demonstrated how development plays a predictive role in children's media use and preferences as well as how media use subsequently impacts development in both positive and negative ways. Our review of the influence of child development on media usage and preferences highlights the consistent presence of television in children's lives across developmental stages. We also see that content preferences and preferences for interactive media change dramatically with age. As technology continues to evolve, interactive media are likely to make inroads into children's lives at younger and younger ages. It will be important for researchers to track these changes in use and preference as well as identify how these changes affect children's lives.

This review also highlights how media can affect child development. In particular, it illustrates the importance of media *content* when studying media effects. Violent content and advertising content are certainly reasons for parental concern and public policy initiatives. Yet on the contrary, developmentally appropriate media content designed with the explicit intent to support healthy outcomes in children can be beneficial for children's cognitive, emotional, and social developments. Efforts to help families achieve a healthy media diet that balances both quantity and quality are worthwhile.

Lastly, this chapter presents three important theories to explain the negative and positive effects that media can have on child development. Social learning theory and the capacity model tend to focus on how children, in general, are likely to be affected by the media. It is becoming increasingly important, however, for researchers to pay more attention to conditional media effects. The DSMM offers a promising direction for understanding conditional effects as it identifies several susceptibility factors that can determine media exposure and preferences as well as strengthen or weaken media effects. Only by identifying for whom and when effects occur can we obtain a true understanding of the role of media in child development.

FUTURE DIRECTIONS IN MEDIA AND CHILDREN'S RESEARCH

From this review, we can see that there is a wealth of research on both the positive and negative effects of media use on children's behavior. However, this review has also illuminated several critical gaps in the literature. These gaps highlight two major directions for future research. First, when investigating media effects, it is crucial not only to determine whether media has an effect but also to investigate *how* media influences children's behavior. To date, although researchers have proposed underlying mechanisms to explain media effects, empirical evidence to support these underlying mechanisms is largely missing. This gap is particularly notable in the research on the effects of media on ADHD-related behaviors, school readiness, and core knowledge skills. Second, the existing research has shown that media's influence on children is small to moderate in size and not always consistent. These small to moderate effect sizes are likely indicative of the limited attention paid to individual differences. Too many research studies disregard the important influence of individual differences, yet is quite reasonable that certain children may be particularly susceptible to the influence of media while others may be less susceptible (Valkenburg & Peter, 2013a, b). It is critical that future research investigate the moderating roles of individual difference variables to identify which variables may increase or decrease media's influence on children. Such research will help us better understand the true size and nature of media's influence on children.

REFERENCES

American Psychiatric Association (Ed.). (2000). *Diagnostic and statistical manual of mental disorders: DSM-IV-TR®*. American Psychiatric Pub.

Anderson, C., & Maguire, T. (1978). The effect of TV viewing on the educational performance of elementary school children. *Alberta Journal of Educational Research, 24*(3), 156–163.

Anderson, C. A., & Bushman, B. J. (2001). Effects of violent video games on aggressive behavior, aggressive cognition, aggressive affect, physiological arousal, and prosocial behavior: A meta-analytic review of the scientific literature. *Psychological Science, 12*(5), 353–359. doi:10.1111/1467-9280.00366

Anderson, C. A., & Bushman, B. J. (2002). Human aggression. *Annual Review of Psychology, 53*(1), 27–51.

Anderson, C. A., & Dill, K. E. (2000). Video games and aggressive thoughts, feelings, and behavior in the laboratory and in life. *Journal of Personality and Social Psychology, 78*(4), 772. doi:10.1037//0022-3514.78.4.772

Anderson, D. R., & Lorch, E. P. (1983). Looking at television: Action or reaction. In J. Bryant & D. R. Anderson (Eds.), *Children's understanding of television: Research on attention and comprehension* (pp. 1–33). San Diego, CA: Academic Press.

ARC Consulting LLC. (1995). *Research findings: The magic school bus* (Vol. 1, *Executive Summary*, and Vol. 2, *Comprehensive Report*). New York: Author.

Ardac, D., & Akaygun, S. (2004). Effectiveness of multimedia-based instruction that emphasizes molecular representations on students' understanding of chemical change. *Journal of Research in Science Teaching, 41*(4), 317–337. doi:10.1002/tea.20005

Bandura, A. (1965). Influence of models' reinforcement contingencies on the acquisition of imitative responses. *Journal of Personality and Social Psychology, 1*(6), 589.

Bandura, A. (1977). *Social learning theory.* New York, NY: General Learning Press.

Bandura, A. (1986). *Social foundations of thought and action: A social cognitive theory.* Englewood Cliffs, NJ: Prentice-Hall.

Bandura, A. (2001). Social cognitive theory of mass communication. *Media Psychology, 3,* 265–299. doi:10.1207/S1532785XMEP0303_03

Beentjes, J. W. J., Koolstra, C. M., Marseille, N., & van der Voort, T. H. A. (2001). Children's use of different media: For how long and why? In S. Livingstone & M. Bovill (Eds.), *Children and their changing media environment: A European comparative study* (pp. 85–112). Mahwah, NJ: Erlbaum.

Borzekowski, D. L., & Robinson, T. N. (2001). The 30-second effect: An experiment revealing the impact of television commercials on food preferences of preschoolers. *Journal of the American Dietetic Association, 101*(1), 42–46. doi:10.1016/S0002-8223(01)00012-8

Buijzen, M., & Valkenburg, P. M. (2003). The unintended effects of television advertising A parent-child survey. *Communication Research, 30*(5), 483–503. doi:10.1177/0093650203256361

Buijzen, M., & Valkenburg, P. M. (2012). The intended and unintended effects of advertising on children. In E. Scharrer (Ed.), *The international encyclopedia of media studies.* Oxford, England: Blackwell. doi:10.1002/9781444361506.wbiems132

Bukatko, D. (2007). *Child and adolescent development: A chronological approach.* Florence, KY: Cengage Learning.

Bushman, B. J., & Huesmann, L. R. (2001). Effects of televised violence on aggression. In D. G. Singer & J. L. Singer (Eds.), *Handbook of children and the media* (pp. 223–254). Thousand Oaks, CA: Sage. doi:10.1001/archpedi.160.4.348

Bushman, B. J., & Huesmann, L. R. (2006). Short-term and long-term effects of violent media on aggression in children and adults. *Archives of Pediatrics & Adolescent Medicine, 160*(4), 348.

Christakis, D. A. (2009). The effects of infant media usage: What do we know and what should we learn? *Acta Pædiatrica, 98,* 8–16. doi:10.1111/j.1651-2227.2008.01027.x

Christakis, D. A., & Zimmerman, F. J. (2007). Violent television viewing during preschool is associated with antisocial behavior during school age. *Pediatrics, 120*(5), 993–999. doi:10.1542/peds.2006-3244

Council on Communications and Media. (2013). Children, adolescents, and the media. *Pediatrics, 132*(5), 958–961. doi:10.1542/peds.2013-2656; 10.1542/peds.2013-2656

Doty, D. E., Popplewell, S. R., & Byers, G. O. (2001). Interactive CD-ROM storybooks and young readers' reading comprehension. *Journal of Research on Computing in Education, 33,* 374–384.

Eysenck, H. J. (1997). Personality and the biosocial model of anti-social and criminal behaviour. In A. Raine, P. A. Brennan, D. P. Farrington, & S. A. Mednick (Eds.), *Biosocial bases of violence* (pp. 21–37). New York: Plenum.

Ferguson, C. J., San Miguel, C., Garza, A., & Jerabeck, J. M. (2011). A longitudinal test of video game violence influences on dating and aggression: A 3-year longitudinal study of adolescents. *Journal of Psychiatric Research, 26*(2), 141–146. doi:10.1016/j.jpsychires.2011.10.014,

Field, J., Muir, D., Pilon, R., Sinclair, M., & Dodwell, P. (1980). Infants' orientation to lateral sounds from birth to three months. *Child Development, 51*(1), 295–298.

Fisch, S. M. (2000). A capacity model of children's comprehension of educational content on television. *Media Psychology, 2,* 63–91. doi:10.1207/S1532785XMEP0201_4

Fisch, S. M. (2003). *The impact of cyberchase on children's mathematical problem solving* (No. 1). Teaneck, NJ: MediaKidz Research & Consulting.

Fisch, S. M. (2004). *Children's learning from educational television.* Mahwah, NJ: Erlbaum.

Fisch, S. M., Lesh, R., Motoki, E., Crespo, S., & Melfi, V. (2010). *Children's learning from multiple media in informal mathematics education.* (No. 1). Teaneck, NJ: MediaKidz Research & Consulting.

Fisch, S. M., & Truglio, R. T. (Eds.). (2001). *"G" is for growing: Thirty years of research on children and "Sesame Street."* Mahwah, NJ: Erlbaum.

Gantz, W., Schwartz, N., Angelini, J. R., & Rideout, V. (2007). *Food for thought: Television food advertising to children in the United States* (No. 1). Washington, DC: Henry J. Kaiser Family Foundation.

Gentile, D. A., Anderson, C. A., Yukawa, S., Ihori, N., Saleem, M., Lim Kam Ming, … Sakamoto, A. (2009). The effects of prosocial video games on prosocial behaviors: International evidence from correlational, longitudinal, and experimental studies. *Personality and Social Psychology Bulletin, 35*(6), 752–763. doi:10.1177/0146167209333045

Halford, J. C., Gillespie, J., Brown, V., Pontin, E. E., & Dovey, T. M. (2004). Effect of television advertisements for foods on food consumption in children. *Appetite, 42*(2), 221–225. doi:10.1016/j.appet.2003.11.006

Henry, A. E., & Story, M. (2009). Food and beverage brands that market to children and adolescents on the Internet: A content analysis of branded web sites. *Journal of Nutrition Education and Behavior, 41*(5), 353–359. doi:10.1016/j.jneb.2008.08.004

Huesmann, L. R., Moise-Titus, J., Podolski, C. L., & Eron, L. D. (2003). Longitudinal relations between children's exposure to TV violence and their aggressive and violent behavior in young adulthood. *Developmental Psychology, 39*, 201–221. doi:10.1037/0012-1649.39.2.201

Huizinga, M., Nikkelen, S. W. C., & Valkenburg, P. M. (2013). Children's media use and its relation to attention, hyperactivity, and impulsivity. In D. Lemish (Ed.), *The Routledge international handbook on children, adolescents and media* (p. 179). London, England: Taylor & Francis.

Jordan, A. B. (2007). Heavy television viewing and childhood obesity. *Journal of Children and Media, 1*(1), 45–54. doi:10.1080/17482790601005124

Kirkorian, H. L., & Anderson, D. R. (2011). Learning from educational media. In S. L. Calvert & B. J. Wilson (Eds.), *The handbook of children, media, and development* (pp. 190–213). Oxford, England: Wiley-Blackwell.

Koolstra, C. M., van Zanten, J., Lucassen, N., & Ishaak, N. (2004). The formal pace of *Sesame Street* over 26 years. *Perceptual and Motor Skills, 99*(1), 354–360.

Kronenberger, W. G., Mathews, V. P., Dunn, D. W., Wang, Y., Wood, E. A., Giauque, A. L., … Li, T. (2005). Media violence exposure and executive functioning in aggressive and control adolescents. *Journal of Clinical Psychology, 61*(6), 725–737. doi:10.1002/jclp.20022

Lang, A. (2000). The limited capacity model of mediated message processing. *Journal of Communication, 50*(1), 46–70. doi:10.1111/j.1460-2466.2000.tb02833.x

Linebarger, D. L., Kosanic, A. Z., Greenwood, C. R., & Doku, N. S. (2004). Effects of viewing the television program *Between the Lions* on the emergent literacy skills of young children. *Journal of Educational Psychology, 96*(2), 297–308. doi:10.1037/0022-0663.96.2.297

Linebarger, D. L., & Piotrowski, J. T. (2009). TV as storyteller: How exposure to television narratives impacts at-risk preschoolers' story knowledge and narrative skills. *British Journal of Developmental Psychology, 27*, 47–69. doi:10.1348/026151008X400445

Mares, M., & Pan, Z. (2013). Effects of *Sesame Street*: A meta-analysis of children's learning in 15 countries. *Journal of Applied Developmental Psychology, 34*, 140–151. doi:http://dx.doi.org/10.1016/j.appdev.2013.01.001

Mares, M., & Woodard, E. (2007). Positive effects of television on children's social interaction: A meta-analysis. In R. W. Preiss, B. M. Gayle, N. Burrell, M. Allen, & J. Bryant (Eds.), *Mass media effects research: Advances through meta-analysis* (pp. 281–300). Mahwah, NJ: Erlbaum. doi:10.1207/S1532785XMEP0703_4

McKenna, M. C., Reinking, D., & Bradley, B. A. (2003). The effects of electronic trade books on the decoding growth of beginning readers. In R. M. Joshi, C. K. Leong, & B. L. K. Kaczmarek (Eds.), *Literacy acquisition: The role of phonology, morphology, and orthography* (pp. 193–202). Amsterdam, The Netherlands: IOS Press.

Nigg, J. T. (2009). *What causes ADHD? Understanding what goes wrong and why.* New York, NY: Guilford Press.

Oliver, M. B., Kim, J., & Sanders, M. S. (2006). Personality. In J. Bryant & P. Vorderer (Eds.), *Psychology of entertainment* (pp. 329–341) Mahwah, NJ: Erlbaum.

Opree, S. J., Buijzen, M., van Reijmersdal, E. A., & Valkenburg, P. M. (in press). Children's advertising exposure, advertised product desire, and materialism: A longitudinal study. *Communication Research.*

Paik, H., & Comstock, G. (1994). The effects of television violence on antisocial behavior: A meta-analysis. *Communication Research, 21*, 516–546. doi:10.1177/009365094021004004

Pecora, N., Murray, J. P., & Wartella, E. (Eds.). (2007). *Children and television: Fifty years of research.* Mahwah, NJ: Erlbaum.

Rideout, V., Foehr, U. G., & Roberts, D. F. (2010). *Generation M²: Media in the lives of 8- to 18-year-olds.* (No. 1). Menlo Park, CA: Henry J. Kaiser Family Foundation.

Rockman et al. (1996). *Evaluation of the "Bill Nye the Science Guy" television series and outreach: A report to KCTS-TV.* San Francisco, CA.

Rushton, J. P. (1979). Effects of prosocial television and film material on the behavior of viewers. In L. Berkowitz (Ed.), *Advances in experimental social psychology* (pp. 321–351). New York, NY: Academic Press.

Saleem, M., Anderson, C. A., & Gentile, D. A. (2012). Effects of prosocial, neutral, and violent video games on children's helpful and hurtful behaviors. *Aggressive Behavior, 38*(4), 281–287. doi:10.1002/ab.21428

Singer, J. L., & Singer, D. G. (1994). *"Barney & Friends" as education and entertainment: Phase 2. Can children learn through preschool exposure to "Barney & Friends"?* (No. 2). New Haven, CT: Yale University Family Television Research and Consultation Center.

Slater, M. D. (2007). Reinforcing spirals: The mutual influence of media selectivity and media effects and their impact on individual behavior and social identity. *Communication Theory, 17*(3), 281–303.

Swing, E. L., Gentile, D. A., Anderson, C. A., & Walsh, D. A. (2010). Television and video game exposure and the development of attention problems. *Pediatrics, 126*(2), 214–221. doi:10.1542

Szybist, J. (2011). Is TV on the decrease? *Televizion, 24*, 26.

Thomas, R. M. (2005). *Comparing theories of child development* (6th ed.). Belmont, CA: Thomson Wadsworth.

Valkenburg, P. M. (2004). *Children's responses to the screen: A media psychological approach.* Mahwah, NJ: Erlbaum.

Valkenburg, P. M., & Cantor, J. (2000). Children's likes and dislikes of entertainment programs. In D. Zillman & P. Vorderer (Eds.), *Media entertainment: The psychology of its appeal* (pp. 135–152). Hillsdale, NJ: Erlbaum.

Valkenburg, P. M., & Peter, J. (2013a). The differential susceptibility to media effects model. *Journal of Communication, 63*, 221–243. doi:10.1111/jcom.12024

Valkenburg, P. M., & Peter, J. (2013b). Five challenges for the future of media-effects research. *International Journal of Communication, 7*, 19. doi:1932–8036/2013FEA0002

Valkenburg, P. M., & Vroone, M. (2004). Developmental changes in infants' and toddlers' attention to television entertainment. *Communication Research, 31*, 288–311. doi:10.1177/0093650204263435

Wartella, E., Rideout, V., Lauricella, A., & Connell, S. (2013). *Parenting in the age of digital technology: A national survey*. Report of the Center on Media and Human Development, School of Communication, Northwestern University, Evanston, IL.

Wilson, B. J., Smith, S. L., Potter, W. J., Kunkel, D., Linz, D., Colvin, C. M., & Donnerstein, E. (2002). Violence in children's television programming: Assessing the risks. *Journal of Communication, 52*(1), 5–35.

CHAPTER SIX

Children's Peer Relationships Outside the Family

ROBERT L. DURAN AND DIANE T. PRUSANK

" ... the world of peers constitutes a challenging and sometimes unforgiving environment."
—HAY, PAYNE, & CHADWICK (2004, P. 100)

Research on toddlers as young as 18 months indicates that they are developing the requisite prosocial skills for creating friendships (Svetlova, Nichols, & Brownell, 2010). By preschool, children's friendships benefit them by extending their peer acceptance and enhancing teachers' evaluation of their competence (Lindsey, 2002). Preschoolers are in tune enough to social relationships with their peers that observers note that their "*best* friendships" are distinguishable from their "friendships" in providing more support and companionship (Sebanc, Kearns, Hernandez, & Galvin, 2007). These early peer relationships set the stage for childhood friendships, the lack of which can lead to negative consequences spanning both internalizing and externalizing behaviors (e.g., Engle, McElwain, & Lasky, 2011; Nangle, Erdley, Newman, Mason, & Carpenter, 2003).

This chapter will briefly review research that demonstrates the importance of children's friendships to their immediate and long-term social and mental health. The main focus, however, will be upon the research that discusses communication activities within peer relationships (including peer groups, friendships, and best friendships). We will look at communication activities that both attract (e.g., initiating get-togethers, self-disclosure) and repel (aggression, negative emotional displays) peers within the childhood years (e.g., Asher, Parker, & Walker, 1996;

Burgess, Wojslawowicz, Rubin, Rose-Krasnor, & Booth-LaForce, 2006; Gottman, Gonso, & Rasmussen, 1975; Sebanc, 2003; Rose & Asher, 2004).

Of special interest will be the recent explosion of research in the area of "bullying." This work highlights the "darker" side of peer relationships as they develop in childhood. Although the media may have created a monolithic image of the "school bully," the research in this area indicates that bullies come in all "shapes and sizes" and function within a context that serves to normalize their behavior. In some studies bullies have been found to be popular and socially skilled, and further, their behavior has been recognized as socially functional, while in others bullies are perceived as socially incompetent and themselves the targets of bullying (Guerra, Williams, & Sadak, 2011; Powell & Ladd, 2010; Witvliet et al., 2009).

Another set of peer relationships we will discuss includes those within the special needs community. Given the axiom that similarity breeds attraction, it is not surprising to see that often children with disabilities befriend children with disabilities (Estell, Jones, Pearl, & Van Acker, 2009). Some research indicates that within certain communities, the stability of these friendships is problematic (e.g., see Mikani, 2010, on friendships among children with ADHD). Other researchers have started to elucidate the actual behaviors enacted in friendship among developmentally disabled children (Freeman & Kasari, 2002), noting the similarities and differences with regard to friendships forged by typically developing children. Further, attempts at inclusivity have opened the door to extend this work to initiate an understanding of characteristics of friendships developed between children with developmental disorders and typically developing children (Webster & Carter, 2007).

We believe that integrating the research on both bullying and friendships of the developmentally disabled has the potential to significantly alter the theoretical and empirical work looking at the relationship between communication behaviors and friendship development in childhood. Prior to discussing "atypical" peer relationships it is important to review the requisite communication behaviors of "typical" peer relationships.

TYPICALLY DEVELOPING CHILDREN'S PEER RELATIONSHIPS

The development of relationships outside of one's family is the beginning of a child's move towards independence. Taking the social skills one has learned within the family and testing their efficacy outside the home is a major step for children. Audiences outside the family may not be as forgiving of social errors, may provide negative feedback, seek their own social goals, and require new levels of perspective taking. Relationships with peers develop with the assumption of equal status, require negotiation, conflict management, coordination, competition, appropriate use of humor, and at some point, and in the case of best friends, disclosure of intimate information. Haslett and Samter (1997) note that interactions with friends provide a unique opportunity to learn about mutuality, reciprocity, and negotiation—concepts believed to be the foundation on which successful adult relationships are built. In this sense, then, friends shape children's social and emotional growth in ways parents cannot (p. 193).

The research on peer relationships outside the family looks at peer acceptance, friendship, and best friendship (Socha & Stamp, 2009). Acceptance has been defined as being generally well liked by peers, while friendship entails participation in a close dyadic relationship (Lindsey, 2002, p. 146). Research supports the contention that these constructs, while not synonymous, are related. Lindsey (2002) found that in preschool, high-accepted children were more likely to have a friend, and further, children who reported more friends were likely to be rated by both teachers and peers as being competent (p. 152). Noting that best friendships are considered to be of higher quality (greater support, companionship, and exclusivity) and more stable than friendships, Sebanc et al. (2007) found that peer acceptance also predicts having a best friend (p. 92). Given the importance of peer acceptance to the development of peer relationships, researchers have looked at the correlates of acceptance, and data indicate a correlation between prosocial behavior and peer acceptance (Sebanc et al., 2007, p. 88). Prosocial behaviors consist of actions like sharing toys and "being nice." Other prosocial behaviors, like being responsive and reciprocal, differentiate children who have friends from those who don't have friends (Howes, 1988). In a classroom setting, children in reciprocated relationships initiate more interactions and are more frequently the target of visual cues from peers than are children without reciprocated relationships (Vaughn et al., 2000).

However, just as children's temperaments and skills vary, so do their friendships. Research indicates that the quality of children's friendships vary, and consequently, not all friendships are equally useful for children. Engle, McElwain, and Lasky's (2011) longitudinal and extensive study of children across the spectrum of friendship quality relationships conclude that low quality friendships (i.e., low positive interaction, high conflict) place children at risk for developing externalizing behaviors as a consequence of the negative relational behaviors enacted within the friendship. Children's high quality friendships, on the other hand, are their own breeding ground for the development of positive social skills. Specifically, Engle, McElwain, and Lasky (2011) found that children in high quality friendships were rated by teachers as having high social skills, which included cooperation, self-control, assertion, and responsibility (p. 372). In addition, children in low-quality friendships exhibited more externalizing behaviors.

Importantly, they also found that friendships remained stable, including the quality level of friendships from kindergarten through grade 3 (Engle, McElwain, & Lasky, 2011, p. 382).

There are gender differences in the research on the development of children's relationships outside the family. Males are likely to have fewer best friends than females (Ladd, Kochenderfer, & Coleman, 1996; Sebanc et al., 2007), and boys form large, extensive social networks while girls tend to form a series of smaller, exclusive, intensive networks of friends (Baines & Blatchford, 2009). In the Sebanc et al. (2007) study, boys were more likely to have high scores on aggression, which was then related to peer rejection.

Nangle, Erdly, Newman, Mason, and Carpenter's (2003) study indicated that more high quality friendships were the best defense against loneliness, which would lessen the risk of depression (p. 553). This finding points to problems with earlier research and training programs that focused more generically on increasing the social skills of children in an effort to decrease peer rejection and increase peer acceptance. As we will see later in this chapter, researchers in the area of friendships of both the victims of bullies and the developmentally disabled have come to a similar conclusion, recognizing that the development of friendships may be both more possible and more effective as a barrier against a variety of social ills.

BULLYING AND PEER VICTIMIZATION

Researchers have argued that a primary developmental activity in infancy and toddlerhood is attachment (e.g., see Haslett and Samter, this volume). That is, parents and family in general provide infants with a sense of attachment and nurturing, requisite scaffolding to experience and develop effectance motivation, and further form attachments within and outside of the family. Childhood, the next major phase of development, is also concerned with attachment. However, the child is concerned about who the attachments are with. In other words, the child is concerned about where they fit with regard to peer hierarchies. Which group does the child belong to, where is he/she within that group, and how does that social group compare to other groups?

The desire for social status serves as the organizing principle of social relationships. As some attain status, others necessarily lose status; it is the ultimate zero-sum game. As with all hierarchies they are in constant flux and certainly will recalibrate at the next significant life stage, high school, if not sooner. Communication skills (or the lack thereof) are the mechanism by which status and place/rank is determined.

Late elementary school is a time when students form hierarchical social structures in which some children and social groups are more popular and powerful than others (Adler & Adler, 1996). Children engage in a number of aggressive behaviors, such as name-calling, teasing, confrontations, and physical attacks, to assert their dominance and maintain their position in the social hierarchy (Adler & Adler, 1996; Farmer, 2000; Rodkin & Hodges, 2003). There is a distinction, however, between physical aggression and aggressive behavior. The former results in social isolation, victimization, and unpopularity (Asher & Coie, 1990), while the latter is associated with popularity and social status (Rose & Asher, 2004).

Bullying is one way that children, particularly at this age, work out their place in the social hierarchy. Bullying tends to increase during childhood, peak during early adolescence, and decline during the late adolescent years (Nansel et al., 2001). The same downward trend with regard to age holds for victims because older children often bully younger ones.

Sex differences exist with regard to the means and strategies employed to attain position in the social hierarchy, but they are not a factor in the ultimate goal of attaining status and avoiding low status. Boys are more likely to demonstrate physical and verbal bullying behaviors, while girls are more likely to engage in exclusionary behaviors and spreading rumors (Olweus, 1993; Peskin, Tortolero, & Markham, 2006). Witvliet, Olthof, Hoeksma, Goossens., Smits, and Koot (2009) found that girls engage in more relational bullying than boys, but boys use both physical and relational bullying. Physical dominance is more important in boys' groups than in girls'. However, physical bullying becomes a less effective strategy as children grow older.

Research indicates that the number of children who report having been bullied is extremely large and actually may be underreported due to embarrassment, fear of retaliation, and/or rejection (Powell & Ladd, 2010). Further, the frequency of bullying varies depending on the wording of the question. If children are asked whether they have ever been bullied, 60% say yes. If children are asked whether they have experienced persistent bullying, the percentage ranges from 10% to 25% (Olweus & Limber, 2002).

Bullying is defined as a distinct type of aggression characterized by a power imbalance and involves repetitive acts (Olweus, 1999; Solberg & Olweus, 2003). Bullying is conceptualized by Olweus (1993) as a behavior that leaves a child "exposed, repeatedly and over time, to negative actions on the part of one or more other students" (p. 9). Negative action is behavior that "intentionally inflicts, or attempts to inflict, injury or discomfort upon another" (p. 9). Negative actions can be verbal, such as teasing, threatening, name-calling, or physical, such as hitting, kicking, pushing, and shoving. There are two types of bullying activities: direct and indirect bullying. Direct bullying is open and physical attacks on the victim. Indirect, also referred to as relational aggression, includes social isolation and exclusion from groups. Olweus (1993) stated that there must be three characteristics present for behavior to be labeled bullying: harmful intent, imbalance of power and strength, and repetition of negative actions (p. 190).

There are different subtypes and roles children enact in bullying episodes. The different types of roles are (1) actively avoiding all involvement in bullying (outsider); (2) providing help to victims (defending); and, (3) providing bullies with an approving audience even when not participating (reinforcing; Hawkins, Pepler, & Craig, 2001). Salmivalli, Lagerspetz, Bjorkqvist, Osterman, and Kaukiainen (1996) offered two correlated but different types of bullying behavior: *initiating* acts of bullying and assisting or *following* a leading bully.

Gasser and Keller (2009) investigated differences in the interpersonal abilities between bullies and bully-victims with regard to social competency and moral motivations. Previous research has found that bullies are sociable, assertive, popular, good leaders, and integrated into the peer group (Estell, Farmer, & Cairns, 2007). Bullies have also been found to have superior theory-of-mind skills (Gini, 2006), which enable them to anticipate the thoughts and actions of others and manipulate social contexts. This skill set can be contrasted with the bully-victim (Olweus, 1993; Solberg, Olweus, & Endresen, 2007). Bully-victims respond aggressively to social challenges. They tend to react impulsively. The aggression literature distinguishes between proactive and reactive aggression (Coie & Dodge, 1998). Proactive aggression is goal directed, calculated, and is not linked to a stimulus. Reactive aggression is affective, impulsive, defensive, and hostile responses to perceived threats and has been linked to peer rejection. Crick and Dodge (1999) define bullying as a form of proactive aggression "in which aggressive acts are employed to achieve interpersonal dominance over another" (p. 129). Proactive aggression is related to many aspects of social adaptation and social competence, like popularity, dominance, and communicative skills (Poulin & Boivin, 2000). Bullies are more likely to engage in proactive aggression while bully-victims are more likely to engage in reactive aggression.

Investigating other characteristics of bullies and victims, Estell, Farmer, Irvin, Crowther, and Akos (2009) examined differences among students with mild disabilities, academically gifted students, and general education students on ratings of victimization and bullying. Students who receive remedial student services and are integrated into the general education population make up 10% to 20% of the student population. "Students involved in bullying and victimization are more likely to have academic and social adjustment problems" (Estell et al., 2009, p. 136).

Guerra, Williams, and Sadek (2011) investigated the causes of bullying and victimization utilizing both quantitative and qualitative (focus groups) methods. The sample for the study consisted of 59 schools (21 elementary, 30 middle schools, and 8 high schools) across Colorado. Approximately 2,300 middle school students completed questionnaires and served in focus groups. The focus groups provided some interesting results. Bullying starts at home for some children, with older siblings bullying younger ones. Some children noted that bullying is a way of life in school; it is what kids do. Bullying from this perspective is seen as normative. It was also noted that bullying varies by school. Children noted that bullying is a function of whether their school tolerates it or not. Some motives for bullying were that it is fun and that sometimes it is a form of entertainment. Other motives were that it comes from jealousy and a desire for status. "Participants also noted that some kids bully because they are popular, some kids bully because they want to be popular ('wannabes'), and some kids bully because they are unpopular" (Guerra et al., 2011, p. 305).

Further, the focus groups revealed that victims had low self-esteem and were perceived as weak, timid, vulnerable, socially isolated, physically smaller, "different," and annoying. Those children labeled as annoying engaged in "strange" behaviors, such as chewing with the mouth open. Of particular importance is that many of the "strange" behaviors identified were communication behaviors, such as talking too loud, saying the wrong thing, and not standing up for themselves.

Two interesting motivators for bullying emerged from the data: it is fun, and it is related to sexuality. In middle school bullying was linked to popularity and sexuality in somewhat different ways for boys and for girls. For boys dominance is a way to show status and power and therefore desirability. "Boys were seen as dominating and elevating their status as desirable mates through demonstration of physical force against other males, and by lowering the status of girls 'they like' by labeling them as 'sluts' and posting lewd messages about their sexual conquests in public places (particularly bathrooms), cell phones, and the Internet" (Guerra et al., 2011, p. 308). "For girls, bullying was seen as a way to enhance their physical and sexual appeal—by limiting competition through rumors, gossip, and exclusion, also in public places, cell phones, and the Internet" (Guerra et al., 2011, p. 308). Focus groups showed the goals for the girls were to enhance their sexual status and access to the most desirable (popular) males. This is consistent with recent gender theories of teenage bullying and violence that suggests girls gain social power by elevating their status as a sex object (Brown, Chesney-Lind, & Stein, 2007).

Related to the motivation to capture the interest of the opposite sex, Olthof and Goossens (2008) contended that "children's bullying behavior is partly motivated by their desire to be accepted by other bullying children and by members of the opposite sex" (p. 25). The authors agree with Maslow's (1970) belief that this motivation comes from an inherent need to belong. Baumeister and Leary (1995) claim that the need to belong is so strong that it might even motivate antisocial behavior. As a result, bullying may stem from a desire to belong to a group of others who engage in antisocial behaviors while also reflecting a desire not to be associated with those whom the bullies victimize. "Our motivational account implies that bullying children's desire to be accepted by other bullying children motivates them to behave as a bully, and that the resulting behavioral similarity might or might not lead the other bullying children to actually accept them" (Olthof & Goossens, 2008, p. 26).

Bullying was assessed by a peer report procedure, similar to Salmivalli et al.'s (1996) participant role scale. Children were assigned continuous scores of their bullying-related behavior on the basis of how many classmates nominate them in response to items describing a particular type of behavior (continuous as opposed to categorical: bully, victim, follower, defender, outsider, etc.). Involvement in bullying was measured by the 32-item New Participant Role Scale (NPRS; Goossens, Olthof, & Dekker, 2006). The NPRS consists of five subscales: bully ("is in charge when someone is bullied and starts bullying"); follower ("joins when others are bullying and incites bully by shouting"); outsider ("takes care not to get involved," "leaves the scene when someone's being bullied"); defender ("comforts victim," "stays with victim during recess"); and victim ("is laughed at by others," "gets bullied by other children").

Descriptive statistics showed boys engaged in significantly more bullying and following behaviors than did girls. Girls were victims more often than boys. As compared to boys, girls displayed more outsider and defender behaviors. Children generally desired and received more acceptance from same-sex classmates than from opposite-sex, which is consistent with gender segregation among early adolescents (Maccoby, 2000).

Results indicated that children's bullying behavior was positively related to their desire to be accepted by other bullying children, while being unrelated or negatively related to their desire to be accepted by non-bullying children. This was true for boys but not girls. Girls' bullying/following behavior was related to a desire to be accepted by bullying and non-bullying boys. Olthof and Goossens (2008) concluded that their hypothesis was supported with the caveat that antisocial girls seek the acceptance of antisocial boys, not necessarily other antisocial girls. Further, although bullying boys sought the acceptance of other bullying boys by engaging in similar bullying behavior, in reality this was not a good strategy because they were not accepted by other bullies. With regard to the opposite sex, girls engaged in bullying behaviors to be accepted by the opposite sex (bullies or non-bullies)—the more bullying behaviors girls demonstrated, the more they wanted to be accepted by the opposite sex. This was not the case for boys; they did not engage in bullying behavior to be accepted by the opposite sex.

Further investigating motives for bullying behaviors, Gini (2006) tested two competing explanations for bullying behavior. One explanation suggested that bullies have a social skills deficit and hence act out aggressively. Another explanation suggested bullies are socially skilled but lack empathy to relate to their victims' emotional pain. Further, the study sought to evaluate the skills of different types of children involved in bullying episodes: bullies, victims, and defenders.

Results indicated victimized children showed deficits in social skills, social problem solving, assertiveness, and motivational recognition. Defenders scored high on social cognition, demonstrating high level social abilities and well-developed understanding of both cognitive and emotional states of others. Bullies had similar scores to defenders, so the difference in behaviors resides in a "moral compass." Defenders have high moral sensibility and empathic reactivity, which may be one of the motivations for prosocial behavior.

Yet another study investigating competing explanations for bullying behavior was conducted by Witvliet, Olthof, Hoeksma, Goosserns, Smits, and Koot (2009), who investigated three explanations for the configuration and construction of 4th–7th grade peer groups: the Behavioral Similarity Hypothesis, the Likeability Explanation, and the Perceived Popularity Explanation.

The Behavioral Similarity Hypothesis suggests behavioral similarity among peer group members is not only a function of socialization (association among group members mirroring the behaviors of the other members of the group), but also a function of selection in which members select those who display similar behaviors. Hence, bullies associate with bullies and victims with victims. However, research has shown that bullies dislike other bullies (Olthof & Goossens, 2008), and that aggressive children do not accept other aggressive children.

The Likeability Explanation suggests that bullies are not well liked and often rejected. As a result they form a peer group not out of attraction but rather by default. "Their rejected social status may be a reason to affiliate with other rejected children. What is more, belonging to a rejected peer group may provide bullying children a social context in which their rejected status is sustained and their bullying is reinforced" (Witvliet et al., 2009, p. 287). This explanation still doesn't explain why the bullying group affiliates as opposed to staying isolated.

The Perceived Popularity Explanation suggests that bullying behavior is just a communication strategy employed by popular, high status children to attain and maintain social status and dominance. Adler and Adler (1998) showed that adolescents who are members of dominant peer groups often use bullying as a technique to maintain their exclusive position at the top of the social hierarchy. Eder, Evans, and Parker (1995) found that children in high status peer groups tend to gossip and pick on lower status children as a way to maintain their sense of superiority. "When dominant children affiliate with each other they can also be expected to be somewhat similar in terms of bullying, because such behavior reflects one of the strategies that they may use to acquire or maintain dominance" (Witvliet et al., 2009, p. 287).

Results showed that "peer groups high in perceived popularity and low in likeability tend to show a large amount of bullying, whereas groups low in perceived popularity and high in likeability tend to show little bullying" (Witvliet et al., 2009, p. 297). The Perceived Popularity Explanation received the most support for bullying behavior; as a result, bullying is seen as a social strategy to obtain and maintain membership of a perceived popular peer group.

Regardless of the causes or motives of bullying, the effects can be devastating to young children resulting in feeling of shame, depression, embarrassment, insecurity, low self-esteem, and fear of school. Children develop psychosomatic illnesses such as headaches or stomachaches as a result of the stress and anxiety. Long-term effects include difficulty keeping a job, greater financial problems, depression, and anxiety disorders such as social phobia and fear of evaluation as adults (Wolke, Copeland, Angold, & Costello, 2013). Bullies and bully-victims also report experiencing long-term consequences such as engaging in risky or illegal behaviors, regular smoking, substance and alcohol abuse, and experiencing psychiatric problems (Wolke et al., 2013).

Approximately 10% of children are severely or repeatedly victimized, with substantially more reporting the occasional victimization (Hanish & Guerra, 2000; Storch & Ledley, 2005). Peer victimization has been defined as "the experience among children of being a target of the aggressive behavior of other children, who are not siblings and not necessarily age-mates" (Hawker & Boulton, 2000, p. 441). Victimizing manifests itself in behaviors such as teasing, deliberate exclusion, being the target of gossip, and threats of physical violence.

Bullied children experience both short- and long-term consequences: depression (Neary & Joseph, 1994), anxiety (Olweus, 1978; Slee, 1994), low self-esteem (Boulton & Smith, 1994), loneliness (Boulton & Underwood, 1992), school absenteeism (Reid, 1983), and relationship problems later in life (Gilmartin, 1987). Hawker and Boulton (2000) performed a meta-analysis of studies looking at peer victimization and measures of psychosocial difficulties. They reported that victimized children had higher levels of depression, loneliness, and anxiety and lower levels of self-esteem and social self-concept.

"The picture of the typical victim of peer bullying is a nonassertive social isolate with low self-esteem who is an easy target and does not stand up to bullies" (Guerra et al., 2011, p. 297). Victims are also less socially skilled (Schwartz, 2000) and more socially isolated from peer networks (Nansel et al., 2001). The relationship of self-esteem and bullies is less clear; some have low self-esteem, while others have high self-esteem. However, some scholars have differentiated types of victims as they have types of bullies.

Passive victims are usually anxious, insecure, cautious, quiet, and more likely to react by crying or withdrawing. Sometimes they have low self-esteem; see self as failure; and feel stupid, ashamed, and unattractive (Olweus, 1993). Boys who are victims are usually physically weaker and not popular, poor at sports, possess poor physical coordination, report being lonely, don't have peers as close friends, and relate better to adults than to peers. "Overall, the passive victim is characterized by anxious or submissive reaction patterns and somehow seems to signal to other students they are insecure individuals who will not fight back if attacked" (Powell & Ladd, 2010, p. 193).

A less frequent type of victim is the proactive victim (Olweus, 1978) who is characterized as both anxious and aggressive. Sometimes they are ADHD with behavioral problems; some label them as bully/victims because they act out both sets of behaviors. They are more likely than bullies to use physical aggression, and they have low self-esteem (Scaglione & Scaglione, 2006). They are not acting out to gain power or dominance; rather they are acting out of rage, anger, and revenge. They are higher on relational loneliness, have peer relational problems, and have internalized antisocial behavioral beliefs. They have more negative affect and greater use of destructive coping strategies than pure victims.

One factor that mitigates the occurrence of victimization by bullies is the presence of friends. Fox and Boulton (2006) investigated the moderating effect of friendship on behavioral problems (poor social skills) and victimization. A secondary purpose was to look "at the effect of the identity of the very best friend, i.e. the victimization of the very best friend, the social skills problems of the very best friend, and the peer acceptance (social preference) of the very best friend" (Fox & Boulton, 2006, p. 113). Basically, it was proposed that if one's very best friend is skilled, well liked, "cool," etc., the less skilled friend is not likely to be the target of victimization.

Therefore, results suggest it is not only the presence of friends who lessen the likelihood of bullying but *who* the friends are. That is, the popularity and social skills of one's friends are an important factor in preventing victimization. Basically, bullies don't pick on popular children, or the friends of those popular children. It was further observed that a friend helps mitigate victimization by occupying the potential victim's time and thus s/he is not alone and a target of bullying. Further, a friend can provide verbal and physical defense from a bully and can provide the victim with counsel to avoid confrontations with bullies.

CHILDREN WITH DEVELOPMENTAL DISABILITIES

Thus far we have looked at the communication skills and the development of relationships within typically developing populations as well as the burgeoning research on bullies and peer victims. Over the past two decades, as a consequence of increased movement to inclusive classrooms, a body of research has emerged which explicates the challenges faced by children with developmental disabilities (DD) as they attempt to engage in relationships with typically developing (TD) children (Webster & Carter, 2007). Unfortunately, the research indicates the failures to develop a social network of friends and/or succeed in acquiring a stable best friend have serious consequences for this population. DD children are at a higher risk than TD children for missing out on the many benefits of a social network and close friends, due to disorders like Attention Deficit Hyperactivity Disorder (ADHD) or Autism Spectrum Disorder (ASD). In this section, we begin with a description of the cognitive and behavior characteristics of children with specific developmental disabilities that are essential to social interaction and the development of friendship. Next, we discuss research that demonstrates the impact of these skills deficits in the social world of children. Finally, we review features of and research about various skills training programs designed specifically to help DD children develop friendships.

Two specific developmental disorders have received a great deal of attention in the literature and so we will focus on these: ADHD and ASD. By definition, each of these disorders carries developmental disabilities that impact the capacity to create and sustain social relationships, and as a consequence, the symptoms of these disorders include impaired social connections. According to the American Psychiatric Association (APA), ADHD is characterized as follows: "People with ADHD typically have trouble getting organized, staying focused, making realistic plans and thinking before acting. They may be fidgety, noisy and unable to adapt to changing situations. Children with ADHD can be defiant, socially inept or aggressive" (http://www.apa.org/topics/adhd/).

In their review of research on ADHD children's social relationships, Frankel and Feinberg (2002) noted that these children were described as more "socially 'busy' and more negative" than TD children (p. 130). The negative behaviors come in the form of hostility, aggression, and disruptive behavior that results from poor impulse control. Thus some ADHD children who are in social settings are likely to produce a lot of behavior but the behavior that is exhibited is not prosocial or attractive.

For example, Merrell and Wolfe (1998) noted in their study that ADHD children were assessed as significantly less socially cooperative (i.e., sharing toys, compromising, taking turns) than their TD counterparts as early as kindergarten. It is difficult for children with ADHD to contribute positively to the development of friendships as a consequence of deficits in the ability to modulate emotions and arousal coupled with issues in processing information. These core issues likely contribute to lowered abilities to connect emotionally or to demonstrate perspective-taking skills (Mikami, 2010). Maedgen and Carlson (2000) found that ADHD Combined (displaying both inattentive and hyperactivity-impulsivity symptoms) were more likely to be aggressive than their TD counterparts. Even when processing interactions, the issue of aggressiveness arises. Stormont (2001) notes that when asked what should be done in a hypothetical social situation, children with ADHD propose more aggressive solutions and have problems understanding how to adjust their behavior based on the situation. Similarly, Frankel and Feinberg (2002) noted that children diagnosed with ADHD "tend to attribute hostile intent" (p. 132), anticipating aggression in interactions while gathering information before deciding on how to behave. The negative perceptions of others and the hostile, aggressive, and disruptive behaviors exhibited by ADHD children lead to findings like Mikami's (2010) that "any friendships that children with ADHD do have may be less stable, and also of lower quality, relative to friendships of comparison children" (p. 183). Given the research we have reviewed on bullying and the link between aggressiveness and ADHD, the conclusion by Unnever and

Cornell (2003) that ADHD children are more likely to be victims of bullying and bully others as well is not surprising.

Difficulty in forming peer relationships is one of the diagnostic criteria of ASD (Solish, Perry, & Minnes, 2010). The APA Fact Sheet on ASD states:

> People with ASD tend to have communication deficits, such as responding inappropriately in conversations, misreading nonverbal interactions, or having difficulty building friendships appropriate to their age. In addition, people with ASD may be overly dependent on routines, highly sensitive to changes in their environment, or intensely focused on inappropriate items. (http://www.dsm5.org/Documents/Autism%20Spectrum%20Disorder%20 Fact%20Sheet.pdf)

Bellini, Peters, Benner, and Hopf (2007) summarized the research by noting that ASD social skill "deficiencies include difficulties with initiating interactions, maintaining reciprocity, sharing enjoyment, taking another person's perspective, and inferring the interests of others" (p. 153). Unfortunately for the child with ASD, researchers (see Bellini, 2006, for example) believe that the skills deficits contribute to negative interactions with peers, which in turn lead to withdrawing from social situations. Indeed, Solish, Perry, and Minnes (2010) found that TD children were more likely to participate in social and recreational activities than were ASD children. Additionally, ASD children were more likely to participate in social activities with an adult while TD children were more likely to participate in social activities with peers.

The lack of interaction with peers prevents the possibility of remediating one's skills in organic interactions with peers and, as Bellini's (2006) work suggests, contributes to a cycle that includes increasing levels of social anxiety which make social withdrawal a relief. Even when children with ASD may be assumed to have a better chance at developing relationships because they are higher functioning ASD, research does not demonstrate that this is the case. In fact, Mazurek and Kanne (2010) note that stronger cognitive and social skills in an ASD population prove more problematic (p. 1518). Mazurek and Kanne (2010) postulate that higher functioning ASD children are more likely to attempt to initiate friendships but remain inappropriate and because their ASD is less severe, they are more aware of the poor quality of their relationships. Consequently, they are likely to experience negative repercussions such as heightened anxiety and depression, as well as becoming victimized by peers. In fact, data from Mazurek and Kanne's (2010) study demonstrated a negative association between anxiety/depression and ASD severity.

Social skills deficits haunt ASD children and impede them from relationships throughout their school years. Solomon, Bauminger, and Rogers (2011) contend that executive functioning deficits hold back even high functioning ASD children from developing more mature relationships in adolescence because the nature of friendships here shift from the concrete to the abstract—from activities-based affiliations to intimacy-based connections. Intimacy requires skills such as organization, decision making, planning, and, perhaps most important, perspective taking. Heiman's (2005) work supports the notion that children with developmental disabilities are at a disadvantage as the requirements for enacting friendships progress in abstractness. Finally, Frankel et al. (2010) note that the lack of peer relationships in younger years "makes deficits in knowledge of peer etiquette more obvious as the child with ASD gets older" (p. 827).

As was the case with ADHD, it should not be surprising to the reader that children with ASD are four times more likely to be recipients of bullying than are TD children (Little, 2002). The poor social skills of ASD children directly contribute, for example, as one study found that children with ASD tended to have the poorest and least effective defenses against being teased (Frankel et al., 2010). But the skills deficits also contribute indirectly as Cappadocia, Weiss, and Pepler (2012) note of the relationship between bullying and ASD: "Due to their social difficulties, children with ASD likely do not benefit from the protective factor of supportive peers. In fact, they may be at greater risk for victimization due to their marginalization among peers" (p. 267).

It is well established that children with DD, such as ADHD or ASD, are disproportionately peer rejected and additionally are less likely to report having friends or best friends. For example, Solish, Perry, and Minnes (2010) noted that half of their ASD subjects reported having no friends at all, and further, that when compared with TD and/or children with another intellectual disability (e.g., Down's syndrome), ASD children were the least likely to have a best friend (p. 232). Mazurek and Kanne (2010) note that ASD severity has a negative relationship to the number of friends as well. In their study, one-quarter of the ASD sample reported having no peer relationships at all (p. 1518). Hoza, Mrug, Gerdes, Hinshaw, Bukowski, Gold, Kraemer, Pelham, Wigal, and Arnold (2005) found that 52% of their ADHD subjects were peer rejected, 56% of their ADHD subjects had no dyadic friend, and ADHD subjects were most likely to be nominated as nonfriends by peers of high social status. Hoza et al. (2005) note the patterns they found with regard to ADHD and peer relationships started as young as age 7. The persistence of such findings is alarming, particularly considering the bullying research which notes that having at least one friend creates a buffer zone around children who are generally peer rejected, keeping them out of the sightline of bullies. But this is not an easy task either. Thus researchers in this area work to create training programs that will help DD children to develop such a buffer zone.

The success of such programs is varied. What is interesting from our perspective are the skills that serve as the focus for training. Nearly all training programs focus on both the child and the mother. Mothers are seen as integral for two reasons: (1) research is clear in the TD population that mothers' pursuit of play dates has an impact on the quality and number of friendships children have as they age (e.g., Kennedy, 1992; Ladd & Hartt, 1992), and (2) mothers serve a vital role in guiding children before, during, and after interaction with peers. For children with ADHD, use of medications and behavior management strategies can help to increase levels of peer acceptance because these strategies can reduce aggression and target the elimination of other specific disruptive behaviors. Children can be monitored and rewarded for very specific behaviors. Social Skills training programs focus on varied skill sets including entering an existing group, arranging a play date, conversation skills, managing emotions, taking turns, and so forth. Researchers like Mikami (2010) have stated that the mixed results from studies that have tested such interventions speak to the need to develop less generalized social skills programs and more specifically targeted friendship skills programs. Mikami argues that it would be more fruitful for children with ADHD in particular to work at developing a single friendship rather than looking to increase peer acceptance, which requires varied skills that change with age and are modified by gender.

A good example of a program which has been used to enhance skills to develop friendships (as opposed to general increased peer acceptance) is the UCLA Children's Friendship Training (CFT) program (Frankel et al., 2010), which incorporates some of the previously noted skills, but also trains children in "good host behavior" for play dates and expanding and developing friendship networks. In a recent study, Frankel et al. (2010) tested the CFT with ASD children, training them and their mothers over a 12-week period. As part of the program, children were not only trained in general conversation techniques, but also given specific strategies for inviting a child to a play date and hosting the play date, while the mother was trained to listen to the interaction during the play date and intervene when any violations occurred. Rules for the play date included knowing that the "guest is always right" (meaning he/she gets a choice of activities), to praise the guest's behavior and not to criticize the guest, stay with and stay focused on the play date, and try to barter or negotiate with the guest when the host wants to do something different and the guest would rather stay with the same activity (Frankel et al., 2010, p. 834).

Upon review, it is evident that these types of behaviors are designed to enhance theory of the mind, or enact perspective taking. Behaviorally, they create an environment that would emerge organically if the subject of this training were both motivated to connect with the peer and cognitively able to interpret the social cues of the other. These behaviors are not just polite, they are empathetic, and create an environment in which a guest feels welcomed and safe. However, the results seem to indicate that the behaviors do not last. In the Frankel et al. (2010) study looking at high functioning ASD children in the CFT program, measurement after treatment indicated that a majority of the children had demonstrated gains in skills on almost four different measures (out of 15) soon after treatment, but most subjects only sustained these gains on one measure by the next assessment 3 months later, and at no point throughout the program were posttest measurements of the targeted skills perceived higher by their school teachers.

FUTURE RESEARCH DIRECTIONS IN CHILDREN'S PEER RELATIONSHIPS OUTSIDE THE FAMILY

The purpose of this chapter was to review research that demonstrated the importance of children's peer relationships to their immediate and long-term social and mental health. We reviewed communication activities that served to both attract (e.g., initiating get-togethers, self-disclosure) and repel (aggression, negative emotional displays) peers within the childhood years.

Of special interest has been the research in the area of "bullying." Although the media may have created a monolithic image of the "school bully," the research in this area indicates that bullies often have very different motivations and different means of asserting their dominance. In some studies bullies have been found to be popular and socially skilled, with their behavior perceived as socially functional, while others are isolated, angry, and themselves victimized (Guerra, Williams, & Sadak, 2011; Powell & Ladd, 2010; Witvliet et al., 2009).

Another set of peer relationships of interest has been that within the special needs community. Some research indicated that within certain communities the stability of these friendships is problematic. Researchers have started to identify the specific behaviors enacted in friendship among developmentally disabled children (Freeman & Kasari, 2002), noting the similarities and differences with regard to friendships forged by typically developing children. Further, educational inclusivity (mainstreaming) has provided an opportunity to garner a greater understanding of the characteristics of friendships developed between children with developmental disorders and typically developing children (Webster & Carter, 2007).

Deviant case research is predicated on the notion that sometimes the best way to understand and see what is "normal" or typical is to study deviant or atypical behavior. For example, sophisticated skill sets are surely involved in the enactment of being a "defender" of a DD victim of bullying, while maintaining peer acceptance and popularity. We believe that integrating the research on both bullying and the friendships of the developmentally disabled has the potential to inform theoretical and applied work investigating the role of communication in friendship development in childhood.

The literature reveals that many programs have been developed to address the social dynamics and skills deficiencies of special needs children and those who engage in bullying behaviors, but the research clearly demonstrates that "one size doesn't fit all." For example, numerous studies indicate that some bullies are socially skilled and popular, while others are unskilled and themselves the targets of bullying from other students. It appears that some other variables must be mediating the bullying behaviors and social perceptions in such a manner that for some they result in positive outcomes like popularity and social status, while for others they result in negative social evaluations and isolation. A potential mediating variable is cognitive communication competence. Popular children who engage in bullying behavior simply may be more skilled in the application of these behaviors. That is, it is not the behavior itself that is viewed as socially competent or not, but rather how much, when, where, under what circumstances, and to whom the behavior is exhibited that become relevant to judgments of social effectiveness. As a result, school bullying programs may need to focus not only on competent communication behaviors/skills but also on the cognitive processes involved in the selection and enactment of those behaviors within a social interaction/context.

Finally, the literature with regard to bullying illustrates that we, as a society, may not be entirely clear on our feelings concerning "bullying" behaviors. The research seems to suggest that it depends on *who* is doing the bullying as to whether the behaviors are considered functional or dysfunctional. For some children it is an effective strategy to attain and maintain status and popularity and they rise to the top of the social pecking order. For other children it is a maladaptive response to interpersonal stressors and conflict and they pay a social price. Although the behaviors themselves appear to be similar, the personal motivations behind them are not, nor are the social consequences. Some are rewarded with social power and status, while others are further ostracized.

Mills and Carwile (2009) make a similar claim with regard to the functions and perceptions of teasing behaviors. They claim that while teasing is a communication activity that can be perceived as bullying in the form of name-calling, sarcasm, and put-downs, it can also serve a positive function by creating a sense of relational closeness. They claim, "Teasing can be playful and fun, and it can be a prosocial strategy of affiliation, education, and influence" (p. 281). Mills and Carwile (2009) caution those who develop and implement bullying prevention programs in schools to be careful to consider some of the positive, functional aspects of teasing and not "throw the baby out with the bath water." As a result of this concern, future research needs to address not only the differences in the intentions/functions behind bullying behaviors but also the consequences, both negative and positive, of such behaviors. Simply put, why do they work for some and not for others? Research on this question is vitally important because the consequences of bullying behavior, both for the victims and the bully-victims, have far too often proved to be tragic and catastrophic.

REFERENCES

Adler, P. A., & Adler, P. (1996). Preadolescent clique stratification and the hierarchy of identity. *Sociological Inquiry, 66*, 111–142.

Adler, P. A., & Adler, P. (1998). *Peer power: Preadolescent culture and identity.* New Brunswick, NJ: Rutgers University Press.

Asher, S. R., & Coie, J. D. (Eds.). (1990). *Peer rejection in childhood.* New York, NY: Cambridge University Press.

Asher, S. R., Parker, J. G., & Walker, D. L. (1996). Distinguishing friendship from acceptance: Implications for intervention and assessment. In W. M. Bukowski, A.F. Newcomb, & W. W. Hartup (Eds.), *The company they keep: Friendship in childhood and adolescence* (pp. 366–405). New York, NY: Cambridge University Press.

Baines, E., & Blachford, P. (2009). Sex differences in the structure and stability of children's playground social networks and their overlap with friendship relations. *British Journal of Developmental Psychology, 27*, 743–760. doi:10.1348/026151008x371114

Baumeister, R. F., & Leary, M. R. (1995). The need to belong: Desire for interpersonal attachments as a fundamental human motivation. *Psychological Bulletin, 117*, 497–529.

Bellini, S. (2006). The development of social anxiety in high functioning adolescents with autism spectrum disorders. *Focus on Autism and Other Developmental Disabilities, 2*, 138–145.

Bellini, S., Peters, J., Benner, L., & Hopf, A. (2007). A meta-analysis of school-based social skill interventions for children with autism spectrum disorders. *Remedial and Special Education, 28*, 153–162.

Boulton, M. J., & Smith, P. K. (1994). Bully/victim problems in middle-school children: Stability, self-perceived competence, peer perceptions, and peer acceptance. *British Journal of Developmental Psychology, 12*, 315–329.

Boulton, M. J., & Underwood, K. (1992). Bully/victim problems among middle school children. *British Journal of Educational Psychology, 62*, 73–87.

Brown, L. M., Chesney-Lind, M., & Stein, N. (2007). Toward a gendered theory of teen violence and victimization. *Violence Against Women, 13*, 1249–1273.

Burgess, K. B., Wojslawowicz, J. C., Rubin, K. H., Rose-Krasnor, L., & Booth-LaForce, C. (2006). Social information processing and coping strategies of shy/withdrawn and aggressive children: Does friendship matter? *Child Development, 77*, 371–383.

Cappadocia, M. C., Weiss, J. A., & Pepler, D. (2012). Bullying experiences among children and youth with autism spectrum disorders. *Journal of Autism and Developmental Disorders, 42*(2), 266–277. doi:10.1007/s10803-011-1241-x.

Coie, J. D., & Dodge, K. A. (1998). Aggression and antisocial behavior. In W. Damon (Series Ed.) & N. Eisenberg (Vol. Ed.), *Handbook of child psychology: Vol. 3. Social, emotional, and personality development* (pp. 779–862). New York, NY: John Wiley & Sons.

Crick, N. R., & Dodge, K. A. (1999). "Superiority" is in the eye of the beholder: A comment of Sutton, Smith and Swettenham. *Social Development, 8*, 128–131.

Eder, D., Evans, C. C., & Parker, S. (1995). *School talk: Gender and adolescent culture.* New Brunswick, NJ: Rutgers University Press.

Engle, J. M., McElwain, N. L., & Lasky, N. (2011). Presence and quality of kindergarten children's friendships: Concurrent and longitudinal associations with children adjustment in the early school years. *Infant and Child Development, 20*, 365–386.

Espelage, D. L., Holt, M. K., & Henkel, R. R. (2003). Examination of peer-group contextual effects on aggression during early adolescence. *Child Development, 74*, 205–220.

Estell, D. B., Farmer, T. M., & Cairns, B. D. (2007). Bullies and victims in rural African American youth: Behavioral characteristics and social network placement. *Aggressive Behavior, 33*, 145–159.

Estell, D. B., Farmer, T. M., Irvin, M. J., Crowther, A., & Akos, P. (2009). Students with exceptionalities and the peer group context of bullying and victimization in late elementary school. *Journal of Family Studies, 18*, 136–150.

Estell, D. B., Jones, M. H., Pearl, R., & Von Acker, R. (2009). Best friendships of students with and without learning disabilities across late elementary schools. *Exceptional Children, 76*, 110–124.

Farmer, T. W. (2000). The social dynamics of aggressive and disruptive behavior in school: Implications for behavioral consultation. *Journal of Education and Behavioral Consultation, 21,* 194–208.

Fox, C. L., & Boulton, M. J. (2006). Friendship as a moderator of the relationship between social skills problems and peer victimization. *Aggressive Behavior, 32,* 110–121.

Frankel, F., & Feinberg, D. (2002). Social problems association with ADHD vs. ODD in children referred for friendship problems. *Child Psychiatry and Human Development, 32,* 125–146.

Frankel, F., Myatt, R., Sugar, C., Whitham, C., Gorospe, C. M., & Laugeson, E. (2010). A randomized controlled study of parent-assisted children's friendship training with children having Autism Spectrum Disorders. *Journal of Autism and Developmental Disorders, 40,* 827–842. doi:10.1007/s10803-009-0932-z

Freeman, S. F. N., & Kasari, C. (2002). Characteristics and qualities of the play dates of children with Down syndrome: Emerging or true friendships? *American Journal of Mental Retardation, 107,* 16–31.

Gasser, L., & Keller, M. (2009). Are the competent the morally good? Perspective taking and moral motivation of children involved in bullying. *Social Development, 18,* 798–816.

Gilmartin, B. G. (1987). Peer group antecedents of severe love-shyness in males. *Journal of Personality, 55,* 467–489.

Gini, G. (2006). Social cognition and moral cognition in bullying: What's wrong? *Aggressive Behavior, 32,* 528–539.

Gleason, T. R., Gower, A. L., Hohmann, L. M., & Gleason, T. C. (2005). Temperament and friendship in school aged children. *International Journal of Behavioral Development, 29*(4), 336–344.

Goossens, F. A., Olthof, T., & Dekker, P. (2006). The New Participant Role Scales: A comparison between various criteria for assigning roles and indications for their validity. *Aggressive Behavior, 32,* 343–357.

Gottman, J., Gonso, J., & Rasmussen, B. (1975). Social interaction, social competence, and friendship in children. *Child Development, 46,* 709–718.

Guerra, N. G., Williams, K. R., & Sadek, S. (2011). Understanding bullying and victimization during childhood and adolescence: A mixed methods study. *Child Development, 82,* 295–310.

Hanish L. D., & Guerra, N. G. (2000). Predictors of peer victimization among urban youth. *Social Development, 9,* 521–543.

Haslett, B. B., & Samter, W. (1997). Children communicating: The first 5 years. Mahwah, NJ: Erlbaum.

Haslett, B. B., & Samter, W. (2014). Parent–infant communication. In J. F. Nussbaum (Ed.), *Life span communication.* New York, NY: Peter Lang.

Hawker, D. S., & Boulton, M. J. (2000). Twenty years' research on peer victimization and psychological maladjustment: A meta-analytic review of cross-sectional studies. *Journal Child Psychological Psychiatry, 41,* 441–455.

Hawkins, D. L., Pepler, D. J., & Craig, W. M. (2001). Naturalistic observations of peer interventions in bullying. *Social Development, 10,* 512–527.

Hay, D. F., Payne, A., & Chadwick, A. (2004). Peer relations in childhood. *Journal of Child Psychology and Psychiatry, 45,* 84–108.

Heiman, T. (2005). An examination of peer relationships of children with and without attention deficit hyperactivity disorder. *School Psychology International, 26,* 330–339.

Howes, C. (1988). Same- and cross-sex friends: Implications for interaction and social skills. *Early Childhood Research Quarterly, 3,* 21–37.

Hoza, B., Mrug, S., Gerdes, A. C., Hinshaw, S. P., Bukowski, W. M., Gold, J. A., Kraemer, H. C., Pelham, W. E., Jr., Wigal, T., & Arnold, L. E. (2005). What aspects of peer relationships are impaired in children with attention-deficit/hyperactivity disorder? *Journal of Consulting and Clinical Psychology, 73*, 411–423.

Kennedy, J. (1992). Relationship of maternal beliefs and childrearing strategies to social competence in preschool. *Child Study Journal, 22*, 39–61.

Ladd, G. W., & Hartt, C. G. (1992). Creating informal play opportunities: Are parents' and preschoolers' initiations related to children's competence with peers? *Developmental Psychology, 28*(6), 1179–1187. doi:0012-1649/92

Ladd, G. W., Kochenderfer, B. J., & Coleman, C. C. (1996). Friendship quality as a predictor of young children's early school adjustment. *Child Development, 67*, 1181–1197.

Lindsey, E. (2002). Preschool children's friendships and peer acceptance: Links to social competence. *Child Study Journal, 32*, 145–156.

Little, L. (2002). Middle-class mothers' perceptions of peer and sibling victimization among children with Asperger's syndrome and nonverbal learning disorders. *Issues in Comprehensive Pediatric Nursing, 25*, 43–57. doi:10.1080/014608602753504847

Maccoby, E. (2000). Perspectives on gender development. *International Journal of Behavioral Development, 24*, 398–406.

Maedgen, J. W., & Carlson, C. L. (2000). Social functioning and emotional regulation in the attention deficit hyperactivity disorder subtypes. *Journal of Clinical Child Psychology, 29*, 30–42.

Maslow, A. (1970). *Motivation and personality* (2nd ed.). New York, NY: Harper & Row.

Mazurek, M. O., & Kanne, S. M. (2010). Friendship and internalizing symptoms among children and adolescents with ASD. *Journal of Autism and Developmental Disorders, 40*, 1512–1250. doi:10.1007/s10803-010-1014-y

Merrell, K. W., & Wolfe, T. M. (1998). The relationship of teacher-rated social skills deficits and ADHD characteristics among kindergarten-age children. *Psychology in the Schools, 33*, 101–109.

Mikami, A. Y. (2010). The importance of friendship for youth with attention-deficit/hyperactivity disorder. *Clinical Child and Family Psychological Review, 13*, 181–198. doi:10.1007/s10567-010-0067-y

Mills, C. B., & Carwile, A. M. (2009). The good, the bad, and the borderline: Separating teasing from bullying. *Communication Education, 58*, 276–301.

Nangle, D. W., Erdly, C. A., Newman, J. E., Mason, C. A., & Carpenter, E. M. (2003). Popularity, friendship quantity, and friendship quality: Interactive influences on children's loneliness and depression. *Journal of Clinical Child and Adolescent Psychology, 32*, 546–555.

Nansel, T. R., Overpeck, M., Pilla, R. S., Ruan, W. J., Simons-Morton, B., & Scheidt, P. (2001). Bullying behaviors among US youth. *Journal of the American Medical Association, 16*, 2094–2100.

Neary, A., & Joseph, S. (1994). Peer victimization and its relationship to self-concept and depression among schoolgirls. *Personality and Individual Differences, 16*, 183–186.

Olthof, T., & Goossens, F. A. (2008). Bullying and the need to belong: Early adolescents' bullying-related behavior and the acceptance they desire and receive from particular classmates. *Social Development, 17*, 24–46.

Olweus, D. (1978). *Aggression in the schools: Bullies and whipping boys*. Washington, DC: Hemisphere.

Olweus, D. (1993). *Bullying at school: What we know and what we can do*. Cambridge, MA: Blackwell.

Olweus, D. (1999). Sweden. In P. K. Smith, Y. Morita, J. Juger-Tas, D. Olweus, R. Catalano, & P. Slee (Eds.), *The nature of school bullying: A cross-national perspective* (pp. 7–27). Florence, KY: Routledge.

Olweus, D., & Limber, S. (2002). *Bullying prevention program* (Rep. No. Book 9). Boulder: Center for the Study of Prevention and Violence, Institute of Behavioral Science, University of Colorado at Boulder.

Peskin, M. F., Tortolero, S. R., & Markham, C. M. (2006). Bullying and victimization among Black and Hispanic adolescents. *Adolescence, 41*, 467–484.

Poulin, F., & Boivin, M. (2000). Reactive and proactive aggression: Evidence of a two-factor model. *Psychological Assessment, 12*, 115–122.

Powell, M. D., & Ladd, L. D. (2010). Bullying: A review of the literature and implications for family therapists. *The American Journal of Family Therapy, 38*, 189–206.

Reid, K. (1983). Retrospection and persistent school absenteeism. *Education Research, 25*, 110–115.

Reijntjes, A., Kamphuis, J. H., Prinzie, P., Boelen, P. A., van der Schoot, M., & Telch, M. J. (2011). Prospective linkages between peer victimization and externalizing problems in children: A meta-analysis. *Aggressive Behavior, 37*, 215–222.

Rodkin, P. C., & Hodges, E. V. E. (2003). Bullies and victims in the peer ecology: Four questions for psychologists and school professionals. *School Psychology Review, 32*, 384–400.

Rose, A. J., & Asher, S. R. (2004). Children's strategies and goals in response to help-giving and help-seeking tasks within a friendship. *Child Development, 75*, 749–763.

Salmivalli, C., Lagerspetz, K., Bjorkqvist, K., Osterman, K., & Kaukiainen, A. (1996). Bullying as a group process: Participant roles and their relations to social status within the group. *Aggressive Behavior, 38*, 305–312.

Scaglione, J., & Scaglione, A. R. (2006). *Bully-proofing children: A practical, hands-on guide to stop bullying.* Lanham, MD: Rowman & Littlefield.

Schwartz, D. (2000). Subtypes of victims and aggressors in children's peer groups. *Journal of Abnormal Psychology, 28*, 181–192.

Sebanc, A. E., Kearns, K. T., Hernandez, M. D., & Galvin, K. B. (2007). Predicting having a best friend in young children: Individual characteristics and friendship features. *Journal of Genetic Psychology, 168*, 81–95.

Sebanc, A. M. (2003). The friendship features of preschool children: Links with prosocial behavior and aggression. *Social Development, 12*, 249–268.

Slee, P. T. (1994). Situational and interpersonal correlates of anxiety associated with peer victimization. *Child Psychiatry and Human Development, 25*, 97–107.

Socha, T., & Stamp, G. H. (Eds.). (2009). *Parents and children communicating with society: Managing relationships outside the home.* New York, NY: Routledge.

Solberg, M. E., & Olweus, D. (2003). Prevalence estimation of school bullying with the Olweus bully/victim questionnaire. *Aggressive Behavior, 29*, 239–268.

Solberg, M. E., Olweus, D., & Endresen, I. (2007). Bullies and victims at school: Are they the same pupils? *British Journal of Educational Psychology, 77*, 441–464.

Solish, A., Perry, A., & Minnes, P. (2010). Participation of children with and without disabilities in social, recreational and leisure activities. *Journal of Applied Research in Intellectual Disabilities, 23*, 226–236. doi:10.1111/j.1468-3148.2009.00525.x

Solomon, M., Bauminger, N., & Rogers, S. J. (2011). Abstract reasoning and friendship in high functioning preadolescents with autism spectrum disorder. *Journal of Autism and Developmental Disorders, 41*, 32–43.

Storch, E. A., & Ledley, D. R. (2005). Peer victimization and psychological adjustment in children: Current knowledge and future directions. *Clinical Pediatrics, 44*, 29–38.

Stormont, M. (2001). Preschool family and child characteristics associated with stable behavior problems in children. *Journal of Early Intervention, 24*, 241–251. EJ 650 506.

Svetlova, M., Nichols, S. R., & Brownell, C. A. (2010). Toddler's prosocial behavior: From instrumental to empathic to altruistic behavior. *Child Development, 81*, 1814–1827.

Unnever, J. D., & Cornell, D. G. (2003). Bullying, self-control, and ADHD. *Journal of Interpersonal Violence, 81,* 129–147.

Vaughn, B. E., Azia, M. R., Caya, L. R., Newell, W., Krzysik, L., Bost, K. K., & Kazura, K. L. (2000). Friendship and social competence in a sample of preschool children attending Head Start. *Developmental Psychology, 36,* 326–338.

Webster, A. A., & Carter, M. (2007). Social relationships and friendships of children with developmental disabilities: Implications for inclusive settings. A systematic review. *Journal of Intellectual & Developmental Disability, 32,* 200–213. doi:10.1080/13668250701549443

Witvliet, W., Olthof, T., Hoeksma, J. B., Goossens, F. A., Smits, M. S. I., & Koot, H. M. (2009). Peer group affiliation of children: The role of perceived popularity, likeability, and behavioral similarity in bullying. *Social Development, 19,* 285–303.

Wolke, D., Copeland, W. E., Angold, A., & Costello, J. E. (2013). Impact of bullying in childhood on adult health, wealth, crime, and social outcomes. *Psychological Science, 24,* 1958-1970. doi:10.117/0956797613481608.

CHAPTER SEVEN

Communication and Learning

JENNIFER H. WALDECK

Learning is fundamental to human development across the lifespan. Most of our understanding of how people learn is based on research conducted in formal educational contexts; however, learning and education occur through a variety of formal and informal life experiences across the lifespan, including conditioning and reinforcement, the development of hobbies, formal education, employment-related training, and travel.

The purpose of this chapter is to provide an overview of the aspects of communication that impact learning throughout the lifespan in a range of contexts. Toward that end, this chapter examines the concept of learning and its various forms, how learners are socialized to the educational experience; theoretical explanations of how learning occurs; and the role of communication in (a) effective teacher and student behavior, (b) how classrooms are structured and managed, and (c) course-related technology use.

LEARNING AND EDUCATION AS LIFESPAN PROCESSES

Instructional communication is an interdisciplinary field of research that draws on the research conducted by educational psychology, pedagogy, and communication scholars (Mottet & Beebe, 2006). The nature of instructional communication research allows scholars working in this area to focus on the "communicative factors in the teaching-learning process that occur across grade levels, instructional settings, and subject matter" (Myers, 2010, p. 149), making it a lifespan approach to education (since it doesn't focus on a specific grade level or context).

The instructional communication perspective conceptualizes and measures learning in terms of three domains identified by Bloom (1956) and Krathwohl, Bloom, and Masia (1964). Additionally, many educators employ learning models such as Emotional Intelligence (Goleman, 1998) and related Social and Emotional Learning (Norris, 2003).

Bloom's Taxonomy

Cognitive learning. Cognitive learning is concerned with the acquisition, understanding, evaluation, and use of information. At its most base level, cognitive learning refers to the memorization and recollection of information. The second level addresses the ability to move beyond memorization to understanding of class material. The highest orders of cognitive learning refer to application, analysis, synthesis, and evaluation of information.

Cognitive learning is measured by two scales: (1) the Learning Indicators Scale (Frymier & Houser, 1999), which focuses on indicators such as student question asking, volunteering opinions, and discussing course content with others; and (2) most commonly, the Learning Loss Scale (Richmond, McCroskey, Kearney & Plax, 1987). The Learning Loss measure was designed to be used across disciplines, classrooms, and content and overcomes the reliability and validity problems of test scores as indicators of cognition.

Early childhood education, along with lower-division high school and college courses, tends to focus on lower-order cognitive objectives and move to application, analysis, synthesis, and evaluation as the student progresses through a subject. Thus, consistent with lifespan communication theory (Harwood, this volume), learning is nonlinear. For example, college students who have earlier mastered synthesis in one area may be focused on lower comprehension outcomes because they are new to a subject (McCroskey, Richmond, & McCroskey, 2006).

Psychomotor learning. Psychomotor (or behavioral) outcomes are concerned with the performance of specific physical behaviors. At the lowest level, learners focus on developing basic physical behaviors: incorporating hand gestures into an oral presentation, for example. As psychomotor learning goals increase in complexity, learners focus on perfecting behaviors learned at the lower levels and integrating them with others. For example, a student might be asked to combine the use of hand and arm gestures with movement around the classroom, smiling, and eye contact with the audience during a speech.

McCroskey et al. (2006) wrote that behavioral learning is emphasized in the lower grades, but downplayed in later grades and in college. However, the evaluation,

COMMUNICATION AND LEARNING | 137

training, and assessment of physical skills and behaviors assume greater importance again during career-related training and development (Waldeck, Plax, & Kearney, 2010). For example, individuals must refine their customer service skills, or learn culturally appropriate behaviors for international business travel. Psychomotor learning is measured through behavior-specific assessments. Within the communication field, a number of measures assess behaviors such as public speaking, conversation, nonverbal behavior, and overall communication competence.

Affective learning. Affect has to do with an individual's attitudes, beliefs, and values relative to the knowledge and behaviors he or she has learned (Krathwohl, Bloom, & Masia, 1964). Strong affect for a course or subject corresponds to a positive attitude. Lower-order affective learning involves liking for the course and subject matter as a result of the instructional experience; higher-order affective learning involves the likelihood of engaging in behaviors taught in the class. A student's ability to internalize positive attitudes toward the course or subject appears to be a precursor to cognitive learning (Rodriguez, Plax, & Kearney, 1996). Although research indicates that both the affective and cognitive domains are important, educators historically placed little importance on the "liking" component of learning (McCroskey et al., 2006). More recently, though, as research has illustrated the connection between liking for the course/subject matter, student motivation, and cognitive learning (Waldeck, 2007), teachers appear to increasingly value both types of learning. Evidence of the importance of affective learning exists across educational levels and contexts (Martin & Mottet, 2011). Affect is measured using Andersen's (1979) Affective Learning Measure (ALM) or the Revised ALM (Mottet & Richmond, 1998).

Emotional Intelligence

Some schools focus on the development of social skills, emotion management, and self-regulation. These learning outcomes fall under the umbrella of *emotional intelligence*, a construct popularized in the education field by Elias et al. (1997), who argued that cognition and academic performance are important, but insufficient, conditions for success. Elias et al. concluded that when schools programmatically focus on the prevention and awareness of social problems like drug use, violence, and bullying, children have a heightened likelihood of being respectful of others, practicing responsible behavior, making reasoned decisions, and solving problems effectively.

Examples of emotional intelligence education in U.S. schools. One example of an educational program focused on emotional intelligence is Character Counts! (CC). CC is designed to enhance trust, respect, responsibility, fairness, caring, and citizenship across the lifespan. CC promotes acquisition of specific social skills among children through school-based curriculum, sports, and after-school programs. For adults, Josephson's Center for Business Ethics provides consulting designed to help organizations maximize emotional intelligence and develop a culture of ethical behavior.

In another example, a team of communication researchers developed a substance abuse intervention and resistance program for middle schools called *keepin' it REAL*. The *keepin' it REAL* program teaches teenagers resistance strategies when offered alcohol, drugs, tobacco, and other substances. Aware that young people communicate about substance abuse, perceive risk, and make decisions differently depending on their age and grade level, researchers empirically determined that the critical age range for implementing the program is 7th and 8th grades (Pettigrew et al., 2012).

A pedagogical framework for emotional intelligence. Social and Emotional Learning (SEL) is a comprehensive approach to the development of self-awareness, self-regulation of emotion, self-monitoring, empathy and perspective taking, responsible decision making, and relational communication skills among K–12 children. These competencies may influence later-life job satisfaction and performance (Norris, 2003).

Socialization: The Foundation for a Lifetime of Learning

Early childhood socialization: The family-of-origin. Relationships and the messages exchanged within them play an important role in education. One of the strongest influences on an individual's attitudes toward education is his or her family (Kranstuber, Carr, & Hosek, 2012). Attitudes formed in early childhood as a result of parental influence predict a number of outcomes later in college (Kranstuber et al.) and in the workplace (Medved, Brogan, McClanahan, Morris, & Shepherd, 2006).

Socialization refers to an ongoing process by which people learn the values, norms, and behaviors that will help them to participate and succeed in new, unfamiliar contexts, including school. Whenever humans encounter situations for which they have limited cognitive and experiential referents, they rely on the socialization process for reducing uncertainty (Waldeck & Myers, 2007). Children are socialized to education through observation (e.g., watching an older sibling study); obtaining educational and occupational information from others (e.g., college entrance requirements); and memorable parental messages about education (e.g., the importance of studying and preparing for college).

Memorable messages are verbal messages that people hear early in life, remember, and consider influential. Overall, parent-child relationships, the messages parents transmit to their children about education, and the way children make sense of those messages are related to several important student outcomes, including motivation, college satisfaction, motivation to learn, and cognitive learning indicators (Kranstuber et al.. 2012). Kranstuber et al found no evidence of a linear re ~~memorable messages are verbal~~ ombination of them) and stu ~~messages that people hear early in~~ communicated in a ~~life, remember + consider influential.~~

positive and meaningful way by a parent with whom the child reports having a satisfying relationship, and when children perceive the parent as having their best interests in mind when delivering the message, memorable messages have a potent socializing impact on young people in the areas of motivation, empowerment, college satisfaction, and cognitive learning indicators.

Researchers have further examined the types of socialization that occur in other educational contexts. For instance, confidence and self-efficacy beliefs resulting from parental messages play a significant role in performance in STEM (science, technology, engineering, and mathematics) courses, and the pursuit of related careers (DiBenedetto & Bembenutty, 2013). Students with earlier positive experiences communicating and forming relationships online perform better on tasks like planning and small talk in digital collaborations (Sherman, Michikyan, & Greenfield, 2013). Further, socially appropriate face-to-face behaviors learned in childhood predict effective communication in online learning environments (Reich, Black, & Korobkova, in press).

Additionally, memorable messages are imparted by on-campus mentors and have an especially strong impact on first-generation college students (Wang, 2012). The importance of socialization continues in the workplace, where variables such as training effectiveness, job satisfaction, assimilation, and retention are positively impacted by effective formal and informal educational practices (Waldeck, Seibold, & Flanagan, 2004).

THEORIZING ABOUT COMMUNICATION AND LEARNING FROM A DEVELOPMENTAL PERSPECTIVE

The instructional communication literature is theoretically rich with developmental frameworks. Developmental theories emphasize how people learn and grow as they age. The theories overviewed in this section are representative of those employed in communication research which highlights learning and education as lifespan activities in which both the content of learning and the relationships learners have with their teachers and one another are important. Although a number of theoretical frameworks help explain education, those selected for discussion address the role of communication in instruction and development.

Piaget's Developmental Theory

Piaget (1977) illustrated that as children age, they are able to differentiate among stimuli and respond in increasingly sophisticated ways. Kline and Clinton (1998) used this framework to examine how children develop communication competence and learn persuasive skills. They found "systematic age changes in persuasive message practice" (p. 120); specifically, with increasing age, children are more proficient at designing messages that are motivating, positively framed, and correspond to the views and preferred positions of others. Piaget's work also drives studies of how children learn to interpret and assign meaning to television and film portrayals. For example, older children perceive, interpret, and respond to fear- and anger-inducing television scenes in more sophisticated and discriminating ways than younger ones (Weiss & Wilson, 1998).

Expectancy Learning/Learned Helplessness

This perspective suggests that people learn to expect positive or negative outcomes of their own behavior over time, and that learned helplessness results when consequences are random and impossible to predict. McCroskey and Richmond (1987) used this theoretical framework in examining communication apprehension and anxiety as learned behaviors in the educational context. When people's experiences with and resulting expectations about communication are unpredictable, they lose confidence and become anxious; when outcomes are negative, they become fearful. These learned responses have documented negative influences on affective, cognitive, and psychomotor learning. Expectancy learning also helps us understand phenomena such as how people learn to use new technologies in school and at work (Turner, Turner, & Van de Walle, 2007) and adapt to perceived "difficult" subjects in school, such as math and computer science (Wilson & Schrock, 2001).

Approach/Avoidance Theory

As people develop, they acquire preferences for what they like or prefer and dislike. Approach/avoidance theory formalizes the proposition that as we discover these preferences, we move toward what we like, evaluate positively, and prefer; we avoid, or move away from, what we dislike, evaluate negatively, and do not prefer (Mehrabian, 1971). Researchers have illuminated how approach/avoidance may predict the impact of teacher immediacy and student communication apprehension on student outcomes. For instance, apprehensive students are more likely to avoid classroom discussions than students who have low communication apprehension (Neer, 1990). Waldeck, Kearney, and Plax (2001b) used approach/avoidance theory in a study of digital out-of-class communication and found that students who evaluate digital media positively, even if they haven't used them to communicate with instructors, are likely to use them to contact professors outside of class. More recently, Witt and Kerssen-Griep (2011) made recommendations for encouraging student "approach" reactions to instructional feedback, including avoiding or mitigating (through the use of immediacy cues, for instance) feedback which may be face-threatening to students.

Social Cognitive Theory

This theory articulates how individuals learn over time by observing how other people deal with similar situations (Bandura, 2009). Learners watch how others either in their immediate environment or in the media react to stimuli and repeat the responses, particularly when the models are emulated. In an empirical test of this proposition, Cantor and Omdahl (1999) found that children who viewed dramas of accidents with negative consequences were more likely to subsequently demonstrate safety guidelines for avoiding accidents delivered in an age-appropriate instructional format. Martins and Wilson (2012) applied this theory to explain the empirical relationship between viewing social aggression on television and elementary school children's tendency to display such behaviors in the classroom.

Rhetorical/Relational Goal Theory

This perspective suggests that students have both academic and relational needs that may change over time (Mottet, Frymier, & Beebe, 2006). Academic needs are related to a student's desire to acquire information and ideas and achieve goals such as learning or obtaining a particular grade. Relational needs involve feeling confirmed as a student and a person and are met through interactions with instructors and other students. Similarly, instructors have both rhetorical (content-related) and relational goals and may emphasize one of these over the other through their communication with students. Instructional communication researchers are particularly interested in the interplay between a focus on academic content and the benefits of context-appropriate developmental relationships that form across time among instructors and students. The nature of instructor goals and student needs varies according to grade level, the student's stage of personal and academic development, and educational context. In an application, Claus, Booth-Butterfield, and Chory (2012) found that students employ fewer antisocial communication behaviors when their instructors are antisocial (i.e., instructors display actions that interfere with the instructional process, such as boring lectures, giving unfair tests, or being late to class) if they perceive the instructor as interpersonally attractive and humorous, and report a high level of relational closeness with the instructor.

OVERVIEW OF THE ROLE OF COMMUNICATION VARIABLES IN LEARNING

What follows is a review of instructional communication research using a classification developed by Waldeck, Kearney, and Plax (2001b): Student variables, instructor variables, instructor/student interaction, classroom variables, and technology use. Space limitations preclude an exhaustive review; this section focuses on those constructs and studies which update older reviews; emphasize the developmental/lifespan nature of learning and education; and meet the criteria of being (a) programmatic and heuristic, (b) theoretically framed, and (c) valuable to scholars, training and development practitioners, and instructors across disciplines and grade levels.

Student Communication

Noncommunication and communication apprehension. Noncommunicative individuals tend to suffer in the areas of learning and achievement, and despite no meaningful relationship between measures of quietness and IQ, others often perceive them as unintelligent (Richmond & McCroskey, 1998). Unfortunately, the perception of quiet people as unintelligent becomes a self-fulfilling prophecy, posing a serious problem for learning and development across the lifespan. As a result of heredity, modeling, reinforcement, or expectancy learning, more than 80% of the population either identifies as a shy person in general or can identify at least one period in their lives during which they felt shy (Zimbardo, 1977).

One of the most studied aspects of shyness is *communication apprehension* (CA), the fear of actual or anticipated communication. About one in five suffer from CA (Richmond & McCroskey, 1998); some experience their anxiety across situations, and others only in certain settings. High CA learners will make different choices within the educational context than low CA learners, such as selecting large lecture classes which require little or no interaction and avoiding courses with oral presentation requirements. Low CA students prefer "learning by doing," whereas high CAs prefer more passive learning—both in school and at work (Johnson, 2003; Russ, 2012). High CAs tend to be highly sensitive to instructor feedback, prefer to receive it privately, and do not often evaluate it as useful to their learning (Malachowski, Martin, & Vallade, 2013).

Apprehensive students may take longer than low CA students to complete their degrees or may not complete them at all (Ericson & Gardner, 1992). And, high apprehensives are less likely to engage in important out-of-class communication (OCC) with their instructors than low CAs (Martin & Myers, 2006). OCC is an important facet of education that high CAs miss out on, as it is positively related to student motivation, higher grades, and cognitive learning (Dobransky & Frymier, 2004).

Student motivation. Academic success results from student engagement (Mazer, 2013b), which is driven by state *motivation* (Mazer, 2013a). Motivation is a process that engages students to do something because they want to, rather than because someone else wants them to, even though they would prefer not to. Motivation involves cultivating particular behaviors (such as reading and attending classes) within learners and prompting them to use these consistently (Richmond, 1990).

Interestingly, Christophel (1990) determined that *state* motivation is a more important predictor of learning in a course than a trait-like predisposition to be motivated across learning contexts. Instructor communication, course material, assessments, projects, and media employed in individual courses can all be modified to influence student state motivation. Additionally, out-of-class teacher/student communication increases student state motivation (Jones, 2008), as do teacher confirmation behaviors and student perceptions of a classroom community (Edwards, Edwards, Torrens, & Beck, 2011). Antisocial instructor communication behaviors such as verbal aggression (Myers, 2002) and teacher misbehaviors (Wanzer & McCroskey, 1998) can demotivate students.

Pedagogical strategies also influence motivation. Course-related activities that challenge students to work hard and to their highest potential have a direct positive impact on levels of student motivation (Bolkan, Goodboy, & Griffin, 2011). When challenged by their instructors, students appear to work in "deep and strategic ways" (p. 344) and are less likely to study superficially. Course-related technology such as micro-blogs and social media can motivate students when learners perceive the medium as relevant to their coursework, have confidence in using it, and are satisfied with the outcome (Waldeck & Dougherty, 2012).

Student resistance and power. Resistance refers to student use of oppositional behaviors, with the goal of avoiding instructor influence and classroom management (Burroughs, Kearney, & Plax, 1989). Resistance interferes with an instructor's ability to structure and maximize time spent on-task (Plax, 2008) and is related to lowered levels of cognitive and affective learning (Burroughs, 2007). Instructors are better served by utilizing polite, encouraging, motivating messages and strategies for shaping desired student behaviors which will endure over time, than by employing antisocial, negative tactics which result in short-lived compliance (Zhang & Sapp, 2013).

Students demonstrate a range of verbal and nonverbal, passive and direct, and public and private strategies to resist and exert power over their instructors when requesting grade changes, extended deadlines, extra credit, and other exceptions to course policies (Golish & Olsen, 2000). These messages can diminish learning, particularly when students resort to verbal or online aggression. Antisocial messages are not only detrimental to the sender's learning, but are also perceived by other students as an obstacle to learning (Bjorklund & Rehling, 2010). Waldeck (2013b) found a self-serving bias apparent in student reports of resistance and challenge behavior; students are much more likely to recall and report other students' resistance than their own, particularly when the communication was antisocial.

Instructor Communication

Clarity. Teacher clarity refers to "a cluster of teacher behaviors that contributes to the fidelity of instructional messages" (Chesebro & Wanzer, 2006, p. 950). Instructors can enhance clarity by defining major concepts, answering student questions directly, providing explicit project guidelines and learning objectives, teaching in a step-by-step manner at an appropriate pace, using relevant examples, and responding to deficiencies in student understanding (Chesebro, 2003). Clear instructor communication enhances student motivation, affect, and cognitive learning; reduces student receiver apprehension in the classroom; and increases student achievement (Chesebro).

Immediacy. Immediacy refers to verbal and nonverbal behaviors that enhance perceived physical and psychological closeness between communicators. *Nonverbal* immediacy (NVI) cues include smiling, nodding, movement around the classroom, forward body leaning, and eye contact (Andersen, 1979). Researchers have identified positive associations between student perceptions of instructor NVI and affective learning, perceived cognitive learning, test scores, and course grades across age groups, cultures, and contexts (Witt, Wheeless, & Allen, 2004). NVI remains important at work, with implications for training and development. Nonverbally immediate supervisors are perceived by employees as credible and interpersonally attractive, and they positively influence employee motivation (Richmond & McCroskey, 2000).

Confirmation. Confirmation refers to ways instructors communicate to students that they are valued and significant (Ellis, 2004). Confirmation occurs when instructors (1) respond to questions in ways that show interest and availability; (2) view students as individuals; (3) use teaching strategies that make students feel valued (e.g., creating special activities to help students who are struggling); and (4) avoid embarrassing students. Ellis found that confirmation is positively related to state motivation, cognitive learning, and affective learning. Moreover, students' perceptions of instructor confirmation impact their evaluations of the instructor's credibility and overall teaching (Schrodt, Turman, & Soliz, 2006) and help shape positive predictions about the outcome value of interacting with an instructor (Horan, Houser, Goodboy, & Frymier, 2011).

Misbehaviors. Instructors may communicate in ways that irritate, demotivate, or distract students from learning. Misbehaviors are classified in terms of incompetence (actions that illustrate the instructor's lack of concern for either the course or students), offensiveness (mean or rude behavior that humiliates or embarrasses students), and indolence (irresponsible or lazy behavior such as neglecting to grade assignments) and are linked to negative student reactions to school, the instructor, and learning (Kearney, Plax, Hays, & Ivey, 1991). Further, they influence student motives to communicate with their instructors (Goodboy, Myers, & Bolkan, 2010), resistance to teacher influence (Kearney et al., 1991), motivation (Zhang, 2007), and perceptions of instructor credibility (Myers, 2001). Although nonverbal immediacy helps teachers overcome many negative student perceptions, students hold teachers responsible for their negative communication behaviors and typically do not consider any plausible mitigating "excuses" why instructors might communicate antisocially (Kelsey, Kearney, Plax, Allen, & Ritter, 2004).

Power. Power involves the use of persuasive communication strategies known as Behavior Alteration Techniques (BATs) to elicit desired student task-related behaviors (Kearney, Plax, Richmond, & McCroskey, 1984). Good instructors recognize that students respond to influence differentially, understand the range of influence messages available, and are skilled at appropriately selecting and using all of them. Instructors are most influential when they emphasize rewards associated with student compliance (through the use of prosocial BATs) and avoid antisocial BAT (which threaten punishment for resistance; Kearney et al.). Prosocial BATs positively influence student interest in courses (Weber, 2004), perceptions of instructor fairness (Horan & Myers, 2009), positive affect (McCroskey, Richmond, Plax, & Kearney, 1985), and account for up to 36% of the variance in cognitive learning (Richmond et al., 1987). In research highly relevant to the contemporary instructional environment, Finn and Ledbetter (2013) found that teachers' policies toward wireless communication device use during class influence student perceptions of their credibility and influence. Specifically, instructors are advised to encourage device use at least for educational purposes during class to enhance student perceptions of their credibility, and reward and referent power.

Humor. Teachers sometimes communicate to intentionally "elicit laughter, chuckling, and other forms of spontaneous behavior taken to mean pleasure, delight and/or surprise in the receiver" (Booth-Butterfield & Booth-Butterfield, 1991, p. 206). Humorous instructors are aware of the appropriateness of a funny message in a given situation, possess the skills to be funny, and are motivated to be funny for strategic instruction-related reasons (e.g., cultivating immediacy). And they positively influence student perceptions of their clarity and learning (Wanzer, Frymier, & Irwin, 2010), and quality of out-of-class communication (Aylor & Oppliger, 2003).

Instructor-Student Interaction

Out-of-class communication (OCC). OCC refers to teacher/student interaction that takes place outside of formal instruction (e.g., phone, office hour visits, running into each other on- or off-campus, and in the classroom before or after class). Typically initiated by students, reported topics of OCC include course-related information, self-disclosure, seeking advice, course-related ideas, asking for favors, and career plans (Jaasma & Koper, 2001). Reasons for seeking digital OCC are similar (Waldeck, Kearney, & Plax, 2001a), and course-related policies and procedures are the most common topic of OCC in both environments. OCC positively impacts student cognitive and affective development (Terenzini, Pascarella, & Blimling, 1996). Instructors can encourage it by using affinity-seeking strategies (Myers, Martin, & Knapp, 2005), creating perceptions of personalized education (Waldeck, 2007), and being assertive, responsive, and humorous (Aylor & Oppliger, 2003), as well as immediate (Jaasma & Koper, 1999). Immediacy cues can be communicated online as well as in traditional education contexts, eliciting digitally mediated OCC and related positive outcomes (Waldeck et al., 2001a).

Mentoring. Faculty mentors counsel, guide, and tutor student protégés in academic, career, and social areas (Waldeck, Orrego, Plax, & Kearney, 1997). Mentoring affords students opportunities for OCC, which positively enhances retention rates and academic progress. Undergraduate, graduate, and non-student protégés tend to be more self-confident, empowered, and well connected in important communication networks than their non-mentored counterparts (Styhre, Josephson, & Knauseder, 2006). Although academic mentoring relationships can be difficult to develop (Waldeck et al., 1997), prospective mentors and protégés with high levels of communication competence and self-esteem are most likely to engage in mentoring (Kalbfleisch, 2002) and obtain the most benefits and satisfaction from doing so (Waldeck et al., 1997).

Personalized education. This framework for providing students with positive attention and to prioritize their unique needs has been studied at all educational levels. Calling for a rigorous analysis of its definition and outcomes, Waldeck (2007) found college student perceptions of personalized education are heightened when students have instructors who share their time outside of class, provide counsel to students about personal problems, exhibit competent communication, promote instructor/student equality, exhibit flexibility with course requirements, and provide special favors and exceptions to course policies. "Competent [instructor] communication that demonstrates warmth, goodwill, friendliness, and sincerity" (Waldeck, 2007, p. 438) is critically important to perceptions of personalized education and a productive teacher/student relationship.

Classroom Variables

Classroom management. Classroom management refers to instructor behaviors that "produce high levels of student involvement in classroom activities, minimal amounts of student behaviors that interfere with the teacher's or students' work, and efficient use of instructional time" (Emmer & Evertson, 1981, p. 342). There is a significant relationship between time spent on task and student learning (Woolfolk, 2001). Traditional classroom management strategies include structuring the classroom with clear rules and procedures; time management; defined curricular goals and corresponding lesson plans; and use of prompts, structured transitions, questioning techniques, motivational statements, and persuasive Behavior Alteration Techniques.

A well-managed classroom encourages student interest, perceptions of classroom justice and fairness, motivation, and learning outcomes; simultaneously, students are less likely to be resistant and aggressive when instructors employ effective management strategies (Roach, Richmond, & Mottet, 2006).

Leadership. Finding evidence that traditional classroom management techniques and behavior alternation techniques may lack effectiveness in the contemporary classroom, Waldeck (2013a, 2013b) argued for a new paradigm of instructor leadership that is characterized by promoting student engagement (rather than short-lasting compliance with instructor requests) both in and out of the classroom. Additionally, leadership may involve building student commitment to involvement in their courses and the ideas exchanged there, and less concern about micro-managing student attention and time (typical of the traditional classroom management perspective).

Other work suggests support for this thinking. Studies of engagement (student investment in learning which involves incorporating the material into their lives beyond the class) indicate that teacher communication behavior may be the single most powerful influence on how the potential for student application of their learning in their everyday experiences (Mazer, 2013a). Suggesting that instructors can be transformational leaders (Bass & Riggio, 2005) who engage students in charismatic ways, Bolkan and Goodboy (2011) delineated a number of recommended teacher behaviors, including availability, demonstrating content relevance and attitude homophily, immediacy, equality, self-disclosure, individualized feedback, challenging students, encouraging independent thinking, and promoting class participation.

Classroom justice. When students perceive injustice or unfairness related to a course, they may engage in a number of negative behaviors, including evaluating their instructor poorly and verbal aggression. Horan, Chory, and Goodboy (2010) investigated student experiences with justice and classroom conditions that may promote it. First, in assessing justice, students compare an outcome (such as a grade) to some standard or referent (e.g., the grade they felt they deserved or the grades received by peers). Second, students evaluate the perceived fairness of classroom procedures (e.g., instructional format, workload, teacher grading practices, and policies). Finally, students assess how instructors treat them in the implementation of course policies and communication, rejecting racist and sexist remarks, implication of student wrong-doing, and singling out students. Students perceive highest levels of classroom justice in classes in which instructors provide and follow a clear syllabus, offer multiple grading opportunities, present information clearly, and provide effective feedback. Moreover, competent and caring instructors can heighten student perceptions of justice (Chory, 2007). Students who perceive classroom injustice may become angry, and engage in dissent or withdrawal (Horan et al., 2010), with clear negative implications for their learning.

Learning-Related Technology

As new media have impacted the ways in which people learn, socialize, and work, researchers have examined how technology facilitates education and aids in the development and maintenance of important instructional relationships across the lifespan. Although learners expect and appreciate the use of technology associated with their courses, research indicates that instructors must be cautious in how they integrate it. First, instructors should employ technology for strategic reasons clearly related to instructional objectives and not for the sake of simply using the latest technologies (Turman & Schrodt, 2005). Millennials report lower self-confidence with using technology than their instructors and employers assume (Beyond.com, 2013) and can easily become demotivated and uninterested when they perceive technology requirements of a course as busywork or too complex (Waldeck & Dougherty, 2012). Second, there is a point of diminishing returns for the use of technology (Turman & Schrodt, 2005): affective learning is highest when instructors use minimal or moderate amounts. Intense technology use "becomes a distraction and students' internal motivation … suffers" (p. 120). The threshold for diminishing returns appears to be slightly higher for females than males.

Technology further enables social interaction among teachers and students. Instructors who engage in high levels of self-disclosure to students through their Facebook profiles positively impact motivation, affect, and class climate; however, relatively few students interact with their instructors on Facebook and nearly a third believe that it is inappropriate to do so (Mazer, Murphy, & Simonds, 2007). Instructors should use social media to interact with students cautiously. Moreover, students should consider their online communication with instructors carefully. Instructors have negative reactions to student emails that they perceive as overly casual, careless, or demanding (Stephens, Houser, & Cowan, 2009).

Education is characterized by new applications of technology such as Flipped Instruction (in which students learn new content via online videos outside of the classroom and work on what was traditionally "homework" during class interactively with other students and the instructor) and Active Learning Classrooms (which facilitate in-class technology use and student collaboration). Although research suggests that these innovations may facilitate student engagement and learning, the communication discipline has yet to weigh in with empirical findings.

Future Research Directions in Communication and Learning

This chapter has firmly established learning as a developmental process typically facilitated by formal and informal educational activities that occur within childhood and post-secondary institutionalized learning, and through adulthood workplace training and development opportunities. However, the learning experiences of older adults remain understudied in the communication studies discipline. For example, research suggests that aging brings about physiological (Merriam, 2001) and psychological/self-image (Knowles, 1980) changes which in turn impact aspects of learning including cognitive processing rates and styles, the degree of learner self-direction, and primary and secondary mental abilities. Communication researchers could profitably examine the experiences of older learners in both formal educational settings, work, and post-retirement opportunities such as study and travel in order to build a body of literature focused on learning that is as broad as it is deep. Learning is one of the true developmental, lifespan activities of the human experience—yet our formal understanding of it is mostly limited to the experiences of traditional students in formal educational settings. A greater understanding of the needs, modes of expression and inquiry, and learning goals of older adults would aid both instructors and other learners in facilitating a learning community that is meaningful for all participants.

Additionally, the memorable message construct reviewed in this chapter has interesting implications for a number of student populations beyond those already studied. Memorable messages have documented profound influences on how individuals react to later life experiences, and these may be particularly important for vulnerable learners at risk for attrition, lowered self-confidence, and problematic learning experiences and outcomes—as already documented in the work on first generation students. Other groups whose attitudes about learning, and experiences with it, may be affected by memorable messages and may include women, returning war veterans, and those with a history of physical or emotional illness.

This chapter also revealed the changing nature of instructor power in the classroom. The literature on student power, anecdotal evidence, as well as preliminary empirical data which revisit the teacher power construct indicate a dynamic interplay between the content- and relational-goals of both instructors and students. Continued research should focus on the changing student perceptions of their instructors' power, and the leadership that students require in order to balance their somewhat conflicted and chaotic communicative lives as they relate to learning. Waldeck (2013a) offered some practical suggestions to instructors wishing to better direct student attention to course-related tasks without alienating them (e.g., integrating social media into assignments, sharing the research suggesting that our ability to multitask may be exaggerated in our own minds, and creating realistic rules and boundaries for communication device use in the classroom). Future research should empirically validate ways that instructors influence a new generation of "connected" students.

Finally, instructional communication scholarship would be enhanced by a stronger emphasis on unique pedagogical strategies and technologies such as Flipped Instruction and Active Learning Classrooms; collaborative testing; the meaningful integration of social media, wikis, blogging, and microblogging into courses; and group experiences that promote learning rather than frustration. Many of these newer and nontraditional strategies and technologies meet with teacher and/or student resistance, despite evidence that they are effective. Research from the communication field, and particularly that framed from a developmental perspective, would enhance the base of support for approaching learning and instruction in new ways for new learners. For example, a number of empirical studies conducted outside the discipline have concluded that allowing students to collaborate on quizzes and exams enhances the degree to which they engage with content and develop communication and cooperation skills, and decreases the anxiety that cripples some students surrounding the testing experience (Kapitanoff, 2009; Pandey & Kapitanoff, 2011; Rao, Collins, & DiCarlo, 2002). In short, well-executed collaborative testing has numerous strong potential benefits for learners. Because the act of collaboration is by its nature a communicative process, these conclusions would be made more robust if further questions were asked from a communication perspective. Further, these questions should be framed with an interest in whether the learner's lifespan developmental level impacts the success of collaborative learning and testing experiences.

CONCLUSION

This chapter has framed education as a communicative, developmental, and lifespan phenomenon. In it, we defined learning and examined how various learning outcomes are measured. We identified developmental theories associated with instructional communication research, and reviewed the communication variables which impact human learning and development. Instructional communication is a flourishing area of relevant, rigorous, and heuristic research with numerous lifespan implications and linkages to other areas of the communication discipline. Scholars interested in these issues should continue to examine learning not only as a childhood or early life experience, but also as one that is critical across the lifespan for growth, development, and accomplishment of our highest human potential.

REFERENCES

Andersen, J. F. (1979). Instructor immediacy as a predictor of teaching effectiveness. In D. Nimmo (Ed.), *Communication yearbook 3* (pp. 543–559). New Brunswick, NJ: Transaction Books.

Aylor, B., & Oppliger, P. (2003). Out-of-class communication and student perceptions of instructor humor orientation and socio-communicative style. *Communication Education, 52*, 122–134.

Banchero, S. (2012, May 8). School standards pushback. *The Wall Street Journal.* http://online.wsj. com/article/SB10001424052702303630404577390431072241906.html

Bandura, A. (2009). Social cognitive theory of mass communication. In J. Bryant & M. B. Oliver (Eds.), *Media effects: Advances in theory and research* (2nd ed., pp. 94–124). Mahwah, NJ: Erlbaum.

Bass, B. M., & Riggio, R. E. (2005). *Transformational leadership* (2nd ed.). Mahwah, NJ: Erlbaum.

Beyond.com. (2013, May 28). Beyond.com survey uncovers how veteran HR professionals really feel about job seekers from the Millennial generation. http://about.beyond.com/press/ releases/20130528-Beyondcom-Survey-Uncovers-How-Veteran-HR-Professionals-Really- Feel-about-Job-Seekers-from-Millennial-Generation

Bjorklund, W. L., & Rehling, D. L. (2010). Student perceptions of classroom incivility. *College Teaching, 58,* 15–18.

Bloom, B. S. (Ed.). (1956). *Taxonomy of educational objectives: Handbook I. Cognitive domain.* New York, NY: McKay.

Bolkan, S., & Goodboy, A. K. (2011). Behavioral indicators of transformational leadership in the college classroom. *Qualitative Research Reports in Communication, 12,* 10–18.

Bolkan, S., Goodboy, A. K., & Griffin, D. J. (2011). Teacher leadership and intellectual stimulation: Improving students' approaches to studying through intrinsic motivation. *Communication Research Reports, 28,* 337–346.

Booth-Butterfield, S., & Booth-Butterfield, M. (1991). The communication of humor in everyday life. *Southern Communication Journal, 56,* 205–218.

Brady, M. (2012, August 8). Eight problems with common core standards. *The Washington Post.* http://www.washingtonpost.com/blogs/answer-sheet/post/eight-problems-with-common- core-standards/2012/08/21/821b300a-e4e7-11e1-8f62-58260e3940a0_blog.html

Burroughs, N. F. (2007). A reinvestigation of the relationship of teacher nonverbal immediacy and student compliance-resistance with learning. *Communication Education, 56,* 453–475.

Burroughs, N. F., Kearney, P., & Plax, T. G. (1989). Compliance-resistance in the college classroom. *Communication Education, 38,* 214–229.

Cantor, J., & Omdahl, B. L. (1999). Children's acceptance of safety guidelines after exposure to televised dramas depicting accidents. *Western Journal of Communication, 63,* 57–71.

Chesebro, J. L. (2003). Effects of teacher clarity and nonverbal immediacy on student learning, receiver apprehension, and affect. *Communication Education, 52,* 135–147.

Chesebro, J. L., & Wanzer, M. B. (2006). Instructional message variables. In T. P. Mottet, V. P. Richmond, & J. C. McCroskey (Eds.), *Handbook of instructional communication* (pp. 89–116). Boston, MA: Pearson.

Chory, R. M. (2007). Enhancing student perceptions of fairness: The relationship between instructor credibility and classroom justice. *Communication Education, 56,* 89–105.

Christophel, D. M. (1990). The relationships among teacher immediacy behaviors, student motivation, and learning. *Communication Education, 39,* 323–340.

Claus, C. J., Booth-Butterfield, M., & Chory, R. M. (2012). The relationship between instructor misbehaviors and student antisocial behavior alteration techniques: The roles of instructor attractiveness, humor, and relational closeness. *Communication Education, 61,* 161–183.

DiBenedetto, M. K., & Bembenutty, H. (2013). Within the pipeline: Self-regulated learning, self-efficacy, and socialization among college students in science courses. *Learning and Individual Differences, 23,* 218–224.

Dobransky, N. D., & Frymier, A. B. (2004). Developing teacher-student relationships through out-of-class communication. *Communication Quarterly, 52,* 211–223.

Edwards, C., Edwards, A., Torrens, A., & Beck, A. (2011). Confirmation and community: The relationships between teacher confirmation, classroom community, student motivation, and learning. *Online Journal of Communication and Media Technologies, 1,* 17–43.

Elias, M. J., Zins, J. E., Weissberg, R. P., Frey, K. S., Greenberg, M. T., Haynes, N. M., … Shiver, T. P. (1997). *Promoting social and emotional learning: Guidelines for educators.* Alexandria, VA: Association for Supervision and Curriculum Development.

Ellis, K. (2004). The impact of perceived instructor confirmation on receiver apprehension, motivation, and learning. *Communication Education, 53,* 1–20.

Emmer, E. T., & Evertson, C. M. (1981). Synthesis of research on classroom management. *Educational Leadership, 38,* 342–347.

Ericson, P. M., & Gardner, J. W. (1992). Two longitudinal studies of communication apprehension and its effects on college students' success. *Communication Quarterly, 40,* 127–137.

Finn, A. N., & Ledbetter, A. M. (2013). Teacher power mediates the effects of technology policies on teacher credibility. *Communication Education, 62,* 26–47.

Frymier, A. B., & Houser, M. L. (1999). The revised learning indicators scale. *Communication Studies, 50,* 1–12.

Goleman, D. (1998). *Working with emotional intelligence.* New York, NY: Bantam.

Golish, T. D., & Olson, L. N. (2000). Students' use of power in the classroom: An investigation of student power, teacher power, and teacher immediacy. *Communication Quarterly, 48,* 293–310.

Goodboy, A. K., Myers, S. A., & Bolkan, S. (2010). Student motives for communicating with instructors as a function of perceived instructor misbehaviors. *Communication Research Reports, 27,* 11–19.

Hines, C., Cruickshank, D., & Kennedy, J. (1985). Teacher clarity and its relationship to student achievement and satisfaction. *American Educational Research Journal, 22,* 87–99.

Horan, S. M., Chory, R. M., & Goodboy, A. K. (2010). Understanding students' classroom justice experiences and responses. *Communication Education, 59,* 453–474.

Horan, S. M., Houser, M. L., Goodboy, A. K., & Frymier, A. B. (2011). Students' early impressions of instructors: Understanding the role of relational skills and messages. *Communication Education, 28,* 74–85.

Horan, S. M., & Myers, S. A. (2009). An investigation of college instructors' use of classroom justice, power, and behavior alteration techniques. *Communication Education, 58,* 483–496.

Jaasma, M. A., & Koper, R. J. (1999). The relationship of student-faculty out-of-class communication to instructor immediacy and trust and to student motivation. *Communication Education, 48,* 41–47.

Jaasma, M. A., & Koper, R. J. (2001, May). *Talk to me: An examination of the content of out-of-class interactions between students and faculty.* Paper presented to the Instructional and Developmental Communication Division of the International Communication Association, Washington, DC.

Johnson, D. I. (2003). The relationship between student learning mode and changes in thoughts about communication in the basic oral communication course. *Communication Research Reports, 20,* 251–259.

Jones, A. C. (2008). The effects of out-of-class support on student satisfaction and motivation to learn. *Communication Education, 48,* 41–47.

Kalbfleisch, P. J. (2002). Communicating in mentoring relationships: A theory for enactment. *Communication Theory, 12,* 63–69.

Kapitanoff, S. H. (2009). Collaborative testing: Cognitive and interpersonal processes related to enhanced test performance. *Active Learning in Higher Education, 10,* 56–70.

Kearney, P., Plax, T. G., Hays, E. R., & Ivey, M. (1991). College instructor misbehaviors: What students don't like about what instructors say and do. *Communication Quarterly, 39,* 309–324.

Kearney, P., Plax, T. G., Richmond, V. P., & McCroskey, J. C. (1984). Power in the classroom IV: Alternatives to discipline. In R. Bostrom (Ed.), *Communication yearbook 8* (pp. 724–746). Beverly Hills, CA: Sage.

Kearney, P., Plax, T. G., Richmond, V. P., & McCroskey, J. C. (1985). Power in the classroom III: Teacher communication techniques and messages. *Communication Education, 34*, 19–28.

Kelsey, D. M., Kearney, P., Plax, T. G., Allen, T. H., & Ritter, K. J. (2004). College students' attributions of instructor misbehaviors. *Communication Education, 53*, 40–55.

Kline, S. L., & Clinton, B. L. (1998). Developments in children's persuasive practices. *Communication Education, 47*, 120–136.

Knowles, M. S. (1980). *The modern practice of adult education.* Chicago, IL: Follet.

Kranstuber, H., Carr, K., & Hosek, A. M. (2012). "If you can dream it, you can achieve it." Parent memorable messages as indicators of college student success. *Communication Education, 61*, 44–66.

Krathwohl, D. R., Bloom, B. S., & Masia, B. B. (1964). *Taxonomy of educational objectives: Handbook II. Affective domain.* New York, NY: McKay.

Malachowski, C. C., Martin, M. M., & Vallade, J. I. (2013). An investigation of students' adaptation, aggression, and apprehension traits with their instructional feedback orientations. *Communication Education, 62*, 127–147.

Martin, L., & Mottet, T. P. (2011). The effect of instructor nonverbal immediacy behaviors and feedback sensitivity on Hispanic students' affective learning outcomes in ninth-grade writing conferences. *Communication Education, 60*, 1–19.

Martin, M. M., & Myers, S. A. (2006). Students' communication traits and their out-of-class communication with instructors. *Communication Education, 23*, 283–289.

Martins, N., & Wilson, B. J. (2012). Social aggression on television and its relationship to children's aggression in the classroom. *Human Communication Research, 38*, 48–71.

Mazer, J. P. (2013a). Associations among teacher communication behaviors, student interest, and engagement: A validity test. *Communication Education, 62*, 86–96.

Mazer, J. P. (2013b). Validity of the student interest and engagement scales: Associations with student learning outcomes. *Communication Studies, 64*, 125–140.

Mazer, J. P., Murphy, R. E., & Simonds, C. J. (2007). I'll see you on "Facebook": The effects of computer-mediated teacher self-disclosure on student motivation, affective learning, and class climate. *Communication Education, 56*, 1–17.

McCroskey, J. C., & Richmond, V. P. (1987). Willingness to communicate. In J. C. McCroskey & J. A. Daly (Eds.), *Personality and interpersonal communication* (pp. 129–156). Newbury Park, CA: Sage.

McCroskey, J. C., Richmond, V. P., & McCroskey, L. L. (2006). *An introduction to communication in the classroom: The role of communication in teaching and training.* Boston, MA: Allyn & Bacon.

McCroskey, J. C., Richmond, V. P., Plax, T. G., & Kearney, P. (1985). Power in the classroom V: Behavior alteration techniques, communication training, and learning. *Communication Education, 34*, 214–227.

Medved, C. E., Brogan, S. M., McClanahan, M. A., Morris, J. F., & Shepherd, G. J. (2006). Family and work socializing communication: Messages, gender, and ideological implications. *Journal of Family Communication, 6, 161–180.*

Mehrabian, A. (1971). *Silent messages.* Belmont, CA: Wadsworth.

Merriam, S. B. (2001). *The new update on adult learning theory.* San Francisco, CA: Jossey-Bass.

Mottet, T. P., & Beebe, S. A. (2006). Foundations of instructional communication. In T. P. Mottet, V. P. Richmond, & J.C. McCroskey (Eds.), *Handbook of instructional communication: Rhetorical and relational perspectives* (pp. 3–32). Boston, MA: Allyn & Bacon.

Mottet, T. P., Frymier, A. B., & Beebe, S. A. (2006). Theorizing about instructional communication. In T. P. Mottet, V. P. Richmond, & J. C. McCroskey (Eds.), *Handbook of instructional communication: Rhetorical and relational perspectives* (pp. 255–282). Boston, MA: Allyn & Bacon.

Mottet, T. P., & Richmond, V. P. (1998). New is not necessarily better: A reexamination of affective learning measurement. *Communication Research Reports, 15*, 370–378.

Myers, S. A. (2001). Perceived aggressive instructor credibility and verbal aggressiveness in the college classroom. *Communication Research Reports, 18*, 354–364.

Myers, S. A. (2002). Perceived aggressive instructor communication and student state motivation, learning, and satisfaction. *Communication Reports, 18*, 354–364.

Myers, S. A. (2010). Instructional communication: The emergence of a field. In D. L. Fassett & J. T. Warren (Eds.), *Sage handbook of communication and instruction*. Thousand Oaks, CA: Sage.

Myers, S. A., Martin, M. M., & Knapp, J. L. (2005). Perceived instructor in-class communicative behaviors as a predictor of student participation in out of class communication. *Communication Quarterly, 53*, 437–450.

Neer, M. R. (1990). Reducing situational anxiety and avoidance behavior associated with classroom apprehension. *Southern Communication Journal, 56*, 49–61.

Norris, J. A. (2003). Looking at classroom management through a social and emotional learning lens. *Theory Into Practice, 42*, 313–318.

Pandey, C., & Kapitanoff, S. (2011). The influence of anxiety and quality of interaction on collaborative test performance. *Active Learning in Higher Education, 12*, 163–174.

Pettigrew, J., Miller-Day, M., Shin, Y., Hecht, M. L., Krieger, J. R., & Graham, J. W. (2012). Describing teacher-student interactions: A qualitative assessment of teacher implementation of the 7th grade *keepin' it REAL* substance abuse intervention. *American Journal of Community Psychology, 51*, 43–56.

Piaget, J. (1977). *The development of thought: Equilibration of cognitive structures*. New York, NY: Viking.

Plax, T. G. (2008). Classroom management techniques. In W. Donsach (Ed.), *The international encyclopedia of communication*. Blackwell Reference Online. http://www.communicationencyclopedia.com/subscriber/tocnode?id=g9781405131995_yr2010_chunk_g97814051319958_ss33-1

Rao, S. P., Collins, H. L., & DiCarlo, S. E. (2002). Collaborative testing enhances student learning. *Advances in Physiology Education, 26*, 37–41.

Reich, S. M., Black, R. W., & Korobkova, K. (in press). Establishing connections and community in virtual worlds for children. *Journal of Community Psychology*.

Richmond, V. P. (1990). Communication in the classroom: Power and motivation. *Communication Education, 39*, 181–195.

Richmond, V. P., & McCroskey, J. C. (1998). *Communication apprehension, avoidance, and effectiveness* (5th ed.). Needham Heights, MA: Allyn & Bacon.

Richmond, V. P., & McCroskey, J. C. (2000). The impact of supervisor and subordinate immediacy on relational and organizational outcomes. *Communication Monographs, 67*, 85–95.

Richmond, V. P., McCroskey, J. C., Kearney, P., & Plax, T. G. (1987). Power in the classroom VII: Linking behavior alteration techniques to cognitive learning. *Communication Education, 36*, 1–12.

Roach, K. D., Richmond, V. P., & Mottet, T. P. (2006). Teachers' influence messages. In T. P. Mottet, V. P. Richmond, & J. C. McCroskey (Eds.), *Handbook of instructional communication: Rhetorical and relational perspectives* (pp. 117–139). Boston, MA: Allyn & Bacon.

Rodriguez, J. I., Plax, T. G., & Kearney, P. (1996). Clarifying the relationship between teacher nonverbal immediacy and student cognitive learning: Affective learning as the central causal mediator. *Communication Education, 45*, 293–305.

Russ, T. L. (2012). The relationship between communication apprehension and learning preferences in an organizational setting. *Journal of Business Communication, 49*, 312–331.

Schrodt, P., Turman, P. D., & Soliz, J. (2006). Perceived understanding as a mediator of perceived instructor confirmation and students' ratings of instruction. *Communication Education, 55*, 370–388.

Sherman, L., Michikyan, M., & Greenfield, P. (2013, April). *Digital bonds: Online and offline connectedness in emerging adults.* Paper presented at the biennial meeting of the Society for Research in Child Development, Seattle, WA.

Stephens, K. K., Houser, M. L., & Cowan, R. L. (2009). RU able to meat me: The impact of students' overly casual email messages to instructors. *Communication Education, 58*, 303–326.

Styhre, A., Josephson, P. E., & Knauseder, I. (2006). Organizational learning in non-writing communities. *Management Learning, 37*, 83–100.

Terenzini, P. T., Pascaraella, E. T., & Blimling, G. S. (1996). Students' out of class experiences and their influence in learning and cognitive development: A literature review. *Journal of College Student Development, 37*, 149–162.

Turman, P. D., & Schrodt, P. (2005). The influence of instructional technology use on students' affect: Do course designs and biological sex make a difference? *Communication Education, 56*, 109–129.

Turner, P., Turner, S., & Van de Walle, G. (2007). How older people account for their experiences with interactive technology. *Behaviour and Information Technology, 26*, 287–296.

Waldeck, J. H. (2007). Answering the question: Student perceptions of personalized education and the construct's relationship to learning outcomes. *Communication Education, 56*, 409–432.

Waldeck, J. H. (2013a). Managing the contemporary learning experience: Reflections and new directions for instructional leadership. *Spectra, 49*(3), pp. 14–17.

Waldeck, J. H. (2013b, June). Student perceptions of instructor power in the contemporary classroom. Paper presented to the Instructional Developmental Division of the International Communication Association, London, England.

Waldeck, J. H., & Dougherty, K. (2012). Collaborative communication technologies and learning in college courses: Which are used, for what purposes, and to what ends? *Learning, Media, and Technology, 36*, 1–24.

Waldeck, J. H., Kearney, P., & Plax, T. G. (2001a). Instructor email message strategies and student willingness to communicate online. *Journal of Applied Communication Research, 29*, 54–70.

Waldeck, J. H., Kearney, P., & Plax, T. G. (2001b). The state of the art in instructional communication research. In W. R. Gudykunst (Ed.), *Communication yearbook 24* (pp. 207–230). Thousand Oaks, CA: Sage.

Waldeck, J. H., & Myers, K. K. (2007). Organizational assimilation theory, research, and implications for multiple areas of the discipline: A state of the art review. In C. Beck (Ed.), *Communication yearbook, 31* (pp. 322–367). Mahwah, NJ: Erlbaum.

Waldeck, J. H., Orrego, V. O., Plax, T. G., & Kearney, P. (1997). Graduate student/faculty mentoring: Who gets mentored, how it happens, and to what end. *Communication Quarterly, 45*, 93–109.

Waldeck, J. H., Plax, T. G., & Kearney, P. (2010). Philosophical and methodological foundations of instructional communication research. In D. L. Fassett & J. T. Warren (Eds.), *Handbook of communication and instruction* (pp. 161–179). Thousand Oaks, CA: Sage.

Waldeck, J. H., Seibold, D. R., & Flanagan, A. J. (2004). Organizational assimilation and communication technology use. *Communication Monographs, 71*, 161–183.

Wang, T. R. (2012). Understanding the memorable messages first generation college students receive from on-campus mentors. *Communication Education, 61*, 335–357.

Wanzer, M. B., Frymier, A. B., & Irwin, J. (2010). An explanation of the relationship between instructor humor and student learning: Instructional humor processing theory. *Communication Education, 59*, 1–18.

Wanzer, M. B., & McCroskey, J. C. (1998). Instructor socio-communicative style as a correlate of student affect toward instructor and course material. *Communication Education, 47*, 43–52.

Weber, K. (2004). The relationship between student interest and teacher's use of behavior alteration techniques. *Communication Research Reports, 21*, 428–436.

Weiss, A. J., & Wilson, B. J. (1998). Children's cognitive and emotional responses to the portrayal of negative emotions in family-formatted situation comedies. *Human Communication Research, 24*, 584–609.

Wilson, B. C., & Schrock, S. (2001). Contributing to success in an introductory computer science course: A study of twelve factors. *Proceedings of the thirty-second SIGCSE technical symposium on computer science education, 33*, 184–188.

Wilson, B. C. (2002). A study of factors promoting success in computer science including gender differences. *Computer Science Education, 12*, 141–164.

Witt, P. L., & Kerssen-Griep, J. (2011). Instructional feedback I: The interaction of facework and immediacy on students' perception of instructor credibility. *Communication Education, 60*, 75–94.

Witt, P. L., & Wheeless, L. R. (2001). An experimental study of teachers' verbal and nonverbal immediacy and students' affective and cognitive learning. *Communication Education, 50*, 327–342.

Witt, P. L., Wheeless, L. R., & Allen, M. (2004). A meta-analytical review of the relationship between teacher immediacy and student learning. *Communication Monographs, 71*, 184–207.

Woolfolk, A. (2001). *Educational psychology* (8th ed.). Boston, MA: Allyn and Bacon.

Zhang, Q. (2007). Teacher misbehaviors as learning demotivators in college classrooms: A cross-cultural investigation in China, Germany, Japan, and the United States. *Communication Education, 56*, 209–227.

Zhang, Q., & Sapp, D. A. (2013). Psychological reactance and resistance intention in the classroom: Effects of perceived request politeness and legitimacy, relationship distance, and teacher credibility. *Communication Education, 62*, 1–25.

Zimbardo, P. G. (1977). *Shyness: What it is, what to do about it.* Reading, MA: Addison-Wesley.

PART FOUR

Adolescent Communication

CHAPTER EIGHT

The Digital Bridge into Adulthood

Media Uses and Effects in Adolescence

PIOTR S. BOBKOWSKI AND AUTUMN SHAFER

Occupying the transition between childhood and emerging adulthood, adolescence is marked by considerable biological, cognitive, emotional, and social development (Susman & Rogol, 2004). With pubertal changes—linear growth, sexual maturation, brain development, and so on—taking place in the backdrop, adolescents negotiate their identities, aspirations, and shifting positions within familial, peer, environmental, and cultural spheres. Media constitute one source on which adolescents rely to better understand themselves, the world around them, and their place in it. This chapter focuses on some of the ways in which the media influence well-being during adolescence.

Adolescents spend much of their out-of-school time using media. A 2009 study showed that U.S. youth (8- to 18-year-olds) used media an average of 11 hours each day (Rideout, Foehr, & Roberts, 2010). This included four daily hours of watching television, more than three hours of listening to music, and nearly two hours using the phone (i.e., texting and talking). To accomplish all this, adolescents engaged in media multitasking 29% of the time. Adolescents have been among the early adopters of social media. According to 2012 data, 95% of American adolescents (12 to 17 years old) used the Internet, and of these, 76% had a Facebook account (Madden, Lenhart, Cortesi, et al., 2013). Teens' media use may continue to rise as mobile media devices become ubiquitous. In 2012, 37% of 12- to 17-year-olds owned smartphones, and 25% said that they accessed the Internet primarily through cell phones (Madden, Lenhart, Duggan, Cortesi, & Gasser, 2013).

THEORETICAL MODELS OF MEDIA EFFECTS

Traditional and popular notions of media effects conceive of direct and uniform influence of the media on audiences. News commentary surrounding instances of youth violence often speculates about the perpetrators mimicking violent video games, for instance. While there is no doubt that the media influence young people, media researchers take a more measured approach to understanding media's role in adolescent development. The reinforcing spirals theory (Slater, 2007) underscores the heterogeneity of media effects. According to this perspective, media's influence is situated within broader networks of socializing agents (e.g., parents, peers, neighborhoods), which can stimulate media exposure and lessen or reinforce the lessons young people draw from the media. One study linking violent media exposure with subsequent aggression illustrated the importance of the environment for media effects. The study showed that the association between violent media use and aggression was more pronounced among adolescents who felt alienated and victimized by their peers than among those without such social challenges (Slater, Henry, Swaim, & Cardador, 2004). Another study showed that an interest in music, evidenced by the consumption of music-oriented websites, magazines, and television, led middle school students to associate with others who shared this interest, and to the adoption of behaviors shared by this group, including risky substance use (Slater & Henry, 2013). This theory emphasizes the contextual elements that shape media usage and effects.

We organize the discussion of media effects in the present chapter around the adolescent media practice model (Brown, 2000; Shafer, Bobkowski, & Brown, 2012). Like the reinforcing spirals theory, the media practice model emphasizes the importance of context for understanding the effects of media on adolescent development. The model's central tenet is that adolescents "choose media and interact with media based on who they are and who they want to be" (Brown, 2000, p. 35). The model comprises three sets of media practices—selection, engagement, and application—that structure adolescents' interactions with media. These three sets of practices constitute a cyclical process, with adolescents exerting a degree of agency in their media *selections*, in how they *engage* with the media, how they interpret the media's meanings, and how they *apply* these interpretations to their identities and identity aspirations. The cyclical process continues with adolescents' identities subsequently influencing their media selections.

Although media can exert a positive influence on adolescent development (e.g., Greitemeyer & Osswald, 2010), in this chapter we focus on four potentially detrimental intersections between media and adolescent well-being: violence and aggression, sexual health, body image and eating disorders, and risky substances. Each of the following sections discusses the prevalence of media that represent these content domains, and adolescents' selections, interactions with, and applications of these media.

VIOLENCE AND AGGRESSION

Most television programs, movies, and video games portray some violence. More than half (61%) of the prime-time television programs broadcast in the United States in the 1990s contained violence (Signorielli, 2003). Among the most popular films (1950–2006), 89% contained violence (Bleakley, Jamieson, & Romer, 2012). Although quantifying the volume of violence in video games is more challenging, a study of video game advertisements in magazines showed that 56% of the ads contained violent images or language (Scharrer, 2004). Violence appeared less frequently in music videos and in popular online videos (Smith & Boyson, 2002; Weaver, Zelenkauskaite, & Samson, 2012).

Some adolescents are more predisposed than others to using violent media. Adolescent sensation seekers, that is, those who exhibit a higher need for stimulating experiences (Zuckerman, 1994), use more violent media than their peers who score lower on sensation seeking (Slater, 2003). There is also evidence that more aggressive youth are more likely to use violent media than their less-aggressive peers (Slater, 2003), although this effect has not been consistent (Huesmann, Moise-Titus, Podolski, & Eron, 2003; Krahé, Busching, & Möller, 2012).

What happens at the time of engagement with violent media? One review identified three processes that can be triggered through engagement in violent media: priming of aggressive behavioral scripts, mimicking, and arousal (Bushman & Huesmann, 2006). First, violent media activate aggressive behavioral scripts stored in individuals' cognitions, prompting individuals exposed to violent media to react more aggressively than they would otherwise. Second, imitation is a fundamental human behavior, and seeing violent actions in the media can trigger an imitation response. Third, engagement in violent media leads to physiological arousal as marked by an increased heart rate, for instance. Dehumanization also may mediate the effect of violent video game play on aggression (Greitmeyer & McLatchie, 2011). Study participants who played a violent video game rated fictional experiment partners as less human than those who played a neutral or prosocial video game. A burgeoning literature examines the neurological activity that accompanies engagement in violent media, especially violent video games (e.g., Bailey, West, & Anderson, 2011; Wang et al., 2009). These studies illustrate the brain functions that accompany game play and manifest behaviorally in documented behavioral effects of violent gaming such as increased arousal and anxiety and a decreased ability to regulate emotion (Wang et al., 2009).

A large literature examines the long-term implications of violent media. Repeated exposures to violent media can result in desensitization. Habitual users of violent media exhibit less distressed reactions to violent portrayals than individuals who use less violent media (Carnagey, Anderson, & Bushman, 2007). Increased aggression is a well-documented outcome of violent media use. A recent study of

German high school students showed, for instance, that the use of violent media was associated with increased self- and teacher-reported rates of aggression two years later (Krahé et al., 2012). Studies also link violent media use in adolescence with adult aggression. One study showed that recent aggression among emerging adults (20 to 22 years old), as reported by the respondent and his/her family member or friend, was associated with the respondents' violent media habits in childhood (6 to 10 years old; Huesmann et al., 2003). Another study showed an association between television viewing in adolescence (14 years old) and adult aggression (22 years old), as indicated by self-reports and police records (Johnson, Cohen, Smailes, Kasen, & Brook, 2002).

One recently developed subgenre of media violence research focuses on the antecedents and effects of violent pornography among adolescents. Approximately 5% of 10- to 15-year-olds reported exposure to violent pornography in the previous 12 months (Ybarra, Mitchell, Hamburger, Diener-West, & Leaf, 2011). The actual exposure to violent pornography may be underreported because the majority (88%) of the most popular pornography videos contain some form of physical aggression (Bridges, Wosnitzer, Scharrer, Sun, & Liberman, 2010). Exposure to violent pornography is linked to engaging in sexual aggression. Youth who reported viewing violent pornography were six times more likely to engage in a sexually aggressive act than those who reported viewing non-violent pornography (Ybarra et al., 2011).

In sum, violence saturates much of the media that adolescents consume and research evidence documents both short-term and long-term effects of violent media on adolescents' cognitions and behaviors. The link between exposure to violence and aggressive outcomes is not direct, however. Personal and environmental factors combine to shape adolescents' exposure to violent media, and how they process and apply these media in their lives.

SEXUAL HEALTH

Much of the media adolescents consume is sexual. In one study, about 90% of television shows that featured teenage characters included some sexual content (Aubrey, 2004). In another study, more than two-thirds of all television shows contained some talk about sex and more than one-third included depictions of sexual behavior (Kunkel, Eyal, Finnerty, Biely, & Donnerstein, 2005). Only about 10% of television shows with sexual content mentioned risks associated with sex (Kunkel et al., 2005), and less than 1% included sexual health information (Pardun, L'Engle, & Brown, 2005). Popular teen music (especially rap and hip hop) and movies tend to feature sexual content even more frequently and explicitly than television (Gunasekera, Chapman, & Campbell, 2005; Pardun et al., 2005). Video games regularly portray sexualized characters and situations (Scharrer, 2004), and one estimate suggests that 37% of all websites feature sexually explicit content (Optenet, 2010). Only about 10% of American adolescents reported intentionally seeking out online pornography (Ybarra et al., 2011), but about 28% said they came across sexually explicit online content (Wolak, Mitchell, & Finkelhor, 2007).

A fairly consistent script characterizes much of the sexual media youth consume, portraying willingly objectified women being actively and aggressively pursued by men (Aubrey, 2004; Ferris, Smith, Greenberg, & Smith, 2007; Primack, Gold, Schwarz, & Dalton, 2008). Male characters are shown to have many sexual partners and to associate sex with pleasure and recreation (Farvid & Braun, 2006). Adolescents learn in what situations sex is expected, how to behave in romantic relationships, and what characteristics potential partners may find attractive (Ferris et al., 2007; Segrin & Nabi, 2002).

Biological and developmental evidence provides insights about when and why adolescents are drawn to sexual media. One study found that teenage girls who entered puberty earlier than their peers were more interested in sexual media than later maturing girls (Brown, Halpern, & L'Engle, 2005). For males, high-testosterone levels have been associated with increased likelihood to engage in sexual intercourse (Udry, 1990), and it is possible that testosterone levels also may be associated with sexual media selection. Longitudinal studies also have noted that adolescents begin to pay more attention to sexual media as they enter puberty (Bleakley, Hennessy, Fishbein, & Jordan, 2008; Kim et al., 2006). Family and environmental values may moderate this link between physical maturation and interest in sexual media. For instance, adolescents' religiosity and less permissive attitudes about premarital sex were inversely associated with liking television shows that contained mature content, including sexual content (Bobkowski, 2009).

Just as not all adolescents uniformly consume sexual media, adolescents' engagement with selected sexual media also varies. Mediating the relationship between exposure and effects, engagement encompasses young people's psychological, interpretative, and physical interactions with sexual media content. Engagement can manifest in both conscious and non-conscious processing and include such factors as attention, interaction, reactance, counterarguing, character identification, narrative transportation, and arousal. Multitasking, for example, which entails the simultaneous use of two or more media and is common among adolescents (Jeong & Fishbein, 2007), affects media engagement and shapes the effect of sexual media consumption. One study found that watching television while surfing the Internet increased the effects of sexual media (Collins, 2008). Another study examined the relationship between media and non-media multitasking (e.g., watching television and cooking dinner) and found that heavy media/non-media multitaskers were less affected by sexual media exposure (Jeong, Hwang, & Fishbein, 2010).

Adolescents draw on relatively little personal sexual experience to interpret and evaluate the sexual media they consume. Greater involvement in a television program and its characters can make the experience feel more real or personal and thus amplify the effects of sexual media for adolescents. In one study, involvement fully mediated the effects of watching a dating reality television show on the consistency between viewers' beliefs about dating and the show's themes (e.g., the importance of physical appearance when dating; Zurbriggen & Morgan, 2006). Involvement mediated the relationship between sexual beliefs and values and exposure to sexual online content for girls (Peter & Valkenburg, 2010). Physical and emotional arousal constitutes another example of a processing mediator for sexual media effects. Engaging with sexual media may create a sexual or general physiological arousal among adolescents (Hansen & Krygowski, 1994). Arousal may increase focus on and memory for the media content, thus increasing the potential of effects. One study found arousal to mediate the relationship between exposure to online pornography and sexual preoccupancy (Peter & Valkenburg, 2008).

Once a young person engages with sexual media he or she may apply the sexual attitudes, norms, beliefs, and expectations to his or her sexual behaviors. Studies have found that sexual media exposure is associated with sexual attitudes, norms, self-efficacy, expectations, and behaviors that are consistent with the consumed sexual content (e.g., attitudes that sex is recreational; Ward & Friedman, 2006; feeling peer pressure to have sex; Bleakley et al., 2008; and expectations to have sex earlier; Aubrey, Harrison, Kramer, & Yellin, 2003; see Wright, 2011 for overview). Longitudinal studies also have found evidence of a causal link between greater sexual media exposure and sexual behavior among adolescents (e.g., earlier sexual debut, greater number of sexual partners, lower rates of contraception use, higher rates of teen pregnancy) (Brown et al., 2006; Chandra et al., 2008; Fisher et al., 2009).

As was the case with violence, adolescent media are filled with sexual images, ideas, and scripts. Adolescents seek information and guidance from sexual media about what is appropriate, inappropriate, and expected, as they develop a sense of who they are sexually. The media's influence on adolescent sexual socialization is not a strictly linear process: adolescents rely on idiosyncratic reasons for using sexual media, engaging these media, and appropriating precepts from the media into their sexual identities.

BODY IMAGE AND EATING DISORDERS

The media adolescents consume may encourage and reinforce a distorted body image, low appearance self-esteem, depression, and eating disorders. Body types typically represented on television are skewed toward thinness for females and fitness for males (White, Brown, & Ginsburg, 1999). Studies also have found that the thin ideal—thinness as the ultimate desired body shape and as a condition for social and personal success and happiness—is pervasive in video games, in magazines, and on the Internet (Downs & Smith, 2010; Tiggemann & Miller, 2010). Not only do media portray an unrealistic body shape (overly thin for women and overly muscular for men), but also an unrealistic standard of beauty—straight white teeth, unblemished skin, and thick, styled hair (Want, 2009). This media image of beauty may be impossible for most adolescents to achieve (Levine & Murnen, 2009). Researchers have consistently found a link between media exposure and negative body image (Anschutz, Engels, Becker, & Van Strien, 2008; Grabe, Ward, & Hyde, 2008; Want, 2009). Negative body image is a psychological discrepancy between a person's perceived body and his or her ideal body that is particularly salient (Halliwell & Dittmar, 2006).

An adolescent's body and body image may be a particularly important aspect of his or her identity, given the natural physical changes (e.g., growth, body shape) that occur during this period. Adolescent girls seem especially vulnerable to thin-ideal media (Groesz, Levine, & Murnen, 2002), which may result from developmental changes that increase the importance of being perceived as attractive to potential mates (Halpern, 2003) and socially accepted by peers (Lloyd, 2002). Internalization of the thin ideal may occur before adolescence and then continue to affect adolescent identity (e.g., Sands & Wardle, 2003). A meta-analysis found that females with preexisting body dissatisfaction issues were more likely to be affected negatively by thin-ideal media exposure than women without preexisting issues (Ferguson, 2013).

Engagement with media, once again, plays an important role in the extent to which the consumption of thin-ideal media influences one's self-perceptions. Three key engagement factors have been identified: social comparison, parasocial relationship, and wishful identification with media characters. Social comparison, in this context, involves the active comparison between the body image represented in media with an adolescent's self-perception of his or her body (Eyal & Te'eni-Harari, 2013). When presented with an image of thinness in magazines, women who had a tendency to self-compare were more likely to engage in social comparison with the thin models (Tiggemann & McGill, 2004). Parasocial relationship, meanwhile, describes a media viewer's perception that a media character is like a companion to the viewer (Eyal & Te'eni-Harari, 2013). Media characters may act as peer-like socialization agents for adolescents. In a study of middle school boys and girls, parasocial relationship with characters partially mediated the relationship between media exposure and body image perceptions, in such a way that greater parasocial relationships led to more negative body image (Eyal & Te'eni-Harai, 2013). Wishful identification—liking and desire to emulate a media character—also may explain how body image media effects occur. While the amount of television, music videos, or magazines that high school girls consumed did not predict body and appearance dissatisfaction, their identification with female characters in those media was significantly related with their body dissatisfaction (Bell & Dittmar, 2011).

Adolescents' engagement with thin-ideal media likely affects how they interpret and incorporate the information and values communicated in the media into their body image attitudes, beliefs, and behaviors. A drive for thinness developed from media may lead to negative and obsessive thoughts about food, diet, and appearance (Holmstrom, 2004; Maor, Sayag, Dahan, & Hermoni, 2006). This negative thinking also may be present even when a person's body weight is within a healthy range (Myers & Biocca, 1992). Negative body image is a known risk factor for a number of physical and mental health problems, including disordered eating (Grogan, 2008).

The popularity and potency of pro–eating disorder websites illustrates the reciprocal nature of media uses and effects proposed by the media practice model (Shafer et al., 2012). Adolescents (primarily young women) whose negative body image and eating disorders often stem from exposure to the body ideals promoted in the media can reinforce their unhealthy beliefs and behaviors by participating in online "pro-ana" (pro–anorexia nervosa) and "pro-mia" (pro–bulimia nervosa) communities. Pro–eating disorder online search terms are used more than 13 million times annually to find pro–eating disorder websites and "thinspiration" (Lewis & Arbuthnott, 2012). Using pro–eating disorder websites is associated with increased duration and hospitalization rates for adolescents diagnosed with eating disorders (Wilson, Peebles, Hardy, & Litt, 2006).

RISKY SUBSTANCES

The media that adolescents consume consistently depict individuals using and abusing alcohol, tobacco, and illicit substances. The most popular television shows regularly feature alcohol use, with tobacco and drug use portrayed less often (Christenson, Henriksen, & Roberts, 2000). Considerable numbers of underage viewers are regularly exposed to television alcohol advertising despite industry standards limiting alcohol advertising to younger audiences (Center on Alcohol Marketing and Youth, 2008). References to alcohol and illicit drugs are on the rise in song lyrics. While only 12% of top-rated songs in 1988 mentioned alcohol and 2% referenced drugs, in 2008, 30% referenced alcohol and 12% drugs (Christenson, Roberts, Bjork, 2012). An average urban ninth-grader hears 27 references to marijuana in the music he or she consumes daily (Primack, Douglas, & Kraemer, 2010).

Of the most popular movies released between 1998 and 2003, 83% contained alcohol use (Wills, Sargent, Gibbons, Gerrard, & Stoolmiller, 2009). The average adolescent viewed 594 instances of tobacco use in these movies (Wills, Sargent, Stoolmiller, Gibbons, & Gerrard, 2008). Teen characters regularly model substance use for their audiences in popular movies (Stern, 2005) and in teen-oriented best-selling books (Coyne, Callister, & Phillips, 2011). The Internet also exposes youth to substances. YouTube, for example, offers youth easy access to media that normalize and glamorize substance use, including smoking fetish videos that combine smoking with erotic appeals (Kim, Paek, & Lynn, 2010).

Research on the influence of tobacco and alcohol advertising and promotional items illustrates how young people's engagement with substance-rich media mediates the effect of substance marketing on substance use. In a cross-sectional study, middle school students who were more receptive to tobacco marketing in the form of in-store displays or branded promotional products were more likely to express an interest in smoking than those who were less receptive to tobacco marketing (Feighery, Borzekowski, Schooler, & Flora, 1998). Longitudinal work showed that adolescents (12 to 15 years old) who had a favorite cigarette ad, or who owned or were willing to own a tobacco-related promotional product, were more likely to smoke six years later than adolescents who were not receptive to these forms of tobacco marketing (Gilpin, White, Messer, & Pierce, 2007).

In terms of attitudes and beliefs, risky substance portrayals can affect adolescents' perceptions of how acceptable and desirable it is to use substances. An experiment compared alcohol-related perceptions and behavioral intentions of youth who viewed fictional social media profiles portraying alcohol abuse by slightly older peers, against those of teens who viewed profiles lacking alcohol references (Litt & Stock, 2011). Teens exposed to the drinking profiles had more positive perceptions of youth who drink, more positive attitudes toward drinking, and considered teen alcohol use to be more normative than the teens who viewed non-alcohol profiles. These cognitive perceptions mediated the effect of the profiles on teens' intentions to drink. Those viewing alcohol-containing profiles expressed higher willingness to drink than those in the non-alcohol condition.

Reflecting the reinforcing spirals perspective (Slater, 2007) and the reciprocal nature of media uses and effects of the media practice model (Shafer et al., 2012), longitudinal studies have linked teens' exposure to alcohol and tobacco in movies and music with smoking and drinking in their social groups and their own drinking and smoking behaviors. Two related studies (Wills et al., 2008, 2009) measured teens' (10 to 14 years old) exposure to tobacco and alcohol use portrayals in popular movies. Baseline exposure to smoking and drinking was related to the teens' smoking and drinking expectancies eight months later, that is, their views that smoking and drinking would be enjoyable and that smoking would be relaxing. Baseline exposure was also related to the proportion of smokers and drinkers in the teens' peer groups eight months later and to their own smoking and drinking. Exposure to drinking at the follow-up was further associated with experiencing drinking-related problems eight months later (Wills et al., 2009). Another national survey showed that adolescents who viewed more music television at baseline (mean age 13.4 years) were more likely to increase the number of smoking friends and more likely to start smoking themselves over the course of three years than youth who consumed less music television at baseline (Slater & Hayes, 2010). These studies illustrate that exposure to media that glamorize alcohol and tobacco are related to environmental shifts that support and further reinforce the substance-positive media messages and adolescents' own substance use.

Many of the media that adolescents consume suggest that alcohol, tobacco, and illicit substances are necessary to fully enjoy oneself and one's relationships. While not all adolescents are equally open to this media script, the extent to which they engage with ads and promotional items may mold their eventual substance use. Substance-promoting media may affect not only adolescents' substance use, but also the peer groups that can support their continued use of both the media and risky substances.

FUTURE RESEARCH DIRECTIONS IN ADOLESCENT MEDIA USES AND EFFECTS

Developments and trends in communication technologies challenge media researchers to continually produce theoretically sound research that addresses timely and meaningful problems. We identify three research directions that reflect what we perceive to be important current needs within the field of adolescent media effects. Given the media landscape's rapid pace of change, however, we concede that these research paths may evolve in unforeseen ways with future technological advancements.

First, research must reflect that today's youth operate in a mobile media world, with many experiencing a ubiquitous connection to their friends and other media content through smartphones, tablets, and wearable media devices (e.g., Google Glass). We expect the volume of media use to continue increasing, and with it the media's socializing influence on young people's development. A constant connection also allows for a more individualized media experience. While political communication scholars debate the implications of increased availability of politically polarized news sources (e.g., Iyengar & Hahn, 2009), what are the parallel effects of customized risky media among adolescents? For example, a young woman inclined to wishful comparison and a negative body image can individualize the content of her media experience to exclude any messages that could influence positively her self-perception. We do not know yet the extent to which young people engage in such customized media experiences. In examining the influence of risky media, however, researchers should consider the myriad ways in which young people today can use the media to reinforce (but also to inhibit) the media messages they consume.

Mobile media also facilitate increased media multitasking as young people simultaneously engage in several phone applications, for example, or split their attention between a television set, a laptop, and a mobile phone. We anticipate that media multitasking will continue rising (Rideout et al., 2010), and that young people will increasingly experience media in a more fragmentary way than previous generations. Researchers should strive to incorporate this reality into their investigations. A deep engagement with any one medium may become less frequent, with fleeting and superficial media consumption becoming the norm (Webster & Ksiazek, 2012). Increased engagement in sexual media may be predicted by arousal, for example, and engagement in content that reinforces conventional body ideals by wishful comparison. As researchers examine the influence of specific content, it is advisable that they examine and account for the relevant engagement factors determining the extent to which youth actively consume the media in question. The possibility that some types of multitasking may enhance engagement or contribute to a cumulative effect also should be examined.

Finally, as media become more participatory and young people increasingly act as produsers—both users and producers—of media (Bruns, 2008), it may be appropriate for more media effects research to focus on the effects of producing risky media. Questions surrounding the psychological implications of creating and distributing digital content remain unexamined. To what extent, for instance, does the act of posting a sexual music video in one's social media profile affect one's sexual self-concept? And how does creating a YouTube cigarette review video influence one's resolve to smoke? Research suggests that by publicly asserting attitudes or performing behaviors, individuals internalize these attitudes and behaviors (Gonzales & Hancock, 2008). Given the ubiquity of media production and distribution tools, adolescents' engagement in these processes, and the risks associated with specific content domains, adolescents' production of risky media deserves considerable research attention.

CONCLUSION

In this chapter we outlined how the media can influence adolescent development in myriad ways. Violent media can increase adolescents' aggression, sexual media can accelerate sexual debut, thin-ideal media can inspire a negative body image, and alcohol advertising can promote underage drinking. We also underscored that elements of adolescents' environments and the adolescents themselves can strengthen or diminish these effects through their own media selections, their interactions with the media, and the extent to which they appropriate attitudes and behaviors from the media into their lives. In place of the conventional linear media effects model, we advocated a cyclical approach to understanding how adolescents' identities and environments shape their media uses and are, in turn, influenced by the media. Media's ubiquity, the pervasiveness of their content, and the ever-evolving media technologies ensure the continued need for media research to reveal and clarify media's role in adolescent development.

REFERENCES

Anschutz, D. J., Engels, R. E., Becker, E. S., & Van Strien, T. (2008). The bold and the beautiful: Influence of body size of televised media models on body dissatisfaction and actual food intake. *Appetite, 51*, 530–537.

Aubrey, J. S. (2004). Sex and punishment: An examination of sexual consequences and the sexual double standard in teen programming. *Sex Roles, 50*(7), 505–514.

Aubrey, J. S., Harrison, K., Kramer, L., & Yellin, J. (2003). Variety versus timing. Gender differences in college students' expectations as predicted by exposure to sexually oriented television. *Communication Research, 30*, 432–460.

Bailey, K., West, R., & Anderson, C. A. (2011). The association between chronic exposure to video game violence and affective picture processing: An ERP study. *Cognitive, Affective, and Behavioral Neuroscience, 11*, 259–276.

Bell, B. T., & Dittmar, H. (2011). Does media type matter? The role of identification in adolescent girls' media consumption and the impact of different thin-ideal media on body image, *Sex Roles, 65*, 478–490.

Bleakley, A., Hennessy, M., Fishbein, M., & Jordan, A. (2008). It works both ways: The relationship between exposure to sexual content in the media and adolescent sexual behavior. *Media Psychology, 11*(4), 443–461.

Bleakley, A., Jamieson, P. E., & Romer, D. (2012). Trends of sexual and violent content by gender in top-grossing U.S. films, 1950–2006. *Journal of Adolescent Health, 51*(1), 73–79.

Bobkowski, P. S. (2009). Adolescent religiosity and selective exposure to television. *Journal of Media and Religion, 8*, 55–70.

Bridges, A. J., Wosnitzer, R., Scharrer, E., Sun, C., & Liberman, R. (2010). Aggression and sexual behavior in best-selling pornography videos: Content analysis update. *Violence Against Women, 16*(10), 1065–1085.

Brown, J. D. (2000). Adolescents' sexual media diets. *Journal of Adolescent Health, 27*(2), 35–40.

Brown, J. D., Halpern, C. T., & L'Engle, K. L. (2005). Mass media as a sexual super peer for early maturing girls. *Journal of Adolescent Health, 36*(5), 420–427.

Brown, J. D., L'Engle, K. L., Pardun, C. J., Guo, G., Kenneavy, K., & Jackson, C. (2006). Sexy media matter: Exposure to sexual content in music, movies, television, and magazines predicts black and white adolescents' sexual behavior. *Pediatrics, 117*(4), 1018–1027.

Bruns, A. (2008). *Blogs, "Wikipedia," "Second Life," and beyond: From production to produsage.* New York, NY: Peter Lang.

Bushman, B. J., & Huesmann, L. R. (2006). Short-term and long-term effects of violent media on aggression in children and adults. *Archives of Pediatric and Adolescent Medicine, 160*, 348–362.

Carnagey, N. L., Anderson, C. A., & Bushman, B. J. (2007). The effect of video game violence on physiological desensitization to real-life violence. *Journal of Experimental Social Psychology, 43*, 489–496.

Center on Alcohol Marketing and Youth. (2008). *Youth exposure to alcohol advertising on television, 2001 to 2007*. Washington, DC: Author.

Chandra, A., Martino, S. C., Collins, R. L., Elliot, M. N., Berry, S. H., Kanouse, D. E., & Miu, A. (2008). Does watching sex on television predict teen pregnancy? Findings from a national longitudinal survey of youth. *Pediatrics, 122*, 1047–1054.

Christenson, P. G., Henriksen, L., & Roberts, D. F. (2000). *Substance use in popular prime-time television*. Washington, DC: Office of National Drug Control Policy.

Christenson, P., Roberts, D. F., & Bjork, N. (2012). Booze, drugs, and pop music: Trends in substance portrayals in the Billboard Top 100—1968–2008. *Substance Use & Misuse, 47*, 121–129.

Collins, R. L. (2008). Media multitasking: Issues posed in measuring the effects of television sexual content exposure. *Communication Methods and Measures, 2*, 65–79.

Coyne, S. M., Callister, M., & Phillips, J. C. (2011). Getting boozy in books: Substance use in adolescent literature. *Health Communication, 26*, 512–515.

Downs, E., & Smith, S. L. (2010). Keeping abreast of hypersexuality: A video game character content analysis. *Sex Roles, 62*, 721–733.

Eyal, K., & Te'eni-Harari, T. (2013). Explaining the relationship between media exposure and early adolescents' body image perceptions: The role of favorite characters. *Journal of Media Psychology, 25*(3), 129–141.

Farvid, P., & Braun, V. (2006). "Most of us guys are raring to go anytime, anyplace, anywhere": Male and female sexuality in *Cleo* and *Cosmo*. *Sex Roles, 55*, 295–310.

Feighery, E., Borzekowski, D. L., Schooler, C., & Flora, J. (1998). Seeing, wanting, owning: The relationship between receptivity to tobacco marketing and smoking susceptibility in young people. *Tobacco Control, 7*(2), 123–128.

Ferguson, C. J. (2013). In the eye of the beholder: Thin-ideal media affects some, but not most, viewers in a meta-analytic review of body dissatisfaction in women and men. *Psychology of Popular Media Culture, 2*(1), 20–37.

Ferris, A. L., Smith, S. W., Greenberg, B. S., & Smith, S. L. (2007). The content of reality dating shows and viewer perceptions of dating. *Journal of Communication, 57*, 490–510.

Fisher, D. A., Hill, D. L., Grube, J. W., Bersamin, M. M., Walker, S., & Gruber, E. L. (2009). Televised sexual content and parental mediation: Influences on adolescent sexuality. *Media Psychology, 12*, 121–147.

Gilpin, E. A., White, M. M., Messer, K., & Pierce, J. P. (2007). Receptivity to tobacco advertising and promotions among young adolescents as a predictor of established smoking in adulthood. *American Journal of Public Health, 97*, 1489–1495.

Gonzales, A. L., & Hancock, J. T. (2008). Identity shift in computer-mediated environments. *Media Psychology, 11*, 167–185.

Grabe, S., Ward, M. L., & Hyde, J. S. (2008). The role of the media in body image concerns among women: A meta-analysis of experimental and correlational studies. *Psychological Bulletin, 134*, 460–476.

Greitmeyer, T., & McLatchie, N. (2011). Denying humanness to others: A newly discovered mechanism by which violent video games increase aggressive behavior. *Psychological Science, 22*(5), 659–665.

Greitmeyer, T., & Osswald, S. (2010). Effects of prosocial video games on prosocial behavior. *Journal of Personality and Social Psychology, 98*(2), 211–221.

Groesz, L. M., Levine, M. P., & Murnen, S. K. (2002). The effect of experimental presentation of thin media images on body satisfaction: A meta-analytic review. *The International Journal of Eating Disorders, 31*, 1–16.

Grogan, S. (2008). *Body image: Understanding body dissatisfaction in men, women and children.* New York, NY: Routledge.

Gunasekera, H., Chapman, S., & Campbell, S. (2005). Sex and drugs in popular movies: An analysis of the top 200 films. *Journal of the Royal Society of Medicine, 9,* 464–470.

Halliwell, E., & Dittmar, H. E. (2006). Associations between appearance-related self-discrepancies and young women and men's affect, body satisfaction, and emotional eating: A comparison of fixed-item and participant generated self-discrepancies. *Personality and Social Psychology Bulletin, 32,* 447–458.

Halpern, C. T. (2003). Biological influences on adolescent romantic and sexual behaviour. In P. Florsheim (Ed.), *Adolescent romantic relations and sexual behavior: Theory, research, and practical implications* (pp. 57–84). Mahwah, NJ: Erlbaum.

Hansen, C. H., & Krygowski, W. (1994). Arousal-augmented priming effects: Rock music videos and sex object schemas. *Communication Research, 21,* 24–47.

Holmstrom, A. J. (2004). The effects of the media on body image: A meta-analysis. *Journal of Broadcasting & Electronic Media, 48,* 196–217.

Huesmann, L. R., Moise-Titus, J., Podolski, C., & Eron, L. D. (2003). Longitudinal relations between children's exposure to TV violence and their aggressive and violent behavior in young adulthood: 1977–1992. *Developmental Psychology, 39,* 201–221.

Iyengar, S., & Hahn, K. S. (2009). Red media, blue media: Evidence of ideological selectivity in media use. *Journal of Communication, 59*(1), 19–39.

Jeong, S. H., & Fishbein, M. (2007). Predictors of multitasking with media: Media factors and audience factors. *Media Psychology, 10*(3), 364–384.

Jeong, S. H., Hwang, Y., & Fishbein, M. (2010). Effects of exposure to sexual content in the media on adolescent sexual behaviors: The moderating role of multitasking with media. *Media Psychology, 13*(3), 222–242.

Johnson, J. G., Cohen, P., Smailes, E. M., Kasen, S., & Brook, J. S. (2002). Television viewing and aggressive behavior during adolescence and adulthood. *Science, 295,* 2468–2471.

Kim, J. L., Collins, R. L., Kanouse, D. E., Elliott, M. N., Berry, S. H., Hunter, S. B., ... Kunkel, D. (2006). Sexual readiness, household policies, and other predictors of adolescents' exposure to sexual content in mainstream entertainment television. *Media Psychology, 8*(4), 449–471.

Kim, K., Paek, H-J., & Lynn, J. (2010). A content analysis of smoking fetish videos on YouTube: Regulatory implications for tobacco control. *Health Communication, 25*(2), 97–106.

Krahé, B., Busching, R., & Möller, I. (2012). Media violence and aggression among German adolescents: Associations and trajectories of change in a three-wave longitudinal study. *Psychology of Popular Media Culture, 1*(3), 152–166.

Kunkel, D., Eyal., K., Finnerty, K., Biely, E., & Donnerstein, D. (2005). *Sex on TV 4: A biennial report to the Kaiser Family Foundation.* Menlo Park, CA: Kaiser Family Foundation.

Levine, M. P., & Murnen, S. K. (2009). "Everybody knows that mass media are/are not [pick one] a cause of eating disorders": A critical review of evidence for a causal link between media, negative body image, and disordered eating in females. *Journal of Social & Clinical Psychology, 28,* 9–42.

Lewis, S. P., & Arbuthnott, A. E. (2012). Searching for thinspiration: The nature of Internet searches for pro-eating disorder websites. *Cyberpsychology, Behavior, and Social Networking, 15*(4), 200–204.

Litt, D. M., & Stock, M. L. (2011). Adolescent alcohol-related risk cognitions: The roles of social norms and social networking sites. *Psychology of Addictive Behavior, 25*(4), 708–713.

Lloyd, B. T. (2002). A conceptual framework for examining adolescent identity, media influence and social development. *Review of General Psychology, 6,* 73–91.

Madden, M., Lenhart, A., Cortesi, S., Gasser, U., Duggan, M., Smith, A., & Beaton, M. (2013). *Teens, social media, and privacy*. Washington, DC: Pew Research Center's Internet & American Life Project. Available at: http://pewinternet.org/Reports/2013/Teens-Social-Media-And-Privacy.aspx.

Madden, M., Lenhart, A., Duggan, M., Cortesi, S., & Gasser, U. (2013). *Teens and technology 2013*. Washington, DC: Pew Research Center's Internet & American Life Project. Available at: http://www.pewinternet.org/Reports/2013/Teens-and-Tech.aspx.

Maor, N., Sayag, S., Dahan, R., & Hermoni, D. (2006). Eating attitudes among adolescents. *Israeli Medical Association Journal, 8*, 627–629.

Myers, P. N., & Biocca, F. A. (1992). The elastic body image: The effect of television advertising and programming on body image distortion in young women. *Journal of Communication, 42*(3), 108–133.

Optenet. (2010). *More than one third of web pages are pornographic*. Available at: http://www.optenet.com/en-us/new.asp?id=270.

Pardun, C. J., L'Engle, K. L., & Brown, J. D. (2005). Linking exposure to outcomes: Early adolescents' consumption of sexual content in six media. *Mass Communication and Society, 8*(2), 75–91.

Peter, J., & Valkenburg, P. M. (2008). Adolescents' exposure to sexually explicit Internet material and sexual preoccupancy: A three-wave panel study. *Media Psychology, 11*(2), 207–234.

Peter, J., & Valkenburg, P. M. (2010). Adolescents' use of sexually explicit Internet material and sexual uncertainty: The role of involvement and gender. *Communication Monographs, 77*(3), 357–375.

Primack, B., Douglas, E. L., & Kraemer, K. L. (2010). Exposure to cannabis in popular music and cannabis use among adolescents. *Addiction, 105*, 515–523.

Primack, B. A., Gold, M. A., Schwarz, E. B., & Dalton, M. A. (2008). Degrading and non-degrading sex in popular music: A content analysis. *Public Health Reports, 123*(5), 593–600.

Rideout, V., Foehr, U. G., & Roberts, D. F. (2010). *Generation M²: Media in the lives of 8- to 18-year-olds*. Menlo Park, CA: The Henry J. Kaiser Family Foundation.

Sands, E. R., & Wardle, J. (2003). Internalization of ideal body shapes in 9–12-year-old girls. *International Journal of Eating Disorders, 33*, 193–204.

Scharrer, E. (2004). Virtual violence: Gender and aggression in video game advertisements. *Mass Communication & Society, 7*, 393–412.

Segrin, C., & Nabi, R. (2002). Does television viewing cultivate unrealistic expectations about marriage? *Journal of Communication, 52*, 247–263.

Shafer, A., Bobkowski, P., & Brown, J. D. (2012). Sexual media practice: How adolescents select, engage with, and are affected by sexual media. In K. E. Gill (Ed.), *The Oxford handbook of media psychology* (pp. 223–251). New York, NY: Oxford University Press.

Signorielli, N. (2003). Prime-time violence 1993–2001: Has the picture really changed? *Journal of Broadcasting & Electronic Media, 47*, 36–57.

Slater, M. D. (2003). Alienation, aggression, and sensation seeking as predictors of adolescent use of violent film, computer, and website content. *Journal of Communication, 53*, 105–121.

Slater, M. D. (2007). Reinforcing spirals: The mutual influence of media selectivity and media effects and their impact on individual behavior and social identity. *Communication Theory, 17*, 281–303.

Slater, M. D., & Hayes, A. F. (2010). The influence of youth music television viewership on changes in cigarette use and association with smoking peers: A social identity, reinforcing spirals perspective. *Communication Research, 37*, 751–773

Slater, M. D., & Henry, K. L. (2013). Prospective influence of music-related exposure on adolescent substance-use initiation: A peer group mediation model. *Health Communication: International Perspectives, 18*(3), 291–305.

Slater, M. D., Henry, K. L., Swaim, R. C., & Cardador, J. M. (2004). Vulnerable teens, vulnerable times: How sensation seeking, alienation, and victimization moderate the violent media content-aggressiveness relation. *Communication Research, 31,* 642–668.

Smith, S. L., & Boyson, A. R. (2002). Violence in music videos: Examining the prevalence and context of physical aggression. *Journal of Communication, 52,* 61–83.

Stern, S. R. (2005). Messages from teens on the big screen: Smoking, drinking, and drug use in teen-centered films. *Journal of Health Communication, 10,* 331–346.

Susman, E. J., & Rogol, A. (2004). Puberty and psychological development. In R. M. Lerner & L. Steinberg (Eds.), *Handbook of Adolescent Psychology* (2nd ed., pp. 15–44). Hoboken, NJ: John Wiley & Sons.

Tiggemann, M., & McGill, B. (2004). The role of social comparison in the effect of magazine advertisements on women's mood and body dissatisfaction. *Journal of Social & Clinical Psychology, 23,* 23–44.

Tiggemann, M., & Miller, J. (2010). The Internet and adolescent girls' weight satisfaction and drive for thinness. *Sex Roles, 63,* 79–90.

Udry, J. (1990). Hormonal and social determinants of adolescent sexual initiation. In J. Bancroft & J. Reinisch (Eds.), *Adolescence and puberty* (pp. 70–87). New York, NY: Oxford University Press.

Wang, Y., Mathews, V. P., Kalnin, A. J., Mosier, K. M., Dunn, D. W., Saykin, A. J., & Kronenberg, W. G. (2009). Short-term exposure to a violent video game induces changes in frontolimbic circuitry in adolescents. *Brain Imaging and Behavior, 3,* 38–50.

Want, S. C. (2009). Meta-analytic moderators of experimental exposure to media portrayals of women on female appearance satisfaction: Social comparisons as automatic processes. *Body Image, 6,* 257–269.

Ward, L. M., & Friedman, K. (2006). Using TV as a guide: Associations between television viewing and adolescents' sexual attitudes and behavior. *Journal of Research on Adolescence, 16,* 133–156.

Weaver, A. J., Zelenkauskaite, A., & Samson, L. (2012). The (non)violent world of YouTube: Content trends in web video. *Journal of Communication, 62,* 1065–1083.

Webster, J. G., & Ksiazek, T. B. (2012). The dynamics of audience fragmentation: Public attention in an age of digital media. *Journal of Communication, 62,* 39–56.

White, S. E., Brown, N. J., & Ginsburg, S. L. (1999). Diversity of body types in network television programming: A content analysis. *Communication Research Reports, 16,* 386–392.

Wills, T. A., Sargent, J. D., Gibbons, F. X., Gerrard, M., & Stoolmiller, M. (2009). Movie exposure to alcohol cues and adolescent alcohol problems: A longitudinal analysis in a national sample. *Psychology of Addictive Behaviors, 23*(1), 23–35.

Wills, T. A., Sargent, J. D., Stoolmiller, M., Gibbons, F. X., & Gerrard, M. (2008). Smoking exposure and smoking onset: A longitudinal study of mediation processes in a representative sample of U.S. adolescents. *Psychology of Addictive Behaviors, 22*(2), 269–277.

Wilson J. L., Peebles, R., Hardy, K. K., & Litt, I. F. (2006). Surfing for thinness: A pilot study of pro–eating disorder Web site usage in adolescents with eating disorders. *Pediatrics, 118,* e1635–e1643.

Wolak, J., Mitchell, K. J., & Finkelhor D. (2007). Does online harassment constitute bullying? An exploration of online harassment by known peers and online-only contacts. *Journal of Adolescent Health, 41,* 51–58.

Wright, P. (2011). Mass media effects on youth sexual behavior: Assessing the claim for causality. In C. T. Salmon (Ed.), *Communication Yearbook* (pp. 343–386). New York, NY: Routledge.

Ybarra, M. L., Mitchell, K. J., Hamburger, M., Diener-West, M., & Leaf, P. J. (2011). X-rated material and perpetration of sexually aggressive behavior among children and adolescents: Is there a link? *Aggressive Behavior, 37*, 1–18.

Zuckerman, M. (1994). *Behavioral expressions and biosocial bases of sensation-seeking.* New York, NY: Cambridge University Press.

Zurbriggen, E. L., & Morgan, E. M. (2006). Who wants to marry a millionaire? Reality dating television programs, attitudes towards sex, and sexual behaviors. *Sex Roles, 54*, 1–17.

CHAPTER NINE

Adolescent Identity and Substance Use Prevention

MICHAEL L. HECHT

Adolescence is a time of growth and attendant risks such as substance use, criminal activity, and poor school performance. As a result, this developmental period presents unique challenges for the health promotion community, including substance use prevention, some of which are associated with identity issues. Both popular and developmental research literature paint adolescence as a key period in identity development. While it seems clear that much of who we are is shaped by early development and identity, development generally continues at least into the 20s (Arnett, 2000) and probably throughout the lifespan (Logan, Ward, & Spitze, 1992). Both physical changes (e.g., onset of puberty) and social changes (e.g., increased freedom of movement and peer associations) that occur during adolescences are pivotal in long-term life directions. Indeed, one of the central tasks of the teen years is to figure out who you are and who you can become in the important social domains of adolescence—school/work, family, and friends (Oyserman, Bybee, & Terry, 2006). This is reflected in iconic cultural representations such as films like *Fast Times at Ridgemont High*, *Breakfast Club*, and, more recently, the *Wimpy Kids* and the *Twilight* series, as well as televised representations like the *Cosby Show* and *Pretty Little Liars*. And, of course, we followed Harry Potter through his tween and teen years. As early as James Dean in *Rebel Without a Cause* these media representations largely present this period as emerging identity often rife with angst and struggle.

Clearly one of the key factors in adolescent identity development is the increased independence most teens experience (Collins & Steinberg, 2007). During this period youths typically experiment with a diversity of romantic relationships, career directions, and perspectives and opinions without making a firm commitment (Arnett, 2000). As the transitional state on the way to adulthood, this process has always made sense and yet has often been a struggle. Starting with later bed times, increased unsupervised after school activities, and leading up to physical mobility through mass transit and driver's licenses, adolescence tends to be marked by the transition from a life guided by adults to one of choice and volition. More recently, as more and more youths move onto semi-independence in college, we see the emergence of "helicopter parents" and "drone parents" who remain present in their children's lives, often aided by electronic means. College professors note students texting their parents as they emerge from tests, voluntarily continuing to subject themselves to parental influence even as they exercise independence through electronic and transportation technology never before experienced by their developmental peers. Regardless of these nuances, adolescence is typically a time to develop a stronger sense of identity and greater peer influence while separating from family.

Along with identity development come risks. In general, risks are needed for healthy development; it is how people learn and grow. However, while the risks of earlier developmental periods can be consequential, involving activities that result in bruises and hurt feelings, those encountered during adolescence can result in life-shaping and even life-threatening consequences such as criminalization, early family obligations, and occupational limitations. While adolescent risks tend to be highly interrelated (Jessor, Donovan, & Costa, 1991), one of these substantive risks is early substance experimentation and use (Newcomb & Bentler, 1988). Many youths are experimenting with substances by the end of high school, with the overwhelming majority having tried at least one drug (Johnston, O'Malley, Bachman, & Schulenberg, 2013). Not only do their identities influence decisions to experiment, but also, at the same time, emerging "substance identities" (e.g., "user" and "non-user") shape their sense of self as well as subsequent substance use and other risky behaviors. These processes have implications for substance use prevention that are reflected in the substance use prevention intervention.

CONCEPTUALIZING IDENTITY AND SUBSTANCE USE: THE COMMUNICATION THEORY OF IDENTITY

While there are many ways to conceptualize identity, the author typically invokes the many forms of identity articulated in the Communication Theory of Identity (CTI; Hecht & Choi, 2012). CTI integrates other approaches but is unique in its focus on multiple frames, one of which is the communication of identity. Specifically, the theory articulates personal, relational, enacted, and communal frames as well as their interpenetration.

We turn next to examining how these frames help us understand why adolescents use substances. A number of explanations for substance use have emerged. These can be understood in terms of the frames and their interpenetration. We start with the personal frame, the one most closely aligned with personality psychology and self-concept.

Personal Layer

The personal frame involves how individuals conceptualize themselves. Personal identity does not assume a core self; rather, it assumes individuals have multiple personal identities, some of which are more salient than others. In related research, Oyserman and Fryberg (2006) argue that self-concepts are what we think when we think about ourselves, and this includes future or possible selves. It is clear that for some, the identity of "druggie" or "non-users" is highly salient and influences choices. The distinction between youths who see themselves through the lens of user or non-user emerged most clearly in our work among rural adolescents (Pettigrew, Miller-Day, Krieger, & Hecht, 2012). Similarly, Oyserman, Terry, and Bybee (2002) identify an academically oriented identity that is associated with less risky behaviors.

Personal identity also includes how people feel about themselves. While most have both positive and negative feelings, some tend to fixate on the negative. People with these pronounced and perhaps obsessively negative feelings about self are said to use drugs to "medicate" themselves or find an antidote for negative feelings (Khantzian, 1997). Some addicts even come to prefer the identity they see in themselves when they are high, and this is an obstacle to treatment. Recent brain research suggests that other addictions, such as alcoholism, may be associated with modifying the brain structure, especially the centers that produce dopamine (Spanagel & Weiss, 1999). Without the ability to experience pleasure from experiences when not drunk, people become increasingly tied to use and abuse.

Gender and ethnicity tend to be particularly salient personal identities. Historically, girls were less likely to use substances than boys (Johnston et al., 2013), and those girls who did use were initiated by males (Miller, Alberts, Hecht, Krizek, & Trost, 2000). One explanation may be the generally lower self-esteem reported by girls during this period that correlates with their substance use (Wild, Flisher, Bhana, & Lombard, 2004). In addition, ethnic identity has been identified as a moderator of psychosocial risk and adolescent alcohol and marijuana use (Marsiglia, Kulis, & Hecht, 2001). Conversely, these identities can be protective under some conditions. For example, African Americans and Mexican Americans with stronger identities are less likely to use substances, while risks increase for individuals who have weaker identities (Marsiglia et al., 2001).

Relational Layer

Relational identities involve defining self in terms of others (e.g., as friend) or in relation to other identities (e.g., leader/follower). Clearly the emerging influence of peers (Jessor et al., 1991) invokes a relational identity (i.e., in terms of peer relationships). Adolescence can be a time of wanting to be like others and fitting in, and when the reference group consumes substances this promotes a user identity and use. Research demonstrates social conformity to peer drug use (Marks, Graham, & Hansen, 1992), and exposure and attachment to substance-using peers are strongly predictive of increased risk for early initiation (Kosterman, Hawkins, Guo, Catalano, & Abbott, 2000; Marks et al., 1992). It has long been recognized that merely believing many of your peers are using substances (descriptive norms) is associated with initiation and use, while peer injunctive norms (i.e., what others think is right or wrong) also matter (Elek, Miller-Day, & Hecht, 2006). It has been suggested that consuming some drugs is itself "social" (e.g., marijuana, alcohol). For example, labeling someone a "social drinker" implies a relational identity. Recent research on social networks extends this notion (Choi & Smith, in press.).

Relational identities also include ascriptions, and this, too, plays a role in substance use and other risk behaviors. In general, the image of substance users is quite positive, including perceptions of them as rebellious, acting older, cool, sociable, and intelligent, and other youths' self-images tend to align with users (Aloise-Young, Hennigan, & Graham, 1996). Other research suggests that adolescents are more likely to use substances when their peers ascribe positive qualities to drug users (Barger & Gallo, 2008), and that people who are more sensitive to others' opinions and fear social rejection may be at higher health risks in general (Cole, Kemeny, & Taylor et al., 1997).

Enacted Layer

Enacted identity is one of the areas in which CTI differs from other approaches. Enactments, such as communication, are seen as a frame or layer of identity rather than merely the outcome or expression of identity. That is, how we behave is an element of who we are. For some youths the act of using or not using drugs is in itself an identity. Other aspects of enacted identities speak directly to reasons some people consume drugs. Some research suggests that for many, the prime motivation behind substance use is fun (Steinberg, 2005). This is likely to be enhanced when associated with identities such as "fun loving," "life of the party," and "party animal." In addition, socio-emotional learning theory highlights the role of self-control in substance use. Recent research suggests that some drug use (e.g., smoking) is associated with the inability to delay gratification, while other substance use (e.g., cocaine) may be more closely associated with the draw of risky behaviors (Ert, Yechiam, & Arshavsky, 2013). Other work shows that youths may engage in a particular deviant behavior as a means of enacting an identity, either because it eases entry into a particular social group and the attendant social group-based identity, or because it is self-symbolizing in other ways (Oyserman & Saltz, 1993).

One of the more interesting studies of enacted identity was conducted longitudinally by Barber, Eccles, and Stone (2001). They theorized that leisure activities socialize identity development or, in CTI terms, enacted identities. They then define adolescent identities through personal and enacted frames (12% Brain, 28% Jock, 40% Princess, 11% Basket Case, 9% Criminal) and find links between these identities and substance use. Moreover, the activities (e.g., performing arts and school involvement) that enact these identities are linked to substance use/nonuse as well as school completion.

Conceptually, Schwartz (2001) suggests that enactments may be of self-discovery and self-construction. On one hand, discovery would focus on enactments in the process of identity development and might include adolescents trying out new identities. Construction would, on the other hand, occur as enactments of identities that are in place. This distinction might prove useful in examining adolescent identity enactments that are likely to include both types. Drug experimentation, for example, is likely to be a discovery enactment, while regular use would fall under construction. Future research might address this distinction to determine its usefulness in explaining these two behaviors as well as in the design of prevention interventions.

Communal Layer

The final frame is communal identity that transcends individuals and conveys a societal or at least social level of identity. These identities are most commonly seen in media portrayals. For example, the adolescent identity "druggie" was glorified by the character Spicoli, played by Sean Penn, in *Fast Times at Ridgemont High*. These characters also convey social norms about substance use (Sargent, Wills, Stoolmiller, Gibson, & Gibbons, 2005). Regulations on advertising and portrayals of substance use in content directed to children are based on this notion. Conversely, a large portion of prevention dollars goes to media campaigns or PSAs despite their very modest, at best, effects (Hornik, Jacobsohn, Orwin, Piesse, & Kalton, 2008).

Communal substance identities are, of course, culture bound. In U.S. history we can see prohibition, for example, as an attempt to criminalize alcohol use identities. When prohibition ended we see the criminalization of marijuana and with the emergence of very strict drug laws an exploding prison population based on substance use. The new millennium has seen a reversal in the treatment of marijuana, with medical marijuana gaining increasing acceptance and legalization of recreational use, too, becoming, it seems, increasingly acceptable. As these communal representations of marijuana and marijuana users shift, one can anticipate attendant changes in personal, relational, and enacted identities. This, however, remains for another day and another analysis when more information is available about these trends.

Interpenetration

One of the key assumptions of CTI is that the layers or frames "interpenetrate" each other. Interpenetration is a term borrowed from cultural studies to indicate that the layers are meant as analytical frames, not distinct identity types. Conceptually this means that they are infused within each other and/or overlapping. Empirically, this would mean that they interact. For example, as discussed earlier, a personal identity of "druggie" would interpenetrate a relational identity of being part of a network of drug users and an enacted identity of getting together and using drugs.

Evidence for this phenomenon is available from a number of identity studies (Narváez, Meyer, Ketrzner, Ouellette, & Gordon, 2009), particularly gender and ethnic identities (Perry & Pauletti, 2011). For example, Barger and Gallo (2008) report complex interactions between and among Latina/o ethnic self-labeling, degree of ethnic identification, and other sociodemographic identities in their effects on health risks such as smoking.

Prominent public health theoretical approaches are based on the notion of interpenetration, probably foremost among which is the Ecological Risk and Resiliency Approach (Bogenschneider, 1996). The approach conceptualizes multi-level ecologies that include the interrelationships between and among the individual, social relationships, and context. Increasing recognition of brain neuroscience and other biological factors suggest these interpenetrations are even more complex than suspected (Link, Northridge, Phelan, & Ganz, 1998). For example, brain science suggests that alcoholism influences the brain centers that produce dopamine, which allows humans to experience pleasure (Dettling et al., 1995). As a result, alcoholics have trouble obtaining pleasure out of social relations and activities while sober and, in fact, may not "feel like themselves" without the aid of this substance.

Interpenetrations emerge in a number of ways. In contrast to the view that there is some central or essential self-concept, CTI argues for multiple, emergent, and negotiated identities. At any moment there are likely to be more than one salient identity an individual calls upon, and unless the individual suffers from an identity-related deficit, he or she is likely to be at least somewhat integrated. CTI argues that identities are negotiated between and among people in various situations. Identities emerge and recede in salience based on whom we are with, where we are, and what we are doing. My identity as teacher is more salient in the classroom than at home, and my identity as parent more salient among my children and grandchildren. A conversational partner can invoke an identity through ascription, including invoking stereotypes.

CTI conceptualizes identity as naturally dynamic and emergent, predicting a movement between confusion and synthesis based on ongoing negotiation. These negotiations and the shifting terrain of identities can lead to inconsistencies and disconnections between and among layers. For example, silencing the self theory discusses how women are kept from expressing themselves in various situations (Jack, 1991). Family who remember us at an earlier age may still treat us in ways that contradict how we currently see ourselves. Jung and Hecht (2008) labeled these identity gaps and a series of studies demonstrate that these gaps produce negative outcomes as mild as dissatisfying conversations and as detrimental as depression (Jung & Hecht, 2008). Gaps also emerge within layers. For example, youths are more likely to be involved in delinquent activities if they are experiencing difficulties negotiating the separation-individuation tasks of adolescence (Oyserman & Saltz, 1993).

Many questions remain about how identity gaps and adolescent substance use are related. For example, which gaps are most salient—those between how we see ourselves and how we are seen and treated by peers, near peers, or parents? Do identity gaps mediate the relationship between norms and drug use? Do people differ in their acceptance and comfort with gaps as they do with levels of uncertainty (Afifi, 2009) and how is this related to substance use decisions? Oyserman and Destin (2010), for example, assume that identity congruent behaviors are favored. What happens when people have a wide range of behaviors that are congruent or are tolerant of incongruence? Finally, can identity gaps be used in health promotion messages to drive or motivate change in a prosocial direction? This last question leads to consideration of how this knowledge of identity can be used in adolescent substance use prevention.

ADOLESCENT IDENTITY AND DRUG USE PREVENTION

The central role of adolescent identity in drug use demonstrated in this literature review has influenced the design of prevention interventions. Early on, with the self-concept model firmly in place, these focused on self-esteem training. Interventions were designed to boost esteem under the belief that adolescents who felt positively about themselves would be less likely to use drugs. Unfortunately, not all drug use arises out of a deficit model (e.g., medication for negative feelings), and even when it does, the physiological changes associated with heavy use and addiction may limit the utility of interventions that focus on esteem. As a result, esteem interventions proved largely unsuccessful.

General identity-based interventions have played a somewhat minor role in prevention interventions. Most interventions have utilized social cognitive, socio-emotional learning, or other models based on changing norms and attitudes while teaching life skills. One prominent curriculum, called "School-to-Jobs" (STJ), was based on the identity work of Markus and Nurius (1986). The basic assumption of this intervention is that changing an adolescent's perspective on future selves that can be attained leads to positive change in a wide array of behaviors including academic performance and better mental health (Oyserman et al., 2002; Oyserman, Bybee, & Terry, 2006). STJ systematically addresses different elements of possible selves. The sessions begin by linking school-based possible selves to important social identities. Next these are linked to positive possible selves in the near future such as graduating from eighth grade and then to more distant adult possible selves. The final sessions promote behaviors that youths can use to obtain future positive possible selves, including plans for coping with obstacles. The intervention has proved successful in improving long-term academic performance (Oyserman et al., 2002) as well as reducing depressive symptoms (Oyserman, Bybee, & Terry, 2006) and protecting the youth from risks such as low parent involvement (Oyserman, Brickman, & Rhodes, 2007). These outcomes have proved relatively enduring, holding promise to impact co-occurring problems such as substance use.

Other identity-based interventions have been designed with a treatment focus and will not be reviewed in detail. It is not uncommon for therapy to address identity issues. Moral Recognition Therapy, for example, addresses positive identity formation among youthful offenders and has produced some evidence of reduced recidivism and delinquency (Wilson, Bouffard, & MacKenzie, 2005).

Cultural Identities and Interventions

The prominent role that culture plays in drug use as well as the political implications of drug enforcement suggested that cultural identity should be taken into account in intervention design. Shifting patterns of substance use such as earlier ages of initiation and differing "drugs of choice" among ethnically diverse adolescents created the perceived need to develop culturally based substance use prevention frameworks (Guthrie & Low, 2000), particularly for those with a higher degree of cultural sensitivity (Hecht & Miller-Day, 2009; Hecht, Marsiglia et al., 2003). This is supported by research demonstrating that health messages that are congruent with one's identity tend to be more impactful (Appiah, 2001; Korzenny, McClure, & Rzyttki, 1990; Oyserman & Destin, 2010). The result was a line of work focused on cultural sensitivity, adaptation, competence, and so on that creates messages appealing to personal, relational, enacted, and communal identities.

Approaches to Culturally Based Interventions

A number of different approaches to culturally based interventions have been proposed. One key dimension along which they differ is whether they start with mainstream culture, create an intervention with no assumption of cultural grounding (i.e., that mainstream culture is ubiquitous or invisible), and then look to add a "cultural" dimension or whether cultural grounding is the goal from the start. They also differ in whether the goal is to target a specific cultural identity or infuse identities into a multicultural intervention. The use of various terms such as sensitivity, appropriateness, adaptation, competence, and grounding hint at some of these differences but all speak to the need for cultural identity to be considered in the development and adaptation of interventions and all inform intervention design. Overall, meta-analyses demonstrate moderately strong benefits of cultural adaptation across mental health interventions (Griner & Smith, 2006). Culture-specific adaptations provide other benefits, including enhanced recruitment and retention among ethnic minorities (Castro, Barrera, & Martinez, 2004; Griner & Smith, 2006; Kumpfer, Alvarado, Smith, & Bellamy, 2002).

Early approaches to cultural sensitivity were articulated by Resnicow, Baronowski, Ahluwalia, and Braithwaite (1999) and Kreuter, Lukwago, Bucholtz, Clark, and Sanders-Thompson (2003). Resnicov and colleagues utilized a linguistic metaphor of deep and surface cultural structures. On one hand, surface structures are the more visible and superficial aspects of culture including art, food, and clothing that can be infused into a curriculum. Deep structure, on the other hand, reflects the underling complexity of a culture such as ideology, values, and beliefs. A health message reflecting the deep structure of Latino/a culture might base its appeal on familism, a cultural orientation in which the family of origin is of primary importance, even after marriage (Suarez-Orozco & Suarez-Orozco, 1995). Kreuter and colleagues developed a more specific taxonomy of techniques for achieving culture sensitivity describing peripheral strategies (e.g., packaging through images), evidential strategies (e.g., presenting evidence about how it impacts that group), linguistic strategies (e.g., accessibility through native language), constituent-involving (e.g., strategies drawing on experiences of the group), and sociocultural strategies (e.g., Resnicow et al.'s concept of deep structure).

In an attempt to shift the focus and "center" culture in message development, Hecht and Krieger (2006) articulated the principle of cultural grounding to guide health message design. We felt this was important because the techniques suggested sometimes result in a target audience feeling "singled out," especially when the behavioral issues are stigmatizing, such as crime or obesity. In a sense, messages can be seen as "over accommodating" by going too far in adjusting to a particular cultural identity, a strategy that often produces dissatisfying communication outcomes (Harwood, Giles, Fox, Ryan, & Williams, 1993; Hecht, Jackson, & Ribeau, 2003).

Emerging from the Communication Theory of Identity, cultural grounding argues that messages should be grounded in the identities salient to the audience. The diverse interplay and interpenetration of these identities (e.g., race, gender, SES, occupation, age) make it unlikely that a message would target a single identity. Instead, the strategy entails identifying the salient cross-cutting audience identities in order to reach out to or activate one or more identities for each person. As a result, message development starts with and from the perspective of group members. The principle is closely aligned with multiculturalism (Banks & Banks, 2010) based on the premise that inclusive grounding maximizes impact and both exclusive focus and exclusion diminish effect. We turn, next, to strategies for grounding messages.

Methods of Cultural Grounding

One of the primary methods for achieving cultural grounding is community-based participatory research (Minkler & Wallerstein, 2008). At its heart, CBPR involves a partnership approach to intervention design. Community members and prevention scientists work together as a team in all steps in the intervention design, development, and implementation. This requires a balancing of the needs of all partners and recognition that all have contributions to make.

When CBPR first emerged it represented a shift in focus from the researcher conducting research and implementing a curriculum on a group who were viewed as recipients. Akin to the move in conceptualizing the people involved in our research as participants rather than subjects, CBPR involves relinquishing total control or power. The community is seen as a full and equal partner in some versions of CBPR. Less extreme stances still acknowledge differences in skills or expertise. For example, in grounding a school-based prevention curriculum, teachers are experts on their classroom, students are experts on their experiences, and prevention scientists are experts in prevention strategies.

One of the issues with CBPR is how to define communities. Airhihenbuwa's (2007) PEN-3 model was developed in order to guide the interventionist working in Africa to focus on three elements of culture: cultural identity (person, extended family, neighborhood), relationships and expectations (perceptions, enablers, nurturers), and cultural empowerment (positive and negative factors). This approach is particularly noteworthy for its focus on the positive as well as negative elements of culture and health and its application across a range of public health issues (cancer, hypertension, diabetes, smoking, diet, and obesity).

My colleagues and I have argued that narrative research is an important method for defining cultures and culturally grounding prevention messages (Colby et al., 2013; Hecht & Krieger, 2006; Larkey & Hecht, 2010; Miller-Day & Hecht, 2013). Narratives are not only a universal communicative form but, as well, a method of interpreting and understanding the world (Miller-Day & Hecht, 2013).

In other words, people communicate using narratives but, at the same time, store information and events through narrative structures. This means, of course, that while narratives themselves are a pan-cultural form of communication, specific narratives express or enact cultural values and identities. One has only to think about children's books such as *Cinderella* to understand how narratives convey a sense of good and evil as well as family roles in European ancestry cultures. Family narratives convey not only history but, as well, teach children how they belong and how they should behave. My mother's stories of signs in Brooklyn, New York, during the 1920s that read "no Jews or dogs allowed" was meant to convey who I was and how I needed to relate to people she said saw us as "others."

Based on this rich personal and scholarly history of narratives, colleagues and I articulated what we have come to call narrative engagement theory to explain how culturally grounded, narrative prevention messages can be developed (Colby et al., 2013; Hecht & Krieger, 1996; Larkey & Hecht, 2010; Miller-Day & Hecht, 2013). The theory argues that effective health promotion plots are seen as realistic and interesting, and the audience needs to identify with the characters. These narratives are not only effective in impact norms and social cognitions as well as substance use and other health behaviors, but also result in social proliferation of the stories through networks that can amplify effects.

The messages design method that emerged from this theorizing culturally grounds health messages. Evolving from Miller-Day's thesis work (Miller-Rassulo & Hecht, 1988), we argue that collecting personal narratives, identifying themes in those narratives, and then working with community members to create performances of prototypical narratives all ground the messages in the target culture and are impactful (Miller-Day & Hecht, 2013). Our data support this conclusion (Lee, Hecht, Miller-Day, & Elek, 2011; Miller-Day et al., 2000).

Culturally Based Substance Use Prevention Interventions

Two of the most prominent culturally sensitive, school-based interventions are Life Skills Training and Project Alert. Both started as a mainstream cultural intervention without self-consciously attending to culture in their initial intervention work. In essence, both targeted the identities of mainstream (i.e., white) youth culture by considering the development needs as well as constructing images and narratives that would appeal to the culture. The mere fact that these are drug prevention interventions targeted at younger adolescents in order to intervene before or during early experimentation reflects a perception of adolescent identities as risk taking and increasingly independent. The focus on issues like peer pressure and social norms reflects relational identity and strategies such as teaching drug offer resistance skills invoke enacted identities. The interventions themselves reflect communal identities as cultural representations of how the prevention community perceives adolescent identities. Thus, even the "generic" (read mainstream white) interventions target adolescent identities.

One of the most widely disseminated middle school drug prevention interventions, Life Skills Training, was culturally based and adapted by Botvin and colleagues (1992). Their prevention curriculum was originally developed for and tested with a predominantly white, suburban sample. Later it was adapted for an urban, Hispanic population using a process that involved psychologists, Hispanic health educators, experts on Hispanic cultural issues, reading specialists, and urban, non-white students who reviewed the original curriculum and made suggestions. While the underlying prevention strategy changes remained, adaptations were made to the reading level, examples illustrating program content, and behavioral rehearsal exercises (Botvin et al., 1992). Similar modifications were made to accommodate African American youth. We turn, next, to an intervention, *keepin' it REAL*, that was self-consciously constructed to target adolescent identities.

KEEPIN' IT REAL: A CASE-STUDY IN IDENTITY-BASED SUBSTANCE USE PREVENTION

As the most widely disseminated school-based prevention curriculum in the world, *keepin' it REAL* (kiR) is grounded in CTI and youth identities. kiR was adopted by D.A.R.E. for national and international dissemination resulting in distribution to 2 million youths in the United States as well as those in 47 other countries. The remainder of this chapter examines how identity research was used to develop the prevention messages that influence adolescent health choices and behaviors.

At its origins, *keepin' it REAL* was developed for middle schools in Phoenix, Arizona. Calling upon narrative theory and cultural grounding, research was conducted to identify salient cultural identities and practices of adolescents in that school system. The curriculum is grounded in earlier work focused on African American and Mexican American identities and communication practices (Hecht & Ribeau, 1987; Hecht, Ribeau, & Sedano, 1990) and leading to both qualitative (Miller et al., 2000) and quantitative (Marsiglia et al., 2001; Matsunaga, Hecht, Elek, & Ndaiye, 2010) studies of adolescent identities and drug-related communication practices. The findings of these studies, along with a literature review of the respective cultures and adolescent development (Colby et al., 2013), provided the framework for the curriculum. As with other prevention programs, our focus on peer pressure and social norms invoked relational identities and teaching drug offer resistance skills enacted their identities. What was different was the grounding of our curriculum in these cultural identities through narratives and our process of message development collected during this process (Miller et al., 2000) as well as our process of message construction.

The philosophy of *keepin' it REAL* is to develop a "kid-centric" curriculum through culturally grounding the curriculum in engaging narratives. The lessons are structured around youth narratives that operationalize identity by drawing upon their own experiences to present problems that must be solved. Youths are engaged actively through interaction in which they, not the implementer or teacher, are centered. Adolescent identities are necessarily invoked in this "from kids through kids to kids" approach. At the heart of this process are the narratives we identified that are integrated into curriculum in the form of video scenarios, role-playing, decision-making scenarios, and other materials. The "through kids" component was the role youths played in producing videos that presented drug offer situations and modeled resistance skills as well as shaping the other narrative elements. Hecht and Lee (2008) argue that the curriculum develops a non-use branded identity through these strategies and analyses demonstrate the curriculum was successful at developing such a brand identity (Lee & Hecht, 2011). Narrative engagement theory argues that identification with the people involved in the intervention is key, and presenting prosocial models of behaviors moves beyond problematic identity stories demonizing drug users and drug offers (Miller-Day & Hecht, 2013).

One of the key findings of this line of research was that multiculturalism was a more effective strategy than cultural targeting (Hecht, Graham, & Elek, 2006). We argue that people wish to be included rather than targeted, with the latter strategy running the risk of stigmatizing the targeted group. For example, a drug prevention curriculum targeting African Americans may imply that these youths are in greater need of an intervention, when in reality demographically these adolescents in general are less likely to use substances (Johnston et al., 2013). By extension, other types of identities, including social roles such as biker, skater, and so on must be included. Materials cannot portray only a narrow range of adolescent identities but, rather, be inclusive through presentation of the diversity of youth identities beyond culture and gender.

CONCLUSION

As noted in the opening of this chapter, adolescence is a time of immense change and growth, the period between childhood and adulthood. During this period, identities are developed that play determining roles in our future. It is of no doubt that many adolescents will experiment with alcohol, tobacco, marijuana, and sexual experiences. However, when these behaviors become associated with one's own identity, they can become problematic and detrimental. Through review of many scientific articles related to adolescent identity development and risky behaviors, we can identify several links within peer groups, ethnic identity, desire for experimentation, and self-esteem. When adolescents feel accepted by a peer group, they are likely to be happier and therefore seek this acceptance through whatever means they feel necessary, including through risky behaviors. This is similar for ethnic groups, and the strength with which one identifies with his or her own ethnicity can be a determining factor. Desire to "try on" an identity can also lead to delinquent behavior, but this can be reversed if the adolescent does not find the kind of acceptance he or she desires. Low self-esteem is also linked to these kinds of identities and, furthermore, to acceptance. It would appear that identity development for adolescents relies heavily on finding acceptance even if that means one participates in risky behaviors. These characteristics of identity form the core of substance abuse prevention interventions, ranging from those that take a more generic cultural approach to adolescence to those more self-consciously focused on adolescent cultural and other identities.

The research described in this chapter is but a start. Little is known, for example, about the processes of identity negotiation between and among adolescents and the attendant identity gaps that may serve as motivation for risky behavior as well as for healthy and responsible choices. Schwartz (2001) raises the question about whether interventions should invoke discovery of identity (e.g., search for information about new or changing identities) or self-construction (e.g., search for more information about existing identities). Moreover, little is known about the implementer role in these processes—what identity/ies are invoked in this process? Elsewhere we argue that it is essential to understand not only how designers create and adapt curriculum but, as well, the role of implementers (Colby et al., 2013; Pettigrew et al., 2013). When discussing the co-branding of *keepin' it REAL* and D.A.R.E., we discuss how the kiR philosophy required law enforcement officers implementing the program to see themselves differently in order to enact the kid-centric philosophy (Hecht & Lee, in press). Does this involve a modification of identities? During the development process various D.A.R.E. constituencies were heard to question whether kiR was consistent with a D.A.R.E. brand identity. Ultimately, most came to accept the collaboration, but tensions still exist (Hecht & Lee, in press). We hypothesized that teacher implementers would modify the curriculum to adapt to their classes but learned that most adapted to fit their own style and identity (Pettigrew et al., 2013). Thus, one must consider a complex nexus of identities when constructing and implementing adolescent interventions, a journey we have begun but must continue just as the youths, themselves, work through this developmental period. As I write this, ahead lies a new generation. The Millennials are older now, and their younger siblings will form a new cultural cohort. What will their identities be like? What will that require?

REFERENCES

Afifi, W. A. (2009). Uncertainty and information management in interpersonal contexts. In S. Smith & S. Wilson (Eds.), *New directions in interpersonal communication research* (pp. 94–114). Thousand Oaks, CA: Sage.

Airhihenbuwa, C. O. (2007). *Healing our differences: The crisis of global health and the politics of identity.* Lanham, MD: Rowman and Littlefield.

Airhihenbuwa, C. O. (2010). Culture matters in global health. *The European Health Psychologist, 12,* 52–55.

Aloise-Young, P. A., Hennigan, K. M., & Graham, J. W. (1996). Role of the self-image and smoker stereotype in smoking onset during early adolescence: a longitudinal study. *Health Psychology, 15,* 494–497.

Appiah, O. (2001). Black, white, Hispanic, and Asian American adolescents' responses to culturally embedded ads. *The Howard Journal of Communication, 12,* 29–48.

Arnett, J. J. (2000). Emerging adulthood: A theory of development from the late teens through the 20's. *American Psychologist, 55,* 469–480.

Banks, J. A., & Banks, C. A. M. (2010). *Multicultural education: Issues and perspectives* (7th ed.). Danvers, MA: John Wiley & Sons

Barber, B. L., Eccles, J. S., & Stone, M. R. (2001). Whatever happened to the jock, the brain, and the princess? Young adult pathways linked to adolescent activity involvement and social identity. *Journal of Adolescent Research, 16,* 429–455.

Barger, S. D., & Gallo, L. C. (2008). Ability of ethnic self-identification to partition modifiable health risk among US residents of Mexican ancestry. *American Journal of Public Health, 98,* 1971–1978.

Bogenschneider, K. (1996). An ecological risk protective theory for building prevention programs, policies, and community capacity to support youth. *Family Relations, 45,* 127–138.

Botvin, G. J., Dusenbury, L., Baker, E., James-Ortiz, S., Botvin, E. M., & Kerner, J. (1992). Smoking prevention among urban minority youth: Assessing effects on outcome and mediating variables. *Health Psychology, 11,* 290–299.

Castro, F. G., Barrera, M., Jr., & Martinez, C. R., Jr. (2004). The cultural adaptation of prevention interventions: Resolving tensions between fidelity and fit. *Prevention Science, 5,* 41–45.

Choi, H. J., & Smith, R. (in press). Members, isolates, and liaisons: Meta-analysis of adolescents' network positions and their smoking behavior. *Substance Use & Misuse.*

Colby, M., Hecht, M. L., Miller-Day, M., Krieger, J. R., Syverstsen, A. K., Graham, J. W., & Pettigrew, J. (2013). Adapting school-based substance use prevention curriculum through cultural grounding: An exemplar of adaptation processes for rural schools. *American Journal of Community Psychology, 51,* 190–205. doi:10.1007/s10464-012-9524-8

Cole, S., Kemeny, M. E., Taylor, S. E., Visscher, B. R., & Fahey, J. L. (1997). Social identity and physical health: Accelerated HIV progression in rejection-sensitive gay men. *American Journal of Public Health, 87,* 1434–1439.

Collins, W. A., & Steinberg, L. (2007). Adolescent development in interpersonal context. *Handbook of Child Psychology.* Wiley Online Library.

Dettling, M., Heinz, A., Dufeu, P., Rommelspacher, H., Gräf, K-J., & Schmidt, L. G. (1995). Dopaminergic responsivity in alcoholism: Trait, state, or residual marker? *American Journal of Psychiatry, 152,* 1317–1321

Elek, E., Miller-Day, M., & Hecht, M. L. (2006). Influences of personal, injunctive, and descriptive norms on early adolescent substance use. *Journal of Drug Issues, 36,* 147–171.

Ert, E., Yechiam, E., & Arshavsky, O. (2013). Smokers' decision making: More than mere risk taking. *PLoS ONE, 8,* e68064.

Griner, D., & Smith, T. B. (2006). Culturally adapted mental health intervention: A meta-analytic review. *Psychotherapy: Theory, Research, Practice, Training, 43,* 531–548. doi:10.1037/0033-3204.43.4.531

Griner, D., & Smith, T. B. (2006). Culturally adapted mental health interventions: A meta-analytic review. *Psychotherapy: Theory, Research, Practice, Training, 43*, 531–548.

Guthrie, B. J., & Low, L. K. (2000). A substance use prevention framework: Considering the social context for African American girls? *Public Health Nursing, 17*, 363–373. doi:10.1046/j.1525-1446.2000.00363.x

Harwood, J., Giles, H., Fox, S., Ryan, E. B., & Williams, A. (1993). Patronizing young and elderly adults: Response strategies in a community setting. *Journal of Applied Communication Research, 21*, 211–226.

Hecht, M., & Choi, H. J. (2012). The Communication Theory of Identity as a framework for health message design. In H. Cho & M. Byrnie. (Eds.), *Health communication message design: Theory, research, and practice* (pp. 137–152). Thousand Oaks, CA: Sage.

Hecht, M. L., Graham, J. W., & Elek, E. (2006). The Drug Resistance Strategies Intervention: Program effects on substance use. *Health Communication, 20*, 267–276.

Hecht, M. L., Jackson, R. L., & Ribeau, S. (2003). *African American communication: Exploring identity and culture.* Mahwah, NJ: Erlbaum.

Hecht, M. L., & Krieger, J. K. (2006). The principle of cultural grounding in school-based substance use prevention: The Drug Resistance Strategies Project. *Journal of Language and Social Psychology, 25*, 301–319.

Hecht, M. L., & Lee, J. K. (2008). Branding through cultural grounding: The *keepin' it REAL* curriculum. In W. D. Evans & G. Hastings (Eds.), *Public health branding: Applying marketing for social change* (pp. 161–179). Oxford, England: Oxford University Press.

Hecht, M. L., & Lee, J. K. (in press). Brand alliance of D.A.R.E. and *keepin' it REAL*: A case study in brand dissemination practices. In W.D. Evans (Ed.), *Psychology of branding*. Hauppauge, NY: Nova Science.

Hecht, M. L., Marsiglia, F. F., Elek-Fisk, E., Wagstaff, D. A, Kulis, S., Dustman, P., & Miller-Day, M. (2003). Culturally grounded substance use prevention: An evaluation of *the keepin' it R.E.A.L.* curriculum. *Prevention Science, 4*, 233–248.

Hecht, M. L., & Miller-Day, M. (2009). The Drug Resistance Strategies Project: Using narrative theory to enhance adolescents' communication competence. In L. Frey & K. Cissna (Eds.), *Routledge handbook of applied communication* (pp. 535–557). New York, NY: Routledge.

Hecht, M. L., & Ribeau, S. (1987). Afro-American identity labels and communicative effectiveness. *Journal of Language and Social Psychology, 6*, 319–326.

Hecht, M. L., Ribeau, S., & Sedano, M. V. (1990). A Mexican-American perspective on interethnic communication. *International Journal of Intercultural Relations, 14*, 31–55.

Hornik, R., Jacobsohn, L., Orwin, R., Piesse, A., & Kalton, G. (2008). Effects of the National Youth Anti-Drug Media Campaign on youths. *American Journal of Public Health, 98*, 2229–2236.

Jack, D. C. (1991). *Silencing the self: Women and depression.* Cambridge, MA: Harvard University Press.

Jackson, R. L. (2002). Cultural contracts theory: Toward an understanding of identity negotiation. *Communication Quarterly, 50*, 359–367.

Jessor, R., Donovan, J. E., & Costa, F. M. (1991). *Beyond adolescence: Problem behavior and young adult development.* New York, NY: Cambridge University Press.

Johnston, L. D., O'Malley, P. M., Bachman, J. G., & Schulenberg, J. E. (2013). *Monitoring the future national results on drug use: 2012 Overview, key findings on adolescent drug use.* Ann Arbor: Institute for Social Research, the University of Michigan.

Jung, E., & Hecht, M. L. (2008). Identity gaps and level of depression among Korean American immigrants. *Health Communication, 23*, 313–325.

Khantzian, E. J. (1997). The self-medication hypothesis of substance use disorders: A reconsideration and recent applications. *Harvard Review of Psychiatry, 4,* 231–244. doi:10.3109/10673229709030550

Korzenny, F., McClure, J., & Rzyttki, B. (1990). Ethnicity, communication, and drugs. *Journal of Drug Issues, 20,* 87–98.

Kosterman, R., Hawkins, J. D., Guo, J., Catalano, R. F., & Abbott, R. D. (2000). The dynamics of alcohol and marijuana initiation: Patterns and predictors of first use in adolescence. *American Journal of Public Health, 90,* 360–366.

Kreuter, M. W., Lukwago, S. N., Bucholtz, D. C., Clark, E. M., & Sanders-Thompson, V. (2003). Achieving cultural appropriateness in health promotion programs: Targeted and tailored approaches. *Heath Education and Behavior, 30,* 133.

Kumpfer, K. L., Alvarado, R., Smith, P., & Bellamy, N. (2002). Cultural sensitivity in universal family-based prevention interventions. *Prevention Science, 3,* 241–244.

Larkey, L. K., & Hecht, M. L. (2010) A model of effects of narrative as culture-centric health promotion. *Journal of Health Communication, 15,* 114–135.

Lee, J. K., & Hecht, M. L. (2011). Examining protective effects of brand equity in the *keepin' it REAL* substance use prevention curriculum. *Health Communication, 26,* 1–10. NIHMS291746

Lee, J. K., Hecht, M. L., Miller-Day, M. A., & Elek, E. (2011). Evaluating mediated perception of narrative health messages: The perception of narrative performance scale. *Communication Methods and Measures, 5,* 126–145. NIHMS291724

Link, B. G., Northridge, M. E., Phelan, J. C., & Ganz, M. L. (1998). Social epidemiology and fundamental cause concept. *The Milbank Quarterly, 76,* 375–402.

Logan, J. R., Ward, R., & Spitze, G. (1992). As old as you feel: Age identity in middle and later life. *Social Forces, 71,* 451–467.

Marks, G., Graham, J. W., & Hansen, W. B. (1992). Social projection and social conformity in adolescent alcohol use: A longitudinal analysis. *Personality and Social Psychology Bulletin, 18,* 96–101.

Markus, H. R., & Nurius, P. (1986). Possible selves. *American Psychologist, 41,* 954–969.

Marsiglia, F. F., Kulis, S., & Hecht, M. L. (2001). Ethnic labels and ethnic identity as predictors of drug use among middle school students in the Southwest. *The Journal of Research on Adolescence, 11,* 21–48.

Matsunaga, M., Hecht, M. L., Elek, E., & Ndiaye, K. (2010). Ethnic identity development and acculturation: A longitudinal analysis of Mexican-Heritage youth in the southwest United States. *Journal of Cross-Cultural Psychology, 41,* 410–427. NIHMS200062

Miller, M. A., Alberts, J. K., Hecht, M. L., Krizek, R. L., & Trost, M. (2000). *Adolescent relationships and drug abuse.* Hillsdale, NJ: Erlbaum.

Miller-Day, M., & Hecht, M. L. (2013). Narrative means to preventative ends: A narrative engagement approach to adolescent substance use prevention. *Health Communication. 28,* 657–670.

Miller-Rassulo, M., & Hecht, M. L. (1988). Performance as persuasion: Trigger scripting as a tool for education and persuasion. *Literature in Performance, 8,* 40–55.

Minkler, M., & Wallerstein, N. (2008). *Community-based participatory research for health from process to outcomes.* Hoboken, NJ: John Wiley & Sons.

Narváez, R. F., Meyer, I. H., Kertzner, R. M., Ouellette, S., & Gordon, A. R. (2009). A qualitative approach to the intersection of sexual, ethnic, and gender identities. *Identity: An International Journal of Theory and Research, 9,* 63–86.

Newcomb, M. D., & Bentler, P. M. (1988). Impact of adolescent drug use and social support on problems of young adults: A longitudinal study. *Journal of Abnormal Psychology, 97,* 64–75. doi:10.1037/0021-843X.97.1.64

Oyserman, D., Brickman, D., & Rhodes, M. (2007). School success, possible selves and parent school-involvement. *Family Relations, 56,* 479–489.

Oyserman, D., Bybee, D., & Terry, K. (2006). Possible selves and academic outcomes: How and when possible selves impel action. *Journal of Personality and Social Psychology, 91,* 188–204.

Oyserman, D., & Destin, M. (2010). Identity-based motivation: Implications for intervention. *The Counseling Psychologist, 38,* 1001–1043.

Oyserman, D., & Fryberg, S. A. (2006). The possible selves of diverse adolescents: Content and function across gender, race and national origin. In J. Kerpelman & C. Dunkel (Eds.), *Possible selves: Theory, research, and applications* (pp. 17–39). Huntington, NY: Nova.

Oyserman, D., & Saltz, E. (1993). Competence, delinquency, and attempts to attain possible selves. *Journal of Personality and Social Psychology, 65,* 360–374.

Oyserman, D., Terry, K., & Bybee, D. (2002). A possible selves intervention to enhance school involvement. *Journal of Adolescence, 25,* 313–326.

Perry, D. G., & Pauletti, R. E. (2011). Gender and adolescent development. *Journal of Research on Adolescence, 21,* 61–74.

Pettigrew, J., Miller-Day, M., Krieger, J., & Hecht, M. (2012). The rural context of illicit substance offers: A study of Appalachian rural adolescents. *Journal of Adolescent Research, 27,* 523–550. doi:10.1177/0743558411432639

Pettigrew, J., Miller-Day, M., Shin, Y., Hecht, M. L., Krieger, J. L., & Graham, J. W. (2013). Describing teacher-student interactions: A qualitative assessment of teacher implementation of the 7th grade *keepin' it REAL* substance use intervention. *American Journal of Community Psychology, 51,* 43–56. doi:10.1007/s10464-012-9539-1

Resnicow, K., Baronowski, T., Ahluwalia, J. S., & Braithwaite, R. L. (1999). Cultural sensitivity in public health: Defined and demystified. *Ethnicity and Disease, 9,* 10–21.

Sargent, J. D., Wills, T. A., Stoolmiller, M., Gibson, J., & Gibbons, F. X. (2005). Alcohol use in motion pictures and its relation with early-onset teen drinking. *Journal of Studies on Alcohol and Drugs, 67,* 54–65.

Schwartz, S. J. (2001). The evolution of Eriksonian and, neo-Eriksonian identity theory and research: A review and integration. *Identity: An International Journal of Theory and Research, 1,* 7–58.

Spanagel, R., & Weiss, F. (1999). The dopamine hypothesis of reward: Past and current status. *Trends in neuroscience, 22,* 521–527.

Steinberg, L. (2005). Cognitive and affective development in adolescence. *TRENDS in Cognitive Sciences, 9,* 69–74.

Suárez-Orozco, C., & Suárez-Orozco, M. 1995. *Transformations: Immigration, family life, and achievement motivation among Latino adolescents.* Palo Alto, CA: Stanford University Press.

Whitbourne, S. K., & Tesch, S. A. (1985). A comparison of identity and intimacy statuses in college students and alumni. *Developmental Psychology, 21,* 1039–1044.

Wild, L. G., Flisher, A. J., Bhana, A., & Lombard, C. (2004). Associations among adolescent risk behaviors and self-esteem in six domains. *Journal of Child Psychology and Psychiatry, 45,* 1454–1467.

Wilson, D. B., Bouffard, L. A., & MacKenzie, D. L. (2005). A quantitative review of structured, group-oriented, cognitive-behavioral programs for offenders. *Criminal Justice and Behavior, 32*(2), 172–204.

CHAPTER TEN

Adolescent Online Friendship and Peer Relationships

KEVIN B. WRIGHT AND SHAWN KING

New communication technologies, such as the Internet, smartphones, tablets as well as a variety of social media platforms, including Facebook, Twitter, You-Tube, and text messaging, have increased in popularity among adolescents in the United States in recent years (Pierce, 2009; Valkenburg & Peter, 2011). For example, over 65% of adolescents in 2009 had at least one social network site profile compared to only 35% of online adults (Jones & Fox, 2009). Not only are young people the early adopters of most new technologies, they are also among the more sophisticated users of it as well. While during the 1990s adolescents tended to use the Internet more for entertainment, since 2005 they have increasingly been using it primarily for interpersonal relationships (Pierce, 2009; Valkenburg & Peter, 2007, 2011). Moreover, the proliferation of the wireless Internet and social media platforms has given adolescents new ways to talk with their friends or make new friends.

This has led to a relatively large amount of research on adolescent social media use and relational development/maintenance over the past decade by communication scholars and other social scientists (boyd, 2007; Davis, 2010; Lenhart, Madden, Macgill, & Smith, 2007; Valkenburg & Peter, 2007, 2011). These studies indicate that these technological innovations have impacted friendship-peer relationships among adolescents in a multitude of ways. For example, new communication technologies are often associated with a number of positive aspects for adolescents. These include online contexts for the development and maintenance of friendship and peer relationships, including those that begin in face-to-face contexts, connections between peers who share mutual interests and concerns, a platform for obtaining peer social support online, and numerous opportunities for social learning and connections to a wider social network than is typically possible in the face-to-face world (Dwyer, 2007; Ellison, Steinfield, & Lampe, 2007; Lee, 2009; Subrahmanyam & Greenfield, 2008; Valkenburg & Peter, 2011).

From a developmental perspective, adolescents use online interactions to establish their identity and self-esteem with friends and members of their larger peer social network (Lee, 2009; Valkenburg & Peter, 2011). Establishing meaningful social relationships and fitting in with a group of peers are basic stages for the healthy development of the adolescent (Harter, 2003). Success in facing these developmental tasks can induce satisfaction with the control one is able to exercise over his/her own life, while failure can lead to poor adjustment. New communication technologies appear to help adolescents develop and practice advanced social skills within their peer groups (Subrahmanyam & Lin, 2007; Valkenburg & Peter, 2011). Yet, researchers have also found that new technologies can facilitate darker sides of interpersonal communication behavior among adolescents, including cyberbullying (Agatson, Kowalski, & Limbert, 2007; Beran & Li, 2007; Schrock & boyd, 2011), which may negatively affect adolescents in a variety of ways.

In addition, researchers have found that the type and quality of interpersonal interactions among adolescents that take place via social media are linked to a number of important positive and negative psychological outcomes that may impact developmental processes (Mitchell, Ybarra, & Finkelhor, 2007; Valkenburg & Peter, 2007, 2011; Valkenburg, Peter, & Schouten, 2006; Ybarra, 2004). For example, positive online interactions with friends and peers (including social support) tend to be linked to reduced stress and increased psychological well-being while negative interactions (such as cyberbullying and online harassment) can lead to increased stress, difficulty adjusting to social situations, loneliness, depression, and other negative outcomes (such as substance abuse, poor grades, etc.).

The purpose of this chapter is to present the current state of research regarding adolescent friendship-peer relationships and new communication technology usage. Specifically, it focuses on adolescent social media use and its impact on the development and maintenance of friendship-peer relationships. In addition, it focuses on research dealing with positive aspects of computer-mediated adolescent friendship-peer relationships (e.g., online social support) and psychological outcomes, as well as more negative aspects of adolescent technology usage (e.g., cyberbullying) and related outcomes. The chapter draws upon relevant theories and research from communication and developmental psychology. In addition, it discusses current limitations to theory and research in this area as well as fruitful directions for future scholarship.

NEW TECHNOLOGIES, FRIENDSHIP-PEER RELATIONSHIPS, AND ADOLESCENTS

Adolescents make up one of the largest age cohorts who regularly use social media (boyd, 2007; Jones & Fox, 2009; Valkenburg & Peter, 2011). What distinguishes social media sites (e.g., Facebook) from other forms of virtual communities is that they allow users to articulate and make visible their social connections. In this way our connections potentially become the connections of our "friends." boyd and Ellison (2007) suggest that "friending" behaviors through social network sites can result in more and different types of connections between individuals that would not otherwise be made. The appeal of interactions with friends and peers among adolescents using social networking sites appears to be based on the speed, convenience, inexpensive nature, and user-friendly features they offer (boyd, 2007). Moreover, other features, such as the ability to communicate with friends and peers without their conversations being overheard by parents or siblings and the ability for socially unskilled or shy individuals to better manage impressions of themselves in the messages they construct, have also been linked to the popularity of social networking sites among adolescents (Blais, Craig, Pepler, & Connolly, 2008; Parks & Archey-Ladas, 2003).

Characteristics of Online Communication

While early studies of computer-mediated communication tended to portray online relationships as being inferior to face-to-face interactions (Kiesler, Siegel, & McGuire, 1984; Sproull & Kiesler, 1986), computer-mediated communication scholars have documented that, on the contrary, online communication can be *hyperpersonal,* or even more friendly, social, and intimate than face-to-face communication (Walther, 1996, 2007; Walther & Parks, 2002). This is due to the reduction of social cues and disconfirming nonverbal cues that often lead to the development of negative perceptions of relational partners in the face-to-face world. Message senders portray themselves in a socially favorable manner to draw the attention of message receivers and foster anticipation of future interaction. Message receivers, in turn, tend to idealize the image of the sender due to overvaluing minimal, text-based cues. Idealized perceptions and optimal self-presentation in the computer-mediated communication process tend to intensify in the feedback loop during online interactions.

Moreover, the asynchronous nature of computer-mediated communication when using social media appears to enhance identity construction, self-presentation, and relationship formation for many individuals (Jones, Millermaier, Goya-Martinez, & Schuler, 2008; Madell & Muncer, 2007). For example, according to Valkenburg and

Peter (2008), asynchronicity can stimulate the controllability of self-presentation and self-disclosure skills among adolescents. In other words, the asynchronous nature of computer-mediated communication allows individuals more time to compose messages about the self before sending them to their larger social network. This may reduce apprehension in terms of communicating ideas with others as well as allowing increased time to develop more competently written messages (Walther, 2007; Wright, 2000). The enhanced controllability of message construction in online communication can create a sense of security in adolescents, which allows them to feel freer in their interpersonal interactions on the Internet than in face-to-face situations (Valkenburg & Peter, 2011). Both self-presentation and self-disclosure need to be learned, practiced, and rehearsed in adolescence, and they both are vital for the development of identity, intimacy, and sexuality (Schlenker, 1986).

The relative anonymity (or at least the ability to remain partially anonymous) of communicating with peers when using various forms of computer-mediated communication (e.g., chat rooms, message boards, tweets) may lead adolescents to have less concern about their physical appearance, which may increase their online self-disclosure, and, as a result, their opportunities for approval and social acceptance (Valkenburg et al., 2006). However, online anonymity may also stimulate impulsive reactions, which may result in increased "flaming" (e.g., disinhibited, aggressive, and insulting comments), as well as in cyberbullying and online harassment of peers (Valkenburg et al., 2006; Walther, 1996). Furthermore, while physical constraints such as the body, biological sex, race, or age can have a profound effect on self-definition and self-presentation in the face-to-face world, many of these attributes become flexible in online environments. In a virtual world, adolescents have the ability to construct their online identities in ways that would not be possible in the face-to-face world. The anonymity afforded to youth within virtual worlds allows adolescents more flexibility in exploring their identity through their language (Calvert, 2002; Huffaker & Calvert, 2006; Subrahmanyam, Smahel, & Greenfield, 2006).

These characteristics of computer-mediated communication may facilitate the development and maintenance of friendships and peer relationships in unique ways or lead to increased antisocial communication depending upon the context of the interaction (Walther, 2007). For example, social media provide adolescents with opportunities to control the richness of the cues they wish to convey to other members of their online social network, such as deciding whether to present only text-based information or whether they enrich this information with photographs or audio/visual information. Individuals appear to be selective in the types of information they present to others when using social media, reserving richer aspects of media social (video/voice) for more intimate friends and relying on leaner media (text, tweets) to communicate with less intimate online network members, although this may vary depending upon the context (Walther, 2007). However, leaner forms of online communication can have a depersonalizing, low social presence, which may lead an adolescent to become less inhibited, which may lead him or her to feel more comfortable engaging in negative behaviors such as cyber-bullying or harassment of a peer.

Facebook appears to be the most popular social media platform for maintaining and developing new friendship relationships among adolescents (boyd & Ellison, 2007; Jones & Fox, 2009). Since its creation in 2004, Facebook reached 100 million active users in August 2008 and surpassed 200 million active users by April 2009 (Facebook, 2012). Part of its popularity can be linked to how Facebook (and similar social media sites) appears to facilitate relational initiation and development, relational maintenance, and relational reconnection (Acquisti & Gross, 2006; Ellison et al., 2007; Lampe, Ellison, & Steinfield, 2007), all of which may extend the size of and quality of one's social support network (Walther & Boyd, 2002; Wright & Bell, 2003; Ye, 2006). Social media also appear to enhance or extend face-to-face support networks in terms of providing greater access to the increased social capital available in a larger, easier to maintain network of individuals who are often geographically separated (Lampe et al., 2007; Ye, 2006).

Importance of Friendship for Adolescents

Feeling connected with peers is especially important to adolescents (Hellenga, 2002). Adolescents maintain a higher number of friends than do adults and interact with friends more than do adults (Berndt, Hawkins, & Hoyle, 1986), and belonging to desirable peer groups appears to be extremely important, particularly those that have a high status (e.g., popular students). The quantity of peer interactions and the intimacy in friendships rise dramatically during adolescence. Furthermore, the peer relationship development patterns established in early adolescence become critical in early adulthood as peers become primary sources of support. Several long-term, longitudinal studies find that characteristics of peer interactions in childhood and early adolescence are repeated in young adult relationships with romantic partners (see Berndt et al., 1986). Interaction with peers provides vital information for an adolescent to make social comparisons to similar others and to receive verification for his or her own feelings, thoughts, and actions, which is crucial to self-identity formation (Eccles & Bryan, 1994; Harter, 1999). With one-to-many communication, an adolescent's connectedness to a group creates a feeling of group belonging, which is very important to one's social identity formation (Harter, 1999, 2003). Yet, despite the ease and convenience of social media to connect adolescents to friends and peers more frequently, increased accessibility to friends online may not predict relational closeness (Johnson & Becker, 2011).

Research on adolescents has also found that feeling close and connected to others on a daily basis is associated with higher daily well-being, and in particular, feeling understood and appreciated and sharing pleasant interactions are especially strong predictors of well-being (Valkenburg et al., 2006). The expectations and meanings of friendships remain constant throughout adolescence and adulthood. In other words, close and meaningful interactions with peers tend to be at least as important to adolescent well-being as they are to adult well-being. Indeed, research affirms that close peer relationships contribute positively to adolescent self-esteem and well-being, whereas peer relationship problems such as peer rejection and a lack of close friends are among the strongest predictors of depression and negative self-views (see Hartup, 1996).

Yet, despite adolescents' extensive use of the Internet to maintain friendships, research has not sufficiently examined how online communication affects adolescents' closeness to their existing friends. This lack of research is remarkable because forming and maintaining close friendships in adolescence are imperative to healthy cognitive, emotional, and social development (Valkenburg & Peter, 2007). Moreover, most of the theoretical explanations of online friendship (including adolescent friendship) have drawn upon traditional relationship frameworks that were developed to explain friendship in the face-to-face world. Developing theories that take into account the effects of the online environment (as well as features of a specific online platform) may help scholars to better understand adolescent friendship in this context.

Adolescents and Online Romantic Relationships

While the focus of this chapter is on friendship and peer relationships, it is also important to consider how adolescents are using new media to communicate with romantic partners, especially since romantic relationships often develop through interactions with others in larger friendship circles within social network sites like Facebook. Finding a romantic partner and establishing a romantic relationship are important adolescent developmental tasks. Related to these tasks are adolescents' developing sexuality and their construction of their sexual identity. Adolescents appear to use social media to reinforce existing romantic relationships, just as they do friendships. Research suggests that online romantic relationships are highly prevalent among adolescents (Subrahmanyam & Greenfield, 2008; Subrahmanyan et al., 2006). Facebook serves as a context for "checking out" potential romantic partners as well as a forum for initial interactions between individuals who are sexually attracted to each other. Social media sites appear to allow teenagers to conveniently search the profiles of numerous potential dating partners anonymously (a practice that is not really possible in the face-to-face world).

In addition, the convergence of adolescent social networks within sites like Facebook allows teenagers to observe the online profiles of "friends of friends." In addition, mobile Facebook applications allow adolescents to engage in conversations with romantic partners without parents or siblings finding out, and this may help shy teenagers or those who might be embarrassed revealing that they are engaged in a romantic relationship to their family or peers. Online forums may also provide sexual minority adolescents with a safe haven for sexual exploration without the prejudice and harassment that gay, lesbian, and bisexual adolescents sometimes face at the hands of peers and adults.

Adolescent Friendship-Peer Relationships and Online Social Support

Social support is an umbrella term for a variety of communication behaviors that "link involvement with social relationships to health and well-being" (Goldsmith & Albrecht, 2011, p. 335). Social support involves the provision of resources such as information, tangible assistance, validation, and emotional comforting (Albrecht & Goldsmith, 2003). Social support is an important component of friendship throughout the lifespan, and it has been found to be essential to adjustment to stressful life situations and psychological well-being (Nussbaum, 1994). Nussbaum (1994) also contends that friends are particularly well suited for giving and receiving social support because they are voluntary, they are less likely to have as stringent role obligations as they do in relationships with parents or siblings, and support from friends and other peers tends to be evaluated positively compared to support in family relationships (Pecchioni, Wright, & Nussbaum, 2005).

In addition, adolescents often feel more comfortable self-disclosing sensitive topics to peers as opposed to family members, and so peers may serve an important supportive function for adolescents who perceive that their parents might not understand or have negative reactions to problems they may be facing (e.g., issues with romantic partners, drug use). Although the size of an adolescent's friendship support network may vary, researchers have found that the perception of receiving support tends to be more important than the actual support a person may or may not receive (Cutrona, Suhr, & MacFarlane, 1990; Goldsmith, 2004). Despite a long-standing interest in social support among social sciences, relatively few studies have examined social support behaviors across the lifespan or social support among adolescents specifically.

Internet use may increase social interaction, the size of social networks, and closeness with others as a means of maintaining social ties and creating new ones, and it often connects people to a wider social network by overcoming the barriers of time and place (Walther, 2007; Walther & Boyd, 2002; Walther & Parks, 2002). For example, Valkenburg and Peter (2007) found that online communication among adolescents enhanced the quality of friendships directly and indirectly through increased time with friends (even when online interaction supplemented face-to-face interaction). This extended network of friends and peer relationships has the potential to provide adolescents with a larger social support network (Desjarlais & Willoughby, 2010; Haythornthwaite, 2002; McKenna & Bargh, 2000; Valkenburg &

Peter, 2007; Walther & Boyd, 2002). However, the meaning of "friend" connections within social network sites may differ from traditional conceptualizations of "friendship" offline. According to boyd (2006), social network site "friendship" can mean a variety of different relationships to individuals, such as actual close friend, lover, acquaintance, schoolmate, family member, public figure, or anyone else whose network you want to access.

Yet, some scholars contend that even acquaintances within an adolescents' online social network can lead to increases in informational support (Bryant, Sanders-Jackson, & Smallwood, 2006; Valkenburg & Peter, 2011). For example, weak ties are typically acquaintances, as opposed to strong ties that might be close friends or family members. People who have more weak ties as part of their social network are likely to have access to greater amounts of information, because the weak ties will bring in novel information (whereas their strong ties are likely to have duplicate information (Grannovetter, 1973). According to Bryant et al. (2006), although many online relationships are generally less intimate than offline relationships, they can provide adolescents with increased information and may enlarge their perspective on the world around them. For example, the interpersonal connections with weaker ties made possible by social media may be particularly valuable for youths suffering from illnesses, such as HIV, eating disorders, and self-injurious behavior, about which they may not feel comfortable talking with their friends in person. In fact, adolescents have been found to prefer online communication over face-to-face communication to talk about intimate topics, such as love, sex, and things they are ashamed about (Schouten, Valkenburg, & Peter, 2007).

However, these interactions could potentially lead to both positive and negative experiences, which may moderate the perceptions of supportive information. For example, several researchers (e.g., Kraut et al., 1998; Locke, 1998; Morgan & Cotten, 2003) believe that online communication hinders adolescents' well-being because it displaces valuable time that could be spent with existing friends in the face-to-face world. Adherents of this displacement hypothesis assume that the Internet motivates adolescents to form online contacts with strangers rather than to maintain friendships with their offline peers. Because online contacts are seen as superficial weak-tie relationships that lack feelings of affection and commitment, the Internet is believed to reduce the quality of adolescents' existing friendships and, thereby, their well-being.

Social support has been linked in numerous studies to important outcomes for individuals, including reduced psychological and physical stress, increased coping, psychological and emotional well-being, improved quality of life, improved immune system response, and reduced morbidity for stress-related illnesses (Aneshensel & Stone, 1982; Berkman & Syme, 1979; Billings & Moos, 1984). A number of researchers have argued that online social networks have the potential to foster increased social support and social capital, particularly among people who use it for interpersonal and community-building purposes (Drentea & Moren-Cross, 2005; Haythornthwaite & Wellman, 2002; Szreter, 2000). Social capital can be defined as "resources embedded in a social structure that are accessed and/or mobilized in purposive actions" (Lin, 2001, p. 29). Social capital is facilitated by strong interpersonal ties, reciprocity norms, interpersonal trust, and shared values. Putnam (2000) posits that there are abilities, resources, and values embedded in social networks and relationships that can potentially create emotional, informational, and instrumental benefits, but that the realization of these benefits may depend upon the types of individuals with whom a person interacts on a regular basis and how well he or she can capitalize on these resources.

In terms of adolescent friendships, online communication with friends may contribute to important health outcomes faced by this population, such as depression. According to Aseltine, Gore, and Colten (1994), friendships take on increased importance for late adolescents with family problems, as adolescents seek greater social distance from family members by "turning to peer relationships as their primary sphere of social participation and emotional investment" (p. 253). These researchers found that social support from friends significantly predicted lower levels of depression (in both asymptomatic and chronic depression cases), whereas support from family members was not related to depression scores.

However, the relationship between online social support and depression can be difficult to interpret depending upon a host of factors. According to Cai (2004), time invested online may detract individuals from investing in face-to-face relationships by reducing contact, network size, density, or quality of interaction. Several early computer-mediated communication studies reported slight but significant increases in loneliness and depression over time (Kraut et al., 1998) and decreases in social and familial involvement (Kraut et al., 1998; Nie & Erbring, 2000) with increasing Internet use. Later studies (see McKenna, Green, & Gleason, 2002) revealed that Internet use and depression were related in more complex ways. These studies found that depression is mediated by appraisals of social support offered by online network members. Although face-to-face support network mobilization often decreases with increased online use, heavy Internet users often turn to computer-mediated support to compensate for more traditional face-to-face supportive interactions (Ellison et al., 2007; McKenna et al., 2002; Xie, 2008).

In short, the benefits of online social support are likely dependent upon the frequency and degree to which adolescents use new communication technologies for obtaining social support. This is consistent with the uses-and-gratifications perspective (Courtois, Merchant, De Marez, & Verleye, 2009; Ebersole, 2006), which posits that individuals use media to fulfill a variety of needs and motives. For example, among adolescents who have strong needs to be connected with their friends, social interaction will be one of the most primary motives for online communication. These interactions may include supportive behaviors, such as emotional support and informational support. However, for other adolescents, their primary motive for using new media may be entertainment (e.g., games or browsing websites) as opposed to social interaction and peer friendship development.

In addition to needs and motives for using new media, personality traits appear to impact the degree and quality of online interaction for adolescents. For example, Kraut et al. (2002) found that Internet use was associated with better outcomes for extroverts and worse outcomes for introverts. For extroverts, using the Internet was related to increases in well-being and self-esteem, as well as decreases in loneliness. In contrast, introverts showed declines in well-being associated with these same variables. Gross, Juvonen, and Gable (2002) found that extroverted adolescents who had strong connections to school-based peers reported that they used the Internet to seek out additional opportunities to interact with them, while teens who were socially anxious were more likely to attempt interactions with strangers online than to interact with peers. Similarly, Valkenburg and Peter (2005) found that online communication contributes to the solidarity of peer group networks for sociable adolescents, but not necessarily for socially anxious teens. Lee (2009) found that extroverted adolescents who already had strong social relationships at an earlier age were more likely to use online communication, which in turn predicted more cohesive friendships, and furthermore better connectedness to school. However, even for shy adolescents, the Internet may contribute to positive well-being for introverted individuals with low social resources who are willing to use online platforms to meet others (Bessiere, Kiesler, Kraut, & Boneva, 2008).

Research on Facebook usage in particular reveals that adolescents can obtain various types of social support (e.g., information, emotional support, connection) through the maintenance of relationships with others on Facebook (Ellison et al., 2007). Facebook also helps adolescents maintain connections with peers outside of their school, as well as friends who are geographically dispersed. Specific to Facebook, researchers have looked at the relationship between the size of one's social network and perceived social support (Kim & Lee, 2011; Manago, Taylor, & Greenfield, 2012). In one study, participants who reported larger networks and larger audiences for status updates predicted social support (Manago et al., 2012). However, the size of the social network can reach an optimal number of Facebook friends (Tong, Van Der Heide, Langwell, & Walther, 2008). Kim and Lee (2011) found that the number of Facebook friends is positively associated with perceived social support only up to a point and suggest that it is the point at which one cannot dedicate sufficient time and effort to maintain so many connections. Ballantine and Stephenson (2011) described active social support as participants interacting with others in the social network through posting on a "wall" or commenting on someone's message. Conversely, individuals can receive support passively as well simply by reading posts that provide helpful information or a sense of connection.

NEGATIVE ASPECTS OF ONLINE ADOLESCENT PEER INTERACTIONS: THE RISE OF CYBERBULLYING ADOLESCENCE AND AGGRESSION

Prior to discussing the phenomenon of cyberbullying, it is helpful to examine more general conceptions of aggression among adolescents. For example, researchers have found that aggressive behavior with peers can lead to social rejection (Carlson, Lahey, Frame, Walker, & Hynd, 1987; Dodge, 1983; Patterson, 1982) and symptoms of depression among adolescents (Hodgens & McCoy, 1989; Kovacs, Paulauskas, Gatsonis, & Richards, 1988). Mayeux and Cillessen (2008) argued that during adolescence individuals engage in relationally aggressive behaviors as a way to maintain popularity and/or gain social status (Sijtsema, Veenstra, Lindenberg, & Salmivalli, 2009). Based on the results of a relatively large number of longitudinal studies, researchers have concluded that one of the strongest predictors of adolescent aggression is childhood aggression (Coie & Dodge, 1988; Lindemann, Harakka, & Keltikangas-Jarvinen, 1997; Reiss & Roth, 1993).

Cyberbullying. In recent years, the advent of new communication technologies and the growth of social media use among adolescents have led to the phenomenon of cyberbullying (Roberto & Eden, 2010; Schrock & boyd, 2011). Cyberbullying can be defined as intentional aggression toward another person online (Roberto & Eden, 2010; Ybarra & Mitchell, 2004) or repeated aggression toward others through the use of computers, cell phones, or other electronic devices (Hinduja & Patchin, 2008). Similar to offline bullying, cyberbullying involves intentional repetitive actions and psychological violence (Valkenburg & Peter, 2011). However, research suggests that victims of cyberbullying typically have negative interactions (i.e., additional bullying) with those who harass them in face-to-face contexts as well (Schrock & boyd, 2011). These acts also typically lead to the person who is being targeted by the bully to feel threatened, embarrassed, or humiliated (Schrock & boyd, 2011), particularly when the bullying occurs in a public computer-mediated forum, such as Facebook or a chat room. In these cases, victims of cyberbullying may experience the added embarrassment of having a larger number of their peers witness or join the harassment than would typically be possible in face-to-face contexts. Moreover, social media allow cyberbullies to harass their victims from a distance and outside the temporal limitations of face-to-face contexts, such as school or after school activities (Ybarra, Diener-West, & Leaf, 2007). Cyberbullying appears to be a very common behavior among adolescents, with reports of up to 46% of adolescents reporting being cyberbullied (Agatston et al., 2007; McQuade & Sampat, 2008). Cyberbullying can be undertaken by an individual or a group (Roberto & Eden, 2010).

Adolescents who are cyberbullied report serious psychological and emotional distress and may experience increased social isolation and loneliness (Patchin &

Hinduja, 2006). In addition, youth who are cyberbullied are at greater risk for a variety of negative outcomes, including drug and alcohol abuse, depressive symptomology, poor academic performance, a higher likelihood of assaulting others or damaging property, and suicidal thoughts (Hinduja & Patchin, 2008; Mitchell & Ybarra, 2007). In addition, similar to face-to-face bullying, victims of cyberbullies may experience low self-esteem, bulimic symptoms in women (Werner & Crick, 1999), and impaired emotional development (Roberto & Eden, 2010).

FUTURE RESEARCH DIRECTIONS IN ADOLESCENT ONLINE RELATIONSHIPS

While online friendship-peer relationships appear to offer a variety of benefits to adolescents in terms of psychological well-being, as we have seen, social media also have the potential to facilitate negative interactions between adolescents, such as cyberbullying. Yet, despite the important work on adolescent friendship-peer relationships to date, considerably more research is needed in this area. Since social media are ubiquitous today, it is easy to forget that Facebook, YouTube, and texting are relatively recent innovations. As with studying the impact of any technological innovation on human beings, it is often difficult for researchers to keep up with emerging technological trends and the multitude of ways that they may impact psychological processes and behaviors.

Clearly, the empirical evidence to date demonstrates that adolescent use of various communication technologies is highly prevalent, and the ways in which these technologies have altered adolescent friendships and peer relationships appear to impact psychological well-being in both positive and negative ways. Given that adolescence is an important developmental stage which impacts adult relationships, communication researchers and other social scientists should continue to investigate the impact of friendship-peer relationships vis-à-vis computer-mediated technologies on important outcomes, such as psychological and physical well-being, identity development, relational stability. The proliferation of online interaction and its impact on adolescents is particularly interesting to explore from a developmental perspective since the majority of online interactions among adolescents circumvent traditional sources of socialization, such as parents and schools (Valkenburg & Peter, 2011). This section explores several future directions for researchers to consider in terms of gaining a better understanding of the influence of social media use on adolescents' well-being.

Future investigators would benefit from adopting a media convergence perspective and moving away from investigating the impact of isolated technologies (e.g., computers, cell phones) and specific social media platforms (e.g., Facebook, YouTube, texting) on adolescent friendship-peer relationships. As we have witnessed in recent years, smartphones and similar devices allow users to communicate in multiple ways, such as sending text messages, accessing social network sites, and talking via phone. Moreover, these devices also allow users to access information via the wireless Internet and locate others in the face-to-face world via GPS technology. As these devices evolve, the interactions between these modalities will most likely combine in unique ways that will alter the way we communicate. For example, a cyberbully using GPS can go beyond harassing his or her victim with text messages and photos on Facebook. Now he or she can also track the physical location of his or her target (which may lead to a physical confrontation). On the positive side, GPS may allow teens to physically locate friends, which may lead to supportive interactions in the physical, face-to-face world. In the future, we are likely to see interesting interactions between individuals who can simultaneously interact with others within face-to-face and mediated landscapes.

Future studies of adolescent new media use would also benefit from research that is focused on characteristics of computer-mediated modalities that may potentially enhance positive and negative psychological outcomes, such as well-being and stress. For example, Sticca, Ruggieri, Alsaker, and Perren (2013) found that adolescents perceive cyberbullying to be more severe when it is more public and more anonymous. New communication technologies vary in their degree of publicity and anonymity, which has important consequences for cyberbullying. For example, Smith et al. (2008) found that bullying through chat rooms, websites, and email were comparable to face-to-face bullying. However, more private channels such as text messages and phone calls were viewed as less severe than face-to-face bullying. YouTube, for example, contains many of the characteristics that foster cyberbullying and has a reputation for attracting bullies. The video-sharing site is popular, highly trafficked, and allows users to leave asynchronous comments on others' videos and pages. YouTube also affords more anonymity than most online social networks as many users use pseudonyms. Not surprisingly, the site has a notable reputation for a disproportionate amount of critical and hateful comments.

In addition, more research is needed to gain a better understanding of the role of social media use in the process of adolescent identity formation. For example, Davis (2010) found that online adolescents communicating with their peers in person-to-person channels, such as instant messaging, increased opportunities for self-disclosure while one-to-many channels, such as posting on a friend's Facebook wall, fostered a sense of connection and belongingness. Self-disclosure and belongingness are both vital to adolescent identity formation, but more research is needed to understand the role that new communication technology channels/modalities play in terms of the identity formation.

In terms of methodological concerns, as with many programs of research in the social sciences, few longitudinal studies exist that examine the relationship between new communication technology, patterns of friendship, and outcomes among adolescents. Far fewer studies examine transitions from preadolescence to adolescence and from adolescence to adulthood. However, such lifespan developmental approaches could shed light on long-term relational processes and their impact on how adolescent relationships develop and impact the lives of teenagers in various ways. Moreover, previous research has suffered from sampling biases, including an overreliance on online convenience samples and the practice of making generalizations about adolescence based on college undergraduate samples (who are often in different developmental stages than adolescents). Future researchers should consider focusing on adolescent-specific processes and behaviors within the context of online relationships.

Furthermore, while the studies in this review draw on a variety of theoretical perspectives, the overall picture of new communication technologies and adolescent friendship-peer relationships would benefit from a larger coherent theoretical framework that helps to explain the various relationships among characteristics of computer-mediated communication, friendship relationship behaviors, relational processes, and outcomes. Communication researchers tend to examine these elements as separate areas of research as opposed to studying them in a more comprehensive way. While the development of such a framework is challenging, it would certainly be useful for understanding the interactions among these elements in a more sophisticated manner. In addition, it may help scholars gain greater precision in terms of predicting important positive and negative behaviors and psychological outcomes for this population. In the meantime, technological innovations in computer-mediated communication will certainly move forward, and adolescents will likely be at the forefront in terms of adopting these new technologies and integrating them into their peer relationships.

REFERENCES

Acquisti, A., & Gross, R. (2006, June). *Imagined communities: Awareness, information sharing, and privacy on the Facebook.* Paper presented at the Privacy Enhancing Technologies workshop. Cambridge, England.

Agatston, P. W., Kowalski, R., & Limbert, S. (2007). Students' perspectives on cyber bullying. *Journal of Adolescent Health, 41*, S59–S60.

Albrecht, T. L., & Goldsmith, D. J. (2003). Social support, social networks, and health. In T. L. Thompson, A. M. Dorsey, K. I. Miller, & R. Parrott (Eds.), *Handbook of health communication* (pp. 263–284). Mahwah, NJ: Erlbaum.

Aneshensel, C. S., & Stone, J. D. (1982). Stress and depression: A test of the buffering model of social support. *Archives of General Psychiatry, 39*, 1392–1396.

Aseltine, R. H., Gore, S., & Colten, M. E. (1994). Depression and the social developmental context of adolescence. *Journal of Personality and Social Psychology, 67*, 252–263. doi:10.1037//0022-3514.67.2.252

Ballantine, P. W., & Stephenson, R. J. (2011). Help me, I'm fat! Social support in online weight loss networks. *Journal of Consumer Behaviour, 10*, 332–337. doi:10.1002/cb.374

Beran, T., & Li, Q. (2007). The relationship between cyberbullying and school bullying. *Journal of Student Wellbeing, 1*, 15–33.

Berkman, L. F., & Syme, L. S. (1979). Social networks, host resistance, and mortality: A nine-year follow-up study of Alameda County residents. *Journal of Epidemiology, 109*, 186–204.

Berndt, T. J., Hawkins, J. A., & Hoyle, S. G. (1986). Changes in friendship during a school year: Effects on children's and adolescents' impressions of friendship and sharing with friends. *Child Development, 57*, 1284–1297.

Berndt, T. J., & Perry, T. B. (1986). Children's perceptions of friendships as supportive relationships. *Developmental Psychology, 22*, 640–648.

Bessiere, K., Kiesler, S., Kraut, R., & Boneva, B. (2008). Effects of Internet use and social resources on changes in depression. *Information, Communication & Society, 11*, 47–70.

Billings, A. G., & Moos, R. H. (1984). The role of coping responses and social resources in attenuating the impact of stressful life events. *Journal of Behavioral Medicine, 4*, 139–157.

Blais, J. J., Craig, W. M., Pepler, D., & Connolly, J. (2008). Adolescents online: The importance of Internet activity choices to salient relationships. *Journal of Youth & Adolescence, 37*, 522–536.

Blumler, J. G., & Katz, E. (1974). *The uses of mass communication.* Newbury Park, CA: Sage.

boyd, d. (2006, December). Friends, friendsters, and top 8: Writing community into being on social network sites. *First Monday, 11*(12). Retrieved October 15, 2008, from http://www.firstmonday.org/issues/issue11_12/boyd/

boyd, d. (2007). Why youth (heart) social network sites: The role of networked publics in teenage social life. In D. Buckingham (Ed.), *MacArthur series on digital learning—youth, identity, and digital media* (pp. 119–142). Cambridge, MA: MIT Press.

boyd, d. m., & Ellison, N. B. (2007). Social network sites: Definition, history, and scholarship. *Journal of Computer-Mediated Communication, 13*, 210–230.

Bryant, J. A., Sanders-Jackson, A., & Smallwood, A. M. K. (2006). IMing, text messaging, and adolescent social networks. *Journal of Computer-Mediated Communicaton, 11*, 577–592.

Cai, X. (2004). Is the computer a functional alternative to traditional media? *Communication Research Reports, 21*, 26–38.

Calvert, S. L. (2002). Identity construction on the Internet. In S. L. Calvert, A. B. Jordan, & R. R. Cocking (Eds.), *Children in the digital age: Influences of electronic media on development* (pp. 57–70). Westport, CT: Praeger.

Carlson, C. L., Lahey, B. B., Frame, C. L., Walker, J., & Hynd, G. W. (1987). Sociometric status of clinic-referred children with attention deficit disorders with and without hyperactivity. *Journal of Abnormal Child Psychology, 15*, 537–548.

Coie, J. D., & Dodge, K. A. (1998). Aggression and antisocial behavior. In W. Damon & N. Eisenberg (Eds.), *Handbook of child psychology: Social, emotional, and personality development* (Vol. 3, pp. 779–862). Toronto, Ontario, Canada: Wiley.

Courtois, C., Merchant, P., De Marez, L., & Verleye, G. (2009). Gratifications and seeding behavior of on-line adolescents. *Journal of Computer-Mediated Communication, 15*, 109–137.

Cutrona, C. E., Suhr, J. A., & MacFarlane, R. (1990). Interpersonal transactions and the psychological sense of support. In S. W. Duck & R. C. Silver (Eds.), *Personal relationships and social support* (pp. 30–45). London, England: Sage.

Davis, K. (2010). Coming of age online: The developmental underpinnings of girls' blogs. *Journal of Adolescent Research, 25*, 145–171.

Desjarlais, M., & Willoughby, T. (2010). A longitudinal study of the relation between adolescent boys' and girls' computer use with friends and friendship quality: Support for the social compensation or the rich-get-richer hypothesis? *Computers in Human Behavior 26*, 896–905.

Dodge, K. A. (1983). Behavioral antecedents of peer social status. *Child Development, 54*, 1386–1399.

Drentea, P., & Moren-Cross, J. L. (2005). Social capital and social support on the web: The case of an Internet mother site. *Sociology of Health & Illness, 27*, 920–943.

Dwyer, C. (2007). Digital relationships in the "MySpace" generation: Results from a qualitative study. *Proceedings of the 40th Hawaii International Conference on System Sciences, USA*, 1–10.

Ebersole, S. (2006). Uses and gratifications of the web among students. *Journal of Computer-Mediated Communication, 6*. Retrieved from http://www3.interscience.wiley.com/cgi-bin/fulltext/120837804/HTMLSTART

Eccles, J. S., & Bryan, J. (1994). Adolescence: Critical crossroad in the path or gender-role development. In M. R. Stevenson (Ed.), *Gender roles through the life span: A multidisciplinary perspective* (pp. 111–147). Muncie, IN: Ball State University.

Ellison, N. B., Steinfeld, C., & Lampe, C. (2007). The benefits of Facebook "friends": Social capital and college students' use of online social network sites. *Journal of Computer-Mediated Communication, 12*. Retrieved July 15, 2009, http://jcmc.indiana.edu/vol12/issue4/ellison.html.

Facebook. (2012, October 4). One billion people. *Newsroom*. Retrieved October 5, 2012, from http://newsroom.fb.com/ImageLibrary/detail.aspx?MediaDetailsID=4227

Goldsmith, D. J. (2004). *Communicating social support*. Cambridge, England: Cambridge University Press.

Goldsmith, D. J., & Albrecht, T. L. (2011). Social support, social networks, and health: A guiding framework. In T. L. Thompson, R. Parrott, & J. F. Nussbaum (Eds.), *The Routledge handbook of health communication* (2nd ed., pp. 335–348). New York, NY: Routledge.

Granovetter, M. (1973). The strength of weak ties. *The American Journal of Sociology, 78*, 1360–1380.

Gross, E. F., Juvonen, J., & Gable, S. L. (2002). Internet use and well-being in adolescence. *Journal of Social Issues, 58*, 75–90.

Harter, S. (1999). *The construction of the self: A developmental perspective*. New York, NY: Guilford Press.

Harter, S. (2003). The development of self-representation during childhood and adolescence. In M. R. Leary & J. P. Tangney (Eds.), *Handbook of self and identity* (pp. 611–642). New York, NY: Guilford Press.

Hartup, W. W. (1996). The company they keep: Friendships and their developmental significance. *Child Development, 67*, 1–13.

Haythornthwaite, C. (2002). Strong, weak, and latent ties and the impact of new media. *The Information Society, 18*, 385–401.

Haythornthwaite, C., & Wellman, B. (2002). The Internet in everyday life: An introduction. In B. Wellman & C. Haythornthwaite (Eds.), *The Internet in everyday life* (pp. 3–42). Oxford, England: Blackwell.

Hellenga, K. (2002). Social space, the final frontier: Adolescents on the Internet. In J. T. Mortimer & R. W. Larson (Eds.), *The changing adolescent experience: Societal trends and the transition to adulthood* (pp. 208–249). Cambridge, England: Cambridge University Press.

Hinduja, S., & Patchin, J. W. (2008). Cyberbullying: An exploratory analysis of factors related to offending and victimization. *Deviant Behavior, 29*, 129–156.

Hodgens, J. B., & McCoy, J. F. (1989). Distinctions among rejected children on the basis of peer-nominated aggression. *Journal of Clinical Childhood Psychology, 18*, 121–128.

Huesmann, L. R., Eron, L. D., Lefkowitz, M. M., & Walder, L. O. (1984). Stability of aggression over time and generations. *Developmental Psychology, 20*, 1120–1134.

Huffaker, D. A., & Calvert, S. L. (2006). Gender, identity, and language use in teenage blogs. *Journal of Computer-Mediated Communication, 10.*

Johnson, A. J., & Becker, J. A. H. (2011). CMC and the conceptualization of "friendship": How friendships have changed with the advent of new methods of interpersonal communication. In K. B. Wright & L. M. Webb (Eds.), *Computer-mediated communication in personal relationships* (pp. 225–243). New York, NY: Peter Lang.

Jones S., & Fox, S. (2009). *Generations online in 2009.* Washington, DC: Pew Internet and American Life Project.

Jones, S., Millermaier, S., Goya-Martinez, M., & Schuler, J. (2008). Whose space is MySpace? A content analysis of MySpace profiles. *First Monday, 13*(9). Retrieved October 5, 2008, from http://www.uic.edu/htbin/cgiwrap/bin/ojs/index.php/fm/article/view/2202/2024

Kiesler, S., Siegel, J., & McGuire, T. W. (1984). Social psychological aspects of CMC. *American Psychologist, 39*, 1123–1134.

Kim, J., & Lee, J. E. (2011). The Facebook paths to happiness: Effects of the number of Facebook friends and self-presentation on subjective well-being. *Cyberpsychology, Behavior, and Social Networking, 6*, 359–364. doi: 10.1089/cyber.2010.0374

Kovacs, M., Paulauskas, S., Gatsonis, C., & Richards, C. (1988). Depressive disorders in childhood: III. A longitudinal study of comorbidity and risk for conduct disorders. *Journal of Affective Disorders, 15*, 205–217.

Kraut, R., Kiesler, S., Boneva, B., Cummings, J., Helgeson, V., & Crawford, A. (2002). Internet paradox revisited. *Journal of Social Issues, 58*, 49–74.

Kraut, R., Patterson, M., Lundmark, V., Kiesler, S., Mukhopadhyay, T., & Scherlis, W. (1998). Internet paradox: A social technology that reduces social involvement and psychological well-being? *American Psychologist, 53*, 1017–1031.

Lampe, C., Ellison, N., & Steinfield, C. (2007, April). A familiar face(book): Profile elements as signals in an online social network. *Proceedings of the SIGCHI conference on human factors in computing systems, San Jose, CA* (pp. 435–444). New York, NY: ACM.

Lee, S. J. (2009). Online communication and adolescent social ties: Who benefits more from Internet use? *Journal of Computer-Mediated Communication, 14*, 509–531.

Lenhart, A., Madden, M., Macgill, A. R., & Smith, A. (2007). *Teens and social media: The use of social media gains a greater foothold in teen life as they embrace the conversational nature of interactive online media.* Washington, DC: Pew Internet & American Life Project.

Lin, N. (2001). *Social capital: A theory of social structure and action.* Cambridge, England: Cambridge University Press.

Lindeman, M., Harakka, T., & Keltikangas-Jarvinen, L. (1997). Age and gender differences in adolescents' reactions to conflict situations: Aggression, prosociality, and withdrawal. *Journal of Youth and Adolescence, 26*, 339–351.

Locke, J. L. (1998). *The de-voicing of society: Why we don't talk to each other anymore.* New York, NY: Simon & Schuster.

Madell, D. E., & Muncer, S. J. (2007). Control over social interactions: An important reason for young people's use of the Internet and mobile phones for communication. *Cyberpsychology & Behavior, 10*, 137–140.

Manago, A. M., Taylor, T., & Greenfield, P. M. (2012). Me and my 400 friends: The anatomy of college students' Facebook networks, their communication patterns, and well-being. *Developmental Psychology, 48*(2), 369–380. doi:10.1037/a00226338

Mayeux, L., & Cillessen, A. (2008). It's not just being popular, it's knowing it, too: The role of self-perceptions of status in the associations between peer status and aggression. *Social Development, 17*, 871–888.

McKenna, K. Y. A., & Bargh, J. A. (2000). Plan 9 from cyberspace: The implications of the Internet for personality and social psychology. *Personality and Social Psychology Review, 4,* 57–75.

McKenna, K. Y. A., Green, A. S., & Gleason, M. E. J. (2002). Relationship formation on the Internet: What's the big attraction? *Journal of Social Issues, 58,* 9–32.

McQuade, S. C., & Sampat, N. M. (2008). *Survey of Internet and at-risk behaviors: Undertaken by school districts of Monroe country New York.* Retrieved August 12, 2013, from http://www.rrsei. org/RITCyberSurvey20FinalReport.pdf

Mitchell, K. J., & Ybarra, M. (2007). Online behavior of youth who engage in self-harm provides clues for prevention intervention. *Preventative Medicine, 45,* 392–396.

Mitchell, K. J., Ybarra, M., & Finkelhor, D. (2007). The relative importance of victimization in understanding depression, delinquency, and substance abuse. *Child Maltreatment, 12,* 314–324.

Morgan, C., & Cotten, S. R. (2003). The relationship between Internet activities and depressive symptoms in a sample of college freshmen. *Cyberpsychology & Behavior, 6,* 133–142.

Nie, N. H., & Erbring, L. (2000). *Internet and society: A preliminary report.* Retrieved from the Stanford Institute for the Quantitative Study of Society website http://www.stanford.edu/group/ siqss/press_release/preliminary_report.pdf

Nussbaum, J. F. (1994). Friendship in older adulthood. In M. L. Hummert, J. M. Wiemann, & J. F. Nussbaum (Eds.), *Interpersonal communication in older adulthood* (pp. 209–225). Thousand Oaks, CA: Sage.

Parks, M., & Archey-Ladas, T. (2003). *Communicating self through personal homepages: Is identity more than screen deep.* Paper presented to the annual International Communication Association Convention, San Diego, CA.

Patchin, J., & Hinduja, S. (2006). Bullies move beyond the schoolyard: A preliminary look at cyberbullying. *Youth Violence and Juvenile Justice, 4,* 148–169.

Patterson, G. R. (1982). *A social learning approach to family intervention: III. Coercive family process.* Eugene, OR: Castalia.

Pecchioni, L. L., Wright, K. B., & Nussbaum, J. F. (2005). *Life-span communication.* Mahwah, NJ: Erlbaum.

Pierce, T. (2009). Social anxiety and technology: Face-to-face communication versus technological communication among teens. *Computers in Human Behavior, 25,* 1367–1372.

Putnam, R. D. (2000). *Bowling alone.* New York, NY: Simon & Schuster.

Reiss, A. J., & Roth, J. A. (Eds.). (1993). *Understanding and preventing violence.* Washington, DC: National Academy Press.

Roberto, A. J., & Eden, J. (2010). Cyberbullying: Aggressive communication in the digital age. In T. A. Avtgis & A. S. Rancer (Eds.), *Arguments, aggression, & conflict* (pp. 198–216). New York, NY: Routledge.

Schlenker, B. R. (1986). Self-identification: Toward the integration of the private and public self. In R. F. Baumeister (Ed.), *Public self and private self* (pp. 21–62). New York, NY: Springer-Verlag.

Schouten A. P., Valkenburg, P. M., & Peter, J. (2007). Precursors and underlying processes of adolescents' online self-disclosure: Developing and testing an "Internet-attribute-perception" model. *Media Psychology, 10,* 292–314.

Schrock, A. R., & boyd, d. (2011). Problematic youth interactions online: Solicitation, harassment, and cyberbullying. In K. B. Wright & L. M. Webb (Eds.), *Computer-mediated communication in personal relationships* (pp. 368–396). New York, NY: Peter Lang.

Sijtsema, J., Veenstra, R., Lindenberg, S., & Salmivalli, C. (2009). Empirical test of bullies' status goals: Assessing direct goals, aggression, and prestige. *Aggressive Behavior, 35,* 57–67.

Smith, P. K., Mahdavi, I., Carvalho, M., Fisher, J., Russell, S., & Tippett, N. (2008). Cyberbullying: Its nature and impact in secondary pupils. *The Journal of Child Psychology and Psychiatry, 49*(4), 376–385.

Sproull, L., & Kiesler, S. (1986). Reducing social context cues: Electronic mail in organizational communication. *Management Science, 32*, 1492–1512.

Sticca, F., Ruggieri, S., Alsaker, F., & Perren, S. (2013). Longitudinal risk factors for cyberbullying in adolescence. *Journal of Community & Applied Social Psychology, 23*, 52–67.

Subrahmanyam, K., & Greenfield, P. (2008). Online communication and adolescent relationships. *Future Child, 18*, 119–146.

Subrahmanyam, K., & Lin, G. (2007). Adolescents on the net: Internet use and well-being. *Adolescence, 42*, 659–677.

Subrahmanyam, K., Smahel, D., & Greenfield, P. M. (2006). Connecting developmental processes to the Internet: Identity presentation and sexual exploration in online teen chatrooms. *Developmental Psychology, 42*, 1–12.

Szreter, S. (2000). Social capital, the economy, and education in historical perspective. In S. Baron, J. Field, & T. Schuller (Eds.), *Social capital: Critical perspectives* (pp. 56–77). New York, NY: Oxford University Press.

Tong, S. T., Van Der Heide, B., Langwell, L., & Walther, J. B. (2008). Too much of a good thing? The relationship between number of friends and interpersonal impressions on Facebook. *Journal of Computer-Mediated Communication, 13*, 531–549.

Valkenburg, P. M., & Peter, J. (2005). Adolescents' identity experiments on the Internet: Consequences for social competence and self-concept unity. *Communication Research, 35*, 208–231.

Valkenburg, P. M., & Peter, J. (2007). Online communication and adolescent well-being: Testing the stimulation versus displacement hypothesis. *Journal of Computer-Mediated Communication, 12*, 1169–1182.

Valkenburg, P. M., & Peter, J. (2011). Online communication among adolescents: An integrated model of its attraction, opportunities, and risks. *Journal of Adolescent Health, 48*, 121–127.

Valkenburg P. M., Peter J., & Schouten A. P. (2006). Friend networking sites and their relationship to adolescents' well-being and social self-esteem. *Cyberpsychology & Behavior, 9*, 584–590.

Walther, J. B. (1996). CMC: Impersonal, interpersonal, and hyperpersonal interaction: A relational perspective. *Communication Research, 23*, 3–43.

Walther, J. B. (2007). Selective self-presentation in computer-mediated communication: Hyperpersonal dimensions of technology, language, and cognition. *Computers in Human Behavior, 23*, 2538–2557.

Walther, J. B., & Boyd, S. (2002). Attraction to computer-mediated social support. In C. A. Lin & D. Atkin (Eds.), *Communication technology and society: Audience adoption and uses* (pp. 153–188). Cresskill, NJ: Hampton Press.

Walther, J. B., & Parks, M. R. (2002). Cues filtered out, cues filtered in: Computer-mediated communication and relationships. In M. L. Knapp & J. A. Daly (Eds.), *Handbook of interpersonal communication* (pp. 529–563). Thousand Oaks, CA: Sage.

Werner, N. E., & Crick, N. R. (1999). Relational aggression and social-psychological adjustment in a college sample. *Journal of Abnormal Psychology, 108*, 615–623.

Wright, K. B. (2000). Social support satisfaction, on-line communication apprehension, and perceived life stress within computer-mediated support groups. *Communication Research Reports, 17*, 139–147.

Wright, K. B., & Bell, S. B. (2003). Health-related support groups on the Internet: Linking empirical findings to social support and computer-mediated communication theory. *Journal of Health Psychology, 8*, 37–52.

Xie, B. (2008). Multimodal computer-mediated communication and support among older Chinese Internet users. *Journal of Computer-Mediated Communication, 13,* 728–750.

Ybarra, M. (2004). Linkages between depressive symptomology and Internet harassment among young regular Internet users. *Cyberpsychology & Behavior, 7,* 247–257.

Ybarra, M., Diener-West, M., & Leaf, P. J. (2007). Examining the overlap in Internet harassment and school bullying: Implications for school intervention. *Journal of Adolescent Health, 41,* S42–S50.

Ybarra, M. L., & Mitchell, K. J. (2004). Online aggressor/targets, aggressors, and targets: A comparison of associated youth characteristics. *Journal of Child Psychology and Psychiatry, 45,* 1308–1316.

Ye, J. (2006). Traditional and online support networks in the cross-cultural adaptation of Chinese international students in the United States. *Journal of Computer-Mediated Communication, 11,* 863–876.

PART FIVE

Emerging Adulthood Communication

CHAPTER ELEVEN

Emerging Adults in College

Communication, Friendships, and Risky Sexual Behaviors

ALYSSA ANN LUCAS

"Eventually, it was time to grow up, be healthy and be responsible. You can't live like a kid forever, you know?"

—JONAH HILL, ACTOR

Movies like *Animal House, Revenge of the Nerds, Dead Man on Campus,* and *Old School* demonstrate the role college plays in a young person's participation in risky behaviors such as partying, drinking, drug use, and sexual experimentation while navigating the journey to find one's self. This journey of self-exploration is reflected in a unique life stage called Emerging Adulthood, including the subsample of college students, with members aged 18 to 28 (e.g., Arnett, 2000; Collins & van Dulmen, 2006). Emerging adults are no longer considered children or minors under the thumb of their parents, and emerging adults are not yet taking on the responsibilities, obligations, and permanence of being adults. Instead, they are focused on their identity exploration (Arnett, 2004a, 2006). Their freedom from adult responsibilities and journey to establish identity within the college environment can put emerging adults at risk for lifelong detrimental consequences such as sexually transmitted infections (STIs), infertility, and other emotional, mental, and financial difficulties.

College provides many academic and social events that enrich one's personal and professional growth; however, it also offers dangerous opportunities to try and/or continue risky sexual behaviors that are often fueled by alcohol and drug usage. For example, the college environment is ripe for casual sex interactions through hooking up, one-night stands, and friends with benefits relationships (FWBRs; Bogle, 2008; Hughes, Morrison, & Asada, 2005; Lefkowitz & Gillen, 2006). Moreover, emerging adults' college friendships and interactions within those relationships during college set the stage for a supportive atmosphere that accepts and encourages risky sexual behaviors. Therefore, this chapter provides an overview of the dangers emerging adults experience when attending college. The first section of the chapter outlines Emerging Adulthood with a special focus on friendships, sexual conversations, and the support they provide one another. Focus then shifts to the sexual risks and behaviors that are frequently experienced while attending college. Finally, the chapter concludes with a discussion of future research focusing on the intervention opportunities for improving emerging adults' communication, health, and knowledge.

EMERGING ADULTHOOD

Over the lifespan, individuals experience many transitions and changes. However, with changes to the timing of significant life events in recent decades, like marriage, schooling, children, and career, Arnett (2000, 2006) has determined this is a unique time period for individuals. This period between adolescence (under 18) and adulthood (30s and above) Arnett labeled Emerging Adulthood (approximately 18–25 or 18–28; see also Collins & van Dulmen, 2006). This section offers an overview of the Emerging Adulthood life period and friendships during this time.

Overview of Emerging Adulthood

The trajectory to becoming an adult is now delayed (Arnett 2000, 2004a, 2006). Historically, adulthood started at a young age, almost immediately after high school or college, but now young individuals are postponing marriage, children, and careers, allowing them to enjoy the freedom of more time in making decisions about life goals and plans (Arnett, 2000, 2004a). However, by delaying adulthood they also experience uncertainty "because the lives of young people are so unsettled, and many of them have no idea where their explorations will lead" (Arnett, 2004a, p. 3). The delay can produce both positive and negative experiences for college students.

Arnett (2004a, 2006) describes emerging adulthood as an age of identity exploration, instability, being self-focused, feeling in-between, and experiencing a number of possibilities. During this time, emerging adults focus on themselves because there are few obligatory bonds with others. Also, they want to figure out their identity through various venues, including relational and sexual experimentation, before "settling down" into adulthood (Arnett, 2004a, 2004b). For example, emerging adults are free to search for love and sex. For those in college, hooking up, one-night stands,

FWBRs, and causal dating are normative behaviors (e.g., Bogle, 2008; Hughes et al., 2005; Lefkowitz & Gillen, 2006). The college environment allows for various romantic and sexual experiences because there is no pressure of marriage (Arnett, 2000), and friends likely support such behaviors (e.g., Lucas & Nussbaum, 2011; Morgan & Korobov, 2011). Indeed, the focus on the self can be fun, productive, and useful, but emerging adulthood can also be difficult considering the uncertainty of the future (who and what will they become?) and the ambiguity of the present (in-between restrictions of being a child and the responsibilities of an adult).

Before reaching Emerging Adulthood, adolescents start to increase autonomy from their parents and create bonds with friends that, in addition, help them prepare for future romantic connections (Rawlins, 1992). One's relational life journey continues in Emerging Adulthood by making new friends in college and participating in various romantic relationships and sexual explorations. In the past, women may have attended college to obtain their M-R-S degree (Arnett, 2004a), but now emerging adults, both men and women, have more freedom and time to discover themselves sexually and identify the type person they may want a long-term relationship with in adulthood (Arnett, 2004b). Hooking up, FWBRs, and other casual dating situations allow relational and sexual "auditions" to help dictate the qualities they desire in a potential life partner. In fact, hooking up may be a prime way college students try to start relationships (Owen & Fincham, 2011b). "Sowing one's wild oats" may be normative and accepted, for both men and women, in Emerging Adulthood and they are aware that when adulthood comes, their "fun" is over (Arnett, 2004a). Thus, previously stated life periods may not reflect young people's current experiences of relational and sexual life decisions.

When considering the life cycle of a friendship, researchers and scholars have focused on what happens in friendships during childhood, adolescence, and young adulthood (e.g., Brown, 1981). Brown (1981) notes, "At no other life stage are conditions so ripe for extensive, intensive friendship ties [than adolescence]" (p. 35). However, the significance of friendships on personal growth and individual development is not clear past this specific life period (Hartup & Stevens, 1997). Then, in young adulthood, individuals make a dramatic shift to the responsibilities of adulthood such as marriage, children, and career while time with friends diminishes (Brown, 1981; Collins & Laursen, 2000). Considering the monumental adjustments to "the life event schedule" young people today experience as they move onto the responsibilities of adulthood, Emerging Adulthood is a useful tool for understanding individuals' platonic and romantic relational development during this point in life.

Friendships and Sex Talk in Emerging Adulthood

Over the life course, emerging adults experience some very distinct yet important relationships (e.g., Collins & Laursen, 2000). The first major influence in one's life is family, specifically, one's parents. During adolescence, peers become more important, and there are often contradictory influences from parents and peers (Mirande, 1968). For example, at this age, adolescents begin to move away from parents toward their peers and friends (Duck, 1983). Adolescents are trying to find autonomy, and peers provide guidance in this journey. Friends become the standard to which everything is compared and peers' opinions are important and parents' opinions may be rejected (Brown, 1981). Friendships also play a significant role in creating interpersonal relationships, including romantic relationships (Rawlins, 1992). However, Emerging Adulthood provides an extended amount of years for creating and maintaining friendships than in previous decades. With marriage, spouses become the central relationship in one's life, and friendships may fall by the wayside (Brown, 1981; Collins & Laursen, 2000). Certainly, marriage may bring new friendships such as "couples friends," and with technology like texting and social media individuals may be able to maintain friendships into adulthood. However, with emerging adults delaying marriage (see Chapter 12 this volume), friendships remain important relationships for an extended period of time.

Friendships offer a number of benefits for the individuals involved, like companionship, acceptance, trust, respect, emotional support, intimacy, help, and enjoyment (Hartup & Stevens, 1997; Reohr, 1991), which are likely appreciated during Emerging Adulthood. Specifically, talking and disclosing to someone was rated as the most beneficial feature of friendship (Duck & Wright, 1993; Monsour, 1992; Parks & Floyd, 1996). Both men and women are likely to spend time together "just talking" (Duck & Wright, 1993), and friendships are marked by a benefit of trust (Hartup & Stevens, 1997; Reohr, 1991). Thus, it is not surprising that emerging adults in college spend time self-disclosing sexual information to each other. Indeed, with friends in general one can openly and comfortably discuss sex (Lefkowitz, Boone, & Shearer, 2004).

Young individuals feel most comfortable speaking to their friends about intimate topics like sex (DiIorio, Kelley, & Hockenberry-Eaton, 1999; Rittenour & Booth-Butterfield, 2006) as compared to their parents (Herold & Way, 1988; Papini, Farmer, Clark, Micka, & Barnett, 1990). The key to comfortably talking about sex lies with the emerging adult's perception of openness in the relationship (Papini, Farmer, Clark, & Snell, 1988; Papini et al., 1990), which is likely in friendships. Emerging adults also see these conversations with friends as high in quality (Lefkowitz et al., 2004). The conversations' fun nature may also develop solidarity or relational closeness between the friends (Lucas & Afifi, 2006; Wheeless, 1976). Indeed, the benefits of friendship facilitate and allow for sexual conversations to occur between friends, yet these conversations may have both positive and negative consequences for emerging adults.

Sex-related conversations between college friends are both helpful and hurtful. Through sex talk, emerging adults are able to fulfill the function of what it means to be a friend (Burleson & Samter, 1994), such as listening to their friends, providing social support, and offering sexual advice (Lucas & Nussbaum, 2011; Morgan & Korobov, 2011). Emerging adults are navigating a self-exploration in college, and friends are part of the journey by "being there" during a friend's times of need. In fact, when experiencing a crisis, friends are the ones called upon for assistance (Barnes & Duck, 1994; Finken, 2005). Certainly, as emerging adults become closer and intensify their friendships, more situations to provide support arise (Albrecht & Adelman, 1987).

However, sexual conversations between friends can be problematic. Although the support friends provide during sex talks can feel good, the support may, in fact, be harmful. Instead of dispensing appropriate advice or warnings to combat sexual health risks (e.g., Rittenour & Booth-Butterfield, 2006), friends may trade information, advice, and personal experiences perpetuating misinformation (Rozema, 1986). Furthermore, friends can encourage risky sexual behavior by avoiding conversations about sexual health issues (e.g., Rittenour & Booth-Butterfield, 2006) and focusing on topics that are more fun and enjoyable like sexual positions and sexual likes and dislikes (Lucas & Afifi, 2006). Rittenour & Booth-Butterfield (2006) asked college students about discussing sexual health issues, while Lucas and Afifi (2006) asked college students for the topics they normally discussed with their friends, which they primarily listed as "fun" topics. Despite the differences in the studies, overall it was found that college students are comfortable talking to their friends about sex no matter what the topic may be.

Lucas and Nussbaum (2011) found that college-student emerging adults focused their sexual discussions primarily on what they labeled as "whether or not to participate in a sexual behavior" (e.g., whether or not to have a one-night stand, hook up, or have sex with an ex). If emerging adult friends frequently discuss participating in sexual behavior and not about protecting one's self against the risk, they may be focusing on topics that could cause harmful physical, emotional, and even financial consequences.

During conversations about sexual behavior, friends also may provide social support that encourages or enables the risky rather than risk-adverse sexual behavior (e.g., Hughes et al., 2005; Lucas & Nussbaum, 2011, 2012). For example, friends may provide social support during conversations about sex to assist in maintaining their friendship (Burleson & Samter, 1996), including statements validating the friend's risky sexual behaviors (Lucas & Nussbaum, 2011, 2012). In two studies with a combined 572 college-student emerging adults, Lucas and Nussbaum (2011, 2012) found same-sex friends provided esteem (ego) support (e.g., making the individual feel good about themselves and sexual decisions through showing interest), emotional (e.g., "being there," listening), and informational (e.g., providing information and advice about sexual decisions) social support. Esteem support was the most common form of support that friends provided, which included messages such as encouraging the emerging adult to participate in a hookup by telling him or her to "go for it," and showing approval through praise and nonverbal cues (e.g., thumbs-up) (Lucas & Nussbaum, 2011, 2012). Similarly, Morgan and Korobov (2011) found that through conversations about dating relationships emerging adults provided supportive "social feedback" like sharing similar experiences, providing validation and encouragement, joking, and providing advice. This suggests college students' conversations contribute to identity formation related to interpersonal relationships. Being a good friend during Emerging Adulthood involves providing social support during sexual conversations, which assists with identity development. But supportive responses may encourage risky sexual behaviors, like hooking up.

Emerging Adulthood is a unique life period that addresses new trends of major life events for those aged 18 to 28, including college students (Arnett, 2000; Collins & van Dulmen, 2006). They are concerned with "finding themselves" rather than with the obligations and responsibilities of adulthood. The journey to self-discovery, which entails relational and sexual experimentation, can be both fun and problematic, and friends may impact the journey through sexual conversations, support, and encouragement.

SEXUAL RISK, BEHAVIORS, AND CONSEQUENCES

As young people move into Emerging Adulthood, especially those heading to college, they are excited to have a new start. Emerging adults gain new freedoms that adolescence does not offer, but what they do not leave behind is sexual risk. By far, those aged 15 to 24 (which includes emerging adults in college) are the most at-risk for sexually transmitted infections (STIs) and unplanned pregnancies (Finer & Zolna, 2014). Of the 20 million new cases of STIs each year, over half are diagnosed in late adolescence and Emerging Adulthood individuals (Centers for Disease Control and Prevention, 2013). Similarly, 49% of unintended pregnancies each year occur in late adolescence (Finer & Zolna, 2014) and Emerging Adulthood (Lefkowitz & Gillen, 2006). Although these risks begin in adolescence, it continues into Emerging Adulthood as young people explore their sexuality, audition relational partners, and have peers' support in participating in these risky behaviors.

Risky sexual behaviors that can set up a lifetime of unhealthy decisions and behaviors begin in adolescence (Reyna & Farley, 2006). Adolescents may be at-risk while under their parents' watchful eye; however, in some cases, those friends who do not participate in risky sexual behaviors protect adolescents from participating in these behaviors (Crosenoe, Erickson, & Dornbusch, 2002). These risky behaviors are prolonged through Emerging Adulthood because of the exploratory nature of the developmental period and compounded by the college environment, which is ripe for risky behaviors. Many college emerging adults are living apart from parents, friends are prevalent, individuals are sexually active, and sexual behavior, like hooking up, is frequent (Lefkowitz & Gillen, 2006).

Risk-taking research suggests that younger individuals are more likely to take risks than adults (Gardner & Steinberg, 2005). There are numerous reasons emerging adults take more risks, but perhaps two important explanations include peer influence (e.g., Mirande, 1968) and identity exploration (e.g., Arnett, 2000, 2004a, 2004b). Gardner and Steinberg (2005) found older individuals (older than 24 years) engage in fewer risks, which would suggest that individuals have figured out who they are, what they want to be, and who they want to be with by their late 20s, and thus are ready to transition to adulthood (Arnett, 2004a). Previous generations transitioned from adolescence directly into adulthood, thereby limiting risky behaviors. However, today's prolonged development into adulthood through Emerging Adulthood extends the time period for engaging in risky sexual behaviors, which raises concerns regarding the consequences of these behaviors.

Unintended pregnancy and STI statistics suggest emerging adults may be setting themselves up for lifelong consequences. Although having children is financially costly, living with STIs, like herpes, may have significant long-term effects on emerging adults' health and finances given the financial cost of treatment (Institute of Medicine, 1997). In fact, the CDC (2013) estimates the cost of treating curable STIs is $742 million per year, while the cost of treating eight of the most common STIs for a lifetime is $15.6 billion per each year. This demonstrates the significant financial burden and health risk associated with curing or treating STIs. Additionally, acquiring STIs may also cause infertility and pregnancy problems when emerging adults reach adulthood (Westrom, 1992). For instance, HIV/AIDS transmission becomes a concern (UNAIDS, 2009), and human papillomavirus (HPV; CDC, n.d.) can lead to cervical cancer, making pregnancy difficult to impossible (American Cancer Society, 2008; CDC, n.d.). Clearly, risky sexual behavior leads to financial and physical consequences that could make life within and beyond Emerging Adulthood difficult to manage, for example, discovering infertility when an individual has settled down into marriage.

Additionally, emerging adults may deal with emotional consequences from participating in risky sexual behaviors. While numerous positive and negative emotions are associated with sexual behavior, the negative experiences and regret may take a toll on sexually active emerging adults. Emerging adults are most likely to have relational regrets (Jokisaari, 2004), and sexual regret (Bachtel, 2013; Oswalt, Cameron, & Koob, 2005; Paul, 2006). Specifically, college students experienced regret in response to negative sexual experiences like participating in behaviors that were not aligned with their personal beliefs, allowing alcohol to influence their sexual decision making, not using a condom, and feeling pressured by partners (Oswalt et al., 2005). Further, negative emotional reactions to hooking up were associated with symptoms of depression and loneliness, suggesting that the sexual act of hooking up may be related to young people's "psychological functioning" (Owen & Fincham, 2011b).

Conversely, the experience of positive emotional responses and the void of negative emotional experiences may lead emerging adults to participate in, rather than avoid, risky sexual behaviors. For example, Beike, Markman, and Karadogan (2009) suggested experiences of regret are impacted by the thought of losing an opportunity. If Emerging Adulthood is about the opportunities for self-discovery and relational and sexual experimentation (Arnett, 2000), emerging adults may anticipate the negative emotions they might experience if they miss out on any opportunities to explore. In general, individuals try to avoid negative experiences and the possibility of a "lost opportunity" may be perceived as more negative than potential consequences like unintended pregnancies and STIs. Furthermore, some sexual behaviors that college students participate in may create positive experiences and emotions, leading them to believe there is nothing to regret. Owen and Fincham (2011b) suggested college students find hooking up attractive because of the positive emotions experienced after the hookup. Lucas (2009) and Lucas and Nussbaum (2012) found college-age participants experienced very little regret in response to hooking up, which led them to conclude that hooking up is not a sexual behavior that college students perceive to be regretful. Instead, the sexual regrets emerging adults have noted in other studies are *after* the experiences take place, and, thus, a lack of anticipated regret may be what increases college students' risk. Perhaps anticipating regret due to risky sexual behaviors would help college students protect themselves from unnecessary risk (e.g., Janis & Mann, 1977; Richard et al., 1998; van der Pligt & Richard, 1994). College students may not experience sexual regret at all during Emerging Adulthood, but, rather, regret may be a negative emotion that is experienced later in life.

Sexual Behaviors

Nearly every emerging adult is sexually active by the age of 25 (Lefkowitz & Gillen, 2006), which is not surprising when considering the welcoming environment college provides for the participation in casual sex (e.g., Bogle, 2008; Hughes et al., 2005; Lefkowitz & Gillen, 2006). This section provides an overview of perceptions of normative sexual behavior and moves into discussion of three common sexual relationships.

Perceptions of normative sexual behavior. Sexual behavior before marriage is socially acceptable for emerging adults. Therefore, they may not be concerned about the outcomes of participating in potentially risky sex or they may not believe their behaviors are risky. "Because they are more independent of their parents than adolescents are, and because there is no social stigma against them having sex the way there is for adolescents, emerging adults have less reason to be furtive and anxious about sex" (Arnett, 2006, p. 90). Moreover, peers and friends may influence emerging adults' sexual behaviors, attitudes, and perceptions of norms. Mirande (1968) notes that emerging adults in college go through a process of reconsidering their personal beliefs and ideas, but it is their peers who help confirm their new beliefs and ideas. Peers validating ideas regarding sexual behaviors may create perceptions of what is considered "normal," "typical," and "common" sexually. In fact, college students who perceive peers to be participating in particular sexual behaviors are more likely to be sexually involved (Page, Hammermeister, & Scanlan, 2000). Perhaps emerging adults perceive their peers to be participating in the same types and frequencies of sexual behaviors as they do.

Common Sexual Behaviors. Three main sexual relationships emerging adults have are hooking up, FWBRs, and romantic relationships. "A hookup is a brief sexual encounter between two youths who either don't know each other at all or who are just acquainted" (Paul, 2006, p. 141). Because hooking up refers to a range of behaviors including kissing, touching, oral sex, and sexual intercourse, hooking up can be ambiguous term (Bogle, 2008; Lucas, 2009; Owen & Fincham, 2011b; Paul, 2006). Representative of college students' sexual experiences, hooking up happens frequently on college campuses (Owen & Fincham, 2011b; Paul, 2006). The college environment makes hooking up so "easy" because finding a hookup partner entails situations a college campus creates, including identifying and accepting individuals with similar features, being in close proximity to potential partners, and paying attention to what others are doing (Bogle, 2008). More important, Bogle (2008) outlines how dating has morphed into the "hookup era" in which the hookup is likely to be the first event in courtship instead of the historically common date. If college students are no longer "dating," they may be hooking up as a way to experiment and/or start a relationship (Owen & Fincham, 2011b). Hooking up may be attractive to college students because of the positive emotions that result (Owen, Rhoades, Stanley, & Fincham, 2010); therefore, they may enjoy hooking up and believe it is a normative college experience. But problems may arise if friends encourage and/or pressure emerging adults into hooking up (Lucas & Nussbaum, 2011, 2012; Paul, 2006), if alcohol clouds decision making (Bachtel, 2013; Downing-Matibag & Geisinger, 2009; Oswalt et al., 2005), or if condoms are not available (Downing-Matibag & Geisinger, 2009).

FWBRs are a common way to experience sex and relationships in college (Hughes et al., 2005; Owen & Fincham, 2011a). Like hookups, FWBRs are ambiguous sexual relationships highlighting a temporary situation with a "no strings attached" attitude and are born out of existing friendships (Hughes et al., 2005). Many college students (50% or more) have had sex with a friend at some point (Afifi & Faulkner, 2000; Owen & Fincham, 2011a). Several rules may be critical for the maintenance of FWBRs, such as non-permanence, sexual safety and protection, a focus on remaining friends, communication expectations, and secrecy (Hughes et al., 2005). However, discussions of explicit rules does not seem to take place (Bisson & Levine, 2009). College students seem to participate in FWBRs because, like hookups, the positive outcomes outweigh any negative consequences (Owen & Fincham, 2011a). Emerging adults also enter into FWBRs because of alcohol use and interest in starting a romantic relationship with the FWBR, acting as an "audition" for a long-term relational situation (Owen & Fincham, 2011a).

Emerging adult college students also are looking for romantic relationships, and through their experiences may determine the type of partner they would like to marry and share the responsibilities of adulthood with (Arnett, 2004a). Though they may be the outcome of hooking up or FWBRs (e.g., Owen & Fincham, 2011b), romantic relationships may also develop from the academic and social experiences in which people meet (Arnett, 2004b). Romantic relationships may be a way to decrease sexual risk because the partners are committed to each other; however, commitment may also increase emerging adults' risk. Lefkowitz and Gillen (2006) noted that emerging adults more often use condoms with new partners, while they do not necessarily use condoms in their committed relationships. In some cases, emerging adults use perceptions to determine sexual risk: if someone looks safe, like their romantic partner, a condom is not necessary (Williams et al., 1992). Similarly, Umphrey and Sherblom (2007) found individuals with high relational commitment were less likely to wear a condom. Committed partners were likely to use condoms for protection against pregnancy rather than protection against STIs (Lefkowitz & Gillen, 2006). When condoms were not used, in some cases women had partners who resisted condom use (Roberts & Kennedy, 2006). Open-ended data showed that college-age individuals feel comfortable in committed relationships, and, therefore, did not need to use condoms (Lucas, 2009). Yet, emerging adults may face risks with the absence of or inconsistent use of condoms.

Overall, the way in which young people form relationships has changed (Bogle, 2008) from dating to a "hooking up era" in which emerging adults participate in hookups, FWBRs, as well as more traditional romantic relationships while navigating their identity, relational, and sexual exploration. With the goals of Emerging Adulthood and college campus experiences, young people may be exposed to prolonged sexual risks; thus, appropriate intervention must be implemented to minimize the risk potential of college students.

FUTURE RESEARCH: INTERVENTION

Research on sexual communication among friends is limited (Halpern-Felsher et al., 2004; Holtzman & Rubinson, 1995; and Lefkowitz et al., 2004); thus, in general, this phenomenon is ripe for researchers to investigate and provide a more nuanced perspective of the influence of friends in and communication during the sexual decision-making process. In particular, one path of future research that could assist in tackling the stark STI and unintended pregnancy rates affecting emerging adults is intervention. This section will highlight the focus that intervention research should take in the future.

Several criteria are critical when considering intervening with college students who are at risk and should address the long-term outcomes for college students (Reyna & Farley, 2006) and promote responsible sexual decision making (Weiss, 2007). First, sexual risk intervention ought to focus on communication. Students can learn specific communication skills to assist them in discussing sex in their relationships, problem solving, and decision making (e.g., Powell & Segrin, 2004). Emerging adults are likely to discuss sexual experiences and issues with their friends (Lucas & Nussbaum, 2011, 2012; Morgan & Korobov, 2011; Rittenour & Booth-Butterfield, 2006), and these conversations should be at the forefront of intervention. If friends are emerging adults' primary sexual information sources (Spanier, 1977), consultants during sexual decision making (e.g., Finken, 2005), and supporters of potentially risky behaviors (Hughes et al., 2005; Lucas & Nussbaum, 2011, 2012), then friendships should be a critical focus for improving emerging adults' sexual information, decision making, and social support skills.

Powell and Segrin (2004) found that emerging adults who spoke with their friends about sex were also likely to talk to their romantic partners about sex. This finding would be critical in addressing the concern that emerging adults in romantic relationships may be less likely to use condoms in their committed relationships (Lefkowitz & Gillen, 2006; Roberts & Kennedy, 2006; Umphrey & Sherblom, 2007). But sexual communication research would warn us that just because people are discussing sex does not mean they are discussing safer sex (e.g., Cline, Johnson, & Freeman, 1992) or that communication leads to practicing safer sex (e.g., Desiderato & Crawford, 1995). In fact, research has shown friends can pressure others into hooking up (Paul, 2006), and during sexual conversations encourage hooking up through esteem support (Lucas & Nussbaum, 2011; Morgan & Korobov, 2011).

Second, because emerging adults no longer participate in "dating," intervention could focus on ambiguous sexual activities like hooking up and FWBRs. While emerging adults view these as normative and attractive (Bogle, 2008; Owen et al., 2010; Owen & Fincham, 2011b), ambiguous sexual activities create difficulties including a lack of condom availability during hookups and impaired decision making due to the influence of alcohol (e.g., Bachtel, 2013; Downing-Matibag & Geisinger, 2009; Oswalt et al., 2005). Additionally, many sexual conversations friends have together focus on whether or not to participate in a hookup (Lucas & Nussbaum, 2011). The positive, encouraging support friends often provide may reinforce and increase the likelihood of risky behaviors, like hooking up without a condom (Lucas & Nussbaum, 2012; Morgan & Korobov, 2011). Friends' support also may be perceived as pressure to participate in hooking up (Paul, 2006). Perception of sexual behaviors, including frequency of hookups, may be overestimated, leading college students to believe behaviors are more normative than they actually are (Page et al., 2000). Misperceptions can lead emerging adults to participation in risky behaviors so that they are within the social norms of their peers (Mirande, 1968). Intervention messages should clarify the actuality of hooking up behavior while addressing dangers like not using a condom, alcohol, and harmful social support from friends.

Finally, sexual intervention with college students should highlight the negative emotions (Oswalt et al., 2005; Owen & Fincham, 2011b; Richard et al., 1998) and positive emotions experienced with sexual activity. For example, the absence of regret is one of the reasons emerging adults participate in risky sexual behaviors (Lucas, 2009; Owen et al., 2010), yet sexual regret is more likely experienced after sexual activity (Bachtel, 2013; Oswalt et al., 2005). Although emerging adults experienced relational regret (Jokisaari, 2004), college students were unlikely to note regrets resulting from sexual activity (e.g., Lucas, 2009). In fact, emerging adults, who are on the search for "self," are more likely to anticipate regretting missed opportunities in romantic and sexual experiences than the actual risky sexual behavior (Beike et al., 2009). It is difficult to assess regret when in comparison of one's risk to a peer's risk one feels "safe" (van der Pligt & Richard, 1994). Besides the obvious health-related consequences of sexual activity, young people may also experience negative emotions, leading to symptoms of depression and loneliness (Owen & Fincham, 2011b). Intervention messages should address negative emotions, like sexual regret, that emerging adults may experience, but also provide the skills necessary to anticipate regret during the sexual decision-making process. Richard et al. (1998) tested strategies that have effectively focused on emotions such as messages that suggest unsafe sex can lead to negative feelings while safe sex can lead to positive feelings. Additionally, anticipated regret may be a tool used in intervention messages. Individuals who anticipate regret likely prolong the decision-making process and make decisions based on the outcomes they believe will happen after making a specific decision (e.g., Janis & Mann, 1977).

Emerging adults are at high sexual risk. Messages focusing on communication, hooking up, and the negative emotions associated with sexual activity would be a good first start to diminishing risk and having emerging adults enter adulthood sexually healthy. Other concerns for intervention may include what counts as sexual education in college. Simply put, how are college-student emerging adults going to receive intervention messages and develop skills necessary to manage sexual experiences during Emerging Adulthood? To ensure students receive the information and skill enhancement opportunities they need, the location and timing of interventions must be considered. While many colleges offer Human Sexuality classes, not everyone on campus is required to enroll. Dormitory and other student organizations' sex programming is often limited to start of the semester or to a handful of events during an academic year. Other sexual informational messages are only sporadically posted in dormitory hallways or bathroom stalls. Intervention at the college level needs to consider that emerging adults are no longer minors and may choose what classes and programs they attend. Programs, campaigns, sex education, and messages should be geared toward members of this lifespan period. Keller and Brown (2002) suggest using media as a way to disseminate messages about responsible sexual behavior messages. They note that many media interventions have been effective internationally and could be successful in the United States. Considering the target audience, it is logical to use media, including social media sites, to reach college students and to send a consistent wave of sexual health messages. Broadening the venues for message dissemination (whether programs/campaigns/messages on campus or via media) may help execute interventions directed at emerging adults.

CONCLUSION

Emerging Adulthood is a relatively new and important life period that includes members, whether in or out of college, aged 18 to 28 (Arnett, 2000; Collins & van Dulmen, 2006). They have delayed adulthood by postponing responsibilities and obligations of adulthood and focusing on self-exploration and personal development (Arnett, 2000). Although romantic and sexual exploration related to romantic and sexual experiences can be useful for personal growth and young people spend more focused time with friends, emerging adults face a number of dangers. Friends' social support and encouragement, the nature of the "hooking up" dating era, and the stark statistics of sexual risk suggest emerging adults have a prolonged exposure to risk before becoming adults. The sexual risks taken in Emerging Adulthood may contribute to the physical, emotional, and financial costs in adulthood. Therefore, future research focusing on interventions should look at the sexual communication among friends, the dangers of hooking up, and the negative emotions associated with risky sexual behavior; these are important steps toward promoting lifelong sexual health for emerging adults.

REFERENCES

Afifi, W. A., & Faulkner, S. L. (2000). On being "just friends": The frequency and impact of sexual activity in cross-sex friendships. *Journal of Social & Personal Relationships, 17*, 205–222.
Albrecht, T. L., & Adelman, M. B. (1987). *Communicating social support.* Newbury Park, CA: Sage.
American Cancer Society. (2008). *Overview: Cervical cancer.* Retrieved June 23, 2009, from http://www.cancer.org/docroot/CRI/CRI_2_1x.asp?rnav=criov&dt=8

Arnett, J. J. (2000). Emerging adulthood: A theory of development from the late teens through the twenties. *American Psychologist, 55*, 469–480.

Arnett, J. J. (2004a). *Emerging adulthood: The winding road from late teens through the twenties* (pp. 3–25). New York, NY: Oxford University Press.

Arnett, J. J. (2004b). *Emerging adulthood: The winding road from late teens through the twenties* (pp. 73–95). New York, NY: Oxford University Press.

Arnett, J. J. (2004c). *Emerging adulthood: The winding road from late teens through the twenties* (pp. 119–141). New York, NY: Oxford University Press.

Arnett, J. J. (2006). Emerging adulthood: Understanding the new way of coming of age. In J. J. Arnett & J. L. Tanner (Eds.), *Emerging adults in America: Coming of age in the 21st century* (pp. 3–19). Washington, DC: American Psychological Association.

Bachtel, M. K. (2013). Do hookups hurt? Exploring college students' experiences and perceptions. *Journal of Midwifery & Women's Health, 58*, 41–48.

Barnes, M. K., & Duck, S. (1994). Everyday communicative contexts for social support. In B. R. Burleson, T. L. Albrecht, & I. G. Sarason (Eds.), *Communication of social support: Messages, interactions, relationships, and community* (pp. 175–194). Thousands Oak, CA: Sage.

Beike, D. R., Markman, K. D., & Karadogan, F. (2009). What we regret most are lost opportunities: A theory of regret intensity. *Personality and Social Psychology Bulletin, 35*, 385–397.

Bisson, M. A., & Levine, T. R. (2009). Negotiating a friends with benefits relationship. *Archives of Sexual Behavior, 38*, 66–73.

Bogle, K. A. (2008). *Hooking up: Sex, dating, and relationships on campus.* New York, NY: NYU Press.

Brown, B. B. (1981). A life-span approach to friendship: Age-related dimensions of an ageless relationship. In H. Z. Lopata & D. Maines (Eds.), *Research in the interweave of social roles: Friendship* (vol. 2) (pp. 23–50). Greenwich, CT: Jai Press.

Burleson, B. R., & Samter, W. (1994). A social skills approach to relationship maintenance: How individual differences in communication skills affect the achievement of relationship functions. In D. J. Canary & L. Stafford (Eds.), *Communication and Relational Maintenance* (pp. 61–90). San Diego, CA: Academic Press.

Burleson, B. R., & Samter, W. (1996). Similarity in the communication skills of young adults: Foundations of attraction, friendship, and relationship satisfaction. *Communication Reports, 9*, 125–139.

Centers for Disease Control and Prevention. (n.d.). Genital HPV fact sheet. Retrieved August 27, 2013, from http://www.cdc.gov/std/hpv/stdfact-hpv.htm

Centers for Disease Control and Prevention. (2013). *Sexually transmitted disease SURVEILLANCE 2012.* Atlanta, GA: U.S. Department of Health and Human Services. Retrieved January 14, 2014, from http://www.cdc.gov/std/stats12/Surv2012.pdf

Centers for Disease Control and Prevention. (2013). *CDC fact sheet: Incidence, prevalence, and cost of sexually transmitted infections in the United States.* Retrieved August 27, 2013, from http://www. cdc.gov/std/stats/STI-Estimates-Fact-Sheet-Feb-2013.pdf

Cline, R. J. W., Johnson, S. J., & Freeman, K. E. (1992). Talk among sexual partners about AIDS: Interpersonal communication for risk reduction or risk enhancement? *Health Communication, 4*, 39–56.

Collins, W. A., & Laursen, B. (2000). Adolescent relationships: The art of fugue. In C. Hendrick & S. S. Hendrick (Eds.), *Close relationships: A sourcebook* (pp. 59–69). Thousand Oaks, CA: Sage.

Collins, W. A., & van Dulmen, M. (2006). *Friendships and romance in emerging adulthood: Assessing distinctiveness in close relationships.* In J. J. Arnett & J. L. Tanner (Eds.), *Emerging adults in*

America: Coming of age in the 21st century (pp. 219–233). Washington, DC: American Psychological Association.

Crosnoe, R., Erickson, K. G., & Dornbusch, S. M. (2002). Protective functions of family relationships and school factors on the deviant behavior of adolescent boys and girls: Reducing the impact of risky friendships. *Youth & Society, 33*(4), 515–544.

Desiderato, L. L., & Crawford, H. J. (1995). Risky sexual behavior in college students: Relationships between number of sexual partners, disclosure of previous risky behavior, and alcohol use. *Journal of Youth and Adolescence, 24*(1), 1995.

DiIorio, C., Kelley, M., Hockenberry-Eaton, M. (1999). Communication about sexual issues: Mothers, fathers, and friends. *Journal of Adolescent Health, 24,* 181–189.

Downing-Matibag, T. M., & Geisinger, B. (2009). Hooking up and sexual risk taking among college students: A health belief model perspective. *Qualitative Health Research, 19*(9), 1196–1209.

Duck, S. (1983). *Friends, for life: The psychology of close relationships.* Sussex, England: Harvester Press.

Duck, S., & Wright, P. H. (1993). Reexamining gender differences in same-gender friendships: A close look at two kinds of data. *Sex Roles, 28,* 709–727.

Finer, L. B., & Zolna, M. R. (2014). Shifts in intended and unintended pregnancies in the United States, 2001–2008. *American Journal of Public Health, 104*(S1), S44–S48.

Finken, L. L. (2005). The role of consultants in adolescents' decision making: A focus on abortion decisions. In J. E. Jacobs & P. A. Klaczynski (Eds.), *The development of judgment and decision making in children and adolescents* (pp. 255–278). Mahwah, NJ: Erlbaum.

Gardner, M., & Steinberg, L. (2005). Peer influence on risk taking, risk preference, and risky decision making in adolescence and adulthood: An experimental study. *Developmental Psychology, 41*(4), 625–635.

Halpren-Felsher, B. L., Kropp, R. Y., Boyer, C. B., Tschann, J. M., & Ellen, J. M. (2004). Adolescents self-efficacy to communicate about sex: Its role in condom attitudes, commitment, and use. *Adolescence, 39,* 443–456.

Hartup, W. W., & Stevens, N. (1997). Friendships and adaptation in the life course. *Psychological Bulletin, 121,* 355–370.

Herold, E. S., & Way, L. (1988). Sexual self-disclosure among university women. *The Journal of Sex Research, 24,* 1–14.

Holtzman, D., & Rubinson, R. (1998). Parent and peer communication effects on AIDS-related behavior among U.S. high school students. *Family Planning Perspectives, 27,* 235–240.

Hughes, M., Morrison, K., & Asada, K. J. K. (2005). What's love got to do with it? Exploring the impact of maintenance rules, love attitudes, and network support on friends with benefits relationships. *Western Journal of Communication, 69,* 49–66.

Institute of Medicine. (1997). Committee on prevention and control of sexually transmitted diseases. In T. R. Eng & W. T. Butler (Eds.), *The hidden epidemic: Confronting sexually transmitted diseases.* Washington, DC: National Academy Press.

Janis, I. L., & Mann, L. (1977). *Decision making: A psychological analysis of conflict, choice, and commitment.* New York, NY: The Free Press.

Jokisaari, M. (2004). Regrets and subjective well-being: A life course approach. *Journal of Adult Development, 11,* 281–288.

Keller, S. N., & Brown, J. D. (2002). Media interventions to promote responsible sexual behavior. *The Journal of Sex Research, 39*(1), 67–72.

Lefkowitz, E. S., Boone, T. L., & Shearer, C. L. (2004). Communication with best friends about sex-related topics during emerging adulthood. *Journal of Youth and Adolescence, 33,* 339–351.

Lefkowitz, E. S., & Gillen, M. M. (2006). "Sex is just a normal part of life": Sexuality in emerging adulthood. In J. J. Arnett & J. L. Tanner (Eds.), *Emerging adults in America: Coming of age in the 21st century* (pp. 235–255). Washington, DC: American Psychological Association.

Lucas, A. A. (2009). *The role of friendship support in emerging adults' risky sexual decision-making: A test of the regret regulation theory* (Unpublished doctoral dissertation). The Pennsylvania State University, University Park, PA.

Lucas, A. A., & Afifi, W. A. (2006, November). *"We talk about that and everything in between": Exploring patterns of sexual communication in college-aged friendships.* Paper presented at the Interpersonal Communication Division of the National Communication Association, San Antonio, TX.

Lucas, A. A., & Nussbaum, J. F. (2011). *An exploration of friendship support and sexual decisions in college-aged individuals' sexual conversations.* Paper presented at the Interpersonal Communication Division of National Communication Association Convention, New Orleans, LA.

Lucas, A. A., & Nussbaum, J. F. (2012). *The (dark) role of friendship support and anticipated regret in college-aged individuals' risky sexual decision-making.* Panel paper presented for the Interpersonal Communication Division of National Communication Association Convention, Orlando, FL.

Mirande, A. M. (1968). Reference group theory and adolescent sexual behavior. *Journal of Marriage and the Family, 30,* 572–577.

Monsour, M. (1992). Meanings of intimacy in cross- and same-sex friendships. *Journal of Social and Personal Relationships, 9,* 277–295.

Morgan, E. M., & Korobov, N. (2011). Interpersonal identity formation in conversations with close friends about dating relationships. *Journal of Adolescence, 35*(6), 1–12.

Oswalt, S. B., Cameron, K. A., & Koob, J. J. (2005). Sexual regret in college students. *Archives of Sexual Behavior, 34,* 663–669.

Owen, J., & Fincham, F. D., (2011a). Effects of gender and psychosocial factors on "friends with benefits" relationships among young adults. *Archives of Sexual Behavior, 40*(2), 311–320.

Owen, J., & Fincham, F. D. (2011b). Young adults' emotional reactions after hooking up encounters. *Archives of Sexual Behavior, 40(2),* 321–330.

Owen, J. J., Rhoades, G. K., Stanley, S. M., & Fincham, F. D. (2010). "Hooking up" among college students: Demographic and psychosocial correlates. *Archives of Sexual Behavior, 39*(3), 653–663.

Page, R. M., Hammermeister, J., & Scanlan, A. (2000). Everybody's not doing it: Misperceptions of college students' sexual activity. *American Journal of Health Behavior, 24,* 387–394.

Papini, D. R., Farmer, F. L., Clark, S. M., Micka, J. C., & Barnett, J. K. (1990). Early adolescent age and gender differences in patterns of self-disclosure to parents and friends. *Adolescence, 25,* 959–976.

Papini, D. R., Farmer, F. L., Clark, S. M., & Snell, W. E. (1988). An evaluation of adolescent patterns of sexual self-disclosure to parents and friends. *Journal of Adolescent Research, 3,* 387–401.

Parks, M. R., & Floyd, K. (1996). Meanings for closeness and intimacy in friendship. *Journal of Social and Personal Relationships, 13,* 85–107.

Paul, E. L. (2006). Beer goggles, catching feelings, and the walk of shame: The myths and realities of the hookup experience. In D. C. Kirkpatrick, S. Duck, & M. K. Foley (Eds.), *Relating difficulty: The processes of constructing and managing difficult interaction* (pp. 141–160). Mahwah, NJ: Erlbaum.

Powell, H. L., & Segrin, C. (2004). The effect of family and peer communication on college students' communication with dating partners after HIV and AIDS. *Health Communication, 16,* 427–449.

Rawlins, W. K. (1992). *Friendship matters: Communication, dialectics, and the life course.* New York, NY: Aldine de Gruyter.

Reohr, J. R. (1991). *Friendship: An exploration of structure and process.* New York, NY: Garland.

Reyna, V. F., & Farley, F. (2006). Risk and rationality in adolescent decision making: Implications for theory, practice, and public policy. *Psychological Science in the Public Interest, 7*(1), 1–44.

Richard, R., de Vries, N. K., & van der Pligt, J. (1998). Anticipated regret and precautionary sexual behavior. *Journal of Applied Social Psychology, 28(15)*, 1411–1428.

Rittenour, C. E., & Booth-Butterfield, M. (2006). College students' sexual health: Investigating the role of peer communication. *Qualitative Research Reports in Communication, 7,* 57–65.

Roberts, S. T., & Kennedy, B. L. (2006). Why are young college women not using condoms? Their perceived risk, drug use, and developmental vulnerability may provide important clues to sexual risk. *Archives of Psychiatric Nursing, 20*(1), 32–40.

Rozema, H. J. (1986). Defensive communication climate as a barrier to sex education in the home. *Family Relations, 35,* 531–537.

Spanier, G. B. (1977). Sources of sex information and premarital sexual behavior. *The Journal of Sex Research, 13,* 73–88.

Umphrey, L., & Sherblom, J. (2007). Relational commitment and threats to relationship maintenance goals: Influences on condom use. *Journal of American College Health, 56,* 61–67.

UNAIDS. (2009). AIDS epidemic update. Retrieved November 30, 2013, from http://data.unaids.org/pub/Report/2009/JC1700_Epi_Update_2009_en.pdf

van der Pligt, J., & Richard, R. (1994). Changing adolescents' sexual behaviour: Perceived risk, self-efficacy and anticipated regret. *Patient Education and Counseling, 23,* 187–196.

Weiss, J. A. (2007). Let us talk about it: Safe adolescent sexual decision making. *Journal of the American Academy of Nurse Practitioners, 19,* 450–458.

Westrom, L. (1992). Pelvic inflammatory disease and fertility. *Sexually Transmitted Diseases, 19,* 185–192.

Wheeless, L. R. (1976). Self-disclosure and interpersonal solidarity: Measurement, validation, and relationships. *Human Communication Research, 3,* 47–61.

Williams, S. S., Kimble, D. L., Covell, N. H., Weiss, L. H., Newton, K. J., Fisher, J. D., & Fisher, W. A. (1992). College students use implicit personality theory instead of safer sex. *Journal of Applied Social Psychology, 22,* 921–933.

CHAPTER TWELVE

Commitment and Marriage

TARA G. McMANUS

The most public and socially acknowledged expression of commitment is marriage. With women's average age at marriage being 25.8 years and men's average age being 28.3 years in the United States, women and men are marrying later in life than were generations in the past century (Copen, Daniels, Vespa, & Mosher, 2012). This is not to say that marriage is viewed as undesirable; adolescents and emerging adults in the United States still perceive marriage as a life goal (Sassler, 2010; Willoughby, Olson, Carroll, Nelson, & Miller, 2012). Rather, Americans are delaying marriage. Today, the typical age of first marriage coincides with the approximate age that individuals transition from emerging adulthood to young adulthood (Arnett, 2000).

By delaying marriage, emerging adults may forgo several benefits of long-term commitment until later in life. For instance, married emerging adults and adults were physically and psychologically healthier and engaged in fewer risky behaviors (Schoenborn, 2004). Earlier marriage also contributed to less drug and alcohol use (Willoughby et al., 2012). However, remaining single also is associated with several benefits. Emerging adults reported fewer emotional problems (Meeus, Branje, van der Valk, & de Wied, 2007). Also, because they likely have one or more serious romantic relationships prior to marriage (Sassler, 2010), their pre-marital relationships provide opportunities to cultivate the skills and abilities necessary for maintaining long-term committed romantic relationships (Cate, Levin, & Richmond, 2002). Through these committed non-marital relationships, emerging adults learn how to nurture relationships and care for others. The communicative behaviors used to express, reinforce, and alter commitment are critical, and it is these interpersonal abilities that emerging adults develop through committed non-marital romantic relationships.

This chapter seeks to provide an understanding of emerging adults' romantic commitment and the primary communicative behaviors used. First, commitment in emerging adulthood is explored in order to understand what commitment means and how emerging adults experience non-marital commitment. Then, several communicative behaviors used to express, maintain, or alter commitment are discussed followed by an examination of how they manage the uncertainty often experienced while dating. Finally, a discussion of emerging adults' conflict experiences is presented. The research presented within this chapter reflects the experiences of heterosexual college dating relationships because the vast majority of scholarship focuses on this subpopulation.

COMMITMENT IN EMERGING ADULTHOOD

Commitment is one's desire to continue a relationship over an extended period of time. Regardless of whether commitment is conceptualized unidimensionally (e.g., Rusbult & Buunk, 1993) or multidimensionally (e.g., Johnson, Caughlin, & Huston, 1999), both imply a dependence on and a long-term orientation toward the relationship. Dependence refers to the degree to which partners mutually or equally need and rely on one another to achieve outcomes and goals (Rusbult & Buunk, 1993). Long-term orientation contributed to emerging adults' relational quality and influenced whether they stayed in or ended romantic relationships (Arriaga & Agnew, 2001). The primary distinction between unidimensional and multidimensional definitions is that multidimensional definitions include personal desire for the relationship along with moral and social constraints, whereas unidimensional definitions focus solely on personal desire for the relationship.

When defined unidimensionally, commitment is viewed as a personal choice (Arriaga & Agnew, 2001; Le & Agnew, 2003). In essence, it is how much a person wants to maintain the relationship (Ramirez, 2008). It represents past and expected future experiences for the relationship (Rusbult & Buunk, 1993) and encompasses experiences of closeness, trust, devotion, and affection and love (Cate et al., 2002; Ramirez, 2008). Personal commitment has been associated with the quality of romantic relationships. Among emerging adults, commitment was a strong predictor of relational dissolution (Sprecher, 2001) and was strongly positively associated with relational satisfaction (Lin & Rusbult, 1995). Further, for emerging adult dating couples, commitment and partners' commitment mutuality was associated with healthy functioning relationships (Drigotas, Rusbult, & Verette, 1999).

In essence, an emerging adult's choice to continue a relationship involves past and anticipated future experience of closeness, affection, and love, all of which should positively contribute to relational quality.

While individuals choose to maintain a relationship, several constraints also influence a relationship's continuation (Johnson et al., 1999; Ramirez, 2008). A multidimensional definition of commitment includes personal, moral, and structural commitment (Johnson et al., 1999; Ramirez, 2008). Moral commitment is experienced internally based on one's felt obligations to the relationship and partner, such as religious beliefs, personal values, and attitudes toward divorce (Johnson et al., 1999), and need for consistency among one's values (Ramirez, 2008). Structural commitment refers to the external obstacles one perceives to leaving the relationship, including past and present tangible and intangible barriers to terminating a relationship (Johnson et al., 1999; Ramirez, 2008). For instance, structural commitment may consist of pressure from social network members, difficulty and expense of separation procedures, irretrievable investments (e.g., time, memories), and perceptions of available acceptable alternatives to the relationship (Cate et al., 2002; Johnson et al., 1999). Structural commitments typically do not exert influence unless personal and moral commitments are low (Johnson et al., 1999).

Although related, personal, moral, and structural commitments are conceptually distinct and meaningful dimensions of romantic commitment (Johnson et al., 1999; Ramirez, 2008). In their meta-analysis, Le and Agnew (2003) found satisfaction explained significantly more variance in personal commitment than alternatives and investment (i.e., structural commitment). Yet, alternatives and investments explained a significant proportion of variance beyond what satisfaction alone explained (Le & Agnew, 2003). Personal commitment was positively associated with perceived rewards and investment in romantic relationships (Sprecher, 2001) and negatively associated with perceived alternatives (Lin & Rusbult, 1995; Sprecher, 2001). Lack of perceived alternatives and lack of support from social network members likely act as barriers to ending a relationship, yet these barriers are less constraining in nonmarital relationships than in marriages (Sprecher, 1988), making emerging adults' dating relationships easier to end. As a whole, personal commitment plays a strong role in whether individuals stay or leave romantic relationships; however, moral and structural commitment may be more important for emerging adult relationships than marriages.

Emerging adults' developmental demands influence their willingness and ability to be in committed relationships. Emerging adulthood involves developing the ability to care for oneself (Arnett, 2000). With 60% believing that "fully experiencing the single life" was necessary in order to be ready for marriage (Carroll et al., 2009), it is not surprising emerging adults characterized this period as a time of "self-focused freedom" (Arnett, 2007). During this time, they are building personal and interpersonal skills, including self-reliance, resourcefulness (Gottlieb,

Still, & Newby-Clark, 2007), acceptance of responsibility, independent decision making (Arnett, 2000), problem-solving skills, and conflict management (Carroll et al., 2009; Gottlieb et al., 2007). Emerging adulthood also involves developing the ability to care for others. Indeed, emerging adults viewed the development of interpersonal skills, the ability to prioritize a spouse and children over oneself (Carroll et al., 2009), and the ability to care for a family as critical factors indicating "marriage readiness" (Willoughby et al., 2012). Given these developmental needs, it is not surprising that emerging adults' timing orientation toward goals for and behaviors within and outside of committed relationships are unlike those of adolescents and adults (Sassler, 2010).

Although they are not ready for marriage, emerging adults accumulate a wide range of relational experiences to build these skills (Arnett, 2000; Carroll et al., 2009). Compared to adolescents' romantic relationships, emerging adults' relationships often are longer in duration, more serious, and reflect a wider breadth of emotional and physical intimacy experiences (Arnett, 2000). This may be because of differing relational goals. Emerging adults desire trust and support, while adolescents seek companionship and affiliation from romantic relationships (Sassler, 2010). In the wake of relational breakup, emerging adults can experience positive personal growth, such as gaining confidence, a better ability to cope with relational problems, and improved communication and relational skills (Tashiro & Frazier, 2003). Thus, developing and ending romantic relationships can contribute to the development of critical skills for emerging adults.

Although emerging adults' romantic experiences can be numerous and intense, they are not always positive and enjoyable (Arnett, 2000). Struggles may occur within relationships that help emerging adults build interpersonal skills. For instance, infidelity, dating and flirting with a third party, physical threats, and devaluing statements by a romantic partner were memorable, hurtful events (Bachman & Guerrero, 2006). Emerging adults also report having cyclical "on-again, off-again" experiences with dating partners. Nearly half of college students reported their current or most recent relationship broke up and then later got back together an average of two times (Dailey, Hampel, & Roberts, 2010). The cyclical nature of dating relationships may be due to individuals' commitment. Those in "on-again, off-again" relationships were less committed to their partners than those who were continuously dating (Dailey et al., 2010). Emerging adults are more likely than others to engage in novel or risky romantic and sexual behaviors (Arnett, 2000). These risky behaviors can contribute to a variety of relational and sexual problems, such as starting and/or staying in unsatisfying relationships, fertility issues (e.g., pregnancy, abortion), concerns about contraception, sexual health (e.g., STIs), and safety (e.g., rape; Lefkowitz, Boone, & Shearer, 2004; Morgan & Korobov, 2012). However, those who believed marriage would occur in their near futures engaged in fewer risky behaviors (e.g., drinking and driving, drug use, sexual behaviors) compared to those who believed marriage was in their distant futures (Willoughby et al., 2012). Overall, accumulating relational experiences may improve interpersonal skills, but the experiences may also introduce many difficulties.

Cohabitation is increasingly common among emerging adults in committed dating relationships. Between one-fourth to one half of U.S. men and women cohabit prior to marriage (Goodwin, Mosher, & Chandra, 2010; Kennedy & Bumpass, 2008). Although common, the function of cohabitation differs among emerging adults. Cohabitation can be an alternative to marriage for those who want to share significant amounts of time and space but are not ready to marry (e.g., Manning & Smock, 2005). Supporting this explanation, Clarkberg (1999) argued that cohabitation may be preferable for couples who have rewarding and high-earning careers because it allows them to enjoy the benefits of couplehood without damaging their career success. Yet, some couples view cohabitation as a lifelong alternative to marriage (Manning & Smock, 2005), which is consistent with Clarkberg's contention of cohabitation as a viable option when the couple feels they do not have sufficient financial or career stability. Given that one-third of emerging adults indicated cohabitation was necessary prior to marriage (Willoughby et al., 2012) and its frequency among emerging adults, cohabitation likely functions primarily as a path to marriage for emerging adults (Sassler, 2010).

Emerging adults' unique developmental needs impact their views and behaviors regarding romantic commitment and marriage. During this time, they are improving skills relevant for caring for themselves and others (Carroll et al., 2009). By maintaining relationships that provide trust and support (Sassler, 2010) and experiencing relational difficulties in these romantic relationships (Arnett, 2000; Bachman & Guerrero, 2006), emerging adults develop the necessary personal and interpersonal skills needed for long-term commitment and marriage. Several communication efforts are critical to emerging adults' romantic relationship commitment.

COMMUNICATION AND COMMITMENT

Increased commitment occurs through the communication that partners utilize. While several communication processes have been linked to commitment, the most commonly investigated ones in emerging adulthood include relational maintenance, uncertainty management, and conflict behaviors.

Relational Maintenance Behaviors

Relational maintenance involves the thoughts, emotions, and actions that sustain (Canary & Dainton, 2006), escalate, or terminate relationships (Guerrero, Eloy, & Wabnick, 1993). Although relational maintenance includes cognitive, affective, and behavioral dimensions (Dindia, 2000), the current discussion focuses on behaviors because behaviors are how individuals express or imply their desired commitment. The vast majority of scholarship focuses on prosocial behaviors, or constructive acts that benefit the relationship.

Prosocial maintenance behaviors include actions such as assurances, positivity, task sharing, social network inclusion, and openness. In both dating and marital relationships, these were positively associated with commitment (Ramirez, 2008; Stafford & Canary, 1991). However, the frequency and importance of shared tasks (Dainton & Stafford, 1993; Stafford & Canary, 1991), assurances, and social networking (Stafford & Canary, 1991) were greater for married couples than non-married romantic couples. Individuals who were seriously dating reported greater use of openness and positivity than married individuals (Stafford & Canary, 1991).

Across relationship types, openness promoted the relationship and created positive feelings (Sprecher & Hendrick, 2004). Because openness includes sharing thoughts, feelings, meta-relational communication, advice, and empathy (Dainton & Stafford, 1993; Stafford & Canary, 1991), it likely functions to aid relational development early in emerging adults' relationship and reinforces commitment decisions. In addition to increasing commitment (Guerrero et al., 1993), several turning points characterized by openness (passion, exclusivity, making up after conflict or relational difficulty, deciding to increase commitment) led to relational growth (Baxter & Bullis, 1986). Though openness contributes to commitment, constantly increasing openness may not be necessary. Satisfied committed couples' self-disclosure remained stable over an eight-month period (Sprecher & Hendrick, 2004). And, although self-disclosure was positively associated with relational satisfaction, emerging adult couples whose self-disclosure increased over a two-month period were more likely to have ended their relationship than those whose self-disclosure did not increase (Hendrick, Hendrick, & Adler, 1988). This suggests openness is important, but moderation may be critical for maintaining commitment in emerging adulthood.

Openness functions in conjunction with several other maintenance behaviors. Emerging adults who experienced increased commitment over an eight-week period evidenced greater openness and assurances; those whose commitment remained stable over the eight-week period reported no changes in their use of openness, assurances, positivity, or task sharing (Guerrero et al., 1993). However, those whose commitment decreased over eight weeks reported decreased positivity, assurances, and task sharing (Guerrero et al., 1993). This suggests that while openness may help maintain intimacy and closeness, assurances may be especially notable and meaningful for emerging adults' long-term view of their romantic relationships. Although social network inclusion was more important for married couples' commitment levels (Stafford & Canary, 1991), it may also decrease the turbulence and difficulties experienced by emerging adult couples over time. Over the course of a year, social network integration contributed to stable, committed relationships

(Surra & Hughes, 1997). Those who were in continuously dating relationships experienced more social network inclusion compared to those who were "on-again" in an "on-again, off-again" relationship (Dailey et al., 2010). Further, a meta-analysis of 137 studies between 1973 and 2007 showed social network integration was as strong a predictor for relational breakup as relational satisfaction, investment, and perceived alternatives (Le, Dove, Agnew, Korn, & Mutso, 2010). Thus, positivity, assurances, task sharing, and social networking in addition to openness are important for emerging adults' romantic relationship commitment.

The degree of intentionality for enacting maintenance behaviors also is associated with commitment. Strategic maintenance behaviors are those enacted thoughtfully with the intent to impact the relationship, and routine maintenance behaviors are employed without the mindful purpose to affect the relationship (Dainton & Stafford, 1993). Dindia (2000) argues the distinction between strategic and routine may be arbitrary because some behaviors may be enacted routinely and strategically within a single relationship, some may be used routinely in some relationships while strategically in others, and some behaviors may start as strategic but become routine over the course of a relationship. However, there is evidence indicating this may be an important distinction. Compared to strategic efforts, routine behaviors were stronger predictors of commitment and relational satisfaction (Dainton & Aylor, 2002). However, Weigel (2008) argued that the more committed individuals were to their romantic partner, the more strategic behaviors they used. Among romantic couples of all ages, positivity and task sharing were employed much more routinely than strategically, while advice, assurances, conflict, social network integration, and openness were used both strategically and routinely (Dainton & Aylor, 2002). It may be that doing daily, necessary tasks makes individuals want to continue their romantic relationships, which in turn make them want to go out of their way to intentionally do something to benefit the relationship.

Overall, existing research shows the exchange of prosocial maintenance contributes to greater commitment. This supports Sprecher's (2001) contention that commitment is positively related to the perceived benefits and investments in relationships. As with marriage, non-marital relationships require openness, assurances, and social network inclusion; however, the importance and balance of these may be different for non-marital committed relationships. The foregoing research, however, focused on prosocial maintenance behaviors. Avoidance and destructive conflict also may be important anti-social behaviors affecting commitment in emerging adults' romantic relationships.

Relational Uncertainty

Uncertainty may provoke openness or avoidance among relational partners. Within romantic relationships, relational uncertainty is common, especially during transitional periods in which couples are considering altering their levels of intimacy and commitment (Knobloch & Solomon, 2004; Solomon & Knobloch, 2001). Relational uncertainty refers to the degree of confidence (vs. doubts) individuals have about membership and participation in an intimate relationship (Knobloch & Carpenter-Theune, 2004; Knobloch & Solomon, 2002). As Knobloch and Carpenter-Theune (2004) and Knobloch and Solomon (2002) explain, relational uncertainty encompasses confidence about one's own participation in the relationship (i.e., self-uncertainty), the partner's participation (i.e., partner uncertainty) as well as concerns about the relationship itself (i.e., relationship uncertainty). Regardless of the form it may take, relational uncertainty impacts the relationship maintenance behaviors used and emerging adults' avoidance.

Relational uncertainty affects the maintenance behaviors that individuals use. Uncertainty about one's romantic relationship was associated with fewer prosocial maintenance behaviors (Dainton & Aylor, 2002) and greater avoidance (Knobloch & Solomon, 2002). Advice, assurances, conflict, social network inclusion, openness, positivity, and task sharing were moderately to strongly negatively associated with uncertainty about behaviors that were appropriate for the relationship, the current status of the relationship, relationship uncertainty, and the long-term likelihood for the relationship (Dainton, 2003). The influence of uncertainty and maintenance on commitment is emphasized by scholarship comparing continuously dating and "on-again, off-again" dating relationships. Individuals in "on-again, off-again" relationships were more committed and less relationally uncertain when there was more disclosure and information sharing (Dailey et al., 2010). Yet, for those in continuously dating relationships, individuals were more committed and more certain when they were integrated into their partners' social network (Dailey et al., 2010). The increased relational stability experienced by continuously dating couples may allow these emerging adults to feel more comfortable with one another's social networks (Dailey et al., 2010). Openness may be needed more when individuals feel less secure about the future of their relationship, although, as discussed earlier, this may not benefit the relationship long term.

The relational turbulence model offers an explanation for how uncertainty and avoidance influence intimacy and commitment. The model argues that as couples transition from a casual to committed relationship they increase their interdependence. The increased interdependence creates both interference and facilitation from partners in accomplishing daily tasks and contributes to experiences of relational uncertainty (Knobloch & Solomon, 2004; Solomon & Knobloch, 2001). If the couple successfully manages this turbulent transition, the relationship enjoys continued growth and interdependence, increased facilitation and decreased interference in daily tasks, and goal achievement (Knobloch & Solomon, 2004). Relational uncertainty and interference from partners were associated with negative emotions (Knobloch, Miller, & Carpenter, 2007) and irritations (Theiss &

Solomon, 2006) at transitional periods in dating. As partner and relationship uncertainty increased, couples communicated less directly (Theiss & Solomon, 2006). As relational uncertainty increased, couples were less likely to talk about their relationships (Knobloch & Solomon, 2005). Emerging adults avoided topics such as past relationships and sexual experiences, conflict-inducing topics, relational norms (which included nonverbal affectionate behaviors and infidelity), the state of the relationship, and negative life experiences (Anderson, Kunkel, & Dennis, 2011). And, dating couples had an average of two taboo topics in their relationships (Roloff & Ifert, 1998). Overall, avoidance is common when experiencing relational uncertainty.

Uncertainty may increase avoidance because of the valence of the information that emerging adults anticipate receiving from partners (Afifi, Dillow, & Morse, 2004). For instance, information exchanged during transitional periods may be personally or relationally threatening (Knobloch & Carptenter-Theune, 2004). Those who expected to receive negative information reported small decreases in commitment over a three-week time period, whereas no change in commitment was observed for those who anticipated receiving positive information (Afifi et al., 2004). Not only does anticipation of negative information decrease commitment, but receipt of negative information also may damage the relationship. When individuals received negative information about their romantic partners, those who were lower in commitment became less satisfied with their romantic relationship than those who were higher in commitment (Arriaga, Slaughterbeck, Capezza, & Hmurovic, 2007). Although avoidance is sometimes motivated by a desire to protect the relationship (Afifi & Guerrero, 2000), in these cases, this explanation may not be the case; rather, the negative information may be what individuals desire distance from.

Topic avoidance may also be motivated by a desire to protect, destroy, or deescalate the relationship, manage one's own identity, maintain privacy and autonomy, or because the information would be unhelpful or the recipient would be unresponsive and discussion futile (Afifi & Guerrero, 2000; Anderson et al., 2011). However, the salience of these reasons depends upon the context (Afifi & Guerrero, 2000). Among emerging adults who were considering increasing romantic commitment, the number of topics avoided decreased as intimacy increased; yet, their reasons for topic avoidance moderated this association (Knobloch & Carpenter-Theune, 2004). At moderate levels of intimacy and commitment, the greatest topic avoidance occurred. The avoidance occurred because they believed discussing the issue would threaten themselves or the relationship, or because the issue was beneficial or important to the relationship (Knobloch & Carpenter-Theune, 2004). Thus, several of the reasons Afifi and Guerrero (2000) identified as motivating factors for topic avoidance influence emerging adults' romantic commitment.

Although avoidance may be privileged and openness infrequent when emerging adults transition toward greater commitment, Knobloch and colleagues (2007) suggest that during times of increasing commitment, engaging in more direct, open communication may help manage the negativity and turbulence experienced. Part of this openness, especially when discussing differences, may lead to conflict. Open collaborative and compromising efforts by emerging adults can benefit the relationship and commitment (Sanderson & Karetsky, 2002) and contribute to a greater sense of interdependence not previously experienced (Siegert & Stamp, 1994). Conversely, conflict, especially the "first big fight," may create uncertainty about the partner and relationship (Siegert & Stamp, 1994).

Conflict, Aggression, and Violence

Although often viewed as negative (see Wilmot & Hocker, 2011, for discussion), conflict in romantic relationships can be beneficial. Conflict management can lead to shared meaning between the individuals because they acknowledge differences and find ways to overcome or address incompatible goals and scarce resources (Masuda & Duck, 2002; Wilmot & Hocker, 2011). As Masuda and Duck (2002) explain, conflict signals that the relationship needs "realignment."

Although the vast majority of conflict research focuses on married couples, recent scholarship suggests emerging adults' conflict experiences may be worthy of attention. Conflict in romantic relationships increased throughout emerging adulthood and began to decrease around age 25 (Chen et al., 2006). The frequency of conflict was negatively associated with relational satisfaction and commitment (Campbell, Simpson, Boldry, & Kashy, 2005). The increase may occur because emerging adults are developing interpersonal and problem-solving skills (Chen et al., 2006; Gottlieb et al., 2007), and, therefore, they may struggle managing conflict in mutually satisfying ways. Although they may engage in frequent conflict, emerging adults expected romantic partners to use high levels of affiliative and moderately low levels of dominate behaviors during conflict episodes (Ebesu Hubbard, 2001). Further, the outcome of conflict, especially the first "big" conflict, may "reaffirm and strengthen a couple's commitment ... through increased understanding and acceptance of their differences ... [or, it] may push people apart by bringing to the surface basic incompatibilities in attitudes, beliefs, and/or expectations" (Siegert & Stamp, 1994, p. 346). Given the timing of these changes and the impact conflict can have for relationship satisfaction, understanding conflict behaviors can provide insight into romantic commitment during emerging adulthood.

As with relational maintenance behaviors, constructive conflict positively affects emerging adult relationships. Constructive strategies, including openness and compromise, were more likely and denial was less likely when emerging adults desired intimate romantic relationships (Sanderson & Karetsky, 2002). Emerging adults' intimacy increased the likelihood they would resolve the conflict and maintain the relationship (Sanderson & Karetsky, 2002). Perceptions of resolvability also were positively associated with relational assurances and negatively associated with relational harm (Johnson & Roloff, 2000). Emerging adults who employed optimistic comparisons between serial arguments were more likely than those who did not make optimistic comparisons to perceive conflicts as resolvable and less likely to experience relational harm (Johnson & Roloff, 2000). Additionally, affiliation may be important during conflict. Perceptions of affiliation during conflict were positively correlated with communication satisfaction (Ebesu Hubbard, 2001). Communication satisfaction was also more likely when partners were perceived to be relationally responsive (i.e., they met or positively exceeded expectations for dominance; Ebesu Hubbard, 2001). Further, affiliative humor (i.e., witty banter and amusing or funny statements intended to amuse others, facilitate relationships, or reduce tension) was associated with lower distress after conflict episodes and increased closeness and perceived resolvability among emerging adult romantic dating partners (Campbell, Martin, & Ward, 2008).

Conversely, and consistent with marital conflict, avoidance and aggression hurt emerging adults' romantic relationships, and women may be more sensitive to relational difficulties than men. Compared to men, women reported more problems within romantic relationships (Chen et al., 2006). Also, while men's and women's relational satisfaction prior to conflict episodes was negatively related to their use of avoidance during conflict, only women's use of avoidance and their perceptions of partners' avoidance contributed to decreased relational satisfaction after a conflict conversation (Afifi, McManus, Steuber, & Coho, 2009). For both men and women, anger and aggression were both detrimental. Men and women who believed partners were angry and believed the anger to be a reason for a partner's avoidance tended to use more avoidance (Afifi et al., 2009). Aggressive humor (i.e., hurtful, disparaging, or manipulative comments such as sarcasm, teasing, and ridicule intended to enhance the speaker at the expense of the target) during conflict decreased closeness and increased emotional distress (Campbell, Martin, & Ward, 2008). Prolonged aggression may increase negative relational and personal consequences.

Aggression and violence can be experienced across the lifespan, but they may be more prevalent in emerging adulthood. Between one-quarter and one-third of college freshmen had experienced violence in their romantic relationships, ranging from pushing and throwing objects, to pinning or being pinned down, to lethal threats (Gryl, Stith, & Bird, 1991). In a more recent sample of nearly 500 emerging adults, aggression was commonly reported by both males and females in dating relationships, with less than 10% never being victimized and only 4% reporting never engaging in relational aggression toward a romantic partner (Goldstein, Chesir-Teran, & McFaul, 2008). Males were the victim of relational aggression more often than the women (Goldstein et al., 2008). Women used more physical aggression but were more likely to be seriously injured by violent acts compared to men (Archer, 2000). Further, among those who have experienced aggression or violence, they report it occurs about twice a year, and women tend to report greater frequencies of aggression and violence occurring in relationships than men (Olson, 2002b). The prevalence of aggression and violence may be due in part to emerging adults' lack of interpersonal and conflict management skills.

As with conflict, more broadly, the vast majority of research investigating aggression and violence in romantic relationships has focused on married couples. Olson's work (e.g., 2002a, 2002b) interviewed individuals who self-identified as being in aggressive or violent romantic relationships, and about half her sample included emerging adults and dating couples. Her research suggests that aggression takes several forms. Aggression consisted of verbal and noncontact physical actions (e.g., throwing items) that typically were enacted equally and reciprocated between men and women when power within the relationship was shared (Olson, 2002b). Physical violence and verbal abuse were also symmetrically enacted by men and women and involved a greater degree of aggression such as grabbing the partner and dangerous one-up, verbally aggressive cycles of negative reciprocity that could escalate into physical violence (Olson, 2002b). Finally, abusive relationships were characterized by unilateral control by one partner over the other and no reciprocation of violent acts (Olson, 2002a). In a follow-up study, Olson (2002a) found that remaining calm and being direct and tactful allowed them to achieve their goals; however, being aggressive and violent was viewed as communicatively competent in some situations. For instance, some explained their aggression was justifiable and appropriate because it was a form of self-defense or fitting to the context and specific relationship (Olson, 2002a). Participants believed their aggression to be effective when partners become increasingly angry or if they needed to get their partner's attention (Olson, 2002a).

The frequency of aggression or violence and the possibility that it may occur several times, escalate, and desensitize individuals to aggression or violence (Olson, 2002b) raises concerns for emerging adults who are developing conflict management skills. Emerging adults' ability to learn and use prosocial and relationally healthy conflict management strategies may be minimized. Further, victims of relational aggression and abuse may experience a "chilling effect" in which they withdraw from conflict and fail to voice concerns out of fear of retaliation by the partner (Solomon & Samp, 1998). Individuals in abusive relationships often remain committed to and stay in the relationship, even when they view it as unsatisfying, which can perpetuate and prolong the victimization (Rusbult & Martz, 1995).

FUTURE DIRECTIONS

While existing research provides an understanding of commitment in emerging adulthood, additional research is needed. First a broader operationalization of commitment may be insightful. Although commitment primarily is defined and studied as a personal desire, moral and structural commitments also are influential. For instance, social pressures and expectations may be stronger among emerging adults, affecting their decisions to be "on-again" in a romantic relationship or to engage in risky sexual behaviors (see Chapter 11). Thus, acknowledging the constraints involved in commitment can improve our understanding of the reasons that emerging adults continue or end romantic relationships. Further, while many comparisons are made between married and nonmarried couples and between college-age and adult couples regarding their communication behaviors within their relationships, with few exceptions (e.g., Huston, Caughlin, Houts, Smith, & George, 2001) it is unknown how those behaviors continue or change as individuals enter into marriage and mature. Therefore, longitudinal research would be beneficial for understanding how early commitment experiences influence communication and commitment in adulthood.

More attention to sampling also may improve knowledge of commitment in emerging adulthood. Scholarship tends to group all dating couples together. Thus, emerging adults are either studied in conjunction with adolescents or with adults rather than recognizing the different developmental demands individuals across the lifespan have and the influence of these demands on how individuals experience and communicate commitment. Further, nonheteronormative relationships need to be examined. For instance, four of the five most frequent maintenance behaviors that committed couples used differed between heterosexual and same-sex committed individuals (Haas & Stafford, 2005). Notably metarelational communication was used predominately among same-sex couples; Haas and Stafford argued communicative connections are the sole means of bonding and same-sex couples may feel the need to "take the pulse of the relationship" more often than in heterosexual relationships (p. 56). This suggests that how nonheterosexual relationships create and maintain commitment may vary, but whether this occurs within emerging adulthood or develops as individuals mature is unknown.

CONCLUSION

As a whole, prosocial, constructive communication contributes to greater personal commitment in emerging adulthood, and anti-social, destructive communication hurts commitment. What seems to be especially noteworthy during emerging adulthood is that by engaging in committed romantic relationships, individuals develop the skills necessary for healthy, rewarding committed relationships that they hope to obtain during adulthood. Conversely, they may learn and reinforce anti-social behaviors, which may contribute to unhealthy or unrewarding romantic relationships. In essence, emerging adult romantic relationships are a "testing ground" for marriage and commitment. This is reflected both in how they use cohabitation as a part of the courtship as well as in how they practice relationship maintenance and manage relational uncertainty and conflict. While an understanding of communication and commitment within emerging adulthood is outlined, much work is needed to better clarify our understanding and improve our ability to assist emerging adults as they transition out of adolescent and into adult romantic relationships.

REFERENCES

Afifi, T. D., McManus, T., Steuber, K., & Coho, A. (2009). Verbal avoidance and dissatisfaction in intimate conflict situations. *Human Communication Research, 35,* 357–383. doi:10.1111/j.1468-2958.2009.01355.x

Afifi, W. A., Dillow, M. R., & Morse, C. (2004). Examining predictors and consequences of information seeking in close relationships. *Personal Relationships,* 429–449. doi:10.1111/j.1475-6811.2004.00091.x

Afifi, W. A., & Guerrero, L. K. (2000). Motivations underlying topic avoidance in close relationships. In S. Petronio (Ed.), *Balancing the secrets of private disclosures* (pp. 165–179). Mahwah, NJ: Erlbaum.

Anderson, M., Kunkel, A., & Dennis, M. R. (2011). "Let's (not) talk about that": Bridging the past sexual experiences taboo to build healthy romantic relationships. *Journal of Sex Research, 48,* 381–391. doi:10.1080/00224499.2010.482215

Archer, J. (2000). Sex differences in aggression between heterosexual partners: A meta-analytic review. *Psychological Review, 126,* 651–680. doi:10.1037/0033-2909.126.5.651

Arnett, J. J. (2000). Emerging adulthood: A theory of development from the late teens through the twenties. *American Psychologist, 55*(5), 469–480. doi:10.1037//0003-066x.55.5-469

Arnett, J. J. (2007). Emerging adulthood: What is it and what is it good for? *Child Development Perspectives, 1,* 68–73. doi:10.1111/j.1750-8606.2007.00016.x

Arriaga, X. B., & Agnew, C. R. (2001). Being committed: Affective, cognitive, and conative components of relationship commitment. *Personality and Social Psychology Bulletin, 27,* 1190–1203. doi:10.1177/0146167201279011

Arriaga, X. B., Slaughterbeck, E. S., Capezza, N. M., & Hmurovic, J. L. (2007). From bad to worse: Relationship commitment and vulnerability to partner imperfections. *Personal Relationships, 14,* 389–409. doi:10.1111/j.1475-6811.2007.00162.x

Bachman, G. F., & Guerrero, L. K. (2006). Relational quality and communicative responses following hurtful events in dating relationships: An expectancy violations analysis. *Journal of Social and Personal Relationships, 23,* 943–963. doi:10.1177/0265407506070476 10.1177/0265407506070476

Baxter, L. A., & Bullis, C. (1986). Turning points in developing romantic relationships. *Human Communication Research, 12,* 469–493. doi:10.1111/j.1468-2958.1986.tb00088.x

Campbell, L., Martin, R. A., & Ward, J. R. (2008). An observational study of humor use while resolving conflict in dating couples. *Personal Relationships, 15,* 41–55. doi:10.1111/j.1475-6811.2007.00183.x

Campbell, L., Simpson, J. A., Boldry, J., & Kashy, D. A. (2005). Perceptions of conflict and support in romantic relationships: The role of attachment anxiety. *Journal of Personality and Social Psychology, 88,* 510–531. doi:10.1037/0022-3514.88.3.510

Canary, D. J., & Dainton, M. (2006). Maintaining relationships. In A. L. Vangelisti & D. Perlman (Eds.), *The Cambridge handbook of personal relationships* (pp. 727–743). New York, NY: Cambridge University Press.

Carroll, J. S., Badger, S., Willoughby, B. J., Nelson, L. J., Madsen, S. D., & McNamara Barry, C. (2009). Ready or not? Criteria for marriage readiness among emerging adults. *Journal of Adolescent Research, 24,* 349–375. doi:10.1177/0743558409334253

Cate, R. M., Levin, L. A., & Richmond, L. S. (2002). Premarital relationship stability: A review of recent research. *Journal of Social and Personal Relationships, 19,* 261–284. doi:10.1177/0265407502192005

Chen, H., Cohen, P., Kasen, S., Johnson, J. G., Ehrensaft, M., & Gordon, K. (2006). Predicting conflict within romantic relationships during the transition to adulthood. *Personal Relationships, 13,* 411–427. doi:10.1111/j.1475-6811.2006.00127.x

Clarkberg, M. (1999). The price of partnering: The role of economic well-being in young adults' first union experiences. *Social Forces, 77,* 945–968. doi:10.1093/sf/77.3.945

Copen, C. E., Daniels, K., Vespa, J., & Mosher, W. D. (2012). *First marriages in the United States: Data from the 2006–2010 National Survey of Family Growth.* National Health Statistics Reports, 49. Hyattsville, MD: National Center for Health Statistics.

Dailey, R. M., Hampel, A. D., & Roberts, J. B. (2010). Relational maintenance in on-again/off-again relationships: An assessment of how relational maintenance, uncertainty, and commitment vary by relationship type and status. *Communication Monographs, 77,* 75–101. doi:10.1080/03637750903514292

Dainton, M. (2003). Equity and uncertainty in relational maintenance. *Western Journal of Communication, 67,* 164–186. doi:10.1080/10570310309374765

Dainton, M., & Aylor, B. (2002). Routine and strategic maintenance efforts: Behavioral patterns, variations associated with relational length, and the prediction of relational characteristics. *Communication Monographs, 69,* 52–66. doi:10.1080/03637750216533

Dainton, M., & Stafford, L. (1993). Routine maintenance behaviors: A comparison of relationship type, partner similarity and sex differences. *Journal of Social and Personal Relationships, 10,* 255–271. doi:10.1177/026540759301000206

Dindia, K. (2000). Relational maintenance. In C. Hendrick & S. S. Hendrick (Eds.), *Close relationships: A sourcebook* (pp. 287–300). Thousand Oaks, CA: Sage.

Drigotas, S. M., Rusbult, C. E., & Verette, J. (1999). Level of commitment, mutuality of commitment and couple well-being. *Personal Relationships, 6,* 389–409. doi:10.1111/j.1475-6811.1999.tb00199.x

Ebesu Hubbard, A. A. (2001). Conflict between relationally uncertain romantic partners: The influence of relational responsiveness and empathy. *Communication Monographs, 68,* 400–414. doi:10.1080/03637750128071

Goldstein, S. E., Chesir-Teran, D., & McFaul, A. (2008). Profiles and correlates of relational aggression in young adults' romantic relationships. *Journal of Youth and Adolescence, 37,* 251–265. doi:10.1007/s10964-007-9255-6

Goodwin, P. Y., Mosher, W. D., & Chandra, A. (2010). *Marriage and cohabitations in the United States: A statistical portrait based on cycle 6 (2002) of the National Survey of Family Growth.* DHHS Publication No. (PHS) 2010-1980. Hyattsville, MD: Centers for Disease Control and Prevention, U.S. Department of Health and Human Services.

Gottlieb, B. H., Still, E., & Newby-Clark, I. R. (2007). Types and precipitants of growth and decline in emerging adulthood. *Journal of Adolescent Research, 22,* 132–155. doi:10.1177/0743558406298201

Gryl, F. E., Stith, S. M., & Bird, G. W. (1991). Close dating relationships among college students: Differences by use of violence and by gender. *Journal of Social and Personal Relationships, 8,* 243–264. doi: 0.1177/0265407591082005

Guerrero, L. K., Eloy, S. V., & Wabnik, A. I. (1993). Linking maintenance strategies to relationship development and disengagement: A reconceptualization. *Journal of Social and Personal Relationships, 10,* 273–283. doi:10.1177/026540759301000207

Haas, S. M., & Stafford, L. (2005). Maintenance behaviors in same-sex marital relationships: A matched sample comparison. *The Journal of Family Communication, 5,* 43–60. doi:10.1207/s15327698jfc0501_3

Hendrick, S. S., Hendrick, C., & Adler, N. L. (1988). Romantic relationships: Love, satisfaction, and staying together. *Journal of Personality and Social Psychology, 54,* 980–988. doi:10.1037/0022-3514.54.6.980

Huston, T. L., Caughlin, J. P., Houts, R. M., Smith, S. E., & George, L. J. (2001). The connubial crucible: Newlywed years as predictors or marital delight, distress, and divorce. *Journal of Personality and Social Psychology, 80,* 237–252. doi:10.1037//0022-3514-80.2.237

Johnson, K. L., & Roloff, M. E. (2000). Correlates of the perceived resolvability and relational consequences of serial arguing in dating relationships: Argumentative features and the use of coping strategies. *Journal of Social and Personal Relationships, 17,* 676–686. doi:10.1177/0265407500174011

Johnson, M. P., Caughlin, J. P., & Huston, T. L. (1999). The tripartite nature of marital commitment: Personal, moral, and structural reasons to stay married. *Journal of Marriage and Family, 61,* 160–177. doi:10.2307/353891

Kennedy, S., & Bumpass, L. L. (2008). Cohabitation and children's living arrangements: New estimates from the United States. *Demographic Research, 19,* 1663–1692. doi:10.4054/DemRes.2008.19.47

Knobloch, L. K., & Carpenter-Theune, K. E. (2004). Topic avoidance in developing romantic relationships: Associations with intimacy and relational uncertainty. *Communication Research, 31,* 173–205. doi:10.1177/0093650203261516

Knoboch, L. K., Miller, L. E., & Carpenter, K. E. (2007). Using the relational turbulence model to understand negative emotion within courtship. *Personal Relationships, 14,* 91–112. doi:10.1111/j.1475-6811.2006.00143.x

Knobloch, L. K., & Solomon, D. H. (2002). Intimacy and the magnitude and experience of episodic relational uncertainty within romantic relationships. *Personal Relationships, 9,* 457–478. doi:10.1111/1475-6811.09406

Knobloch, L. K., & Solomon, D. H. (2004). Interference and facilitation form partners in the development of interdependence within romantic relationships. *Personal Relationships, 11,* 115–130. doi:10.1111/j.1475-6811.2004.00074.x

Knobloch, L. K., & Solomon, D. H. (2005). Relational uncertainty and relational information processing: Questions without answers? *Communication Research, 32,* 349–388. doi:10.1177/0093650205275384

Le, B., & Agnew, C. R. (2003). Commitment and its theorized determinates: A meta-analysis of the investment model. *Personal Relationships, 10,* 35–57. doi:10.1111/1475-6811.00035

Le, B., Dove, N. L., Agnew, C. R., Korn, M. S., & Mutso, A. A. (2010). Predicting nonmarital romantic dissolution: A meta-analytic synthesis. *Personal Relationships, 17,* 377–390. doi:10.1111/j.1475-6811.2010.01285.x

Lefkowitz, E. S., Boone, T. L., & Shearer, C. L. (2004). Communication with best friends about sex-related topics during emerging adulthood. *Journal of Youth and Adolescence, 33,* 339–351. doi:10.1023/B:JOYO.0000032642.27242.c1

Lin, Y-H. W., & Rusbult, C. E. (1995). Commitment to dating relationships and cross-sex friendship in America and China. *Journal of Social and Personal Relationships, 12,* 7–26. doi:10.1177/0265407595121002

Manning, W. D., & Smock, P. J. (2005). Measuring and modeling cohabitation: New perspectives from qualitative data. *Journal of Marriage and Family, 67,* 989–1002. doi:10.1111/j.1741-3737.2005.00189.x

Masuda, M., & Duck, S. (2002). Issues in ebb and flow: Management and maintenance of relationships as a skilled activity. In J. H. Harvey & A. Wenzel (Eds.), *A clinician's guide to maintaining and enhancing relationships* (pp. 13–41). Mahwah, NJ: Erlbaum.

Meeus, W. H. J., Branje, S. J. T., van der Valk, I., & de Wied, M. (2007). Relationships with intimate partner, best friend, and parents, in adolescents and early adulthood: A study of the saliency of the intimate partnership. *International Journal of Behavioral Development, 31,* 569–580. doi:10.1177/0165025407080584

Morgan, E. M., & Korobov, N. (2012). Interpersonal identity formation in conversations with close friends about dating relationships. *Journal of Adolescence, 35,* 1471–1483. doi:10.1016/j.adolescence.2011.09.005

Olson, L. N. (2002a). "As ugly and painful as it was, it was effective:" Individuals' unique assessment of communication competence during aggressive conflict episodes. *Communication Studies, 53,* 171–188. doi:10.1080/10510970209388583

Olson, L. N. (2002b). Exploring "common couple violence" in heterosexual romantic relationships. *Western Journal of Communication, 66,* 104–128. doi:10.1080/10570310209374727

Ramirez, A. (2008). An examination of the tripartite approach to commitment: An actor-partner interdependence model analysis of the effect of relational maintenance behavior. *Journal of Social and Personal Relationships, 25,* 943–965. doi:10.1111/j.1741-3737.2007.00442.x

Roloff, M. E., & Ifert, D. (1998). Antecedence and consequences of explicit agreements to declare a topic taboo in dating relationships. *Personal Relationships, 5,* 191–205. doi:10.1111/j.1475-6811.1998.tb00167.x

Rusbult, C. E., & Buunk, B. P. (1993). Commitment processes in close relationships: An interdependence analysis. *Journal of Social and Personal Relationships, 10,* 175–204. doi:10.1177/026540759301000202

Rusbult, C. E., & Martz, J. M. (1995). Remaining in an abusive relationship: An Investment Model analysis of nonvoluntary dependence. *Personality and Social Psychology Bulletin, 21,* 558–571. doi:10.1177/0146167295216002

Sanderson, C. A., & Karetsky, K. H. (2002). Intimacy goals and strategies of conflict resolution in dating relationships: A mediational analysis. *Journal of Social and Personal Relationships, 19,* 317–337. doi:10.1177/0265407502193002

Sassler, S. (2010). Partnering across the life course: Sex, relationships, and mate selection. *Journal of Marriage and Family, 72,* 557–575. doi:10.1111/j.1741-3737.2010.00718.x

Schoenborn, C. A. (2004). *Marital status and health: United States, 1999–2002 advanced data from vital and health statistics.* Publication No. 351. Hyattsville, MD: Centers for Disease Control and Prevention, U.S. Department of Health and Human Services. National Center for Health Statistics.

Siegert, J. R., & Stamp, G. H. (1994). "Our first big fight" as a milestone in the development of close relationships. *Communication Monographs, 61,* 354–360. doi:10.1080/03637759409376342

Solomon, D. H., & Knobloch, L. K. (2001). Relationship uncertainty, partner interference, and intimacy within dating relationships. *Journal of Social and Personal Relationships, 18,* 804–820. doi:10.1177/0265407501186004

Solomon, D. H., & Samp, J. A. (1998). Power and problem appraisal: Perceptual foundations of the chilling effect in dating relationships. *Journal of Social and Personal Relationships, 15,* 191–209. doi:10.1177/0265407598152004

Sprecher, S. (1988). Investment model, equity, and social support determinants of relationship commitment. *Social Psychology Quarterly, 51*, 318–328. doi:10.2307/2786759

Sprecher, S. (2001). Equity and social exchange in dating couples: Associations with satisfaction commitment and stability. *Journal of Marriage and Family, 63*, 599–613. doi:10.1111/j.1741-3737.2001.00599.x

Sprecher, S., & Hendrick, S. S. (2004). Self-disclosure in intimate relationship: Associations with individual and relationship characteristics over time. *Journal of Social and Clinical Psychology, 23*, 857–877. doi:10.1521/jscp.23.6.857.54803

Stafford, L., & Canary, D. J. (1991). Maintenance strategies and romantic relationship type, gender and relational characteristics. *Journal of Social and Personal Relationships, 8*, 217–242. doi:10.1177/0265407591082004.

Surra, C. A., & Hughes, D. K. (1997). Commitment processes in accounts of the development of premarital relationships. *Journal of Marriage and the Family, 59*, 5–21. doi:10.2307/353658

Tashiro, T., & Frazier, P. (2003). "I'll never be in a relationship like that again": Personal growth following romantic relationship break ups. *Personal Relationships, 10*, 113–128. doi:10.1111/1475-6811.00039

Theiss, J. A., & Solomon, D. H. (2006). A relational turbulence model of communication about irritations in romantic relationships. *Communication Research, 33*, 391–418. doi:10.1177/0093650206291482

Weigel, D. J. (2008). A dyadic assessment of how couples indicate their commitment to each other. *Personal Relationships, 15*, 17–39. doi:10.1111/j.1475-6811.2007.00182.x

Willoughby, B. J., Olson, C. D., Carroll, J. S., Nelson, L. J., & Miller, R. B. (2012). Sooner or later? The marital horizons of parents and their emerging adult children. *Journal of Social and Personal Relationships, 29*, 967–981. doi:10.1177/0265407512443637

Wilmot, W., & Hocker, J. (2011). *Interpersonal conflict*. New York, NY: McGraw-Hill.

CHAPTER THIRTEEN

Communication and Workplace Socialization

A Lifespan Examination of the Work-Life Interface

MICHAEL W. KRAMER AND KAREN K. MYERS

Most adults spend significant time working in organizations during their lifetime. It would be impossible to gain a thorough understanding of workplace socialization by examining only the communication that occurs in the organizations during those years. Instead, this chapter takes a lifespan perspective to explore how workplace communication is influenced by the interface of communication at work and outside of work. The chapter is organized similarly to Jablin and Krone's (1994) lifespan perspective on task/work relationships based on socialization/assimilation models (e.g., Jablin, 1987, 2001; Kramer, 2010). The chapter examines communication as part of the work-life interface during four general periods: (1) the time growing up prior to individuals entering the workforce as full-time employees, often called anticipatory socialization; (2) the time when individuals first become full-time employees, often called entry or encounter; (3) the time throughout their working years when individuals experience various work-life issues, sometimes called role management or metamorphosis; and (4) the time when individuals leave employment, commonly called exit.

EARLY WORK-LIFE INTERFACE

Individuals begin the process of organizational socialization long before their first jobs. Through *anticipatory socialization* individuals develop beliefs and expectations "concerning how people communicate in particular occupations and work settings"

(Jablin, 1982, p. 680). Composed of communication and non-interactional experiences, anticipatory socialization is a continuous learning and interpretive process. The beliefs and values acquired through socialization guide individuals' general choices, behaviors, and expectations about organizational membership. More narrowly, *anticipatory role socialization* involves communication and experiences that shape individuals' interest and pursuit of particular vocations, careers, jobs, or roles (Kramer, 2010). Both processes continue across the lifespan. This section highlights the correlates and consequences of those processes in workers' early lives.

Children and Work Habits

Anticipatory socialization begins early in life. Some experts believe that children as young as three years old know that bosses tell workers what to do (Goldstein & Oldham, 1979). Although childhood experiences differ, children often learn about the value of work and its relationship to earning income by doing chores for parents and receiving pay or an allowance (Goodnow, 1988). This money-for-work exchange is further engrained when adolescents and teens begin working for pay by mowing, babysitting, or performing other odd jobs. Through these early experiences, youths begin to understand the relationship between work and income even before they are eligible to take their first part-time jobs.

Society influences youths' impressions about what is considered reputable work. In most cultures, being a physician or educated professional translates into higher incomes and prestige. Many children are encouraged to study hard to enter selective universities to prepare for those careers. Some careers and jobs are colloquially labeled "real jobs" based on characteristics that are valued by society— full-time, benefits package, and advancement opportunities (Clair, 1996). These qualities are such a part of American ideology that most American college students can define "real jobs" and admit to measuring their success by these standards. Other jobs are not considered "real jobs" because they require little skill, pay poorly, and offer few advancement opportunities (Clair, 1996). Some jobs (e.g., mortician, slaughter-house worker, janitor) are even considered "dirty work" because they are physically, morally, or socially tainted, and, although valuable for the well-being of society, many individuals avoid dirty jobs because individuals who perform them are also socially stigmatized by the work (Ashforth & Kreiner, 1999).

The Family Role in Career Aspirations

Family communication is one of the most influential forms of anticipatory socialization. Children begin developing perceptions and attitudes about work based on their parents' discourse about the meaning of work in general, as well as their attitudes about their specific jobs. For example, children who hear parents complain about overbearing supervisors and unfair work practices are likely to be less trusting of employers and to believe that workers need to watch out for themselves (Levine & Hoffner, 2006). If adults in their households did not hold steady jobs, children are less likely to anticipate steady employment as a necessity (Goodnow, 1988). Conversely, parents who speak joyfully about work and encourage their children to pursue fulfilling careers likely instill in them eager anticipation about future jobs and careers (Langellier & Peterson, 2006).

Parents often directly influence their children's broad vocational choices and even their organizational assimilation experiences. In some families, girls are expected to prioritize family obligations and are not encouraged to seek white-collar careers (Myers, Jahn, Gailliard, & Stoltzfus, 2011). Through family exposure and interaction, children often follow their parents into blue-collar or white-collar jobs (Lucas, 2011) and pursue their parents' careers (Myers et al., 2011). When parents appear to like their work environment, tasks, and associates, their children often feel drawn into those careers because they are already familiar and they think that they might enjoy them. Communication within families enables children to acculturate into particular industries or organizations more effortlessly. Gibson and Papa (2000) found that children whose parents worked for the community's largest employer were familiar with and accepting of norms of working extra-long shifts, working through sickness, and forgoing vacations. When they joined the organization as adults, they were not shocked by the harsh working conditions. They expected those working conditions as the sacrifice they must make to be good workers and provide for their families.

Parents also influence children's educational pursuits. Not surprisingly, parents with baccalaureate and graduate degrees more often encourage and even expect their children to graduate from college (Schlechter & Milevski, 2010). Since many careers require at least some college education, this too socializes youth indirectly toward certain careers.

The Role of Educational Institutions and Peers in Work/Career Attitudes

In addition to teaching basic skills, educational institutions prepare children to be responsible and knowledgeable citizens. In schools, typically the first organizations in which they are members, youths experience the need to follow rules, take directions from adult authority figures other than their parents, and complete tasks in a satisfactory manner with deadlines (Jablin, 2001; Wentzel & Looney, 2007). At advanced levels, institutions of higher education socialize youths to organizational membership and prepare them for future employment. Higher education moves youths into vocational-career paths by requiring they select courses or majors generally designed to prepare students for particular industries or careers. Classes help students learn about their interests and skills. Students who are gifted writers may choose careers in journalism or public relations, whereas students who excel in science may choose careers in biology or medicine. Students' choice of a college major can be influenced by many factors including their academic interests, career goals, social connections, and interactions with family, friends, teachers, and other influential people (e.g., Galotti et al., 2006). However, Malgwi, Howe, and Burnaby (2005) report that women and men may choose majors for different reasons. They found women choose majors based on their interest in the subject, followed by the potential for career advancement and the major's potential job opportunities, whereas men rate the level of pay in the field, the potential for career advancement, and the potential job opportunities as their most important criteria. Their research does not explore how interaction with teachers, practicing professionals, or peers influenced interest in the subject (Myers et al., 2011).

School also socializes children for work by giving them opportunities to interact with peers, thus creating friendships, competitors, and conflict partners, much like they will experience with coworkers (Jablin, 2001). Peers are an important source of information about occupations; they share information about what they have personally witnessed, what they have viewed in the media, and what they know based on interactions with parents and other adults (Jablin, 2001). Adolescents judge and discuss their friends' parents' careers based on the perceived financial status of their friends' families (Peterson & Peters, 1983). Peers also critique their friends' and classmates' planned vocational pursuits (Myers et al., 2011). They may laugh at or tease others whose jobs or careers do not fit their definition of real jobs (Clair, 1996) or seem inappropriate for the individual's gender or socioeconomic status (Willis, 1977). They may also encourage vocational pursuits, although this appears to be less common and less influential (Peterson & Peters, 1983).

The Socializing Effect of Media

Many studies examine media's socializing effect on adolescents' consumerism (e.g., Dotson & Hyatt, 2005), political awareness (e.g., Warren & Wicks, 2011), and sexuality (Fuchs, 2002; Moore, Raymond, Mittelstaedt, & Tanner, 2002), but only a few have investigated how media socialize adolescents' and young adults' career interests. In the communication field, Hymlö (2006) investigated movies targeted toward pre-teen and teenage girls and the effect on girls' vocational socialization. Hymlö found that these movies communicate to girls that glamorous, high-paying careers are easy to enter, but educators and teachers often interfere with girls' ambitions. Furthermore, the movies conveyed that girls should rely on fathers and boyfriends to protect and rescue them with emotional and financial support. In Myers and colleagues' (2011) study, some adolescents reported becoming interested in careers in law, medicine, or crime investigation because of movies such as *Legally Blonde* or television series such as *Grey's Anatomy* and *CSI: Crime Scene*

Investigation. Most admitted that these career depictions were unrealistic, but their interests were piqued nevertheless.

Summary

During anticipatory socialization individuals develop attitudes and behaviors that influence their work experiences throughout their lives. Communication with family members, peers, educators, and the media, along with early work experiences, influence individuals' choices of careers and organizations as they end their formal education.

ENCOUNTER

As individuals reach their late teens or early 20s, many first enter the workforce full-time. This transition is delayed for those who pursue advanced degrees or become stay-at-home parents. When the transition occurs, it involves leave-taking—letting go of previous roles and adapting to new roles (Louis, 1980). For example, college students may move from as few as 12 to 15 hours per week of structured time to a 40-hour workweek. They may need to let go of late nights and last-minute cramming to work early mornings and be prepared to be constantly evaluated. During this transition, the interface of work and life communication has a number of important influences.

Communication with family members frequently influences job searches or *anticipatory organizational socialization.* Some children begin working in the family business at a young age and are groomed to take management positions when they become full-time employees (Botero & Litchfield, 2013). Immediate family members may help their children find work in the same industry or even the same organization (Gibson & Papa, 2000). In other cases, more distant relatives or acquaintances, known as weak links in social networks, provide important job leads (Granovetter, 1973). Job and company information from family members and friends likely serves as a substitute for realistic job previews (e.g., Phillips, 1998) and reduces unmet expectations that lead to newcomer turnover (e.g., Wanous, Poland, Premack, & Davis, 1992). The more realistic information from these sources helps newcomers adjust more quickly to new jobs and probably explains why employees hired through job referrals typically have higher satisfaction and lower turnover (Ryan & Tippins, 2004). So, in addition to influencing occupational choices, communication with family and friends influences job opportunities and adjustment to those jobs.

New full-time employees must manage a range of uncertainties concerning their role, their task, the organization's culture and norms, organizational power and politics, relationships to coworkers, and how they will be appraised (Morrison, 1995). Although they rely heavily on organizational sources to manage these uncertainties, such as peers, supervisors, subordinates, written materials, and customer/clients (Miller & Jablin, 1991), they also manage uncertainty by talking to friends, partners, and family members (Teboul, 1994). These non-work sources provide certain advantages. Newcomers may safely vent about work without consequences, gain the benefit of an outside perspective in making sense of their experiences, or find greater understanding based on a longer-term relationship history. Thus, communication outside of work helps individuals gain understanding of their work.

Employees, new or established, also benefit from social support. This includes emotional support, which builds esteem through listening or empathy; appraisal support, which provides feedback or social comparison; information support, which provides advice or suggestions; and instrumental support, which provides assistance or resources (House, 1981). Social support from coworkers and supervisors assists employees as they deal with work stress (e.g., Ray, 1987). Recent research demonstrates the mutual importance of both supervisor and life partner/spousal support on reducing work-family conflicts and strains (Seiger & Wiese, 2009). Overall, communication of social support both at work and away from work assists newcomers and established employees in adjusting to work and life situations.

LONG-TERM WORK-LIFE ISSUES

Anticipatory socialization continues to affect individuals long after they have joined organizations. One of the most significant ways that a lifetime of communication socializes and affects organizational members is how it shapes workplace values, behaviors, and relationships. This section discusses how individuals' socialization also is affected by distinctive facets of the era in which they grew up. In particular, it specifies how their cohort's socialization affects their workplace experience and their interaction with workplace colleagues in and out of their generational cohort.

The Cohort Effect

Generational cohorts are collectives of individuals who share similarities because they were born within a distinct era and socialized by its events and values. Cohort theory proposes that experiences during childhood and adolescence "coalesce into a natural view of the world" (Mannheim, 1952, p. 113), and these early impressions explain some differences in generational perspectives. Historical events, societal trends and perspectives, technological advances, the economy, and a host of other influences socialized them to particular values and ways of thinking during their life stages (Howe & Strauss, 2007; Myers & Sadaghiani, 2010). These socializing forces are especially influential during key developmental stages such as early adulthood when shared experiences shape, define, and eventually differentiate individuals between cohorts (Noble & Schewe, 2003). These distinctive values and perspectives can affect cohort members' workplace performance, relationships, and expectations.

Baby Boomers (born 1946–1960), children of parents raised during the depression and World War II, grew up during a time of social change in a healthy postwar economy in which jobs and opportunity fostered optimism (Lancaster & Stillman, 2005). Their cohort's large size caused many to become competitive, particularly in the workplace. For many Boomers their careers became an essential component of their identities (Collinson & Hearn, 1994). They exhibit strong loyalty to employers (Jacobson, 2007), value hard work, expect to pay their dues to get ahead, look for ways to get a leg up on the competition, and often work 60 or more hours a week (McGuire, By, & Hutchings, 2007). They thrive on social recognition, value meetings as an important means of accomplishing work, and prefer face-to-face communication in part because they spent much of their lives without computers (Myers & Sadaghiani, 2010).

Generation Xers (born 1960–1980) grew up during the computer revolution and corporate downsizing that included massive layoffs (Bova & Kroth, 2001). A much smaller cohort, they grew up in a depressed economy in the early 1980s. They experienced the introduction of cable television, home computers, and early commercial and private Internet use (Smola & Sutton, 2002). Many Generation Xers came from households in which both parents worked, causing them to become self-reliant. Generation Xers also watched workaholic parents lose jobs, causing them to distrust institutions. They are skeptical, have limited loyalty to employers, and frequently change jobs (Smola & Sutton, 2002). Unlike Boomers, they think meetings are a waste of time (McGuire et al., 2007). Generation Xers prioritize balancing work with family and personal life (Stauffer, 1997). These qualities can generate clashes of values, misunderstandings, and conflicts in the workplace between Generation Xers and Baby Boomers.

Millennials (a.k.a. *Generation Yers*, born 1980–1994) have been the object of intense parental and societal attention (Cara, 2009). They are largely Baby Boomers' children raised in an era of structured activities, overprotection, and over-involved helicopter parents who hover over them (Howe & Strauss, 2007). They are the "always connected" generation with most preferring to have their electronic devices always at hand (Pew Research Center, 2010), but they are more diverse and more accepting of diversity than past generations (Pew Research Center, 2007). They can see problems and opportunities from fresh perspectives and are more comfortable working in teams than previous generations (Myers & Sadaghiani, 2010). Many Millennials were greatly affected when the Great Recession caused a delay in securing their first career jobs and attaining financial independence (Shaputis, 2004). Millennials have a high need for recognition and achievement, and many have a high level of self-esteem (Jayson, 2011). They are willing to challenge authority, which can cause more senior colleagues to feel disrespected (Gorman, Nelson, & Glassman, 2004). Millennials prefer to integrate work and personal life. They strive to attain balance between learning and playing, between academic life and social life, and between work life and family life (Howe & Strauss, 2007). Like Generation Xers, they believe in *working to live* rather than *living to work* (Loughlin & Barling, 2001). Many Baby Boomers who have devoted their lives to their employers and to their careers have difficulty understanding Gen Xers' and Millennials' unwillingness to make similar sacrifices.

Work-Life Balance

Most working adults face *work-life balance* issues, or how to manage work with other life demands (Greenhaus & Powell, 2006; Parker & Wang, 2013). Sometimes referred to as *work-family balance*, many of the issues originally emerged as women entered the workplace and searched for ways to meet obligations between childrearing and employment. Researchers often draw on *Border Theory* as a lens for explaining how individuals manage the boundaries between areas of their lives, shifting between two distinctive domains such as work and family life (Clark, 2000). Since the 1980s, new organizational policies and federal laws, such as the Family and Medical Leave Act (FMLA), have given many workers opportunities for more flexible work schedules and opportunities to take leave to accommodate childbirth or adoption. While these laws and policies were well intended, many workers, such as those who work for smaller employers or who cannot afford to take unpaid leave, are not able to take advantage of FMLA (United States Department of Labor, 2012). Others feel they cannot take advantage of FMLA or flexible work schedules because of workplace pressures and concerns over how coworkers and supervisors will react (Buzzanell & Liu, 2005; Kirby & Krone, 2002).

A primary difficulty is that even when programs are available to employees, workers frequently are required to negotiate work flexibility or leave time with their supervisors. Workers often dread doing so because they fear it will create an impression that they are less committed, which could have long-term negative career consequences (Miller, Jablin, Casey, Lamphear-Van Horn, & Ethington, 1996). To make matters worse, many supervisors are reluctant to offer time off for fear of lost productivity and fear of creating a precedent causing more employees to request leave or flexible work hours (Buzzanell & Liu, 2005).

Work-life balance has long been seen as a women's issue. Since the 1970s, when women began to participate in greater numbers in the workplace, women have continued to struggle with integrating work and personal life. Women are still expected to undertake the primary caregiving responsibilities (Tracy, 2008), and thus many have been encouraged to delay starting a family until after they have established their careers. The message has become so ingrained that many women encounter fertility issues related to increased age and identity issues because they have not allowed themselves to imagine becoming mothers earlier in their careers (Hallstein, 2008). Some argue that their protective mother role is carried into their profession. For example, female professors at small colleges often are expected to mother their Millennial students (Varallo, 2008).

The era in which work-life balance issues were considered only a women's issue may be fading. Many Generation X and Millennial women and men consider work-life balance a primary goal and wish to fully participate in their role as caregiving parents in addition to pursuing their careers (Dorment, 2013). Frequently men are not afforded the support offered to women to achieve this balance. Females are more likely than males to be socialized by their parents to value balancing work with family (Medved, Brogan, McClanahan, Morris, & Shepherd, 2006). Males are socialized to provide for their family's financial security above all else. While women are supported in taking maternity leave because it is gender normative, few men take much leave following the birth of a child because they fear a *feminine stigma* with others thinking them less masculine (Dorment, 2013). A Pew Research Foundation study found that half of all working fathers feel stress managing work and family life demands, and that 46% of working fathers say that they are not able to spend enough time with their children (Parker & Wang, 2013).

There are strong perceptual differences in the workplace on work and life issues. In some occupations, such as the professoriate, workplace accommodations are common (e.g., reduced teaching loads or semester/quarter leaves of absence). Some believe that the status quo must continually be challenged to provide more support for parents of newborns and children (Sotirin, 2008). Others suggest that providing extra support through time off or reduced workloads negatively affects their colleagues when the organization and workgroup miss out on their contributions or when others must take on extra work to cover for them (Dow, 2008). They perceive that working parents should not expect peers to have their workplace disrupted by the presence of children or to accept that their new-parent colleagues rarely spend time in the office or participate in meetings after they return to full-time work (Dow, 2008). Administrators face the difficult task of balancing support for parents with equitable treatment of other full-time employees facing other non-work issues (Kramer, 2008).

Although these examples underscore work-life issues among university employees, these are concerns shared by workers and management in all sectors. Implementing formal initiatives designed to provide work-life balance has not provided the relief desired by all parties (Myers, Gailliard, & Putnam, 2012). Organizations have tried a number of initiatives such as *results only work environments* in which workers are not held accountable for when and where they work, only for the results they produce (Ressler & Thompson, 2008). Others have implemented *adaptable workplaces* in which managers and employees operate with a shared understanding of all workers' roles in order to adapt to one another's fluctuating needs (Burud & Tumolo, 2004). Although such initiatives may improve some workers' work-life balance, some argue that these programs are mostly designed to placate while doing little to actually improve workers' situations (Myers et al., 2012).

Summary

Research indicates that one's age-group cohort has a significant effect on work attitudes and experiences throughout a career. Differences in attitude about work and how to properly balance work-life issues can lead to workplace conflict between employees. The nature of these conflicts likely changes as one cohort exits the workforce and is replaced by a new one.

EXIT FROM WORK

Exit is an inevitable part of organizational experience. Exit is generally divided into voluntary turnover, such as maternity leaves, career changes, or retirement, and involuntary turnover, such as being fired or laid off. The communication interaction between work and non-work sources is quite different for these two different processes.

Voluntary Exit

Although once it was common to have lifetime employment in one particular career and even within one organization, now people typically have multiple careers working for different organizations (Brown, 2000). Voluntary exit generally occurs for one of three reasons: (1) planned exits due to events outside of work, such as finishing a degree, pregnancy, spousal job changes, or reaching retirement age; (2) shocks at work, such as not receiving an expected promotion, being harassed, or finding differences with new management after a merger; and (3) experiencing gradual dissatisfaction, such as finding work conditions less acceptable over time (Lee, Mitchell, Wise, & Fireman, 1996). Individuals sometimes wait until they have secured a new position before resigning or may resign without one depending on the severity of the shock, the level of dissatisfaction, and the availability of alternatives.

The voluntary exit process typically follows three phases: (1) pre-announcement, during which individuals make decisions to exit; (2) announcement, at which individuals publically announce they are leaving until they depart; and (3) exit, when they no longer have an official organizational capacity (Jablin, 1987, 2001). Throughout this process, work and outside-of-work communication interact. During pre-announcement individuals communicate with other employees, but also family and friends as they develop reasons for leaving. For example, Tan and Kramer (2012) found that individuals considering career changes spoke to various work colleagues as well as family members and friends as they reached their decisions. Some received encouragement from coworkers to find more satisfying work while others discussed reasons for leaving with family members. Similarly, Avery and Jablin (1988) found that individuals increased their communication to spouses and family members as they made decisions to retire and developed post-retirement plans. Not surprising, individuals considering voluntary exit did not always communicate the same to everyone. They may talk to close coworkers while leaving supervisors unaware that they are considering changes (Klatzke, 2008). People considering taking lower-paying or lower-status jobs, such as from lawyer to teacher, primarily discussed the issues with people they felt would support their career changes but spoke to those less likely to be supportive, including parents in some instance, only after the change was finalized (Tan & Kramer, 2012). In this way, the intersection of work and non-work contacts influenced exit decisions.

During announcement, individuals often develop different messages for different audiences (Klatzke, 2008). For example, the official reasons for leaving that they communicate to company officials might include career opportunities or family-related issues, while reasons given to family and workplace friends might include mistreatment by supervisors or unsatisfactory work conditions. They may also be contacted by both close workplace friends and more distant employees throughout the organization who want to know the reason they are leaving so that they can determine whether they should also consider options like transferring or seeking employment elsewhere (Kramer, 1989). Individuals often feel concern for their current coworkers and want to make sure that work will continue with little disruption after they leave (Jablin, 1987). As a result, they try to pass on information about their work duties to those who may be assuming their position or affected by their leaving. This can be anything from important ideas about ongoing work projects to simple matters like who makes sure that the coffee machine supply does not run out. In addition, there is usually some sort of exit-recognition event (Kramer, 2010). These may range from something simple like a final lunch with close friends to something elaborate with a banquet and gifts in a rented hall.

During exit, communication to previous coworkers usually dramatically changes despite intentions to stay in touch. In many cases, work confidentiality issues make it difficult for employees to discuss many topics with someone who has left, resulting in reduced contact (Klatzke, 2008). Even individuals who transfer to another area within a company report quickly losing contact with former coworkers and supervisors (Kramer, 1989). Given the importance of proximity in maintaining communication networks (Allen, 1970), a drop-off of communication still typically occurs after an employee exits a work location, even with the availability of electronic communication today, as former coworkers become busy and involved with others.

Retirement is a special case of voluntary exit in that future employment is not involved, although many individuals take on part-time work either for the supplemental income, the need to structure their lives, or the satisfaction of continuing to be productive. Many retirees find that they lose contact with former coworkers because they no longer have mutual work topics to discuss, and so they instead increase communication to family members or other community members with similar hobbies or interests (Avery & Jablin, 1988). Overall, it is not surprising that during voluntary exit there are dramatic decreases in the communication with former work colleagues and increases in the communication with family and friends.

Involuntary Exit

Involuntary exit can be divided into two broad categories: (1) dismissals due to poor performance (e.g., absenteeism, inadequate effort) or inappropriate behaviors (e.g., sexual harassment, unprofessional behavior); and (2) dismissals due to organizational issues such as mergers, layoffs, or realignments. The difference is important in terms of attributions that others make about the dismissal, which affects the resulting communication.

When poor performance dismissals occur, supervisors attribute the problem to individuals' traits, such as lack of ability or effort, rather than situations, such as lack of training or support (Fairhurst, Green, & Snavely, 1984). Owing to these attributions, communication focuses on documenting problems, corrective efforts, and warnings, culminating in dismal meetings at which employees are confronted with evidence and either resign or are dismissed (Cox & Kramer, 1995). Prior to the dismissal, peers and even supervisors may actively encourage employees to leave on their own, such as suggesting they would be happier elsewhere or that another organization offers better opportunities (Cox, 1999). Collectively, work communication becomes largely professional and distant rather than supportive to ineffective employees, although some close coworkers likely remain supportive.

By contrast, when organizational issues (e.g., downsizing) are the cause of dismissals, it is easy to attribute the problem to the situation rather than the individual. As a result, under the best scenarios, management communicates support for employees by providing advanced warning of possible layoffs, open communication concerning the reasons for the layoffs in general and for specific individuals, and institutional support such as outplacement to reduce unemployment periods (Eby & Buch, 1998). In addition, supportive communication from supervisors is important in reducing uncertainty, increasing satisfaction, and reducing turnover for those who survive layoffs (Johnson, Bernhagen, Miller, & Allen, 1996). Of course, some organizations remain secretive and do not provide outplacement support, approaches which usually negatively affect current and former employees.

Although we are unaware of research that directly addresses how family members communicate to employees before and after they are dismissed for either poor performance or organizational causes, it seems likely that family members make attributions that affect their communication. Family members are likely to initially attribute either type of dismissal to the organization and join in blaming the situation (the company), and thus they communicate positive support during job searches. The attributions are likely to change if the person is repeatedly dismissed for cause or if the job search is unsuccessful for a long period of time. Then, the attributions likely change to personal traits, which will likely lead to negative communication of blaming and belittling the individual who is already experiencing low self-esteem for his or her lack of employment. These are work-life communication issues that need further research.

FUTURE RESEARCH ON WORK-LIFE INTERFACE

Additional areas of anticipatory socialization should be explored. Since many people change not just jobs but careers multiple times during their lives, the impact of previous careers and work on new careers requires further examination. "New" employees with 20 years of experience in other careers have different communication expectations, experiences, and skills than recent 23-year-old college graduates. It is also important to study how new communication technologies are changing how people enter the workforce. These changes include easy access to organization-sponsored information that is primarily positive (e.g., company websites) and sources outside the company that provide alternative and sometimes negative perspectives (e.g., Glassdoor.com). Scholars should explore how individuals investigate and choose jobs and careers when they are seeking a second/third career or when they choose to reenter the workforce after a voluntary leave.

Most investigations of work-life balance have focused on couples with children. Additional research needs to explore the same issues as they relate to single people, single parents, empty nesters, and the sandwich generation (taking care of both children and elderly parents). Exploring various age cohorts' differing expectations and experiences related to these issues may also provide useful insights.

Career paths have also become more varied. For example, working at a distance has become more common as technology and flexible work arrangements allow for transitions to telecommuting and dispersed teams. Some transitions may be voluntary, such as when a parent chooses to work or stay at home for a number of years or when a grown child makes a similar choice to care for an aging parent.

Other career transitions may be involuntary due to layoffs from economic downturns or mergers and acquisitions. It will be important to explore how individuals communicate and develop work relations in these various work arrangements as they enter and exit workplaces. In addition, because life expectancy has increased significantly over the last century, research should explore how people's new expectations for longer retirements, second careers, part-time work, or increases in volunteer activity influence transitions in and out of the workforce.

Finally, communication scholars have virtually ignored the important role of social class on the work-life interface. Dougherty (2011) examines some of the ways that social class differences affect work-life experiences, particularly for those she terms body workers (mostly blue collar) rather than text workers (white collar). Similarly, individuals of lower social class enter the workplace after having significantly different experiences in higher education than those with greater means as they try to blend up to their middle- and upper-class peers. Individuals aspiring to higher status jobs than their parents have more difficulty assimilating into the workforce than those who can learn from their parents already in those occupations. Workers in higher level positions have more opportunities for maintaining work-life balance and job loss experiences are more common among those of lower social class. Since race is often related to social class, future research needs to explore how race and social class permeate and affect the work-life interface throughout a lifetime.

CONCLUSIONS

Throughout an individual's life, communication interacts between work and life to influence the experience of both. As people grow and mature, communication influences career choices and impacts organizational choices and expectations. During the years of full-time work, communication at work and away from work influences the experience of joining organizations and then balancing work-life issues. Communication at work and outside of work influences the process of voluntarily or involuntarily exiting organizations. In this way, work-related communication interacts with other life experiences throughout the lifespan.

REFERENCES

Allen, T. J. (1970). Communication networks in R & D laboratories. *R&D Management, 1*, 14–21. doi:10.1111/j.1467-9310.1970.tb01193.x

Ashforth, B. E., & Kreiner, G. (1999). "How can you do it?" Dirty work and the challenge of constructing a positive identity. *Academy of Management Review, 24*, 413–434. doi:10.5465/AMR.1999.2202129

Avery, C. M., & Jablin, F. M. (1988). Retirement preparation programs and organizational communication. *Communication Education, 37*, 68–80. doi:10.1080/03634528809378704

Botero, I. C., & Litchfield, S. R. (2013). Exploring human resource management in family firms: A summary of what we know and ideas for future development. In P. Z. Poutziouris, K. X. Smyymios, & S. Goel (Eds.), *Handbook of research on family business* (2nd ed., pp. 371–405). Northampton, MA: Edward Elgar.

Bova, B., & Kroth, M. (2001). Workplace learning and generation X. *Journal of Workplace Learning, 13*, 57–65. doi:10.1108/13665620110383645

Brown, B. L. (2000). Changing career patterns. *ERIC Digest, 219*, 1–2. Retrieved from http://www.calpro-online.org/eric/docs/dig219.pdf

Burud, S., & Tumolo, M. (2004). *Leveraging the new human capital: Adaptive strategies, results achieved, and stories of transformation*. Mountain View, CA: Davies-Black.

Buzzanell, P. M., & Liu, M. (2005). Struggling with maternity leave policies and practices: A post-structuralist feminist analysis of gendered organizing. *Journal of Applied Communication Research, 33*, 1–25. doi:10.1080/0090988042000318495

Cara. (2009). Millennials want work/life balance…. Oh, the horror! Retrieved from http://careers.washington.edu/Blog/2009/02/Millennials-Want-WorkLife-Balance-Oh-The-Horror

Clair, R. P. (1996). The political nature of the colloquialism, "a real job": Implications for organizational socialization. *Communication Monographs, 63*, 249–267. doi:10.1080/03637759609376392

Clark, S. (2000). Work/family border theory: A new theory of work/family balance. *Human Relations, 53*, 747–770. doi:10.1177/0018726700536001

Collinson, D., & Hearn, J. (1994). Naming men as men: Implications for work, organization and management. *Gender, Work & Organization, 1*, 2–22. doi:10.1111/j.1468-0432.1994.tb00002.x

Cox, S. A. (1999). Group communication and employee turnover: How coworkers encourage peers to voluntarily exit. *Southern Communication Journal, 64*, 181–192. doi:10.1080/10417949909373133

Cox, S. A., & Kramer, M. W. (1995). Communication during employee dismissals. *Management Communication Quarterly, 9*, 156–190. doi:10.1177/0893318995009002002

Dorment, R. (2013, June–July). Why men still can't have it all. *Esquire*. Retrieved from http://www.esquire.com/features/why-men-still-cant-have-it-all-0613

Dotson, M. J., & Hyatt, E. M. (2005). Major influence factors in children's consumer socialization. *Journal of Consumer Marketing, 22*, 35–42. doi:10.1108/0736376051057361

Dougherty, D. S. (2011). *The reluctant farmer: An exploration of work, social class & the production of food*. Leicestershire, England: Troubador.

Dow, B. J. (2008). Does it take a department to raise a child? *Women's Studies in Communication, 31*, 158–165. doi:10.1080/07491409.2008.10162528

Eby, L. T., & Buch, K. (1998). The impact of adopting an ethical approach to employee dismissal during corporate restructuring. *Journal of Business Ethics, 17*, 1253–1264. doi:10.1023/A:1005758628414

Fairhurst, G. T., Green, S. G., & Snavely, B. K. (1984). Managerial control and discipline: Whips and chains. In R. N. Bostrom & B. H. Westley (Eds.), *Communication yearbook 8* (pp. 558–593). Beverly Hills, CA: Sage.

Fuchs, C. (2002). Too much of something is bad enough: Success and excess in Spice World. In F. Gateward & M. Pomerance (Eds.), *Sugar, spice, and everything nice: Cinemas of girlhood* (pp. 342–359). Detroit, MI: Wayne State University Press.

Galotti, K. M., Ciner, E., Altenbaumer, H. E., Geerts, H. J., Rupp, A., & Woulfe, J. (2006). Decision-making styles in a real-life decision: Choosing a college major. *Personality and Individual Differences, 41*, 629–639. doi:10.1016/j.paid.2006.03.003

Gibson, M. K., & Papa, M. J. (2000). The mud, the blood, and the beer guys: Organizational osmosis in blue-collar work groups. *Journal of Applied Communication Research, 28*, 68–88. doi:10.1080/00909880009365554

Goldstein, B., & Oldham, J. (1979). *Children and work: A study of socialization.* New Brunswick, NJ: Transaction Books.

Goodnow, J. J. (1988). Children's household work: Its nature and functions. *Psychological Bulletin, 103,* 5–26. doi:10.1037/0033-2909.103.1.5

Gorman, P., Nelson, T., & Glassman, A. (2004). The Millennial generation: A strategic opportunity. *Organizational Analysis, 12,* 255–270.

Granovetter, M. S. (1973). The strength of weak ties. *American Journal of Sociology, 78,* 1360–1380. doi:10.2307/2776392

Greenhaus, J. H., & Powell, G. N. (2006). When work and family are allies: A theory of work-family enrichment. *Academy of Management Review, 31,* 72–92. doi:10.5465/AMR.2006.19379625

Hallstein, L. O. (2008). Silences and choice: The legacies of white second wave feminism in the new professorate. *Women's Studies in Communication, 31,* 143–150. doi:10.1080/07491409.2008.1016252

House, J. S. (1981). *Work stress and social support.* Boston, MA: Addison-Wesley.

Howe, N., & Strauss, W. (2007). *Millennials go to college.* Great Falls, VA: LifeCourse Associates.

Hymlö, A. (2006). Girls on film: An examination of gendered vocational socialization messages found in motion pictures targeting teenage girls. *Western Journal of Communication, 70,* 167–185. doi:10.1080/10570310600843488

Jablin, F. M. (1982). Organizational communication: An assimilation approach. In M. Roloff & C. Berger (Eds.), *Social cognition and communication* (pp. 255–286). Newbury Park, CA: Sage.

Jablin, F. M. (1987). Organizational entry, assimilation, and exit. In F. M. Jablin, L. L. Putnam, K. H. Roberts, & L. W. Porter (Eds.), *Handbook of organizational communication: An interdisciplinary perspective* (pp. 679–740). Thousand Oaks, CA: Sage.

Jablin, F. M. (2001). Organizational entry, assimilation, and disengagement/exit In F. M. Jablin & L. L. Putnam (Eds.), *The new handbook of organizational communication: Advances in theory, research, and methods* (pp. 732–818). Thousand Oaks, CA: Sage.

Jablin, F. M., & Krone, K. (1994). Task/work relationships: A life-span perspective. In M. L. Knapp & G. R. Miller (Eds.), *Handbook of interpersonal communication* (2nd ed., pp. 621–675). Thousand Oaks, CA: Sage.

Jacobson, W. S. (2007). Two's company, three's a crowd, and four's a lot to manage: Supervising in today's intergenerational workplace. *Popular Government, 73,* 18–23.

Jayson, S. (2011, January 11). Youths prefer praise to sex, booze: Study: Self-esteem takes precedence, *USA Today,* p. 3.

Johnson, J. R., Bernhagen, M. J., Miller, V., & Allen, M. (1996). The role of communication in managing reductions in work force. *Journal of Applied Communication Research, 24,* 139–164. doi:10.1080/00909889609365448

Kirby, E., & Krone, K. (2002). "The policy exists but you can't really use it": Communication and the structuration of work-family policies. *Journal of Applied Communication Research, 30,* 50–77. doi:10.1080/00909880216577

Klatzke, S. R. (2008). *Communication and sensemaking during the exit phase of socialization* (Unpublished doctoral dissertation). University of Missouri, Columbia.

Kramer, M. W. (1989). Communication during intraorganization job transfers. *Management Communication Quarterly, 3,* 219–248. doi:10.1177/0893318989003002004

Kramer, M. W. (2008). The year of the newborns: A department chair's reflections. *Women's Studies in Communication, 31,* 196–202. doi:10.1080/07491409.2008.10162532

Kramer, M. W. (2010). *Organziational socialization: Joining and leaving organizations.* Cambridge, England: Polity.

Lancaster, L. C., & Stillman, D. (2005). *When generations collide: Who they are. Why they clash. How to solve the generational puzzle at work.* New York, NY: HarperCollins.

Langellier, K. M., & Peterson, E. E. (2006). "Somebody's got to pick eggs": Family storytelling about work. *Communication Monographs, 73,* 468–473. doi:10.1080/03637750601061190

Lee, T. W., Mitchell, T. R., Wise, L., & Fireman, S. (1996). An unfolding model of voluntary employee turnover. *Academy of Management Journal, 39,* 5–36. doi:10.2307/256629

Levine, K. J., & Hoffner, C. A. (2006). Adolescents' conceptions of work. *Journal of Adolescent Research, 21,* 647–669. doi:10.1177/0743558406293963

Loughlin, C., & Barling, J. (2001). Young workers' work values, attitudes, and behaviors. *Journal of Occupational and Organizational Psychology, 74,* 543–558. doi:10.1348/096317901167514

Louis, M. R. (1980). Surprise and sense making: What newcomers experience in entering unfamiliar organizational settings. *Administrative Science Quarterly, 25,* 226–251. doi:http://www.jstor.org/stable/2392453

Lucas, K. (2011). Socializing messages in blue-collar families: Communicative pathways to social mobility and reproduction. *Western Journal of Communication, 75,* 95–121. doi:10.1080/10570314.2010.536964

Malgwi, C. A., Howe, M. A., & Burnaby, P. A. (2005). Influences on students' choice of college major. *Journal of Education for Business, 80,* 275–282. doi:10.3200/JOEB.80.5.275-282

Mannheim, K. (1952). The problem of generations. In P. Kecskemeti (Ed.), *Essays on the sociology of knowledge* (pp. 113, 276–320). London, England: Routledge.

McGuire, D., By, R. T., & Hutchings, K. (2007). Towards a model of human resource solutions for achieving intergenerational interaction in organizations. *Journal of European Industrial Training, 31,* 592–608. doi:10.1108/03090590710833651

Medved, C. E., Brogan, S. M., McClanahan, A. M., Morris, J. F., & Shepherd, G. J. (2006). Family and work socializing communication: Messages, gender, and ideological implications. *Journal of Family Communication, 6,* 161–180. doi:10.1207/s15327698jfc0603_1

Miller, V. D., & Jablin, F. M. (1991). Information seeking during organizational entry: Influences, tactics, and a model of the process. *Academy of Management Review, 16,* 92–120. doi:10.2307/258608

Miller, V. D., Jablin, F. M., Casey, M. K., Lamphear-Van Horn, M., & Ethington, C. (1996). The maternity leave as a role negotiation process. *Journal of Managerial Issues, 8,* 286–309. doi:http://www.jstor.org/stable/40604108

Moore, J. N., Raymond, M., Mittelstaedt, J. D., & Tanner, J. F., Jr. (2002). Age and consumer socialization agent influences on adolescents' sexual knowledge, attitudes, and behavior: Implications for social marketing initiatives and public policy. *Journal of Public Policy & Marketing, 21,* 37–52. doi:http://dx.doi.org/10.1509/jppm.21.1.37.17612

Morrison, E. W. (1995). Information usefulness and acquisition during organizational encounter. *Management Communication Quarterly, 9,* 131–155. doi:10.1177/0893318995009002001

Myers, K. K., Gailliard, B. M., & Putnam, L. L. (2012). Reconsidering the concept of workplace flexibility: Is adaptability a better solution? In C. T. Salmon (Ed.), *Communication yearbook* (Vol. 36, pp. 195–230). Mahwah, NJ: Erlbaum.

Myers, K. K., Jahn, J. L. S., Gailliard, B. M., & Stoltzfus, K. (2011). Vocational anticipatory socialization (VAS): A communicative model of adolescents' interests in STEM. *Management Communication Quarterly, 25,* 87–120. doi:10.1177/0893318910377068

Myers, K. K., & Sadaghiani, K. (2010). Millennials in the workplace: A communication perspective on millennials' organizational relationships and performance. *Journal of Business and Psychology, 25,* 225–238. doi:10.1007/s10869-010-9172-7

Noble, S. M., & Schewe, C. D. (2003). Cohort segmentation: An exploration of its validity. *Journal of Business Research, 56*, 979–987. doi:http://dx.doi.org/10.1016/S0148-2963(02)00268-0

Parker, K., & Wang, W. (2013). Modern parenthood: Roles of moms and dads converge as they balance work and family. Retrieved from http://www.pewsocialtrends.org/2013/03/14/modern-parenthood-roles-of-moms-and-dads-converge-as-they-balance-work-and-family/

Peterson, G. W., & Peters, D. F. (1983). Adolescents' construction of social reality: The impact of television and peers. *Youth and Society, 15*, 67–85. doi:10.1177/0044118X83015001005

Pew Research Center. (2007). *Millennials in adulthood.* Available at: http://www.pewsocialtrends.org/2014/03/07/millennials-in-adulthood/

Pew Research Center. (2010). *Internet and American life project April 29–May 30, 2010 tracking survey.* Available at: http://www.pewinternet.org/search/internet+and+american+life+project+april+29%E2%80%93may+30%2c+2010/

Phillips, J. M. (1998). Effects of realistic job previews on multiple organizational outcomes: A meta-analysis. *Academy of Management Journal, 41*, 673–690. doi:10.2307/256964

Ray, E. B. (1987). Supportive relationships and occupational stress in the workplace. In T. L. Albrecht & M. B. Adelman (Eds.), *Communicating social support* (pp. 172–191). Newbury Park, CA: Sage.

Ressler, C., & Thompson, J. (2008). *Why work sucks and how to fix it.* New York, NY: Portfolio.

Ryan, A. M., & Tippins, N. T. (2004). Attracting and selecting: What psychological research tells us. *Human Resource Management, 43*, 305–318. doi:10.1002/hrm.20026

Schlechter, M., & Milevski, A. (2010). Parental level of education: Associations with psychological well-being, academic achievement and reasons for pursuing higher education in adolescence. *Educational Psychology, 30*, 1–10. doi:10.1080/01443410903326084

Seiger, C. P., & Wiese, B. S. (2009). Social support from work and family domains as an antecedent or moderator of work–family conflicts? *Journal of Vocational Behavior, 75*, 26–37. doi:http://dx.doi.org/10.1016/j.jvb.2009.03.001

Shaputis, K. (2004). *The crowded nest syndrome: Surviving the return of adult children.* Olympia, WA: Clutter Fairy.

Smola, K. W., & Sutton, C. D. (2002). Generational differences: Revisiting generational work values for the new millennium. *Journal of Organizational Behavior, 23*, 363–382. doi:10.1002/job.147

Sotirin, P. (2008). Academic momhood: In for the long haul. *Women's Studies in Communication, 31*, 258–267. doi:10.1080/07491409.2008.10162541

Stauffer, D. (1997). For generation Xers, what counts isn't work or all play. *Management Review, 86*, 7–19. doi:http://search.proquest.com/docview/206680976?accountid=12964

Tan, C. L., & Kramer, M. W. (2012). Communication and voluntary downward career changes. *Journal of Applied Communication Research, 40*, 87–106. doi:10.1080/00909882.2011.634429

Teboul, J. B. (1994). Facing and coping with uncertainty during organizational encounter. *Management Communication Quarterly, 8*, 190–224. doi:10.1177/0893318994008002003

Tracy, S. J. (2008). Care as common good. *Women's Studies in Communication, 31*, 166–174. doi:10.1080/07491409.2008.10162529

United States Department of Labor. (2012). *The Family and Medical Leave Act.* Fact Sheet No. 28. Retrieved from http://www.dol.gov/whd/regs/compliance/whdfs28.htm.

Varallo, S. M. (2008). Motherwork in academe: Intensive caring for the Millennial student. *Western Journal of Communication, 31*, 151–157. doi:10.1080/07491409.2008.10162527

Wanous, J. P., Poland, T. D., Premack, S. L., & Davis, K. S. (1992). The effects of met expectations on newcomer attitudes and behaviors: A review and meta-analysis. *Journal of Applied Psychology, 77*, 288–297. doi:10.1037/0021-9010.77.3.288

Warren, R., & Wicks, R. H. (2011). Political socialization: Modeling teen political and civic engagement. *Journalism & Mass Communication Quarterly, 88*, 156–175. doi:10.1177/107769901108800109

Wentzel, K. R., & Looney, L. (2007). Socialization in school settings. In J. E. Grusec & P. D. Hastings (Eds.), *Handbook of socialization: Theory and research* (pp. 382–403). New York, NY: Guilford Press.

Willis, P. E. (1977). *Learning to labour: How working class kids get working class jobs.* London, England: Gower.

CHAPTER FOURTEEN

Friend Me, Poke Me, Then Comfort Me

An Exploration of Supportive Communication in Online Social Networking Sites

ANDREW C. HIGH

Adolescence, the developmental period approximating the teenage years and early twenties, is a troubling time characterized by stressful events, complicated transitions, and conflicted feelings (Arnett, 2000). Scholars have reported that adolescents perceive limits to their social skills and doubt their ability to develop mature relationships (Martin, 2000). Symptoms of depression also peak during adolescence, particularly among college students who are isolated from their normal social networks (Morgan & Cotten, 2003). To experiment and help cope with the changes in their lives, the use of alcohol and marijuana peaks in late adolescence, and cigarette use increases during this time (Bates & Labouvie, 1997). Arnett (2000) argued that these risky behaviors are the result of coping with changes in identity. Because adolescence is characterized by change and uncertainty, adolescents require assistance to help them navigate this phase of the lifespan.

To help them cope with the traumatic events and emotions associated with a perceived life in transition, adolescents can turn to members of their social networks. The benefits of social support have been documented in prior research, and some scholars assert that receiving support from others is a core requirement of social relationships (Turner, 1981). In particular, social support helps people manage physical, mental, social, and personal stressors, which arise in a multitude of situations (Burleson & MacGeorge, 2002). Supportive communication promotes heightened social competence, improved coping skills, reduced emotional distress, and enhanced positive affect (Bodie, Burleson, & Jones, 2012; Jones & Burleson, 2003).

Of particular importance to adolescents, social support decreases the stress caused by both academic and social problems (Burleson, Holmstrom, & Gilstrap, 2005). This chapter explores the influence of social support in helping adolescents cope with the stressors in their lives. I concentrate on online supportive communication and explore how mediated social networks can benefit and hinder three phases of the support process: support seeking, support provision, and support reception/evaluation. To achieve these goals, this chapter begins by reviewing research on social support. Next, social networks are described with an emphasis on how they shape the support people receive. The paper concludes with a discussion of how social network and social support may be influenced by computer-mediated communication (CMC).

SOCIAL SUPPORT

According to Burleson and MacGeorge (2002), social support is "verbal and non-verbal behavior produced with the intention of providing assistance to others perceived as needing that aid" (p. 374). As previously mentioned, social support buffers people against the stresses that accompany major and minor life events (Jones & Burleson, 2003; Servaty-Seib & Burleson, 2007). It can help people reappraise traumas, manage emotional upset, and generally feel better about themselves (Bodie et al., 2012; Burleson, 2003; Burleson & MacGeorge, 2002). Scholars have determined that social support improves people's ability to cope with stressful events, facilitates psychological adjustment, and promotes self-efficacy (Bodie et al., 2012; Burleson & MacGeorge, 2002). Conversely, low quality social support can lead to relational consequences, reduced affect improvement, negative evaluations of supportive messages, and even increased incidence of nervous disorders and insomnia (Bodie et al., 2012; Hanson & Östergren, 1987; Servaty-Seib & Burleson, 2007).

Xu and Burleson (2001) devised a typology of social support that represents a range of comforting messages people receive from their friends and family. *Emotional support* includes messages that assess or repair a support seeker's affective state. Efforts to manage, suppress, or ameliorate an emotional reaction to an incident constitute emotional support. *Informational support* provides perspective, facts, or advice to individuals in need. The provision of informational support increases people's ability to independently solve problems. *Esteem support* attempts to reaffirm people's self-image in the face of hardship. This type of support reminds people that they are worthwhile individuals, despite their problems. People can also provide *tangible support* by supplying others with material aid. For instance, loaning money, driving people on errands, and helping around the house exemplify tangible support. *Network support* involves bolstering a person's social contacts. This type of support is enacted by initiating social memberships or expanding interpersonal resources.

Optimal matching theory contends that people are comforted most effectively when they receive the type of support that best matches the stressors or emotions they experience (Cutrona & Russell, 1990). As Barbee and Cunningham (1995) concluded, "The number of helpful behaviors that a person receives after a stressful event may not matter as much as the specific fit of the helpful behavior to the problem or emotion at hand" (p. 408). Whereas participants frequently report that emotional support messages are the most sensitive and effective type of support they receive (Burleson, 2003; Burleson & MacGeorge, 2002; Sullivan, 1996), other types of support are instrumental in certain situations. Informational support, for example, is highly valued when support providers possess expertise or exert control over a situation (Sullivan, 1996). Tangible support is favorably evaluated in some contexts (Dunkel-Schetter, Blasband, Feinstein, & Herbert, 1992), and High and Solomon (2008) observed that esteem and network support benefit adolescents transitioning into college. Thus, distinct types of support are most effective when they match the demands of a stressor.

This section cites research asserting the existence of several different types of social support. The challenge for someone in need of comfort lies in accessing the type of support that will most sensitively or effectively manage his or her distress. Adding to this complexity, social support is not universally accessible. Rather, social network structures influence people's ability to receive comfort.

SOCIAL SUPPORT AND SOCIAL NETWORKS

People mobilize their social networks to provide social support after they experience a traumatic event; greater amounts of distress elicit more reliance on social network members for coping assistance (Ensel & Lin, 1991). The different types of assistance people acquire from their networks can then shelter them from the impact of the stressor and reduce their felt distress (Miller, Smerglia, Gaudet, & Kitson, 1998). According to Hanson and Östergren (1987), differences in people's social networks underlie variations in the support they receive.

One influential characteristic of a social network is its size. Although Stokes (1983) documented a curvilinear association between network size and social support, most studies conclude that large networks provide greater access to comfort. Large, diverse networks provide quality social support because they entail numerous social contacts that can help people cope (Fiori, Antonucci, & Cortina, 2006). For example, Haines, Hurlbert, and Beggs (1996) reported that large social networks increase people's involvement in comforting interactions. Individuals with large, diverse networks often receive more emotional and instrumental support than do people with fewer contacts (Fiori, Smith, & Antonucci, 2007; Litwin & Landau, 2000). Similarly, maintaining strong bonds within marriages and across larger familial networks produces stable and robust ties for supportive communication (Birditt & Antonucci, 2007; McIlvane, Ajrouch, & Antonucci, 2007). Conversely, people with smaller networks perceive less support (Litwin & Landau, 2000). In particular, maintaining fewer social contacts equates to receiving low levels of emotional support (Hanson & Östergren, 1987). Thus, the size of a social network determines the availability of supportive communication.

The density and quality of the ties within a network also influence the support conveyed therein. Belonging to a dense network improves a person's chances of receiving support in both routine and emergency situations (Haines et al., 1996). Stokes (1983) highlighted the importance of quality connections within a social network when he observed that having at least one confidant in a network is a powerful predictor of available support. People who are integrated into a network and maintain ties with individuals who share similar characteristics report better resources for social support than individuals who have less dense or more dissimilar networks (Haines et al., 1996). Indeed, networks that curtail people's social participation limit their access to comfort (Hanson & Östergren, 1987). This research documents that both the quantity and the quality of social network ties are instrumental in determining available comfort.

In addition to studying structural characteristics, researchers have classified the different types of social networks people inhabit. The concept of network type describes the composition or category of the groupings in which people are embedded (Litwin & Landau, 2000). These analyses have produced network typologies with various names, including the high quality network, the high family/friend network, the high spouse/family network, the family-intensive network, the kin network, the family-focused network, the neighbor-focused network, the friend-focused network, and the restricted network (Birditt & Antonucci, 2007; Fiori et al., 2007; Litwin, 2001; Litwin & Landua, 2000). Despite differences in nomenclature, the networks uncovered by researchers exhibit marked similarity. Glossing over minor differences, some people maintain diverse networks in which they possess many connections and frequently associate with a variety of people. There are also specialized networks characterized by contact with friends, family, children, or neighbors. Finally, several studies document restricted networks that are smaller and lack quality connections.

Of particular concern are the restricted networks that constitute few and infrequent social contacts. Lally, Black, Thornock, and Hawkins (1979) asserted that restrictive networks do not possess sufficient resources to buffer people from the stresses of prolonged or multiple troubles. People with few social resources report insufficient levels of tangible, informational, and emotional support (Hanson & Östergren, 1987). Similarly, Birditt and Antonucci (2007) observed that people with low quality social networks report lower life satisfaction and lower levels of self-esteem than do people with more robust networks. Several reports also document the lowest levels of well-being among people in restricted networks

(Fiori et al., 2006; Fiori et al., 2007; Litwin, 2001). In fact, a 10-year study of mortality in California suggested that the highest rates of death occurred among people with few social contacts (Berkman, 1977). Thus, restricted networks are unable to support individuals in times of stress and are associated with a number of physical and psychological problems.

Kahn and Antonucci (1980) proposed the concept of a support convoy to describe the social support people receive from social networks throughout their lives. A support convoy consists of three hierarchically organized levels, conceptualized as concentric circles. The outer level consists of the sources of support who are only capable of providing specific role-based comfort. Membership in the outer region is context dependent, unstable, and vulnerable to change. The middle circle consists of relationships that are interpersonally closer than those in the outer circle; however, associations in this region are still somewhat contingent upon social roles. Individuals in the middle region are often substituted as people vacate social positions and undergo transition. Lastly, the inner circle consists of close sources of support, typically family members and best friends. Rather than being contingent on social roles, membership in the inner region entails providing sensitive support in a variety of situations.

The three levels of a support convoy correspond with both relational closeness and utility in times of stress. A convoy's three levels represent permeable boundaries in such a way that people can pass in and out of the levels, and the convoy as a whole, throughout life. Furthermore, everyone's convoy differs according to the size, composition, or type of network, and these differences produce distinct outcomes related to social support (McIlvane et al., 2007). People benefit by maintaining robust convoys with sufficient numbers of support providers in all three levels (Kanh & Antonucci, 1980). Individuals limited by a restricted network may, however, lack confidants in every level of the convoy, including the inner circle (Kahn & Antonucci, 1980).

This section reviewed research relating social support to the social networks in which people reside. Specifically, the concept of a support convoy was reviewed as a mechanism to conceptualize people's changing social networks. Despite the benefits of robust support convoys, convoy membership varies throughout the lifespan and many people lack adequate membership in their convoys during times of stress (Kahn & Antonucci, 1980). People, especially those struggling with stressors, would benefit by taking advantage of any tools that enable them to maintain or expand access to their support convoys.

CMC AND SOCIAL SUPPORT

A recent report by the Pew Internet and American Life Project indicated that 95% of teenagers use the Internet (Madden, Lenhart, Duggan, Cortesi, & Gasser, 2013).

Beyond this, scholars and the general public have both begun to appreciate the advantages CMC has for communication. For example, CMC represents a novel means for sustaining support convoys. Although support convoys were traditionally thought to change as a result of progressing social roles and life stages, CMC allows people to maintain cohesive convoys despite temporal and physical disruptions. In fact, there are fewer socially isolated individuals among Internet users than non-users (Katz & Aspden, 1997), and e-mail improves people's connections to family and friends (Rainie & Horrigan, 2002). Whereas scholars traditionally conceived of support convoys as variable networks, CMC represents a resource for people to assemble cohesive networks throughout the lifespan.

Prior research has uncovered mixed opinions about the utility of CMC as a context for supportive communication. Fahy (2003) observed that people feel compelled to compensate for the paucity of nonverbal cues online, thereby increasing the cognitive effort required to exchange supportive messages. Other scholars cite the lack of physicality and social context as two of the biggest disadvantages of online supportive communication (Colvin, Chenoweth, Bold, & Harding, 2004). Because of these hindrances, some people who receive support via CMC report more disruption to their lives following a stressor than do people who receive support through face-to-face (FtF) interactions (Lewandowski, Rosenberg, Parks, & Siegel, 2011). Other scholars disagree with these negative assessments and assert that CMC is a valuable context for comforting interactions. Indeed, Walther and Parks (2002) claimed that CMC "must be judged as a fabulously successful medium for social support" (p. 545). CMC removes impediments to maintaining support convoys because of its unlimited temporal availability and lack of geographic constraints (Turner, Grube, & Meyers, 2001; Wright, 2000). Other scholars cite the large number of people communicating, variety of support options, greater control over interactions, and increased anonymity as advantages of online supportive communication (High & Solomon, 2010; Turner et al., 2001; Walther & Boyd, 2002; Wright, 2000). Rains and Young (2009) also highlighted the availability of multiple communication modalities and the ease of sustaining interactions as benefits of social support conveyed online.

People value online supportive communication because it enhances their ability to cope with emotions and enact a changing identity (Love et al., 2012). Scholars have also observed instances of effective informational, emotional, esteem, network, and tangible support online (Love et al., 2012; Robinson & Turner, 2003). Some people who receive mediated informational or emotional support indicate that they are more satisfied with the messages they receive online than FtF (Wright, 1999). Based on the results of a meta-analysis, Rains and Young (2009) reported that receiving support online resulted in decreased depression combined with heightened perceptions of social support, quality of life, and self-efficacy. Similarly, Wright (2002) observed a negative correlation between emotional support conveyed online and cancer patients' stress levels. This research confirms that people employ CMC to seek and receive social support and that doing so can be rewarding. The main CMC contexts adolescents use to maintain and expand their social networks, thereby enhancing their support convoys, are social networking sites (SNS), such as Facebook, MySpace, and Twitter. Recent estimates suggest that 80% of adolescents use online SNS, and the majority of adolescents have profiles on multiple SNS (Lenhart et al., 2011). This chapter highlights online SNS because of their focus on users' social networks. More specifically, the remainder of this chapter focuses on the ways adolescents may use online SNS for social support. The majority of research on online supportive communication has examined online support groups; however, examining the process of supportive communication in online SNS taps a relatively informal channel of support provision (Lewandowski et al., 2011). The subsequent discussion of social support in SNS focuses on three phases of the support process: support seeking, support provision, and support reception/evaluation.

Seeking Social Support in CMC

To initiate the process of social support, people requiring advice or assistance seek comfort from members of their social networks. Little research has examined the process of seeking social support, and this is especially true in the context of online SNS. To provide a preliminary account of the process of seeking support in an online SNS, Bellur, High, and Oeldorf-Hirsch (2008) conducted a study involving several fictitious Facebook profiles in which the owner of the profile exhibited varying support-seeking behaviors. The authors reasoned that profiles that effectively employ the features of Facebook to directly seek social support had a greater likelihood of receiving support from viewers of the profiles.

Contrary to predictions, the participants disliked the Facebook profiles that displayed a clear need for social support, and participants reported a greater willingness to provide support to profiles that indirectly communicated distress. Only people who possessed certain personal qualities were willing to provide support after viewing the high emotional bandwidth profile. In other words, explicitly seeking support by using several technological features on Facebook was not successful. Seeking social support may be a difficult process to enact, at least by manipulating wall posts, status updates, and profile pictures, in an online SNS.

These seemingly counterintuitive results may be explained by considering the social norms of online SNS. Fulk, Schmitz, and Steinfeld's (1990) social influence model of technology use recognizes that CMC occurs in an active and influential social context. Although the normative behaviors and possibilities for communication within an online medium are determined to some extent by its objective features, they are also formed by the attitudes and behaviors of its users. Fulk et al. (1990)

contended, "A realistic understanding of behavior requires knowledge not simply of objective features of the environment, but also the social milieu that alters and adjusts perceptions of that environment" (p. 127). The social norms surrounding media use can have profound effects on the behavior that is deemed normal or appropriate.

The normative behavior of Facebook emphasizes positive expression and unassuming, if not frivolous, self-disclosure. For example, 68% of SNS users say they had an experience in these venues that made them feel good about themselves, and 85% of users say people frequently post kind comments (Rainie, Lenhart, & Smith, 2012). The social influence model of technology use and these observations from Facebook suggest that openly communicating distress counters the norms of online SNS. Facebook contains features that can be used to directly seek supportive communication; however, such communication may oppose norms of positivity and contradict conventional modes of behavior in this context.

Providing Social Support in CMC

Online SNS may not be effective contexts for seeking support; however, there are several reasons to suspect that support provision could be enhanced therein. Whereas seeking support may counter the norms of an online SNS, there is a stronger norm in society to help friends in need. Moreover, the qualities of online SNS facilitate the provision of effective social support.

Walther's (1996) hyperpersonal perspective to online communication suggests that people can be more effective communicators online than FtF. Walther (1996) described hyperpersonal communication as CMC that is more positive or effective than people's normal FtF interactions. According to the hyperpersonal perspective, communicators can adapt to and exploit the diminished nonverbal cues online in ways that enhance their ability to attain interpersonal goals (Walther, 1996, 2006). Specifically, message senders are able to engage in selective self-presentation online. Because CMC requires people to type their comments before sending them, a communicator is able to revise or abandon unfavorable messages before they are sent (Walther, 1996, 2006). Consistent with this idea, people adapt to the lack of nonverbal cues online by carefully and strategically constructing their verbal messages (Henderson & Gilding, 2004). Walther (2006) reported that people mindfully edit their statements online, with greater editing leading to higher levels of immediacy and affection. Thus, CMC provides users with greater control over message construction than is possible FtF (Walther & Parks, 2002).

The absence of many nonverbal demands and temporal commitments in CMC also enables communicators to redirect cognitive resources to where they can be applied most effectively (Walther, 1996, 1997). Because online communicators do not have to expend cognitive resources on several nonverbal behaviors (e.g., physical appearance, posture, gestures, vocalics), these extra resources can be reallocated to verbal message construction. In other words, people who provide support in online SNS can dedicate greater cognitive resources to the messages they send, thereby enabling them to create more effective comforting messages than are possible FtF.

Several studies have reported that interacting in CMC can increase people's efficacy. For example, shy and non-shy individuals tend to be significantly different on measures of rejection sensitivity, willingness to initiate relationships, and self-disclosure; however, such differences disappear in mediated interpersonal interactions (Stritzke, Nguyen, & Durkin, 2004). Interacting via text-based CMC, including online SNS, increases people's confidence and alleviates social fears by lending them increased control over their self-disclosure and greater confidence to achieve their social goals (Shepherd & Edelmann, 2005). High (2012) adopted the logic of the hyperpersonal perspective and argued that CMC can benefit certain people who are tasked with providing support. According to predictions, some support providers, most notably those who normally struggle in FtF supportive interactions, achieved more positive outcomes online than FtF. These results suggest that CMC may elicit hyperpersonal outcomes for some support providers.

Online interactions may be most advantageous for people who lack the confidence, skill, or resources to achieve success FtF. Men, in particular, have difficulty providing effective comfort in FtF contexts. Compared to women, men exhibit a reduced likelihood of providing emotional support (Burleson et al., 2005), seeking support (Ashton & Fuehrer, 1993), and producing sensitive comfort (Samter, 2002). Men exhibit an especially pronounced dislike of providing sensitive messages to other men (Burleson et al., 2005). An important caveat to these gender difference is that all of these findings have been produced in FtF interactions. The factors that are particularly consequential for male support providers, such as anxiety, face threat, and uncertainty (see Burleson, 2003), may, however, be lessened online. When they interact via CMC, men experience a buffer between themselves and their partners (O'Sullivan, 2000). This perceptual space not only shields males from their partners' reactions but also lends them more time to compose and edit messages so that they convey effective support. Consistent with these predictions, High (2012) observed that men provided higher quality emotional support to both male and female receivers when these interactions occurred online than FtF.

This section integrated theory and research related to social support and CMC to conclude that support provision is enhanced in online SNS. Guided by the principles of the hyperpersonal perspective, there is reason to suspect that support providers carefully edit their messages in online SNS to create higher quality comfort than they normally provide FtF. The unique features of CMC, such as cognitive reallocation, the buffer between communicators, and relaxed temporal demands, also facilitate the process of support provision.

Receiving and Evaluating Social Support in CMC

The final stage in the process of social support is the reception and evaluation of comforting messages. Like the provision of support discussed in the previous section, the evaluation of social support may be enhanced online. This stage is contingent upon the quality of the messages people receive, and if support providers produce effective supportive messages online, support receivers should create positive evaluations of those messages.

The hyperpersonal perspective not only predicts benefits for message senders, but it also posits positive outcomes for receivers, such as idealized impressions of conversational partners. People who receive messages in CMC engage in a process of over-attribution based on the limited information they possess. In the absence of nonverbal cues that can detract from otherwise positive messages, receivers focus on whatever information they do receive and "fill in" the gaps of their impressions with desired or relevant information (Walther, 1996). Individuals have also been found to compensate for the lack of nonverbal cues online by trusting their partners more than people who interact FtF (Kock, 2005). In a telling example of over-attribution in CMC, Walther (1997) reported that long-term CMC groups rated their partners to be more physically attractive than did groups who interacted FtF, despite the fact that the members of the online groups never saw each other. CMC interactants form idealized impressions based on the limited cues they encounter, and subsequently over-attribute, online.

Situations requiring social support are often cognitively demanding, involve painful emotions, and are face threatening endeavors for support receivers (Burleson, 2003; Burleson & MacGeorge, 2002). The combination of these factors makes supportive interactions among the most cognitively complex situations people encounter (Burleson, 2003). Yet, when people receive support online, they are distanced from both their problems and support providers, and this distance can enhance their evaluation of comforting messages. O'Sullivan's (2000) buffer effect contends that the perceptual space between communicators can lessen some of the complexities of interpersonal interaction. Indeed, people prefer the buffer of mediated communication when they are concerned with their self-presentation or have to communicate sensitive information (O'Sullivan, 2000). CMC allows people to evaluate messages in a time and space removed from a demanding social encounter; therefore, people may process these messages more thoroughly online than FtF.

Mediated interactions provide receivers with extended time to process and evaluate supportive messages, and these resources may allow people to more fully appreciate supportive messages than is possible FtF. Scholars also contend that interacting online is less physiologically arousing than communicating FtF. The facial expressions, body language, and oral comments uttered in FtF interactions heighten physiological arousal (Bates & Cleese, 2001). Conversely, the suppression of those expressions decreases the arousal of communication (Reinig, Briggs, Shepherd, Yen, Nunamaker, 1995). Although some scholars criticize CMC for reducing the arousal of conversation, some people recognize its utility. As Kock (2005) observed, "Decreases in physiological arousal may arguably influence task outcome quality positively under the appropriate circumstances" (p. 124). Reduced arousal may allow receivers of support to engage in thoughtful, focused processing of the messages they receive. To the extent that support receivers carefully evaluate comforting messages, especially high quality messages that were generated, in part, due to the affordances of CMC, they should achieve more positive outcomes online than FtF.

Prior research has validated this theorizing by reporting a number of psychosocial benefits to receiving support online (see Eastin & LaRose, 2005; Rains & Young, 2009; Wright, 1999, 2002). Receivers of informational and emotional support online report that the messages they receive affirm important aspects of their identity and their experience with a stressor (Love et al., 2012). Wright (1999) also noted that people who receive mediated informational or emotional support are more satisfied with the support they receive from online sources than FtF interactions. Facebook users, in particular, receive higher levels of social support than other Internet users (Hampton, Goulet, Rainie, & Purcell, 2011). Beyond that, greater investment, more time spent on the site, and a large network of Facebook friends elicit stronger feelings of support and satisfaction with received support (Wright et al., 2013). Thus, prior research confirms that support receivers can benefit by interacting online.

This section suggests that support receivers can experience favorable outcomes online. If support providers are able to communicate more effective messages online than FtF, people who obtain support online should, in turn, have greater odds of receiving effective support. Moreover, support receivers can devote more effort to carefully processing comforting messages in CMC contexts that are removed from stressors, the demands of FtF interaction, and the face threat associated with receiving support. As long as high quality messages are transmitted, online SNS should be effective venues for the reception of comforting messages.

FUTURE RESEARCH DIRECTIONS FOR ONLINE SUPPORTIVE COMMUNICATION WITHIN SOCIAL NETWORKING SITES

This chapter asserts that online SNS are useful for helping users preserve and expand their support convoys (see also Eastin & LaRose, 2005). Although little prior research has directly investigated the process of supportive communication on networks like Facebook, MySpace, and Twitter, this chapter asserts that the benefits of CMC are contingent upon the stage of supportive communication under consideration.

One fruitful direction for future research is investigating the types of social support that are most commonly or effectively communicated in different SNS. To do this, scholars need to appreciate the technological features of specific online venues (see High & Solomon, 2010). Prior research has concluded that features of CMC contexts, such as synchronicity, anonymity, and customization, influence users' experiences of communication (Matsunaga, 2010; Sundar, 2008). Online SNS are unique contexts because they entail options for asynchronous public or private communication. Some SNS also contain a chat feature that users can employ to exchange synchronous messages. The levels of customization and anonymity in these venues are set according to a user's discretion by carefully manipulating the features on a profile page. The choices people make regarding these affordances may influence the experience of support for both support providers and receivers. By taking these factors, and their ability to shape interactions, into account, not only can researchers document the different types of support that occur in different contexts but they can also explain why certain outcomes occur. For example, it may not be that online SNS yield different outcomes than do online discussion boards. Rather, it may be that differences in anonymity that exist across these platforms create different experiences and outcomes of supportive communication. There may not be an inherent quality of CMC that alters communication; however, the technological affordances of different channels deserve attention for their ability to influence supportive interactions. By thoroughly considering the affordances that both help to define certain channels and that exist across channels, scholars interested in CMC can propose research questions that might not have a counterpart in FtF interactions.

Beyond investigating the specific types of support people receive in online SNS, research could consider whether the support people receive in these contexts is adequate. Some research describes support adequacy as the extent to which people's desires for certain types of support are met in a given interaction (Brock & Lawrence, 2009; Dehle, Larsen, & Landers, 2001; High & Steuber, 2014). To the extent that people's desires are met, support is considered to be adequate. In contrast, when people's desires are not met, negative outcomes result from inadequate support. Although some researchers contend that any form of inadequate support is harmful, other scholars assert that distinct negative outcomes result from either desiring more support than is received or receiving more support than is desired (Brock & Lawrence, 2009). Adolescents, and people throughout the lifespan, will likely continue to turn to SNS for supportive communication as access to these contexts spreads throughout the lifespan and more potential support providers can be reached via SNS. People develop desires for the amounts and types of supportive communication they hope to receive online, and researchers can document whether these desires are met, why desires are not met, and what the consequences of unmet desires seem to be. Some preliminary research indicates that people desire more network support than they receive from online sources (High & Steuber, 2014); however, that study examined online sources in general, rather than asking about people's desires in different contexts of CMC. People likely desire different amounts and types of support from different online venues, and the reasons and outcomes for these desires across different contexts of CMC can be better understood.

CONCLUDING THOUGHTS

The process of supportive communication is evolving as more and more people seek, provide, and subsequently receive support online. In the past, membership in support convoys was tenuous, and disruption frequently occurred following life events. This chapter contends that online SNS can maintain or even expand adolescents' support convoys, thereby providing them with increased access to sources of social support. If adolescents do not realize this potential, the friends in an online SNS may equate to a collection of people whose lives a person can follow and vicariously experience. If used to their full potential, however, these friends represent a strengthened support convoy and a source of profoundly helpful, yet otherwise untapped supportive communication.

REFERENCES

Arnett, J. J. (2000). Emerging adulthood: A theory of development from the late teens through the twenties. *American Psychologist, 55*, 469–480. doi:10.1037/0003-066X.55.5.469

Ashton, W. A., & Fuehrer, A. (1993). Effects of gender and gender-role identification of participants and type of social support resource on support seeking. *Sex Roles, 28*, 461–476. doi:10.1007/BF00289608

Barbee, A. P., & Cunningham, M. R. (1995). An experimental approach to social support communications: Interactive coping in close relationships. In B. R. Burleson (Ed.), *Communication yearbook 18* (pp. 381–413). Thousand Oaks, CA: Sage.

Bates, B., & Cleese, J. (2001). *The human face*. New York, NY: Dorling Kindersley.

Bates, M. E., & Labouvie, E. W. (1997). Adolescent risk factors and the prediction of persistent alcohol and drug use into adulthood. *Alcoholism: Clinical and Experimental Research, 21*, 944–950. doi:10.1111/j.1530-0277.1997.tb03863.x

Bellur, S., High, A. C., & Oeldorf-Hirsch, A. (2008, May). *Misery doesn't love company: An exploration of bandwidth in online social networks.* Paper presented at the International Communication Association conference, Montreal, Canada.

Berkman, L. F. (1977). *Social networks, host resistance, and mortality: A follow-up study of Alameda County residents* (Unpublished doctoral dissertation). University of California, Berkeley.

Birditt, K. S., & Antonucci, T. C. (2007). Relationship quality profiles and well-being among married adults. *Journal of Family Psychology, 21*, 595–604. doi:10.1037/08933200.21.4.595

Bodie, G. D., Burleson, B. R., & Jones, S. M. (2012). Explaining the relationships among supportive message quality, evaluations, and outcomes: A dual-process approach. *Communication Monographs, 79*, 1–22. doi:10.1080/03637751.2011.646491

Brock, R. L., & Lawrence, E. (2009). Too much of a good thing: Underprovision versus overprovision of partner support. *Journal of Family Psychology, 23*, 181–192. doi:10.1037/a0015402

Burleson, B. R. (2003). Emotional support skill. In J. O. Greene & B. R. Burleson (Eds.), *Handbook of communication and social interaction skills* (pp. 551–594). Mahwah, NJ: Erlbaum.

Burleson, B. R., Holmstrom, A. J., & Gilstrap, C. M. (2005). "Guys can't say *that* to guys": Four experiments assessing the normative motivation account for deficiencies in the emotional support provided by men. *Communication Monographs, 72*, 468–501. doi:10.1080/03637750500322636

Burleson, B. R., & MacGeorge, E. L. (2002). Supportive communication. In M. L. Knapp and J. A. Daly (Eds.), *Handbook of interpersonal communication* (3rd ed., pp. 374–424). Thousand Oaks, CA: Sage.

Colvin, J., Chenoweth, L., Bold, M., & Harding, C. (2004). Caregivers of older adults: Advantages and disadvantages of Internet-based social support. *Family Relations, 53*, 49–57. doi:10.1111/j.1741-3729.2004.00008.x

Cutrona, C. E., & Russell, D. W. (1990). Types of social support and specific stress: Toward a theory of optimal matching. In B. R. Burleson, I. G. Sarason, & G. R. Pierce (Eds.), *Social support: An interactional view* (pp. 319–366). New York, NY: John Wiley & Sons.

Dehle, C., Larsen, D., & Landers, J. L. (2001). Social support in marriage. *The American Journal of Family Therapy, 29*, 307–324. doi:10.1080/01926180126500

Dunkel-Shetter, C., Blasband, D., Feinstein, L., & Herbert, T. (1992). Elments of supportive interactions: When are attempts to help effective? In S. Spacapan & S. Oskamp (Eds.), *Helping and being helped: Naturalistic studies* (pp. 83–114). Newbury Park, CA: Sage.

Eastin, M. S., & LaRose, R. (2005). Alt. support: Modeling social support online. *Computers in Human Behavior, 21*, 977–992. doi:10.1016/j.chb.2004.02.024

Ensel, W. M., & Lin, N. (1991). The life stress paradigm and psychological distress. *Journal of Health and Social Behavior, 32*, 321–341. doi:10.2307/2137101

Fahy, P. J. (2003). Indicators of support in online interaction. *The International Review of Research in Open and Distance Learning, 4*(1).

Fiori, K. L., Antonucci, T. C., & Cortina, K. S. (2006). Social network typologies and mental health among older adults. *The Journals of Gerontology, 61B*, 25–32. doi:10.1093/geronb/61.1.P25

Fiori, K. L., Smith, J., & Antonucci, T. C. (2007). Social network types among older adults: A multidimensional approach. *The Journals of Gerontology, 62B*, 322–330. doi:10.1093/geronb/62.6.P322

Fulk, J., Schmitz, K., & Steinfield, C. (1990). A social influence model of technology use. In J. Fulk & C. Steinfield (Eds.), *Organizations and communication technology* (pp. 117–140). Newbury Park, CA: Sage.

Haines, V. A., Hurlbert, J. S., & Beggs, J. J. (1996). Exploring the determinants of support provision: Provider characteristics, personal networks, community contexts, and support following life events. *Journal of Health and Social Behavior, 37*, 252–264. doi:10.2307/2137295

Hampton, K., Goulet, L. S., Rainie, L., & Purcell, K. (2011). Social networking sites and our lives. *Pew Internet & American Life Project*. Retrieved from http://www.pewinternet.org/Reports/2011/Technology-and-social-networks/Summary.aspx.

Hanson, B. S., & Östergren, P. O. (1987). Different social network and social support characteristics, nervous problems and insomnia: Theoretical and methodological aspects on some results from the population study 'Men born in 1914', Malmö, Sweden. *Social Science & Medicine, 25*, 849–859. doi:10.1016/0277-9536(87)90043-8

Henderson, S., & Gilding, M. (2004). 'I've never clicked this much with anyone in my life': Trust and hyperpersonal communication in online friendships. *New Media & Society, 6*, 487–506. doi:10.1177/146144804044331

High, A. C. (2012). *The production and reception of verbal person-centered social support in face-to-face and computer mediated dyadic conversations* (Unpublished doctoral dissertation). The Pennsylvania State University, State College.

High, A. C., & Solomon, D. H. (2008, July). *Making college feel like home: The role of computer-mediated and face-to-face support in the transition to college.* Paper presented at the International Association of Relationship Research conference, Providence, RI.

High, A. C., & Solomon, D. H. (2010). Locating computer-mediated social support within online communication environments. In K. B. Wright & L. M. Webb (Eds.), *Computer-mediated communication in personal relationships* (pp. 119–136). New York, NY: Peter Lang.

High, A. C., & Steuber, K. R. (2014). An examination of support (in)adequacy: Types, sources, and consequences of social support among infertile women. *Communication Monographs.* doi: 10.1080/03637751.2013.878868

Jones, S. M., & Burleson, B. R. (2003). Effects of helper and recipient sex on the experience and outcomes of comforting messages: An experimental investigation. *Sex Roles, 48*, 1–19. doi:10.1023/A:1022393827581

Kahn, R. L., & Antonucci, T. C. (1980). Convoys over the life course: Attachment, roles, and social support. In P. B. Baltes & O. Brim (Eds.), *Life span development and behavior* (pp. 253–286). New York, NY: All Academic Press.

Katz, J., & Aspden, P. (1997). Motivations for and barriers to Internet usage: Results of a national public opinion survey. *Internet Research, 7*, 170–188. doi:10.1108/10662249710171814

Kock, N. (2005). Compensatory adaptation to media obstacles: An experimental study of process redesign dyads. *Information Resources Management Journal, 18*, 41–67. doi:10.4018/irmj.2005040103

Lally, M., Black, E., Thornock, M., & Hawkins, J. D. (1979). Older women in single room occupant (SRO) hotels: A Seattle profile. *The Gerontologist, 19*, 67–73. doi:10.1093/geront/19.1.67

Lenhart, A., Madden, M., Smith, A., Purcell, K., Zickuhr, K., & Rainie, L. (2011). Teens, kindness and cruelty on social network sites. *Pew Internet and American Life Project.* Available at http://pewinternet.org/Reports/2011/Teens-and-social-media.aspx

Lewandowski, J., Rosenberg, B. D., Parks, M. J., & Siegel, J. T. (2011). The effect of informal social support: Face-to-face versus computer-mediated communication. *Computers in Human Behavior, 27*, 1806–1814. doi:10.1016/j.chb.2011.03.008

Litwin, H. (2001). Social network type and morale in old age. *The Gerontologist, 41*, 516–524. doi:10.1093/geront/41.4.516

Litwin, H., & Landau, R. (2000). Social network type and social support among the old-old. *Journal of Aging Studies, 14*, 213–228. doi:10.1016/S0890-4065(00)80012-2

Love, B., Crook, B., Thompson, C. M., Zaitchik, S., Knapp, J., LeFebvre, L., … & Rechis, R. (2012). Exploring psychosocial support online: A content analysis of messages in an adolescent and young adult cancer community. *Cyberpsychology, Behavior, and Social Networking, 15*, 555–559. doi:10.1089/cyber.2012.0138

Madden, M., Lenhart, A., Duggan, M., Cortesi, S., & Gasser, U. (2013). *Teens and technology 2013.* The Pew Internet and American Life Project. Available at: http://www.pewinternet.org/Reports/2013/Teens-and-Tech.aspx.

Martin, L. (2000). The relationship of college experiences to psychosocial outcomes in students. *Journal of College Student Development, 41*, 292–301.

Matsunaga, M. (2010). Testing a mediational model of bullied victim's evaluation of received support and post-bullying adaptation: A Japan-U.S. cross cultural comparison. *Communication Monographs, 77*, 312–340.

McIlvane, J. M., Ajrouch, K. J., & Antonucci, T. C. (2007). Generational structure and social resources in mid-life: Influences on health and well-being. *Journal of Social Issues, 63*, 759–773. doi:10.1111/j.1540-4560.2007.00535.x

Miller, N. B., Smerglia, V. L., Gaudet, D. S., & Kitson, G. C. (1998). Stressful life events, social support, and the distress of widowed and divorced women a counteractive model. *Journal of Family Issues, 19*, 181–203. doi:10.1177/019251398019002004

Morgan, C., & Cotten, S. R. (2003). The relationship between Internet activities and depressive symptoms in a sample of college freshman. *CyberPsychology & Behavior, 6*, 133–142. doi:10.1089/109493103321640329

O'Sullivan, P. B. (2000). What you don't know won't hurt me: Impression management functions of communication channels in relationships. *Human Communication Research, 26*, 403–431. doi:10.1093/hcr/26.3.403

Rainie, L., & Horrigan, J. (2002). Getting serious online: As Americans gain experience online, they pursue more serious activities. *Pew Internet and American Life Project.* Available at http://www.pewinternet.org/~/media//Files/Reports/2002/PIP_Getting_Serious_Online3ng.pdf.pdf.

Rainie, L., Lenhard, A., & Smith A. (2012). The tone of life on social networking sites. *The Pew Internet and American Life Project.* Available at http://pewinternet.org/Reports/2012/Social-networking-climate.aspx.

Rains, S. A., & Young, V. (2009). A meta-analysis of research on formal computer-mediated support groups: Examining group characteristics and health outcomes. *Human Communication Research, 35*, 309–336. doi:10.1111/j.1468-2958.2009.01353.x

Reinig, B. A., Briggs, R. O., Shepherd, M. M., Yen, J., & Nunamaker, J. F., Jr. (1995). Affective reward and the adoption of group support systems: Productivity is not always enough. *Journal of Management Information Systems, 12*, 171–185.

Robinson, J. D., & Turner, J. (2003). Impersonal, interpersonal, and hyperpersonal social support: Cancer and older Adults. *Health Communication, 15*, 227–234. doi:10.1207/S15327027HC1502_10

Samter, W. (2002). How gender and cognitive complexity influence the provision of emotional support: A study of indirect effects. *Communication Reports, 15*, 5–16. doi:10.1080/08934210209367748

Servaty-Seib, H. L., & Burleson, B. R. (2007). Bereaved adolescents' evaluations of the helpfulness of support-intended statements: Associations with person centeredness and demographic, personality, and contextual factors. *Journal of Social and Personal Relationships, 24*, 207–223. doi:10.1177/0265407507075411

Shepherd, R. M., & Edelman, R. J. (2005). Reasons for Internet use and social anxiety. *Personality and Individual Differences, 39*, 949–958. doi:10.1016/j.paid.2005.04.001

Stokes, J. P. (1983). Predicting satisfaction with social support from social network structure. *American Journal of Community Psychology, 11*, 141–152. doi:10.1007/BF00894363

Stritzke, W. G. K., Nguyen, A., & Durkin, K. (2004). Shyness and computer-mediated communication: A self-presentational theory perspective. *Communication Research, 14*, 1–22.

Sullivan, C. F. (1996). Recipients' perceptions of support attempts across various stressful life events. *Communication Research Reports, 13*, 183–190. doi:10.1080/08824099609362085

Sundar, S. S. (2008). The MAIN model: A heuristic approach to understanding technology effects on credibility. In M. J. Metzger & A. J. Flanigan (Eds.), *Digital media, youth, and credibility* (pp. 73–100). Cambridge, MA: MIT Press.

Turner, J. W., Grube, J. A., & Meyers, J. (2001). Developing an optimal match within online communities: An exploration of CMC support communities and traditional support. *Journal of Communication, 51*, 231–251. doi:10.1111/j.1460-2466.2001.tb02879.x

Turner, R. J. (1981). Social support as a contingency in psychological well-being. *Journal of Health and Social Behavior, 22*, 357–367. doi:10.2307/2136677

Walther, J. B. (1992). Interpersonal effects in computer-mediated interaction: A relational perspective. *Communication Research, 19*, 52–90. doi:10.1177/009365092019001003

Walther, J. B. (1996). Computer-mediated communication: Impersonal, interpersonal, and hyperpersonal interaction. *Communication Research, 23*, 3–43. doi:10.1177/009365096023001001

Walther, J. B. (1997). Group and interpersonal effects in international computer-mediated collaboration. *Human Communication Research, 23*, 342–369. doi:10.1111/j.1468-2958.1997.tb00400.x

Walther, J. B. (2006). Nonverbal dynamics in computer-mediated communication, or:(and the net: ('s with you:) and you:) alone. In V. Manusov & M. L. Patterson (Eds.), *The Sage handbook of nonverbal communication* (pp. 461–480). Thousand Oaks, CA: Sage. doi:10.4135/9781412976152.n24

Walther, J. B., & Boyd, S. (2002). Attraction to computer-mediated social support. In C. A. Lin & D. Atkins (Eds.), *Communication technology and society: Audience adoption and uses of the new media* (pp. 133–167). New York: Hampton Press.

Walther, J. B., & Parks, M. R. (2002). Cues filtered out, cues filtered in: Computer-mediated communication relationships. In M. L. Knapp, J. A. Daly, & G. R. Miller (Eds.), *The handbook of Interpersonal Communication* (3rd ed., pp. 529–559). Thousand Oaks, CA: Sage.

Wright, K. B. (1999). Computer-mediated support groups: An examination of social support, perceived stress, and coping strategies. *Communication Quarterly, 47*, 402–414. doi:10.1080/01463379909385570

Wright, K. B. (2000). Perceptions of on-line support providers: An examination of perceived homophily, source credibility, communication, and social support within on-line support groups. *Communication Quarterly, 48*, 44–59. doi:10.1080/01463370009385579

Wright, K. B. (2002). Social support within an on-line cancer community: An assessment of emotional support, perceptions of advantages and disadvantages, and motives for using the community from a communication perspective. *Journal of Applied Communication Research, 30*, 195–209. doi:10.1080/00909880216586

Wright, K. B., Rosenberg, J., Egbert, N., Ploeger, N. A., Bernard, D. R., & King, S. (2013). Communication competence, social support, and depression among college students: A model of Facebook and face-to-face support network influence. *Journal of Health Communication, 18*, 41–57. doi:10.1080/10810730.2012.688250

Xu, Y., & Burleson, B. R. (2001). Effects of sex, culture, and support type on perceptions of spousal social support: An assessment of the "support gap" hypothesis in early marriage. *Human Communication Research, 24*, 535–566. doi:10.1111/j.1468-2958.2001.tb00792.x

PART SIX

Middle Adulthood Communication

CHAPTER FIFTEEN

Sandwich Relationships

Intergenerational Communication

JORDAN SOLIZ AND CRAIG FOWLER

Although we celebrate birthdays on an annual basis and our chronological age serves important legal and pragmatic purposes (e.g., determining when we can start driving and claim social security), our progression through the lifespan is marked more by the age *group* with which we identify (or are identified with by others) than by our chronological age. Until Erikson (1968) introduced the lifespan perspective on human development, conventional approaches to human development focused almost exclusively on the path from birth to young adulthood. We still see remnants of this thinking today evidenced by the numerous age groups that represent development in early life (e.g., infant, toddler, child, pre-teen/"tweener," teenager, emerging adult, young adult) compared to the limited age categories beyond this life stage. As Erikson argued, human development continues across the entirety of the lifespan. Everyone experiences physiological changes as part of the aging process, and aging is often discussed in terms of these biological and physiological variations. Yet, aging across the lifespan also includes the emergence of and adaptation to different roles in personal and professional lives. Whereas younger adulthood and older adulthood have somewhat socially defined parameters, middle adulthood (also referred to as "midlife" or "middle-aged") is more nuanced (Fingerman, Nussbaum, & Birditt, 2004).

Although there is some consensus on the age range constituting middle adulthood (40 to 60 or 65 years old), these often change depending on the lifespan position of individuals. That is, notions of middle-aged vary based on where we are in the lifespan as a way to "cognitively" position ourselves into a more sought-after life position (Williams & Garrett, 2002). For instance, older adults may increase the top end of the age range to still be considered "middle-aged" as they progress in their years. Further, the experiences of middle adulthood are anything but homogenous in terms of the relationships, roles, responsibilities, and experiences (Fingerman et al., 2004). Thus, although the terms "middle adulthood" and "middle-aged" may be part of our everyday discourse, there is a great deal of variation on what demarcates this part of the lifespan. More than the age range, middle adulthood is defined by the expectations, experiences, and, often, demands associated with professional and personal roles. In the current chapter we focus on the personal roles and, specifically, the changing family ties and corresponding familial roles that often define middle adulthood. In previous research and in popular culture, the familial roles and responsibilities associated with middle adulthood have evoked the label "sandwich generation."

MIDDLE ADULTHOOD AS THE "SANDWICH GENERATION"

Discussing family roles across the lifespan, Barbato and Perse (1999) state, "The relationship roles remain constant as both travel through life together; however, how one enacts or recreates the roles may change as the family experiences changes" (p. 148). In other words, one is always a child, and, if one has children, one is always a parent. Yet, the parent-child roles are always in flux and, perhaps, never more so than in middle adulthood when many individuals are simultaneously a parent to an adolescent child or young adult and an adult child to an aging parent or parents. As Grundy and Henretta (2006) point out, Attias-Donfut (1995) labeled this middle generation the *pivot generation* because they are the lynchpin in this "three-generation configuration," often enacting important and changing roles as both a parent and an adult child.

Invoking the same concept, the term "sandwich generation" was coined by Miller (1981) as a metaphor to describe middle-aged adults' relational "position" between younger and older generations. Historically, research on the sandwich generation has assumed that that middle-aged adults are serving both as a parent to an adolescent (or young adult) and also carry burdens associated with the changing roles as an adult child to the aging parent (Horowitz, 1985). Thus, the "sandwich generation" implies that the middle-aged adult is caught between two generational pulls, and that the stress of being responsible for multiple generations can affect financial security, personal well-being, and career development. A great deal of scholarly attention has been devoted to understanding, identifying, and developing coping mechanisms for members of this sandwich generation (Riley & Bowen, 2005). For instance, researchers have attempted to quantify exactly how many people are members of the sandwich generation and the degree to which membership is actually problematic.

A summary of a nationally representative survey from the Pew Research Center provides an overview of the sandwich generation today (Parker & Patten, 2013). Approximately half of all adults in their 40s and 50s have at least one young child or young adult child that they are supporting as well as an older parent over 65. Although a small proportion of these individuals are providing financial support to *both* the younger and older generation, these adults indicate that they provide emotional and other instrumental support (e.g., household chores, daily living tasks, health care needs) more frequently. In contrast to much of the discourse surrounding the sandwich generation and, specifically, the potential burden of caring for aging parents, middle-aged adults report that, although there are pressures and obligations associated with providing support to *both* generations, more of the burden emerges from responsibilities associated with young adult children. Perhaps one of the more surprising aspects of the sandwich generation today is that although they deal with similar demands as in the past, they appear to have as much life satisfaction as younger and older adults who are not part of the sandwich generation.

Several recent sources suggest that relatively few middle-aged adults can truly be described as "sandwiched." Pierret (2006) noted that the adoption of different membership criteria resulted in estimates ranging from 1% to 33% of women aged 45 to 56 qualifying as a member of the sandwich generation, but stressed that only "9% of these women are giving a significant amount of care ... to both their children and their parents" (p. 4). Finding similar trends in their inquiry, Rosenthal, Martin-Matthews, and Matthews (1996) argued that "the image of the 'sandwich generation' may become an entrenched myth that will contribute to the growing lore about the 'burden' on modern societies of 'too many' elderly people" (p. S282). They also stress that while "being caught [in the middle] is not a typical experience, when it does occur its impact may be severe" (p. S282).

Although the prevalence of the sandwich generation may be exaggerated, there is still evidence that being "caught" or "sandwiched" can be problematic. For instance, adults who provided care to both parents and children were less likely than non-caregivers or those providing care to only one generation to engage in a variety of health-promoting behaviors (Chassin, Macy, Seo, Presson, & Sherman, 2010). Likewise, Malach Pines, Neal, Hammer, and Icekson (2011) demonstrated that among persons who had a co-resident child and who were providing at least three hours per week caring for a parent, the stress of caring for that parent was associated with burnout at work. Still, contrary findings arise in Rubin and White-Means's (2009) study, which suggested that work lives actually reduced the stress and burden experienced by sandwiched caregivers. Loomis and Booth (1995) firmly argued that "multigenerational caregiving responsibilities have little to no effect on caregivers' well-being" (p. 139), while Ward and Spitze (1998) concluded that "strains of intergenerational assistance implied by the 'sandwich generation' are neither common nor pronounced, and we find little evidence that they reduce the generally high levels of marital quality reported by middle-aged couples" (p. 663). Thus, despite Rosenthal et al.'s (1996) caution that the effects of being caught may be so problematic, it does not appear that members of the sandwich generation are *inevitably* destined for caregiving burdens and stressors as a result of having multiple familial and role responsibilities.

In short, there is a great deal of variability in the experiences of middle-aged persons who are simultaneously parents and children, and there are multiple factors that affect the kinds of outcomes associated with assuming the varied family roles and responsibilities of middle adulthood (e.g., value and cultural orientations, general family climate, personality, health of caregivers and family members). An often-ignored piece of the puzzle is the communication that occurs within these relationships which undoubtedly facilitates more positive relational and personal well-being in the family. As Williams and Nussbaum (2001) point out, "Middle-aged adults who are raising adolescent children while they continue a very active relationship with their own parents inhabit a fascinating communicative niche" (p. 195). Our objective in the remainder of this chapter is to focus on the role of communication in (re)creating and enacting relational roles in middle adulthood. We focus primarily on (a) parenting in middle adulthood and (b) the role of the adult child in middle adulthood. We conclude with a focus on the interdependence of these three generations.

PARENT-CHILD COMMUNICATION IN MIDDLE ADULTHOOD: MIDDLE-AGED ADULTS AS PARENTS

Although the sandwich generation metaphor implies that middle-aged adults have responsibilities for *both* younger and older family members, a majority of the research and, we would argue, social discourse focuses *solely* on the relational dynamics with the older generation (e.g., aging parents). Not only does this potentially reinforce the negative attitudes toward older adults (Kite, Stockdale, Whitley, & Johnson, 2005) by focusing on *negative* aspects of changing relational roles or caregiving burden with the aging parents (i.e., the older generation), but it also obscures the fact that many middle-aged adults perceive the stressors associated with the younger generation as more salient than those associated with the older parents (Parker & Patten, 2013).

Middle-aged adults are likely parenting adolescents and/or, what Arnett (2000) labels, emerging adults. A great deal of scholarly attention has been devoted to debating markers of adolescence (e.g., Moshman, 2011; Smetana, 2011). Although outlining the various perspectives is beyond the scope of this chapter, what we can agree on is that adolescence is a stage in the formative process toward adulthood in which physiological, cognitive, and emotional changes couple with cultural norms and are reflected in changes in sense of self (i.e., identity) and relationships with others. In the family, one of the most salient dimensions of adolescence is a (re)negotiation of the roles and corresponding responsibility in parent-adolescent relationships as family members balance the desire for autonomy and independence while maintaining the established parent-child bond. In addition to adolescence, emerging adulthood has recently been recognized as a salient developmental stage for many individuals following adolescence (Arnett, 2000).

Typically conceived in the 18- to 25-year range, emerging adults experience fewer physical changes than adolescents and are not in the midst of influences from social aspects of secondary education. Yet, they are still developing a sense of self and identity as well as establishing new parameters in the parent-child relationship. Likewise, much as they were during their offspring's adolescence, parents are still concerned with socializing values and attitudes to their adult children and, perhaps, opening up conversational topics (e.g., sex) that were taboo or avoided in adolescence (Willoughby & Arnett, 2013). Whereas some scholars argue that parent-child communication during the emerging adult stage is influenced by the nature of communication in adolescence (e.g., Willoughby & Arnett, 2013), others assert that research demonstrates discontinuity from adolescence to younger adulthood (Fingerman, Cheng, Tighe, Birditt, & Zarit, 2012), suggesting that this is still a formative time period in the parent-child relationship.

Understanding the dynamics of the parent-child relationship at this stage in the lifespan also necessitates recognizing the role of age identity of family members. Adolescence and emerging adulthood are marked in many ways by the communicative behaviors and expectations associated with this age group (Williams & Thurlow, 2005) compared to middle-aged and older adults. Moreover, an array of studies and theorizing has demonstrated potential problematic aspects of intergenerational communication stemming from various communicative styles of age group and age-based stereotypes toward "other" age groups (Barker, Giles, & Harwood, 2004). Whereas much of the research and commentary on problematic aspects of intergenerational communication is based on non-intimate others, we can assume that many age-based attitudes and communication carry over into the family.

For many middle-aged adults, parenting is a complex communicative context as their adolescent or adult children are developing an independent sense of self and managing new emerging identities while remaining emotionally and, at times, financially dependent on their parents. Moreover, motives for communicating with children are likely shifting as individuals move from young parents to middle-aged parents. For instance, communicating for affection and pleasure was less of a motive for middle-aged (ages 40–49) and older parents (50–78) compared to young parents (age 20–39), although as parents age, they are more driven to talk to children by controlling motives (Barbato & Perse, 1999). This suggests that there is a recognition or expectation that the parent role is changing at this point in the lifespan. Although the parental role during adolescence to young adulthood is ambiguous and experiences vary from family to family, one of the more salient aspects of parenting in this stage of life centers on appropriate *parental involvement*.

Parental Involvement in Middle Adulthood

On the whole, middle-aged parents appear to be happy in their role as parents (Mitchell, 2010). Their satisfaction is often attributed to the perception that children are "on track" developmentally, are good people, and are a source of unconditional love. Conversely, parental dissatisfaction is frequently attributed to a lack of consensus (e.g., holding different values and having clashing personalities), a child's personality flaws (e.g., a sense of entitlement or selfishness), or being developmentally "behind schedule" (Mitchell, 2010).

Recent trends point to increased parental involvement in middle adulthood in the lives of children even as children enter emerging and young adulthood. Although this change can be attributed, in part, to an increase in the number of individuals attending university during which parental financial and emotional support and overall involvement are often necessary, there also seems to be more general cultural shift, especially in the United States. In and of itself, increased parental involvement for lengthier periods is not necessarily a negative trend. As Fingerman, Cheng, Tighe et al. (2012) point out, what often differentiates positive and negative aspects of increased parental involvement in emerging and young adulthood is whether or not parents attribute their involvement to normative or non-normative aspects of relational and career development.

Perhaps this is no more clear than with the growing trend of parental involvement in the lives of "boomerang children," i.e., young adults who return home after living outside of the house. A recent Pew Center report (Parker, 2012) found that 29% of 25- to 34-year-old adults fit the profile of a boomerang child. Obviously, during the period when the child was not residing in the household, adult children experience more independence from parent influence and regulations. For parents, there were likely fewer financial and time constraints as they were no longer serving as a primary caregiver for the child. In general, parents and children likely have become accustomed to living somewhat independently from the other family member. As such, re-entry into the parental home is a complex process and, as Vogl-Bauer (2009) points out, requires discussions concerning household responsibilities and division of labor as well as recognizing and adjusting to the different parent-child expectations regarding topics of conversation, household rules, and lifestyles of an adult child compared to adolescence. Further, adult children returning home often do so out of financial necessity, and, thus, discussions and expectations about financial support are often intertwined with re-entry into the home.

As previously noted, and contrary to much of the social commentary surrounding the sandwich generation, a great deal of stress and burden experienced by middle-aged adults is due to demands associated with the younger generation as opposed to the older generation (i.e., aging parents). It is likely that the growing trend in "boomerang children" has a great deal to do with this finding. Yet, we know little about why managing the changing roles and responsibilities in one's relationship with children may be perceived as more stressful than experiencing changes in one's relationship with parents as they age. One reason is that middle-aged parents may internalize any issues or struggles with adult children as they view this as a negative reflection of their parenting. Further, whereas children may appreciate such assistance, recent work suggests that parental assistance to grown children is sometimes viewed negatively. For example, Fingerman, Cheng, Cichy, Birditt, and Zarit (2013) reported that 15% to 17% of adult children reported that they felt parental assistance came with strings attached, expectations spoken or unsaid, or was intrusive. Thus, parental involvement and assistance may create tensions in the relationship. Finally, society seems to provide more support and understanding for those who provide care to older parents than it does for people who are still caring for young adult children (Parker & Patten, 2013). One of the unique communicative dynamics in this situation is how parents talk about, disclose, and, at times, defend parental involvement and support in the lives of their young adult children.

PARENT-CHILD COMMUNICATION IN MIDDLE ADULTHOOD: MIDDLE-AGED ADULTS AS ADULT CHILDREN

By the time adult children enter middle adulthood, their parents will typically be at the upper boundary of what might be considered middle-aged or, in many cases, have entered older adulthood. Although parents may not yet require ongoing care, they are perhaps beginning to experience ongoing, chronic conditions that have implications for how each generation experiences the parent-child relationship. Yet, the changes in the parent-child relationship are not inherently negative. Rather, evidence suggests that middle-aged children find their relationship with aging parents rewarding. For instance, findings from the third wave of the *National Survey of Families and Households* (Sweet & Bumpass, 2002)[1] demonstrate that a majority of middle-aged adults had weekly contact with mothers (approximately 40% with fathers) and, perhaps more important, nearly two-thirds of participants rated the quality of their relationship extremely positively. Similar accounts emerge from the AARP's *Intergenerational Linkages Survey*, in which 80% of respondents considered their relationship with parents to be emotionally close (Lawton, Silverstein, & Bengtson, 1994) and in Umberson's (1992) study, in which more than 90% of middle-aged adults reported that their mother made them feel loved and cared for (82% for fathers).

The quality of midlife child-parent relationships seems to vary as a function of sex, however, and there are consistent reports that the closest intergenerational ties tend to be between mothers and their adult daughters, with the father-son relationship being typically lower in affectional closeness throughout the life course (Lawton et al., 1994; Rossi, 1989; Rossi & Rossi, 1990; Suitor & Pillemer, 1988).

Although the relationships middle-aged children have with their parents seem to be in robust health, it is likely that the parents themselves perceive the relationship as even healthier than do their adult children. The intergenerational stake hypothesis (Bengtson & Kuypers, 1971) accounts for the fact that parents often provide more favorable evaluations of the parent-child relationship than do their children. Because parents are concerned with "the continuity of values they have found important in life, and with close relationships in the family they have founded" (Giarrusso, Stallings & Bengtson, 1995, p. 228), they are motivated to overreport the degree of family closeness and consensus, and to underreport the degree of disagreement and conflict in their relationship. Conversely, children are motivated more by the drive for autonomy and therefore have a weaker incentive to view the relationship favorably. Consequently, they are prone to underreport closeness and consensus and to overstate the amount of conflict in the relationship, as this differentiation furthers the goal of autonomy seeking. Giarrusso et al. (1995) found that this trend remained quite stable across a twenty-year period, and even in later life, mothers and daughters perceive their relationship in ways consistent with the intergenerational stake hypothesis.

Contrary to popular thought and discourse surrounding the "sandwich generation," the parent-adult child relationship is characterized as one with minimal conflict (Baruch & Barnett, 1983). For parents and children who maintain regular contact yet live essentially independent lives, this may not be surprising. Yet, even in contexts in which older parents share a home with adult children, overt disagreement is remarkably rare (Suitor & Pillemer, 1988). Whereas the adolescent-parent relationship is often perceived as conflictual and problematic, research indicates that as children grow older and mature, their relationships with parents improve (Rossi, 1989; Rossi & Rossi, 1990) and are characterized by increases in frequency of interaction, affective closeness, and satisfaction with the relationship (Troll & Fingerman, 1996). An important question, however, is *why* is this the case?

One explanation—and, perhaps, the simplest—is that as parents and adult children share more in common in terms of life experiences (e.g., social and familial roles), they often form a stronger, closer bond (Aquilino, 1997; De Goede, Branje, & Meeus, 2009; Lefkowitz, 2005). Prior to this convergence, parents have had experiences that children have not yet encountered, which limits the common ground on which a relationship can be forged (Fingerman, 2003), inhibits family members' ability to understand one another, and serves as a barrier to developing close relationships. Moreover, by being at fundamentally different life stages, each generation may see interaction (or a lack thereof) as a means to fulfilling incommensurate goals (e.g., connectedness/generativity vs. autonomy). However, as role similarity increases, the "developmental schism" (Fingerman, 2003) narrows, allowing greater potential for relational intimacy. In other words, adult children in middle adulthood attain "filial maturity," which allows them to view their mother and father as individuals who transcend the parental role and have their own "past histories" (Birditt, Fingerman, Lefkowitz, & Kamp Dush, 2008, p. 1). In this sense, adult children are more likely to accept their parents as people with weaknesses and to perceive them as persons with whom they can "engage in an empathetic, compassionate, and reciprocal ... relationship" (Birditt et al., 2008, p. 2). Not surprisingly, parents *also* describe their adult children as becoming more and more like age peers and friends (Blieszner & Mancini, 1987; Fingerman, Hay, Kamp Dush, Cichy, & Hosterman, 2007). As these "developmental schisms" lessen, the communication and interactions (e.g., frequency, topics of conversation) between adult children and their parents, at times, mirror conversation between friends more so than intergenerational family relationships.

Of course, despite the increasingly peer-like nature of the relationship, parents are *still* parents. As such, adult children who might be considered members of the sandwich generation and who are providing care for parents still report being on the receiving end of parental support via financial, emotional, informational, and instrumental support (Ingersoll-Dayton, Neal, & Hammer, 2001). Interestingly, just over a quarter of adult children experience intergenerational ambivalence toward parents and parents-in-law, reporting "contradictory emotions and cognitions" with respect to these persons (Willson, Shuey, & Elder, 2003, p. 1056). Although we caution against overgeneralizations that position the sandwich generation as caregivers for aging parents, we also realize that this is the case for many middle-aged adults. As such, we now turn our attention to how health of aging parents can affect the dynamics of the parent-child relationship.

Parental Health and Adult Child–Older Parent Relationships

As the parents of middle-aged children age, they are not necessarily in a state of poor or debilitating health. Even among those aged 85 or older, fewer than one-fifth of persons report needing help with activities of daily living (e.g., getting around one's home, dressing, eating, toileting, and bathing), although a third of people in this age group report needing some help with tasks such as household chores, shopping, or getting around (CDC, 2009). Nonetheless, older parents may frequently experience some sort of decline in functioning, such as hearing loss or visual impairment, and poorer parental health has been linked to elevated feelings of intergenerational ambivalence among relationships with adult children (Willson et al., 2003). Recognizing the potential for these sorts of health issues to influence the quality of the parent-child relationship, Fingerman and colleagues (2007) examined perceptions of continuity and change in the parent-child relationship in situations in which the older parent experienced significant and irreversible vision loss, hearing loss requiring a hearing aid, or had neither impairment. Although almost half of the adult children studied reported that their parent's health was declining, most participants nevertheless described positive changes in the parent-child relationship, such as greater closeness. As Fingerman et al. (2007) put it, "Parents and offspring report that their relationships have been good for years, but are getting better" (pp. 298–299), even when there are potential barriers (e.g., hearing loss) to smooth social interaction.

Many middle-aged children and older parents are, perhaps, more concerned about what might happen if and when one or more parents are unable to maintain independence. Reflecting this concern, Cicirelli (1988) coined the term "filial anxiety" to capture a child's dual concerns of being capable of caring for a parent and of his or her parent's well-being. Although we have noted the generally rosy status of relationships between middle-aged children and their parents, this may come at a price, for children's filial anxiety appears to peak during their 50s (Murray, Lowe, & Horne, 1995) and is experienced more severely by adult children who are closer to their parents (Cicirelli, 1988). At the back of many middle-aged children's minds will be the prospect of facing the relational, financial, and health challenges documented in studies of caregiver strain (Archbold, 1983; Sorensen, Mak, & Pinquart, 2011; Turner, Killian, & Cain, 2004; Wakabayashi & Donato, 2005).

Unfortunately, for many middle-aged children, the "back of the mind" is where considerations of their parent(s)' possible future care needs will stay. Bromley and Blieszner (1997) found that although 80% of the adult children recognized that parent(s) might need future assistance, fewer than 40% had discussed the topic with parents. Pecchioni (2001) similarly found that 55% of the adult daughters had experienced little to no discussion about caregiving arrangements with parents. It is difficult to be sure precisely how many children engage their parents in discussion about future care needs, but even optimistic reports acknowledge that only a minority has formed concrete plans for addressing those needs (AARP, 2007). Although some children may simply prefer to avoid dwelling on the topic of declining parental health, Pecchioni learned that 90% of the mother-daughter dyads she studied thought such conversations unnecessary and considered their shared life history and closeness a sufficient basis for intuiting parental preferences and implementing them if need be. Thus, it appears that adult children tend to *react* to sudden deteriorations in parental health rather than proactively preparing for such declines (Hansson et al., 1990). As such, care-related decisions that have profound consequences for parents and children must often be made quickly, under stressful circumstances that might impair good judgment, and without much (if any) consultation between children and those affected most by these choices—the parents themselves (Pinquart & Sorensen, 2002; Van Meter & Johnson, 1985). Although families may develop tacit understandings of how to address future care needs (Pecchioni, 2001) rather than addressing the topic overtly, when explicit conversations about eldercare arrangements *do* occur, parents and children are quite satisfied with how decisions are made (Carpenter & Mulligan, 2009; Pratt, Jones, Shin, & Walker, 1989). There is growing understanding of what constitutes effective preparation for and discussion of parental care. For instance, effective preparation occurs prior to a parental health crisis and addresses topics such as the kind and amount of assistance that may be needed, the point at which assistance needs to be offered, and the preferred source of such help (Cicirelli, 1993; Hummert & Morgan, 2002). Moreover, while children should avoid seizing control of eldercare arrangements, they *should* seize the chance to advocate for their parents by helping them with research and assist their parents in exercising autonomy by accepting responsibilities that are delegated to them. Even if middle-aged adults are not actively caring for older parents, the discussions about future life plans—or, at minimum, the groundwork for these discussions—is (or should be) a normative feature of middle adulthood.

Blieszner and Mancini (1987) noted that while families acknowledged the need to plan for the future, they did not always feel capable of doing so, or know how to begin conversations about caregiving. It is understandable, then, that Fowler and Afifi (2011) learned that adult children's feelings of communication efficacy predicted their discussion of eldercare arrangements with parents. A recent study explored how middle-aged children's encoding of attempts to broach discussion of future care needs with parents was perceived by a sample of older adults, working on the premise that such information has the potential to enhance these feelings of communication efficacy. In this study, Fowler, Fisher, and Pitts (in press) learned that children's use of positive and negative politeness shaped perceptions among parents that the children were trying to be supportive, which subsequently increased their feeling that they would be responsive to similar efforts by their children to engage them in a similar decision.

COMMUNICATION AND MULTIGENERATIONAL INTERDEPENDENCE

Researchers and practitioners often discuss parent-child relationship in middle adulthood in terms of dyads without consideration that these relationships often occur in a relational system. Our previous discussion has followed this trend by segmenting this "sandwich generation" into the relationships with the younger and older generations, respectively. More extant research, however, has highlighted the interdependence of these three generations. For instance, Miller-Day (2004) moved beyond the mother-daughter dyad to investigate the experiences of the (grand) daughter-mother-(grand)mother *triad*, demonstrating the complexity and nuances of multigenerational family processes. Not only must mother balance dual roles as parent and adult child, but, often, this middle generation serves as a lynchpin for the relationships between other generations. For instance, both Soliz and Harwood (2006) and Whitbeck, Hoyt, and Huck (1993) demonstrate that a key facilitating factor in positive grandparent-grandchild relationships is encouragement and support from parents.

In investigating three-generation family relationships, Hamill and colleagues (Hamill, 1994; Hamill & Goldberg, 1997) support the significance of intergenerational independence in that relationships and the quality of communication are influenced, in part, by individual and relational dynamics of other family members. For instance, communication in the father-adolescent child relationship suffers when fathers are experiencing dissatisfaction with transitions and changes occurring during midlife. Further emphasizing the interdependence of family relationships, the quality of communication in mother-daughter relationships was associated both with mothers' general perceptions of their relationships with their own parents, and with their perceptions of the burden created by caring for their parents (Hamill, 1994). Moreover, as Fingerman, Cheng, Birditt, and Zarit (2012) demonstrate, many middle-aged adults have multiple children. Understanding potential stress and burdens and their subsequent effect on well-being for middle-aged adults necessitates accounting for experiences and relationships with all children.

Given the range of ages that constitute middle adulthood and general demographics of grandparents, the onset on grandparenthood can occur in later middle adulthood and, thus, is an important aspect of middle adulthood. In fact, an additional example of interdependence of multiple generations is evident in Dun's (2010) work on the onset of grandparenthood in which the parent-adult child relationship often changes as the child becomes a parent and the parent takes on a grandparent identity. Whereas the new generation typically creates a connection between parents and their adult children, one of the more intriguing findings was the nature of communication, which can often be tainted with face-threatening advice and conflict over different values and beliefs about (grand)parenting. And, often, these changing roles lead to more disclosure and frequency of communication in a positive and negative manner. Finally, and fitting with the idea of shared experiences, individuals may reflect on their parents as they see them in this new role. Although the grandparent aspect of middle adulthood is not as heavily focused, it seems like an integral part of sandwich generation.

CONCLUSION AND DIRECTIONS FOR FUTURE RESEARCH

In middle adulthood, most individuals have dynamic and changing roles as parents and as adult children. Although the stage in parenthood can vary based on age of becoming a parent, it is likely that parental relationships in middle adulthood largely center on adolescent or emerging adult children. In terms of the role as an adult child, parents are likely entering the stage with their parents at which roles, responsibilities, and relational expectations are shifting. In both cases, middle-aged adults are likely (re)negotiating their involvement and relational goals with each generation. At the heart of negotiating these changes in a constructive manner are the family communication processes, and, thus, this remains an important context of inquiry for researchers and practitioners. In this vein, we see four important trajectories for future scholarly endeavors. First, as we address in this chapter, more attention should be devoted to identifying and understanding stressors (and ways to ameliorate these stressors) tied to the younger generation. A shift away from an overemphasis on the family dynamics associated with aging parents will not only better reflect the actual lived experiences of middle-aged adults but will also minimize the perception of aging parents (and older adults, in general) as the sole cause of familial burden and obligation in middle adulthood. Second, most family scholars conceptualize families from a systems perspective, understanding the interdependence of multiple family members. However, intergenerational relationships in middle adulthood are still researched primarily on the dyadic level. Although we allude to examples in which this is not the case in our discussion of multigenerational interdependence, system-level analyses remain atypical. Focusing on family relationships between and within (e.g., adult siblings) generations will provide a more holistic understanding of family and relational factors associated with gratifying and potentially stressful experiences in middle adulthood. Third, we believe there are both an opportunity and a necessity to investigate how families interact with institutions, programs, and resources outside of the family that may assist in addressing any challenges that arise in relationships with younger and older generations as one enters middle adulthood. These could include formal programs such as those that assist with caregiving for aging parents or more informal resources such as online forums that provide guidance and support for parents in managing changes that occur when adult children return home. Finally, for too long scholarship on middle-aged family members has accepted the premise that this period of life is accompanied solely by difficulties resulting from being sandwiched between generations. Although future scholarship should not ignore the unique challenges that family members may face during midlife, we believe it is time to move beyond this emphasis, and to explore aspects of family relationships that may be particularly rewarding during this phase of life.

REFERENCES

AARP. (2007). *Are Americans talking with their parents about independent living? A 2007 study among boomer women.* Washington, DC: L. Skufca.

Aquilino, W. S. (1997). From adolescent to young adult: A prospective study of parent-child relations during the transition to adulthood. *Journal of Marriage and the Family, 59,* 670–686.

Archbold, P. G. (1983). Impact of parent-caring on women. *Family Relations, 32,* 39–45.

Arnett, J. J. (2000). Emerging adulthood: A theory of development from the late teens through the twenties. *American Psychologist, 55,* 469–480.

Attias-Donfunt, C. (1995). *Intergenerational solidarity: Ageing, families, and the state.* Paris, France: Nathan.

Barbato, C. A., & Perse, E. M. (1999). "I don't care if you are 65, you are still my baby!" Examining parents' communication motives throughout the lifespan. *Communication Research Reports, 16,* 147–156.

Barker, V., Giles, H., & Harwood, J. (2004). Inter- and intragroup perspectives on intergenerational communication. In J. F. Nussbaum & J. Coupland (Eds.), *Handbook of communication and aging research* (pp. 139–166). Mahwah, NJ: Erlbaum.

Baruch, G., & Barnett, R. C. (1983). Adult daughters' relationships with their mothers. *Journal of Marriage and the Family, 45,* 601–606.

Bengtson, V. L., & Kuypers, J. A. (1971). Generational difference and developmental stake. *Aging and Human Development, 2,* 249–260.

Birditt, K. S., Fingerman, K. L., Lefkowitz, E. S., & Kamp Dush, C. M. (2008). Parents perceived as peers: Filial maturity in adulthood. *Journal of Adult Development, 15,* 1–12.

Blieszner, R., & Mancini, J. (1987). Enduring ties: Older adults' parental role and responsibilities. *Family Relations, 36,* 176–180.

Bromley, M. C., & Blieszner, R. (1997). Planning for long term care: Filial behavior and relationship quality of adult children with independent parents. *Family Relations, 46,* 155–162.

Carpenter, B. D., & Mulligan, E. A. (2009). Family, know thyself: A workbook-based inter-generational intervention to improve parent care coordination. *Clinical Gerontologist, 32,* 147–163.

CDC. (2009). Limitations in activities of daily living and instrumental activities of daily living, 2003–2007. Retrieved from http://www.cdc.gov/nchs/health_policy/ADL_tables.htm

Chassin, L., Macy, J. T., Seo, D.-C., Presson, C. C., & Sherman, S. J. (2010). The association between membership in the sandwich generation and health behaviors: A longitudinal study. *Journal of Applied Developmental Psychology, 31,* 38–46.

Cicirelli, V. G. (1988). A measure of filial anxiety regarding anticipated care of elderly parents. *The Gerontologist, G4, 28,* 478–482.

Cicirelli, V. G. (1993). Intergenerational communication in the mother-daughter dyad regarding caregiving decisions. In N. Coupland & J. F. Nussbaum (Eds.), *Discourse and lifespan identity* (pp. 215–236). Newbury Park, CA: Sage.

De Goede, I. H. A., Branje, S. J. T., & Meeus, W. H. J. (2009). Developmental changes in adolescents' perceptions of relationships with their parents. *Journal of Youth and Adolescence, 38,* 75–88.

Dun, T. (2010). Turning points in parent-grandparent relationships during the start of a new genera-tion. *Journal of Family Communication, 10,* 196–210.

Erikson, E. H. (1968). *Identity: Youth and crisis.* New York, NY: Norton.

Fingerman, K. L. (2003). *Mothers and their adult daughters: Mixed emotions, enduring bonds.* New York, NY: Prometheus Books.

Fingerman, K. L., Cheng, Y. P., Birditt, K. S., & Zarit, S. (2012). Only as happy as the least happy child: Multiple grown children's problems and successes and middle-aged parents' well-being. *Journal of Gerontology: Psychological Sciences, 67,* 184–193.

Fingerman, K. L., Cheng, Y. P., Tighe, L., Birditt, K. S., & Zarit, S. (2012). Relationships between young adults and their parents. In A. Booth, S. L. Brown, N. Landale, W. Manning, & S. M. McHale (Eds.), *Early adulthood in a family context* (pp. 59–85). New York, NY: Springer.

Fingerman, K. L., Cheng, Y., Cichy, K. E., Birditt, K. S., & Zarit, S. (2013). Help with "strings attached": Offspring perceptions that middle-aged parents offer conflicted support. *Journals of Gerontology, Series B: Psychological and Social Sciences, 68*, 902–911.

Fingerman, K. L., Hay, E. L., Kamp Dush, C. M., Cichy, K. E., & Hosterman, S. J. (2007). Parents' and offspring's perceptions of change and continuity when parents experience the transition to old age. *Advances in Life Course Research, 12*, 275–306.

Fingerman, K. L., Nussbaum, J., & Birditt, K. S. (2004). An exploration of the marital and family issues of the later-life adult. In A. Vangelisti (Ed.), *The handbook of family communication* (pp. 153–176). Mahwah, NJ: Erlbaum.

Fowler, C. A., & Afifi, W. A. (2011). Applying the theory of motivated information management to decisions to seek information about parent-care preferences. *Journal of Social and Personal Relationships, 28*, 507–535.

Fowler, C. A., Fisher, C. L., & Pitts, M. J. (in press). Older adults' evaluations of middle-aged children's attempts to initiate discussion of care needs. *Health Communication.*

Giarrusso, R., Stallings, M., & Bengtson, V. L. (1995). The "intergenerational stake" hypothesis revisited: Parent-child differences in perceptions of relationships 20 years later. In V. L. Bengtson, K. W. Schaie, & L. M. Burton (Eds.), *Adult intergenerational relations: Effects of social change* (pp. 227–263). New York, NY: Springer.

Grundy, E., & Henretta, J. C. (2006). Between elderly parents and adult children: A new look at the intergenerational care provided by the sandwich generation. *Ageing and Society, 26*, 707–722.

Hamill, S. B. (1994). Parent-adolescent communication in sandwich generation families. *Journal of Adolescent Research, 9*, 458–482.

Hamill, S. B., & Goldberg, W. A. (1997). Between adolescents and aging grandparents: Midlife concerns of adults in the "Sandwich Generation." *Journal of Adult Development, 4*, 135–147.

Hansson, R., Nelson, E., Carver, M., NeeSmith, D., Dowling, E., Fletcher, W., & Suhr, P. (1990). Adult children with elderly parents: When to intervene? *Family Relations, 39*, 153–158.

Horowitz, A. (1985). Sons and daughters as caregivers to older parents: Differences in role performance and consequence. *The Gerontologist, 25*, 612–617.

Hummert, M. L., & Morgan, M. (2002). Negotiating decisions in the aging family. In M. L. Hummert & J. F. Nussbaum (Eds.), *Aging, communication, and health* (pp. 177–201). Hillsdale, NJ: Erlbaum.

Ingersoll-Dayton, B., Neal, M. B., & Hammer, L. B. (2001). Aging parents helping adult children: The experience of the sandwiched generation. *Family Relations, 50*, 262–271.

Kite, M. E., Stockdale, G. D., Whitley, B. E., Jr., & Johnson, B. T. (2005). Attitudes toward older and younger adults: An updated meta-analysis. *Journal of Social Issues, 61*, 241–266.

Lawton, L., Silverstein, M., & Bengtson, V. (1994). Affection, social contact, and geographic distance between adult children and their parents. *Journal of Marriage and the Family, 56*, 57–68.

Lefkowitz, E. S. (2005). "Things have gotten better": Developmental changes among emerging adults after the transition to university. *Journal of Adolescent Research, 20*, 40–63.

Loomis, L. S., & Booth, A. (1995). Multigenerational caregiving and well-being: The myth of the beleaguered sandwich generation. *Journal of Family Issues, 16*, 131–148.

Malach Pines, A. M., Neal, M., Hammer, L. B., & Icekson, T. (2011). Job burnout and couple burnout in dual-earner couples in the sandwiched generation. *Social Psychology Quarterly, 74*, 361–386.

Miller, D. (1981). The "sandwich" generation: Adult children of the aging. *Social Work, 26*, 419–423.

Miller-Day, M. (2004). *Communication among grandmothers, mothers, and adult daughters: A qualitative study of maternal relationships.* Mahwah, NJ: Erlbaum.

Mitchell, B. A. (2010). Happiness in midlife parental roles: A contextual mixed methods analysis. *Family Relations, 59,* 326–339.

Moshman, D. (2011). *Adolescent rationality and development: Cognition, morality, and identity* (3rd ed.). New York, NY: Psychology Press.

Murray, P. D., Lowe, J. D., & Horne, H. L. (1995). Assessing filial maturity through the use of the filial anxiety scale. *Journal of Psychology, 129,* 519–529.

Parker, K. (2012, March). *The boomerang generation.* Washington, DC: Pew Research Center Social & Demographic Trends Project. Retrieved from http://www.pewsocialtrends.org/files/2012/03/PewSocialTrends-2012-BoomerangGeneration.pdf.

Parker, K., & Patten, E. (2013). The sandwich generation: Rising financial burdens for middle-aged Americans. *Pew Research Center Social & Demographic Trends.*

Pecchioni, L. (2001). Implicit decision-making in family caregiving. *Journal of Social and Personal Relationships, 18,* 219–237.

Pierret, C. R. (2006). The "sandwich generation": Women caring for parents and children. *Monthly Labor Review, 129,* 3–9

Pinquart, M., & Sorensen, S. (2002). Psychological outcomes of preparation for future care needs. *Journal of Applied Gerontology, 21,* 452–470.

Pratt, C. C., Jones, L. L., Shin, H. Y., & Walker, A. J. (1989). Autonomy and decision making between single older women and their caregiving daughters. *The Gerontologist, 29,* 792–797.

Riley, L. D., & Bowen, C. (2005). The sandwich generation: Challenges and coping strategies of multigenerational families. *The Family Journal, 13,* 52–58.

Rosenthal, C. J., Martin-Matthews, A., & Matthews, S. H. (1996). Caught in the middle? Occupancy in multiple roles and help to parents in a national probability sample of Canadian adults. *Journal of Gerontology: Social Sciences,* 51B, S274–S283.

Rossi, A. (1989). A life-course approach to gender, aging, and intergenerational relations. In K. W. Schaie & C. Schooler (Eds.), *Social structure and aging: Psychological processes* (pp. 207–236). Hillsdale, NJ: Erlbaum.

Rossi, A. S., & Rossi, P. H. (1990). *Of human bonding: Parent-child relations across the life-course.* New York, NY: Aldine de Guyter.

Rubin, R., & White-Means, S. (2009). Informal caregiving: Dilemmas of sandwiched caregivers. *Journal of Family and Economic Issues,* 30, 252–267.

Smetana, J. G. (2011). *Adolescents, families, and social development: How teens construct their worlds.* Malden, MA: Wiley-Blackwell.

Soliz, J., & Harwood, J. (2006). Shared family identity, age salience, and intergroup contact: Investigation of the grandparent-grandchild relationship. *Communication Monographs, 73,* 87–107.

Sorensen, S., Mak, W., & Pinquart, M. (2011). Planning and decision making for care transitions. *Annual Review of Gerontology and Geriatrics, 31,* 111–142.

Suitor, J. J., & Pillemer, K. (1988). Explaining intergenerational conflict when adult children and elderly parents live together. *Journal of Marriage and Family, 50,* 1037–1047.

Sweet, J. A., & Bumpass, L. L. (2002). *The National Survey of Families and Households—Waves 1, 2, and 3: Data Description and Documentation.* Center for Demography and Ecology, University of Wisconsin–Madison (http://www.ssc.wisc.edu/nsfh/home.htm)

Troll, L. E., & Fingerman, K. L. (1996). Connections between parents and their adult children. In C. Magai & S. H. McFadden (Eds.), *Handbook of emotion, adult development, and aging* (pp. 185–205). San Diego, CA: Academic Press.

Turner, M. J., Killian, T. S., & Cain, R. (2004). Life course transitions and depressive symptoms among women in midlife. *International Journal of Aging and Human Development, 58*, 241–265.

Umberson, D. (1992). Relationships between adult children and their parents: Psychological consequences for both generations. *Journal of Marriage and Family, 54*, 664–674.

Van Meter, M. K., & Johnson, P. (1985). Family decision making and long term care for the elderly: Part II. *Journal of Religion and Aging, 1*, 59–72.

Vogl-Bauer, S. (2009). When the world comes home: Examining internal and external influences on communication exchanges between parents and their boomerang children. In T. J. Socha & G. H. Stamp (Eds.), *Parents and children communication with society: Managing relationships outside of home* (pp. 285–304). New York, NY: Routledge.

Wakabayashi, C., & Donato, K. M. (2005). The consequences of caregiving: Effects on women's employment and earnings. *Population Research and Policy Review, 24*, 467–488.

Ward, R. A., & Spitze, G. (1998). Sandwiched marriages: The implications of child and parent relations for marital quality in midlife. *Social Forces, 72*, 647–666.

Whitbeck, L. B., Hoyt, D. R., & Huck, S. M. (1993). Family relationship history, contemporary parent-grandparent relationship quality, and the grandparent-grandchild relationship. *Journal of Marriage and the Family, 55*, 1025–1035.

Williams, A., & Garrett, P. (2002). Communication evaluations across the life span: From adolescent storm and stress to elder aches and pains. *Journal of Language and Social Psychology, 21*, 101–126.

Williams, A., & Nussbaum, J. (2001). *Intergenerational communication across the lifespan*. Mahwah, NJ: Erlbaum.

Williams, A., & Thurlow, C. (Eds.). (2005). *Talking adolescence: Perspectives on communication in the teenage years*. New York, NY: Peter Lang.

Willougby, B. J., & Arnett, J. J. (2013). Communication during emerging adulthood. In A. Vangelisti (Ed.), *Handbook of family communication* (pp. 287–301). New York, NY: Routledge.

Willson, A. E., Shuey, K. M., & Elder, G. H. (2003). Ambivalence in the relationship of adult children to aging parents and in-laws. *Journal of Marriage and Family, 65*, 1055–1072.

NOTE

1 Data from this study were analyzed using the online tool *BADGIR* provided at https://nesstar. ssc.wisc.edu/webview/index.jsp

CHAPTER SIXTEEN

Communicating in Professional Life

The Nature and Evolution of Superior-Subordinate Interactions

DENNIS S. GOURAN

Early adulthood is a time of uncertainty, exploration, change, and search for stability. By the time individuals reach middle adulthood, they typically have settled on particular types of career choices, identified with the sorts of organizations that they perceive as enabling them to pursue their careers and fulfill their professional aspirations, and actively sought to be members of particular ones. It is at this point that professional interactions become a dominant component of one's day-to-day life. These interactions, moreover, are largely both defined and governed by the sorts of formal relationships in which one finds him- or herself within the organization or institution of which he or she has become a part, namely, ones in which he or she is a superior, subordinate, or peer. The interactions that transpire also have much to do with the evolution of such relationships in respect to mutual expectations, role enactment, relative status, motivations, duration, importance to the parties, and the like. The focus of this chapter is superior-subordinate relationships and the impact that interactions within them have on how one negotiates various aspects of his or her professional life, performs, and derives such satisfactions as he or she may experience during the period ranging from middle to later adulthood.

Most of the scholarship relevant to superior-subordinate interactions reflects a concern with the more general subject of organizational leadership even though, strictly speaking, the two domains are not completely overlapping. Much of what we know about the former, however, is informed by scholarly inquiry in the latter. In fact, the lion's share of what this chapter reveals about superior-subordinate interactions draws heavily, even primarily, from research and theory concerning leadership. The literature dealing with leadership, of course, is enormous (see Bass, 2008), and I have had to be more selective in consulting it than I would have liked. Conversely, the selectivity has contributed to a more focused overview of perspectives that appear to add substantially to our understanding of those influences that perhaps most conspicuously govern the communicative exchanges that occur between superiors and their subordinates throughout organizational life. Of the perspectives that are applicable in illuminating superior-subordinate interactions in organizational settings, the ones I find to be especially helpful and, hence, have chosen to consider in this chapter include the personality, stylistic, motivational, exchange, transformational, and authentic views. My task here is to demonstrate more precisely why they are helpful and in what respects.

THEORETICAL PERSPECTIVES OF VALUE IN UNDERSTANDING SUPERIOR-SUBORDINATE INTERACTIONS IN ORGANIZATIONS

For each of the six perspectives that follow, I begin with a general overview of what it entails and discuss how it applies to particular aspects of superior-subordinate interactions. After citing some of the relevant research findings, I point to limitations in the extent to which the perspective enables one to enhance his or her understanding of the nature, evolution, and consequences of such communicative exchanges. It is this aspect of the coverage that perhaps makes most evident the necessity of drawing on multiple perspectives for achieving a reasonably complete understanding of the interactions of interest. The limitations, moreover, suggest possibilities and directions for further research.

The Personality Perspective

The early to mid-twentieth century in social science brought with it great interest in the personal qualities that distinguish those in positions of leadership and authority from others and, by implication, superiors from subordinates. Such qualities, many presumed, were genetic in nature. In two different surveys of research emanating from this tradition, Ralph Stogdill (1948, 1974) established there was not much justification for the assumption. This is not to suggest that little of significance emerged from the hundreds of studies conducted, but merely that consistently distinguishing characteristics were few and far between. The list reduced primarily to five: intelligence, self-confidence, determination, integrity, and sociability (Northouse, 2013a). In light of such a small set, Stogdill (1974) was of the view that the significance of the findings was the revelation that different situations may call for different personal attributes, regardless of whether they are inherited or not. More important for purposes of this exploration, however, is whether or not such characteristics matter in regard to superior-subordinate, or leader-follower, interactions. One could, on speculative grounds, make a case that each of the variables noted and others like them would be manifested in interactions of superiors with their subordinates and could have something to do with quality of relationships that evolve. For instance, an exceptionally intelligent supervisor could prove to be intimidating to many of his or her supervisees and induce fear in them, or a highly sociable boss could elicit positive reactions from his or her subordinates as a result of the tone of his or her utterances. Unfortunately, those doing the research that led to leader profiles such as the one mentioned above emerged from perceptual rather than behavioral data and, consequently, failed to provide much basis for understanding specifically how personal qualities enter into the formation and development of superior-subordinate relationships.

In the latter stages of the twentieth century, there was a renaissance of interest in personality characteristics but as acquired, not innate, with consequent interest in how they contribute to interpersonal relationships involving superiors and their subordinates in the workplace. Noteworthy was the identification of the "Five-Factor Model of Personality," which includes neuroticism (more appropriately, positive adjustment), extraversion, openness, agreeableness, and conscientiousness (Goldberg, 1990; McCrea & Costa, 1987), as well as work involving social intelligence (Cantor & Kihlstrom, 1987; Zaccaro, Gilbert, Thor, & Mumford, 1991) and emotional intelligence (Goleman, 1995, 1998). Social intelligence refers to one's capacity "to determine the requirements for leadership in a particular situation and select an appropriate response" (Yukl, 2010, p. 213), whereas emotional intelligence has reference to "the ability to perceive and express emotions, to use emotions to facilitate thinking, to understand and reason with emotions, and to effectively [sic] manage emotions within oneself and in relationships with others" (Northouse, 2013a, pp. 27–28). Individuals possessing these and the "Big Five" characteristics, research suggests, tend to be more effective in working with others and developing positive relationships with them than those lacking such qualities and, hence, function better in superior-subordinate relationships in particular. It is worth noting here, however, that extraversion and sociability are not necessarily assets, nor are introversion and other attributes indicative of less outgoingness always the liabilities that some people are prone to assume, as Susan Cain (2012) has amply demonstrated in her recently published book concerning the upside of introversion.

Historically, those identified with the personality perspective have been in search of the positive qualities that enable individuals to perform well in their interactions with others when they are in positions of authority, leadership, and other superior-subordinate structures, as the preceding overview should make clear

(Kellerman, 2004, 2012). However, as anyone who has spent more than a modicum of time in organizations is aware, superior-subordinate relationships are frequently far from positive and/or functional. Research involving personal qualities, although less plentiful for toxic than for positive relationships, serves to reveal why.

One attribute beginning to receive attention in this connection is narcissism. Michael Maccoby (2003, 2007) has done much to advance the view that organizations often have so-called "productive narcissists," who can be forces for good. The evidence for this view would seem to suggest the opposite—at least at a relational level (see, for example, Chatterjee & Hambrick, 2007; Nevicka, Ten Velden, De Hoogh, & Van Vianin, 2011; Rosenthal & Pittinsky, 2006; Twenge & Campbell, 2009). The extreme sense of entitlement to which narcissists (especially ones who qualify as "malignant") are given, as well as their often complete insensitivity to the feelings and well-being of others (in this case, subordinates), have provided fodder for three recent books concerning this related cluster of similar aspects of personality (see James, 2012; Sutton, 2012a, 2012b).

Further contributing to poor and often dysfunctional superior-subordinate relationships, as well as consistent with the preceding discussion of narcissism and the qualities it embodies, are four of the seven factors Kellerman (2004) has identified as contributing to bad leadership: rigidity, intemperateness, callousness, and insularity. The remaining three (incompetence, corruptness, and evilness), while personal qualities in certain senses, do not appear to qualify as the sorts of attributes on which those examining superior-subordinate relationships from the personality perspective have been focusing and entail consideration of numerous other factors for coming to grips with precisely what they represent.

Although the personality perspective and the scholarly inquiries it has engendered provide interesting insights into the development of superior-subordinate relationships in organizational settings, the understanding to which it has led to date is far from complete. Among other things, it is not clear how the sorts of personal qualities noted manifest themselves, behaviorally speaking, as the relationships of interest evolve. In addition, the focus of inquiry has been the superior, with little or no attention to the personal characteristics of the subordinate (see Kellerman, 2008). Fuller understanding requires the addition of other perspectives and what they have uncovered. The first of these to which I now turn is the stylistic perspective.

The Stylistic Perspective

As interest in the determination of what specific personal qualities and attributes enable individuals to move into positions of authority and to function effectively once in them began to wane during the mid-twentieth century, the accent in theory and research shifted to behavior, or perhaps more accurately, manner of behavior. A seminal study that facilitated the shift was one that Lewin, Lippitt, and White (1939) conducted, and in which they were interested in the impact of three styles of leaders on subordinates: democratic, autocratic, and *laissez-faire*. As those concerned with personality had been, Lewin et al. and those who followed them were interested in determining whether or not there exist universal modes of behavior that when in evidence contribute to the emergence of both performance-based and relational outcomes of interest.

A good deal of the research emanating from the stylistic perspective initially addressed the matter of whether or not individuals in positions of authority, responsibility, and leadership behave while enacting their roles in a consistent fashion. Two early programs, one at Ohio State and the other at the University of Michigan, focused on this matter. Working with an inventory called the Leader Behavior Description Questionnaire, those in the OSU group came to the conclusion that that there are two general types of behavior that leaders exhibit: initiating structure (or task-oriented behavior) and consideration (or relationally oriented behavior; see Stogdill, 1974). One could be high or low in respect to either or both. Those at the University of Michigan were less concerned, however, about the development of measures and more interested in how leaders' behavior related to the performance of subordinates in groups and organizations (see the collection of pertinent inquiries in Cartwright & Zander, 1968). Like their OSU counterparts, members of the Michigan group identified leader behavior in terms of two categories: production orientation (which places the accent on task performance) and employee orientation (which places the accent on relationships). However, they presumed the two to lie at different ends of the same continuum—a view they later came to reject (Northouse, 2013b). This led to a set of four combinations of high and low standing on each dimension of behavior comparable to the four stemming from the OSU program. Both groups of scholars took as the dependent variables of interest subordinate satisfaction and productivity. Findings from hundreds of studies they conducted or stimulated others to undertake proved to be inconclusive. Emerging was some limited support for the view that the high-high combination of style leads to better outcomes than any other combination (Yukl, 2010).

Despite the data revealing the sometimes superiority of the high-high combination of task-related and relationally oriented styles, it may not be the combination per se, but instead the appropriate reading of the circumstances in which one enacts this combination, versus one of the others, that is critical to success and in the case of this exploration the quality of the superior-subordinate relationship. This seems to be the message in work by Robert Blake, Jane Mouton, and Anne McCanse (see Blake & McCanse, 1991; Blake & Mouton, 1985) and Kenneth Blanchard and his associates (see Blanchard, Zigarmi, & Nelson, 1993; Blanchard, Zigarmi, & Zigarmi, 1985). Research from both programs suggests that mismatching of a leader's style to a particular set of circumstances in which subordinates find themselves vis-à-vis their level of development, for instance, being overly supportive when directiveness is desired, sought, and appropriate or delegating responsibility when the situation calls more for coaching, can, and does, contribute to a reduction in relational quality. It can even lead to dissolution of a relationship.

Further supportive of the notion that proper matches of style to circumstances is key to effective performance and positive relationships is Fred Fiedler's (1967) long-term study of the interaction of a leader's style and orientation toward co-workers in respect both to subordinates' performance and their level of satisfaction, showing that mismatches have a negative impact on both. I should point out that Fiedler was not a proponent of behavioral flexibility, that is, changing one's style, even though he acknowledged that most leaders have a secondary style to which they can and do resort in the face of a mismatch of the primary style (see Fiedler, 1995). In the long run, however, identifying the proper match in the first place proves to be of greater value.

As in the case of the personality perspective, the stylistic perspective through-out its evolution, especially in its early stages, has been predominantly leader-centered. More recent research, on the other hand, exhibits some effort to take into consideration characteristics of subordinates and the situation in which they are interacting with superiors that have a bearing on the exchanges that occur and how they, in turn, may affect both performance and the health of the relationships they (the subordinates) have with their superiors. The next perspective, the one I previously labeled as "motivational," reveals a significant advance in scholarly attention to both characteristics of subordinates and the situation in which they interact with their superiors. Even though the research is closely identified with one individual, namely, Robert House, it was influenced by Martin Evans (1970), who developed an earlier version of the perspective from which House profited.

The Motivational Perspective

From the perspective of path-goal theory, key to the successful exercise of influence, as well as the development of good relations between superiors and their subordi-nates, is what the former do to help the latter overcome constraints on their levels of motivation (Yukl, 2010). The perspective is partially grounded in another body of work called "expectancy theory" (see Georgopoulos, Mahoney, & Jones, 1957; Vroom, 1964; Vroom & Jago, 1978). When individuals lack motivation to perform a given task, there is typically one of three explanations: they perceive themselves as lacking the skill necessary to perform the task successfully; they see a low proba-bility of the task's being completed for reasons unrelated to their own competence; or the payoff does not appear to be proportionate to the effort the task requires for successful completion (Yukl, 2010).

When any of these constraints is operative among one's subordinates, the challenge for the superior is to remove the obstacle the constraint presents, to assist the subordinates in getting around it, or to enable them otherwise to surmount it. As House (1971) put it in an early formulation of the theory:

> The motivational function of the leader consists of increasing personal payoffs to subordinates for work-goal attainment and making the path to these payoffs easier to travel by clarifying it, reducing roadblocks and pitfalls, and increasing the opportunities for personal satisfaction en route. (p. 324)

Moreover, "[L]eader behavior will be viewed as acceptable to subordinates to the extent that the subordinates see such behavior as either an immediate source of satisfaction or as instrumental to future satisfaction" (House & Dessler, 1974, p. 13).

In both the original version of path-goal theory (House, 1971) and a subsequently revised version (House, 1996), House examined situational factors, for instance, the ambiguity, repetitiveness, and complexity of a task, as well as such characteristics of subordinates as authoritarianism, need for affiliation, and desire for control as sources of diminished motivation. At least as important as the factors themselves, he posited, is how they combine to suggest appropriate styles of interaction by superiors to raise the level of motivation and, thereby, to improve the prospects for successful completion of particular tasks and the likelihood of the subordinates' satisfaction with the result—not to mention their relationships with their superiors. Although House (1996) expanded the categories of style from four to eight in the reformulated version of the theory, in both it and the original, the focus is on four: directive, supportive, participative, and achievement oriented.

Research growing from the theory has in general revealed limited support (see summaries by Podsakoff, MacKenzie, Ahearne, & Bommer, 1995; Wofford & Liska, 1993). In part, this has been a result of researchers having focused primarily on the situational variables relating to only two categories of leader behavior in the original four: directive and supportive. In each case, moreover, only some of the moderating task and subordinate variables expected to favor these particular styles have proved to be predictive of either performance or satisfaction. It may be that the genuinely crucial situational variables have yet to be identified. Note the title of the article by Podsakoff et al. (1995): "Searching for a Needle in a Haystack: Trying to Identify the Illusive Moderators of Leadership Behaviors." Nevertheless, the findings to date have provided sufficient reason for believing that the performance and satisfaction of subordinates improve when superiors engage in behavior that can raise levels of motivation.

On the other hand, the same behavior is not equally well suited for overcoming all constraints on subordinates' motivation in the execution of different types of tasks, particularly when they themselves vary in respect to what they experience as frustrating about undertaking those tasks. If, for instance, one is not motivated to perform a task because he or she finds it to be boring, what might be necessary for a superior to create interest and enthusiasm could be quite different from what is most efficacious in dealing with another individual lacking in motivation as a consequence of feeling insufficiently competent to perform the task successfully. The motivational perspective has served to make this level of complexity clear. As Gary Yukl (2010) points out, "[P]ath-goal theory has made an important contribution to the study of leadership by providing a conceptual framework to guide researchers in identifying potentially relevant situational variables" (p. 233).

A lesson for superiors deriving from the motivational perspective is that relationships with subordinates are likely to be better, not to mention their performance, when one makes conscious efforts to raise motivation if it seems to be waning and recognizes that succeeding not only requires careful identification of the influences that may be operative, including characteristics of both tasks and those being asked to perform them, but also a willingness to alter his or her manner of interacting, as appropriate to the constraints. In line with this thinking in many respects is another theoretical view that for purposes of this chapter I refer to as the "exchange" perspective. This body of work, however, has as its central concern not what superiors can do generally (e.g., behaving democratically) or how to adapt to particular configurations of circumstances (e.g., using a delegating style with mature individuals versus a directive style with immature individuals) in their interactions with subordinates, but instead recognizing differences and establishing a high-quality, albeit unique relationship with each. Although many scholars have been attracted to this perspective (often referred to as Leader-Member Exchange Theory, LMX), it is perhaps more strongly associated with George Graen and Fred Dansereau than anyone else.

The Exchange Perspective

In its original formulation, the LMX perspective carried the label "Vertical Dyad Linkage Theory" (Danserseau, Graen, & Haga, 1975). The perspective was purportedly descriptive in nature and acknowledged that in organizations, it is common for those in positions of authority to develop a different relationship with each of their subordinates. The nature of these relationships is an outgrowth of personal compatibility, relative competence of the subordinates, and dependability (Graen & Cashman, 1975). Differential patterns of exchange serve a twofold function. First, they provide a means by which superiors and subordinates mutually arrive at an understanding of the latter's role. Second, they lead to the formation of in-groups and out-groups. Those in in-groups curry favor with superiors, are motivated to go beyond their job descriptions, and more easily advance than others. In contrast, those in out-groups tend to behave in accordance with formal role requirements but fail to develop much of a sense of identification with their respective organizations or strong positive relationships with their superiors. In fact, the perception of preferential treatment by superiors of those comprising the in-groups presumably appears to be a source of resentment and disaffection among those in the out-groups. Or so the early research suggested.

The exchange perspective underwent revision in the last fifteen years of the twentieth century. Not only did it acquire a new designation ("Leader-Member Exchange Theory"), but it also began to take on a more prescriptive character, with the accent on superiors' needing to make efforts to establish high-quality exchange relationships with all subordinates through a process called "leadership-making" as a means of overcoming some of the difficulties associated with the formation of in-groups and out-groups that can arise in the absence of any sort of preventive or inhibitory interventions (Graen & Uhl-Bien, 1991, 1995). The process of leadership-making has superiors' moving, or at least attempting to move, subordinates through three relational stages: stranger, acquaintance, and mature partnership. In principle, every subordinate could reach the third stage by virtue of his or her superior's having engaged in high-quality communication, but, in fact, the likelihood of this occurring is rather remote.

Although the research emanating from the exchange perspective has not been as rigorous as one might like, and there are methodological problems about which he or she should be concerned, especially ones involving the measurement of quality of relationships, leadership-making, and relational satisfaction (see Arnand, Hu, Liden, & Vidyarthi, 2011; Yukl, 2010), there are indications that efforts by superiors to engage in high-quality downward communication have a positive relationship to subordinates' perceptions of role clarity, relational satisfaction, performance, and organizational commitment (Graen, Novak, & Sommerkamp, 1982; Yukl, 2010). Dirks and Ferrin (2002), moreover, determined that such actions correlate positively with the development of subordinates' trust in their superiors.

It is noteworthy in this review of the evidence that despite what Graen et al. (1982) had uncovered while the theory still carried the label "Vertical Dyad Linkage" and had an allegedly descriptive character, it encouraged those in positions of authority to continue contributing to the formation of in-groups and out-groups, with attendant deliberate cultivation of the former. It would be more than a decade later before proponents came to appreciate the damage such encouragement could do and the potential good that it tended to prevent. If there is a lesson for those in positions of authority in organizations in the earlier research and the later body of scholarship ensuing with the shift from an exclusively descriptive character of the exchange perspective to a more prescriptive view, it is that becoming resigned to in-group and out-group formation as a fact of organizational life is likely not a good idea and that taking steps to prevent that from happening is.

The original version of the exchange perspective embodied in Vertical Dyad Linkage Theory had a decidedly transactional character as related to superior-subordinate interactions, inasmuch as it portrayed them as involving behavior having as its aim the achievement of superiors' desired outcomes, principally by means of *quid pro quo* measures. Subordinates who knew how to "play the game," as it were, could benefit in a variety of ways, whereas those who did not, or did not wish to, were apt to function in such a manner that they could retain membership but with relatively few of the privileges accorded to those in superiors' in-groups. As a result of the shift in emphasis on the desirability, if not need, for superiors to engage in leadership-making in a deliberately conscious way, the exchange perspective now bears a much stronger relationship to the next view of superior-subordinate interaction I consider, that is, the transformational perspective, which emphasizes contributing to the collective good, not specifically to the achievement of one's personal objectives and well-being.

The Transformational Perspective

In 1978, James MacGregor Burns published his now well-known and frequently cited book *Leadership*. Although James Downton (1973) preceded Burns in introducing the concept of transformational leadership, Burns's treatment of it was the one that caught on and found its way into the scholarly agenda of Bernard Bass and many of his associates who, contrary to the views of those who considered it elusive at best, saw transformational leadership as measurable, something actually in evidence in many organizations, and a form of influence that those in positions of authority and others could learn and master (see Avolio, Bass, & Jung, 1999; Bass, 1985, 1990, 1998; Bass & Avolio, 1990a, 1990b, 1994; Bass & Riggio, 2006). Although others have developed different formulations of the transformational perspective and written extensively about them (see, for example, Bennis & Nanus, 1985; Kouzes & Posner, 2012), the examination that follows reflects the conceptualization of transformational leadership that Bass and his associates were primarily responsible for developing because their version is the one that has fostered the most empirical studies and tests of hypotheses concerning the leadership/outcome relationship.

Transformational leadership is difficult to characterize. At least, the most recent view, as articulated in the volume by Bass and Riggio (2006), is. Various aspects of the perspective lead one to think of transformational leadership as a set of intangible personal qualities. This is understandable in respect to the first two of the defining characteristics: idealized influence, which equates to charisma, and inspirational motivation, which equates to vision. However, the remaining two characteristics, that is, intellectual stimulation and individualized consideration, appear to represent more overt forms of directly observable behavior. In contrast, charisma and vision are attributes one can only infer from another's manifest behavior. We often have difficulty determining what precisely it is that makes an individual come across as charismatic. Similarly, when one articulates and explains a vision, we do not know whether, in fact, it is an accurate representation of what he or she actually sees as a possible future state that we can and/or should endorse.

Further complicating the picture is that transformational leaders also from time to time engage in behavior that would qualify as transactional by virtue of their including in their interactions rewards and promises, as well as punishments and threats, both immediate and delayed, as depicted in Bass and Riggio's (2006) "Full Range of Leadership Model" (p. 7). They additionally at times are apt to behave in a *laissez-faire* fashion, even though proponents of the transformational perspective generally regard this as "non-leadership."

Conceptual issues surrounding what exactly qualifies one as transformational notwithstanding, individuals who fit the profile seem to have a capacity for stimulating their subordinates to look beyond themselves and commit first and foremost to the collective good (Bass, 1985, 1990), as well as to do so willingly. Evidence of this type of impact has surfaced in studies by Brown and Mashavi (2002); Koh (1990); Koh, Steers, and Terborg (1995); Pitman (1993); Rai and Sinha (2000); and Zohar (2002).

Beyond having powerful effects on subordinates' commitment to, and identification with, the organization, the Bass brand of transformational leader also seems to have considerable facility in eliciting levels of satisfaction among subordinates with his or her leadership (see meta-analyses by DeGroote, Kiker, & Cross, 2000; Dundrum, Lowe, & Avolio, 2002; Lowe, Kroeck, Sivasubramaniam, 1996), as well as trust (Conger & Kanungo, 1998; House & Shamir, 1993), because of the apparent self-sacrificial behavior to which such individuals are prone. This resonates with observations Adam Grant (2013) has made on the basis of a series of studies in which he was involved and that drew into serious question the widespread assumption in organizational life that compared to "takers," individuals who place self at the center of their lives and individual goals above the collective good, so-called givers, that is, those who subordinate self-interest to the well-being of others, have little chance of even acceding to positions of authority, let alone exercising much influence. Grant's work shows this thinking and the dubious view of altruistic behavior it encourages to be wrong on both counts. To be other-oriented as an organizational member, then, is to preclude neither opportunities for assuming positions of authority nor being successful in them.

Finally, subordinates seem to perform well under conditions in which their superiors qualify as transformational. Bass and Riggio (2006) summarize a good deal of research supportive of this claim in such diverse areas as sales, military operations, not-for-profit organizational work, and athletics. A reason for enhanced performance appears to be that transformational leaders have an impact on subordinates' sense of self-efficacy as a result of their own (Hoyt, Murphy, Halverson, & Watson, 2003; Yukl, 1993). Apparently, one's belief that he or she is capable of making a positive difference can have a contagious effect on others and in the case of transformational leaders does.

Behaving in line with the description of transformational leaders that has emerged from the scholarly activity that Bernard Bass, his associates, and others have noted can do much to create positive superior-subordinate relationships that additionally foster a climate in which both superior and subordinate alike place self-interest below collective well-being in priority, encourage them to become increasingly collaborative in their orientation toward task performance, strengthen their mutual identification with the organization, enhance performance beyond expectations, otherwise facilitate the achievement of collective goals, and, in the process, become both better organizational citizens and individuals more generally. These are reasons, among others, that the label of "transformational leadership" has come into increasingly common use in the past quarter century.

Not everyone, of course, is able to acquire or cultivate the qualities and enact the patterns of behavior that set transformational leaders apart from others, no matter how hard he or she might try. Those who are able, however, have a clear, if not substantial, edge when it comes to developing superior-subordinate relationships that are mutually gratifying and, in the long run, beneficial.

Unfortunately, there also reside among us individuals who come across as transformational when, in fact, they are not. Bass and Riggio (2006) refer to such figures as "pseudotransformational" (p. 40). Beneath a projected veneer of concern for their subordinates in these cases lurks a level of disingenuousness that over time can bring out some of the most unadmirable of human qualities. Among the terms that Bass and Riggio use to characterize pseudotransformational leaders are "authoritarian," "self-aggrandizing," "exploitative," "narcissistic," "impetuous," and "impulsively aggressive" (p. 40). They resort to manipulation, threats, and promises to exact compliance while at the same time attempting to preserve the false image they have with those to whom they have not revealed their actual selves and to whom their duplicity is not yet apparent. It was the presence of these types individuals in positions of authority and others sharing some of the characteristics noted that gave rise, in part, to the last of the perspectives I cover in this chapter—what has come to be known as the authentic leadership perspective.

The Authentic Perspective

The authentic perspective on leadership is of recent origin and, as noted, appears to have developed in response to corporate and political corruption, disservice to the public, and other forms of troubling, often patently unethical, behavior, among many people in positions of authority and leadership. As with pseudotransformational leaders, there is an abundance of those who qualify as inauthentic in contemporary organizational and public life. With each revelation that carries some degree of notoriety, the feeling that our institutions are failing and that our leaders have let us down becomes more and more pronounced. Such feelings lead further to widespread cynicism and mistrust. Yet, there are many authentic leaders among us. They are individuals whom we admire for their honesty, freedom from pretence, transparency, and dependability. From the authentic perspective, confidence in leaders is a product of their genuineness and trustworthiness, particularly in the realm of superior-subordinate relationships. We want people in leadership roles who say what they mean and mean what they say. A person in a position of authority whose subordinates perceive him or her to be deficient in these respects is apt to have low-quality relationships with them, if not outright antagonistic, or even hostile, ones.

Individuals from the business and corporate world, such as Bill George (2003) and Robert Terry (1993), have made efforts to identify the elements of authentic leadership from a practitioner's point of view. There is interest value in what they have to say. However, for purposes of the present discussion, there is possibly greater illumination stemming from social-scientific inquiries by Fred Walumbwa and his associates (see Walumbwa, Avolio, Gardner, Wernsing, & Peterson, 2008; Walumbwa, Wang, Wang, Schaubroeck, & Avolio, 2010), who consider it as a developmental process that evolves over time via a variety of factors, all of which serve to shape others' perceptions of a leader's trustworthiness, the patterns of interaction in which the parties engage, and ultimately the quality of their relationship.

Authenticity, research suggests, is a manifestation of several psychological capacities (confidence, hope, optimism, and resilience), moral reasoning, and critical life events. These factors combine in ways that contribute over time to the development of greater self-awareness, a clearly structured moral perspective, objectivity in the assessment of information, and transparency in relationships (Luthans & Avolio, 2003). The implication of scholarly inquiries relating to authentic leadership is that to the extent one acquires such behavioral dispositions as a result of the antecedent factors, the trust that others place in the individual will enhance his or her prospects for developing positive collaborative superior-subordinate relationships.

Even though the authentic perspective on leadership lacks a substantial enough foundation in research to warrant very many claims concerning its contribution to our understanding of the formation, development, and quality of superior-subordinate relationships, an individual in a position of authority or leadership would be well advised to recognize that inauthenticity can be a serious impediment to working constructively and effectively with his or her subordinates. Even if there were no morally compelling reasons for being authentic (even though I think that this is definitely not the case), there surely are pragmatically sound ones for trying to cultivate authenticity and to display it in all of one's interactions with his or her subordinates.

DIRECTIONS FOR FUTURE RESEARCH

As I noted earlier, limitations in what we have learned from the several perspectives I have discussed open avenues for further inquiries into how communication enters into the development of superior subordinate-relationships in professional life. Following are several one might consider pursuing. I address these in the same order in which I introduced each of the six perspectives above. Before proceeding, however, I should point out that all converge on a common theme, that is, the general neglect of the subordinate in scholarly examinations and discussions of superior-subordinate relationships. This is a deficiency in examinations of leadership to which Barbara Kellerman (2008) has eloquently called attention in *Followership: How Followers Are Creating Change and Changing Leaders*.

In the spirit of Kellerman's indictment of scholarly inquiry into leadership, the personality perspective might be of greater value if those interested in it were to devote more attention to the personal qualities in subordinates they have associated with leaders. It would even be of interest if those doing research from this perspective were to explore whether or not superiors and subordinates having similar personality profiles develop better or worse relationships than those whose profiles differ and, if so, how that is manifested in their communicative behavior. It is conceivable that similarity is a source of dysfunction rather than an asset in respect to the quality of exchanges that occur.

As to the stylistic perspective, neglect of subordinates' preferences for how they believe superiors should behave versus do behave in their interactions with them might tell us a good deal more than we currently know concerning what distinguishes the development of positive versus negative relationships between the two. That such preferences exist and seem to make a difference at a relational level has garnered some support in the "Global Leadership and Organizational Behavior Effectiveness" program of research in which House, Hanges, Javidan, Dorfman, and Gupta (2004) have been involved.

Those doing research from the motivational perspective have done better than those associated with the first two in considering subordinate characteristics vis-à-vis styles of interactions. Lacking, however, is sufficient concern with how particular constraints on motivation (e.g., perceived competence, assessed likelihood of completing a task, and anticipated payoff) may mediate the impact of given styles of leadership. Efforts to become more definitive in this respect could add considerably to what we know about how superior-subordinate interactions contribute to relationship development as well as quality.

Like those studying superior-subordinate interactions and the relationships they foster, exponents of the exchange perspective have concerned themselves with the subordinate side, but not to the extent that we have much understanding of what makes for successful "leadership-making" or qualifies as high-quality interaction from the point view of subordinates insofar as their moving through the stranger, acquaintance, and mature partnership stages (see Graen & Uhl-Bien, 1991; Nahrang, Morgeson, & Ilies, 2009) is concerned. Specifics would do much to enhance the value of this perspective both at a theoretical and practical levels.

The transformational perspective holds as important the need for critical thought and reaction when it comes to leaders' articulation of their visions, yet there is evidence to suggest that followers (in our case, subordinates) are often given to passive acceptance in this regard. It would be of value to identify what it is about subordinates in some instances that leads them to respond to intellectual challenges posed by superiors who by all accounts appear to be transformational in this way rather than in the manner that Bass and Riggio (2006), among others, portray as lying in large measure at the base of genuinely transformational leadership.

A parallel concern arises in relation to the authentic leadership perspective. What precisely is it that enables some subordinates to detect authenticity in their superiors successfully when others do not or possibly cannot? A related question has to do with why some subordinates seem to be so easily fooled into perceiving their superiors as authentic when, objectively speaking, they clearly would not qualify. Answers to these questions could do much to advance the status of the perspective, as well as provide guidance to the gullible to be wary of possibilities for seeing as authentic superiors who are not.

CONCLUSION

None of the six perspectives on leadership (personality, stylistic, motivational, exchange, transformational, or authentic) that I have examined in these pages is sufficient to account for how interaction unfolds and evolves in superior-subordinate relationships. Despite the fact that each offers a different way of accounting for some of what occurs, as well as provides unique clues as to how one might profit from the knowledge to which the perspective exposes him or her and how he or she consequently could begin thinking more seriously about how to engage in superior-subordinate interactions to increase the likelihood of positive outcomes and minimize that for negative outcomes, in combination, they afford one even greater possibilities for success. At least, that is my hope.

REFERENCES

Arnand, S., Hu, J., Liden, R. C., & Vidyarthi, P. R. (2011). Leader-member exchange: Recent research findings and prospects for the future. In A. Bryman, D. Collinson, K. Grint, G. Jackson, & M. Uhl-Bien (Eds.), *The Sage handbook of leadership* (pp. 311–325). London, England: Sage.
Avolio, B. J., Bass, B. M., & Jung, D. I. (1999). Re-examining the components of transformational and transactional leadership using the multifactor leadership questionnaire. *Journal of Occupational and Organizational Psychology, 72*, 441–462.
Bass, B. M. (1985). *Leadership and performance beyond expectations.* New York, NY: Free Press.

Bass, B. M. (1990). From transactional to transformational leadership: Learning to share the vision. *Organizational Dynamics, 18,* 19–31.

Bass, B. M. (1998). The ethics of transformational leadership. In J. Ciulla (Ed.), *Ethics: The heart of leadership* (pp. 169–192). Westport, CT: Praeger.

Bass, B. M. (with Bass, R.). (2008). *The Bass handbook of leadership: Theory, research, & managerial applications* (4th ed.). New York, NY: Free Press.

Bass, B. M., & Avolio, B. J. (1990a). The implications of transactional and transformation leadership for individual, team, and organizational development. *Research in Organizational Change and Development, 4,* 231–272.

Bass, B. M., & Avolio, B. J. (1990b). *Multifactor leadership questionnaire.* Palo Alto, CA: Consulting Psychologists Press.

Bass, B. M., & Avolio, B. J. (1994). *Improving organizational effectiveness through transformational leadership.* Thousand Oaks, CA: Sage.

Bass, B. M., & Riggio, R. E. (2006). *Transformational leadership* (2nd ed.). Mahwah, NJ: Erlbaum.

Bennis, W. G., & Nanus, B. (1985). *Leaders: The strategies for taking charge.* New York, NY: Harper & Row.

Blake, R. R., & McCanse, A. A. (1991). *Leadership dilemmas: Grid solutions.* Houston, TX: Gulf.

Blake, R. R., & Mouton, J. S. (1985). *The managerial grid.* Houston, TX: Gulf.

Blanchard, K., Zigarmi, D., & Nelson, R. (1993). Situational leadership after 25 years: A retrospective. *Journal of Leadership Studies, 1,* 22–36.

Blanchard, K., Zigarmi, P., & Zigarmi, D. (1985). *Leadership and the one minute manager: Increasing effectiveness through situational leadership.* New York, NY: Morrow.

Brown, F. W., & Mashavi, D. (2002). Herding academic cats: Faculty reactions to transformational and contingent reward leadership by department chairs. *Leadership Studies, 8,* 79–94.

Burns, J. M. (1978). *Leadership.* New York, NY: Harper & Row.

Cain, S. (2012). *Quiet: The power of introverts in a world that can't stop talking.* New York, NY: Crown.

Cantor, N., & Kihlstrom, J. F. (1987). *Personality and social intelligence.* Englewood Cliffs, NJ: Prentice-Hall.

Cartwright, D., & Zander, A. (Eds.). (1968). *Group dynamics: Theory and research* (3rd ed.). New York, NY: Harper & Row.

Chatterjee, A., & Hambrick, D. C. (2007). It's all about me: Narcissistic chief executive officers and their effects on company strategy and performance. *Administrative Science Quarterly, 52,* 351–387.

Conger, J. A., & Kanungo, R. N. (1998). *Charismatic leadership in organizations.* Thousand Oaks, CA: Sage.

Dansereau, F., Jr., Graen, G., & Haga, W. J. (1975). A vertical dyad linkage approach to leadership within formal organizations: A longitudinal investigation of the role-making process. *Organizational Behavior and Human Performance, 13,* 46–78.

DeGroote, T., Kiker, D. S., & Cross, T. C. (2000). A meta-analysis to review organizational outcomes related to charismatic leadership. *Canadian Journal of Administrative Sciences, 17,* 356–371.

Dirks, K. T., & Ferrin, D. L. (2002). Trust in leadership: Meta-analytic findings and implications for research and practice. *Journal of Applied Psychology, 87,* 611–628.

Downton, J. V. (1973). *Rebel leadership: Commitment and charisma in a revolutionary process.* New York, NY: Free Press.

Dundrum, U. R., Lowe, K. B., & Avolio, B. J. (2002). A meta-analysis of transformational and transactional leadership correlates of effectiveness and satisfaction: An update and extension.

In B. J. Avolio & F. J. Yammarino (Eds.), *Transformation and charismatic leadership: The road ahead* (pp. 35–66). Oxford, England: JAI/Elsevier.

Evans, M. G. (1970). The effects of supervisory behavior on the path-goal relationship. *Organizational Behavior and Human Performance, 5,* 277–298.

Fiedler, F. E. (1967). *A theory of leadership effectiveness.* New York, NY: McGraw-Hill.

Fiedler, F. E. (1995). Reflections by an accidental theorist. *Leadership Quarterly, 6,* 453–461.

George, B. (2003). *Authentic leaders: Rediscovering the secrets to creating lasting value.* San Francisco, CA: Jossey-Bass.

Georgopoulos, B. S., Mahoney, G. M., & Jones, N. W., Jr. (1957). A path-goal approach to productivity. *Journal of Applied Psychology, 41,* 345–353.

Goldberg, L. R. (1990). An alternative "description of personality": The big-five factor structure. *Journal of Personality and Social Psychology, 59,* 1216–1229.

Goleman, D. (1995). *Emotional intelligence. Why it can matter more than IQ.* New York, NY: Bantam Books.

Goleman, D. (1998). *Working with emotional intelligence.* New York, NY: Bantam Books.

Graen, G. B., & Cashman, J. F. (1975). A role-making model of leadership in formal organizations: A developmental approach. In J. G. Hunt & L. L. Larson (Eds.), *Leadership frontiers* (pp. 143–166). Kent, OH: Kent State University Press.

Graen, G. B., Novak, M. A., & Sommerkamp, P. (1982). The effects of leader-member exchange and job-design on productivity and satisfaction: Testing a dual attachment model. *Organizational Behavior and Human Performance, 30,* 109–131.

Graen, G. B., & Uhl-Bien, M. (1991). The transformation of professionals into self-managing and partially self-designing contributors: Toward a theory of leadership-making. *Journal of Management Systems, 3*(3), 33–48.

Graen, G. B., & Uhl-Bien, M. (1995). Relationship-based approach to leadership. Development of leader-member exchange (LMX) theory of leadership over 25 years: Applying a multi-level multi-domain approach. *Leadership Quarterly, 6,* 219–247.

Grant, A. (2013). *Give and take: A revolutionary approach.* New York, NY: Viking.

House, R. J. (1971). A path-goal theory of leader effectiveness. *Administrative Science Quarterly, 16,* 321–339.

House, R. J. (1996). Path-goal theory of leadership: Lessons, legacy, and a reformulated theory. *Leadership Quarterly, 7,* 323–352.

House, R. J., & Dessler, G. (1974). The path-goal theory of leadership. In J. G. Hunt & L. L Larson (Eds.), *Leadership: The cutting edge* (pp. 189–207). Carbondale: Southern Illinois University Press.

House, R. J., Hanges, P. J., Javidan, M., Dorfman, P. W., & Gupta, V. (Eds.). (2004). *Culture, leadership, and organizations: The GLOBE study of 62 societies.* Thousand Oaks, CA: Sage.

House, R. J., & Shamir, B. (1993). Toward the integration of transformational, charismatic, and visionary theories. In M. M. Chemers & R. Ayman (Eds.), *Leadership theory and research: Perspective and directions* (pp. 81–107). New York, NY: Academic Press.

Hoyt, C. L., Murphy, S. E., Halverson, S. K., & Watson, C. B. (2003). Group leadership: Efficacy and effectiveness. *Group Dynamics: Theory, Research, and Practice, 7,* 259–274.

James, A. (2012). *Assholes: A theory.* New York, NY: Doubleday.

Kellerman, B. (2004). *Bad leadership: What it is, how it happens, why it matters.* Boston, MA: Harvard Business School Press.

Kellerman, B. (2008). *Followership: How followers are creating change and changing leaders.* Boston, MA: Harvard Business School Press.

Kellerman, B. (2012). *The end of leadership.* New York, NY: Harper Business.

Koh, W. L. (1990). *An empirical validation of the theory of transformational leadership in secondary schools in Singapore* (Unpublished doctoral dissertation). University of Oregon, Eugene.

Koh, W. L., Steers, R. M., & Terborg, J. R. (1995). The effects of transformational leadership on teacher attitudes and student performance in Singapore. *Journal of Organizational Behavior, 16,* 319–333.

Kouzes, J., & Posner, B. (2012). *The leadership challenge: How to make extraordinary things happen in organizations* (5th ed.). San Francisco, CA: Jossey-Bass.

Lewin, K., Lippitt, R., & White, R. K. (1939). Patterns of aggressive behavior in experimentally created social climates. *Journal of Social Psychology, 10,* 271–301.

Lowe, K. B., Kroeck, K. G., & Sivasubramaniam, N. (1996). Effectiveness correlates of transformational and transaction leadership: A meta-analytic review of the MLQ literature. *Leadership Quarterly, 7,* 385–425.

Luthans, F., & Avolio, B. J. (2003). Authentic leadership development. In K. S. Cameron, J. E. Dutton, & R. E. Quinn (Eds.), *Positive organizational scholarship* (pp. 241–258). San Francisco, CA: Berrett-Koehler.

Maccoby, M. (2003). *The productive narcissist: The promise and peril of visionary leadership.* New York, NY: Broadway Books.

Maccoby, M. (2007). *The leaders we need and what makes us follow.* Boston, MA: Harvard Business School Press.

McCrea, R. R., & Costa, P. T. (1987). Validation of the five-factor model of personality across instruments and observers. *Journal of Personality and Social Psychology, 52,* 81–90.

Nahrang, J. D., Morgeson, R. P., & Ilies, R. (2009). The development of leader-member exchanges: Exploring how personality and performance influence leader and member relationships over time. *Organizational Behavior and Decision Processes, 108,* 256–266.

Nevicka, B., Ten Velden, F. S., De Hoogh, A. H. B., & Van Vianin, A. E. M. (2011). Reality at odds with perceptions: Narcissistic leaders and group performance. *Psychological Science, 22,* 1259–1264.

Northouse, P. G. (2013a). Trait approach. In P. G. Northouse (Ed.), *Leadership: Theory and practice* (6th ed., pp. 19–42). Thousand Oaks, CA: Sage.

Northouse, P. G. (2013b). Style approach. In P. G. Northouse (Ed.), *Leadership: Theory and practice* (6th ed., pp. 75–97). Thousand Oaks, CA: Sage.

Northouse, P. G. (2013c). Transformational leadership (pp. 185–217). In P. G. Northouse (Ed.), *Leadership: Theory and practice* (6th ed., pp. 185–217). Thousand Oaks, CA: Sage.

Pitman, B. (1993). *The relationship between charismatic leadership behaviors and organizational commitment among white-collar workers* (Unpublished doctoral dissertation). Georgia State University, Atlanta.

Podsakoff, P. M., MacKenzie, S. B., Ahearne, M., & Bommer, W. H. (1995). Searching for a needle in a haystack: Trying to identify the illusive moderators of leadership behaviors. *Journal of Management, 21,* 423–470.

Rai, S., & Sinha, A. K. (2000). Transformational leadership, organizational commitment, and facilitating climate. *Psychological Studies, 45,* 33–42.

Rosenthal, S. A., & Pittinsky, T. L. (2006). Narcissistic leadership. *Leadership Quarterly, 17,* 617–633.

Stogdill, R. M. (1948), Personal factors associated with leadership: A survey of the literature, *Journal of Psychology, 25,* 35–71.

Stogdill, R. M. (1974) *Handbook of leadership: A survey of theory and research.* New York, NY: Free Press.

Sutton, R. I. (2012a). *Good boss, bad boss: How to be the best ... and learn from the worst* (Rev. ed.). New York, NY: Business Plus.

Sutton, R. I. (2012b). *The no asshole rule: Building a civilized workplace and surviving one that isn't* (Rev. ed.). New York, NY: Business Plus.

Terry, R. W. (1993). *Authentic leadership: Courage in action.* San Francisco, CA: Jossey-Bass.

Twenge, J. M., & Campbell, W. K. (2009). *The narcissism epidemic: Living in the age of entitlement.* New York, NY: Free Press.

Vroom, V. H. (1964). *Work and motivation.* New York, NY: John Wiley & Sons.

Vroom, V. H., & Jago, A. G. (1978). On the validity of the Vroom-Yetton model. *Journal of Applied Psychology, 63,* 151–162.

Walumbwa, F. O., Avolio, B. J., Gardner, W. L., Wernsing, T., & Peterson, S. J. (2008). Authentic leadership: Development and validation of a theory-based measure. *Journal of Management, 34,* 89–126.

Walumbwa, F. O., Wang, P., Wang, H., Schaubroeck, J., & Avolio, B. J. (2010). Psychological processes linking authentic leadership to follower behaviors. *Leadership Quarterly, 21,* 901–914.

Wofford, J. C., & Liska, L. Z. (1993). Path-goal theories of leadership: A meta-analysis. *Journal of Management, 19,* 858–876.

Yukl, G. (1993). A retrospective on Robert House's "1976 theory of charismatic leadership" and recent revisions. *Leadership Quarterly, 4,* 367–373.

Yukl, G. (2010). *Leadership in organizations* (7th ed.). Upper Saddle River, NJ: Prentice Hall.

Zacarro, S. J., Gilbert, J. A., Thor, K. K., & Mumford, M. D. (1991). Leadership and social intelligence: Linking social perspectiveness and behavioral flexibility to leader effectiveness. *Leadership Quarterly, 2,* 317–342.

Zohar, D. (2002). The effects of leadership dimensions, safety climate, and assigned priorities on minor injuries in work groups. *Journal of Organizational Behavior, 23,* 75–92.

CHAPTER SEVENTEEN

Spouse and Parent

Television Images of Major Roles of Adulthood

DIANE T. PRUSANK

"Regardless of whether they are fictional or real, television families are sites of cultural anxieties, where the work of social cohesion is ritually enacted."

—KOMPARE (2009, P. 102)

While recent data indicate that the age of first marriage is increasing and the number of people marrying is declining, it is still the case that the majority of adult Americans marry at least once (Wilcox & Marquardt, 2010), and we still see marriage as "an event of adulthood" (Centers for Disease Control and Prevention, 2010). Additionally, although parenthood is an activity that is rapidly uncoupling from marriage (Wilcox & Marquardt, 2010), it is still another signifier of adulthood. Ultimately, these two roles, spouse and parent, consume both the physical and mental lives of the majority of U.S. adults.

There is a good deal of research that analyzes media products that portend to give advice about relationships—both romantic and parental. For example, a substantial body of research exists that analyzes popular magazines targeted to women and teen girls. Researchers have long criticized these magazines for their emphasis on heteronormative romance and the centrality of males to the lives of females. The sheer plethora of advice on how to capture the eye or the heart of a male in magazines targeted to females attests to the obsession with making sure women know they need a male partner to be complete. Magazines targeted to both girls and grown women consistently portray their readers as essential to the functioning of romantic relationships and emphasize this point by casting males as naturally unskilled, yet mostly benevolent partners (e.g., Ferguson, 1983; Prusank, Duran, & DeLillo, 1993; Schlenker, Caron, & Halteman, 1998; Prusank, 2007a).

Analyses of popular parenting advice reiterate the centrality of women to the relational sphere. Researchers (e.g., Hulbert, 2003; Newson & Newson, 1974; Prusank, 2007b; Prusank & Duran, in press) in this area have traced popular advice and models of parenting promulgated within the culture since the 1700s. While there are clear differences among these models, which are traced to sociohistorical shifts, there are two consistencies among the different models of advice to parents. First, the term "parent" itself rarely applies to fathers. The preponderance of popular parenting materials across the centuries was geared toward mothers. Second, the models all imply that parents (read: mothers) are deficient in their knowledge. "Good mothers" know they don't know enough to be good mothers. Good mothers look to experts for advice. Changes in our culture over the last several decades have expanded the possibilities for enacting the adult roles of mother and father. For example, the increasing instances of working mothers have lead to what has been labeled the "Mommy Wars." The concept characterizes a battle in ideologies of "good mother"—the stay at home traditional mother versus the career mother. Researchers have documented the enactment of this battle in media outlets, such as popular magazines (e.g., Johnston & Swanson, 2003a, 2003b).

Media Dependency Theory (Ball-Rokeach & DeFluer, 1976) argues that changes in previously stable structures (e.g., the roles of husband/wife or roles of mother/father) can increase our dependence on media outlets as we look for clarity and understanding. Indeed, scholars over the past few decades have noted and commented upon our increasing reliance on the media for advice on how to conduct our everyday lives and its impact on us. In the realm of parenting, for example, Postman (1994) notes that

> many parents have lost confidence in their ability to raise children because they believe that the information and instincts they have about child-rearing are unreliable. As a consequence, they not only do not resist media influence, they turn to experts who are presumed to know what is best for children. (p. 150)

Media sold under the guise of educating or informing are not the only important conveyors of the culture's views on marriage and parenting. Our theories of media effects such as Media Dependence, Cultivation Theory, Media Accumulation, Priming, and so forth have demonstrated that media which intend to entertain have a powerful impact on both our perceptions and our behaviors, and in fact a good deal of research exists which has looked at the messages in media about the American family, if not specifically the roles of spouse and parent. This chapter rests on the premise that entertainment media play a significant role in providing adults with images of what it means to be a "good" spouse and a "good" parent and intends to take a closer look at what we may have gathered about these roles as we grow up in a media world.

Television programming serves as the main vehicle for analysis in this chapter. Television use continues to grow (Nielsen, 2013a) despite the diversity of media options available. Gerbner (1998) argued that television was the great storyteller and, as such, had a unique and profound impact on the way we see our world. Kompare (2009) argues that television is "perhaps the media form most suited to promoting and representing familial experience due to its domestic nature" (p. 102). Two specific types of television programming have been the focus of the majority of research on television images of family roles: the situation comedy and reality television. This chapter first explores the research on the images of spouses and parents in situation comedies. The situation comedy's consistent portrayal of stock images in predictable dilemmas with comforting resolutions surely pervades our ideas about how the world works. The second section of this chapter looks at the recent research on how reality television has invested in portraying the family and specifically the roles of spouse and parent. Thus, this chapter brings together two branches of research, which differ first because of the focal point of analysis (i.e., situation comedy versus reality television). Importantly, a majority of the research that has been conducted on the content of situation comedies has been derived from the quantitative tradition, while the majority of the research on the content of reality television is conducted within the critical tradition. Consequently, these two complementary lines of research are rarely discussed in tandem. The work in this chapter creates a space for these two lines of research to inform each other. The chapter concludes with some thoughts on the linkages across the findings in these two lines of the research including the steadfast portrayal of "the family" in situation comedies and reality television.

THE SITUATION COMEDY

Television situation comedies, in particular, have relied on the middle-class nuclear family as their landscape for over 50 years. In doing so, they have reinforced a heteronormative marital state. While there have been portrayals of single-parent families since the 1950s (at that time, single-father families), the marital status of the key parent often changes during the course of the series. In 1990, Cantor noted about single-parent family forms on television, "Given the high value placed on marriage and the nuclear family, it is not surprising that many single parents are shown to marry, remarry or look for lovers in these television shows" (p. 281). Even on a program like *Sex and the City*, which claimed a feminist perspective on the lives of women, the ability to enact alternative family forms is ultimately eschewed.

For example, while praised for its plot lines around alternative perspectives about motherhood, the first character who has a child is portrayed as working to balance work and child while not succumbing to sentimentalization and cultural pressures about babies (e.g., Tropp, 2006) and weddings, *this character* eventually marries the father of the child and buys a home. In fact, when including the storylines from the franchise films, three of the four female characters ultimately marry and two have children. And in its own parody of these cultural standards, *South Park* sequentially portrays the middle-class mother, Sharon, as "the stereotypical mother: she listens to her son, worries over him, and wants the best for him and his sister, Shelly" (Nagy, 2010, p. 6), but after she divorces the father of her children, the character becomes selfish and unconcerned about her children. Nagy notes that Sharon is "redeemed," and her character is restored to ideal motherhood status when she later remarries the father of her children (p. 8).

Interestingly, Skill, Robinson, and Wallace (1987) noted from their analysis that while diverse forms of family (defined in their study as single-parent homes, families who had experienced divorce, families who had adopted, etc.) were increasing in numbers on prime-time network television, programs with conventional families at the center had greater longevity, which they attributed to greater audience attraction (p. 367). It is also the case that television has shifted to reflect the upheaval in gender roles as a consequence of the women's movement and the subsequent entrance of more women into the workforce (see, for example, Layton's [2004] discussion of the emergence of the workaholic single female character in primetime television). Yet working wives on television are almost always women from middle-class families who are working not out of necessity, but by choice as they pursue a career.

Despite some slight variation in the structure of and role enactment in families as well as the public handwringing about the demise of the American family and the efforts of television to lead the way, the conventional two-parent middle-class family is still the mainstay of mainstream prime-time situation comedies. Television situation comedies not only demonstrate a propensity for a traditional structure, but they gravitate consistently to portrayals of middle-class families. In fact, Butsch (2011) notes from his studies over four decades that families on television are clearly demarcated by class with only 10% of the 400 situation comedies analyzed in his research featuring a working-class family.

What do husbands/fathers and wives/mothers look like in prime-time television? For the most part, mothers/wives and fathers/husbands are portrayed in the context of a middle-class family that encounters easily solvable problems. The lives of these families are rarely deterred by serious financial issues, clinical mental health problems, death, or divorce. Rather they are portrayed in ways that reinforce idealized versions of spousal and parent-child relationships. The term "ideal" is intended to reflect mainstream cultural practices that are promoted by "experts" and various media outlets. In the case of parental and spousal relationships, communication scholars will recognize the "ideology of intimacy," rife with open and honest expressions of emotion and an inherent equality void of explicit power struggles or explicit discussions of relational enactments of dominance and submission. In regard to parenting practices, the ideal of the balance of nurturance and control characterized by Baumrind's (1968) *Authoritative* parenting is enacted in a developmentally appropriate way through reasoned conversation and clear and consistent expectations.

Thus, for example, Douglas and Olson (1995) found that the portrayal of the relationship between middle-class spouses in more recent years was characterized by increased egalitarianism as well as higher levels of expressiveness, openness, and mutual trust. The open and expressive style of communication is not lost on the audience. When Reep and Dambrot (1994) asked subjects to rate both the use of instrumental and expressive communication of television fathers and mothers who spanned 30 years on television, subjects rated fathers on television shows in the 1980s as more expressive than they rated characters from earlier decades, and they rated mother characters from the 1980s as more instrumental than they had rated their maternal counterparts of the 1950s and 1960s.

Parents and children often enact an idealized relationship in situation comedies. Butsch (2011) notes in his analyses of domestic comedies over the decades that middle-class parents are portrayed as "wise" and working together "to raise their children in practically perfect families" (p. 102). Jordan (1995), in one of the few studies that has focused exclusively on portrayals of children in situation comedies, notes that the children are portrayed as spending more time talking with adults than with other children, and that their interaction with adults is more positive than it is with children. While the most frequent type of interactions children are likely to have with both adults and children is general banter, the second most frequent type of interaction is children being directed by adults. The relationships are "close" as the researchers note that parents are also likely to confide in their children, and that children provide parents with advice (Jordan, 1995). Such idealistic relationships within families were even found in Larson's (1993) close analysis of the adult cartoon program *The Simpsons*. When coding the utterances of family members in both *The Simpsons* and *The Cosby Show*, Larson notes that 78% of the statements between family members were affiliative, and that *The Simpsons's* family members produced more supportive utterances than were found in the Huxtable family of *The Cosby Show*.

Of course problems and conflicts are an integral part of the situation comedy plot line. Comstock and Strzyzewski (1990) found that instances of conflict occurred more frequently in situation comedies than in family prime-time dramas, but that these conflicts were short lived. In addition, the conflict strategies used by family characters tended to be gender stereotyped so that "wives kindly attended to their husbands' concerns even though husbands generally raise these concerns in a distributive manner. Husbands, on the other hand, often assert their 'authority' or simply avoid discussion of relational concerns initiated by wives" (Comstock & Strzyzewski, 1990, pp. 277–278).

Mazur and Kalbfleisch (2003) found family members in situation comedies lie frequently and are not good at lie detection. However, in their analysis of four popular programs (*The Simpsons, King of the Hill, Home Improvement,* and *Mad About You*), the researchers found that the most common type of lie told was a lie to spare feelings (p. 205). Thus, while deception as a communicative behavior is not advocated by the relational experts, attending to the feelings of others is an important activity in spousal and parent-child relationships. Family members in situation comedies may therefore constrain themselves in their interactions for the good of other family members.

Variations on a Theme

Interestingly, the character most frequently found to be telling a lie is the husband/father and within the family, the mother/wife is the most likely target of lying (Mazur & Kalbfleisch, 2003, p. 204). This crack in the façade of the "perfect family" portrayed in a middle-class context is in line with the work of both Butsch (2011) and Scharrer (2001), who note that by the 1990s, some portrayals of middle-class fathers diverge a bit from the ideal. Scharrer contends that as a consequence of the working wife's more equal status, the middle-class father does become the butt of some jokes. Similarly, Butsch notes the emergence (albeit not the dominant portrayal) of a middle-class father character that is successful at work but at home displays "an insistent adolescent macho maleness" that renders him less than the ideal father (p. 102). However, in their recent inductive analysis of fathers in situation comedies, Pehlke, Hennon, Radina, and Kuvalanka (2009) found that middle-class fathers made up two-thirds of the sample of fathers on prime time situation comedies, and that they were portrayed positively by negotiating with their wives and emotionally supporting their children (p. 130). The working-class fathers, in line with previous research, did not fare as well.

The trope of the dimwitted but goodhearted father had long been the purview of the working-class family in television situation comedies. So persistent has been this character and its connection to his class that Butsch (2011) coined the term "the working class buffoon." In their analysis of fathers in situation comedies, Pehlke et al. (2009) note that "all instances of foolish behavior with the exception of those presented in the program *According to Jim* are credited to working-class fathers" (p. 130). Cantor (1990) claims that while this trope is seen in domestic comedies since their advent, it is also found throughout various forms of women's fiction including movies and comic strips and expands the explanation by noting that it supports a "myth of female dominance and the breakdown of male authority" (p. 283). So there is a duality to this construction in that the buffoonish nature of the male character leaves a space for an oppositional character of strength and maturity, i.e., the good wife/mother. Scharrer (2001), using the analytic lens of humor and its relationship to power, argues that this version of gender relationships is possible specifically in the working-class context because of the conception that working-class males lack capital and thus lack in power.

Indeed research indicates that as audiences view situation comedies, they are aware of how families of different social classes are portrayed. For example, Douglas and Olson (1995) asked subjects to rate various features of family interactions in situation comedies from the 1950s through the early 1990s. Working-class families in this study were perceived by subjects/audience to have the highest levels of distress, characterized by conflict, a closed system, and unsatisfying relationships. Thus consumers of domestic comedies can see that when approaching the enactment of spousal and parenting roles, the best place to situate oneself is minimally within the context of the middle class. In never demonstrating just how these ideal spousal and parenting skill sets are acquired, one is led to believe these are natural consequences of middle-class status.

As noted, the research on prime-time television portrayals has demonstrated some variation in terms of structure and work roles. Importantly, programs have been developed that expand the ethnic/racial diversity of the central characters (e.g., *Good Times, Sanford and Son, The Cosby Show, The Jeffersons*). However, research continues to find that the systematic difference in how spousal and parental roles are portrayed is the socioeconomic class of the central family. This is not to say that television programming does not rely on racial and ethnic stereotypes in the development of husbands/fathers and wives/mothers (e.g., Merskin, 2007), but rather to highlight the fact that class-based stereotypes are a staple of prime-time television that often trump issues of race and ethnicity. The parenting and spousal relationships in the working-class families of *Good Times* and *Sanford and Son* fit neatly into the domestic comedy bumbling husband/father with wise wife who joins with other characters to make him the object of humor. This enactment is also true on *The Jeffersons*, wherein the financially successful father/husband is still treated as a working-class buffoon. His working-class origins, which are an essential feature of his character and often play a role in the plot, stand in contrast to the middle-class origins of the parents on *The Cosby Show*. Here Cantor (1990) notes that Cliff Huxtable "is the traditional middle-class TV father, sympathetic, caring and strong" (p. 282), and Larson's (1993) data reinforce the show's focus on his positive parenting skills. In their recent work, Pehlke et al. (2009) found that non-white fathers portrayed in situation comedies were exclusively middle-class fathers and, as such, were portrayed positively, including being emotionally supportive of both their children and their wives.

As family structures have evolved over the past several decades, the depictions of mothers, fathers, and children in prime-time comedies have evolved on the periphery by incorporating cultural demands to diversify some features of family such as ethnic makeup and role expansion for women, but the texture of these programs in terms of their portrayal of spouses and parents remains remarkably consistent. The middle-class heterosexual family remains the dominant "positive" image in the situation comedy. Antithetical to this ideal are working-class families, characterized by higher levels of conflict and distress. When audiences are engaged with this programming, they are likely to feel as Douglas and Olson (1995) conclude about television families: they "reinforce the desirability of middle class life not simply as a function of domestic artifacts, such as the level of consumption, but as a consequence of the relationships inside the family" (para. 51).

Kompare (2009) notes that domestic comedies present what appears to be "normalilty" because of their nature as a staple of television entertainment. The form of this genre is easily and clearly articulated; the family structure is predictable, the constructed weekly problems are easily manageable, and the loving outcomes are stock. In situation comedies, differences in family structure, gendered labor, or ethnicity of the family ultimately make no real difference at all in the lives of the domestic comedy family.

REALITY TELEVISION

While it is true that situation comedies have a long history of presenting images of the American family, Matheson (2007) notes, "Today, reality television has arguably taken center stage as the genre providing images of American family life" (p. 33). Reality television is of particular interest here because it is a vehicle for presenting the "ordinary" (e.g., marriage and parenting) as extraordinary. Reality television appears in a variety of forms, many of which take "everyday people" and place them in situations that are so far from the norm that any cognitive comparison work we might do while viewing is pure conjecture. Other programs, however, create situations so close to our own existence that comparisons of our lives to those we are viewing seems natural. Sears and Godderis (2011) refer to these as "Lifestyle Surveillance" programs, where the focus is on "documenting ordinary, day-to-day experiences and conventional life transitions" (p. 182).

A subgenre of lifestyle surveillance programs most similar to the situation comedy relies on presenting celebrity families (presumed to be extraordinary) within their daily (read: ordinary) lives. The modern reality television family came about in an effort to create a "different family" for the purposes of entertainment, not as a social statement. Kompare (2009) argues the first modern reality television family, *The Osbournes*, was the embodiment of the extraordinary and the ordinary, which is the essential frame of reality television. The family is extraordinary because of their wealth and privilege and the fame of the father (rock star Ozzy Osbourne), but also because of the crude ways they enact the ordinary. But the ordinary does exist as basic family functioning and is highlighted when family members cook meals, play games, plan trips, go shopping, etc. Ultimately, when looking at the family members as they appear in the program, Kompare recognizes in the father a similarity to iconic "befuddled" fathers like Cliff Huxtable from *The Cosby Show* or Tim Taylor from *Home Improvement*. Sharon Osbourne is similarly portrayed as the iconic situation comedy mother—the "defacto ringleader … taking charge of most situations" (Kompare, 2009, p. 113). Thus, through the analysis of this first modern reality television family, Kompare concludes, "*The Osbournes* stretches the familiar sitcom representational codes to their limits, while still remaining within recognizable normative constructions of dad, mom, son, and daughter" (p. 112).

Many reality programs focusing on the ordinary lives of assumed extraordinary families have aired since *The Osbournes,* and several have followed the lead of focusing on a famous musician. Smith's (2008) analysis of *Run's House* and *Snoop Dogg's Father Hood* provides further evidence of the strength of the situation comedy archetypes of spouse and parenting roles. These two reality programs focus on the home lives of two black rap artists of high acclaim. In her analysis, Smith ultimately equates Run's parenting and spousal style with that of the character Cliff Huxtable of *The Cosby Show* in that both men are seen as successful enough at work that they can spend significant amounts of time outside of work engaging with family. In terms of discipline, both fathers are characterized as being positive and disciplining with discussion wherein parents and children take time to express their thoughts and feelings (Smith, 2008, p. 402). This style is reminiscent of what we see in middle-class families on situation comedies. Interestingly, Smith notes that Run's wife not only disciplines the children, but her husband as well (p. 403). Life in Snoop Dogg's house is different, and I would contend that his reality self reflects more of the working-class buffoon model, as Smith's analysis shows him to be devoid of authority over his children as well as his dogs. Snoop's wife is the lynchpin of the family, and Smith notes that Snoop reinforces this as he refers to her as "Boss Lady."

Thus these celebrity reality families bear a close resemblance to the stock characters of domestic situation comedies. In his analysis of *The Osbournes*, Kompare (2009) notes that the features of the normative fictional television family are so entrenched that they in fact provide constraints on the production of reality television families. These constraints help them to appear as "family" and not as some other form of social grouping. The producers of such reality programs rely heavily on structural and behavioral elements that make easily recognizable parents and spouses out of people who are living, by all standards, extraordinary lives.

A second subgenre of these lifestyle surveillance programs instead relies on "ordinary people" who one presumes "most audience" members see as similar enough to oneself. Unlike the celebrity families just described, these programs are not intended to mimic situation comedies but portend to follow "ordinary" people as they plan for stock life events like marriage and birth. Programs such as *A Wedding Story* and *A Baby Story* promote the normality of being a spouse or parent by emphasizing how the focal couples have planned for marriage and childbirth and wait with great anticipation to take on the new roles of wife/mother and husband/father. Within the programs, coherent narratives display how "ordinary" people navigate these seemingly essential life transitions replete with brief and solvable crises. Maher (2004) notes of programs like *A Wedding Story* or *A Baby Story* that while viewing, women are able either to project themselves into the circumstances or use the programs as a vehicle to relive important moments they have already experienced, and in so doing these shows create a space for viewers to "soothe the pain of the dissimilarity between experience and fantasy by watching another episode that evokes the same romance fantasy and which of course serves to sustain the fantasy" (p. 199).

Researchers argue that the content of these programs reinforces existing media portrayals of the dominance of white middle-class heterosexual families as the ideal situation for marriage and the birth of children (Morris & McInerney, 2010; Sears & Godderis, 2011). It is important to note that while these programs include men to reinforce the heteronormativity of marriage and parenthood, in contrast to the celebrity family stories, males are peripheral to these main events. Most screen time is focused on the soon-to-be wife/mother and most events in the narrative rely on her activity planning and preparing for the life transition. As Engstrom (2003) notes in her analysis of 100 episodes of the program *A Wedding Story*, for the groom, the expectation "is that he simply show up" (p. 13). Engstrom's analysis details the dominant conventions of the "middle-class white wedding" portrayed on reality television, replete with white wedding gown, tiered wedding cake, large bridal party, wedding reception venue, and the employment of a disc jockey or band along with the focus on the detailed activities designed to enhance the physical appearance of the bride as a continual act of hegemony.

The third and final subgenre of lifestyle surveillance reality programming reviewed here takes a darker look at family life than either the celebrity reality programs or the preparation for the life transition reality programs. Researchers (Brancato, 2007; Matheson, 2007) who have analyzed the programs *Wife Swap* and *Trading Spouses* demonstrate that the foundation of these programs is articulating differences between families. Differences that serve as the site for conflict often stem from differences between the families' socioeconomic status, race, religion, or geographic region. Families in these programs are shown to have different beliefs about how spouses and children should behave, how clean or decorated homes should be, how money should be spent, and how much families should invest their time and energy in work, sports, school, and so forth. More often than not, these shows grapple with the cultural struggle over the centrality of motherhood to women and the centrality of the breadwinner role for men.

Add to these programs those that focus on parenting such as *Supernanny* and *Nanny 911*. In these programs self-defined "out of control" families seek help in understanding how to better manage family life. While the premise of these shows is parenting, marital relationships are also shown as strained and in need of attention. Parenting practices promulgated by the expert nannies on these shows are in line with the middle-class authoritative style discussed earlier, where parenting is adapted to stage development, and reasoning with children is a key element. Here, parents balance nurturance and control (e.g., when releasing a child from "time-out in the naughty corner," mother is advised to hug the child and tell him/her, "I love you"). As Brancato (2007) notes, the final message of these shows is that "regardless of your circumstances or background, through the concerted application of the scientific method, love and happiness can be maintained in your home" (p. 54).

The common theme within this subgenre of lifestyle surveillance programs is the overwhelmed family. In the nanny programs, families self-proclaim their chaos by asking to be on the show. In the *Wife Swap* and *Trading Spouses* programs, family problems are revealed by the narrator voice-overs introducing these families of various socioeconomic backgrounds, as well as in the responses of family members as they are exposed to the beliefs, values, and behaviors of the oppositional family. Thus a significant difference in these programs as opposed to fictional situation comedies is that distress and disorder appear to be a part of both middle-class and working-class families, and so settling into a middle-class family does not ensure that spouses and parents will enact "appropriate" skills for a harmoniously functioning family. And in contrast to portrayals of disorder in the celebrity reality family programs, chaos is not a location for humor nor do problems easily dissipate. What the audience does learn through these families-in-crisis programs is that families are fixable.

Critics argue that "fixing" families in reality television first and foremost means "fixing" the wife/mother. Indeed Brancato (2007) notes that the premise of these types of shows, where women are either traded or trained, ultimately focus on wives/mothers who are deficient in the emotional work of women in the home. And while researchers may see some dimensions of the resolutions on these programs differently, they agree that the resolutions presented never approach issues related to structural elements of social class, race, or region. Resolution of family problems in these programs rests assuredly with the mother/wife and changes in her own outlook and behavior, and in so doing they do promote what Hochschild (2003) calls the hypersymbolization of the mother. On the nanny programs she learns to be systematic in approaching her children and communicating more with her husband. On the programs where she is traded to a new home she will invariably take better care of her own home, spend more time with her children and less time on herself, and appreciate her husband more. The resolution to family problems occurs when

342 | DIANE T. PRUSANK

the ordinary female is recreated in the mold of some ideal wife and mother through a constructed experience in which the wife/mother is able to hold up a mirror to herself so she can see her personal failures (Jensen, 2010).

Fact and Fiction

This chapter makes a unique contribution to the literature because it brings together two strains of research that are separated not only by television genre focus, but also by methodology. By and large, the research on the portrayal of families in situation comedies is conducted through quantitative content analysis, while the research on reality television is dominated by a critical/cultural perspective. Reviewing different strains of research on both situation comedies and various types of lifestyle surveillance programs reveals patterns of similarity that cut across program genre and are found regardless of methodology. Specifically, the categories related to social class and gender are essential in defining the nature of how families function.

While some reality programming has indeed diversified the television screen by including families of different backgrounds and belief systems, the well-grounded critique of such reality shows is that the resolution of critical issues of inequality of gender, race, socioeconomic class, and so forth are inevitably presented as mere interpersonal conflicts (Park, 2011). Jensen (2010) notes of the *Supernanny* programs, the question is always "what kind of parent are you" and consequently the question is never "under what conditions are you parenting?" (p. 179). Importantly, Ouellette and Murray (2009) argue that is it not an accident that the proliferation of reality programming which promulgates the idea that fixing families is a private enterprise "emerged at a historical juncture marked by the dismantling of public welfare programs and an emphasis on private and personal initiative as an alternative to the state's role in managing social needs and risks" (p. 9). Domestic comedies also fail to adequately address structural problems that sustain social class distinctions. They too focus on the family as the site for resolving conflict and portray family issues as quickly and easily resolvable within the domestic sphere (Comstock & Strzyzewski, 1990). Working-class families in situation comedies are portrayed as more distressed, and working-class fathers are portrayed as less skillful at managing life.

In these situation comedies, the strong female role is often found in working-class families and stands in contrast to the inept father. Thus problems are often located within the husband/father and fixed by the wife/mother and so issues related to the circumstances within which they parent are also treated as irrelevant. In the reality programs that focus on the family lives of "ordinary" people, regardless of social class, the wife/mother serves as both source of problem and site of solution. A woman's mistakes reverberate throughout the whole family and must be fixed within the family by "fixing" her. In many ways over the past decade, these programs have enacted our latest social battles: the culture wars, the mommy wars, and the social class wars. In their enactment of these battles, these families-in-crisis reality programs are both different (in the lack of reverence for mothers/wives) and the same (in the centrality of women to family and peripheral and inconsequential nature of men in the domestic sphere) as other television versions of families.

Situation comedies and reality television do differ in their portrayal of men in families. While both genres of programming rely greatly on some version of the working-class buffoon, men in middle-class families are portrayed in a positive light in situation comedies as well as in the celebrity reality television families reviewed here. However, the reality programs that portend to follow "ordinary" people in their ordinary lives convey images of males who are essential, but somehow unable to participate fully in spousal and parent-child relationships. Men's importance is negated through the very premise of shows that are based on the idea that women are the planners and strategizers around life events such as marriage and childbirth. Men's importance is also negated in reality programs that proclaim women as the lynchpin of the family. The symbolic nature of simply "trading" or "swapping" a mother affects the homeostasis of the family system. That the *individual mother* matters is exemplified by the fact that a different set of behaviors is the ultimate consequence of replacing the person who fulfills this role. A good deal of the "action" in these programs takes place while the men are at work (even more so in the nanny programs). In all of these programs, it is essential that women change, and the performance of men is ancillary. The portrayal of men in these programs reminds one of Vavrus's (2007) discussion of the term "NASCAR Dads." The enactment of that term in media use is unrelated to men actually spending time in a parenting role, but rather only signifies their location within a private context. So too appear many of the husbands/fathers in reality programs which focus on "ordinary families." Here husbands/fathers are located within the context of family, but not acting in any way of consequence to it. Thus while in the situation comedy, husbands/fathers may be a great help or a great obstacle, in many lifestyle surveillance reality programs, he is simply a required placeholder.

As noted earlier, there are some differences between reality television and situation comedy portrayals of males. However, the consistency in the portrayal of issues related to social class and females across both the genres of programming analyzed and the methodologies used in this research was impossible to ignore. Portrayals of the working-class buffoon in both situation comedies and reality television give weight to the notion that being in a lower socioeconomic group is not conducive to a peaceful family life, and further these portrayals imply that the family's status is a consequence of male incompetence. Across genres, middle-class fathers and husbands on the other hand are not problematic (so much so that they may be practically invisible as is the case in some reality programming). Finally, regardless of the socioeconomic status of the family and genre of programming, mothers/wives are portrayed as the lynchpin of the family. The wife/mother may be incompetent in some reality programming, but she is "fixable" and work on her improves family life. Thus stock characters based on social class and gender cut across programming genres and are highlighted in research results regardless of methodology. The strength of these speaks to their core in our culture's conception of family, social class, and gender. The inability of new forms of television programming to present the enactment of family roles in different configurations is stultifying.

Future Directions in Research on Spouse and Parenting Roles

Past research has focused on programming generated through network television. Our quickly expanding media landscape makes current research more challenging because media outlets have proliferated and the activities we perform as we consume and produce media are far more varied. The suggestions for future research here address both of these issues.

First, current research must acknowledge that the outlets for creation and distribution of television programming include, but are not limited to, streaming services and premium cable and basic cable channels. Expansion of research to programs produced by or for these outlets—which may have lower ratings, but a still substantial audience—can assess whether such programming increases the breadth and depth of stock characters like mothers and fathers and husbands and wives. While the research reviewed here indicates that reality television did not seem to change the portrayal of spouses and parents, it may be that independent producers of programs searching for niche audiences through distribution on cable and streaming services are more likely to expand the boundaries of television characters.

Second, researchers must acknowledge that social media outlets are changing the way we watch television. Nielsen (2013b) reported that "19 million unique people in the U.S. composed 263 million Tweets about live TV" in the second quarter of 2013" (para. 3). Twitter, then, is an excellent location for analysis of the interpretation of the portrayal of roles of spouse and parent. Of particular import are the tweets directed at both actors and writers of programs who are available for live tweeting during programs. These tweets often contain opinions about the characters and their behaviors and consequently are a rich source of unobtrusive data about audience interpretation of media portrayals of spouse and parenting roles.

Further, Nielsen (2013b) estimates that the Twitter TV audience for any given episode is 50 times larger than the unique generators of the tweets. Given that this is the case, our consumption of television portrayals is now mediated in a way that is trackable and analyzable. Researchers should be able to test the impact of the tweets on the audience's view of the characters who are being portrayed by utilizing experimental designs that assess the impact of the "second screen" on the audience's views of media portrayals of spouse and parenting roles.

REFERENCES

Ball-Rokeach, S. J., & DeFleur, M. L. (1976). A dependency model of mass media effects. *Communication Research, 3*(1), 3–21. doi:10.1177/009365027600300101

Baumrind, D. K. (1968). Authoritarian vs. authoritative control. *Adolesence, 3,* 255–272.

Brancato, J. (2007). Domesticating politics: The representation of wives and mothers in American reality television. *Film & History, 37,* 49–56. doi:10.1353/flm.2007.0044

Butsch, R. (2011). Ralph, Fred, Archie, Homer and the King of Queens: Why television keeps recreating the male working-class buffoon. In G. Dines and J. M. Humez (Eds.), *Gender, race and class in media* (3rd ed., pp. 101–109). Thousand Oaks, CA: Sage.

Cantor, M. (1990). Prime-time fathers: A study in continuity and change. *Critical Studies in Mass Communication, 7*(3), 275–285. doi:10.1080/15295039009360179

Centers for Disease Control and Prevention. (2010, February). Marriage and cohabitation in the United States: A statistical portrait based on cycle 6 (2002) of the National Survey of Family Growth. *Vital Health and Statistics, 23*(28).

Comstock, J., & Strzyzewski, K. (1990). Interpersonal interaction on television: Family conflict and jealousy on primetime. *Journal of Broadcasting & Electronic Media, 34*(3), 263–282. doi:10.1080/08838159009386742

Douglas, W., & Olson, B. (1995). Beyond family structure: The family in domestic comedy. *Journal of Broadcasting and Electronic Media, 39*(2), 236. doi:10.1080/08838159509364301

Engstrom, E. (2003). Hegemony in reality based TV programming: The world according to *A Wedding Story. Media Report to Women, 31*(1), 10–14.

Ferguson, M. (1983). *Forever feminine: Women's magazines and the cult of femininity.* London, England: Heinemann.

Gerbner, G. (1998). Cultivation analysis: An overview. *Mass Communication and Society, 1*(3&4), 175–194. doi:10.1086/268608.

Hochschild, A. (2003). *The commercialization of intimate life: Notes from home and work.* Los Angeles: University of California Press.

Holmes, B. M., & Johnson, K. R. (2009). Where fantasy meets reality: Media exposure, relationship beliefs and standards, and the moderating effect of a current relationship. In E. P. Lamont (Ed.), *Social psychology: New research* (pp. 117–133). Hauppauge, NY: Nova Science.

Hulbert, A. (2003). *Raising America: Experts, parents and a century of advice about children.* New York, NY: Knopf.

Jensen, T. (2010). What kind of mum are you at the moment? Supernanny and the psychologizing of classed embodiment. *Subjectivity, 3*(2), 170–192.

Johnston, D. D., & Swanson, D. H. (2003a). Undermining mothers: A content analysis of the representation of mothers in magazines. *Mass Communication and Society, 6*(3), 21–33.

Johnston, D. D., & Swanson, D. H. (2003b). Invisible mothers: A content analysis of motherhood ideologies and myths in magazines. *Sex Roles, 49*(1/2), 21–33.

Jordan, A. (1995). The portrayal of children on prime time situation comedies. *Journal of Popular Culture, 29*(3), 139–147. doi:10.1111/j.0022-3840.1995.00139.x

Kompare, D. (2009). Extraordinarily ordinary: *The Osbournes* as "An American Family." In S. Murray & L. Ouellette (Eds.), *Reality TV: Remaking television culture* (pp. 100–119). New York, NY: NYU Press.

Larson, M. S. (1993). Family communication on prime-time television. *Journal of Broadcasting & Electronic Media, 37*(3), 349–358. doi:10.1080/08838159309364227

Layton, L. (2004). Working nine to nine: The new women of prime time. *Studies in Gender and Sexuality, 5*(3), 351–369. doi:10.1080/15240650509349255

Maher, J. (2004). What do women watch? Tuning into the compulsory heterosexual channel. In S. Murray & L. Ouellette (Eds.), *Reality TV: Remaking television culture* (pp. 197–213). New York, NY: NYU Press.

Matheson, S. A. (2007). The cultural politics of *Wife Swap*: Taste, lifestyle media and the American family. *Film and History, 37*(2), 33–48. doi:10.1353/flm.2007.0057

Mazur, M. A., & Kalbfleisch, P. J. (2003). Lying and deception detection in television families. *Communication Research Reports, 20*(3), 200–207. doi:10.1080/08824090309388818

Merskin, D. (2007). Three faces of Eva: Perpetuation of the hot-Latina stereotype in *Desperate Housewives. The Howard Journal of Communications, 18*, 133–151. doi:10.1080.10646170701309890

Morris, T., & McInerney, K. (2010, June). Media representations of pregnancy and childbirth: An analysis of reality television programs in the United States. *Birth: Issues in Prenatal Care, 37*(2), 134–140. doi:10.1111/j.1523-536X.2010.00393.x

Nagy, V. (2010). Motherhood, stereotypes, and *South Park. Women's Studies, 39*, 1–17, doi:10.1080/00497870903368948

Newson, J., & Newson, E. (1974). Cultural aspects of child rearing in the English-speaking world. In M. P. M. Richards (Ed.), *The integration of a child into a social world* (pp. 52–82). London, England: Cambridge University Press.

Nielsen. (2013a, May). Nielsen's 2014 advance national TV household universe estimate. Retrieved June 14, 2013, from http://www.nielsen.com/us/en/newswire/2013/nielsen-estimates-115-6-million-tv-homes-in-the-u-s---up-1-2-.html

Nielsen. (2013b, October). Nielsen launches "Nielsen Twitter TV Ratings." Retrieved from http://www.nielsen.com/us/en/press-room/2013/nielsen-launches-nielsen-twitter-tv-ratings.html

Ouellette, L., & Murray, S. (2009). Introduction. In S. Murray & L. Ouellette (Eds.), *Reality TV: Remaking television culture* (pp. 1–20). New York, NY: NYU Press.

Park, J. H. (2011). Confronting racial prejudice: The ideological implications of racial conflict on ABC's *Wife Swap. Journal of Media and Cultural Studies, 25*(3), 317–331. doi:10.1080/1030431 2.2010.506948

Pehlke, T. A., II, Hennon, C. B., Radina, M. E., & Kuvalanka, K. A. (2009). Does father still know best? An inductive thematic analysis of popular TV sitcoms. *Fathering, 7*(2), 114–139. http://dx.doi.org/10.3149/fth.0702.114

Postman, N. (1994). *The disappearance of childhood.* New York, NY: Random House.

Prusank, D. T. (2007a). Masculinities in teen magazines: The good, the bad and the ugly. *The Journal of Men's Studies, 15*(2), 160–177. doi:10.3149/jms.1502.160

Prusank, D. T. (2007b). The introduction of communication into popular parenting advice: An analysis of Hiam Ginott's *Between Parent and Child. The Review of Communication, 7*(4), 338–351. doi:10.1080/15358590701596864

Prusank, D. T., & Duran, R. L. (in press). Walking the tightrope: Parenting advice in *Essence* magazine. *Howard Journal of Communications.*

Prusank, D. T., Duran, R. L., & DeLillo, D. A. (1993). Interpersonal relationships in women's magazines: Dating and relating in the 1970s and 1980s. *Journal of Social and Personal Relationships, 10*, 307–320.

Reep, D. C., & Dambrot, F. H. (1994). T.V. parents: Fathers (and now mothers) know best. *Journal of Popular Culture, 28*(2), 13. doi:10.1111/j.0022-3840.1994.2802_13.x

Scharrer, E. (2001). From wise to foolish: The portrayal of the sitcom father, 1950s–1990s. *Journal of Broadcasting and Electronic Media, 45*(1), 23–40. doi:10.1207/s15506878jobem4501_3

Schlenker, J., Caron, S., & Halteman, W. (1998). A feminist analysis of *Seventeen* magazine: Content analysis from 1945 to 1995. *Sex Roles, 38*, 135–149.

Sears, C. A., & Godderis, R. (2011). Roar like a tiger on TV? Constructions of women and childbirth in reality TV. *Feminist Media Studies, 11*(2), 181–195. doi:10.1080/14680777.2010.521626

Segrin, C., & Nabi, R. L. (2002). Does television viewing cultivate unrealistic expectations about marriage? *Journal of Communication, 52*(2), 247–263. doi: 10.1093/joc/52.2.247

Skill, T., Robinson, J. D., & Wallace, S. P. (1987). Portrayal of families on prime-time TV: Structure, type and frequency. *Journalism & Mass Communication Quarterly, 64*(2–3), 360–367, 398. doi:10.1177/107769908706400211

Smith, D. C. (2008). Critiquing reality-based televisual Black fatherhood: A critical analysis of *Run's House* and *Snoop Dogg's Father Hood*. *Critical Studies in Media Communication, 25*(4), 393–412. doi:10.1080/15295030802328020

Stearns, P. M. (2003). *Anxious parents: A history of modern childrearing in America*. New York, NY: NYU Press.

Tropp, L. (2006). "Faking a sonogram": Representations of motherhood on *Sex and the City*. *The Journal of Popular Culture, 39*(5), 861–877.

Vavrus, M. D. (2007). The politics of NASCAR dads: Branded media paternity. *Critical Studies in Media Communication, 24*(3), 245–261. doi:10.1080/07393180701520942

Wilcox, W. B., & Marquardt, E. (2010). When marriage disappears: The new middle America. The State of Our Unions 2010. University of Virginia: The National Marriage Project. http://nationalmarriageproject.org/reports/

PART SEVEN

Older Adulthood Communication

CHAPTER EIGHTEEN

Media Use and Effects in Older Adulthood

JAMES D. ROBINSON AND KATHLEEN B. WATTERS

ADULTS AND TELEVISION

The A. C. Nielsen Company reports that nearly 97% of all homes in the United States have incorporated at least one television set into the décor (as cited in the U.S. Census, 2010). Nearly 85% of these homes had two or more sets, 55% had three or more sets, and 33% had four or more TV sets. Of these 114.7 million, 91% receive TV programming over a cable, 31% subscribe to a premium channel, and 33% have a digital video recorder. And television viewing remains the number one leisure activity in the U.S. with the average adult spending about 34 hours per week watching TV (as cited in the U.S. Census, 2010).

Surprisingly, Nielsen estimates that the number of homes with a TV set has actually dropped 2.2% over the past 20 years (as cited in "Ownership of TV Sets," 2011). This decrease has been attributed to the advent of the Internet, a declining economy, and media convergence (as cited in "Ownership of TV Sets," 2011). Increasingly adults are using the Internet and alternative delivery media systems such as HULU or Apple TV to access movies and TV programming. In fact, Pew (2009) suggests 35% of all U.S. homes have used the Internet or alternative delivery services such as HULU to watch movies or TV programming. This change has encouraged Nielsen to include Internet viewers in their definition of "TV household" (as cited in "Ownership of TV Sets," 2011).

Television viewing remains the number one leisure activity in the U.S. with the average adult spending about 56% of his or her total leisure time watching TV (Bureau of Labor Statistics, 2011). While the U.S. remains a worldwide leader in television viewing, other countries are catching up. Ofcom (as cited in Statista, 2013a) estimates that in contrast to the 293 minutes of TV Americans watch daily, citizens of other countries watch at the following rates: Italy (253), Poland (242), United Kingdom (242), Canada (240), Spain (239), France (227), Germany (225), Brazil (225), and Russia (220) minutes daily.

Older Adults and Television

Nielsen (2009) estimates adults 65+ watched 47 hours of TV per week in 2009—more than any other age cohort (see Table 1). While they watch the most, only 23% of older adults identified TV viewing as their single favorite leisure activity (Gallop-Goodman, 2001), and TV viewing is rated as less enjoyable than other leisure activities (Spring, 1993).

Table 1. Weekly TV Viewing by Age Cohort.

Age	Hours & Minutes per Week
Adults 65+ Years of Age	47:21
Adults 50–64 Years of Age	42:38
Adults 35–49 Years of Age	35:40
Adults 25–34 Years of Age	31:58
Adults 18–24 Years of Age	26:14
Adults 12–17 Years of Age	23:24
Adults 2–11 Years of Age	25:17

Source: Nielsen, 2009.

Robinson, Skill, and Turner (2004) and many, many scholars before them (e.g., Bower, 1985) suggested that the high levels of TV consumption are attributable, in part, to time and opportunity, and that appears to be the case (Mares & Woodward, 2006). More nuanced explanations incorporate financial constraints, reduced mobility, and health issues as contributing factors to such high levels of TV viewing. However, generally speaking older adults are financially better off than their younger counterparts, in relatively good health, socially active, and mobile. Complicating matters is the fact that many older adults have a spouse—who may or may not be in good health or mobile. To date, this caretaking variable has gone relatively unexplored.

Television Content Preferences and Older Adults

Like their younger counterparts, older adults identify entertainment and information as their primary motivations for watching television (Mundorf & Brownell, 1990). Older adults are less likely to watch animated programs (e.g., *The Simpsons* or *Futurama*), situation comedies, and reality programming than younger adults and are more likely to watch game shows, educational programming, history and biography programs, movies, and "How To" programs than younger adults (Simmons Market Research Bureau, 2013). They are also more likely to watch PBS programming than younger adults (see Tables 2 & 3).

Table 2. Network Viewership by Age.

Percentage of Adults Watching Some Programming on Each Network (Past 30 Days)									
Viewer Years of Age									
Network	% Adult Viewers	18–24	25–34	35–44	45–54	55–64	65+	70+	75+
PBS	23.1%	14%	12.9%	14.9%	23.7%	26.3%	41.6%	39.3%	39.9%
ABC	57.7%	50.0%	56.1%	59.6%	60.2%	56.0%	60.5%	61.0%	59.1%
CBS	65.2%	52.9%	60.7%	65.5%	66.5%	69.4%	70.7%	68.6%	66.5%
NBC	47.7%	41.3%	50.2%	50.8%	47.1%	47.2%	47.4%	46.3%	45.3%

Table 3. Programming Type by Age.

Percentage of Adults Watching Some Programming by Type (Past 30 Days)									
Genre	Viewers	18–24	25–34	35–44	45–54	55–64	65+	70+	75+
Comedy/Variety	13.3%	10.2	14.0	14.9	12.5	12.3	14.5	14.0	13.0
Game Show	8.7%	3.4	6.4	7.0	10.1	8.5	14.4	15.6	16.9
Drama	59.2%	52.5	60.9	57.9	61.0	64.3	56.3	50.5	48.3
News/ Documentary	28.4%	15.3	18.4	21.3	28.8	33.5	46.6	45.8	45.5
Reality	46.7%	35.6	51.3	49.0	49.7	45.3	44.9	44.1	42.4
Situation Comedy	35.8%	36.8	41.6	38.8	35.9	34.3	28.7	27.1	26.0
Evening Animation	14.8%	31.7	22.2	17.6	12.2	7.1	6.0	3.0	2.8
History & Biography	6.8%	7.6	3.3	4.7	5.4	7.3	12.7	8.2	7.2
How To/ Instruction	9.3%	1.1	3.9	5.2	11.0	12.4	18.3	18.5	18.8
Movies	7.7%	6.3	5.7	5.5	7.9	7.4	12.6	11.5	12.8

Examination of specific programs suggests *60 Minutes* is appointment viewing for many older adults. Nearly 41% of older adults report watching *60 Minutes* and reported giving the program their full attention. Other popular programs for adults 65+ include *The Good Wife*, *20/20*, *The Mentalist*, and *NCIS* (see Table 4). Older adults watch religious programming when dissatisfied with secular or non-religious programming (Abelman, 1987), but they do not substitute it for actual church attendance as they become less able to get to church (Hays et al., 1998).

Table 4. Some Highly Rated 2010 Prime Time TV Programs (Full Attention).

Program	18–24	25–34	35–44	45–54	55–64	65+	70+	75+
American Idol	7.8%	17.1%	18.7%	20.3%	15.3%	20.8%	10.4%	6.3%
Dancing with the Stars	2.9%	8.8%	9.2%	17.7%	22.4%	14.5%	24.7%	17.7%
NCIS	9.5%	10.0%	15.6%	19.3%	24.1%	21.4%	13.6%	8.0%
The Mentalist	2.1%	5.9%	12.6%	25.8%	29.0%	24.6%	14.9%	8.8%
Criminal Minds	8.4%	11.9%	20.4%	24.5%	18.9%	15.9%	10.0%	6.0%
CSI	11.0%	12.9%	19.8%	20.7%	17.6%	18.0%	18.5%	4.5%
60 Minutes	3.3%	3.9%	9.0%	17.7%	25.3%	40.9%	30%	19.7%
20/20	2.0%	13.1%	11.3%	24%	23%	26.6%	19%	12.5%
Big Bang Theory	7.4%	15.6%	26.0%	23.7%	18.7%	8.7%	4.5%	3.6%
The Good Wife	0.7%	7.5%	10.3%	21.9%	25.8%	33.8%	22.7%	14.9%

The biggest difference in older and younger adults is the likelihood of watching TV news. Goodman (1990) found older males and females identified news and public affairs programming as favorite TV fare, and they pay more attention while watching the news (Simmons Market Research Bureau, 2013). Pew (2012d) reports that 73% of older adults watched TV news the day before they were surveyed, 63% identify themselves as regular viewers of local TV news, and 51% report watching cable news regularly. In contrast, only 55% of adults 18 and older reported watching the news the previous day, 48% report watching local news regularly, and only 34% watch cable news on a regular basis (See Table 5).

Table 5. Adults Watching TV News.

Watched TV News Yesterday	2012	2006
65 Years of Age & Older	73%	69%
50–64 Years of Age	65%	63%
30–49 Years of Age	52%	53%
18–29 Years of Age	34%	49%
Total Adults (18+ Years of Age)	55%	57%

Watch Local TV News Regularly	2012	2006
65 Years of Age & Older	63%	65%
50–64 Years of Age	57%	60%
30–49 Years of Age	46%	51%
18–29 Years of Age	28%	42%
Total Adults (18+ Years of Age)	48%	54%
Watch Cable News Channel Regularly	2012	2006
65 Years of Age & Older	51%	38%
50–64 Years of Age	34%	39%
30–49 Years of Age	33%	31%
18–29 Years of Age	23%	29%
Total Adults (18+ Years of Age)	34%	34%

Adults, Older Adults, and Radio Use

The average U.S. home has eight radios (Bureau of Labor Statistics, 2011). Just over 99% of those homes have at least one radio, and 85% of all adults listen at least once a week (Bureau of Labor Statistics, 2011). In addition, Arbitron (as cited in Statista, 2013b) estimates 25% of all adults listen to satellite radio (e.g., Sirius/XM), 15% stream radio from the Internet at least once a week, and 52% of all adults have streamed Internet radio at one time or another.

The number of people using tertiary radio has not declined significantly since 2002, but time spent listening to AM and FM radio has decreased. Arbitron (as cited in Statista, 2013b) estimates that in 2002, adults listened to 824 hours annually or 2.26 hours per day. By 2008, time spent listening had dropped to 744 minutes per year or about 2 hours per day. In 2012, adults were spending only about 92 minutes per day listening to AM or FM radio in real time.

A number of factors, including satellite radio, digital playback devices such as the iPod, and cellphones that can stream music from the Internet, have contributed to that decline. For example, Arbitron (2013) estimates the percentage of people 18 years of age and older who use media in their cars breaks out as follows: AM/FM radio, 84%, CD player 63%, iPod/MP3 player, 29%, satellite radio, 15%, and online radio (e.g., Pandora or Spotify), 12%. Arbitron (as cited in Pew, 2012c) estimates that 66% of all radio listening occurs away from home, and most of this listening occurs in the car. Katz Marketing Solutions (as cited in Statista, 2013b) suggests that 40% of all radio listening occurs in the car.

HD radio, once believed to be the technology that would rejuvenate radio listenership, has lost ground in recent years. HD radio is a marketing term used to describe a proprietary digital signal and is not "high definition." HD radio is simply a brand name for digital radio developed by a company called iBiquity. Pew (2012c) reports that between 2006 and 2010, the number of adults interested in HD radio never exceeded 8%, and only 2% of all adults report using HD radio in their car.

Simmons Market Research Bureau (2013) research suggests radio usage increases with age until listeners hit their mid-to late 50s and from then on declines. Specifically, 9.4% of all adults 18 to 24 indicated they did listen to the radio during the previous week, and that percentage increased to 16.1% for adults 25 to 34 (Simmons Market Research Bureau, 2013). Just over 20% of all adults 35 to 54 indicated they listened during the previous week, and that percentage declined to 17.8% for the 55 to 64 age cohort. Only 9.9% of all adults 70+ report listening to the radio, and only 6.1% of adults 75+ listened to the radio at some point during the previous week (Simmons Market Research Bureau, 2013).

Arbitron (as cited in Statista, 2013b) estimates that in 2012 the amount of time spent listening by age cohort was as follows: Older adults listened to the radio about 64 minutes per day, Adults aged 35 to 64 listened for 95 minutes, and Adults aged 25 to 54 listened for 98 minutes. Only teenagers aged 13 to 17 listened to the radio less than older adults. Those teens listened to the radio only one hour per day (Arbitron as cited in Statista, 2013b).

While teenagers and young adults listen to music, older adults listen to informative or talk dominant radio programming, and adults 65+ listen to the radio more at home than anywhere else (Arbitron, 2009). In 2009, the top five radio formats for adults 65 years of age and older were News/Talk/Information (28.7%), Country Music (13.9%), Adult Contemporary Music (7.6%), Classical Music (5.6%), and All News (3.2%). Empty cells in Table 6 indicate the format is outside the top ten for that age cohort.

Table 6. Radio Format by Listener Age.

Radio Format/Age Group	25–34	35–44	45–54	55–64	65+
News/Talk/Information	5.7%	9.3%	12.6%	18.6%	28.7%
Country Music	11.9%	11.4%	12.5%	13.7%	13.9%
Adult Contemporary Music	7.2%	8.8%	9.6%	10.0%	7.6%
Classical				2.7%	5.6%
All News				2.1%	3.2%

Adults, Older Adults, and Books

In 2011, 84% of all adults reported reading a book, and 15% read an e-book on the day prior to being the surveyed (Pew, 2013a, b, & c). The amount of time adults spend reading books (105 hours) and the satisfaction derived from reading books have remained relatively stable since 2002. However, the number of voracious readers—those reading more than 50 books in the past year—dropped from 13% in 1978 to 7% in 1990 and finally to 5% by 2011 (Pew, 2013a, b, & c). Similarly, the number of individuals who have not read a single book in the previous year increased from 8% in 1978 to 16% in 1990 and to 19% in 2011 (Pew, 2013a, b, & c).

When asked what they read, 47% of the adults indicated they had read a book they characterized as being in the mystery/thriller/crime category. Other popular types of books and the percentage of people reporting having read them follow: Other Fiction (33%), Biographies (29%), History (27%), Other Non-Fiction (26%), Science Fiction (25%), Religious & Spirituality (24%), Romance (23%), and Self-Help (18%). Finally, when asked about enjoyment, 50% indicated they enjoyed books a lot, 30% enjoyed reading books some, 10% indicated they didn't enjoy reading much, and less than 10% reported not enjoying it all (Pew, 2013).

The conventional wisdom suggests that time spent reading decreases across the lifespan (Gordon, Gaitz, & Scott, 1976; McEnvoy & Vincent, 1980). However, 26% of this decline has been attributed to impaired vision (Ngandu & O'Rourke, 1980), and the most avid of all book readers are older adults. Recent estimates suggest adults 65+ reported reading 23 books in 2011 and this 5 more books than adults 50 to 64, 9 more books than adults 30–49, and 6 more books than adults 18–29 (Pew, 2011, as cited in Statista, 2013a, b, c, d, & f).

For convenience and in response to declining vision, older adults are recognizing that the ability to adjust the contrast of the screen, use backlighting, and increase the font size of the text makes reading on an e-reader easier than reading a book. Preliminary research suggests older adults can read from an iPad significantly faster than they can read from a printed book because of the increased contrast between the text and background (Kretzschmar et al., 2013). Even so, older adults are least likely to read their books on an e-reader (Pew, 2012e). Pew (2012e) reports that in 2011, only 12% of all 65+ adults reported reading a book on an e-reader within the previous year. By 2012 the number of adults 65 or older using an e-reader had increased to 20%. Similarly, the number of adults between 50 and 64 using an e-reader increased from 19% to 23%, the number of adults between 30 and 49 years of age increased from 25% to 41%, and the number of adults 18 to 29 increased from 25% to 31% (Pew, 2012e).

Older adults are also increasingly listening to audio books as a functional alternative to reading. Pew (2013a, b, & c) suggests 11% of all adults reported listening to an audio book in 2011. A report by the Audio Publishers Association (cited in Statista, 2013d) breaks down the consumers within this $1.2 billion industry as follows: Adults 65–74 (17%), 55–64 (20%), 45–54 (18%), 35–44 (23%), 25–34 (18%), and 18–24 (4%).

Adults, Older Adults, and Newspapers

Until 2009 *Editor and Publisher Yearbook* tracked the number of newspapers in the United States. They reported that in 1981 there were 1,730 morning and afternoon newspapers, but by 2009 the number of U.S. dailies had decreased to 1,387 (Editor and Publisher, 2009, as cited in Statista, 2013c). It comes as no surprise that advertising revenue, classified advertising revenue, and newspaper readership have also declined over that time (Pew, 2013c).

Pew (2012a) reported that in the year 2000, 47% of the adults had read a print copy of a newspaper the previous day. By 2010, the number of adults reported having a read a newspaper the previous day had decreased to 26%, and by 2012 the number had fallen to 23%. Pew (2012a) also observed that the number of adults who consider themselves regular newspaper readers has also declined. In 2004 54% of all adults considered themselves regular newspaper readers, but by 2012 that number fell to less than 38% (Pew, 2012a). Similarly, the number of adults indicating they never read a daily newspaper has also increased from 11% to 38% between 2004 and 2012 (Pew, 2012a).

A comparable decline in weekly or local newspaper readership has also been observed. In 2004, 36% of all adults indicated they read the weekly paper regularly, and by 2012 that number had dropped to 30%, and the number of adults indicating they never read the weekly paper increased from 26% to 28% (Pew, 2012a).

Finally, adult readers also spend less time reading the newspaper than they did ten years ago. In 2003, readers spent about 33 minutes a day reading the newspaper, but by 2012, they were spending less than 25 minutes per day (Editor & Publisher, 2013).

Even though newspaper readership has suffered a dramatic decline in recent years, it is still clear that older adults are the most active newspaper readers of any age cohort. Pew (2012a) reports that in 2010 46% of adults 65+ reported they read a newspaper the previous day. The percentages of younger adults reading a printed newspaper on the previous day were as follows: 18–24 (7%), 25–29 (11%), 30–39 (15%), 40–49 (24%), and 50–64 (35%). Younger adults are more likely to access news online. In 2010, only 9% of all adults 65+ accessed a newspaper online on the previous day. The rates for younger adults accessing newspapers online are as follows: 18–24 (16%), 25–29 (18%), 30–39 (22%), 40–49 (19%), and 50–64 (17%). Finally, if we examine online and print editions, the statistics for accessing a newspaper yesterday are as follows: 65+ (50%), 18–24 (20%), 25–29 (25%), 30–39 (33%), 40–49 (37%), and 50–64 (45%).

Older adults also spend more time reading their newspaper. In fact, adults under the age of 65 spend less than half of the time adults 65+ spend with the daily newspaper. Older adults spend almost 45 minutes a day with the newspaper, while adults 35 to 64 spend only 23 minutes and adults 18 to 34 spend only 14 minutes (Pew, 2012a). Finally, even if time spent watching TV news, listening to news on the radio, and reading a printed or online edition of a newspaper are all included, older adults still spend more time with the news. Adults 65+ reported spending about 83 minutes with the news, while adults 18 to 29 spend 45 minutes and adults 30 to 39 spend 68 minutes (Pew, 2012a). Adults 50 to 64 spend nearly as much time with the news (81 minutes) as adults 65+ (Pew, 2012a).

Examination of what older adults read in the newspaper suggests that they are more likely to report reading the entire paper. In fact, 31.5% of adults 65+ read the entire paper, while other age cohorts are far less likely to read every page (Simmons Market Research, 2013). The percentage of adults at various age cohorts reporting they read every page of the newspaper follows: 18–24 (7.6%), 25–34 (9.4%), 35–44 (10.3%), 45–54 (18.0%), and 55–64 (25.1%) (Simmons Market Research, 2013). Finally, more than 24% of all adults 70+ still report reading every page of the daily newspaper (Simmons Market Research, 2013).

When we look at the newspaper sections most likely to be read by adults 65+ we find they are the following: Front Page (35.4%), General News (33.3%), Editorial (23.2%), Sports (18.1%), Comics (16.6%), Entertainment (15.1%), Business Finance (14.4%), Food/Cooking (13.8%), and TV/Radio Listings (13.6%) (Simmons Market Research, 2013). Gender differences exist; older males are more likely to read the Sports section and less likely to read the Food/Cooking sections of the newspaper than their female counterparts (Burnett, 1991; Simmons Market Research, 2013). Similarly, economic differences in reading preferences also exist. Older, affluent male adults read the news section, business section, travel section, and magazine section of the newspaper more than their less affluent male counterparts, and older, less affluent females are more likely to read the advertisements than more affluent female readers (Burnett, 1991; Simmons, 2013).

Adults, Older Adults, and Magazines

The number of adults who reported *never* reading a magazine during 2012 was 75%, and only about 10% indicated they rarely read a magazine. This means only 3% of all adults are regular magazine readers and the remainder read magazines sometimes (Pew, 2012a). Pew (2012a) reports that when asked about reading a magazine the previous day, in 2012 only 19% indicated that they had. In 2000 that number was 26% (Pew, 2012a).

The typical magazine reader is a white female who is about 47 years of age and has a median household income of $63,000 (Pew, 2012a). The average digital magazine reader is 41 years of age, white, and has a median household income of $70,000. Only about 2% of all magazine readers report reading both the print and digital versions of the magazine and demographically more closely resemble the digital readers than they resemble the print readers (Pew, 2012a).

The value of a particular media channel is measured by statistics based on audience reach. Magazine reach refers to how many different people are exposed to one or more magazines within a particular time frame. Television Bureau of Advertising estimated that in 2012 the average daily reach for magazines (adults 18+) was 24.8% (as cited in Statista, 2013e). In other words, on a typical day just under 25% of the adults 18+ were exposed to one or more magazines. Keep in mind that "exposed to" does not mean that an individual actually read an article or examined a specific advertisement in any particular magazine. It just means that this percentage or fraction of people looked at some magazine on an average daily basis.

The Television Bureau of Advertising (2012) reported magazine reach for adults 65+ was 37.4% on a typical day. The reach for adults 18 to 34 years of age was 16%, and the reach for adults 35 to 64 was only 25.6% (Television Bureau of Advertising, 2012, as cited in Statista, 2013e). And while reach is an important statistic—particularly for advertisers—surveying adult readers is another way of determining who is reading magazines. Simmons Market Research Bureau (2013) indicated that in 2010, 18.2% of the 65+ adults typically read one or more English-language magazine. Approximately 10.8% of all adults 18 to 24, 15.4% of all adults 25 to 34, and 17.3% of all adults 55 to 64 indicated they read at least one magazine (Simmons Market Research Bureau, 2013). Adults 35 to 44 (18.6%) and 45 to 54 (19.7%) were slightly more likely to read magazines than their older counterparts (Simmons Market Research Bureau, 2013). It is interesting to note that the only adult age group that is less likely than 18- to 24-year-olds to read a magazine are the 75+ adults (Simmons Market Research Bureau, 2013).

If free or membership magazines are excluded, the seven magazines with the highest circulation are *Better Homes and Gardens*, *Reader's Digest*, *Good Housekeeping*, *National Geographic*, *Family Circle*, *People*, and *Woman's Day*. Table 7 breaks down readership of these magazines by age cohort and illustrates how important the 65+ age cohort is to magazine sales in the United States (Simmons Market Research Bureau, 2013). In terms of time spent reading magazines, adults 65+ spend about 25 minutes each day reading magazines, and adults 18+ spend only about 12 minutes (Television Bureau of Advertising, 2012, as cited in Statista, 2013e).

Table 7. Magazine Readership by Age Cohort.

Magazine Title	Percentage of Readers by Age Cohort				
	65+	70+	75+	18–34	35–49
Better Homes & Gardens	28.5%	19.7%	14.7%	12.3%	28%
Reader's Digest	35.1%	23.9%	15.6%	13.9%	22.2%
National Geographic	25.2%	16.9%	11.5%	19.4%	24.4%
Good Housekeeping	29.7%	21.0%	15.2%	9.8%	24.4%
Woman's Day	27.6%	18.7%	13.3%	9.0%	28.1%
Family Circle	30.8%	20.8%	15.3%	12.1%	27.0%
People	18.2%	11.5%	7.6%	21.7%	30.0%
Time	20.6%	12.6%	9.2%	20.7%	26.9%
Ladies' Home Journal	35.2%	25.3%	18.6%	6.2%	25.3%

Given their interest in news, it comes as no surprise that Pew (2004) examined readership patterns of the three most popular news magazines—*Time, Newsweek,* and *U.S. News and World Reports* (which no longer publishes a print edition). With data gathered in 2003, they report that readers of these popular news magazines are male, older, and affluent. The average reader for each magazine was 43.1, 44.4, and 45 years of age, respectively. The average income level was $65,697, $66,739, and $63,603, respectively, and readers of each magazine were well above the industry average for reader income and above the U.S. adult population average of $50,760 in 2003.

Adults, Older Adults, and Internet Use

In 2010, over 82% of all U.S. households had at least one personal computer, and 71% had Internet access (U.S. Census Bureau, 2010). Close to 80% of all adults between the ages of 18 and 64 have Internet access available from their own home, and nearly 80% of all adults between 18 and 64 also have access to the Internet from some location other than their own home. Only 53% of all adults 65+ have Internet access from their own home, and only 41% have access from somewhere other than their own home. Without a doubt, adults 65+ are less likely to have Internet access than any other age group.

The average adult 18+ years of age spent 156 minutes per day using the Internet in 2010. Adults 18 to 24 used the Internet about 192 minutes per day, while adults 35 to 64 averaged 147 minutes per day. Adults 65+ years of age access the Internet the least. During that same year adults 65 and older spent only about 93 minutes each day on the Internet (U.S. Census Bureau, 2010).

Most of the time Americans 15 years of age and older spend on the computer is used to engage in social intercourse. Americans spend the vast majority of their computer time on social networking sites, communicating via instant messaging, and emailing others (U.S. Census Bureau, 2010). Males and females 15+ spend about 35% and 29% of their time, respectively, interacting with others online. While we tend to think of interaction as being synchronous (e.g., back and forth in real time—such as a telephone conversation), these new technologies also allow interaction to occur asynchronously. Asynchronous communication means people can interact without being available at the same time (e.g., sending email). Table 8 identifies the various Internet activities people involve themselves in by age cohort (U.S. Census Bureau, 2010).

Early research by Adler (1996) suggested the major reason that the elderly adopted personal computers was to send and receive electronic mail. The ability to communicate with their children and grandchildren was identified as a primary motivation for the adoption of the personal computer. This argument is further bolstered by the 2010 census data presented above and by the recent increase in social networking involvement by older adults. Pew (2013) reports that 72% of all adults and 43% of all adults 65+ use social networking sites. This represents a threefold increase in the past four years.

Table 8. Internet Activities by Age.

Typical Daily Activities of Adult Internet Users in the U.S. in 2010 by Age Group				
Activity	18–29	30–49	50–64	65+
Send or read email	62%	67%	60%	55%
Use a search engine to find information	55%	54%	42%	34%
Get news online	44%	45%	42%	34%
Check weather reports and forecasts online	38%	37%	27%	27%
Look for news and information about politics	18%	22%	17%	19%
Do any banking online	27%	30%	22%	19%
Watch a video on a video-sharing site	39%	20%	12%	17%
Use a social networking site	60%	39%	20%	13%
Send instant messages	24%	15%	9%	4%
Buy a product online	7%	10%	6%	6%
Use classified ads sites like Craigslist	14%	13%	6%	5%
Buy or make a reservation for travel	5%	6%	4%	3%
Participate in an online auction	5%	5%	4%	2%

TV Portrayals of Older Adults

Robinson and Skill (1995) reviewed the literature and concluded characters 65 years of age and older have been significantly underrepresented on television since the beginning of television broadcasting. They reported that in nearly every published study of TV characters, fewer than 5% were depicted as 65 years of age or older. This 5% ceiling for older characters was observed in prime-time programming, daytime programming, and children's programming.

Signorielli (2004) conducted the most recent, large-scale, multiple season examination of prime-time television content that is the *de facto* gold standard for this area of research. In analyzing fall and spring samples from the 1993, 1997, 1998, and 1999 seasons and a single sample from the fall during the 1994, 1995, 1996, 2000, 2001, and 2002 seasons she found that only 3% of the characters appearing on six broadcast networks (ABC, CBS, NBC, Fox, UPN, and WB) were elderly.

Recent, smaller-scale investigations yield similar findings. Ye and Ward (2010) report that 5.1% of the characters appearing on two medical dramas (*Grey's Anatomy* and *ER*) between 2000 and 2007 were older; Lauzen, Dozier, and Reyes (2007) found 3.9% of the characters on situation comedies and dramas on five broadcast networks (ABC, CBS, NBC, WB, UPN) aired during the 2003–2004 television season were 60 years of age or older; and Robinson and Anderson (2006) ascertained that 8% (n = 107) of characters in children's animated TV programs aired on the WB, the Cartoon Network, Nickelodeon, Fox, and ABC during October 2003 were older.

In addition to being underrepresented, elderly characters tend to be male and Caucasian (Gerbner, Gross, Signorielli, & Morgan, 1980; Lauzen et al., 2007; Robinson & Anderson, 2006). They generally have no discernible religious affiliation, are more likely to be cast as widowers than other age cohorts (Robinson & Skill, 1995), are unlikely to be cast in central roles (Robinson & Anderson, 2006; Robinson & Skill, 1995), and occupy less prestigious occupations (Signorielli, 2004). They are cast in humorous roles and often not treated with respect (Gerbner et al., 1980), and they are less likely to be leaders, sexually active, and engage in leisure activities than younger characters (Lauzen et al., 2007).

Content analysts examining portrayals of older adults in films report similar levels of underrepresenation. Lauzen and Dozier (2005) report similar findings in the top 100 domestic grossing films of 2002 (U.S.). Similarly, research suggests older adults are underrepresented in other countries including Germany (Kessler, Rakoczy, & Staudinger, 2004) and Taiwan (Shu-Chin, Yan Bing, & Hummert, 2009). While research focusing on the impact of such portrayals is needed (Signorielli, 2004), there is reason to be concerned that audiences dependent on the media for information about older adults are not being well served. Similarly, the impact of such portrayals on older audience members is also sorely lacking.

Older Adults in Advertising

While early research on television advertising suggested older adults were not depicted in a very favorable light (Francher, 1973; Harris & Feinberg, 1977), like television portrayals, underrepresentation is a more common occurence than negative portrayals (Langmeyer, 1984; Robinson, Duet, & Smith, 1995; Swayne & Greco, 1987). For example, Roy and Harwood (1997) conducted an extensive study of television commercials and found older adults underrepresented on commercials aired during prime-time network programming. They report that only 6.9% of the characters appearing on commercials were older adults, and while portrayed in a positive light, again elderly female characters were far less common than older male characters, and the vast majority of these characters were white.

More recently, Lee, Carpenter, and Meyers (2007) examined commercials on five networks (NBC, ABC, CBS, FOX, and WB) throughout the day. By coding 1,977 commercials, they found 15% of the advertisements contained a character 55 or older. They also report that 86% were Caucasian, and that 82% of the characters were male. Finally, commercials featuring older adults were more likely to appear in commercials aired in the afternoon and less likely to be aired during primetime. There was not, however, strong evidence of negative portrayals in the commercials examined (Lee, Carpenter, & Meyers, 2007).

Print Portrayals of Older Adults

Portrayals of older adults in print advertising generally mirror depictions in television programming. Most research suggests underrepresentation, with older males being far more common than older females (England, Kuhn, & Gardner, 1981; Gantz, Gartenberg, & Rainbow, 1980; Hollenshead & Ingersol, 1982). Early studies almost always report fewer than 5% of the characters being older, and fewer than 2% of the characters are older females. More recently Raman, Harwood, Weis, Anderson, and Miller (2008) and Ursic, Ursic, and Ursic (1986) found 9% of advertisements contained representations of adults aged 65 and older—though older women remained dramatically underrepresented relative to older men in U.S. magazine ads. Kvasnicka, Beymer, and Perloff (1982) observed that while older adults were underrepresented in these advertisements, their depictions were more favorable in magazine advertisements targeted toward the elderly.

Research on portrayals of older adults in newspapers suggests that very little space in the daily newspaper is devoted to older adults (Broussard, Blackmon, Blackwell, Smith, & Hunt, 1980) leading Wass, Hawkins, Kelly, Magners, and McMorrow (1985) to conclude that only 1% of the news was devoted to coverage about and/or designed for the elderly. Buchholz and Bynum (1982) examined the *New York Times* and the *Daily Oklahoman* from 1970 to 1978 and concluded "the two newspapers pictured the elderly more favorably than the media critics might lead one to believe" (p. 87). They argue that most of the articles balance negative images with positive images. Buchholz and Bynum suggest that if you consider reader attention factors such as headline size, article length, and page placement, there are more positive than negative stories, and, in addition, the positive stories are more prominently displayed.

Buchholz and Bynum (1982) also report that 97% of the stories about the elderly were obituaries, public policy and legislation pieces, retirement notices, anniversaries, and stories about fraud in government programs for the elderly. Less than 3% of the articles are about significant issues facing the elderly (e.g., health, retirement, housing, crime, employment, transportation, income, or demographic changes in the United States). In contrast, almost 25% of the articles are obituaries, compelling Buchholz and Bynum (1982) to write that "the surest way for the aged to get into the news columns was to die" (p. 86).

CONCLUSION

A surprisingly small amount of research has examined media portrayals of older adults in recent years. But it appears that the elderly continue to be infrequently seen on television, and when they do appear, they occupy lead roles at about one-half the rates of other age groups. Similarly, older adults are unlikely to appear in films, and they are unlikely to be featured in newspaper articles. Hacker (1951) suggested that fictional portrayals are an indication of a group's social status, and if Hacker is right, then much needs to be done about societal attitudes toward older adults.

The consistency in these research findings may be the most interesting finding of all. If television writers are trying to attract audiences of a particular demographic composition that are appealing to advertisers, it makes sense that they would create stories and characters that they believe will attract and hold those viewers. Regardless of whether the information used by the writers and directors comes from their own personal feelings about what the target audience will like, past show successes, or a detailed analysis of the demographic group being targeted, the programs represent the writers' best judgments about what the target audience will watch. As CBS programmer Herman Keld explained, "We always look for programming that appeals to everybody, but that kind of program doesn't exist, really. So the networks tend to program for their core audiences" (Gitlin, 1983, p. 57). It is clear that the networks still do not believe that the prime demographic market is interested in older characters on TV.

In an important work on the narrative form, Gallie (1964) pointed out that skillful storytellers do not provide explicit explanations within the story: "Characters must be presented and described in general terms, so that we can know them as types and are interested in them as individuals; but it is in the latter spirit that we follow their actions" (p. 23). Perhaps less central or peripheral characters that do not develop over the course of the episode may provide a more interesting window into the culture than the central characters since they must comply with accepted stereotypical characteristics of that group to be accepted and not disruptive to the central characters and the storyline. These characters may serve as indicators of the cultural acceptability of particular groups and maybe over time provide insight into cultural change.

In outlining Peripheral Imagery Theory, Robinson and Skill (1993) suggest that because peripheral characters are portrayed in general or stereotypical terms, examination of peripheral character portrayals on successful shows may provide insight into the attitudes and stereotypes of the target audience. In addition, the peripheral characters provide a context for understanding the central characters and provide the audience with the information they need in order to follow the story. It would be interesting for future research to examine whether or not shows that successfully tap into audience stereotypes are more successful than programs that present peripheral characters in a manner that is inconsistent with audience attitudes toward those social groups or individuals.

The work of Dutta-Bergman on media complementarity theory is also an idea that needs to be examined within the realm of older adults and media use. Dutta-Bergman (2004) argues that new media channels (e.g., Twitter) do not necessarily replace older channels (e.g., radio) but instead are adopted and used in a complementary manner. Research by Tian and Robinson (2008a, 2008b) suggests that in the case of health information, adults and older adults do indeed use mass media channels and even interpersonal channels complementarily. This was shown in both intentional health information searches and in incidental health information acquisition. Older adults are increasingly adopting new communication technologies but that has not been the death knell of those communication technologies. The continued use of a media channel or channels seems to be more likely predicated on other factors such as availability and utility.

In terms of media usage, Mares and Cantor (1992) found elderly viewers use the mass media to alter their mood (Zillman, 1988) and for social comparison purposes (Festinger, 1954). These comparisons yield information about the relative abilities and opinions of audience members as well as information that can alter their affective states. Mares and Cantor (1992) suggested that older audience members rated programs that depicted the elderly in a negative fashion more favorably than they rated programs that portrayed the elderly as being happy and socially integrated.

Further, Mares and Cantor (1992) reported that people who are unhappy actually want to find programs with characters similar to themselves and in circumstances that are worse than their own. Consistent with social comparison theory, Mares and Cantor (1982) suggest that such comparisons actually raise audience levels of affect through ego enhancement. Similarly, unhappy, depressed, and lonely audience members may avoid programs with positive portrayals of similar others because they do not want to receive the ego-threatening information such comparisons would yield. If they are right, it may well be that invisibility is more damaging to older adult viewers than the negative portrayals they feared they would find.

Of course Mares and Cantor (1992) were discussing audience use of central characters. Peripheral characters seem less likely to be useful in the social comparison process because audience members need information about specific opinions and abilities to engage in social comparisons. Future research needs to determine whether central characters are used for mood management and peripheral characters are beacons of cultural attitudes and stereotypes.

The plethora of data now available to researchers also needs close examination. Research by Simmons Market Research (2013) illustrates that older adults are more likely to watch movies on TV than their younger counterparts. Of course some of this viewing is the result of more time spent viewing television but it also suggests movies are still interesting to older adults even though they seldom attend them in theaters. Older movies contain familiar characters and story configurations that comfortable and familiar and given the proliferation of cable channels these movies are readily available. And older movies contain actors that are closer in age to the older adult than the most recent box office successes. This is consistent with the findings by Mares and Cantor (1992), who reported audience members do prefer to watch programs containing characters that are similar (in terms of age) to themselves.

Future research on the impact of older adult portrayals needs to focus on priming effects. Both positive and negative portrayals of elderly characters need to be examined as a source of attitudinal and behavioral priming of audience members. Further, this research needs to determine whether young and old audience members access negative stereotypes in their cognitions and if these thoughts impact their ultimate behavior. Similarly, content analytic research needs to focus on the way issues facing the elderly are framed. Identifying health issues associated with growing old is potentially an important role for the media, but it may also serve as a way of encouraging audience members to view these issues as problems of the old and not societal problems. Such research could significantly enhance our understanding of the uses and consequences of media portrayals.

Media Use and Effects in Older Adulthood: Future Research Directions

Relatively little research is done on the media use of older adults and even less is done on the impact of the media on older adults. And more is sorely needed. Older adults provide an extremely important audience for understanding the media. Even though an extended discussion is outside the scope of this chapter, our understanding of the relationship between media use and age could be increased significantly by incorporating spousal caretaking into the picture. Older adults may generally be healthy, wealthy, and mobile, but their ability to participate in other leisure activities may be limited by a spouse with health problems.

REFERENCES

Abelman, R. (1987). Religious television and uses and gratifications. *Journal of Broadcasting and Electronic Media, 31*, 93–107.

Adams, M., & Groen, R. (1975). Media habits and preferences of the elderly. *Journal of Leisurability, 2*(2), 25–30.

Adler, R. (1996). Older adults and computers: Report of a national survey seniornet. Retrieved from http://www.seniornet.org/intute/survey2.html.

Arbitron. (2009). National radio listening trends. http://futureofradioonline.com/wp-content/uploads/2010/12/RadioToday_20101.pdf

Arbitron. (2013). The infinite dial 2013: Navigating digital platforms. http://www.edisonresearch. com/wp-content/uploads/2013/04/Edison_Research_Arbitron_Infinite_Dial_2013.pdf

Ball-Rokeach, S., & DeFleur, M. (1976). A dependency model of mass-media effects. *Communication Research, 3*, 3–21.

Bower, R. T. (1983). *The changing television audience in America.* New York, NY: Columbia University Press.

Broussard, E. J., Blackmon, C. R., Blackwell, D. L., Smith, D. W., & Hunt, S. (1980). News of aged and aging in 10 metropolitan dailies. *Journalism Quarterly, 57,* 324–327.

Buchholz, M., & Bynum, J. E. (1982). Newspaper presentation of America's aged: A content analysis of image and role. *The Gerontologist, 22,* 83–87.

Bureau of Labor Statistics. (2011). American time use survey. http://www.bls.gov/news.release/archives/atus_06222012.pdf

Burnett, J. J. (1991). Examining the media habits of the affluent elderly. *Journal of Advertising Research, 31*(5), 33–41.

Dutta-Bergman, M. J. (2004). Complementarity in consumption of news types across traditional and new media. *Journal of Broadcasting & Electronic Media, 48,* 41–60.

Editor & Publisher Co. (2013). Table 1146: Daily and Sunday newspapers—Number and circulation, 1991 to 2009, and by state, 2009. In ProQuest, *ProQuest statistical abstract of the United States: 2013.* Retrieved from http://statab.conquestsystems.com/sa/abstract.html?tableno=1146&acc-no=C7095-1.24&year=2013&z=8CA9A6F843A665C643C972DF33AF1A-8F73A8A9F5

England, P., Kuhn, A., & Gardner, T. (1981). The ages of men and women in magazine advertisements. *Journalism Quarterly, 58,* 468–471.

Festinger, L. (1954). A theory of social comparison processes. *Human Relations, 7,* 117–140.

Francher, J. (1973). It's the Pepsi generation: Accelerated aging and the television commercial. *International Journal of Aging and Human Development, 3,* 245–255.

Gallie, W. B. (1964). Philosophy and historical understanding. London, UK: Chatto and Windus.

Gallop-Goodman, C. (2001, March). Time off. *American Demographics, 24.*

Gantz, W., Gartenberg, H., & Rainbow, C. (1980). Approaching invisibility: Portrayals of the elderly in magazine advertisements. *Journal of Communication, 30,* 56–60.

Gerbner, G., Gross, L., Signorielli, N., & Morgan, M. (1980). Aging with television: Images on television drama and conceptions of social reality. *Journal of Communication, 30,* 37–48.

Gitlin, T. (1983). Inside Prime Time. New York, NY: Knopf Doubleday Publishing.

Goodman, R. I. (1990). Television news viewing by older adults. *Journalism Quarterly, 67,* 137–141.

Gordon, C., Gaitz, C., & Scott, J. (1976). Leisure and lives: Personal expressivity across the life span. In R. Binstock & E. Shanas (Eds.), *Handbook of aging and the social sciences* (pp. 310–341). New York, NY: Van Nostrand-Reinhold.

Hacker, H. M. (1951). Women as a minority group. *Social Focus, 30,* 39–44.

Harris, A., & Feinberg, J. (1977). Television and aging: Is what you see what you get? *Gerontologist, 17*(5), 464–468.

Harwood, J. (1997). Viewing age: Lifespan identify and television viewing choices. *Journal of Broadcasting & Electronic Media, 41,* 203–213.

Hays, J., Landerman, L., Blazer, D., Koenig, H., Carroll, J., & Musick, M. (1998). Aging, health, and the electronic church. *Journal of Aging and Health, 10*(4), 458–482.

Hollenshead, C., & Ingersol, B. (1982). Middle-aged and older women in print advertisements. *Educational Gerontology, 9,* 111–122.

Kessler, E., Rakoczy, K., & Staudinger, U. (2004). The portrayal of older people in prime time television series: The match with gerontological evidence. *Aging and Society, 24*, 531–552.

Kretzschmar, F., Pleimling, D., Hosemann, J., Fussel, S., Bomkessel-Schlesewsky, I., & Schlesewsky, M. (2013). Subjective impressions do not mirror online reading effort: Concurrent EEG-Eyetracking evidence from the reading of books and digital media. *Plosone.* http://www.plosone.org/article/info%3Adoi%2F10.1371%2Fjournal.pone.0056178

Kvasnicka, B., Beymer, B., & Perloff, R. (1982). Portrayals of the elderly in magazine advertisements. *Journalism Quarterly, 59*, 656–658.

Langmeyer, L. (1984) Senior citizens and television advertisements: A research note. *Current Issues and Research in Advertising, 6*, 167–179.

Lauzen, M., & Dozier, D. (2005). Maintaining the double standard: Portrayals of age and gender in popular television and film. *Sex Roles, 52*, 437–446.

Lauzen, M. M., Dozier, D. M., & Reyes, B. (2007). From adultescents to zoomers: An examination of age and gender in prime-time television. *Communication Quarterly, 55*, 343–357.

Lee, M., Carpenter, B., & Meyers, L. (2007).Representations of older adults in television advertisements. *Journal of Aging Studies, 21*, 23–30.

Mares, M., & Cantor, J. (1992). Elderly viewers' responses to televised portrayals of old age: Empathy and mood management versus social comparison. *Communication Research, 19*, 459–478.

Mares, M. L., & Woodard, E. (2006). In search of the older audience: Adult age differences in television viewing. *Journal of Broadcasting & Electronic Media, 50*, 595–614.

McEnvoy, G., & Vincent, C. (1980). Who reads and why? *Journal of Communication, 30*(1), 134–140.

Mundorf, N., & Brownell, W. (1990). Media preferences of older and younger adults. *The Gerontologist, 30*(5), 685–692.

Ngandu, K. M., & O'Rourke, B. (1980, November). *Reading attitudes, habits, interests, and motivations of the elderly.* Paper presented at the annual meeting of the College Reading Association, Boston, MA.

Nielsen. (2009). Three screen report. http://www.nielsen.com/content/dam/corporate/us/en/newswire/uploads/2010/03/3Screens_4Q09_US_rpt.pdf

Nielsen. (2011). Americans using TV and Internet together. http://www.nielsen.com/us/en/newswire/2010/three-screen-report-q409.html

Ownership of TV sets falls in U.S. (2011, May 3). *The New York Times.* http://www.nytimes.com/2011/05/03/business/media/03television.html?_r=0

Pew. (2009). The audience for online video-sharing sites shoots up. Internet and American life project. http://pewinternet.org/Reports/2009/13--The-Audience-for-Online-VideoSharing-Sites-Shoots-Up.aspx

Pew. (2004). 2004 annual report—magazine audience. http://www.journalism.org/node/575

Pew. (2012a). In changing news landscape, even television is vulnerable. http://www.peoplepress.org/files/legacy-pdf/2012%20News%20Consumption%20Report.pdf

Pew. (2012b). Further decline in credibility ratings for most news organizations. http://www.pewtrusts.org/our_work_report_detail.aspx?id=85899411936

Pew. (2012c). The state of the news media 2012. http://stateofthemedia.org/2012/audio-how-far-will-digital-go/?src=prc-section#hd-radio

Pew. (2012d). Trends in news consumption: 1991–2012. http://www.people-press.org/files/legacy-pdf/2012%20News%20Consumption%20Report.pdf

Pew. (2012e). E-book reading jumps; Pring book reading declines. http://libraries.pewinternet.org/files/legacy-pdf/PIP_Reading%20and%20ebooks_12.27.pdf

Pew. (2013a). Average number of books read in the United States in 2011 by age. http://www.statista. com.libproxy.udayton.edu/statistics/222743/mean-number-of-books-read-in-the-us/

Pew. (2013b). Did you read a daily newspaper yesterday? http://www.statista.com.libproxy.udayton. edu/statistics/243958/newspaper-readership-in-the-us/

Pew. (2013c). Newspapers by the numbers. http://stateofthemedia.org/2013/newspapers-stabilizing-but-still-threatened/newspapers-by-the-numbers/

Raman, P., Harwood, J., Weis, D., Anderson, J. L., & Miller, G. (2008). Portrayals of older adults in U.S. and Indian magazine advertisements: A cross-cultural comparison. *Howard Journal of Communications, 19*, 221–240.

Robinson, J., & Skill, T. (1993, November). *The invisible generation: Portrayals of the elderly on television.* Paper presented to the Speech Communication Association, Miami, FL.

Robinson, J., & Skill, T. (1995). The invisible generation: Portrayals of the elderly on prime-time television. *Communication Reports, 8*(2), 111–119.

Robinson, J., Skill, T., & Turner, J. (2004). Media usage patterns and portrayals of seniors. In J. F. Nussbaum & J. Coupland (Eds.), *Handbook of communication and aging research* (2nd ed., pp. 423–450). Mahwah, NJ: Erlbaum.

Robinson, T., & Anderson, C. (2006). Older characters in children's animated television programs: A content analysis of their portrayal. *The Journal of Broadcasting & Electronic Media, 50*(2), 287–304.

Robinson, T. E., Duet, R., & Smith, T. V. (1995). The elderly in advertising: A content analysis of prime-time television commercials. *Proceedings of the 1995 Conference of the American Academy of Advertising* (pp. 1–11). Waco, TX: Hankamer School of Business, Baylor University.

Roy, A., & Harwood, J. (1997). Underrepresented, positively portrayed: Older adults in television commercials. *Journal of Applied Communication Research, 25*, 39–56.

Shu-Chin, L., Yan Bing, Z., & Hummert, M. (2009). Older adults in prime-time television dramas in Taiwan: Prevalence, portrayal, and communication interaction. *Journal of Cross-Cultural Gerontology, 24*(4), 355–372.

Signorielli, N. (2004). Aging on television: Messages relating to gender, race and occupation in prime time. *Journal of Broadcasting & Electronic Media, 48*(2), 279–301.

Simmons Market Research Bureau. (2013, Spring). NHCS adult study—six months [Computer software]. New York, NY: Author.

Spring, J. (1993). Seven days of play. *American Demographics, 15*(3), 50–55.

Statista. (2013a). Average daily time spent viewing television in selected countries. http://www.statista.com.libproxy.udayton.edu/statistics/169735/television-consumption-daily-viewing-time-worldwide-2010/

Statista. (2013b). Weekly time spent listening to the radio in the U.S. in 2012 by age and gender. http://www.statista.com.libproxy.udayton.edu/statistics/252204/weekly-time-spent-listening-to-the-radio-in-the-us-by-age-and-gender/

Statista. (2013c). Number of daily newspapers in the U.S. http://www.statista.com.libproxy.udayton. edu/statistics/183408/number-of-us-daily-newspapers-since-1975/

Statista. (2013d). Breakdown of the U.S. audiobook listeners by age and format preference as of 2012. http://www.statista.com.libproxy.udayton.edu/statistics/249824/the-age-of-audiobook-listeners-in-the-us-by-format-preferrence/

Statista. (2013e). Daily reading of magazines in the U.S. in 2010 and 2012 by age group. http://www.statista.com.libproxy.udayton.edu/statistics/191535/daily-reach-of-magazines-in-the-us-by-age-group/

Statista. (2013f). Estimated time spent reading newspapers in the United States from 2002—2012. http://www.statista.com.libproxy.udayton.edu/statistics/186934/us-newspaper-reading-habits-since-2002/

Swayne, L. E., & Greco, A. J. (1987). The portrayal of older Americans in television commercials. *Journal of Advertising, 16*, 47–54.

Tian, Y., & Robinson, J. D. (2008a). Incidental health information use and media complementarity: A comparison of senior and non-senior cancer patients. *Patient Education and Counseling, 71*, 340–344.

Tian, Y., & Robinson, J. D. (2008b). Media use and health information seeking: An empirical test of complementarity theory. *Health Communication, 23*, 184–190.

TV Basics. (2012). A report on the growth and scope of television. http://www.tvb.org/media/file/TV_Basics.pdf

Ursic, A. C., Ursic, M. L., & Ursic, V. L. (1986). A longitudinal study of the use of the elderly in magazine advertising. *Journal of Communication Research, 13*, 131–133.

U.S. Census Bureau. (2010). Typical daily Internet activities of adult users 2010. http://www.census.gov/compendia/statab/2011/tables/11s1160.pdf

U.S. Census Bureau. (2011). Newspaper usage. http://www.census.gov/compendia/statab/2011/tables/11s1135.pdf

Villa, J. (2001, May 31). Blockbuster launches DirecTV PPV service. http://www.videostoremag.com/news/html/industry_article.cfm?article_id=1262

Wass, H., Hawkins, L., Kelly, E., Magners, C., & McMorrow, A. (1985). The elderly in Sunday newspapers, 1963 and 1983. *Educational Gerontology, 11*, 29–39.

Ye, Y., & Ward, K. E. (2010). The depiction of illness and related matters in two top-ranked prime-time network medical dramas in the United States: A content analysis. *Journal of Health Communication, 15*(5), 555–570.

Zillman, D. (1988). Mood management through communication choices. *American Behavioral Scientist, 31*, 327–340.

CHAPTER NINETEEN

The Socially and Sexually Active Later-Life Family Member

FRAN C. DICKSON AND PATRICK HUGHES

The role and expectations of the later-life family member are changing in contemporary society. Older family members are living longer, healthier, and far more active lives than at any other time in history. As the Baby Boomers age, they are expected to be in better health and to live longer than any other cohort of older Americans (U.S. Census Bureau, 2001). By 2030, 20% of our population will be between the ages of 60 and 85. In other words, it is estimated that 1 in 5 people will be over the age of 60 in 2030. We are also finding that as we age, the number of divorced people over the age of 60 is on the rise. The divorce rate for those over 50 has doubled since 1990 ("U.S. Population Predictions," 2008). For example, in 1990, 1 in 10 older individuals was divorced; more recently it is 1 in 4 ("U.S. Population Predictions," 2008). As a result, we are seeing the "graying of American divorce," in which later-life divorce has become a more common occurrence. In the past, when we thought of a single older family member, their singlehood was typically a result of widowhood, not divorce. For example, one of the first articles that explored dating among older adults examined dating and remarriage only among individuals who were widowed (Cooney & Dunne, 2001).

Since we are seeing an increase in the number of divorces among later-life adults, we are also seeing an increase in the number of single older adults who are interested in finding companionship and dating. With the change in social mores and the Baby Boomers coming of age, it is more common for older adults to be interested in and involved in dating and romantic relationships

(Alterovitz & Mendelsohn, 2013). In addition, this aging cohort is also comfortable with the technological changes occurring in our society. For example, recent studies exploring online dating have found that the fastest growing segments of online daters are those over the age of 55 (Stephure, Boon, MacKinnon, & Deveau, 2009). We are also seeing an increase in online dating sites for older adults such as ourtime.com, over65dating.com, and seniorpeoplemeet.com.

What does all this mean? Older adults are out in the social world, they are single, they are healthy, they want to date, and they want sex. This desire to be socially active violates many family members' expectations of their later-life family member and presents certain challenges for the family members as a whole (Dickson & Hughes, 2015). This chapter discusses what we know about socially and sexually active single later-life adults and the implications that this new social pattern has on family communication. Traditional views of older adults in lifespan research are becoming irrelevant and need to be modified to include the social trends of single later-life adults seeking out intimacy and romance. This chapter will discuss research on the social and sexual life of the single socially and sexually active aging Baby Boomer cohort.

LATER-LIFE DATING

It has been well documented that social relationships are important for physical and psychological well-being, especially in later life (Antonucci & Akiyama, 1995; Bulcroft & O'Conner, 1986; Carr, 2004; Carstensen, 1992; Dickson-Markman & Shern, 1990; Li & Liang, 2007). In addition, there are significantly more single, unmarried later-life adults today than at any other time in history, and these single adults are at risk for loneliness, isolation, and depression (Carr, 2004; Pinquart & Sorensen, 2001).

While older adults continue to experience the threat of social isolation and poor health, they continue to seek out meaningful friendships (Troll, 1994) and intimate, romantic relationships (Cooney & Dunne, 2001). Older adults also show a need for emotional intimacy (Gibson, 1993). Literature on the subject of intimacy shows that romantic relationships are often viewed as a necessity among older adults post-divorce or widowhood (Aleman, 2003) and as beneficial for their mental health (Carr, 2004; Malt & Farquharson, 2012).

Recent research suggests that adults over the age of 55 have not only been admitting to dating more frequently than in the past, but their participation in modern dating rituals has increased within recent years as well. Stephure, Boon, Mackinnon, and Deveau (2009) report that older single adults are more likely to explore online dating sites to initiate and establish intimate relationships in part due to the difficulty of meeting potential intimate partners.

The benefits of later-life dating are clearly demonstrated in the literature. For example, both men and women who have lost a spouse experience a decline in life satisfaction after the death of their spouse. Conversely, when one gained a partner, life satisfaction significantly increased (Chipperfield & Havens, 2007; Glass & Jolly, 1997). In observing research available on satisfaction in relation to later-life romantic relationships, intimacy and support provided by relationships allow older adults to be better adjusted and satisfied throughout their later life (Dickson, Hughes, & Walker, 2005).

Though the need for romantic relationships is present at all stages of life, patterns of dating choices for older adults differ significantly from those of young and mid-life adults. Researchers such as Malt and Farquharson (2012) have indicted the importance of gender roles of older adults within their dating lives. For example, women frequently have a strong need for independence and do not want to lose financial and social independence. Researchers have found that women avoid cohabitation and marriage more than do men, as they are hesitant to make a large commitment in fear of losing independence and individuality. This is largely owing to roles played in previous romantic relationships (Malt & Farquharson, 2012). For example, many women were expected to be the home keeper, with responsibilities for the children and the upkeep of the household. However, in their later life women have the opportunity to take control of their financial and social independence, some for the first time in their lives (Malt & Farquharson 2012). This newly established strength and freedom are something not easily given up. Dickson, Hughes, and Walker (2005) stated that women have a great need for independence while reporting that they are happy in the romantic relationship but did not want to get married. This is because "women did not want to end up as caretakers, lose their sense of autonomy, nor their financial independence" (p. 73). Conversely, men tend to desire marriage and were more likely to present the idea early in a dating relationship (Aleman, 2003). The reason women agree to relationships as older adults is that they are in need of companionship and enjoy the affection associated with a partner (Dickson et al., 2005). Alterovitz and Mendelsohn (2009) demonstrated that men are more likely to commit to exclusively dating and remarrying, while women are more interested in remaining socially and financially independent These trends also identify reasons later-life women and men want to date.

Communication and desires about later-life romantic relationships give further insight into roles, responsibilities, and expectations of older adults. Aleman (2005) studied participants at a midwestern retirement home in order to identify common conversation topics among dating older adults. The first communication topic identified was sexual activity in the later-life dating relationship. Aleman (2005) found that many participants expressed the desire for sexual relations; however, they felt it was inappropriate for someone their age to participate in such activities based on social constructs and lack of physical ability. The importance of communication surrounding sexual activities among older adults may be a result of the increased sexual activity among married and unmarried older adults in the past 30 years (Beckman, Waern, Gustafson, & Skoog, 2008). As this activity has become more prevalent, attitudes toward sexuality have become more accepted and perceived more positively, resulting in higher levels of sexual satisfaction. The second communication topic Aleman (2005) identified was that older adults discussed how sexual relationships should be heterosexual. In other words, many older adults reported being uncomfortable with the idea of homosexuality. Finally, the third communication topic identified was the idea that commitment should be discussed only in the present and not the future (Aleman, 2005). Many older adults talked about how relationships should not necessarily be future oriented and that they should be enjoyed only in the present. This concept of commitment allows us to better understand relationship expectations and length in later-life romantic relationships.

What is clear is that older adults do indeed desire committed, exclusive, romantic relationships; however, they are often apprehensive to settle down. This desire can conflict with the need to remain independent, which can be a large deterrent to cohabitating or marrying (Malt & Farquharson, 2012). The difficulty to commit not only comes from a desire to remain autonomous (Dickson et al., 2005; Malt & Farquharson, 2012), but also in accordance with social norms of how older adults should act in regard to romance (Aleman, 2003). Dating, however, provides a placeholder for such a commitment while giving emotional support necessary for elderly individuals' life satisfaction (Bulcroft & O'Conner, 1986; William, Locker, Briley, Ryan, & Scott, 2011).

ONLINE DATING AMONG LATER-LIFE ADULTS

It is no secret that social interactions, especially those romantic in nature, are changing as the Internet becomes more prevalent in society coupled with an increased broadmindedness toward sexual activity in the senior years. In addition, as relational support is a critical component of life satisfaction for older adults, the Internet is providing an opportunity for older adults to fulfill this need through seeking romantic partners online. Online dating has opened up a new world for single older adults. For example, Malt (2007) found older adults not only used computers and the Internet, but also that they used it frequently and with the same enthusiasm as most young people. On average older adults spend 5.4 hours a day online, with some spending as much as 8 hours a day online. In addition, while online, many later-life adults were actively involved in multiple online dating sites that resulted in face-to-face, lasting relationships (Malt, 2007).

Alterovitz and Mendelsohn (2009) examined online dating habits through identifying the desirable characteristics that online daters seek out. Most of their findings generalized across all the age groups with one significant difference in that older women continued to be more selective than men in later life. The researchers identified three other key factors in choosing a partner through online dating that were consistent across the lifespan: (1) women will seek older men, and older men will seek younger women, (2) throughout the lifespan, men more than women offer status-related information, while women as compared to men seek status-related information, and (3) throughout the lifespan, women identify physical attractiveness more than men, and men will seek physical attractiveness more than women (Alterovitz & Mendelsohn, 2009). These factors indicate that age does not have a profound effect on attraction or sexual activity among older adults. Finally, it was common across the lifespan for people to communicate as long as 3 months before meeting face-to-face. However, once they met, it was common to engage in sexual relations on the first date (Malt, 2007).

Not only do online relationships develop quickly once they meet face-to-face, but their quality also tends to be high. The meaningful and romantic relationships that many older adults develop online typically last on average for 6 years (Malt, 2007). It was also common for older adults to stay in unsatisfying relationships for about 4 months before officially terminating the relationship (Malt, 2007). This confirms that life stage may not be a factor that differentiates older and young adults who engage in online dating. While this study informs us on what people prefer in initiating later-life relationships, it does not examine how relational termination strategies differ across the life stages.

RELATIONSHIP TERMINATION AMONG ROMANTIC LATER-LIFE RELATIONSHIPS

Much of the termination research on older adults measures their response to interpersonal dilemmas and unpleasant social information in interpersonal encounters (Charles & Carstensen, 2008), not encounters specific to later-life romances. For example, many relationships traverse through Lee's (1984) five stages of relationship breakup including the discovery of dissatisfaction, exposure, negotiation, resolution, and transformation. However, the specific breakup strategies used vary by gender. For example, men are more likely than women to end a romantic relationship because of decreased physical attraction and attention as well as decreased sexual activities with his partner (Conlan, 2007). Conlan (2007) and others (Birditt & Fingerman, 2003) also suggested that women end a romantic relationship based on sensible factors such as a physical relocation and lack of accessibility of supportive resources, lack of perceived time invested by her partner, and a decrease in perceived protection by her partner. Ikkink and Tilbur (1999) suggested that the less support that was exchanged between individuals, the greater the chance of their relationship ending became. While these reasons for relational termination are common, much of the research on communication strategies used to dissolve romantic relationships examines young and middle-aged adults, again excluding older adults.

Similar to the desire for sexual intimacy, older adults also show a need for emotional intimacy. Literature on the subject of intimacy shows that romantic relationships are often viewed as a necessity among older adults post-divorce or in widowhood (Aleman, 2003). However, the reasons for this intimacy are different between the sexes. Alterovitz and Mendelsohn (2009) found men are more likely to commit to exclusively dating and remarrying, while women are more interested in remaining somewhat independent and having various romantic options available to them.

After reviewing all current research on the topic of relationship termination and older adult dating, it has become apparent that there is a lack of research on the strategies and tactics utilized in terminating intimate later-life relationships. The current research on later-life dating tends to focus on the initiation of such dating and the quality of the relationship. Often the research discusses the length of relationships and only briefly touches on strategies used and reasons for termination of the relationship.

A preliminary study has identified common trends in breakup strategies among later-life adults (Dickson, Ziegler, Greathouse, Burke, & Kohler, 2014). Analysis of this small data set indicated that there are clear patterns for how older adults dissolve their intimate relationships. The most common pattern involved a discussion stating that it was not working out and an agreement that the relationship would terminate. All of the descriptions of relationship terminations described a rational, calm encounter with no drama (as a study participant reported). In addition, some of the female study participants reported that having the relationship just wasn't worth it, and they should have just stayed with their female friends. While these results are preliminary, they are consistent with previous research that found that older couples typically do not engage in intense and volatile conflicts (Dickson et al., 2002).

LATER-LIFE SEXUAL ACTIVITY

A common myth portrays the late-life adults as asexual. Recent research, however, suggests that older adults are sexually active (Taylor & Gosney, 2011). Contrary to popular belief, many elderly are, or would like to be, sexually active. In a study by Ward, Disch, Levy, and Schensul (2004), nearly half of their 398 participants reported being sexually active (42%). In addition, Sormanti and Shibusawa (2007) found in their study of 1,280 women over the age of 50 that the majority reported sexual activity in the last 6 months. Ginsberg, Pomerantz, and Kramer-Freely's (2005) study on adults over the age of 60 found that the majority engaged in physical and/or sexual encounters in the last year. In a similar study, it was found that up to 65% of residents in a senior residence home had engaged in sexual intercourse in the last 6 months, and 20% of those over the age of 78 were sexually active (Nusbaum, Lenahan, & Sadovsky, 2005). Finally, Gott (2006) reported that 81.5% of adults over the age of 50 were involved in sexual relations, which also included unprotected sex with prostitutes.

Older adults are also more likely to have fewer reservations about sexual promiscuity once the need and ability to bear children is no longer a concern (Lindau et al., 2007), and they even participate in cybersex with their online partners (Malt, 2007). Current availability of prescription drugs utilized to improve the sex lives of older adults has opened the door to an active sex life, as well as increased knowledge of the sexual activity (Lindau et al., 2007). In addition, Lindau et al.'s (2007) research reported that even among participants between 75 and 85 years of age "54% of sexually active persons reported having sex at least two to three times per month, and 23% reported having sex once a week or more" (p. 768). Addis, Van Den Feden, Wassle-Fyr, Vittinghoff, Brown, and Brown (2006) report that 60% of their sample reported having sexual relations at least monthly while three-fourths of their sample reported that they were sexually active. They also found that women reported that the opportunity to have sex decreased with age, but there was little to no difference between the want for and satisfaction of these encounters (Addis et al., 2006). These studies demonstrate that sexual intimacy is an important component in the older adult's life.

Older single adults also engaged in risky sexual behavior (Coleman & Ball, 2007), such as unprotected sexual relations with multiple partners, putting them at risk for HIV/AIDS (Whipple & Scura, 1996). In addition, recent research has also indicated that irregular condom use, or barrier protection, was related to the amount of information older adults had regarding HIV/AIDS (Love et al., 2008). Therefore, it is not surprising that Simone and Applebaum (2008) found that 25% of those infected with HIV are over the age of 50, while Jacquescoley (2008) reported that for those over the age of 65, the number of HIV/AIDS cases has grown substantially in the last 10 years. These numbers indicate that sexually active later-life adults are not receiving information on HIV/AIDS prevention (Williams & Donnelly, 2002)

In addition to the risk for HIV/AIDS, later-life adults are also at risk for STDs. Emmers-Sommer, Nebel, Allison, Cannella, Cartmill, Ewing, Horvath,

Osborne, and Wojtaszek (2009) found that women age 18 to 60 were more proactive regarding their sexual health, decreasing their risk for STD. Grant and Ragsdale (2008) further posit that physicians report age as a factor for not including HIV/STD testing within the later-life population, in which they are assuming that their older single patients are not sexually active. In conclusion, research conducted by Morton, Kim, and Treise (2009) found that younger women, as compared to older women, are more aware of sexual health, behavior associated with protection, taking responsibility for finding sexual health information, and sexual health maintenance.

These studies demonstrate that older adults are sexually active and willing to participate in non-traditional sexual relations; however, they do not discuss the use of or engage in healthy sex practices, such as using barrier protection with intimate partners. They also do not discuss their activities with their health care providers and/or family members. Discussions of this topic with family members can provide the opportunity for sexual health education and emotional support.

FAMILY ISSUES WITH OLDER ADULTS

Despite the need for intimate relationships among single, later-life family members, many later-life daters face issues of family tension regarding their dating. Socially active later-life adults not only experience resistance and discomfort with their later-life romances from society, they also need to manage the reactions of their immediate family members. Since this is a fairly new phenomenon, few studies have examined the how families, specifically adult children, react to their later-life parents' dating and intimate relationships. An early study (Talbott, 1998) found that adult children create obstacles to their parent's dating and express hostility to the idea that their parent might "replace" the deceased or divorced parent. In addition, adult children had a difficult time viewing their later-life parent as sexually active or romantically involved (Alterovitz & Mendelsohn, 2013).

Through conducting several interviews within a retirement community, Aleman (2003) noted that the main reason later-life daters were hesitant to fully commit to romantic relationships was the result of experiencing thoughts and feelings about how their family might react to their re-partnering in their senior years. Other research supports these findings by documenting that many later-life parents avoid disclosing information about their dating with their family members with the fear that this discussion topic might cause conflict in the family (Miller, 2009). However, when researching how adult children respond to their parent's dating, some research shows that adult children are often more supportive than friends (Dickson et al., 2005). In addition, Hay, Fingerman, and Lefkowitz (2008) found that as adult children age and become more mature, they begin to care significantly more about the well-being and happiness of their later-life parent(s), regardless of the marital status of the parent. In other words, if dating makes their later-life parents happy, they accept that their single parent is involved in an intimate relationship.

Other studies have found that open and honest communication between the later-life dating adult and their adult children may even be beneficial to the health and lifestyle of the child. For example, Shimkowski and Schrodt (2012) found that there is a significant relationship between frequent, honest, and open communication between parents and their adult children's mental well-being and that this relationship becomes stronger as the adult child ages. This research also reported that the more the parent and child communicated effectively, the more understanding they showed for each other (Shimkowski & Schrodt, 2012). Interestingly enough, other research suggests that the more stress parents create for their adult children regarding their own romantic lives, the more likely it will be that the adult child will create a stressful and unhealthy romantic and marital situation for him- or herself later in life (Reczek, Lui, & Umberson, 2010). This idea supports the conclusion that openness and understanding in communication between the later-life parent and adult child is beneficial to the parent and adult child relationship. Everyone involved will experience the idea that the less stress later-life daters experience surrounding their romantic lives, the more beneficial the outcomes will be.

Finally, Dickson, Hsueh, O'Neil, Rapp, Shaw, and Shroyer (2013) conducted a study that examined the relationship between later-life dating parents and their adult children. The specific focus of the study was to examine the communicative reactions adult children expressed when learning about their later-life parent's dating. In this study, the majority of the later-life parents reported that they were extremely uncomfortable discussing their private dating experiences with their adult children despite having good health and a positive relationship with their adult child.

Four themes emerged from the qualitative interview data collected in the Dickson et al. study (2013): acceptance; concern; support; and withholding information. Acceptance was the most common theme that emerged, with older men in the study reporting that they received more acceptance from their adult children than did the older women. The majority of the study participants reported that their adult children said they accept that their parent is dating but that they do not want to know the details. Concern was the next most common theme, and it was a more common reaction among the older women than among the men. For example, adult children were worried about their parent's safety and the financial implications of re-partnering. Adult children made comments such as, "She is with you for your money and we are concerned about that." Or, "You don't want to take care of another man again, do you?" The third most common theme was support.

This theme again was experienced more by the women than the men. For example, older women reported that their adult children wanted to give them dating advice or help them prepare for a date. Both the men and women in the study reported that they felt supported when their adult children asked them about what they did on their dates, what the romantic partner was like, and whether they were ever going to meet this person. The final theme that emerged from the study was withholding information. In this theme, the later-life parents reported that they did not inform their adult children that they were dating or involved with someone. They reported that they were worried about conflict and how their adult children would react to this information. While this study concluded that it is important for later-life family members to feel that they can discuss their personal lives with their adult children and receive support, it is also possible that these kinds of discussions can lead to breaking down negative, inaccurate stereotypes about the single older adult's social and sexual life.

CONCLUSION

Traditionally, lifespan research has viewed the later-life adult as one in his or her decline, with a decrease in social activity. Recent research has shed new light on how to view the single later-life adult. The aging of the Baby Boomers has brought on a whole new definition of one's senior years. Aging Baby Boomers are healthy, active, social, and divorcing. These new socially active older adults are changing the definition of what it means to be aging. Medical professionals and family members need to adjust their views of older adults. As the research has demonstrated, traditional views of the asexual later-life adult are no longer relevant. We need to re-think stereotypes we have as well as negative attitudes about what it means to be old. Today we are finding that there is a new group of later-life adults who plan to live life to its fullest. We need to overcome older-adult stereotypes that limit our understanding of the complexity of intimate relationships in later life.

FUTURE RESEARCH DIRECTIONS

During the writing of this chapter, it became evident that there is a lack of communication-based research that explores interaction associated with and among the socially active later-life adult. For example, we know little about how families react to the socially active older family member and outcomes associated with those interactions. For example, does the older family member become more secretive because of concern over family reactions and does this pattern lead to family isolation? As we experience the graying of divorce, future research needs to examine the ways in which families manage and negotiate older family members' transition into singlehood. While this can be a time of crisis, it is important to understand the communication processes that occur with the older family member and outcomes associated with these processes. Are families providing support and understanding or are they isolating the newly divorced older family member and how does this relate to mental and physical health?

In addition, research can address the developmental process associated with later-life romance. Does it follow the same patterns that occur in younger relationships? In other words, how does life stage impact the ways in which later-life adults experience courtship, dating, romance, and even remarriage? Finally, research has indicated that people over the age of 60 are the group most at risk for STDs and HIV/AIDS. Research is needed on the development of successful health campaigns that can sensitize older adults to the health hazards of unprotected sexual intercourse.

Finally, research needs to examine how traditional attitudes about aging are no longer relevant. Initial research has indicated that the older single adult is healthier and socially active but older stereotypes are preventing them from receiving the support and attention needed from health care providers and family members. For example, medical health care providers typically do not ask the older patient whether he or she is sexually active. This is making the diagnosis of STDs or HIV/AIDS more difficult, resulting in a delay of any necessary treatment.

In conclusion, the communication dynamics associated with the socially and sexually active adult is an understudied area. Research in this area can help us to improve our family relationships, help older adults manage intimate relationships in later life, and improve health care among older adults.

REFERENCES

Addis, I. B., Van Den Feden, S. K., Wassel-Fyr, C. L., Vittinghoff, E., Brown, J. S., Thom, D. H., & Reproductive Risk Factors for Incontinence Study at Kaiser (RRISK) Study Group. (2006). Sexual activity and function in middle-aged and older women. *Obstetric Gynecology, 107*(4), 755–764.

Aleman, M. (2003). "You should get yourself a boyfriend" but "let's not get serious": Communicating a code of romance in a retirement community. *Qualitative Research Reports in Communication, 4*, 31–37.

Aleman, M. (2005). Embracing and resisting romantic fantasies as the rhetorical vision on a Senior-Net discussion board. *Journal of Communication, 55*(1), 5–21.

Alterovitz, S. R., & Mendelsohn, G. A. (2009). Partner preferences across the life span: Online dating by older adults. *Psychology and Aging, 24*(2), 513–517. doi:10.1037/a0015897

Altervoitz, S. R., & Mendelsohn, G. A. (2013). Relationship goals for middle-aged, young-old, and old-old Internet daters: An analysis of online dating adds. *Journal of Aging Studies, 27*, 159–165.

Antonucci, T., & Akiyama, A. (1995). Convoys of social relationships: Family and friendships within a life span context. In R. Blieszner & V. H. Bedford (Eds.), *Handbook of aging and the family* (4th ed., pp. 355–371). Westport, CT: Greenwood Press.

Beckman, N., Waern, M., Gustafson, D., & Skoog, I. (2008). Secular trends in self-reported sexual activity and satisfaction in Swedish 70 year olds: Cross section of four populations. *British Medical Journal, 337*, 1971–2001.

Birditt, K. S., & Fingerman, K. L. (2003). Age and gender differences in adults' descriptions of emotional reactions to interpersonal problems. *Journal of Gerontology, 58*(4), 237–245.

Bulcroft, K., & O'Conner, M. (1986). The importance of dating relationships on quality of life for older persons. *Family Relations, 35*(3), 397–401.

Cali, B. E., Coleman, J. M., & Campbell, C. (2013). Stranger danger? Women's self-protection intent and the continuing stigma of online dating. *Cyberpsychology, Behavior & Social Networking, 16*(12), 853–857. doi:10.1089/cyber.2012.0512

Carr, D. (2004). The desire to date and remarry among older widows and widowers. *Journal of Marriage and the Family, 66*(4), 1051–1068.

Carstensen, L. (1992). Social and emotional patterns in adulthood: Social support for socioemotional selectivity theory. *Psychology and Aging, 7*, 331–338.

Charles, S. T., & Carstensen, L. L. (2008). Unpleasant situations elicit different emotional responses in younger and older adults. *Psychology and Aging, 23*(3), 495–504. doi:10.1037//a0013284

Chipperfield, G., & Havens, B. (2007). Gender differences in the relationship between marital status transitions and life satisfaction in later life. *Journal of Gerontology, 56*(3), 176–186.

Coleman, C. L., & Ball, K. (2007). Determinants of perceived barriers to condom use among HIV-infected middle-aged and older African-American men. *Journal of Advanced Nursing, 60*(4), 368–376.

Conlan, S. K. (2007). *Romantic relationship termination*. Austin: University of Texas Press.

Cooney, T. M., & Dunne, K. (2001). Intimate relationships in later life: Current realities, future prospects. *Journal of Family Issues, 22*(7), 838–858.

Dickson, F. C., & Hughes, P. (2015). Aging families and family communication. In L. H. Turner & R. West (Eds.), *The Sage Handbook of Family Communication* (pp. 263-275). Thousand Oaks, CA: Sage.

Dickson, F. C., Hsueh, S., O'Neil, K., Rapp, G., Shaw, L., & Shroyer, J. (2013). *Difficult conversations between later-life adults and their adult children: An analysis of later-life dating discussions*. Paper presented at the annual meeting of the National Communication Association, Washington, DC.

Dickson, F. C., Hughes, P. C., Manning, L. D., Walker, K. L., Bollis-Pecci, T., & Gratson, S. D. (2002). Conflict in long-term, later-life married couples. *Southern Communication Journal, 67*, 110–121.

Dickson, F. C., Hughes, P. C., & Walker, K. L. (2005). An exploratory investigation into dating among later-life women. *Western Journal of Communication, 69*(1), 67–82.

Dickson, F. C., Zielger, K., Greathouse, L., Burke, B., & Kohler, T. (2014). *Communication strategies used in the termination of later-life romantic relationships*. Manuscript in progress, Chapman University, Orange, CA.

Dickson-Markman, F., & Shern, D. (1990). Social support and health among the elderly. *Journal of Applied Communication Research, 18*, 49–63.

Emmers-Sommer, T. M., Nebel S., Allison, M., Cannella, M. L., Cartmill, D., Ewing, S., Horvath, D., Osborne, J. K., & Wojtaszek, B. (2009). Patient–provider communication about sexual health: The relationship with gender, age, gender-stereotypical beliefs, and perceptions of communication inappropriateness. *Sex Roles, 60*(9), 615–763.

Gibson, H. B. (1993). Emotional and sexual adjustment in later life. In S. Arber & M. Evanrou (Eds.), *Aging, independence and the life course* (pp. 104–118). London, England: Jessica Kingley.

Ginsberg, H. B., Pomerantz, S. C., & Kramer-Feeley, V. (2005). Sexuality in older adults: Behaviors and preferences. *Age and Aging, 34,* 475–480.

Glass, J. J., & Jolly, G. R. (1997). Satisfaction in later life among women 60 or over. *Educational Gerontology, 23*(4), 297.

Gott, M. (2006). Sexual health and the new ageing. *Age and Aging, 35,* 106–107.

Grant, K., & Ragsdale, K. (2008). Sex and the "recently single": Perceptions of sexuality and HIV risk among mature women and primary care physicians. *Culture, Health & Sexuality, 10*(5), 495–511.

Hay, E. L., Fingerman, K. L., & Lefkowitz, E. S. (2008). The worries adult children and their parents experience for one another. *International Journal of Aging and Human Development, 67*(2), 101–127.

Ikkink, K., & Tilburg, T. (1999). Broken ties: Reciprocity and other factors affecting the termination of older adults' relationships. *Social Networks, 21*(2), 131–146.

Jacquescoley, E. (2008). Behavioral prevention study gauges HIV/AIDS and depression in the older US population. *AIDS Care, 20*(9), 1152–1153.

Lee, L. (1984). Sequences in separation: A framework for investigating ending of the personal (romantic) relationship. *Journal of Social and Personal Relationships, 1*(1), 49–73.

Li, L. W., & Liang, J. (2007). Social exchanges and subjective well-being among older Chinese: Does age make a difference? *Psychology and Aging, 22*(2), 386–391.

Lindau, S. T., Schumm, L. P., Laumann, E. O., Levinson, W., O'Muircheartaigh, C. A., & Waite, L. J. (2007). A study of sexuality and health among older adults in the United States. *New England Journal of Medicine, 357*(8), 762–774.

Love, T. I., Heckman, T. G., Sikkema, K. J., Hensen, N. B., Kockman, A., Suhr, J. A., Garske, J. P., & Johnson, C. J. (2008). Patterns and correlates of sexual activity and condom use behavior in persons 50-plus years of age living with HIV/AIDS. *AIDS Behavior, 12*(6), 943–956.

Malt, S. (2007). Love actually! Older adults and their romantic Internet relationships. *Australian Journal of Emerging Technologies & Society, 5*(2), 84–102.

Malt, S., & Farquharson, K. (2012). The initiation and progression of late-life romantic relationships. *Journal of Sociology, 49*(4), 1–15. doi:10.1177/1440783312442254

Miller, A. E. (2009). Revealing and concealing post-marital dating information: Divorced coparents' privacy rule development and boundary coordination processes. *Journal of Family Communication, 9,* 135–149.

Morton, C. R., Kim, H., & Treise, D. (2009). *Sex after 50: A qualitative study on mature women's sexual health attitudes and beliefs.* Paper presented at the meeting of the International Communication Association. Chicago.

Nusbaum, M. R. H., Lenahan, P., & Sadovsky, R. (2005). Sexual health in aging men and women: Addressing the physiologic and psychological sexual changes that occur with age. *Geriatrics, 60,* 18–23.

Pinquart, M., & Sorensen, S. (2001). Influences on loneliness in older adults: A meta-analysis. *Basic and Applied Social Psychology, 23*(4), 245–266.

Reczek, C., Liu, H., & Umberson, D. (2010). Just the two of us? How parents influence adult children's marital quality. *Journal of Marriage and Family, 72*(5), 1205–1219.

Shimkowski, R. J., & Schrodt, P. (2012). Coparental communication as a mediator of interparental conflict and young adult children's mental well-being. *Communication Monographs, 79*(1), 48–71.

Simone, M. J., & Applebaum, J. (2008). HIV in older adults. *Geriatrics, 63*(12), 6–12.

Sormanti, M., & Shibusawa, T. (2007). Predictors of condom use and HIV testing among midlife and older women seeking medical services. *Journal of Aging and Health, 19*, 705–719.

Stephure, R. J., Boon, S. D., MacKinnon, S. L., & Deveau, V. L. (2009). Internet initiated relationships: Associations between age and involvement in online dating. *Journal of Computer-Mediated Communication, 14*, 658–681.

Talbott, M. M. (1998). Older widows' attitudes toward men and remarriage. *Journal of Aging Studies, 12*(4), 429–449.

Taylor, A., & Gosney, M. A. (2011). Sexuality in older age: Essential considerations for healthcare professionals. *Age and Aging, 40*, 538–543.

Troll, L. E. (1994). Family connectedness of older women: Attachment in later life. In B. I. Turner & L. E. Troll (Eds.), *Women growing older*. Thousand Oaks, CA: Sage.

U.S. Census Bureau. (2001). *The 65 years and over population: Census 2000 brief*. Washington, DC: U.S. Government Printing Office.

U.S. population predictions. (2008). Retrieved April 04, 2012, from http://www.census.gov/population/www/projections/summarytables.html

Ward, E., Disch, W. B., Levy, J., & Schensul, J. (2004). Perceptions of HIV/AIDS risk among urban, low-income senior housing residents. *AIDS Education and Prevention, 16*(6), 571–588

Whipple, B., & Scura, K. W. (1996). The overlooked epidemic: HIV in older adults. *American Journal of Nursing, 96*, 123–126.

William, D. M., Locker, L. Jr., Briley, K., Ryan, R., & Scott, A. J. (2011). What do older adults seek in their potential romantic partners? Evidence from online personal ads. *International Journal of Aging and Human Development, 72*(1), 67-82.

Williams E., & Donnelly, J. (2002). Older Americans and AIDS: Some guidelines for prevention. *Social Work, 47*(2), 105–110.

CHAPTER TWENTY

Health Care Interactions in Older Adulthood

CARLA L. FISHER AND MOLLIE ROSE CANZONA

The United States Census Bureau (2010) reported that in the past decade or so, the older adult population (individuals aged 65 and older) grew at a faster rate than the general population. One of the most significant segments of the population, the Baby Boomer generation (children born 1946–1964), began entering "old age" when they turned 65 in 2011. By 2031, the entire cohort will be in their golden years with the early-born Boomers reaching the age of 85. While some media and scholars assert that this generation of aging people will be among the wealthiest, healthiest, most independent, and active in history, others wager that Baby Boomers will tax the health care system by demanding more services to treat a multitude of ailments, chronic illness, and a longer lifespan (Wister, 2005).

What is certain, however, is that one of the largest groups of the world's population is now considered to be "old age," and, regardless of whether or not they are generally healthy, older adults spend more time interacting with health practitioners or within the health care system than any other age group (Hartman, Catlin, Lassman, Cylus, & Heffler, 2008). Moreover, health care interactions are not limited to the health care setting. A significant portion of older adults' everyday talk with friends and family members is centered on health-related issues (Nussbaum, 1989). Family members are often involved in aging loved ones' later-life care, and familial bonds are a source of support critical to their well-being (Edwards, 2001). Given this and the aging Baby Boomer cohort, health care interaction in older adulthood is an especially prominent social issue in today's world.

This chapter explores the nature, importance, and prominence of health care interactions in older adulthood. Both formal (e.g., provider-patient) and informal (e.g., communication in the family) health care interactive experiences in older adults' social network are important to their ability to successfully age or maximize wellness socially, physically, cognitively, and emotionally. Successful aging is in part tied to communication wellness in these multiple health-related contexts (Nussbaum & Fisher, 2011). Accordingly, special attention is also paid to communication competence issues that are critical to successful aging. These include the difficulty of receiving and providing geriatric medicine, challenges associated with intergenerational provider-patient communication, the role of everyday health interactions and intimacy, the importance of family social support, as well as caregiving interactions or future planning for care needs.

INTERACTING WITH PROVIDERS AND THE HEALTH CARE SYSTEM: THE OLDER ADULT PATIENT

The World Health Organization (WHO, 2007) asserts that since Medicare was passed in the 1960s, older adults not only live longer but also are collectively healthier after the age of 65. Even though the majority of older adults in developed countries are in good health, they will deal with more health care issues than other age categories. According to the American Geriatric Society, older adults are hospitalized more often than younger patients and also have extended hospital stays (Pritchett, 2000; see also Thompson, Robinson, & Beisecker, 2004). The Centers for Disease Control and Prevention (CDC) reported in 2012 that in the preceding 12-month period, nearly 25% of adults over the age of 65 had 10 or more health care visits to physicians, emergency rooms, and/or specialists. By and large, older adults comprise a majority of health care interactive encounters.

Formal health care interactions in older adulthood are not only abundant but also complicated. This is partially due to the complexity of providing geriatric care. In addition to having acute health experiences (e.g., diagnosis of a disease or illness; emergent health events like a heart attack), older patients often exhibit more chronic health ailments simultaneously and, therefore, may require ongoing care for a multitude of issues. According to Researchers at Johns Hopkins University, an overwhelming majority (82%) of Medicare beneficiaries manage at least one chronic condition, and the number of conditions they must concurrently cope with increases markedly with age (Wolff, Starfield, & Anderson, 2002). Recent research shows that 52% of patients over the age of 65 report two or more chronic conditions (Chen & Landefeld, 2007), which may necessitate complex treatment regimens. Thus, regardless of whether or not their care is coordinated or interdisciplinary, older adults' health interactions typically overlap multiple systems or types of care.

To ensure they maximize their ability to successfully age, older adults must learn to interact with various providers (e.g., physicians, nurses, nurse practitioners, physician assistants, pharmacists, nutritionists) within multiple organizations, a notably difficult task for a patient of any age. Both older adult patients and their medical providers have difficulty navigating these current, fractured systems of care. Little coordination between various health professionals and the patient is common owing to structural barriers in health care. Furthermore, research has shown that when older adults present multiple chronic conditions within a health care interaction, health professionals can be confused (Gross, 2006). This confusion about older patients' multiple chronic conditions can result in numerous problems that ultimately impede the delivery of quality geriatric care. For instance, misunderstandings and miscommunications during health care interactions can result in misdiagnoses, time delays that cause serious additional consequences, and polypharmacy (i.e., too many drugs being prescribed; Gross, 2006).

Provider training may play a role in these communication challenges in older adults' health interactions. Surprisingly, even though other age segments of the population (for instance, pediatrics) have been recognized as specialties in the medical field for more than a century, the intricacy of geriatric medicine is still underappreciated as it is considered only a subspecialty. As a result, only a minute group of medical schools even require a geriatric rotation (Nussbaum, Baringer, Fisher, & Kundrat, 2007; Nussbaum & Fisher, 2009). While geriatric-focused elective courses, seminars, or continuing education are growing in some disciplines (e.g., nursing), the collective lack of specialized geriatric training for health professionals, most notably physicians, may contribute to a lack of communication competence in providing care for older adults. At the same time, this lack of training can perpetuate providers' inexperience in coordinating a defining and necessary feature of older adults' medical experiences: communication among the various systems involved in geriatric care.

Managing Multiple Providers, Settings, and Organizations

The complicated nature of older adults' health-related needs heightens the value of using an interdisciplinary or multidisciplinary team approach within geriatric medicine. This approach toward team care, a positive feature of the managed care revolution within the United States, is quickly becoming the standard of care for the aging population (Nussbaum, Pecchioni, & Crowell, 2001).

A multidisciplinary approach to care allots professionals at different levels of training from different fields the opportunity to benefit from each other's knowledge (Abramson & Mizrahi, 1996; Edwards & Smith, 1998). This is essential for older adult patients who must cope with multiple and diverse medical issues warranting treatment from different specialists. Moreover, when this approach is competently implemented it aids practitioners' ability to communicate with patients, to communicate with each other within the care system, and to coordinate communication with providers from diverse organizations. Ultimately, when team care approaches involve the older adult patient, the quality of care is positively impacted. The benefits of group decision-making approaches also extend to other care settings like institutionalized living for older adults. A recent study in England demonstrated that when older adult residents of long-term residential homes are included in decision making with regard to their living environment, they not only feel empowered, but they also become more engaged, happier, and healthier (Knight, Haslam, & Haslam, 2010).

Providing interdisciplinary care and being a member of a multidisciplinary health care team can be challenging for both providers and patients. Professionals on health care teams must become individually competent in an entirely new set of communication skills to ensure quality care, including small-group and organizational communication skills in multiparty interactions. Without these intergroup communication skills, the efficacy of the team in providing quality care can be jeopardized. In line with this view, Nussbaum and Fisher (2009) proposed a new model of geriatric care that is patient centered with communication at the forefront of quality care. In this model, proficient delivery of geriatric care is characterized by successful communication among the older adult patient and three intra-dependent systems: health care professionals, health care organizations, and family/friends.

All of the providers involved in older adult patients' care (e.g., physicians, therapists, nurses, social workers, pharmacists) must share information and circumvent barriers to communication caused by medical hierarchy, disciplinary walls, or structural hindrances. Additionally, providing quality care to older patients is predicated upon proficient inter-institutional communication. Medical clinics, hospitals, continuing care facilities, insurance companies, independent therapy clinics, as well as federal, state, and local government agencies each have unique missions and protocols for operating that must be navigated and coordinated on some level. Finally, competent communication is needed with the older adult's family members and other intimate connections. These individuals must be incorporated into formal health care interactions as they are largely involved in older adults' well-being and care, playing roles like health advocate, companion at appointments, caregiver, and decision maker. Ultimately, competent inter-organizational and intra-communication must take place among the geriatric patient and three communication systems.

At the later end of the lifespan, individuals must manage ongoing chronic health issues, both old and new, as well as acute health experiences. Older adult health interactions are exemplified by difficulties associated with managing multiple conditions and a larger, fractured network of care. To ensure successful aging, it is equally important for both providers and older adults to appreciate the unique interpersonal communication dynamics characterizing their interactions.

INTERPERSONAL COMMUNICATION DYNAMICS AMONG PROVIDERS AND OLDER ADULT PATIENTS

A myriad of factors including variant physical or biological changes, physiology, environmental and lifestyle considerations, education, and income impact the nature of health in adulthood and, thus, communication with providers (Merluzzi & Nairn, 1999). While these differences affect the issues older adults present with, some common interpersonal communication dynamics warrant attention to ensure providers and older adults collectively facilitate quality communication.

Aging Losses, Ageist Stereotypes, and Paternalism

Aging is marked for some individuals by losses. Physiological losses with one's senses (e.g., hearing and vision), cognition (e.g., decline in memory or processing speeds), and function (e.g., limited mobility) can complicate older adult-provider interactions (see Thompson, Robinson, & Beisecker, 2004). For instance, information processing and memory retrieval may take longer for older adults (Sparks & Nussbaum, 2008), meaning they may require more interaction time in comparison to younger patients. For older adults who experience dementia or Alzheimer's disease (AD), the communication changes impeding health care interactions are especially noticeable and challenging. Dementia or AD patients tend to rely more on verbal behavior, use fewer statements or longer utterances, and ask more questions (Ripich, Carpenter, & Ziol, 1997), challenges that can be taxing on providers' time but certainly warranted to ensure quality care.

Still, older adults age differently, so not all elderly patients exhibit the same losses. Likewise, it is important that providers not presume all older patients have losses (an aging stereotype) as ageist communication practices like patronizing behavior (e.g., conversing with an older adult patient as one would with a child) may result. Health care workers may be especially susceptible to ageism because of their exposure to ailing older patients (Adelman, Greene, & Charon, 1991; Lookinland & Anson, 1995). Ageism is often examined through the lens of communication accommodation theory (CAT; Giles, Coupland, & Coupland, 1991). This framework is useful in linking aging stereotypes and older patient-provider interaction and indicates that because providers and patients are of two different social groups (and often in different age groups/generations), each party may change their communicative behavior to accommodate the other person because they feel they do not have much in common. Providers who exhibit ageist beliefs, attitudes, or assumptions tend to either overaccommodate older patients (for instance, they assume the patient is cognitively limited and use simplified speech or speak slowly) or underaccommodate them (they stick to "safe topics" and avoid dissatisfying conversations; Wright et al., 2013). Over- and underaccommodating communication results in patients of any age feeling dissatisfied with care or silenced. It is critical that providers be aware of any ageist assumptions they have of older patients to ensure quality care.

Providers may also need to be careful not to assume all older patients prefer an authoritative communication style, and older adults should be aware of the implications linked to this approach. Traditionally, past research shows that elderly patients tend to have paternalistic views of medical providers, particularly physicians (Wright, Sparks, & O'Hair, 2013). They tend to ask fewer questions and express fewer complaints or misunderstandings in comparison to younger patients (Adelman et al., 1991). Given this, older patients may be less assertive during health care interactions and prefer a more authoritative provider.

This approach can be problematic for older adult patients. Assertive behavior in health care interactions (e.g., asking questions) is also associated with getting more information (Beisecker, 1988), something older adults need to effectively manage their often complicated medical needs (and adhere to prescription regimens; Rost, Carter, & Inui, 1989). Unfortunately, even though older adults may want more information they typically do not receive it unless they introduce the topic themselves (Street, 1991). Older adults' paternalistic attitudes about physicians or preferred authoritative communication style likely contribute to these dynamics. Still, this defining characteristic of older adult-provider communication may be changing. Bradley, Spark, and Nesdale (2001) found no significant differences between younger and older patient groups' satisfaction with an authoritative physician communication style. These scholars suggest that as social norms shift, future generations of older adults may be embracing ideas like patient autonomy and empowerment.

Narrative Communication and Disclosure

While losses are a part of aging, so too are gains. Older adults increase their communication competence across the lifespan and can gain new skills to adjust for losses (Baltes, 1987; Nussbaum et al., 2000; Pecchioni, Wright, & Nussbaum, 2005). Undoubtedly, the knowledge older adults gained through years of experience in health care interactions might also be helpful (Woodwell & Cherry, 2004). Older adults also exhibit more narrative competence (e.g., ability to process and recall narrative) in comparison to younger individuals (Sparks & Nussbaum, 2008). Older adults' narrative communication competence seems especially important to a higher quality provider-patient interaction. Studies suggest that older adults want their personal biographies acknowledged and valued as a foundation for their care (Nolan, Davies, & Grant, 2001). This research further supports a need for providers to allow older patients to discuss health issues and concerns using a storied approach or to embed their medical concerns into a larger life story narrative.

Still, this approach may cause problems for older adults when interacting with providers. Since their concerns are often intricately woven into a larger narrative, it can take older adults longer to clarify the reason for their visit, ask questions, or fully voice their concerns (Nussbaum & Fisher, 2009). Appointment lengths vary, but most providers must divide limited clinic time into time slots as short as fifteen minutes (Gupta & Denton, 2008). Restricted appointment times are less conducive to narrative approaches to health interactions and, therefore, may obstruct older patients' ability to express their concerns. This is further concerning given that some research suggests providers typically spend less time with older patients (Haug & Ory, 1987). In Vieder, Krafchick, Kovach, and Galluzzi's (2002) study of older patients, time constraints contributed to feelings of being "rushed" and were cited repeatedly as significant barriers to communication. Older adult patients report feeling less able to express psychosocial concerns with providers (a critical component to successful aging/older adult health), and this is particularly true when they feel rushed or when they perceive physicians are not invested in what they are saying (Greene, Adelman, Friedman, & Charon, 1994). This is problematic given that older adults disclose less personal information in general, and physiological, financial, and social challenges of aging increase vulnerability to depression and associated psychological problems (Williams, Haskard, & DiMatteo, 2007). Collectively this research is suggestive that narrative preferences in later life, providers' time constraints, and the critical need for an interaction in which patients readily disclose all must be carefully negotiated during provider-older adult interactions.

Presence of a Companion

Another social reality of older adult health interactions is the presence of a third party in the medical visit. Older patients often come to appointments with a loved one who is involved in managing their care on some level. The presence of a third party in formal health care interactions can be complex, but loved ones often play a crucial and beneficial role. Family members and loved ones can assist patients by acting as a memory aid and ensuring psychosocial concerns are attended to by providers (Nussbaum & Fisher, 2009). Research has shown that older adults' companions can also function as a "watchdog" (provide more information to providers), as a "significant other" (offer feedback about health care to both patient and provider), and as a "surrogate" patient (talking more during a health care interaction than the patient; Beisecker & Thompson, 1995).

However, third parties in clinical interactions may create complications related to issues of independence and dependence, competing needs, and privacy (Cicirelli, 1992; Hummert & Morgan, 2001; Greene, Adelman, Friedmann, & Charon, 1994). As older adults become less independent, their children, spouse, and other loved ones may begin to guide their medical decision making. Older patients and their family members may have conflicting beliefs about the older adult's care, which can make medical decision making difficult (Cicirelli, 1992). Specifically, attitudes regarding autonomy and paternalism may clash when considering the welfare of the older patient (Hummert & Morgan, 2001). Further, the presence of a third party may inhibit the patient's ability to communicate sensitive medical needs. It is essential that patients have private time with physicians so that they may discuss potentially private matters (Greene et al., 1994).

In their recent review of adult patient-provider-companion scholarship, Laidsaar-Powell and colleagues (2013) translate the research into provider practice implications central to facilitating successful triadic communication. Specifically, providers should be aware of their own behavior toward the companion and encourage older adult patients' companion's involvement in the medical appointment. Providers should, however, begin by clarifying and collectively agreeing on the companion's role and what constitutes helpful medical companion behavior. At the same time, providers should be aware of the patient's preferences for companion involvement, seek opportunities to communicate sensitive information to patients privately, and be aware of the older adult's companion's involvement in medical decisions both in the health care setting and at home.

While the interpersonal dynamics of provider-patient encounters can be challenging to negotiate and manage for both parties, older adults do not experience all health care interactions in the formal health setting or with professional providers. A significant portion of older adults' health care experiences occur in their larger social network or with friends, family, and other loved ones. According to the American Association of Retired Persons (AARP), National Alliance for Caregiving (NAC), and the United Nations (UN), the involvement of family members in the care of older adults is a worldwide reality that cuts across socioeconomic status, race and ethnicity, as well as developed and developing countries (AARP, NAC, & UN Program on Ageing, 2008; UN, 2007).

HEALTH CARE INTERACTION AMONG OLDER PATIENTS AND THEIR LOVED ONES

The informal settings of family and friendship communication should not be overlooked in understanding the complexity of older adults' health care interactions. Socioemotional selectivity theory (SST), a lifespan developmental psychology theory of social behavior, suggests that as we age, our social networks become smaller, and emotional well-being is increasingly important to successful aging (Carstensen, 1991, 1992). Therefore, emotional goals central to wellness are prioritized and attained through communication in close, intimate bonds with which we have a longer relational history, like friends and family (Carstensen, 1991, 1992). A recent study framed by SST indicated that as healthy women age and enter old age, they not only increasingly prefer communication in close relationships, but also prioritize communication specifically with family members rather than other loved ones (Fisher & Nussbaum, in press). The parent-child bond is especially critical to older adults' well-being. Intimacy between parents and children persists into adulthood and well across the lifespan (Nussbaum, Miller-Day, & Fisher, 2009; Pecchioni et al., 2005). The functioning of this tie is critical to their health given it is a source of affect and mutual aid, which is heightened as older adults experience health complications (Pecchioni et al., 2005). The sibling bond can also experience renewed emotional closeness in later life, particularly after the loss of one's spouse (Cicirelli, 1989). Just the availability of these family ties is linked to keeping older adults at home and out of medical institutions (Hanson & Sauer, 1985). The family environment is, thus, both meaningful and critical to older adults' health.

Several areas of informal and often more intimate health care communication are a significant aspect of older adults' ability to successfully age. Everyday talk for later-life adults can be centered on health-related issues, as loved ones are an important source of intimacy, influence, and social support in their lives. Additionally, older adults' intimate relationships play a notable role in medical decision making as well as their later-life care.

Everyday Health Interactions, Care Transitions, and Social Support

Health is a critical element of any aged individual's everyday living or livelihood. Health is a component of our conversational topics, and the family environment is typically the first exposure individuals have to learning health behaviors (Pecchioni et al., 2005). This does not change during later adulthood. Communication with family and loved ones plays a prominent role in older adults' health-related behaviors. For instance, adherence to medical regimens is associated with family cohesion, less family conflict, and living with a family member (DiMatteo, 2004). On a daily basis, family members might also provide older adults with task assistance with basic activities of daily living (ADLs) like bathing, dressing, eating, and mobility as well as instrumental activities of daily living (IADLs) like housework, transportation, and finances. Family members who provide task assistances with ADLs or IADLs also tend to accompany older adults to multiple medical appointments over the long term and are more involved in those health interactions (Wolff et al., 2012).

In essence, these family members are providing social support to older adults in various health contexts. Social support is the giving and receiving of various types of resources like emotional (nurturance, love, concern), informational (knowledge about issues), and instrumental (task-oriented help like financial assistance or transportation) support. Social support is strongly linked to better physical, mental, and social well-being for adults in later adulthood. To ensure that social support enacted by families is health promoting, support should provide older adults with intimacy, cohesion, or a sense of belonging, and should increase their competence or self-efficacy (Berkman, 2005). Helpful social support serves as a protective buffering from stress and is a significant factor in facilitating healthy functioning of older adults (Antonucci & Jackson, 1987; Carstensen, 1993). It is also critical to older adults' ability to remain in their own homes living independently, particularly after experiencing aging-related decline or managing multiple chronic conditions (Hummert & Morgan, 1999, 2001). Given this, one key to successful aging or resiliency in later life are benefits associated with familial and community social support (Nussbaum, Pecchioni, Robinson, and Thompson, 2000).

Social support from family is critical to older adults' ability to manage acute and chronic conditions. Familial emotional support has been linked with older adults' ability to cope with acute health experiences in later life such as a life-threatening breast cancer diagnosis (e.g., Fisher, 2010). Emotional support has even been linked to decreased risk of death in surviving acute threats like a myocardial infarction (e.g., Berkman, Leo-Summers, & Horwitz, 1992). More tangible support from families is also critical to older adults' self-management of chronic conditions like diabetes, arthritis, and heart disease. A recent review showed that the support older adults receive from loved ones in managing such conditions could serve as a motivating factor. Familial support impacted older adults' ability to manage medications, engage in healthy diets and physical activity, make medical decisions, deal with doctor appointments, and psychosocially cope with their ailment (Gallant, Spitze, & Prohaska, 2007).

However, familial support may also hinder older adults' health care. As such, support communication must be carefully enacted. For instance, for later-life adult women diagnosed with breast cancer, emotional support from their adult daughters is particularly helpful to their ability to cope with the illness but only when daughters are also respectful of their mother's need for privacy at times (e.g., not pressuring her to disclose all the time or when she does not want to; Fisher, 2010). The need for privacy among older adult women may be linked to that generation's socialization traditionally being less open or less encouraged to disclose, especially about health, in comparison to younger generations who have grown up in a social world that more often encourages and accepts openness. Additionally, when managing chronic conditions, unhelpful support may be more common from adult children (in comparison to spouses or siblings). Gallant and colleagues (2007) identified a "lack of understanding" on the part of adult children when unhelpful support behavior was enacted. Also, when aging parents observed that their adult child was being overprotective and trying to control their care, they perceived the support as not helpful given it infringed on their independence.

A recent review of scholarship showed that family support is also important during some health care transitions that older adults encounter in later life. Specifically, families play important roles when helping older adults transition from one care environment to a new setting, from one provider to another health professional, and from one level of care needs to another (Gitlin & Wolff, 2011). Family members are typically involved in key tasks associated with these transitions including managing medications and symptoms, advocating and attending provider visits, and preparing for and coordinating care. In their discussion of implications for patients and families, Gitlin and Wolff (2011) also identify communication skills family members need to successfully help facilitate their older loved one's care transitions. These core competencies include communicating effectively, problem solving, advocacy, conflict management, care coordination, and taking care of oneself.

Health Care Decision Making

Older adults' families also play a prominent role in their medical decision making. Older adults engage in informal health decision making with family members about advance care directives, treatment or care plans, residential care transitions, and age-related lifestyle changes (Hummert & Morgan, 2001). Shared decision making can be a bumpy process for families, and the children of older adult patients often have the most involvement in health care decision making (Cicirelli, 1992). Adult children's influence is even more significant when an older parent is single or widowed (Pratt & Jones-Aust, 1993). Issues of control, paternalism, and dependence are always at the forefront of these family discussions. Family members must carefully communicate in ways that do not threaten the older adult's autonomy, as a sense of control and independence is core to their ability to maintain mental health (Cicirelli, 1992; Heckhausen & Schulz, 1995).

Families and older adults should be careful to navigate decision making as a form of negotiation. In their review of previous research and their own aging scholarship, Hummert and Morgan (2001) offer families suggestions about communication strategies to both avoid and implement to better ensure successful interaction results. For instance, the adult child of an older adult parent should not assume all control over decisions as doing so is associated with poorer health for aging adults. Ideally, older adults should make primary decisions before a crisis occurs (e.g., stroke impeding an older adult's cognitive ability to make decisions), and their children should support these decisions by providing social support as the decision is made.

Caregiving Communication

Families are also often involved in providing care to their aging loved ones. While adult daughters or other women in the family are more likely to serve as an informal caregiver in our society, older adults with illness, limited mobility, or chronic conditions that require long-term care typically receive assistance from some member of their family (Bethea, 2002). The number of families providing informal care is expected to increase with the aging population increase.

Providing care to a loved one is rich with rewards, but families must also be prepared to face relational communication challenges and renegotiate relational dynamics. For marital couples, it is not uncommon for their marriage satisfaction to suffer when one partner begins caring for the other (Bethea, 2002; Williams & Nussbaum, 2001). This is likely tied to dyadic communication changes that occur as their relational communication is replaced with health-focused communication (Bethea, 2002). Also, spousal and other familial caregivers are not trained or experienced in the skills required for providing care. It is not surprising then that conflict is not uncommon when adult children assume care of their aging parent, and they must renegotiate issues of power (Nussbaum et al., 2000).

One approach to minimizing the stress associated with caregiving in later adulthood is to plan for a loved one's care well before it is needed. Future planning for care needs can allow families and older adults to be better prepared and ensure the older adult's health care preferences are prioritized and upheld. Unfortunately, most older adults and family members do not engage in discussions about future care needs and preferences prior to imminent need, even though this behavior is strongly advocated for by aging groups like the AARP. Older adults have expressed wanting to avoid such topics because of discomfort, to minimize conflict, or not to be perceived by family as a burden (Cicirelli, 1993). Adult children report wanting to avoid topics associated with their parents' future mortality (Hummert & Morgan, 2001). Fowler and Fisher (2009) found older parents who have engaged in these discussions also expected they would need care in the future, had aging-related anxiety, feared becoming a burden to their children, and preferred to make decisions for themselves independently. Adult children who reported having these discussions held beliefs that parents and children should make important decisions about the parents' future together.

For both older adults and their adult children, communication competence is necessary to initiate and engage in these conversations earlier in the lifespan. Fowler and Afifi (2011) found that adult children were more likely to open conversations about future care with their aging parents when they had higher levels of communication efficacy (or perceived they had the ability to talk about the issue). To explore this communication competency need further, Fowler, Fisher, and Pitts (in press) examined how adults aged 65 and older evaluated an adult child's communication strategies to initiate the discussion and whether their evaluations impacted their willingness to engage in such talk. They found that conversation openers for this discussion can be an important form of supportive communication and that facework and politeness are key to opening the conversation. More specifically, when an adult child uses politeness strategies to protect the parent's positive face (perception of being loved) and negative face (perception of autonomy), parents evaluated opening this discussion as supportive, which in turn predicted their willingness to discuss future care needs with one of their own children if they were to approach the conversation in a similar manner.

CONCLUSION

As the Baby Boomers continue to age and the world's population of older adults continues to rise as the world has never seen before, it will be increasingly important for older adults, their families and loved ones, and health providers to become more competent in the communication dynamics and challenges characterizing their complex health interactions as presented in this chapter. The health care system has become more advanced as science, medicine, and technology progress. Older adults and their loved ones must continuously become adept at navigating the many subsystems of care central to their health. Older adults must also strive to be assertive, engaged, and empowered recipients of care, and their communication preferences in care are worthy of further exploration as a new aging cohort or generation enters the golden years. It is also important to note that the intricacy of providing geriatric care warrants more attention and respect in medical education, training, and practice to better equip practitioners with the communication skills and awareness needed to engage in quality later-life care. Families too should be respectful of their role in an older loved one's health. Families should work with the older adult and his or her providers by planning ahead and making certain that his or her priorities are upheld. Doing so can better ensure their loved one's needs are heard and that quality of life is kept at the forefront of any interactions. Ultimately, health care interactions in later life are complex and critical to wellness across the lifespan. To safeguard older adults' ability to continuously successfully age, health providers, older patients, and their loved ones must equally share responsibility in enriching their communication competence in health care interaction.

FUTURE RESEARCH DIRECTIONS IN HEALTH CARE
INTERACTIONS IN OLDER ADULTHOOD

To further ensure older adults, their loved ones, and providers enhance their health care interactions, several avenues of research are warranted in the future. To begin, more communication scholarship is needed that attends to the wide range of unique care interactions older adults regularly face. In general, research concerning provider–older adult patient communication is largely dominated by dyadically focused studies with physicians or nurses. Given older adults interact with the most expansive range of providers in comparison to other age groups, researchers should concern themselves with care interactions with a more diverse group of providers. Other such medical professionals might include pharmacists (e.g., see Keshishian, Colodny, & Boone, 2008) given pressing concerns with polypharmacy, or optometrists, a health care setting predominated by older adults. Likewise, complementary and alternative medicine (CAM) is growing among Baby Boomers. Yet older adults rarely disclose such use to physicians (Arcury et al., 2013). More research is needed about enhancing older adults' willingness to disclose but also with regard to their interactions with practitioners of Eastern medicine, like yoga, tai chi, acupuncture, and herbal medicines.

At the same time, researchers should further explore connections among successful aging, organizational or environmental communication, and older adults' health care interactions. Older adult patients have distinctive needs—needs that warrant changes in organizational structures and approaches. Specialists in emergency medicine are at the beginning of such groundbreaking changes in geriatric health care. Holy Cross Hospital (Silver Spring, Maryland) offered the nation its first geriatric emergency department (referred to as a geri-ED or seniors emergency department) when it opened its doors in 2008 in the greater Washington, D.C., area. More EDs throughout the United States are following suit, and research supports such a change. Boltz et al. (2013) showed that ED nurses recognized the need for improvement for their geriatric patients, citing concerns about a lack of a good environmental fit and respect for older patients and the care providers as well as issues with procedures, staffing, time, and safety. They specifically argued for the initiation of EDs or ED units designed specifically for geriatric care. These new, specially designed structures for older patients provide scholars an incredible opportunity to explore connections between provider–geriatric patient–family interactions, enhanced care, and environmental considerations.

Finally, research that heightens awareness of the importance of narrative communication in older adults' health care interactions seems critical on many levels. Such an approach has implications for whether or not older adults disclose or request information, and yet storied communication clearly competes with the demands on health care providers and current structures and limitations in place. Researchers could explore ways in which providers and organizational structures can better attend to the need for a narrative approach in older adult patient interactions. Such research could be translated to medical education and training in the future, both for providers of the geriatric population but also for enhancing the communication skills of older patients and their loved ones.

REFERENCES

Abramson, J. S., & Mizrahi, T. (1996). When social workers and physicians collaborate: Positive and negative interdisciplinary experiences. *Social Work, 41*, 270–281.

Adelman, R. D., Greene, M. G., & Charon, R. (1991). Issues in physician-elderly patient interaction. *Aging and Society, 11*, 127–148.

American Association of Retired Persons, National Alliance for Caregiving, & United Nations Program on Ageing. (2008). *IDOP 2008: Global perspectives on family caregiving.* Retrieved from http://www.aarpinternational.org/resourcelibrary/resourcelibrary_ show.htm?doc_id=728810.

Antonucci, T. C., & Akiyama, H. (1987). Social networks in adult life and a preliminary examination of the convoy model. *Journals of Gerontology, 42*, 519–527.

Antonucci, T. C., & Jackon, J. S. (1987). Social support, interpersonal efficacy, and health. In L. L. Carstensen & B. A. Edelstein (Eds.), *Handbook of Clinical Gerontology* (pp. 291–311). New York, NY: Pargamon Press.

Arcury, T. A., Bell, R. A., Altizer, K. P., Grzywacz, J. G., Sandberg, J. C., & Quandt, S. A. (2013). Attitudes of older adults regarding disclosure of complementary therapy use to physicians. *Journal of Applied Gerontology. 32,* 627–645.

Baltes, P. B. (1987). Theoretical propositions of life-span developmental psychology: On the dynamics between growth and decline. *Developmental Psychology, 23*, 611–626.

Beisecker, A. E. (1988). Aging and the desire for information and input in medical decisions: Patient consumerism in medical encounters. *Gerontologist, 28*, 330–335.

Beisecker, A. E., & Thompson, T. (1995). The elderly patient-physician interaction. In J. Nussbaum & J. Coupland (Eds.), *Handbook of communication and ageing research* (pp. 397–416). Mahwah, NJ: Erlbaum.

Berkman, B. (Ed.). (2005). *Oxford handbook of aging and social work.* New York, NY: Oxford University Press.

Berkman, L. F., Leo-Summers, L., & Horwitz, R. I. (1992). Emotional support and survival after myocardial infarction. A prospective, population-based study of the elderly. *Annals of Internal Medicine, 117*, 1003–1009.

Bethea, L. S. (2002). The impact of an older adult parent on communicative satisfaction and dyadic adjustment in the long-term marital relationship: Adult-children and spouses' retrospective accounts. *Journal of Applied Communication Research, 30*, 107–125.

Boltz, M., Parke, B., Shuluk, J., Capezuti, E., & Galvin, J. E. (2013). Care of the older adult in the emergency department: Nurses views of the pressing issues. *The Gerontologist, 53* 441–453.

Bradley, G., Spark, B., & Nesdale, D. (2001). Doctor communication style and patient outcomes: Gender and age as moderators. *Journal of Applied Social Psychology, 31*, 1749–1773.

Carstensen, L. L. (1991). Selectivity theory: Social activity in life-span context. *Annual Review of Gerontology and Geriatrics, 11*, 195–217.

Carstensen, L. L. (1992). Social and emotional patterns in adulthood: Support for socioemotional selectivity theory. *Psychology and Aging, 7*, 331–338.

Carstensen, L. L. (1993). Motivation for social contact across the life span: A theory of socioemotional selectivity. In J. E. Jacobs (Ed.), *Nebraska Symposium on Motivation: 1992, developmental perspectives on motivation* (Vol. 40, pp. 209–254). Lincoln: University of Nebraska Press.

Centers for Disease Control and Prevention. (2012). *Summary health statistics for U.S. adults: National Health Interview Survey 2011.* Washington, DC: U.S. Government Printing Office.

Chen, H., & Landefeld, S. C. (2007). The hidden poor: Care of the elderly. In W. M. King (Ed.), *Medical management of vulnerable and underserved patients.* New York, NY: McGraw-Hill.

Cicirelli, V. G. (1989). Feelings of attachment to *siblings* and well-being in later life. *Psychology and Aging, 4*, 211–216.

Cicirelli, V. G. (1992). *Family caregiving: Autonomous and paternalistic decision-making.* Newbury Park, CA: Sage.

Cicirelli, V. G. (1993). Attachment and obligation as daughters' motives for caregiving behavior and subsequent effect on subjective burden. *Psychology and Aging, 8*, 144–155.

Coupland, N., Coupland, J., Giles, H., & Henwood, K. (1988). Accommodating the elderly: Invoking and extending a theory. *Language in Society, 17*, 1–41.

DiMatteo, M. R. (2004). Variations in patients' adherence to medical recommendations: A quantitative review of 50 years of research. *Medical Care, 42*(3), 200–209.

Edwards, H. (2001). Family caregiving, communication, and the health of care receivers. In M. L. Hummert & J. F. Nussbaum (Eds.), *Aging, communication, and health: Linking research and practice for successful aging* (pp. 203–224). Mahwah, NJ: Erlbaum.

Edwards, J., & Smith, P. (1998). Impact of interdisciplinary education in underserved areas: Health professions collaboration in Tennessee. *Journal of Professional Nursing, 14*, 144–149.

Fisher, C. L. (2010). Coping with breast cancer across adulthood: Emotional support communication in the mother-daughter bond. *Journal of Applied Communication Research, 38*, 386–411.

Fisher, C. L., & Nussbaum, J. F. (in press). Maximizing wellness in successful aging and cancer coping: The importance of family communication from a socioemotional selectivity theoretical perspective. *Journal of Family Communication.*

Fowler, C., & Afifi, W. A. (2011). Applying the theory of motivated information management to adult children's discussions of caregiving with aging parents. *Journal of Social and Personal Relationships, 28*, 507–535. doi:10.1177/0265407510384896.

Fowler, C., & Fisher, C. L. (2009). Attitudes toward decision-making and aging, and preparation for future care needs. *Health Communication, 24*, 691–630.

Fowler, C., Fisher, C. L., & Pitts, M. (in press). Initiating caregiving conversations with aging parents before the need is imminent: Implications of facework strategies. *Health Communication.*

Gallant, M. P., Spitze, G. D., & Prohaska, T. R. (2007). Help or hindrance? How family and friends influence chronic illness self-management among older adults. *Research on Aging, 29*, 375–409.

Giles, H., Coupland, N., & Coupland, J. (1991). Accommodation theory: Communication, context, and consequence. In H. Giles, N. Coupland, & J. Coupland (Eds.), *Contexts of accommodation: Developments in applied sociolinguistics* (pp. 1–68). Cambridge, England: Cambridge University Press.

Gitlin, L. N., & Wolff, J. (2011). Family involvement in care transitions of older adults: What do we know and where do we go from here? *Annual Review of Gerontology and Geriatrics, 31*, 31–64.

Greene, M. G., Adelman, R. D., Friedmann, E., & Charon, R. (1994). Older patient satisfaction with communication during an initial encounter. *Social Science and Medicine, 38*, 1279–1288.

Gross, J. (2006, October 18). Geriatrics lags in age of high-tech medicine. *The New York Times.* Retrieved January 21, 2008, from http://www.nytimes.com/2006/10/18/health/18aged.html?_r=1&scp=1&sq=%22geriatrics+Lags%22&oref=slogin

Gupta, D., & Denton, B. (2008). Appointment scheduling in health care: Challenges and opportunities. *Institute of Industrial Engineers Transactions, 40*, 800–819.

Hanson, S. H., & Sauer, W. G. (1985). Children and their elderly parents. In W. J. Sauer & R. T. Coward (Eds.), *Social support networks and the care of the elderly: Theory, research and practice* (pp. 41–66). New York, NY: Springer.

Hartman, M., Catlin, A. Lassman, D., Cylus, J., & Heffler, S. (2008). U.S. health spending by age, selected years through 2004. *Health Affairs, 27*, w1–w12.

Haug, M. R., & Ory, M. G. (1987). Issues in elderly patient-provider interactions. *Research on Aging, 9*, 3–44.

Heckhausen, J., & Schulz, R. (1995). A life-span theory of control. *Psychological Review, 102*, 284–304.

Hummert, M. L., & Morgan, M. (1999). *Personal and familial identity in later life: Decision-making about lifestyle changes.* Paper presented at the annual meeting of the International Communication Association, San Francisco, CA.

Hummert, M. L., & Morgan, M. (2001). Negotiating decisions in the aging family. In M. L. Hummert & J. F. Nussbaum (Eds.), *Aging, communication, and health: Linking research and practice for successful aging* (pp. 177–201). Hillsdale, NJ: Erlbaum.

Keshishian, F., Colodny, N., & Boone, R. T. (2008). Physician–patient and pharmacist–patient communication: Geriatrics' perceptions and opinions. *Patient Education and Counseling, 71*, 265–284.

Knight, C., Haslam, S. A., & Haslam, C. (2010). In home or at home? How collective decision making in a new care facility enhances social interaction and wellbeing amongst older adults. *Ageing and Society, 30*, 1393–1418.

Laidsaar-Powell, R. C., Butow, P. N., Bu, S., Charles, C., Gafni, A., Lam, W. W. T., … & Juraskova, I. (2013). Physician–patient–companion communication and decision-making: A systematic review of triadic medical consultations. *Patient education and counseling, 91*, 3–13.

Lookinland, S., & Anson, K. (1995). Perpetuation of ageist attitudes among present and future health care personnel: Implications for future care. *Journal of Advanced Nursing, 21*, 47–56

Merluzzi, T. V., & Nairn, M. A. (1999, March). *An exploration of self-efficacy and longevity in persons with cancer.* Paper presented at the 20th annual meeting of the Society of Behavioral Medicine, San Diego, CA.

Nolan, M., Davies, S., & Grant, G. (2001). Integrating perspectives. In M. Nolan, S. Davies, & G. Grant (Eds.), *In working with older people and their families: Key issues in policy and practice* (pp. 160–178), Buckingham, England: Open University Press.

Nussbaum, J. F. (Ed.). (1989). *Life-span communication: Normative processes.* Hillsdale, NJ: Erlbaum.

Nussbaum, J. F., Baringer, D., Fisher, C. L., & Kundrat, A. (2007). Connecting health, communication, and aging: Cancer communication and older adults. In L. Sparks, D. O'Hair, & G. L. Kreps (Eds.), *Cancer communication and aging* (pp. 67–76). Cresskill, NJ: Hampton.

Nussbaum, J., & Fisher, C. L. (2009). A communication model for the competent delivery of geriatric medicine. *Journal of Language and Social Psychology, 28*,190–208.

Nussbaum, J. F., & Fisher, C. L. (2011). Successful aging and communication wellness: Understanding aging as a process of transition and continuity. In Y. Matsumoto (Ed.), *Faces of aging: The lived experiences of the elderly in Japan* (pp. 263–272). Palo Alto, CA: Stanford University Press.

Nussbaum, J. F., Miller-Day, M., & Fisher, C. L. (2009). *Communication and intimacy in older adulthood.* Madrid, Spain: Aresta.

Nussbaum, J. F., Pecchioni, L., & Crowell, T. (2001). The older patient–health care provider relationship in a managed care environment. In M. L. Hummert & J. F. Nussbaum (Eds.), *Aging, communication, and health: Linking research and practice for successful aging* (pp. 23–42). Mahwah, NJ: Erlbaum.

Nussbaum, J. F., Pecchioni, L. L., Robinson, J. D., & Thompson, T. L. (2000). *Communication and aging* (2nd ed.). Mahwah, NJ: Erlbaum.

Pecchioni, L. L., Wright, K., & Nussbaum, J. F. (2005). *Life-span communication.* Mahwah, NJ: Erlbaum.

Pratt, C. C., & Jones-Aust, L. (1993). Decision-making influence strategies of caregiving daughters and their elderly mothers. *Family Relations, 42,* 376–383.

Pritchett, L. M. (2000). New age of medicine. Business first: The weekly business paper of greater Louisville. Retrieved from http://louisville.bcentral.com/louisville/stories/2000/06126/focus4.html

Ripich, D. N., Carpenter, B., & Ziol, E. (1997). Procedural discourse in men and women with Alzheimer's disease: A longitudinal study with clinical implications. *American Journal of Alzheimer's Disease,* 1–14.

Rost, K., Carter, W., & Inui, T. (1989). Introduction of information during the initial medical visit: Consequences for patient follow-through with physician recommendations for medication. *Social Science Medicine, 28,* 315–321.

Sparks, L., & Nussbaum, J. F. (2008). Health literacy and cancer communication with older adults. *Patient Education & Counseling, 71*(3), 345–350.

Street, R. L. (1991). Information-giving in medical consultations: The influence of patients' communicative styles and personal characteristics. *Social Science and Medicine, 32,* 541–548.

Thompson, T. L., Robinson, J. D., & Beisecker, A. E. (2004). The older patient–physician interaction. In J. F. Nussbaum & J. Coupland (Eds.), *Handbook of communication and aging research* (2nd ed., pp. 451–477). Mahwah, NJ: Erlbaum.

United Nations (UN). (2007). *World population ageing 2007.* Retrieved from http://www.un.org/esa/population/publications/WPA2007/wpp2007.htm

U.S. Department of Commerce, Bureau of the Census. (2010). *The older population: 2010* (2010 Census Briefs, Publication No. CB11-CN.192). Washington, DC: U.S. Government Printing Office.

Vieder, J. N., Krafchick, M. A., Kovach, A. C., & Galluzzi, K. E. (2002). Physician-patient interaction: What do elders want? *Journal of American Osteopathic Association, 102,* 73–78.

Williams, A., & Nussbaum, J. F. (2001). *Intergenerational communication across the life span.* Mahwah, NJ: Erlbaum.

Williams, S. L., Haskard, K. B., & DiMatteo, M. R. (2007). The therapeutic effects of the physician-older patient relationship: Effective communication with vulnerable older patients. *Clinical Interventions in Aging, 2,* 453–467.

Wister, A. V. (2005). *Baby boomer health dynamics: How are we aging?* Toronto, Ontario, Canada: University of Toronto Press.

Wolff, J. L., Clayman, M. L., Rabins, F., Cook, M. A., & Roter, D. L. (2012). An exploration of patient and family engagement in routine primary care visits. *Health Expectations.* doi:10.1111/hex.12019

Wolff, J. L., Starfield, B., & Anderson, G. (2002). Prevalence, expenditures, and complications of multiple chronic conditions in the elderly. *Archives of Internal Medicine, 162,* 2269–2276

Woodwell, D. A., & Cherry, D. K. (2004). *National Ambulatory Medical Care Survey: 2002 summary.* Hyattsville, MD: National Center for Health Statistics.

World Health Organization. (2007). *World health statistics 2007.* Retrieved January 21, 2008, from www.who.int/whosis/whostat2007/en/index.html

Wright, K. B., Sparks, L., & Dan, O. (2013). *Health communication in the 21st century.* Hoboken, NJ: John Wiley & Sons.

Wright, K. B., Sparks, L., & O'Hair, H. D. (2013). Health communication in the 21st century (2nd). Oxford, England: Blackwell.

CHAPTER TWENTY-ONE

End-of-Life Interactions

HOWARD GILES, CHAN THAI, AND ABBY PRESTIN

Death is an inevitable reality that marks the end of a lifespan, and hence the topic of this chapter appropriately concludes this *Handbook*. Whether it is the death of a loved one or one's own death, many complex issues are associated with the end of life. Unfortunately, there is a general "lack of willingness to talk about the issue [that] reflects discomfort with the subject and attempts to deny the reality of death.... This communication avoidance then defines death as even more taboo" (Bosticco & Thompson, 2008, p. 1171). In fact, even in families that are reputedly open to discussing sensitive topics, there often appears a discursive reluctance, if not aversion, to talk about information and emotions associated with an impending death (Caughlin, Mikucki-Enyart, Middleton, Stone, & Brown, 2011).

Relatedly, we found, surprisingly and until recently, a fairly limited amount of systematic research by communication scholars on end-of-life issues (see, however, Miller & Knapp, 1986; Nussbaum, Thompson, & Robinson, 1988; Thompson, 1996). Even the *Handbooks of Communication and Aging Research* (Nussbaum & Coupland, 1995, 2001) did not devote a chapter to this theme, although it did feature in the more recent *Handbook of Health Communication* (Goldsmith, Wittenberg-Lyles, Ragan, & Nussbaum, 2011) and in a recent treatise on communication and successful aging (Giles, Davis, Gasiorek, & Giles, 2013). On the other side of the coin and, despite a valued array of disciplines involved from history to mortuary science to psychology, communication scholars were not represented in the two-volume *Handbook of Death and Dying* (Bryant, 2003).

Gratifyingly, there has been, more recently, an outgrowth of interest in our field in this topic (e.g., Keeley & Yingling, 2007; Nussbaum & Giles, in press; Ragan, Goldsmith, Wittenberg-Lyles, & Sanchez-Riley, 2010; Ragan, Wittenberg-Lyles, Goldsmith, & Kelley, 2008; Thompson, 2011). In that constructive spirit, this chapter expresses the firm conviction that people's inability to manage and talk about death can challenge their managing of it. We begin by discussing different perspectives on the meaning of death, when and how it occurs, what can constitute "a good death" (see Pitts, 2011), and its process. Issues of care at the end of life are then considered, including hospice and palliative care, before discussing the challenges and consequences of end-of-life conversations. Finally, we proffer a research agenda in which communication scholars may contribute to this burgeoning area of research.

CONCEPTUAL WOOD-CLEARING: A DEFINITION OF DEATH

What, then, is death? The extant literature offers a variety of definitions for death, each differing by perspective or paradigm (Kastenbaum, 1992). From a biological vantage point, death is the end of the life of an organism. "In humans and animals, death is manifested by the permanent cessation of vital organic functions, including the absence of heartbeat, spontaneous breathing, and brain activity" (Kleinedler, 2005, p. 163). However, with constant advances in medical technology, death has shifted from an event to a *process*: conditions once considered indicative of death are now reversible (de Grey, 2007). Furthermore, definitions of death are no longer solely predicated on biological and physiological parameters; they now include legal parameters. For instance, in the United States, cessation of brain activity (including involuntary activity necessary to sustain life) resulting from total necrosis of the cerebral neurons following loss of blood flow and oxygenation is generally considered a standard legal indicator of death (Randell, 2004). By this definition, the brain is no longer capable of sustaining the body's systems without advanced life support. This view, similar to the bio-physiological view, asserts that if certain measurable criteria are fulfilled, an individual may be declared "dead" (Lock, 1996).

Aside from the scientific and legal definitions, cultural beliefs often guide the determination of whether or not death has occurred. Every society has a way of explaining death (Kalish, 1980) and has developed its own symbolic systems or spiritual beliefs that contribute to how they understand and make meaning of death (Tomer, 2000). In Japanese culture, death is interpreted primarily as a social rather than an individual event, and efforts to scientifically define the end of life as a measurable point in time are rejected (Lock, 1996). Furthermore, among cultures that do not believe in the end of one's life or "spirit," death may not be the event that ends life, but rather a transition to the form of existence thought to prevail after a physical life has ended (Morgan & Laungani, 2002). Culture also shapes beliefs about what constitutes a "good" or "bad" death (Black & Rubinstein, 2013). Ideas about the former have changed in different societies throughout history. Walter (2003) argues that cultural norms about good and bad deaths in modern Western societies are contingent upon three factors: the extent of secularization, the extent of individualism, and the duration of the dying process (see also Ma-Kellams & Blascovich, 2012). Given these complexities in how death is defined and what it means to different people, it is not surprising that there is much hesitance in talking about death, and when it is discussed, there are perhaps many misunderstandings between patients, family members, and health care providers. Furthermore, the nature of the death and the age of the deceased may further complicate matters.

AGES AND WAYS OF DYING

Differences both in age at time of death and in cause of death shape and guide communication about this topic. For instance, the death of a young child would most likely elicit conversations about potential and "a life that could have been" (Ferrell & Coyle, 2008, p. 25), whereas the death of a very elderly person would likely result in conversations reflecting on the life that was (Morgan & Laungani, 2002). Furthermore, deaths resulting from long-term illness may be discussed very differently from those caused by sudden illness, accidents, or suicides and homicides, as there is more time to discuss and process what will happen.

Worldwide, an estimated 56.5 million people die each year (World Health Organization, 2010), with more than 2.4 million deaths per year in the United States alone (CDC, 2010). In the United States, the average life expectancy is at 77.7 years, and approximately 50% of all deaths each year occur among persons aged 75 years and older (CDC, 2010); death rates generally increase with age. The leading causes of death in the United States include: heart disease, cancer, stroke, chronic lower respiratory diseases, accidents, Alzheimer's disease, diabetes, influenza and pneumonia, nephritis, nephrosis, and septicemia (CDC, 2012). The leading causes of death differ by age group; for instance, in 2010, the leading cause of death for people up to 44 years of age was unintentional injury, whereas for adults ages 45 and over it was chronic illness. Tellingly, for those over 70 years of age, the fourth leading cause of death is Alzheimer's disease. Undoubtedly, the cause of death will influence the way people *communicate* about it. As above, if the event was unexpected, it may be unlikely that the deceased had a conversation with loved ones about his or her death or even managing care for his or her latter days (see Fowler & Afifi, 2011). Conversely, if death was impending, and the deceased and his or her loved ones had time to prepare, it is more likely that there may have been conversations about the event, the aftermath, and its consequences; it is to the latter we now turn.

PSYCHOLOGICAL PROCESSES OF DEATH AND DYING

Extant theory centering on the psychological processes involved in death and dying can provide insight into the role of communication before, during, and after the dying process. One of the primary theoretical paradigms in this field that is most relevant to communication is stage theories of death, which focus on the psychological and emotional stages through which one passes when approaching death. These theories provide a deeper understanding of psychological processes involved in death and dying that can enable the provision of improved care for the dying and their loved ones. These theories may also further illuminate the contribution of communication scholars to improve our understanding of the dying process, and to improve the quality of life outcomes for the deceased and their family members, which may include pain management, social and spiritual support, coping with loss and grief, and the opportunity to express their needs and concerns.

The most widely cited stage theory is Kübler-Ross's (1969) stages of grief, which postulates that individuals move sequentially through five psychological phases as they near death: denial, anger, bargaining, depression, and acceptance. Denial is characterized by the individual's refusal to believe that he or she is dying and may be manifest in cognitions, affect, or behavior. Denial gives way to anger, which is rooted in both one's understanding of impending death and unresolved issues that may breed resentment. Once anger subsides, individuals transition into bargaining, wherein they attempt to create situations in which death will be postponed. Bargaining is followed by depression, in which one experiences a sense of great loss in anticipating separation from this world. In the final stage, one comes to accept death and it is often accompanied by an enhanced desire to sleep, an absence of affect, and preference for solitude. Those who have lived full, long lives may be able to come to a sense of meaning and contentment; however, others may need encouragement to express denial, vent anger, and mourn losses to reach acceptance.

This theory is credited with providing a description of the dying process, legitimizing the topic of death, and offering a structure for death that can reduce the anxiety of care providers (Kastenbaum, 1997). It has also been widely adopted in the understanding of the process by which bereaved individuals come to accept loss. Despite empirical support for the theory (see Maciejewski, Zhang, Block, & Prigerson, 2007), there is little evidence from clinical practice in favor of a unidirectional movement through the stages (Copp, 1998). Rather, dying individuals fluctuate between psychological states such as hope, depression, fear, anger, and sadness (Buckman, 1993). These findings have motivated revised stage theories. For instance, Glaser and Strauss (1968) proposed the trajectories of death model, which describes four trajectories of death that vary based on duration (quick, slow, or steady) and form (improvements, relapses). As well, Pattison (1977) offered the "living–dying interval" model wherein knowledge of one's death is an interruption of the "trajectory" a patient has planned for his or her life and necessitates confronting mortality.

What is the role of communication in these process models? It is clear that the communicative needs of patients differ at each stage (see Wittenberg-Lyles, Goldsmoth, Ferrell, & Ragan, 2013), regardless of which theory we consider, and a greater attention to these needs by those surrounding the patient might help facilitate acceptance. In Kübler-Ross's (1969) model, for instance, individuals in the "anger" stage often verbalize this emotion and direct it toward loved ones and caregivers. How might communication research and theory help caregivers to encourage patients to express anger without misdirecting it at family and friends or to work through resentment and ill feelings to repair damaged relationships? When patients reach the stage of depression, caretakers are encouraged to let them express sorrow at their impending loss, which may defy a natural response to make attempts to cheer the patient up or encourage an optimistic mindset. Finally, the stage of acceptance is often silent, as there is "little or no need for words" (Kübler-Ross, 1969, p. 99), which suggests nonverbal communication may be critical to conveying comfort and love. Overall, these stage theories demonstrate that death is not a singular event, but a process in which communication plays vital roles, and ones we consider below.

END-OF-LIFE COMMUNICATION

Despite the importance of communication in improving quality of care and patient and family outcomes, the topic of communication at the end of life has been "largely understudied" in the communication literature (Vora & Vora, 2008, p. 60). Whereas other disciplines such as medicine, nursing, sociology, and anthropology have investigated this issue, Considine and Miller (2010) concluded that though death appears in two key areas of scholarship—delivering bad news and making decisions about medical care at the end of life—extant research often neglects issues that are both "more mundane and more meaningful" (p. 166), such as a patient's concern with comfort or the significance of his or her life. Currently, there are two main bodies of literature in end-of-life communication—one focusing on communication *about* the end of life and another examining communication *at* the end of life.

Communicating *About* the End of Life

When a loved one is diagnosed with a terminal illness, his or her family members are generally uncertain of what they should say (Moller, 1996), and communicating about death and dying is particularly difficult (Bachner, Davidov, & Carmel, 2008). Villagran, Goldsmith, Wittenberg-Lyles, and Baldwin (2010) emphasize that the bad news, should it be conveyed by family members, be in such a way that the individual is comforted and assured that he or she will not be abandoned. In fact, family uncertainty is compounded by the lack of proficiency of medical personnel in communicating bad news. Indeed, it is uncommon for families to discuss terminal disease together and even less common for them to talk about death or dying. Families that do discuss death take many different approaches to these conversations (see Vail et al., 2012). For instance, couples may talk about the possibility of death once, but not return to the topic thereafter (Gray, Fitch, Phillips, Labrecque, & Fergus, 2000; Hinton, 1981). As the illness progresses, family communication typically becomes increasingly intermittent (Hinton, 1998; Salander & Spetz, 2002).

In the final stages of a disease, families may engage in selective communication, discussing only facts, which may be seen as a "safer" option compared to discussing their emotions (Lewis & Deal, 1995; McDonald et al., 2003). Consequently, concerns of the family and their loved one about death are infrequently discussed, even as death approaches (Beach, 1995; McGrath, 2004; Zhang & Siminoff, 2003). This is compounded for families when medical personnel do not share important information with them that could potentially alleviate their anxieties, such as available provisions for hospice care (Stone, Mikucki-Enyart, Middleton, Caughlin, & Brown, 2012).

Relatedly, Kaplowitz, Osuch, Safron, and Campo (1999) interviewed physicians about communicating prognosis information to patients with metastatic cancer. Overall, physicians were more comfortable giving qualitative information, such as telling patients their disease was not curable, than quantitative estimates of survival time. In fact, physicians struggled with the tension between realism and hope. On the one hand, they believed that patients wanted to know their prognoses, and to this end, most physicians provided survival estimates if they were requested. On the other hand, almost half of physicians did not provide survival estimates to those who do not request them, in part, to preserve patients' hope.

In a similar vein, Thompson (2011) reviewed and critiqued research regarding hope conveyed to the terminally ill. She reported on studies indicating that while many of the latter do not wish unrealistic or even false prognoses—and certainly not blunt factual information stripped of empathy and compassion—most do prefer some honest indications of hope for a fulfilling end of life as well as some faint possibility of remission (Kaplowitz, Campo, & Chui, 2002; Kaplowitz et al., 1999). Importantly, Thompson points out that "there is a spectrum of hope in that patients may simultaneously hope for 'cure' while acknowledging the terminal nature of their illness" (p. 185). In this frame, different *kinds* of hope—as well as perhaps optimism (Gillham, Shatté, Reivich, & Seligman, 2000; Peterson, 2000)—evolve and assume relative salience over time, such as the need for dignity, attaining treatment aspirations, finding inner peace, and so forth.

In a similar vein, and underscoring the negotiable nature of the information-sharing process, Kaplowitz et al. (2002) asked cancer patients whether they desired, requested, and received qualitative prognosis information (i.e., whether or not the disease was terminal) and/or a quantitative estimate (i.e., how long they may survive). Eighty percent of patients wanted a qualitative prognosis, but only about half wanted a quantitative prognosis. Of those who wanted a qualitative prognosis, over 90% were given one, whereas only about half of those who wanted a quantitative prognosis were provided one. Furthermore, whereas about 15% of those who wanted a qualitative prognosis did not ask for it, more than 30% of patients who reported wanting quantitative prognosis failed to ask for it.

Overall, this literature demonstrates a "phenomenon of silence" around the topics of disease, death, and dying for families facing a terminal diagnosis. Topic avoidance appears to be driven by three motivations: aversion to discussing psychologically distressing topics, mutually protective emotional buffering, and belief in the power of positive thinking (Zhang & Siminoff, 2003). In the United States, the topic of death is considered both depressing and frightening (Jennings, 2005), and the cultural trend is to avoid talk of death, both publically and privately (Vora & Vora, 2008). Death is hidden away and many people have little or no experience with it (Hines, 2001); as a consequence, families are hesitant to talk about death because they are afraid of it. Interestingly, although cross-cultural studies demonstrate that Asian cultures are more accepting of death, this does not always translate into willingness to discuss it. For example, in China, death is viewed as a continuous and integral part of life, and there is comparatively less fear associated with death. However, Chinese people seldom talk about death or death-related issues because of a belief that it is bad luck to speak the words with the same phoneme as the Chinese word for death (Wu, Tang, & Kwok, 2002).

Because death can be a frightening topic, family members also worry that by discussing it, they will bring distress to their dying loved one and/or themselves (Yingling & Keeley, 2007). Thus, patients and their families are likely to avoid talking about death to mutually prevent distress in what is termed "protective buffering" (Gray et al., 2000). For instance, spouses might conceal their fear that their terminally ill partners may not beat the disease (Zhang & Siminoff, 2003).

This reluctance to openly address death is exacerbated by a general social reluctance to talk about the negative. As noted by McGrath, Montgomery, White, and Kerridge (2006), in the face of adversity (e.g., terminal illness) there exists the cultural expectation that one must think positively and not voice potential negative outcomes. Zhang and Siminoff (2003) found that 15% of family members of terminal lung cancer patients refused to discuss the possibility that their family member would not make it for fear that such talk would accelerate the patient's death (Caughlin et al., 2011). The influence of this mandate for positive thinking may be such that it impedes or prevents important conversations between a dying person and his or her loved ones (McGrath et al., 2006). This topic avoidance may contribute to distance that often grows between couples during the end stages of a terminal illness (Metzger & Gray, 2008).

Given the empirical evidence demonstrating topic avoidance around death, we may ask whether and under what conditions discussions about death could be beneficial to the patient and/or family. For instance, conversations about death can have psychological or social benefits. For the bereaved, increased acceptance of an impending loss is related to improved post-death adjustment, such as decreased distress (Kramer, 1997) and increases in post-traumatic growth and coping efficacy (Vachon et al., 1977). However, findings are mixed as to whether communication with a dying loved one about impending death helps the bereaved accept the death, and especially so if they have sidestepped talking about, or asking for, prognoses themselves. Higher amounts of communication are associated with more positive coping outcomes following a loss (Beach, 1995), though feelings of regret may increase over time (Hinton, 1998).

In contrast, communicating about death has also been associated with greater post-loss distress (Metzger & Gray, 2008). One study found that those with higher levels of depression before the death of a loved one were likely to discuss dying with that individual more frequently than non-depressed participants. This suggests that those who were more psychologically distressed prior to the loss discussed topics related to dying more often and continued to exhibit higher levels of grief and depression following their loss (Hinton, 1998). It may also be the case that the content of these conversations played a role in producing varied outcomes. Although less is known about the social benefits of communicating about death for the family, these conversations can enhance family cohesion or feelings of closeness (Johnston & Abraham, 2000) and can help ease the dying individual's fears of abandonment (Vora & Vora, 2008).

In sum, scholarship on the topic of communicating about death has found that though families often avoid this topic, even when death is near, these conversations may have psychological benefits, such as facilitating survivors' adjustment to the death of their loved one. Scholars have espoused the important role of practitioners and hospice workers in generating conversation between patients with terminal disease and their loved ones about death and dying (e.g., Yingling & Keeley, 2007). These conversations may help family members or caregivers begin to accept and understand their impending loss and experience improved psychological outcomes during bereavement. They may also help families resolve unfinished business, plan for the future, and work through difficult emotions surrounding the impending loss (Metzger & Gray, 2008). However, though communication between family members about death and dying is important and likely beneficial, families may need guidance from health care or palliative support workers who can share with them the specifics of what kinds of communication may occur at the end of life and how this communication can function positively for the family (Yingling & Keeley, 2007).

Communication *At* the End-of-Life

As noted, there is also a growing literature on communication at the end of life. In particular, the work of Keeley and colleagues (see below) has explored final conversations between survivors and their loved ones who have since passed away (see also Callanan & Kelley, 1997). Retrospective interviews with survivors have uncovered five key themes common during final conversations: messages of love, identity, spirituality, routine talk, and difficult relationship issues. Each theme is discussed in greater detail below.

Love. The most prominent themes of final conversations revolve around love. Final conversations represent a communication act wherein unconditional love may be more readily exchanged because a sense of impending separation removes barriers that typically prevent love and intimacy (Keeley, 2004a). Messages of love are often repeated, may be conveyed both verbally and nonverbally, and emphasize connectedness and closure or completion of a relationship (Keeley, 2007).

In a deeper analysis, Keeley (2004a) found that affirmations of love between a dying person and a loved one confirmed the connection between the two, strengthened their bond, and aided in the survivor's healing process during bereavement. In circumstances in which relationships were strained, messages of love could be difficult to convey, but were rewarding in that they promoted reconciliation (Keeley, 2007). Of note, nonverbal communication of love served an important altruistic function by letting the dying individual know it was okay to go.

Identity. Final conversations often contain messages that reflect the evaluation or construction of the self, both as an individual and as a partner of the relational dyad (Keeley, 2007). These messages alter, bolster, and confirm survivors' personal and relational identities and create opportunities for people to reexamine, reaffirm, and adjust their self-esteem, self-image, and identity (Keeley & Koenig Kellas, 2005).

Spirituality/religious faith. Family members often discuss spiritual or religious beliefs to help provide meaning to death. These messages can take various forms, including direct affirmations of faith, explicit acknowledgment of a higher power, and the expression of the belief that they would be reunited in the next life. Messages also serve to validate religious beliefs, which could mean reaffirming long-held beliefs, restoring lapsed beliefs, or shifting belief systems (Keeley, 2007). The validation of one's spirituality or faith can comfort both the dying individual and his or her loved one (Keeley, 2004b); in particular, many survivors believe that discussions about faith and the afterlife assuaged their loved one's fear of dying.

Communication about faith also provides "rules of conduct" by which survivors should live after the loved one has passed away, which helps survivors cope with challenges during bereavement. Messages about faith, religion, or spiritual beliefs often enhance survivors' ability to enact their spirituality and be more vocal or demonstrative in their beliefs.

Routine talk. Routine talk encompasses messages on a wide range of topics, many of which center on family. These discussions often have a lighthearted quality that preserves a sense of normalcy. Over the course of terminal illness, such talk helps ease the burden of having to say goodbye multiple ways or constructing the best way to say it (Keeley & Koenig Kellas, 2005).

Psychological and Social Consequences of Communicating at the End of Life

Some participants in Keeley's (2007) work discussed difficult interactions with the dying loved one that included criticism, defensiveness, guilt, manipulation, coldness, or contempt. For example, one participant described a final conversation with her dying alcoholic mother in which she was able to work up the courage to talk about troubling issues in their relationship. Ultimately, this discussion helped them to reconcile and move the interaction into a more positive direction. This interaction reflected the "tendency of individuals that have difficult relationships to 'dance around' many of the issues pertaining to their difficult past relationship, while at the same time wanting to engage in a more important, but more difficult final conversation" (Keeley, 2007, p. 243).

Final conversations may result in numerous positive psychological and social consequences for both the dying individual and his or her loved ones. As noted, final conversations can help each conversational partner better understand his or her identity, as well as their relationship with each other and the identities enveloped within that relationship. Many survivors noted that final conversations confirmed the relationship and its importance to the survivor and his or her dying loved one. These conversations could also help to strengthen the relationship by building cohesion or connection, allowing the two to celebrate their relationship, and resolving issues or problems. On a related note, discussion of difficult topics also helped survivors release anger toward dying loved ones and allow for reconciliation of difficult relationships (Keeley, 2007). This is an important aspect of the healing process, as it helped survivors to cope with and make sense of their loss.

Despite a growing literature on conversations and psychological processes at the end of life, this research has been largely removed from the context of caretaking at the end of life. The context of care is important to consider, as the provision of health care, particularly palliative care, is intended to address the psychological needs of patients and their families, and this will be discussed next.

THE ROLE OF COMMUNICATION IN CARING FOR THE DYING

Palliative care—which is both a philosophy of care and a structured system for delivering it—aims to prevent and relieve suffering for patients with life-threatening or debilitating illness (NCP, 2009). It can be delivered concurrently with other life-prolonging treatments or as the main focus of care at any stage of terminal care or life-threatening illness, distinguishing it from hospice, which only applies to care administered when end of life is certain and curative treatment is no longer part of the care plan (Billings, 1998). The goals of palliative care include facilitating decision making, optimizing function, and providing opportunities for personal growth (NCP, 2009). As such, this type of care is crucial to the physical, emotional, and spiritual care of dying persons and their loved ones, and it is in the context of palliative care delivery that the utility of communication scholarship may be illuminated.

Palliative care abides by the principle that ensuring the quality of life for patients and their families includes assisting them with the physical, psychological, social, spiritual, existential, medical, financial, and practical burdens of illness (Enck, 2003; Sulmasy, 2002). This comprehensive care requires provision by Interdisciplinary Care Teams (ICTs) of health care professionals from across disciplines, including medicine, nursing, social work, chaplaincy, nutrition, rehabilitation, and pharmacy, among others (Grant, Elk, Ferrell, Morrison, & von Gunten, 2009). ICTs work together to address the many needs of terminally ill patients and their families. Integration of these professionals into a cohesive and effective team requires skillful leadership, collaboration, and coordination (Otis-Green et al., 2009), and communication is necessary for this to occur (Coffman & Coffman, 1993). Furthermore, all team members are expected to have competence in collaboration, an ability to assess pain and distress, and appreciation of the diverse concerns that might impact care (Larson, 1993).

Although the concept of palliative care is not new, only in the past two decades has the focus of care for terminally ill patients shifted in this direction. The number of hospitals with palliative care programs continues to grow. A 2008 survey of American hospitals reported that 1,299 (31%) have palliative care programs, up from only 632 hospitals in 2000 (Center to Advance Palliative Care [CAPC], 2009). This rapid growth has led to concerns among professional palliative care organizations about the quality of care provided (Grant et al., 2009) and the establishment of guidelines for the provision of care (CAPC, 2009; National Consensus Project [NCP], 2009). In these care guidelines, communication is highlighted as a key area in which health care professionals need proper knowledge and training to effectively address patient issues related to the end of life. Communication is a fundamental tool to assess the medical status of patients, develop goals of care for patients and their families, and establish relationships

(Coffman & Coffman, 1993). Effective communication is necessary to elicit the patient's and family's needs, negotiate goals of care, and help patients and families address concerns (Dahlin & Giansiracusa, 2006). One study showed that physicians who received communication training were more likely to use techniques such as open-ended questions, expressions of empathy, and appropriate responses to patients' cues, leading to greater patient satisfaction and psychological outcomes (Fallowfield et al., 2002).

Communication also facilitates interdisciplinary collaboration between health care professionals in their efforts to reach a common understanding of how best to care for patients and their families. This dynamic can be problematic given the potential for (and reality of) medical "turf wars" when multiple sub-specialties are involved, and these competing identities have, sadly, been shown to have negative repercussions for the timely treatment of patients (e.g., Watson, Hewett, & Gallois, 2012). Independently, Villagran et al. (2010) have underscored the need for "cohesive team communication ... [as] ... a way to reinforce and recognize best practices in patient communication and practice to be used by all team members" when conveying terminal diagnoses. Further, they contend "that most bad news diagnosis requires a *concerted coordinated* health care team to respond to the issue" (p. 232, our italics).

While training programs exist to teach health care providers how to communicate to best deliver palliative care (Grant et al., 2009), the literature and research that have informed these training programs have yet to sufficiently incorporate perspectives from the discipline of Communication. That said, the latter has cogently addressed these issues in recent years (e.g., Ragan et al., 2008; Nussbaum & Giles, in press), and change is clearly on the horizon (see the COMFORT model for nurses and end-of-life care in Wittenberg-Lyles et al., 2013).

EPILOGUE: TOWARD A COMMUNICATIVE MODEL OF EMPOWERMENT

Whether patient suffering is caused by physical symptoms, unwanted medical intervention, or spiritual crisis, the common pathway to relief is through a provider who is able to elicit these concerns and is equipped to help the patient and family address them (Tulsky, 2005). Much of the literature on this topic views communication as success or failure from the perspective of the provider (Tulsky, 2005). However, the process of dying can take many turns, have many trajectories, involve many individuals, and be enormously complex. Nonetheless, communication is fundamental to effecting what can be "a good death" as well as "a good funeral" (O'Rouke, Spitzberg, & Hannawa, 2011), and, as discussed, serves diverse social and relational functions (see also Byock, 2012; Foster, 2007).

Implicit in this chapter is the value for all involved to feel empowered, be they the dying person, medical practitioners, palliative care providers, family, or friends. Thompson (2011) highlights the power many terminally ill may feel when they consider themselves fully in command of the available information needed about their condition and can plan for the familial consequences of this. Relatedly, she cites Curtis et al. (2008): "Knowledge (about the future) is *empowering*, I think the knowledge of what's going on with you health-wise is the most *empowering* thing you've got" (p. 618; our italics). Across the disciplines, there has been much interest in the construct and process of empowerment, yet in communication it has been confined to its group, community, national, and international parameters (e.g., White, 2008). We contend that the construct—and indeed the process—of empowerment is valuable for further theorizing with respect to our current concerns, and, toward this end, we draw upon and extend Cattaneo and Chapman's (2010) model.

Empowerment for these scholars is conceived of as a process whereby someone "who lacks power sets a personally meaningful goal oriented toward increasing power, takes action toward that goal, and observes and reflects on the impact of this action, drawing on the person's evolving self-efficacy, knowledge and competence related to the goal" (p. 646). As their schematic representation of the model indicates, social context (through cultural norms and practices as well as family and professional networks) impacts all components of the model and the connections between them. Among the features of this model as applied to death and dying are that empowerment is not simply an affective intra-psychic state, but a transactive process; embodied in ever-evolving behavioral and interactional outcomes; goal-driven by personal concerns and hopes; and concerned with social influence.

Tellingly, the *communicative* dynamics of empowerment are not articulated in Cattaneo and Chapman's (2010) model and we would wish to emphasize their potential for our purposes in the following ways. First, cultures vary considerably on the "knowledge" component: in the United States, death issues are often a taboo and people have little information to work off discursively. Second, people's "*self-efficacy*" concerning this existentially angstful topic—wherein people are often looking for the "meaning in life" (for a review, see Steger, 2009)—is often relatively low. Third, "*competence*" and "*goal-oriented actions*" have their *communicative* correlates as well discussed in the foregoing review of end-of-life conversations. Fourth, "*power-oriented goals*" would include actively giving others—and also receiving ourselves—more power in understanding, and planning for, the social dilemmas as well as personal and collective dilemmas about death and dying. Paramount here would be the ever-evolving hope goals (Thompson, 2011) and how the dying and their care providers, who can sometimes have competing hopes for themselves and others, may best negotiate and accommodate to these goals for mutual advantage and joint action. Successfully engaging such power-oriented goals of hope may also bolster, in turn, individuals' knowledge, self-efficacy, and competence on meaningful intra-psychic dimensions. By this means, we see the latter not only as mediators (as they are in Cattaneo & Chapman's model), but also as outcome measures liable to foster personal and network well-being. Albeit embryonic, a communication model of the empowerment process as just sketched out might add theoretical bite to future empirical work and questions derived from it posed in Table 1 that should guide praxis as well. Needless to say, such a framework can be infused and refined by recourse to other communication theories, such as communication accommodation theory (e.g., Giles, 2008). In this regard, accommodation as manifest by physicians seeking common ground uniquely with each of their dying patients has been shown to be effective in providing genuine care for the terminally ill (Janseen, & MacLeod, 2010). Interestingly, lessons on how to manage death are being introduced into British classrooms from age three in the not-too-distant future (Manning, 2013).

Table 1. Components of the Communication Empowerment Process, and Questions for Applying to Death and Dying Issues and Dilemmas.

Model Components	Questions for dying, bereaved, and caring individuals
Personally meaningful, power-oriented goals	What kinds of acceptance and influence (e.g., financial, emotional) is this person seeking, or not? Are these goals *and hopes* congruent with significant others' goals, and are they amenable for re-direction? Does this person prefer mortality topics to be avoided?
Self-efficacy	To what extent does this person believe he/she can achieve goals and have ever-evolving hopes met? Can this person manage death-related information from others? How can this process be optimized?
Knowledge	What is this person's prior history of managing death issues? Can he/she manage uncertainty about the future? How can this be effectively resourced?
Communicative competence	Has this person the communicative and accommodative skills to achieve their influence goals? Does this person have the skills to talk about death-related topics and/or to define the death process positively for others? How can these skills be acquired and extended?
Communicative action	Is this person actively—or sending messages of intent—working toward these goals, and at an appropriate pace given the context and circumstances involved?
Impact	Are this person's messages being recognized, reconciled, and appreciated by significant others? Can this person manage the effects of others' reactions to his/her messages? How can these processes be facilitated?

We challenge colleagues to consider how they may contribute to our understanding and improvement of end-of-life communication processes. By contributing to our collective understanding of the complex process of death and the end of life, we might truly begin to enact the poignant sentiments found in *Tuesdays with Morrie*: "Once you learn how to die, you learn how to live.... Death ends a life, not a relationship" (Albom & Dominiguez, 1997, p. 82).

REFERENCES

Albom, M., & Dominiguez, J. (1997). *Tuesdays with Morrie.* New York, NY: Doubleday.

Bachner, Y. G., Davidov, G. E., & Carmel, S. (2008). Caregivers' communication with patients about illness and death: Initial validation of a scale. *Omega, 57,* 381–397.

Beach, D. L. (1995). Caregiver discourse: Perceptions of illness related dialogue. *Hospice Journal, 10,* 13–25.

Billings, J. A. (1998). What is palliative care? *Journal of Palliative Medicine, 1,* 73–81.

Black, H. K., & Rubinstein, R. L. (2013). A death in the family: Death as a Zen concept. *International Journal of Aging and Human Development, 76,* 79–97.

Bosticco, C., & Thompson, T. L. (2008). Death, dying and communication. In W. Donsbach (Ed.), *International encyclopedia of communication* (Vol. 3, pp. 1171–1173). New York, NY: Wiley/Blackwell.

Bryant, C. D. (Ed.). (2003). *Handbook of death and dying* (2 vols.). Thousand Oaks, CA: Sage.

Buckman, R. (1993). Communication in palliative care: A practical guide. In D. Doyle, G. W. C. Hanks, & N. MacDonald (Eds.), *Oxford textbook of palliative medicine* (pp. 51–86). Oxford, England: Oxford Medical.

Byock, I. (2012). *The best care possible: A physician's quest to transform care through the end of life.* New York, NY: Avery.

Callanan, M., & Kelley, P. (1997). *Final gifts: Understanding the special awareness, needs, and communications of the dying.* New York, NY: Bantam.

Cattaneo, L. B., & Chapman, A. R. (2010). The process of empowerment: A model for us in research and practice. *American Psychologist, 65,* 646–659.

Caughlin, J. P., Mikucki-Enyart, S., Middleton, A. V., Stone, A., & Brown, L. (2011). Being open without talking about it: A rhetorical/normative approach to understanding topic avoidance in families after a lung cancer diagnosis. *Communication Monographs, 78,* 409–436.

Center to Advance Palliative Care (CAPC). (2009). New analysis shows hospitals continue to implement palliative care programs at rapid pace. New medical subspecialty fills gap for aging population. Retrieved from http://www.capc.org/news-and-events/releases/news-release-4-14-08. Accessed July 9, 2010.

Centers for Disease Control and Prevention (CDC). (2010). *Health, United States, 2009. With special feature on medical technology.* Washington, DC: U.S. Government Printing Office. Retrieved from: http://cdc.gov/nchs/data/hus/hus09.pdf#indextotrendtablesand.

Centers for Disease Control and Prevention (CDC). (2012). Faststats: Death and mortality. Retrieved from: http://www.cdc.gov/nchs/fastats/deaths.htm.

Coffman, S. L., & Coffman, V. T. (1993). Communication training for hospice volunteers. *Omega, 27,* 153–163.

Considine, J., & Miller, K. (2010). The dialectics of care: Communicative choices at the end-of-life. *Health Communication, 25*, 165–174.

Copp, G. (1998). A review of current theories of death and dying. *Journal of Advanced Nursing, 28*, 382–390.

Curtis, J. R., Engelberg, R., Young, J. P., Vig, L. K. Reinke, L. F., Wenrich, M. D., McGrath, B., McCown, E., & Back, A. L. (2008). An approach to understanding the interaction of hope and desire for explicit prognostic information among individuals with severe chronic obstructive pulmonary disease or advanced cancer. *Journal of Palliative Medicine, 11*, 610–620.

Dahlin, C. M., & Giansiracusa, D. F. (2006). Communication in Palliative Care. In B. R. Ferrell & N. Coyle (Eds.), *Textbook of palliative nursing* (2nd ed., pp. 67–93). New York, NY: Oxford University Press.

de Grey, A. D. N. J. (2007). Life-span extension research and public debate: Societal considerations. *Studies in Ethics, Law, and Technology, 1*, 1. Retrieved from http://works.bepress.com/aubrey_de_grey/1

Enck, R. E. (2003). Connecting the medical and spiritual models in patients nearing death. *American Journal of Hospice and Palliative Care, 20*, 88–89.

Fallowfield, L., Jenkins, V., Farewell, V., Saul, J., Duffy, A., & Eves, R. (2002). Efficacy of a Cancer Research UK communication skills training model for oncologists: A randomized controlled trial. *Lancet, 359*, 650–656.

Ferrell, B. R., & Coyle, N. (2008). *The nature of suffering and the goals of nursing.* New York, NY: Oxford University Press.

Foster, E. (2007). *Communicating at the end of life: Finding magic in the mundane.* Mahwah, NJ: Erlbaum.

Fowler, C., & Afifi, W. A. (2011). Applying the Theory of Motivated Information Management to adult children's discussions of caregiving with aging parents. *Journal of Social and Personal Relationships, 28*, 507–535.

Giles, H. (2008). Communication accommodation theory: "When in Rome …" or not! In L. A. Baxter & D. O. Braithewaite (Eds.), *Engaging theories in interpersonal communication* (pp. 161–173). Thousand Oaks, CA: Sage.

Giles, H., Davis, S., Gasiorek, J., & Giles, J. L. (2013). *Successful aging: A communication guidebook to empowerment.* Barcelona, Spain: Aresta Editorial.

Gillham, J., Shatté, A., Reivich, K., & Seligman, M. (2000). Optimism, pessimism, and explanatory style. In E. Chang (Ed.), *Optimism and pessimism: Implications for theory, research, and practice* (pp. 53–75). Washington, DC: American Psychological Association.

Glaser, B. G., & Strauss A. L. (1968). *Time for dying.* Chicago, IL: Aldine.

Goldsmith, J., Wittenberg-Lyles, E., Ragan, S., & Nussbaum, J. F. (2011). Lifespan and end-of-life health communication. In T. L. Thompson, R. Parrott, & J. F. Nussbaum (Eds.), *Handbook of health communication* (pp. 441–454). New York, NY: Routledge.

Grant, M., Elk, R., Ferrell, B., Morrison, R. S., & von Gunten, C. F. (2009). Current status of palliative care—clinical implementation, education, and research. *CA: A Cancer Journal for Clinicians, 59*, 327–335.

Gray, R. E., Fitch, M., Phillips, C., Labrecque, M., & Fergus, K. (2000). To tell or not to tell: Patterns of disclosure among men with prostate cancer. *Psycho-Oncology, 9*, 273–282.

Hines, S. C. (2001). Coping with uncertainties in advance care planning. *Journal of Communication, 51*, 498–513.

Hinton, J. (1981). Sharing or withholding awareness of dying between husband and wife. *Journal of Psychosomatic Research, 25*, 337–343.

Hinton, J. (1998). An assessment of open communication between people with terminal cancer, caring relatives, and others during home care. *Journal of Palliative Care, 14*, 15–23.

Janseen, A. L., & MacLeod, R. D. (2010). What can people approaching death teach us about how to care? *Patient Education and Counseling, 81*, 251–256.

Jennings, L. (2005). Finding better ways to die. *Futurist, 39*, 43–47.

Johnston, G., & Abraham, C. (2000). Managing awareness: Negotiating and coping with a terminal prognosis. *International Journal of Palliative Nursing, 6*, 485–494.

Kalish, R. (1980). Preface. In R. Kalish (Ed.), *Death and dying: Views from many cultures* (pp. 1–2). Amityville, NY: Baywood.

Kaplowitz, S. A., Campo, S., & Chiu, W. T. (2002). Cancer patients' desires for communication of prognosis information. *Health Communication, 14*, 221–241.

Kaplowitz, S. A., Osuch, J. R., Safron, D., & Campo, S. (1999). Physician communication with seriously ill cancer patients: Results of a survey of physicians. In B. DeVries (Ed.), *End of life issues: Interdisciplinary and multidimensional perspectives* (pp. 205–227). New York, NY: Springer.

Kastenbaum, R. J. (1992). *The psychology of death* (2nd ed.). New York, NY: Springer.

Kastenbaum, R. J. (1997). *Death, society, and human experience* (10th ed.). Columbus, OH: Merrill.

Keeley, M. P. (2004a). Final conversations: Messages of love. *Qualitative Research Reports, 5*, 48–57.

Keeley, M. P. (2004b). Final conversations: Survivors' memorable messages concerning religious faith and spirituality. *Health Communication, 16*, 87–104.

Keeley, M. P. (2007). "Turning toward death together": The functions of messages during final conversations in close relationships. *Journal of Social and Personal Relationships, 24*, 225–253.

Keeley, M. P., & Koenig Kellas, J. (2005). Constructing life and death through final conversation narratives. In L. M. Harter, P. M. Japp, & C. S. Beck (Eds.), *Narratives, health, and healing: Communication theory, research, and practice* (pp. 365–390). Mahwah, NJ: Erlbaum.

Keeley, M. P., & Yingling, J. M. (2007). *Final conversations: Helping the living and the dying talk to each other.* Action, MA: Van de Wyk & Burnham.

Kleinedler, S. (Ed.). (2005). *American Heritage science dictionary* (p. 163). Boston, MA: Houghton Mifflin.

Kramer, D. (1997). How women relate to terminally ill husbands and their subsequent adjustment to bereavement. *Omega, 34*, 93–106.

Kübler-Ross, E. (1969). *On death and dying.* New York, NY: Macmillan.

Larson, D. G. (1993). The caring team. In D. G. Larson (Ed.), *The helper's journey* (pp. 199–227). Champaign, IL: Research Press.

Lewis, F., & Deal, L. (1995). Balancing our lives: A study of the married couple's experience with breast cancer recurrence. *Oncology Nursing Forum, 22*, 943–953.

Lock, M. (1996). Death in technological time: Locating the end of meaningful life. *Medical Anthropology Quarterly, 10*, 575–600.

Maciejewski, P. K., Zhang, B., Block, S. D., & Prigerson, H. (2007). An empirical examination of the stage theory of grief. *Journal of the American Medical Association, 297*, 716–723.

Ma-Kellams, C., & Blascovich, J. (2012). Enjoying life in the face of death: East-West differences in responses to mortality salience. *Journal of Personality and Social Psychology, 103*, 773–786.

Manning, S. (2013, June). Schools to offer pupils "lessons on death" from the age of three. *The Independent, 17*, 21.

McDonald, D. D., Deloge, J., Joslin, N., Petow, W. A., Severson, J. S., Votino, R..., & Del Signore, E. (2003). Communicating end-of-life preferences. *Western Journal of Nursing Research, 25*, 652–666.

McGrath, C., Montgomery, K., White, K., & Kerridge, I. H. (2006). A narrative account of the impact of positive thinking on discussions about death and dying. *Support Care Cancer, 14,* 1246–1251.

McGrath, P. (2004). The burden of the "RA RA" positive: Survivors' and hospice patients' reflections on maintaining a positive attitude to serious illness. *Support Care Cancer, 12,* 25–33.

Metzger, P. L., & Gray, M. J. (2008). End-of-life communication and adjustment: Pre-loss communication as a predictor of bereavement-related outcomes. *Death Studies, 32,* 301–325.

Miller, V. D., & Knapp, M. L. (1986). The *post-nutio* dilemma: Approaches to communicating with the dying. In M. McLaughlin (Ed.), *Communication yearbook 9* (pp. 723–738). Beverly Hills, CA: Sage.

Moller, D. W. (1996). *Confronting death: Values, institutions, and human morality.* New York, NY: Oxford University Press.

Morgan, J. D., & Laungani, P. (2002). General introduction. In J. D. Morgan & P. Laungani (Eds.), *Death and bereavement around the world.* (Vol. 1., pp. 1–4). Amityville, NY: Baywood.

National Consensus Project (NCP). (2009). *Clinical practice guidelines for quality for palliative care* (2nd ed). Pittsburgh, PA: Author.

Nussbaum, J. F., & Coupland, J. (Eds.) (1995 & 2001). *Handbook of communication and aging research.* (1st & 2nd eds.). Mahwah, NJ: Erlbaum.

Nussbaum, J. F., & Giles, H. (Eds.). (in press). *Communication at the end of life.* New York, NY: Peter Lang.

Nussbaum, J. F., Thompson, T. L., & Robinson, J. D. (1988). *Communication and aging.* New York, NY: Harper & Row.

O'Rouke, T., Spitzberg, B. H., & Hannawa, A. F. (2011). The good funeral: Toward an understanding of funeral participation and satisfaction. *Death Studies, 35,* 729–750.

Otis-Green, S., Ferrell, B., Spolum, M., Uman, G., Mullan, P., Baird, P., & Grant, M. (2009). An overview of the ACE project—advocating for clinical excellence: Transdisciplinary palliative care education. *Journal of Cancer Education, 24,* 120–126.

Pattison, E. M. (1977). *The experience of dying.* New York, NY: Simon & Schuster.

Peterson, C. (2000). The future of optimism. *American Psychologist, 55,* 44–55.

Pitts, M. (2011). Dancing with the spirit: Communicating family norms for positive end-of-life transition. In M. Miller-Day (Ed.), *Family communication, connections, and health transitions* (pp. 377–404). New York, NY: Peter Lang.

Ragan, S. L., Goldsmith, J., Wittenberg-Lyles, E. M., & Sanchez-Riley, S. (2010). *Dying with comfort: Illness narratives and early palliative care.* New York, NY: Hampton.

Ragan, S. L., Wittenberg-Lyles, E. M., Goldsmith, J., & Kelley, S. S. (2008). Communication as comfort: Multiple voices in palliative care. New York, NY: Routlege.

Randell, T. (2004). Medical and legal considerations of brain death. *Acta Anaesthesiologica Scandinavica, 48,* 139–144.

Salander, P., & Spetz, A. (2002). How do patients and spouses deal with the serious facts of malignant glioma? *Palliative Medicine, 16,* 305–313.

Steger, M. F. (2009). Meaning in life. In S. J. Lopez (Ed.), *Oxford handbook of positive psychology* (2nd ed., pp. 679–687). Oxford, England: Oxford University Press.

Stone, A. M., Mikucki-Enyart, S., Middleton, A. V., Caughlin, J. P., & Brown, L. (2012). Caring for a parent with lung cancer: Caregivers' perspectives on the role of communication. *Qualitative Health Research, 22,* 957–970.

Sulmasy, D. P. (2002). A biopsychosocial-spiritual model for the care of patients at the end-of-life. *Gerontologist, 42,* 24–33.

Thompson, T. L. (1996). Allowing dignity: Communication with the dying. In E. B. Ray (Ed.), *Communication with the disenfranchized* (pp. 387–404). Hillsdale, NJ: Erlbaum.

Thompson, T. L. (2011). Hope and the act of informed dialogue: A delicate balance of end-of-life. *Journal of Language and Social Psychology, 30,* 177–192.

Tomer, A. (2000). *Death attitudes and the older adult: Theories, concepts, and applications.* Philadelphia, PA: Taylor & Francis.

Tulsky, J. A. (2005). Interventions to enhance communication among patients, providers, and families. *Journal of Palliative Medicine, 8,* S95–S102.

Vachon, M. L., Freedman, K., Formo, A., Rogers, J., Lyall, W. A., & Freeman, S. J. (1977). The final illness in cancer: The widow's perspective. *Canadian Medical Association Journal, 117,* 1151–1154.

Vail, K. E., III, Juhl, J., Arndt, J., Vess, M., Routledge, C., & Rutjens, B. T. (2012). When death is good for life: Considering the positive trajectories of terror management. *Personality and Social Psychology Review, 16,* 303–329.

Villagran, M., Goldsmith, J., Wittenberg-Lyles, E. M., & Baldwin, P. (2010). Creating COMFORT: A communication-based model for breaking bad news. *Communication Education, 59,* 220–234.

Vora, E., & Vora, A. (2008). A contingency framework for listening to the dying. *International Journal of Listening, 22,* 59–72.

Walter, T. (2003). Historical and cultural variants on the good death. *British Medical Journal, 327,* 218–220.

Watson, B. M., & Hewett, D. G., & Gallois, C. (2012). Intergroup communication and health care. In H. Giles (Ed.), *The handbook of intergroup communication* (pp. 293–305). New York, NY: Routledge.

White, R. A. (2008). Communication strategies for empowerment. In W. Donsbach (Ed.), *International encyclopedia of communication* (Vol. 3, pp. 821–825). New York, NY: Wiley/Blackwell.

Wittenberg-Lyles, E., Goldsmoth, J., Ferrell, B., & Ragan, S. L. (2013). *Communication in palliative nursing.* New York, NY: Oxford University Press.

World Health Organization. (2010). *World health statistics 2010.* Geneva, Switzerland: Author.

Wu, A. M. S., Tang, C. T. S., & Kwok, T. C. Y. (2002). Death anxiety among Chinese elderly people in Hong Kong. *Journal of Aging and Health, 14,* 42–56.

Yingling, J., & Keeley, M. P. (2007). A failure to communicate: Let's get real about improving communication at the end-of-life. *American Journal of Hospice and Palliative Medicine, 24,* 95–97.

Zhang, A. Y., & Siminoff, L. A. (2003). Silence and cancer: Why do families and patients fail to communicate? *Health Communication, 15,* 415–429.

About the Editors and Contributors

Editor

Jon F. Nussbaum is Professor of Communication Arts and Sciences and Human Development and Family Studies at the Pennsylvania State University

Editorial Assistant

Amber K. Worthington is a doctoral candidate within the Department of Communication Arts and Sciences at the Pennsylvania State University

Contributors

Piotr S. Bobkowski is Assistant Professor at the William Allen White School of Journalism and Mass Communications at the University of Kansas

Mollie Rose Canzona is a doctoral candidate within the Department of Communication at the George Mason University

Laura S. DeThorne is Associate Professor of Speech and Hearing Science at the University of Illinois, Urbana-Champaign

Fran C. Dickson is Professor and Chair of Communication Studies at Chapman University

Robert L. Duran is Professor of Communication at the University of Hartford

Carla L. Fisher is Assistant Professor of Communication at George Mason University

Craig Fowler is Senior Lecturer in Communication at Massey University, New Zealand

Howard Giles is Professor of Communication, Psychology, and Linguistics at the University of California, Santa Barbara

Dennis S. Gouran is Professor of Labor Studies and Employment and Communication Arts and Sciences at the Pennsylvania State University

Jake Harwood is Professor of Communication and Director of Graduate Studies at the University of Arizona

Beth Booniwell Haslett is Professor of Communication at the University of Delaware

Michael L. Hecht is Distinguished Professor of Communication Arts and Sciences at the Pennsylvania State University

Andrew C. High is Assistant Professor of Communication Studies at the University of Iowa

Patrick Hughes is Associate Professor of Communication Studies and Associate Vice Provost for Undergraduate Education at Texas Tech University

Mary Lee Hummert is Professor of Communication Studies at the University of Kansas

Shawn King is a graduate research assistant at the University of Oklahoma

Michael W. Kramer is Professor and Chair of Communication at the University of Oklahoma

Alyssa Ann Lucas is Assistant Professor at Central Michigan University

Tara G. McManus is Assistant Professor of Communication Studies at the University of Nevada, Las Vegas

Carol A. Miller is Associate Professor of Communication Sciences and Disorders and Linguistics at the Pennsylvania State University

Karen K. Myers is Associate Professor of Communication at the University of California, Santa Barbara

Jessica Taylor Piotrowski is Assistant Professor of Communication Research at the University of Amsterdam

Margaret J. Pitts is Assistant Professor of Communication at the University of Arizona

Abby Prestin is a Cancer Research Training Fellow at the National Cancer Institute

Diane T. Prusank is Professor of Communication at Westfield State University

James D. Robinson is Professor of Communication at the University of Dayton

Wendy Samter is Professor and Chair of Communication at Bryant University

Autumn Shafer is Assistant Professor of Public Relations at Texas Tech University

Jordan Soliz is Associate Professor of Communication Studies at the University of Nebraska, Lincoln

Chan L. Thai is a doctoral candidate in Communication at the University of California, Santa Barbara

Patti M. Valkenburg is Professor of Media, Youth, and Society at the University of Amsterdam

Helen G.M. Vossen is a Postdoctoral Researcher in Communication Research at the University of Amsterdam

Jennifer H. Waldeck is Associate Professor of Communication Studies at Chapman University

Kathleen B. Watters is Associate Professor of Communication at the University of Dayton

Kevin B. Wright is Professor of Communication at George Mason University

Index

F

G

Kvasnicka, B., 364
Kynette, D., 10, 30

L

Labouvie, E.W., 273
Labrecque, M., 410
Ladd, G.W., 82
Ladd, L.D., 114, 116, 117, 122, 126, 128
Lagerspetz, K., 118
Lahey, B.B., 205
Laidsaar-Powell, R.C., 394
Lally, M., 276
Lamb, M.E., 76
Lampe, C., 196, 199
Lampheear-Van Horn, M., 260
Lancaster, L.C., 259
Landers, J.L., 284
Landua, R., 275, 276
Lane, H., 66
Lang, A., 99
Langellier, K.M., 255
Langer, E.J., 15, 18
Langmeyer, L., 363
Langwell, L., 204
language, 53
Larkey, L.K., 186, 187
LaRose, R., 283
Larsen, D., 284
Larson, D.G., 415
Larson, M.S., 335
Lasky, N., 113, 115
Lassman, D., 387
later-life adults, 373–74, 382
    dating and, 374–76
    future research directions on, 382–83
    online dating and, 376–77
    romantic relationship termination among,
        377–78
    sexual activity among, 378–80
Laub, J.H., 43
Laungani, P., 406, 407
Laurent, A.C., 55
Laursen, B., 219
Lauricella, A., 95

Lauzen, M.M., 362, 363
Lawrence, E., 284
Lawton, L., 299, 300
Layton, L., 334
L'Engle, K.L., 162, 163
Le, B., 236, 237, 241
Leader Behavior Description Questionnaire, 315
Leader-Member Exchange Theory, 318, 319
leadership. *See* superior-subordinate interactions
Leaf, P.J., 162, 205
learning
    approach/avoidance theory, 140
    Bloom's taxonomy, 136–37
    classroom variables and, 146–47
    communication and, 135, 139–41
    emotional intelligence, 137–38
    expectancy learning/learned
        helplessness, 140
    future research directions in, 148–50
    instructor communication and, 144–45
    instructor-student interaction and, 145–46
    as a lifespan process, 135–39
    related technology, 148
    rhetorical/relational goal theory, 141
    role of communication variables in, 141–47
    socialization and, 138–39
    social cognitive theory, 141
    student communication and, 142–43
    teacher communication and, 144–45
Learning Indicators Scale, 136
Learning Loss Scale, 136
Leary, M.R., 119
Ledbetter, A.M., 145
Ledley, D.R., 122
Lee, J.K., 187, 189, 190
Lee, L., 377
Lee, M., 363, 364
Lee, S.J., 196, 204
Lee, T.W., 262
Lefkowitz, E.S., 218, 219, 220, 222, 223, 224,
    226, 227, 238, 300, 301, 380
Lenahan, P., 379
Lengua, L., 83
Lenhart, A., 159, 195, 277, 280
Leo-Summers, L., 396
Lesh, R., 106

M

LIFESPAN
COMMUNICATION
Children, Families, and Aging

Thomas J. Socha, *General Editor*

From first words to final conversations, communication plays an integral and significant role in all aspects of human development and everyday living. The Lifespan Communication: Children, Families, and Aging series seeks to publish authored and edited scholarly volumes that focus on relational and group communication as they develop over the lifespan (infancy through later life). The series will include volumes on the communication development of children and adolescents, family communication, peer-group communication (among age cohorts), intergenerational communication, and later-life communication, as well as longitudinal studies of lifespan communication development, communication during lifespan transitions, and lifespan communication research methods. The series includes college textbooks as well as books for use in upper-level undergraduate and graduate courses.

Thomas J. Socha, Series Editor | *tsocha@odu.edu*
Mary Savigar, Acquisitions Editor | *mary.savigar@plang.com*

To order other books in this series, please contact our Customer Service Department at:

> (800) 770-LANG (within the U.S.)
> (212) 647-7706 (outside the U.S.)
> (212) 647-7707 FAX

Or browse online by series at www.peterlang.com